REFERENTIAL
PRACTICE

REFERENTIAL PRACTICE

Language
and
Lived Space
among
the Maya

WILLIAM F. HANKS

The University of Chicago Press \ Chicago and London

WILLIAM F. HANKS is associate professor of anthropology, linguistics, and social sciences at the University of Chicago.

The University of Chicago Press, Chicago 60637
The University of Chicago Press, Ltd., London
© 1990 by The University of Chicago
All rights reserved. Published 1990
Printed in the United States of America
99 98 97 96 95 94 93 92 91 90   5 4 3 2 1

Library of Congress Cataloging in Publication Data

Hanks, William F.
    Referential practice : language and lived space among the Maya /
William F. Hanks.
        p.   cm.
    Includes bibliographical references.
    ISBN 0-226-31545-2 (alk. paper). — ISBN 0-226-31546-0 (pbk.)
    1. Maya language.   2. Language and culture—Yucatán Peninsula.
3. Spatial behavior—Yucatán Peninsula.   4. Mayas—Social
conditions.   I. Title.
PM3969.H36   1990
497'.415—dc20   90-32169
                                                                     CIP

⊗ The paper used in this publication meets the minimum requirements of the
American National Standard for Information Sciences—Permanence of Paper
for Printed Library Materials, ANSI Z39.48-1984.

Contents

Tables, Plates, and Figures

A gallery of photographs follows page 134

Preface and Acknowledgments

This book is the product of research conducted over nearly a dozen years, during which time my thinking has undergone several significant transformations, and my personal and intellectual debts have grown correspondingly. I was first introduced to Maya language when, as a first-year graduate student, I studied it with Norman A. McQuown. As all of his students know, Mac's method is direct; we did close transcriptions (segmental and prosodic) of the spoken language for eight hours per week in class, and for our home assignments, we did more transcription. During the next four years, I took a course every quarter with Mac and worked as his research assistant. Starting then and continuing into the present, he has set a formidable standard of rigor and honesty in handling linguistic data and in resisting reductionist explanations of interaction. During the same period I studied language use with Michael Silverstein, who first drew my attention to indexicality, and with Jerrold Sadock, who kept me focused on the problem of distinguishing language structure from language use. Through his questions and encouragement, John Comaroff helped to orient me to ethnographic description and has since waded through more versions of reference in Maya than either of us cares to recall. I mention these early influences not only out of gratitude but because they have remained generative in my thinking, as will be evident in the following pages. During this first phase, my research was supported by fellowships from the Fulbright Hays Doctoral Dissertation Research program, the Social Science Research Council, the Mrs. Giles Whiting Foundation, and Tinker Travel awards for summer fieldwork from the Center for Latin American Studies, University of Chicago (1977, 1984). Working largely with Prague School linguistics, the ethnography of speaking, and Alfred Schutz's description of interaction, I took a relatively traditional approach to indexical reference in my dissertation, arguing that words like 'this,' 'here,' and 'I' reflect the relation between language structure and the cultural definition of the speaker.

The period between 1984 and 1987 marked a new phase in my thinking about language in context, and this too makes up one of the strata in this book. Having joined the faculty in Anthropology and Linguistics at the University of Chicago, I entered into active dialogue with a number of new interlocutors. Of special importance have been the many insightful critiques and words of encouragement from Terence Turner and Paul Friedrich, both of whom gave long written commentaries on sections of the book. Conversations and several rounds of team teaching with Nancy Munn have influenced my thinking about space, time, and ethnographic description substantially. This book incorporates the conviction that sociocultural systems, including ritual forms and verbal semantics, are ultimately grounded in the everyday activities and values of native actors, not in some disembodied realm of ideas churning along on its own logic. Although I had not yet arrived at the practice framework deployed in this work, which few of my collegues would adopt themselves, these intermediate developments prepared the ground intellectually for it.

During the same period I became increasingly active in seminars at the Center for Psychosocial Studies in Chicago. Long, intense discussions there with excellent scholars have made contributions to my development that it would be difficult to pinpoint but impossible to overlook. My special thanks go to Benjamin Lee, friend and colleague, who has provided detailed commentaries on most of the final manuscript, as well as several versions leading up to it. Richard Bauman, Don Brenneis, James Collins, John Haviland, Judith Irvine, John Lucy, Richard Parmentier, Michael Silverstein, and Greg Urban have been a core group of interlocutors through several seminars in which ideas were pushed to the limit (and often beyond).

These concurrent developments led me to seriously rethink the direction of my analysis and to question more pointedly the notion of subjectivity as I had developed it in earlier writings. At this time, I undertook to reread most of the philosophy of language that I had used in earlier versions and to pursue recent theories of reference, discourse analysis and semantics in more depth. The difference between treating reference as an act performed by a solitary speaker and treating it as an interactive production became clearer, at the same time that the ethnographic and social theoretic stakes of this distinction also became evident. This was something of a crisis period intellectually, during which I came to doubt the validity of the approach to demonstrative reference that I had adopted in my dissertation, but I was still unable to see any feasible alternatives to it. Several unsuccessful attempts at publishing papers and securing funding for a return to the field punctuated the turmoil. In dialogue with colleagues and students, my appreciation of the significance of the topic was developing much more rapidly than my ability to synthesize what I was learning. I found myself in a position that most scholars probably face at one time or another—at sea in a morass of possible approaches to a topic that I had studied for too long. In retrospect, I think this period was formative in the research that made the book possible. It was then that I first investigated frame semantics in some depth, developed the relational approach to reference as a figure-ground structure, and undertook comparative study of deictic systems in languages other than Maya. One of the key aims of this book is to spell out an interactive, sociocentric approach to reference, in both theoretical and ethnographic terms.

The third phase began in late 1986 when I was awarded a research grant from the National Endowment for the Humanities (no. RO 21374-86). This was an enormous boost to the project, for which I shall remain deeply grateful. It made it possible for me to return to the field and focus my attention entirely on reanalyzing primary data and formulating a coherent synthesis. When back in the field, I devised the method of note taking that generated most of the examples in this book: I mapped domestic spaces and assigned numbers to their constituent parts. When recording referential exchanges, I used the numbers to plot the locations of both interactants and objects of reference. The result was sufficiently productive that all but a handful of the key examples adduced in the following pages came from this field session. Once I was back from Yucatán, colleagues and students in Chicago continued to play an important role in the development of my thinking, but I was also able to extend my discourse to colleagues elsewhere. Aaron Cicourel and Charles Goodwin both wrote extensive and productive commentaries on portions of the manuscript. Both have changed my thinking about interaction over recent years, and their words of encouragement have been really helpful. Dell Hymes wrote generous commentaries on parts of the manuscript, as well as on separate papers treating related topics. Much appreciated encouragement and intellectual support for the project has come also from Ellen Basso, Keith Basso, John Gumperz, Jane Hill, and my colleague Sharon Stephens.

In winter of 1988 I had the good fortune to visit the École des Hautes Études en Sciences Sociales in Paris. I am deeply grateful to Pierre Bourdieu for this invitation, which proved to be once again transformative. In searching for a synthesis, I had begun to move in the direction of a practice approach to reference, but there were few precedents, and it was less than clear how to proceed. In Paris I benefited greatly from discussions with Bernard Conein, Pierre Encrevé, and Michel de Fornel, as well as the atmosphere of collegiality at the Centre de sociologie européenne and Centre de linguistique théorique.

In the course of this development, I have found it necessary to fashion a somewhat new language in which to describe referential practices. Some aspects of speech which appear to be simple and beyond question in traditional approaches have become very complicated and unfamiliar in this one. Other cases have undergone the inverse process of radical simplification. These shifts have been abetted by my commitment to a form of interdisciplinary research in which different approaches are brought into confrontation and changed in sometimes basic ways rather than being patched together and repaired around the edges. Readers of this book may wonder at times why I doggedly pursue and illustrate one line of reasoning, while leaving another behind. I can only ask for patience and offer the assurance that my purpose is not to set up a programmatic structure that will answer (and thus stifle) all questions but rather to open questions prematurely closed. Indeed, recent discussions with colleagues have already led me to reconsider aspects of the framework employed in this book (as is reflected in Hanks 1989a).

Throughout this process I have benefited from the efforts of two exceptionally capable research assistants. Coby Jones designed the font and prosodic symbols for Maya transcription on a Mac system and helped create the data files without which the organization of examples would have remained clumsy and burdensome. Lynn Ann MacLeod has been my assistant, editor, and production team for five years and has made invaluable contributions to my research, not only by freeing me from administrative tasks but also by pointing out inconsistencies of statement, tracking down bibliographic entries, formatting and organizing computer files, proofing and printing the entire manuscript more than once. For her sheer competence, good judgment, and insightful suggestions I will remain grateful. Diane Zatz-Artz of Amalgamation House, Inc., produced all of the artwork in the book, no small accomplishment given the notes from which she had to work.

Amidst the layers of intellectual history embodied in this text lies another history, with another temporality and another cast of actors. This is the story of my friendship with a group of Maya-speaking campesinos in the southern hills of Yucatán, Mexico. When I first went to Oxkutzcab in 1977, unable to speak either Maya or Spanish, utterly unfamiliar with the realities of life in rural Yucatán, DP and his family accepted me into their home. They taught me how to fetch water for the household, weed the milpa with a coa, sleep in a hammock, work in the searing sun, and give myself over to the quiet beauty of Maya nights. Several years later, when I was pursuing one or another line of tedious questions with DP, something about what it meant to be 'here', or whether it was 'now' yet, I suggested that he might grow impatient with my worries. "No," he said, "years from now when you look back on this, you will say that I was someone whose willingness to teach you never ran out. You will never exhaust my willingness (*voluntad*). And you've got to get it straight, so ask your questions." It was a remarkable assertion from a man in his mid-fifties with a large family to support and much better things to do than indulge my interests. A man with no formal education, who would seem poor to many North Americans, I never have found the limits of his willingness, and I have come to recognize this generosity, pride, and tenacious commitment to doing things right in most of my Maya friends. Without these qualities on the part of the people, whom I will call (for the sake of anonymity) Doña Toni, DP and his wife DA, their son MC and his wife Eli, VC and his wife Pilar, and Milo, DC, a shaman, and his sons Man and Lol, with their respective wives Margot and Fi, VI, Balim, Chio, Is, and his wife Bal, this book would not have been possible. I could not have learned what I have about Maya culture without their active role in teaching me, not just in answering my questions but in showing me what to ask about.

Many other friends and colleagues in Yucatán have helped me over the years and done much to make my fieldwork as enjoyable as it has been fruitful. Here I should like to express special thanks to Joann Andrews, the late Alfredo Barrera-Vasquez, Juan Ramón Bastarrachea Manzano, James Callaghan, Edward Kurjack, Bernd and Cornelia Neugebauer.

I have written this book with a commitment to describing what people do and say in very specific, nitty-gritty detail. My motivation is not objectivist realism of the sort so popular in contemporary North America. This book ultimately undermines realism by eroding the appearance of transparent access to the world, on which it rests. Rather, my motivations lie in the simple notion that by submitting to the world in its multiple versions, developing the craft of clear vision and description, and forcing our modes of theory to come to grips with multiplicity, we will achieve a better, deeper, and more empathetic understanding of human societies. This is my best effort to date.

My final word of thanks is to my family. My mother, Anne M. Hanks, has been a friend and confidant for as long as I can remember. Her advice and support are gifts of enormous proportions. My sisters, Carol Welsh and Deborah Khalil, and their families have been a constant background presence. My daughter Madeleine was born halfway through the manuscript and has kept me on my toes ever since. Finally, my wife Lori Bartman has made incalculable contributions to my life and work through her love and support, her ability to make space for the obsessive behavior of writing, her insightful questions, and her artistic sensibility. I am of course solely responsible for the contents of this book, but my point in all this is that I am not solely to credit.

Abbreviations

Adj	adjective
Adr	addressee
Adv	adverb
Anaph	anaphoric
Ante	antecedent
Anticip	anticipatory
Apro	A-set pronoun
Art	article
Asym	asymmetric
ATTN	attention focus
Aud	auditory
Aux	auxiliary
BACKGRND KN	background knowledge
Br	brother
Caus	causative
Cert	certain
Comp	complementizer
Coref	coreferential
Corp	corporeal
Da	daughter
Dat	dative
def.	definite
Dir	directive
DISC, Disc	discourse
DLOC	deictic locative adverb
DMAN	deictic manner adverb
DMOD	deictic modal auxiliary
DNOM	deictic nominal
DTEMP	deictic temporal adverb

E	event
En, $\mathrm{E^n}$	event narrated
Es, $\mathrm{E^s}$	event of speaking
Es*, $\mathrm{E^{s*}}$	event of speaking, transposed
Esn, $\mathrm{E^{sn}}$	event of speaking narrated
Esn*, $\mathrm{E^{sn*}}$	event of speaking narrated, transposed
EXCL, Excl	exclusive
Expr	expressive
F	communicative function
F	father
fem.	feminine
Hu	husband
I ground, i ground	indexical ground
ID	initial deictic
Immed	immediate
Imper	imperative
Inc	incompletive
INCL, Incl	inclusive
IndPro	independent pronoun
Intj	interjection
Intrns	intransitive particle
$\mathrm{L^n}$	narrated location
lit.	literally
LOC, Loc	locative
M	mother
Man	manner
N	noun
NC	numerical classifier
Neg	negative particle
Non-Part	nonparticipant
NP	noun phrase
Opt	optative
OSTEV	ostensive evidential adverb
P	participant
$\mathrm{P^n}$	participant in narrated event
$\mathrm{P^s}$	participant in speech event
PART	participant deictic
PERC	perception
Periph	peripheral
plur., pl.	plural
Prep	preposition

Pres	presentative
Prft	perfective
Prt	particle
Pst	past
Psv	passive
Q	interrogative particle
Quant	quantifier
Quot	quotative
R value	relational feature
Ref	referential
Rel	relational particle
Restr	restricted
RN	relational noun
S	sentence
Si	sister
Simul	simultaneous
sing., sg.	singular
So	son
Spec	specified
Spkr	speaker
stv	stative
Sym	symmetric
Tact	tactual
TD	terminal deictic
Temp	temporal
Total	totalizing infix
Transp	transposed
Trm	terminal particle
V	vowel
V_i	intransitive verb
V_t	transitive verb
Vb	verb
VC	verb complex
Vis	visual
Voc	vocative
Wi	wife
1 (nonsubscripted)	first person
2 (nonsubscripted)	second person
3 (nonsubscripted)	third person
F.I.A.100	Field recording number 1, side A at 230
B.B.I.100	Field notes, book 1, page 100

Orthographic Conventions

The orthographic and prosodic symbols used in citations of Maya examples in this book have their standard IPA values, with the following exceptions. (Pitch, volume, and tempo symbols may be doubled to indicate increased intensity.)

š		voiceless palatal fricative, as in English sh
β		voiced bilabial continuant, as in Spanish *abeja*
¢		voiceless alveolar affricate, as in English ts
č		voiceless palatal affricate, as in English ch
ʔ		glottal stop
⚲		glottal squeeze, creakiness
ʡ		glottal stop with percussive release
b’		glottalized b
p’		glottalized p
t’		glottalized t
k’		glottalized k
¢’		glottalized ¢
č’		glottalized č
→		level final intonation contour
↑		rising final intonation contour
↓		falling final intonation contour
↑–	–↑	overhigh pitch, domain indicated by placement
↓–	–↓	overlow pitch, domain indicated by placement
^–	–^	overloud volume, domain indicated by placement
ˇ–	–ˇ	oversoft volume, domain indicated by placement
>–	–>	overfast tempo, domain indicated by placement
<–	–<	overslow tempo, domain indicated by placement
◡		clipped pronunciation or transition
⌢		drawled pronunciation or slow transition

₱		extra slow transition
ß-	-ß	breathy voice quality, domain indicated by placement
~-	-~	nasal voice quality, domain indicated by placement
"		heavy stress
⌐		immediately adjacent, nonoverlapping utterances

1 Social Foundations of Reference

Introduction

1.1 ANTHROPOLOGY OF VERBAL REFERENCE

This is an anthropological study of language use in a contemporary Maya community in Yucatán, Mexico.[1] It is focused on the routine linguistic practices by which Maya speakers make reference to themselves and each other, to their immediate contexts, and to their socially constructed world. Scholars in a number of disciplines have shown convincingly that reference is only a part of the full range of functions subserved by language in communication. Speakers express their own alignments to self and situation, order each other around, question, promise, turn verses, spit curses, make moves, save face, keep pace, assert authority, bitch and cajole, pray, and change the world in their utterances. None of these is explainable strictly on the basis of reference.

Reference may of course *contribute to* an indefinite number of other kinds of communicative effects, but the point is that it cannot in and of itself *constitute* them. The traditional linguistic focus on the value of language as a means of making descriptive statements about the world, which can then be judged as true or false, has been shown repeatedly to single out but one piece of the puzzle. At its best, it results in a self-avowedly selective view of language, in which rigor is achieved by limiting play to a narrow field. At its worst, when applied to pragmatics without qualification, it can produce a sterile, unrealistic view of language use. One need only think of the works of Austin, Friedrich, Goffman, Gumperz, Hymes, Jakobson, Labov, Mukařovski, Sapir, and Silverstein to open up a horizon of speech functions far beyond reference.

One finds excessively limiting the assumptions ordinarily (if not always accurately) associated with studies of language that privilege reference and semantic description: Language exists so that people can make statements about an objective reality that exists apart from speech. The meaning of an expression, to the extent that we can talk about it with any precision, is its contribution to such statements. Language is like logic, at least in its most 'interesting' semantic properties. Since we, as analysts, speak English natively and can trade judgments about example sentences, and since naive speakers make all sorts of extraneous errors in everyday talk, it is reasonable to base our theorizing, even 'pragmatics', on hypothetical examples which we think up ourselves. When we are working in a foreign language, referential values of words can be induced through structured interviews in which things like color chips and genealogically defined kinsmen serve as denotata presented by the analyst and labeled by the informant.

Of course, few if any scholars would agree to all of these statements, certainly not without qualification, yet they arise from a perspective on language that is commonly associated with the study of reference. Why undertake such a study, then, just as we have begun to develop a framework in which to describe other, socially significant, aspects of language use?

My reasons are several. The first is quite simply that reference is a socially significant phenomenon. Language in everyday life is used continually to talk about the world, whether it is represented as an objective reality or as a creation of verbal practices. Moreover, such talk **is** action and can constitute social reality, rather than merely reflecting it. A realistic anthropology of language must incorporate reference rather than trying to work around it. (I do not wish to suggest that any of the aforementioned authors have denied this, but rather that if taken in the extreme, some of their arguments can be misconstrued as justifying such a denial.) The second is that once we take seriously the advances made in research on language use, reference itself ceases to be the isolable, privileged object it may have appeared to be in the past. This is the real rub: reference is a kind of communicative action which occurs as part of an interactive manifold. No clean separation will emerge in this book between the extrareferential functions of speech and the purely referential ones. It seems to me that such a dichotomy claims too much for the independence of functions and too little for the social foundations of semantics itself. Significant strides made by anthropologists in the study of performance style, poetics, oratory, ritual, and myth can contribute to a better understanding of reference instead of marginalizing it or consigning it to other disciplines or other decades.

'Language use' is too broad a topic for a focused study, and 'reference' is not much better. We will necessarily concentrate on selected aspects of how Maya speakers use their language to talk about their world. As a paradigm case of reference, the book focuses narrowly on *deixis*, including pronouns and perceptual and spatial adverbs corresponding roughly to

English 'I, you, this, that, here', and 'there'. The term **deictic** in traditional grammar designates (roughly) linguistic elements which specify
the identity or placement in space or time of individuated objects relative
to the participants in a verbal interaction.[2] English 'this', for instance, in
one of its central uses, identifies a specific object given in the immediate
spatial proximity of the speaker who utters the form. This evidently well-
delimited phenomenon, involving a small number of linguistic constructions, gives us the kind of specificity needed in order to address more
general questions. My main thesis is that deixis, both as a linguistic subsystem and as a kind of act, is a *social construction*, central to the organization of communicative practice and intelligible only in relation to a
sociocultural system. Conversely, this broader system is cast in a new and
interesting light when viewed through the prism of deictic reference, a
topic understudied in current ethnographic research but of considerable
import to anthropology.

1.2 DEIXIS AND ITS DOUBLE

The literature on deixis is extensive and spread over several disciplines,
but as Levinson (1983:61) pointed out, there has been relatively little
thorough description of actual deictic usage, and there exists at present no
adequate framework in which to integrate the diverse facets of the phenomenon. Many specific proposals have been put forth and some have
had a significant influence on the approach worked out in this book.
These will be treated in detail in the following pages. At this point, I wish
to call attention to three orienting assumptions that have informed much
of the research on deixis, without attempting to trace their specific histo-
ries or attach them to particular works. These assumptions I call the 'concreteness', 'subjectivity', and 'isolation' of deixis.

The *concreteness* of deixis lies in the immediate, unquestioned character of the sense of 'here-now'. We all live in space, in our bodies, in our
perceptual fields, in motion, engaged in our various everyday activities.
This lived space usually has the appearance of naturalness, given to us the
way our own body is, as the vehicle, the stage, and the object of experience at the same time. We recall the past and anticipate the future,
stretching out in time the here-now that we inhabit, submitting it to succession, duration, and interval. But these facts do not usually call into
question the impression of immediacy that attaches to the 'I-here-now'
and that leads common sense to accord an objective reality to that which
one can see, witness, touch, take in the hand, indicate as 'this', and af-
firm as real 'here and now'.

Paired with the concreteness of body space and deixis is the natural assumption that the center of space, the zero point, is a person; the individual who inhabits the body by which spatial experience is constructed. From this it follows quickly that the immediate space of 'here' takes on a *subjective* appearance. To ponder the construction of 'here-now' is to ask how the subject places himself or herself in the physical world. The subject determines the point of departure of an oriented perspective which can enter into relations of reciprocity with others but which remains unique. Moreover, the action that takes place 'here-now', such as the production of speech, is often executed by a single actor engaged as agent. One says naturally, 'I-here-now', not 'they-here-now' or even 'we-here-now'. The tendency to view immediate experienced space from an individual angle, stronger in some approaches than in others, imports a subjectivity and egocentrism into the notion of 'here'. The real present would be at once concrete and subjective, substantial and individual.

To think about the immediate present is often, perhaps inevitably, to think about speech. Verbal acts constitute discourse space, as Benveniste remarked, creating a speaker, a location, and a moment of utterance that are utterly unique and always changing. All human languages provide systems of deictic terms with which speakers can designate objects in these emerging, utterance-relative dimensions. Thanks to their indexical ground in action, deictic expressions seem to participate in the concreteness and subjectivity of lived space. For a number of reasons, they have been shown to stand apart from other semantic resources in language.[3] For one thing, as Russell (1940:109) put it, a term like 'this' "merely designates an object without in any degree describing it." It has the special property that "it applies on each occasion of its use to only one thing, but to different things on different occasions" (111). From a grammatical perspective, deictics often have distinctive morphological and syntactic distributions in language and belong to closed paradigms. Alongside concreteness and subjectivity, therefore, we can add the property of the *functional isolation* of deictics within language. Benveniste, Bühler, and Jakobson, for instance, all insisted that the structure of deixis in language is basically distinct from that of nondeictic elements. The source of this uniqueness is the indexical foundation of these forms: deictics appear to stand apart from the rest of language the way the concrete space of an experience in process stands apart from the abstract space of a symbolic map.

These three guiding assumptions derive ultimately, in my opinion, from what phenomenologists call the 'natural attitude', that is, the unquestioned apprehension of experience in everyday life. While analysis and evidence may be marshaled in support of one or another of them, the strength of influence exerted by these ideas is due rather to their seductive appeal to common sense. Russell inhabited the perceptual zone that he contrasted to the God's eye view of physics, describing it eloquently as "a region which is specially warm and intimate and bright, surrounded in all directions by gradually growing darkness" (1940:108). Bühler lived in the Zeigfeld he so lucidly analyzed. My treatment of the here-now in this book is inevitably rooted in my commonsense understanding of experiences and interactions here and among Maya people. It would be pointless to repudiate common sense, but fieldwork and anthropological training force one to bracket its ready assumptions.

Throughout this book, I will argue for three alternatives to the preceding views. The proximal zone of an activity has the appearance of concreteness, but it is a false appearance. The relation between an agent, the agent's body, the location of action, and the conventional categories of language and gesture is a social construction par excellence. Far from the simple naturalness of things given as objects in the world, our ways of understanding the body and of inhabiting its spaces rest on an immense stock of social knowledge. Available in the form of unreflective common sense and habit, what Bourdieu calls 'habitus', this knowledge orients and naturalizes action. It serves as a measure of objectivity and provides the categories in which we delimit what is verifiably here-now. The intuition of subjectivity is most productive when encompassed by the recognition that the speaking subject is never more than a part in a social relation, and that the subject is, as they say, social even in his or her solitude. In assuming egocentricity in deixis, one runs the risk of mistaking a part for the whole, overlooking several basic facts: interaction puts in play the reciprocity of perspectives, the production of mutual knowledge, conflict, and asymmetry. Through its engagements, the body is constantly in the process of transcending its own epidermal limits. Moreover, utterances are in significant respects 'dialogically' constructed in Bakhtin's (1981) terms, which erodes the notion that a single utterance naturally corresponds to a single speaker (see also Ducrot 1984:chap. 8).

In place of egocentricity, therefore, this book will return continually to the **sociocentricity** of deictic reference. Not only is the speaking 'ego' a social construction, but the act of deictic reference is in important ways grounded on the relation between interlocutors. When speakers say 'Here it is', he or she unavoidably conveys something like, 'Hey, you and I stand in a certain relation to each other and to this object and this place, right now'. The interactive relation among participants exerts a pervasive and systematic influence on the micro-orientations inherent in deictic reference. In the course of this book, I will try to develop an appropriately precise way of talking about this social mediation.

It is true that 'shifters' are functionally distinct, as most of the major works on the topic have shown (for instance, Bühler [1934] 1967; Jakobson [1957] 1971; Silverstein 1976b), and I have argued elsewhere (Hanks 1989b). We can nonetheless clarify our understanding of deixis by focusing on the fundamental relations that link it to other mechanisms of spatial apprehension and representation and that link the immediate zone of action to the social field beyond it. In order to bring out the full anthropological import of deixis, it is necessary to integrate it as clearly as possible into the larger context of social life. This requires detailed attention to both its uniqueness and its continuity with other semiotic phenomena. In particular, I will try to show that Maya deixis is related in basic and very significant ways to a range of other orientational systems in the Maya world. These include cultural understandings of the human body, the social organization of the household and domestic space, cardinal point orientation, agricultural practices whereby the land is transformed and goods produced, and the ritual enactments corresponding to all of the foregoing.

My ethnographic claim is that these are core spaces in Maya society and culture, whose contours and divisions are a basic part of the use and understanding of the language in general, including deictics. Rather than isolate the phenomenon, therefore, I will try to show the ways in which it serves as a unifying mechanism and a key to understanding apparently disjunct aspects of social life. I want to show that the referential use of a word like 'this' or 'here' in conversation may have as much social and cultural loading as a deference-coded address form, although the loading is different and less obvious. As we work towards a clearer sense of this, the idea of 'space' itself will be modified and partly replaced by action-centric ones like 'copresence', 'participant access', and the 'relative symmetry' of interactive relations.

Another aspect of the relational definition of deixis is its contribution to discourse. Beyond providing the means for individuating particular referents in context, deictic expressions also play an important role in the organization of information within texts. They subserve the cohesion relations explored by Halliday and Hasan (1976) and others by maintaining reference in anaphoric chains, but they also provide means for introducing new referents into discourse. Deictics ground the discourse in which they occur in the broader context of its production, connecting text to participants, circumstances, and the actual conditions of interaction. In so doing, they provide a crucial point of contact between discourse and the sociocultural body. This function has further implications for the description of discourse genres. Genres incorporate characteristic deictic configurations, requiring distinct types of production and reception frameworks (Hanks 1987a, 1989a). Hence, both internal to text and in the embedding of text in context, deixis is a basic mode of articulation. I underscore this relational matrix in order to emphasize that the notions of embodiment and centering needed to describe demonstrative usage can never be reduced to the physical placement of bodies in space. Nor does all discourse rest on a single unifying ground to which deixis could be an anchor. Rather, interactive relations change over time, and with them the grounds of reference change, the two affecting one another in an ongoing fashion. What is compelling about deixis is not that it lays down stakes in the world of objects, but that it is a semiotic resource for aligning and integrating different orders of communicative phenomena.

1.3 LINGUISTIC PRACTICE

The word 'practice' in the title of this book indexes an important orientation in my approach. For heuristic purposes, we can distinguish between the three broad views of language. The first, which Vološinov ([1929] 1986) called 'abstract objectivism', is committed to the view that language is a system unto itself, with an inner logic irreducibly distinct from other social and conceptual systems. Although called into question by linguists as diverse as Bolinger (1965), Friedrich (1979a), and Lakoff (1987) and increasingly attacked in cognitive studies (e.g., Eco et al. 1988; Johnson 1987), the objectivist view is the legacy of Saussure, traditionally preferred by grammarians and semanticists (for obvious reasons). In opposition to objectivism, Vološinov described what he called 'individual subjectivism', which views language as the fleeting creation of subjects engaged in unique acts of expression. While the first view emphasizes rules and systems, the second focuses on the plasticity and potential creativity of language, along with the reducibility of its laws to those of psychology.

The third view is distinct from both of the first two and developed partly out of an attempt to transcend the dichotomies on which they are based. Following Bourdieu, its primary source, I will call this third alternative 'practice'. Unlike objectivism, a practice approach locates language in the situated processes of verbal communication and foregrounds the articulation of speech with other aspects of the social world. Unlike subjectivism, it brackets the notion of freewheeling creativity and rejects the attempt to reduce language to individual psychology. It is because it attempts to treat speech as a form of action fully embedded in the social world that practice theory holds out promise for an anthropology of language. While I will try to develop a detailed perspective on referential practices over the course of the book, by way of preparation, it will be helpful at this point to outline its major components in broad strokes.[4]

Among the key terms in practice theory, the ones most central in this book are the replacement of 'rules' by **schema** and **strategies**, the notion of **habitus**, the orientation of verbal action to the contexts of its **production** and **reception**, and the **embodiment** of language. These ideas are not all unique to the study of practice, and they do not exhaust the approach, but they do form a set of interrelated working concepts that can contribute significantly to the study of language use while joining it more deeply to social theory. While linguists have paid considerable attention to language use, and 'pragmatics' is an expanding subfield within the discipline (see, for instance, Levinson 1983), the concept of 'rules' has until recently exercised considerable influence over pragmatic theorizing.[5] The idea is that the inherent potential of words for achieving certain communicative effects can be described in terms of rules mapping verbal forms (such as 'I promise') into speech acts (such as promising) whose felicitous execution depends upon speakers following preestablished norms. Thus, one finds 'rules of reference' (Searle 1969), 'rules for ritual insults' (Labov 1972b), 'rules of use' (Silverstein 1976b), 'rules' operating on turn units in conversation (Levinson 1983:298). These studies have made significant contributions to our understanding of speech, and there is no doubt that the generalizations incorporated in the metaphor of rules play a significant role in conversational practices.

It seems to me, nonetheless, that in phrasing generalizations about language use in terms of rules, one focuses too narrowly on the conventionalized and automatic correspondences between linguistic forms and contextual variables (however these are defined). Like the rules of grammar, the rules of use constitute a normative system. What they do not constitute is an account of what speakers actually do with language or how they formulate and understand utterances. It is important to distinguish at the outset between several kinds of rules. Grammatical rules describe the linguistic forms that serve as the means of verbal action. These are at a distinct analytic level from the kind of rule one might propose to describe the hierarchical structure of textual units such as the episode, or interactive units such as a conversational opening. Rules of this sort define act types in relation to a larger contextual framework and are sensitive to indirection, stylistic variation, and subtle differences in expressive ends. As Gumperz (1977:196) pointed out (discussing the contributions of Harvey Sacks), processes of conversational inference are quite different from grammatical rules, in that there are many alternative interpretations available at any point in a conversation rather than a single categorial possibility, and interactants often play off and use this multiplicity.

Of course, any good system of rules can be applied to ambiguous, multiple, and extended cases, but the point is that it treats these as departures from the normative patterns, and it leaves us always a step removed from the question of why a speaker says such and such on a specific occasion, and how this saying is interpreted by an interlocutor. By way of rules, so to speak, we can trace out the lines on the playing field and state the regulations precisely, but we never really get to the question of how the game is played from the players' perspectives. We get a script and an empty stage but no action, because the actors remain anonymous and disembodied. Even from a more restricted semantic perspective, the literal meaning of expressions can be securely defined only by taking them together with some larger social framework that includes agents acting out different interests. As soon as one moves to this level, as one must to deal with interaction, a major difference between grammar and practice emerges: whereas it might make sense to describe grammar as an infinitely generative device, since the set of grammatical sentences in any language is infinite, there is no corresponding infinity in the use of those sentences in context. Even if the set of all possible communicative acts were open-ended, the access that agents have to these acts is virtually always constrained, and the constraints are a key part of what must be described.

Grice's theory of implicature retains this anonymity but represents a significant shift away from rules to the concept of 'maxims' (see §2.2). These state very general principles of interaction such as 'make your contribution as informative as is required' and 'be relevant'. Grice's maxims set vague guidelines on talk but do not seek to associate determinate meanings with specific linguistic forms. The calculation of implicatures is almost always multiple and susceptible to being cancelled without resulting in anomaly. Further, implicatures, which are assumed to be ubiquitous in conversation, are only generated when speakers apparently fail to follow the maxims. An 'implicature' is that which connects what is literally said with what is situationally conveyed. In a similar vein, Gumperz's (1982) writings on conversational inference have shifted attention from systematic correspondence rules to strategies whereby conversationalists manipulate social and linguistic categories. Coincident with this shift is a move away from the assumptions that interactants must share a system of rules entirely, that to explain is to predict, that the paths of the establishment of meaning make up a closed set of norms. In place of these assumptions, Gumperz focuses on situated interpretations involving partially shared knowledge, context-specific 'contextualization cues' and the frequently ad hoc ways in which speakers attribute intention and make sense of utterances.

Bourdieu's outline of a theory of practice starts from a critique of objectivism in social science, in which he distinguishes three kinds of rule, "the law constructed by science, the transcendent social norm and the immanent regularity of practices" ([1972] 1977:22). The first is a theoretical model devised to describe facts without altering them, the second an institutional percept or standard constraint on behavior that preexists it, and last a (set of) scheme(s) which "exist in a practical state in agents' practice, and not in their consciousness, or rather, their discourse" ([1972] 1977:27). It is the latter that becomes most central under the designation 'scheme'. Unlike theoretical rules and the determinate structures they generate, schemata are implicit, embedded in actual practices, flexible enough to apply to an open-ended list of changing circumstances, and nonpredictive. Being grounded in what actors actually do and not what they say they do, schemata need not be subject to discussion or conscious regulation. They are nonetheless social facts, since they figure in the socially acquired and distributed *présavoir* that actors mobilize in acting. Gumperz (1982) repeatedly emphasizes the importance of interpretive schemata in understanding conversational inference, and cognitive theorists have increasingly focused on the relation between schematic and local knowledge in understanding.[6] It is clear that while these various authors use the same or related terms—scheme, schema, schematic, image schemas—the terms do not all designate the same concepts.[7] For our purposes however, they converge in moving away from the notion of rule-governed systems as ordinarily invoked in studies of language towards action-centered processes of understanding. In this book, I am concerned with the consistent patterns of Maya language use but propose no rules of use. In stating regularities, I will try to draw out what I take to be fundamental schemata in the culture, implicit patterns embedded in practices of reference, house building and habitation, agriculture, and ritual.

The move away from rules is joined with a move away from the idea that coparticipants in talk are guided by (follow, hold others to the mandates of) abstract systems like grammar which they must share in order to understand each other. What is shared is described instead in terms of habitual ways of acting and evaluating actions, what Merleau Ponty and Bourdieu called 'habitus', the lasting dispositions, perceptions, and appreciations that inform action and can be changed by it (Bourdieu [1972]

1977:82–83). Unlike abstract systems, habitus incorporates the perspectivally centered, embodied, 'quasi-postural' anticipations, proclivities, and unreflective experiences of actors (Bourdieu 1985). More a working concept than an analytic category susceptible of definition in terms of necessary and sufficient properties, habitus makes three contributions that have been decisive in my understanding of deixis. It locates the problem of what speakers share at the level of their actual embodied practices rather than in conceptual models. It incorporates the idea of habitual patterns of speech beyond the 'rule-governed' structures of grammar (a central concern of language in culture studies in the Boas-Sapir-Whorf tradition from their beginning). Finally, habitus embraces linguistic facts along with nonlinguistic aspects of social knowledge, thereby helping to build a bridge between issues of verbal practice and social relations more globally.

The bonds between verbal categories, situated understanding, and the human body are evident in a wide array of linguistic phenomena, as Johnson (1987) and Lakoff (1987) have recently argued at length. They are especially compelling in the organization of deixis, because of its unavoidable indexicality and because of the incorporation of perceptual and other corporeally grounded features. Many aspects of deixis can be described only in a vocabulary of bodily engagements, as Bühler ([1934] 1967), Evans (1982) and others have observed. This is pointedly true in the case of Maya, because of its special elaboration of perceptual and actional categories in the meanings of the deictic forms.

It is important to underline at the outset the scope of the terms **bodily** and **embodiment** as they will be used in this book. While we will explore Maya notions of the human body in some detail, it is the grounding of categories in the engaged, active, physically emergent, and socially meaningful processes of interaction that I want to emphasize with the terms. It is the body as culturally constituted and interactively mediated that I will invoke in describing referential practices. This has of course been an area of considerable concern for anthropologists, and my descriptions of the Maya are intended to contribute to the anthropology of the body (cf. Carrithers, Collins, and Lukes 1985; Comaroff 1985; Douglas 1973; Friedrich [1970] 1979a; Munn 1986; Turner 1980). One of my main reasons for drawing more on practice sociology than on cognitive studies, despite the fact that they both use the concepts of schemata and embodiment, is precisely because the former grew out of a social framework and incorporates aspects of socially oriented phenomenology, whereas the latter addresses more directly individual psychology and has as yet incorporated little anthropology and still less phenomenology.[8] Lacking the proper background in psychology and wary of any attempt to reduce social facts to individual ones, I make no 'cognitive' claims for the schemata and practices I will describe in the following pages. On the other hand, I do claim to be describing social facts with a proper place in the anthropology of language in general and the Maya in particular.

The special contribution of deixis to an anthropology of the body turns on the unusual way it incorporates bodily space: not only do speakers make *reference to the body* with deictics, but, more interestingly, they make *reference to the world relative to the body*. When speakers say 'this is it', or 'put it over there', they may identify objective things in objective places with no immediately apparent engagement of the body. But when we realize that the terms 'this' and 'there' are definable only relative to things like an arm's reach or the shared perceptual experiences of interactants within sight of one another, then it becomes clear that the body is indeed engaged. Not as the thing pointed to or categorized but as the origin of the point and the source of the categories. We will draw out as closely as possible this capacity of corporeal experience to serve as an indexical ground in relation to which objects in the world 'outside' are singled out. Through its embeddedness in deictic reference, the social body becomes a ubiquitous part of talk about the world, and by implication, knowledge of it as well.

The last key concept of a practice approach to language is its focus on the production and reception of speech. In trying to specify the conveyed meanings of utterances, I will repeatedly draw attention to the ways in which utterances play upon and contribute to the momentary alignments of their producers and receivers. This has several aspects, starting with the fact that in this book, we will concentrate heavily on actual attested utterances rather than on hypothetical ones adduced to display distinctions. This does not derive from a rejection of hypothetical examples or of deductive reasoning but rather from a recognition that in order to get an accurate sense of deictic usage, it is imperative that we start from actual cases. Another corollary of focusing on actual instances is that the idea of social **fields** will come into play in our attempts to describe the contexts of linguistic production. Along with habitus, field is one of the main ideas developed in Bourdieu's sociology (see, for instance, Bourdieu 1980, 1984, 1985). Roughly, a field is constituted as an array of positions occupied by actors competing over capital, such as the field of literary production in France or agricultural production in Yucatán. In Bourdieu's writing, discussions of field and strategy are overlain by terminology derived from economics and divisions of class, whereas in the present study, we shall concentrate mainly on small-scale communicative processes and the linguistic resources they embody. The most important point from the perspective of deictic reference and address is that speakers do not exchange words in a vacuum but are oriented to and constrained by the asymmetric distributions of 'cultural capital' (in the form of prestige, knowledge, and sanctioned access to recognized modes of speaking, rights over space and objects). The act of making deictic reference, I will try to show, is in itself a taking up of position in the field in which it is performed, and Maya speakers' choices of deictic terms for reference reflect the tension inherent in all position taking. This tension counterbalances the infinity of linguistic forms defined by grammar, since it sets limits and costs on speakers' access to the forms. But a practice approach also seeks to describe aspects of action that are habituated and enacted unreflectively rather than only known and used for specific purposes. The relations between utterers and their words are mediated by the stock of sociocultural knowledge, by their embodied habits and routinized modes of expression, by the asymmetries characteristic of any field, and by the contingent interactive relations of which talk is a part.

Reference is a social practice, then, and deixis is a species of reference. When Maya speakers use their language interactively to talk about the world, how do they individuate, identify, and describe objects? How do they locate themselves relative to these objects and to each other in the act of reference itself? The study of deixis shows that such self-positioning is an unavoidable part of talk about the world, at least insofar as such talk entails the individuation of objects. Once we bracket the natural attitude for which here-now is concrete, egocentric, and essentially distinct from other mediated representations of reality, interesting questions arise. How do Maya speakers categorize deictic space? How do they occupy it? What are its component dimensions, and what kinds of communicative acts are simultaneously performed in deictic use? How in deixis do they **create** interactive context? In a practice-based anthropology of language, the answers to these questions are sought in the sociocultural schemata with which deictic categories articulate, in the processes of production and reception of deictic messages, in the habitus relative to which the language is understood, and in the embodiment of the system in interaction between actually engaged coparticipants. These overlapping foci offer us a starting point from which to progressively sharpen the approach and work towards at least provisory answers.

1.4 SKETCH OF THE MAYA DEICTIC SYSTEM

The special interest of the Maya deictic system does not derive from the sheer number or complexity of distinctions encoded. Other languages, such as Santali (Bodding 1929; Zide 1972), Malagasy (Anderson and Keenan 1985:292ff; Hanks 1986), Inuktitut Eskimo (Denny 1984), and Nunggubuyu (Heath 1980) encode as many or more oppositions in different categories. The best examples of quantity and mechanical productivity of deictic forms come, not from Mayan, but from the Eskimo Aleut language family (Bergsland 1951; Jacobson 1984:653ff; Reed et al. 1977). Rather, what makes Maya deixis linguistically interesting and important is the combination of three factors: the elaborate grammaticalization of deixis in the language, the kinds of features it encodes beyond spatial and temporal proximity (including three types of perception, certainty, presentative as opposed to referential forms, egocentric versus sociocentric space), and the interactions between the features. We find encoded in the Maya forms communicative effects conveyed only contextually or through periphrasis in languages such as English. These features combine in highly restricted ways, so that, for instance, only Perceptual forms are conventionally Presentative in force; only Spatial Locatives encode Egocentric as opposed to non-Egocentric regions; only Egocentric forms distinguish Inclusion from Exclusion. Such interactions give powerful evidence of the relations between functions and can help shed light on the structure of deictic systems in other languages. They can also teach us about the contextual structures and modes of communicative action that make up referential practice, thereby contributing to the anthropological dimensions of the study.

The specific focus of the book is a subset of the deictic forms displayed in table 1.1. Most of these are composed of two morphemes, a base (displayed on the vertical axis, labeled Initial Deictics), plus a suffixal or enclitic element (displayed across the horizontal axis, labeled Terminal Deictics). These two order classes will henceforth be called ID and TD, respectively. A deictic construction, such as *té?el o?* 'there (non-Immediate)', is a combination of two morphemes, each of which occurs in other constructions as well (cf. *té?el a?*, *hé?el o?*). The recurrence of forms is indicative of a more extensive set of grammatical interrelations that unite them into distinct categories (such as the Ostensive Evidential adverbs, the Locative adverbs, or the Participant deictics) and unite constructions from different categories (compare all forms ending in the TD *a?* or *o?*).

Some of the general features of Maya deictics can be shown by simple examples. There are two main surface shapes in which the constructions occur: *continuous* and *discontinuous*. Sentences (1–2) show the continuous shape, in which ID and TD are immediately adjacent, and (3–4) show the discontinuous, in which they flank some intervening lexical material, a noun phrase in (3) and a prepositional phrase in (4). (Abbreviations are glossed in note *a* to table 1.1 and in the List of Abbreviations.)

(1)   **hé'el a'**
        OSTEV TD
        'Here it is (presenting).'

(2)   ȼ'áah   **té'el o'**
        Vb-Imper DLOC TD
        'Put it there.'

(3)   **hé'el** a   maáskab' **a'**
        OSTEV Pro2 N   TD
        'Here's your machete (presenting).'

(4)   ȼ'áah   **té'** ič   k'oób'en o'
        Vb-Imper DLOC Prep N   TD
        'Put it there in (the) kitchen.'

A second general distinction is the one between pronominal, prolocative, prosentential (etc.) uses and adnominal, adlocative, and adsentential ones. The first two examples are prosentential and prolocative, respectively, because the deictic element is the only one standing for the constituent in question. The third and fourth examples are adsentential and adlocative modifiers, because the deictics are further elaborated by lexical description. Most Maya deictics have in common that they may be used in either *pro-X* or *ad-X* functions, and that they occur in both continuous and discontinuous shapes.

The labels Initial and Terminal Deictic are meant to capture the relative placement of the forms in sentences. IDs always occur in initial position in the constituent for which they are marked, be it the Sentence, the Noun Phrase, or various Circumstantial adverbial phrases, and they always precede TDs, even when the two parts are discontinuous. TDs, on the other hand, always occur in final position in the sentence or topic phrase. So in (3), the sentence is introduced by the OSTEV base, which functions as the sole predicate, and the TD is in final position. In (4), the DLOC base *té'* introduces the locative phrase, and the TD is final. If the locative phrase is focused or otherwise moved in the sentence, the ID base goes with it and may occur in S-initial position, but the TD still occurs S-final, as in (5).

(5)   *té'* ič   k'oób'en kuȼ'á'ab'al   *o'*
        DLOC Prep N   Aux-Pro3-Vb TD
        'There in (the) kitchen (is where) it is put.'

The regularity of these generalizations is prima facie evidence that the deictics in this language are united in a single system. In subsequent

TABLE 1.1 Synopsis of Maya Deictics

ID Base[a]		Terminal Deictics						Gloss
		a?	o?	b'e?	i?	e?	∅	
OSTEV	hé?e(l)	hé?el a?						'Here it is (Tact Pres)'
	hé?e(l)		hé?el o?					'There it is (Vis Dir)'
	hé?e(l)			hé?e b'e?				'There it is (Aud Dir)'
DMOD	hé?e(l)					hé?el e?		'Indeed, for sure'
DLOC	té?e(l)	té?el a?						'Right there, here (Immed)'
	té?e(l)		té?el o?					'There (Non-Immed)'
	ti?				ti?i?			'There (Anaph)'
	way					way e?		'(In) here (Incl)'
	to(l)		tol o?					'(Out) there (Excl)'
DNOM	le(l)	lel a?						'This one (Immed)'
	le(l)		lel o?					'That one (Non-Immed)'
	le				le ti?			'The one'
	le						le	'The (def art)'

Category				Gloss
PART	t-	t-en		'I (1sg)'
	t-	t-eč		'You (2sg)'
	t-	t-ó'on		'We (1pl)'
	t-	t-é'eš		'You (2pl)'
	le		le ti'	'He, she, it, the one (3sg)'
	le		le ti'-ó'ob'	'They, the ones (3pl)'
DTEMP[b]	walakil	walakil a'		'This time (of day)'
	b'eh'òora	b'eh'òora a'		'Now, presently'
	tolakhéak	tolakhéak o'		'Back then (shared, distant past)'
	b'ehé'el a		b'ehé'elae'	'Now, today, nowadays'
	taánt		taánt e'	'Just (immed past)'
	laáyli		laáyli e'	'Still, even, now'
DMAN	b'ey	b'ey a'		'Like this'
	b'ey	b'ey o'		'Like that, so'
	b'èey		b'èey	'So, thus, since'

---

[a]Grammatical categories of IDS: OSTEV (ostensive evidential adverb); DMOD (deictic modal auxiliary); DLOC (deictic locative adverb); DNOM (deictic nominal); PART (participant deictic); DTEMP (deictic temporal adverb); DMAN (deictic manner adverb).

[b]Partial display of DTEMPS.

chapters, we shall examine the systematicity more closely, with an eye to determining both what the categories share and what makes them distinct.

A number of the ID bases in the left-hand column end in a parenthesized *-l-*. This stands for a standard morphophonemic alternation in which all the forms participate: when in continuous shape or when followed by a vowel-initial suffix, the *-l-* is obligatorily present (as in the forms in the table). When the ID is followed by an independent word, whether or not it begins in a vowel, the base-final *-l* is optionally omitted (and usually is omitted in routine conversation; cf. examples 3–5). Thus, (3) could equally well be rendered *hé?a maáskab'a?*, with no base-final *-l*. When followed by a consonant, the final *-l* is obligatorily omitted; hence *hé? maáskab'aa?* 'here's (a) machete,' and not **hé?el maáskab' a?*. $V_1?V_1$ clusters are usually reducible in Maya to $V?$, and the reduction of *é?e* to *é?* follows this rule. When speaking in general of the ID bases as types, I will cite them in the *hé?*, *té?*, *le* variants, for simplicity. When citing attested tokens, obviously, I will transcribe the form as uttered.

Starting at the top of table 1.1, the first three forms, all based on the ID *hé?*, make up the Ostensive Evidential adverbs. These are conventionally directive and presentative in force and differ from one another by the modes of perceptual access they signal, as reflected in the glosses. *hé?el e?* is a modal auxiliary (hence DMOD) signaling speaker certainty without current perceptual evidence. Although neither directive nor even referential, this construction is nevertheless based on the same ID as the others, the abstract meaning of which is evidently 'certain'. The existence of this series of forms is significant, because it challenges the assumption that space and time are always the rudimentary dimensions of deixis. In this case, certainty and perceptual verifiability are basic, and space is a secondary corollary. This shift is one step in a more global move away from traditional accounts of deixis, in which the location of a referent in the objective world is assumed to be primary. In this study, I argue for a more fine-grained and pragmatically revealing approach in which speaker-addressee **Access** to referents is primary. Sometimes the access is indeed spatial, but in other cases it turns on sensory availability, memory, or commonsense knowledge.

There are five locative deictics (DLOCs) in Maya, used for reference to place. The first two, based on the ID *té?*, usually refer to places of restricted extent (points, as opposed to regions; cf. Eskimo 'restricted' versus 'extended'), according to their relative proximity to the locus of utterance. *tol o?* '(out) there' and *way e?* '(in) here' typically refer to regions (not points), according to whether they include or exclude the speaker at the time of utterance. The significance of this division is that it calls into question empirically the assumption that deictic context is naturally egocentric, by showing that egocentricity is available in languages as a distinctive parameter.[9] It also raises the interesting question of why the egocentric forms in Maya refer to regions dichotomously (inside/outside), while nonegocentric ones distinguish points on a scale of relative immediacy. *tí? i?* 'there' neutralizes all of these distinctions and signals only that the location is known by both interactants from prior knowledge.

There are three nominal deictics (DNOMs) in Maya, aside from the definite article *le,* which serves as the ID base for the category. *lel a?* is used for reference to objects visually or tactually available or new in the discourse. *lel o?* is used for reference to objects visible or simply known by both interactants from background knowledge or prior discourse. Like the DLOC *tí? i?, le ti?* signals no distinctions of relative proximity or sensory access but only that the referent is uniquely identifiable.

Like all of the foregoing forms, the lexical pronouns, or Participant Deictics (PART), are composed of two morphemes, an ID base, in this case *ti? ~ t-* 'to, for, from, at', plus a terminal complement. Instead of the ordinary TDS, the complement in this category is a pronominal suffix, signaling person and number. Since Maya predicates (verbs, predicate nouns, adjectives, some particles) are inflected for subject, object, possessor, and equational subject, the use of independent PART forms is usually grammatically optional. Although they are formally distinct from the other deictic categories, they are functionally related to them insofar as ostensive reference is grounded on the relation between participants. Moreover, the DNOM and PART categories share the form *le ti?* 'the one', and the person suffixes display detailed parallels to the TDS. These will be examined in chapters 4 and 10.

Temporal deictics make up the largest and least regular category in Maya. Because of length limitations, they will not be treated in this book. The interest of the forms can nonetheless be briefly indicated. *walakil a?* and several other forms (some not shown) are used to refer to segments of time in relation to the diurnal cycle in Maya everyday life. *b'eh?òora a?* refers to 'now' starting at the moment of utterance and anticipating into the proximate future. *tolakhéak o?,* obviously derived from the DLOC *tol o?,* refers to a stretch of time typically prior to the day of utterance and recalled by both interactants. *b'ehé?el a? e?,* obviously derived from the OSTEV *hé?el a?,* is used to refer to a point in the very near future, to the day of utterance, or more vaguely to 'these days'. These and the remaining temporal deictics pose numerous problems of interpretation and will have to be the object of a future study.

A final category not treated in this book is the Manner adverbial deictics. Based on the ID *b'ey* ~ *b'èey* 'thus, so, like so', these are the least differentiated in the system, and their meanings are multiple and relatively difficult to specify precisely. *b'èey* is used to signal cross-clause relations conveyed by English 'since (because)', as in 'since you cannot go, I will', and 'so', as in 'so you can't go then'. It is also used to signal approximation or uncertainty, as in *b'èey lás ʔòonseh* 'around, about eleven'. *b'èey* and *b'ey oʔ* often summarize preceding discourse, bringing it to a momentary point of closure, as in 'so that's that', 'so then'. *b'ey oʔ* is also used in reference to currently visible states of affairs. In nearly all cases, it conveys that the referent or proposition is already given for both interactants. *b'ey aʔ*, by contrast, is used for new or anticipated referents or ones tactually available to the speaker. Although it will take further research to clarify the functions of these forms, it is clear that they pose questions regarding the boundary between deixis and nondeixis. In fact, forms in all categories have what appear to be nondeictic usages, which suggests that for the purposes of natural language description, deixis may be best seen as a gradient phenomenon.[10]

Thus, the different categories of Maya deixis raise different issues that have consequences for how we describe reference and embodiment. The TDS convey different specific meanings depending upon the ID with which they are combined, but their relative values remain consistent across categories. All *aʔ* constructions signal perceptual, spatial, or temporal immediacy or anticipation of a referent. They are associated with high-focus gestures (presenting in hand, touching, pointing to the referent) referring to unique objects (as opposed to classes or vaguely known ones), with new (as opposed to already shared) information. *oʔ* conveys less immediate spatial, perceptual, or temporal access, accompanied by less exacting gestures (point, wave, glance), maintenance of shared information (anaphora, reference to prior talk), or shared background knowledge. Deictics ending in *oʔ* usually identify unique objects but may be generic (*le ʔok'ot oʔ* 'dancing, that dance') or hypothetical (*le maák oʔ* 'that person', parallel to English 'imagine *this* person comes up to you'). *b'eʔ* is a specialized marker of nontactual, nonvisual perceptual evidence, which usually identifies a referent by its sound. *iʔ* falls outside the perceptual and spatial zones of deictic context entirely and signals only that the referent is known by both interactants. *eʔ* is a semantically empty placeholder that contributes nothing to the identification of the referent.

In this book, I try to relate the conventional meanings of this subsystem of Maya language to patterns of everyday verbal practice and to the sociocultural world in which it takes place. We will explore in detail questions such as, How do speakers constitute the boundaries between here and there in routine talk, relative to other kinds of spatial divisions given in the schematic background of speech? How do they occupy participant roles? What precisely is the role of perceptual experience in ostensive reference? And how is it combined with other aspects of the communicative process? How do linguistic features articulate with specific aspects of extralinguistic context? How do Maya speakers produce and transform the sociocultural relations that we label 'space'? How can we properly characterize the embodiment and cultural definition of deixis without entirely losing the distinction between language and nonlanguage? While we will focus continually on the social saturation of Maya language, the evidence that the grammar of deixis *does* form a bounded system is, in my opinion, overwhelming. It will be the main focus of chapter 10, where we summarize the global properties of deixis in this language and culture.

1.5 SYNOPSIS OF THIS BOOK

The linguistic and anthropological dimensions of this book are therefore merged rather than juxtaposed. The framework for the merger is derived from pragmatics, interactional sociolinguistics, symbolic and practice-based anthropology. Part 1 consists of the first three chapters, which outline the social basis of reference in Maya discourse. In the present chapter, I have tried briefly to indicate the questions to which the study is directed and the potential significance of the topic for an anthropology of language. My reasons for emphasizing communicative practices over structures and rules follow partly from the nature of deixis as a system embodied in action and partly from a desire to contribute to a deeper understanding of verbal reference and semantics as social phenomena.

Chapter 2 makes explicit the theory of reference on which the analysis is based. It outlines reference from three perspectives: as a communicative activity (§2.1), as a functional potential of the semantic system (§2.2), and as a commonsense construct (§2.3). The individuation of objects in conversation is an interactive achievement possible only within a socially constituted world in which coparticipants already share a frame of reference and a sense of typicality. At the same time that they share common sense and many basic value orientations, coparticipants in talk are virtually always asymmetric in some senses. As Brown and Gillman ([1960] 1972), Errington (1988), Friedrich (1966), Silverstein (1976b), and others have shown, shifters tend to be especially sensitive to such asymmetries. For our purposes, what is most significant is the fact that the social asymmetries among coparticipants in talk constrain the kinds of deictic categories they can use in making reference. The linguistic frame-

work of the book is presented as a 'semantics of understanding', akin to
the approach taken by Fillmore (1982). It incorporates the analytic concepts of prototypes, frames, and figure-ground structuring. As a commonsense construct, reference depends upon a background of schematic
knowledge embodied in schemata and stereotypes of the kind described
by Bourdieu, Schutz, and some interpretive sociologists. Such knowledge is brought to bear on local interactive processes in the interpretation
of reference. Cicourel's research on the production and distribution of
knowledge provides a bridge between sociological and semantic uses of
schemata. In the final section (§2.4), my approach to reference is summarized and located in relation to social practice more generally. Basic units
and levels to be developed in subsequent chapters are summarized in
order to orient the discussion.

The indexical foundation of deictics and other shifters links them to the
local frame in which they are used, and thereby to the bodily zones of the
interlocutors (§§3.1–3.2). The human body is a cultural construct par
excellence, a lived material in which collective values, oppositions, and
potentials are embodied. Through their engagements, agents continually
enter into relations with other agents and thereby define themselves, locate themselves, and coordinate themselves relative to a social world. The
act of making reference in conversation is one such engagement, and
body space is not merely a physical place but a socially mediated field of
interaction. This means that it is both greater than any individual and
changing from moment to moment. In contemporary Maya society, the
household is another primary field of interaction, in which the orientations of agents are defined, reproduced, and played out (§3.3). These
facts have interesting consequences for the use of language around the
household, and particularly for deictic usage, since different kinds of
agents position themselves differently relative to the world in referring to
it (§§3.4–3.6)

Part 2 includes chapters 4, 5, and 6, which together present the linguistic representation of participant frames in Maya and the engagement
of agents in these frames. The first step is the personal pronouns, or more
accurately, Participant deictics, and the basic categories of participation
(chapter 4). These are central to the study of deixis, because they define a
basic template of participant categories, and it is relative to participants
that deictics are interpreted in talk. Recent work on 'footing' and participation frames by Goffman, Charles and Marjorie Goodwin, and Levinson, among others, has shown the need to reassess critically the notions
of 'speaker', 'addressee', and 'other'. This is used as a point of departure
for examining the relation between the conventional categories of Maya

Participant deictics and the interactive relations relative to which they may be used. A basic-level description is proposed in which the pronouns encode the features Speaker, Addressee, Other, as well as distinctions of number and inclusivity in the first person plural.

The analysis of participant frames continues in chapter 5 with nonbasic uses of the forms, in which the social context and interpretation of shifters are relatively more complex (§5.1). The phenomena described include a variety of decenterings in Maya speech: quotation, transposition in narrative, certain kinds of creative reference, a pattern of usage described here as 'excluded addressee', native Maya metalinguistic discourse (§5.2), and two genres of ritual performance (§5.3). What these patterns of usage have in common is that they involve an interplay between the indexical grounding of pronouns (and other shifters) and the referential interpretation of utterances. They also demonstrate that while the physical body is a fundamental aspect of deictic reference, the indexical ground and participant access to context are more abstract and variable than any physical factor. A descriptively adequate account of participant frames must provide for such cases, by increasing the inventory of roles, increasing the combinations of roles, or both. These alternatives are explored, and a general analysis of frame embeddings is proposed.

Chapter 6 focuses on the incorporation of the participants' perceptual field in reference. Drawing explicitly on the ethnographic description of the body in chapter 3 and the participant frames in chapters 4 and 5, it is shown that the Maya understanding of the senses and their relation to knowledge has a formative role in the deictic system. The focus of the chapter is a specialized category of adverbial deictics, which I have called Ostensive Evidentials (OSTEV in table 1.1). The conventional meanings of these forms incorporate features designating the sensory modality in which interactants have access to objects of reference; tactual, visual, and auditory-olfactory. Interestingly, these perceptual features are combined in the grammar of Maya with the communicative force of directives, conveying 'Take this! Look! Listen! There it is (take a whiff)!' as well as other particularized effects. Because of their perceptual features and directive force, these deictics focalize the bodily coengagement of participants in acts of ostensive reference. They provide a natural bridge between the participant role configurations of the pronouns and the spatial orientations inherent in locative deictics. In the indexical frame of an ongoing interaction, the perceptual fields of participants relate them as corporeal agents, persons actually copresent and therefore also located spatially relative to one another and some larger context. Although interactants need not always be face to face and attending to one another, the possibility of mutual touch, gaze, or listening in a shared perceptual field is a basic condition of the reciprocity of perspectives described by Schutz.

Chapters 7, 8, and 9 make up part 3 of the book, the theme of which is the constitution of social space in Oxkutzcab, the site of my research. This is the context in which we can understand the various heres in which speech occurs. The central thesis is that spatial form is produced in Maya society according to a limited set of schemata which recur across sociocultural domains, *including deixis*. These schemata are part of the background social knowledge that Maya speakers share in varying degrees and bring to bear in formulating and interpreting utterances (§7.1). The description begins with cardinal orientation, distinguishing two patterns of use, an action-relative one in which the cardinal terms designate directions relative to a speaker-addressee ground, and an absolute usage in which they designate fixed cosmological places (§7.2). The former has the logical properties of body space, being trajectories from a center, while the latter has the properties of a coordinate grid with intersecting dimensions but no privileged center. Regions, paths, and landmarks around Oxkutzcab are described in §7.3, to give the reader a concrete overview of the place and local ways of describing it. Next, domestic space is described in terms of its production over time, perimeters, and internal subdivisions, and ritual transformations in shamanic performance (§7.4). The discussion is explicitly tied back to chapter 3, where the social organization of household coresidents was outlined. Space in the homestead is a concrete embodiment of social processes, the expansion and contraction of residence groups being projected into the development of the places they inhabit. In ritual performance, much of which is focused on the maintenance of well-being in bodily and domestic space, the household is iconically represented on the altar and in the discourse of prayers. By putting bodily, domestic, and ritually defined spatial schemata side by side, we can see basic commonalities among them. These will become powerful tools in explaining the kinds of distinctions and orientations encoded in Maya spatial deictics, as well as the presupposed contexts of their use (chapters 9–10).

The Maya are traditionally farmers, and their construction of lived space cannot be understood in isolation from their agricultural practices. The process of swidden clearing, burning, planting, weeding, and harvesting products of the field embodies an ongoing cycle of activities in which actors locate themselves both spatially and temporally. These processes are described and shown to involve the transformation of space in accordance with regular principles and recurrent schemata (§8.2). Major ritual ceremonies that punctuate and effect aspects of the process are then outlined, again showing that the treatment of ritual altars iconically reproduces the spaces being acted on in the performance (§8.3). The last section of the chapter is a cumulative summary of the spatial schemata and relations uncovered up to this point in the book (§8.4). It brings together body space, cardinal points, elementary spatial configurations in the local environment, ritual representations, domestic spaces, and agricultural spaces in a series of schematic figures. These help us make explicit some of the vast social frame of reference that Maya speakers assume in their speech, and that is embedded in their deictic system.

Chapter 9 analyzes the linguistic forms of spatial deixis in Maya, starting with comparison and contrast between them and other locational descriptors in the language (§9.1). It is argued in §9.2 that the forms encode relatively abstract features on two axes: (i) space as a bounded region centered on the speaking ego, distinguishing Inclusive from Exclusive dichotomously; and (ii) space as an array of segmented parts, distinguishing relatively Immediate from non-Immediate to the interactive ground. These dimensions constitute a basic-level spatial frame that speakers use in routine ways in talk. Section 9.3 summarizes deictic space and compares the schemata embodied in it to the ones in chapter 8. The objective is to motivate the linguistic categories and the routine practices in which they are used by grounding them in the sociocultural system in which the body and the spatial world are constituted.

Chapters 10 and 11 make up part 4 of the book, in which the Participant, Nominal, Ostensive Evidential, and Locative deictics are unified in a single system, which is then situated in referential practice. Chapter 10 builds directly on chapters 4, 5, 6, and 9, relating the linguistic categories to one another and analyzing relatively complex utterances in which shifters are combined and cointerpreted. These construction types include mainly focus, emphasis, and reduplicative structures which are peculiar to deictics in Maya grammar, and which operate systematically on forms of all categories (§10.2). They contribute to the iconicity that binds different categories to one another in the unity of the system, and binds message forms to their communicative effects in the unity of an utterance. In §10.3, the overlapping of deictic categories is examined, and a general account of the Terminal Deictics is proposed. The formal segmentation between Initial (ID) and Terminal (TD) forms corresponds to a functional segmentation between different aspects of the act of demonstrative reference, namely, the orientation of interactants to the character of a referent and its role in a predication (signaled by the ID) and the indexical grounding of the referent in a given portion of the interactive framework (signaled by the TD). In the final section (§10.4), the system is summarized as an aggregate frame of reference whose categories are understood relative to indexical processes in Maya verbal practice.

Chapter 11 concludes the book with a cumulative statement of the main thesis and the consequences that follow from it. The thesis is that reference in natural language is an oriented social engagement, a form (or various forms) of practice. In referring, a speaker takes up a footing in the world, both as it is described and as it is apprehended in the immediate copresent of the utterance. As a conventional verbal resource, deixis is not an isolated peculiarity in the organization of language in culture but rather a core construct, as basic even as body space, domestic space, and other lived spaces in which social reality is produced and reproduced. The very appearance of self-evidence and objectivity that attach to indexical constructs like 'here' is indicative of their embeddedness in common sense and of their potential to structure experience. When one looks closely, here-now really has little of the simple concreteness often accorded it in philosophical and linguistic descriptions. Here is not a place in any straightforward sense but a socially mediated field of experience, in which a vast array of knowledge is brought to bear by interactants. This knowledge figures prominently in the understanding and formulation of speech and so is relevant to the sociopragmatic description of discourse, even narrowly conceived. Conversely, despite its knotty and esoteric appearance, referential deixis in language can serve for anthropologists as a key to fundamental aspects of the social and cultural constitution of experience.

2 A Relational Approach to Demonstrative Reference

The objective of this chapter is to establish a basic language in which to describe and integrate the dimensions of deictic reference. In labeling the approach 'relational', I wish to foreground one of the central characteristics of linguistic practice: the constituents of practice are not reducible to simple objects but are themselves relations. As I pointed out in chapter 1, the impulse to objectify and concretize is especially strong in the case of deictic reference, with its apparently "compulsive" (to borrow Peirce's term) connection to the world. But we need to get beyond this appearance, to examine the semiotic processes that produce it and that anchor reference in sociocultural contexts. These processes have various components, or 'moments', requiring a language of description drawn from a range of theoretical frameworks. They break down into three main parts: reference as a communicative activity (§2.1), as a feature of the conventional semantics of language (§2.2), and as an object of native speaker commonsense reasoning (§2.3). Although the framework will be elaborated further in subsequent chapters, the terms introduced here make up the baseline from which we will work. By way of introduction, it will be useful to make explicit several assumptions which, until further notice, will underlie the discussion.

A pragmatic account of deixis must situate it in relation to three levels of 'meaning': (i) the conceptual structures which it embodies as a linguistic code, (ii) how these structures are mobilized by native actors in the interactive process, and (iii) how they articulate with socially grounded understandings of speech acts. Harman ([1968] 1971) demonstrated the fruitfulness of distinguishing the three, and the problems that can result from confusing them. The first kind of meaning will consist of the conventional values of deictic forms, whereby they represent referential objects according to certain encoded categories. The second engages the interplay between intention and interpretation in situated deictic use, and the third extends the functional matrix beyond mere reference to the ac-

companying and consequent acts that speakers perform. The union of
Harman's three levels make up what Fillmore (1985:222) called a "semantics of understanding." U semantics "takes as its assignment that of
providing a general account of the relation between linguistic texts, the
contexts in which they are instanced and the process and products of their
interpretation. "Such a theory, as Fillmore emphasizes, does not begin
with a body of assumptions about what aspects of the understanding process belong to linguistics proper and what aspects belong to other cooper-
ating systems of belief and reasoning. Rather, it seeks to integrate the
levels of meaning, arriving at the division between language system and
use only after extensive observations. It is towards a U semantics of deictic practice that this book is directed.

With respect to the role of deixis in communication (level 2), we start
from what has come to be called 'speaker reference' (Donnellan [1978]
1979); Kripke [1977] 1979). According to Donnellan ([1978] 1979), a
speaker's reference, as opposed to a semantic reference, consists in what
the person has in mind to talk about in uttering an expression. That is, it is
linked to the individual's intention to uniquely identify some object or set
of objects. Since not all utterances are performed with this kind of intention, and since intention is no guarantee of communicative success,
'speaker reference' so defined should be taken to designate some aspects
of deictic practice, but not all. 'Semantic reference', in contrast, describes the relation between the language and what it represents on a
given occasion (not the language user and what [s]he intends to convey).
This distinction underlies Donnellan's earlier one between referential and
attributive uses of definite descriptions (Donnellan [1968] 1971), both of
which are subcases of speaker's reference. It can be seen as a development of Grice's ([1957] 1971) theory of non-natural meaning.[1]

Grice set apart the intentionally constituted 'meaning' of a speaker
('meaning$_{nn}$') from the 'natural meaning' of such things as 'spots (that)
mean measles', and a 'recent budget (that) means a rough upcoming
year'. Cases of the former can be recognized by five differentiae: (i) the
statement 'x means$_{nn}$ that p' does not entail p (so 'that remark means that
he didn't go' does not entail that he did not in fact go); (ii) we can argue
from 'x means$_{nn}$ that p' to something about 'what was meant$_{nn}$ by x' (from
'that remark means he won't go' to 'what that remark means'.); (iii) from
'x means$_{nn}$ that p' it can be argued that *somebody* meant that p; (iv) what
is meant$_{nn}$ can be paraphrased in (single) quoted speech ("that remark
means 'he won't go'"); (v) they cannot be paraphrased with the construction 'the fact that x means$_{nn}$ (that) p' (Grice [1957] 1971:53–54). The
thrust of these 'tests' is that non-natural meaning derives not from the fac-

tual connection between some sign and a state of affairs but between a verbal utterance and an intentionally oriented speaker. Grice offers the gloss, " 'A meant$_{nn}$ something by x' is (roughly) equivalent to 'A intended the utterance of x to produce some effect in an audience by means of the recognition of this intention'." (58). It is the speaker's intention to individuate a referential object that grounds Donnellan's 'speaker reference' in Grice's non-natural meaning rather than in the verbal code. As Donnellan observes, the existence of speaker's meaning in natural language is evident in such routine questions as 'what do you mean?' and 'what are you talking about?' Such questions usually ask about the intended effect of the utterance.

It is important to clarify the role of intentions in the overall makeup of communicative action. Speaker's meaning as we have defined it accounts for some but not all of the meaning production that takes place through deixis. Zipf (1971) pointed out that Grice's treatment of intention works only when joined to an account of linguistic meaning, that speakers can communicate *despite* their intentions, and that the best of intentions can fail if not communicated in the appropriate manner. We must further distinguish intending, as a speaker might do, from attributing intention, as an addressee or third person might do, and intending in a private sense (which is beyond the pale of this study) from the social recognition of intention (which will concern us). Speakers' anticipation of communicative results, their attention to subtle changes in participation frameworks (chapters 4 and 5), and their habituation of ways of speaking (chapters 3–5) all go beyond the loop of intentionality as Grice defined it, but all make key contributions to the study of deixis. Since 'speaker' is an interactively defined role, 'speaker's meaning' in this context does not isolate the individual but instead the relations of coparticipation in which intentionality takes shape in talk. Like egocentricity in demonstrative reference, that portion of the intentional orientation of action that pertains strictly to the individual can never be more than a component of a larger formation. At the same time, to invoke intention is to reject mechanistic approaches in which action is determined by psychological or social systems whose internal dynamics override human agency. The kind of system needed to describe referential practice is one in which there is a tension between egocentric and sociocentric moments of communicative action. This tension encompasses speakers' intentions but does not erase them.

Given a rough notion of what actors mean in performing utterances, we need further to distinguish between 'direct use' of linguistic expressions and 'mention' of them. Mention is a mode of discourse in which a linguistic expression is named, or presented, without being attributed to any speaker, often for the purpose of commenting on it (Garver 1965, Searle 1969, Hanks 1987a).[2] For instance, ' "this" is a four-letter word' illustrates mention of the demonstrative, whereas 'this book is red (spoken pointing to a book)' is, we will assume, a direct ostensive use. The importance of observing this distinction in semantic description lies in the fact that expressions in the mention mode are not linked to the immediate context of utterance in the same way as those in direct use; ' "this" is a four-letter word' makes no ostensive presentation nor any claim about the spatial or perceptual field of the speaker. While the main focus of discussion here will be the conditions on direct use and interpretation of deixis, we will see that varieties of mention play a role as well.

Whether we formulate reference as a conceptual structure, as the communication of an intention, as a speech act, or as an amalgam of these, we will want to distinguish reference from coreference from synonymy. A linguistic expression used in performing singular definite reference, such as 'the sun' in the utterance, 'the sun is hot', **refers to** an object, such as the sun.[3] We can adopt Linsky's ([1967] 1971:80–81) position that the object referred to necessarily exists, so long as we countenance a variety of modes of existence, as Linsky does. Under the terms of the present discussion, Bullwinkle, Rocky, Mother Goose, the Fountain of Youth, and the category of person can equally well be the objects of individuated reference. **Coreference**, on the other hand, is a relation holding between two or more linguistic expressions which refer to the same object. Take the expressions 'Bullwinkle', 'that crazy moose', 'Rocky's companion', and 'the antlered costar of the Rocky and Bullwinkle show'. If we assume all four of these to pick out the same individual, then they are, in this context, coreferential. Clearly, for expressions to be coreferential is no guarantee that they have the same sense or encoded descriptive value. Given the right context, a proper name, an elaborate description, a pronoun (e.g., 'he'), or a zero anaphor (as in A: Where's Jack? B: 'gone', from which A understands 'Jack is gone') can pick out the same individual. Because it requires a context in which a pair (or more) of referring expressions are linked to the same object, coreference is tied to speaker reference and thereby to the communicative process in which this occurs. By contrast, relations of **synonymy** hold between linguistic expressions in virtue of their similarity of conventional meaning. For example, 'give', 'confer', and 'grant' might be seen as members of a set of synonyms whose encoded meanings differ minimally.[4] Whereas reference and coreference pertain to the communicative process (levels 2 and 3), synonymy pertains mainly to the semantic structure of language (level 1).

A final preliminary distinction which I will assume is the one between **successful** and **fully proper** acts of reference (Linsky [1967] 1971:77). A speaker may succeed in individuating an object in context by uttering an expression that in fact fails to accurately characterize the object, yet suffices to pick it out. Looking at the president, I could say "The vice-president is chipper today," and succeed in communicating to you an evaluation of the individual before us. One can mistakenly name, describe, or entitle an individual object, and interactants can disagree about which characterization is the right one while still successfully making speaker-reference to it. In acts of fully proper reference, on the other hand, the characterization must correspond accurately to the object, at whatever level of definition the context requires; the person referred to as 'the man in the straw hat' must in fact have a straw hat in his possession rather than a plastic look-alike. The divide between proper and successful reference is obviously not a clean one, since speakers routinely disagree, negotiate, and revise their terms. Moreover, accuracy is never a measure of the sheer relation between words and things without the mediating influence of a social context to define the grounds and levels of accuracy. But it is important to recognize that a study of how successful reference is achieved in conversation is basically different from a study of the conditions on proper reference. The latter, but not the former, can provide a basis for determining the conventional semantics of referring expressions.

2.1 REFERENCE AS A COMMUNICATIVE ACTIVITY

In this section we will explore in more detail the components of a pragmatic approach to deictic reference. The main focus will be on the role of the speech situation in securing speaker meaning, that is, how and where contextual knowledge and emergent features of interaction enter into the determination of the referent. The first step will be to outline reference as a collaborative speech act that takes place within a social frame (§2.1.1). This will be followed by the distinctive **relational structure** of deictic reference, whereby a focal object is individuated relative to an indexical ground (§2.1.2). In the third and final part, the idea of **indexical symmetry** is introduced as a way of describing the various participant relations on which deictic reference is grounded.

2.1.1 Priority of the Act

Singular definite reference is usually associated with the stipulations that the object must exist and be uniquely identifiable by the speaker (and addressee, to be successful). Searle (1969:77ff.) treats these as the 'axioms of existence and identifiability' and incorporates them into his 'rules of reference' (94–96). But how is this identification achieved? How is the referent individuated apart from all other objects? One possibility is that the description fits **only** the object in question, to the exclusion of all others. This may be so in some cases, but not in most. It is worth briefly recapitulating why. Linsky ([1967] 1971:77) pointed out that a description like 'the old madman' can be used perfectly well to refer uniquely to a person even though he is not mad and more than one other person is. Proper names like Alfonso and Manuel may pick out individuals but are themselves usually common to many. Donnellan's examples of referential usage make it clear that it is not the descriptive information encoded in an expression that identifies the referent, since this information can be minimal (in the case of a solitary pronoun) or wrong.

In general, the descriptive information encoded in a linguistic expression is insufficient in itself to uniquely identify a referent. Rather, "what secures uniqueness is the user of the expression and the context in which it is used together with the expression" (Linsky [1967] 1971:77). By introducing the user and the context of reference, Linsky and Donnellan invoke both intentionality and the potentially determining role of background knowledge. In a different context, Quine (1971:144, 153) made the related point that individuated reference is impossible apart from the network of terms, predicates, and auxiliary devices that speakers of a language share. Apart from this 'coordinate system' or 'frame of reference', both encoded meaning and extension are nonsense. We can summarize the push towards a contextually available coordinate system by saying simply that verbal reference is possible only in the union of a linguistic expression with an interactive frame. Often, though not always, this frame will include antecedent discourse in which the object has been identified already. Thus, Donnellan ([1978] 1979) distinguishes two kinds of referential use of definite descriptions: (i) those that occur in an 'anaphoric chain', and (ii) those that do not. The former individuate a referent through a relation of coreference with preceding words in the discourse. The latter usually rely on presupposed background knowledge shared by participants: a kind of tacit anaphoric relation in which prior experience secures uniqueness of reference. In chapters 3, 7, and 8, we will return to this background in ethnographic terms. At this point, I want to emphasize that the uniqueness and identifiability of a referential object are not properties of a pure conventional code but of the situated use of a code in a pragmatic frame.

The concept of an 'interpretive frame' lies at the base of U semantics (Fillmore 1985:222) and plays a special role in the description of deictic reference. Fillmore (1978:165) defines 'frame' as a set of lexical items whose members index portions of some actional or conceptual whole. For instance, 'buy' and 'sell' correspond to different portions of a single 'commercial event', and the names Monday, Tuesday, Wednesday, . . . correspond to parts in a single calendric cycle called the 'week'. The key feature of frames is that the individual items that fit into them, the words, are only intelligible to someone who has access to the entire schema. "What holds such word groups together is the fact of their being motivated by, founded on, and co-structured with, specific unified frameworks of knowledge, or coherent schematizations of experience" (Fillmore 1985:223). The relation between frames and words is a subtle one, and Fillmore carefully distinguishes 'frames' from 'lexical fields'. The latter are made up of sets of linguistic items organized in paradigmatic opposition to one another—such that it is the relation between the forms that determines the interpretation of any one and not the relation between the forms and some conceptual or actional whole that exists independent of the language.

Frames are not language-internal objects, characterizable in a level 1 conceptual semantics; they are constituents of the social, cultural, and natural world in which language is used as a means of communication and action (level 2, 3). Unavoidably a semantics based on frames is more like an encyclopedia than a dictionary and incorporates the view that linguistic categories exist in relation to particular 'structured understandings of cultural institutions, beliefs about the world', and so forth (Fillmore 1985:231). Rather than supplying a 'semantic representation', in the form of an object read off as the interpretation of a sentence, frame semantics takes the internal semantic structure of the sentence as a 'blueprint' from which an interpreter constructs a whole understanding. In this kind of theory, both the acting subject and background understandings play a role in interpretation. The divide between 'properly linguistic meaning' and 'speaker's meaning' is maintained in the idea that the former, but not the latter, must figure in all pragmatic contexts.[5] Much as Linsky observed for reference, speaker's meaning is derived from a combination of the words used and the extralinguistic context (Fillmore 1985:233).[6]

It is very unlikely (if not impossible) that any unified, consistent set of frames could be proposed for a language that would suffice to describe all or even most of the interpretations that arise in the use of that language. In effect, the idea of embedding acts of reference and predication in frames is directed towards providing a 'maximally rich' (Fillmore 1985:234) interpretation, not a neatly bounded one. Still, the question arises as to what kinds of frames are most relevant to a given class of uses. This is

mainly an empirical question, but our focus on the actional whole of deictic reference indicates certain directions. Whatever else is included in the
deictic frame, the forms corresponding to different parts of utterance context play a role: 'I', 'you', 'here', 'this', and 'now' are members of a
single set corresponding to the 'proximal frame'. We may or may not decide to include 'there', 'that', 'then', and the third person pronouns in a
single frame with the proximal forms, since they are all defined in relation
to one another, even though they are not all 'proximal'. We will return to
this question in chapter 10. In at least some standard uses, the referential
function of deixis is linked to presentative or directive illocutionary force,
and when it is, the communicative whole of which the deictic is part must
include these extrareferential effects. It has long been recognized that
bodily gestures—such as pointing, directed gaze, and handing over an
object—are a necessary part of (at least some) ostensive reference, and
similarly that the current attentional focus of interactants may play a role
as well (Bühler [1934] 1967; Fillmore 1982; Leonard 1985; Lyons 1977).
Beyond these quite general indications, we need to work through the
details of demonstrative practice in a given cultural setting in order to formulate the relevant frames and properly characterize the multifunctionality of deictic practice.[7] To do so for contemporary Maya conversation is
one of the primary descriptive goals of this book.

2.1.2 Relational Structure of Demonstrative Reference

In order to clarify the kind of frames involved in deictic reference, we
need a more specific statement of the components of the event itself. We
can start from a simple example of ostensive reference, as in:

(1)   **lel a? ha?**
             'This (is) water'. (said pointing to a gourdful)

The boldface portion is the Immediate nominal demonstrative (DNOM; see
table 1.1) used without any descriptive elaboration.[8] Such ostensive presentation and the deictics that contribute to it are often viewed as the epit-
ome of direct reference in language. Searle (1969:80) is one of several
philosophers to observe that ostension can contribute to securing uniqueness of reference, amplifying the description with demonstration. Thus, it
pertains primarily to reference as an act, where the connection between
expressions and situations is in play. It is the indexical basis of deixis that
accounts for its apparent concreteness. Following Gale (1964, 1968),
Morris (1971:31), Peirce (1940:107), and Searle (1969:80), indexicals
are defined as signs (linguistic or not) that stand in a relation of actual
contiguity with their object. Morris (1971:20, 22) and Searle (1969:80)

distinguish indexicals, which indicate, but in no way describe, their object, from characterizing signs that do describe objects, even in their absence.

It is important to recognize that natural language deictics are not pure indexicals under the foregoing definition. A cursory look at Maya, Malagasy (Anderson and Keenan 1985; Hanks 1986), Eskimo (Denny 1984), Santali (Zide 1972), or many other languages shows immediately that deictics *do* have conventional meanings and that they *do* characterize objects. Furthermore, they are heir to the familiar indeterminacies of individuated reference. What exactly is the point individuated by *lel a?* 'this', as opposed to *lel o?* 'that'? What are the conventional structures of ostension in natural languages, and how do they differ from one another? These questions move in the direction of what Kaplan ([1978] 1979:390) called a 'Fregean view' of demonstrative reference, with some modifications. This view holds that the distinction between sense and denotation, which Frege observed for nonindexicals, can be extended to demonstratives. The object indexed corresponds to the denotation, and the manner of indication to the sense.[9] It would be wrong to overstress the similarity between the conventional meaning of a deictic and a 'pure sense' component in the traditional terms (see Kaplan [1978] 1979:385), and we need not claim that the extension of a deictic token stands apart from the proposition in which it occurs. But it does appear necessary to recognize that natural languages have whole repertoires of deictic expressions, precisely because such expressions stand for qualitatively distinct parts of pragmatic frames. For natural language, we need to recognize both an indexical component and a characterizing one, by which the referent is identified relative to utterance context.

Kaplan (1978:401–2) describes an index as the contextual factors relative to which the extension is determined, for a sentence containing demonstratives, such as 'I was happy back then'. He points out that the indexical component cannot be thought of as a simple object, such as a 'world' w, but must be seen as a set of coordinates, such as a time t, a place p (made up of three dimensions x, y, z), and an agent a. Thus, the index i would equal $(w, t, p, a, \ldots)$.[10] Kaplan subsequently revises this formulation, replacing the idea of index by 'content', which is the specific proposition expressed in a context (hence linked to something like an index). On the other hand, the character of a demonstrative is "that complement of the sense of an expression which determines how the content is determined by the context" (403). Thus, in what he calls an 'amplified Fregean account', Kaplan appears to maintain a distinction between a relatively constant semantic component (character) and a dynamic, situa-

tional one (index, content). This distinction is, I believe, a necessary part
of any universal framework for describing deixis.

If we incorporate into U semantics the ideas of speaker reference and
contextually computed semantic reference, then we need to reconsider the
contrast between deictic and nondeictic elements. That is, deictics cannot
be described merely as indexicals, since indexicality is a general feature
of reference, in play in some degree in all language use (for instance, in
the linkage to frames). What is distinctive about deictics and other shifters (Jakobson [1957] 1971; Silverstein 1976b) is that indexical relations
are the very core of their general meanings.[11] In Yucatec, *way e?* 'here'
means roughly, 'The place where I utter this token of *way'e?*'. *Lel a?*
'this' is 'the one immediate to this token of *lela?*'. Similar paraphrase
relations obtain between the corresponding expressions in any language
and their phrasal (near) equivalents, as a number of scholars have observed (Bloomfield 1933:248; Bühler [1934] 1967:175; Collinson
1937:43ff.; Lyons 1977:646; Russell 1940:114).[12]

At the heart of such paraphrases is the observation that deictic categories encode a **relation** (relative proximity, inclusion, etc. Cf. Kaplan's
'character') between some **referent** (the one, the place, etc. Cf. 'content') and the **indexical** context of the speech act (the speaker, addressee, or 'here-now' of the utterance). The relational feature specifies the
pragmatic **dimension** within which the referent is localizable (proximity,
visibility, audibility, . . .). Put somewhat differently, demonstrative reference is a function from the utterance context, which I will call the Indexical Ground or Origo, to the content, which I will call the referential
object. The Relational predicate is the character of the function. Therefore, deictics stand for two objects, not just one, namely, a referent and
an indexical ground, or 'pivot'. The resulting structure can be abbreviated
as 'the x in relation R to y' (or R(x, y) for predicative uses), where x is the
object referred to, and y is the indexical ground (cf. Jakobson [1957]
1971; Lyons 1977:646; Reichenbach 1947:248).

The necessity of distinguishing an indexical from a characterizing
component in the semantics of deixis is also evident when we compare
different expressions. Take Maya *way e?* 'here' and *tol o?* 'there.' Both
of them may be used in a context in which the speaker locates a place
relative to himself. For instance, A and B are walking through the forest,
separated by about ten yards from one another but maintaining verbal
contact. In order to refer to his own present location, either speaker would
use the expression *way e?*, whereas to refer to the location of the other,
either would use *tol o?* (it is perhaps noteworthy that there are three other
locative deictics which would not be used under these circumstances).

TABLE **2.1** Relational Structures of Deictic Reference

Form		Denotatum Type	Relational Type	Indexical Type[a]
This	=	'the one	Proximal to	me'
That	=	'the one	Distal to	you'
That	=	'the one	Distal to	you and me'
This	=	'the one	Visible to	me'
That	=	'the one	Visible to	you and me'
Here	=	'the region	Immediate to	you'
There	=	'the region	Non-Immediate to	you and me'
I	=	'the person	Speaker of	this utterance'
You	=	'the person	Addressee of	this utterance'
Now	=	'the time	Immediate to	this utterance'

[a] Indexical types are abbreviated and stand for participation configurations realized in the utterance and actually occupied in the interactive situation.

The two deictics pick out different parts of a single actional frame. We can capture this by saying that they are indexically equivalent (or at least similar) but encode opposite relational features. As I will try to show in chapter 9, *way e?* encodes the sense component 'inclusive of speaker', and *tol o?* 'exclusive of speaker'. In order to capture the relations between such pairs, we must distinguish the two components. Table 2.1 schematizes the pairing.

But what is the lexical origo of deictic reference, and how is it related to the referential object? In the case of spatial adverbs like the two just cited from Maya, the locus of the speaker serves as origo, giving the impression that the indexical ground can be treated as a sort of egocentric place. This is a potentially misleading impression, however. What grounds the reference is not only the speaker's location but the utterance framework in which the reference is produced. This framework includes the speaker as one of its salient parts, but as Kaplan (1978) pointed out, it is actually a *set of coordinates*. That is, the index is both more complex and more abstract than the speaker's physical location. In the course of this book we will develop an increasingly fine-grained description of the indexical grounds of referential practices in Maya. For instance, chapter 3 will explore the sociocultural constitution of the body, arguing that even egocentric space is socially structured. Chapters 4 and 5 subsume the speaker within increasingly elaborate interactive frameworks, showing how indexical origos are produced and layered in discourse. Chapter 6 then returns to bodily grounded modes of access to referents, analyzing the perceptual and actional features encoded in the Ostensive Evidential forms. The key point for now is that the indexical origo is logically necessary in order to apply the relational features of demonstratives: it is that relative to which the referential object is identified. This relational fact is more basic than any essential characteristic inherent in the index.

The characterizing and indexical components of deictics are not merely paired but are related in an asymmetric way. Referential objects are uniquely identified by relational features such as Proximal, Distal, and Exclusive (taken in union with situational frames). In addition to these, deictics in many languages encode characterizing features, such as Human, Animate, Regional, Extended, Static, and Kinetic. Unlike true relational features, these attribute inherent properties to referential objects, and they do not presuppose the utterance situation in order to be interpreted. Along with the relational component, characterizing features help individuate the denotatum. By contrast, the indexical origo is usually less salient and less precisely defined in the conventional categories of deixis. Languages rarely encode more distinctions among the contexts *in which* a deictic form can be used than among those *in reference to which* it can be used (Hanks 1989b). In general, it is fair to say that whereas the character features make up a large network of specific relation types, indexical grounds can be described in terms of just a few relatively general configurations.

There is a strong parallel between deictic reference, on the one hand, and the asymmetric duality between Figure and Ground, on the other. The discreteness, individuation, definiteness, and singularity that are the hallmarks of deictic reference are all typical Figure characteristics. The diffuseness, variability, and backgrounded character of the indexical 'zero point' is due to its being, in fact, the Ground upon which the referential Figure is defined. Furthermore, there is a material connection between the two frameworks in terms of what they structure. The Figure-Ground relation, as invoked here, organizes visual perception. Deictic reference is by no means limited to visual or even perceptual access to referents, but perceptual distinctions are encoded in deictics in a variety of languages, including Maya (see chapter 5). Clearly, the perceptual field is one coordinate of the broader deictic field in these cultures, and the conventional categories of the language reflect this. Even in languages like English, in which apparently no perceptual distinctions are encoded in deictics, the perceptual corollaries of spatial proximity may still be fundamental to the actual use of the forms. More important than the substantive connection between deixis and Figure-Ground in perception is the structural parallel between the two phenomena. One advantage of the analogy to Figure-

Ground is exactly that it focuses our attention on the fact that deixis is a framework for organizing the actor's **access** to the context of speech at the moment of utterance. Deictic reference organizes the field of interaction into a foreground upon a background, as Figure and Ground organize the visual field.[13]

It is common in the linguistic and philosophical literature to describe deictics as forms whose meanings are based on the place and time of the speaking ego.[14] Lyons (1982:121) gives a clear statement of the view when he says "the basic function of deixis is to relate the entities and situation to which reference is made in language to the spatiotemporal zero-point—the here and now—of the context of utterance. Admittedly, this zero-point is egocentric, as everyone who ever talks about deixis would agree." So deictics relate referents to a spatiotemporal matrix which is based on the speaker, whose position defines ground zero. Russell (1940:108) saw speaker relativity as the very basis of 'egocentric particulars', which include the deictics under discussion. He proposed to derive all such forms from the perceptual-conceptual experience denoted by 'I notice'; 'Here' is where I am, 'this' is what I now notice, 'I' is the biography to which 'this' belongs. Given this approach, the object referred to by an instance of 'this' was not the world object itself for Russell but the sensation of noticing it. The result was to surround reference in an envelop of private experience and merely assume the priority of the first person pronoun over other demonstratives (see Gale 1968:152).

Recently, Evans (1982:chap. 6) proposed a revised Russellian account in which demonstrative identification is based on a special kind of information link between the subject and the referential object. 'Here thoughts', as Evans describes them, are merely the least specific in a system of thoughts about places, which include 'it's F over there', 'it's F up to the left', 'it's F a bit behind me', and so forth (153). All of these rest on the egocentric mode of thought, which is linked to bodily action (157). Evans departs from Russell in making body space basic instead of the person and in his recognition that this egocentric space must be located in a larger public 'map', in order to provide a spatial orientation at all (163).[15] These are interesting innovations consistent with current linguistic work on body space as a basis for a whole range of semantic schemata (Fillmore 1982:45; Lakoff 1987:271ff.). It is therefore worth considering the limits of such a view.

As developed by Russell and Evans, the egocentric thesis is grounded in a level 1 semantics, in which what is at stake is the conceptual structure of a certain kind of thought, not the semiotic constitution of a certain kind of communicative practice. It is at the level of the language as conventional information structure that egocentricity is first applied. Yet deictic systems are **embodied** in the sense that they are explicable only in a vocabulary whose terms derive their meaning from activities that engage bodies (Evans 1982:157). The acting speaker (implying levels 2 and 3) is therefore fundamental to semantic meaning (level 1). But is it the characterizing relational feature R or the indexical ground i that is egocentric? It must be the former, since the indexical ground is an actional framework that includes at least the addressee and his or her relation to the speaker, as well as other coordinates. To describe the frame as egocentric would therefore be to make the very strong and implausible claim that social and cultural contexts revolve fundamentally around the individual. Even if this is so under certain circumstances, it is unrealistic to assume it across the board.[16] As for the relational features, it is surely an empirical question what kinds of features get encoded in languages and whether or not they can be derived from the individual body. A more fruitful approach is to ask when and under what circumstances deictic features and acts are built on body experience and when are they not. I will show in chapter 9 that the Maya construction of spatial 'here' actually includes both egocentric and sociocentric coordinates, which means that a universal theory must have access to both. Finally, egocentricity and the closely related idea of 'subjectivity' in deixis (Lyons 1982) should both be understood as categories whose values derive from the social system in which they are embedded. That is, egocentricity is not an alternative to sociocentricity but a *part* of it. I will spell out in ethnographic terms the role of bodily space in Maya culture in chapters 3 and 8.

In their examination of referring as a collaborative process, Clark and Wilkes-Gibbs (1986) call into question the egocentricity of reference. They propose instead to treat reference in conversation as a joint achievement of the interactants, not a one-man act. They criticize philosophical treatments of speaker reference (per Donnellan, Kripke, and Searle) for what they consider their idealized, 'literary' view: speakers refer as if they were writing to distant readers; the intention to refer is satisfied by issuing a noun phrase; the act is cotemporal with the noun phrase; and the speaker has complete control over the process (Clark and Wilkes-Gibbs 1986:3). While such a view of reference does not follow necessarily from the egocentric thesis, it does summarize a set of 'default' assumptions that deserve to be questioned. Clark and Wilkes-Gibbs demonstrate that the standard kinds of referring expressions are insufficient to describe the utterance forms attested in actual transcripts of conversation. They show eight kinds of nonstandard expressions, such as 'expanded, episodic and installment' noun phrases (4−7) and propose a two-step process of 'presentation' and 'acceptance' through which the reference is jointly established (9). The key point is that the speaker is just one party in a social relation, and reference is produced by this relation, not the individual. Participants in conversation try to establish, roughly by the initiation of each new contribution, the mutual belief that the listeners have understood what the speaker meant in the last utterance, to a criterion sufficient for current purposes (33). This principle, which they call the 'principle of mutual responsibility', reflects the observation that interactants generally prefer to establish a reference before moving on to another.

The 'collaborative' view of reference corresponds most closely to speech under specific circumstances, as the authors recognize (Clark and Wilkes-Gibbs 1986:35). It is a doctrine of successful, rather than proper, practice. The data discussed (10–16) come from an experimental situation in which the parties were separated by a screen blocking vision and charged with the task of identifying and ordering members in a set of twelve Tangram figures. The unfamiliarity of the objects and the lack of visual contact set up what I will call an **asymmetric** interactive frame, in which shared knowledge was lacking but necessary to the task at hand. As a result of these factors, the role of timing in the acceptance process, by which the addressee signals that he has understood, is underplayed. Parties in everyday conversation do not always establish agreement on reference before proceeding but may delay, speed up, or suspend the process. These qualifications notwithstanding, Clark and Wilkes-Gibbs have clarified a major problem area in the pragmatics of reference by showing the consequences of approaching it as an act in context. In the relational structure of deictic reference, we must start from an indexical ground consisting of an interactional whole, not an egocentric one. If in a language egocentricity is singled out and encoded in the characterizing components of a deictic system, then we should examine the cultural context and interactive conditions on this form rather than assume it to be the natural state of affairs.

2.1.3 Symmetry and Asymmetry of Indexical Ground

The collaboration and search for mutuality that Clark and Wilkes-Gibbs (1986) make central in their approach to reference has its roots in the sociological tradition of conversational and interactional studies. This includes many well-known studies of turn taking, sequential organization, conversational inference, and the negotiation of meaning in dialogue (Garfinkel 1967, [1962] 1972; Goffman 1981; Gumperz 1982; Sacks, Schegloff, and Jefferson 1974; Schegloff 1972, 1982; C. Goodwin 1981; M. Goodwin in press; and see the useful review in Levinson 1983:chap.

6; Turner 1974). This literature has begun to work its way into linguistic pragmatics only recently and has a great deal to contribute to the analysis of reference in communication. One of its main premises is that participants must manage their interaction in order to achieve what Schutz (1973) called the 'reciprocity of perspectives'. Rather than assuming the essential equivalence of speaker and addressee as idealized automata who can communicate automatically and without breakdowns, communication is seen to be a complex achievement requiring a joint effort. Language arises out of social experience, and only secondarily out of concepts or bodily experiences as such.

Schutz considered the social relation embodied in face-to-face communication to be the prototype of all social relations. His analysis of it proceeds from the observation that actors have different perspectives, attach different significance to objects, and moreover, that they commonsensically recognize this fact. Not two individuals occupy the same 'I' and 'here' at some level, and no two have identical biographies. It is only by a relatively intricate series of assumptions, mutual orientations, and shared knowledge that communication manages to occur at all. The recognition of intention that philosophers place in the center of 'speaker reference' Schutz explained as a 'reciprocity of motives'. He distinguished an 'in order to' motive from a 'because motive', where the former is the intended, anticipated, goal orientation of an act, and the latter is the antecedent circumstance or disposition which leads up to the act. A question, in the simplest case, is uttered *in order to* elicit a response, and a response is issued *because of* the question to which it is oriented.[17]

Commonsense thought overcomes the differences in individual perspectives by way of twin idealizations, which Schutz (1970:183) called the "interchangeability of standpoints" and the "congruency of the system of relevances." An interactant takes it for granted that if he changes place with another, the world will appear to him as it does to the other, at the same distance and with the same typical features. 'Congruency' denotes the assumption that the differences in perspective separating actors are, until further notice, irrelevant to their activities. What is relevant is that they assume that they are identifying and commenting on the same objects in the same world. Their respective meanings are not absolutely identical but are sufficient for the purposes at hand. In this framework, the level of referential uniqueness sustained by speakers is set relative to their motives; some referential contexts require finer individuation and more precise agreement than others. What secures mutuality and uniqueness of reference is a common body of background knowledge, some already in play in the immediate field of interaction and some accessible as common sense.

From the concern with reciprocity as an ongoing achievement comes the impetus to study breakdowns, repairs, and management techniques in talk. Clark and Wilkes-Gibbs (1986) contribute an empirical demonstration that these studies bear centrally on the practice of reference, not only on the 'organizational' aspects of conversation. For a theory of demonstrative reference, the phenomenon of reciprocity is especially important because of the perspectival orientations inherent in the semantics of the forms: the individual and experiential field which is for one person 'I', 'here', and 'this' is for his or her interlocutor 'you', 'there', and 'that'.[18] The uniqueness of the individual who utters 'I' to some 'you' is subsumed in the fact that this 'you' is himself an 'I', in relation to whom he (the original speaker) is a 'you' (Benveniste [1965] 1974). There appear to be two things going on here: (i) indexical referential expressions have the distinctive feature of 'shifting' their reference systematically when used from different perspectives, as linguists have thoroughly understood; (ii) the object individuated by A's uttering 'this' can be identified by B—is knowable for him, whether or not he refers to it as 'that'—and would be for him a 'this' if he were in A's place. They speak the same language and can make a single 'we'. The first has to do with Schutz's 'interchangeability' of perspectives and the second with the congruency of the categories used by interactants.

The extent to which two people really do have interchangeable perspectives and congruent knowledge bases has a direct impact on their use of deictics. Donnellan's ([1978] 1979) observation that definite descriptions in referential contexts rely on 'anaphoric chains' or background knowledge has application to some deictic use as well. Whether preceded by an overt antecedent or not, many instances of 'there', 'that', 'he', and 'then' are anaphoric in the sense that they require the congruency of shared knowledge of the object, individual, or time referred to. Leonard (1985) showed that Swahili demonstratives, traditionally glossed as 'proximal' and 'distal', actually encode a distinction between high and low focus, with the former used for introducing new information and the latter for maintaining what is already established in the discourse. In Maya, as we shall see, deictic forms differ systematically in terms of what interactants already know or have in their common focus of attention, versus what a speaker presents as novel. Such facts of language structure show that relative congruency among interactants can be significant at the level of the semantics as well as in the practice of reference.

We shall speak of the shared knowledge and experience that links interlocutors as **symmetric** dimensions of speech context, and those that separate or distinguish them as **asymmetric**. This is consistent with the use
of the same terms by Brown and Gillman ([1960] 1972) and Friedrich
(1966) in their classic studies of address. The former introduced the concept of social asymmetry to describe relations among individuals such as
'older than', 'parent of', 'richer than', 'employer of'. The common feature of these is that they are irreversible; if A is richer than B, then B
is not richer than A. In social terms, they involve a dominance relation
which Brown and Gillman summarized as the 'asymmetric power relation' (Brown and Gillman [1960] 1972:257). The symmetric pole applies
to relations like 'attended the same school', 'have the same parent', and
'practice the same profession'. These are reversible—if A has the same
parents as B, then B has the same parents as A—and involve relations of
solidarity and equivalence. While the power dimension divides the interactants, solidarity unifies them. Brown and Gillman extended their use of
'symmetric and asymmetric' from the socially established relations among
people to the linguistic forms they exchange when addressing one another.

For deictic reference, the kinds of relations in play are centered on
the access that speaker and addressee have to the referent at the moment
of utterance. This may derive from common background experience, a
shared perceptual field, a shared focus of attention, or other symmetrical
relations. The point is that the object of reference is accessible to both
parties. To the degree that interactants have differential access to the referent or even to each other as a function of intervening boundaries, the
context is asymmetric. Although these specific relations involve neither
power nor solidarity, they represent a homologous split between factors
that divide and factors that unify parties to an interaction. It is logical that
shared knowledge can be a significant form of solidarity, and asymmetric
knowledge a means of domination.[19] The role of the referent in my formulation of contextual symmetry is motivated by the fact that it is reference, not address, that I am describing.[20] One of the goals of this study is
to demonstrate that social relations are as important in the way people
refer to the world as they are in the way they address one other. Because
the focal object is a referent and not the interlocutor himself, this social
mediation is less obvious but no less necessary.

Friedrich (1966) elaborated the framework proposed by Brown and
Gillman and applied it to nineteenth-century Russian pronoun usage.
Rather than lump the various forms of symmetry and asymmetry into the
abstract dimensions of power and solidarity, he showed that Russian usage
was sensitive to ten, more finely grained dimensions. These included the

topic of discourse, the social context of speech, relative age, generation, gender, genealogical distance, coresidence in a household or village, dialect, and emotional affinity. Together with Friedrich's ([1964, 1970] 1979) description of social structure and household organization in Russian society, this study indicates clearly the kinds of factors that can constitute symmetry for reference, as well as address. In chapters 3, 7, and 8, analogous aspects of Maya social life are sketched.

The relative symmetry of indexical context is therefore a function of the relation between participants. This can be viewed abstractly in terms of how much relevant knowledge and experience they already share and can mobilize to identify the referent. Alternatively, it can be dissolved into the more specific dimensions in which mutual knowledge is embodied—background experience, spatial, perceptual, or attentional immediacy. Contextual frames can be ordered along an abstract continuum of 'sharedness' or 'reciprocity'. Face-to-face talk between brothers who work together daily regarding the household they both inhabit, for instance, is relatively symmetric, whereas strangers communicating from opposite sides of a wall are in an asymmetric context. Clark and Wilkes-Gibbs's experimental subjects were placed in a relatively asymmetric context (with vision blocked and unfamiliar objects) and faced with a task demanding precise individuation.

The more specific view of symmetry focuses on the concrete parameters in which the relation is embodied. Interactants can be separated spatially and perceptually but share highly determinate knowledge of the referent based on experience prior to the speech event. Hence two indexical contexts could be equally asymmetric but qualitatively distinct in terms of *what* is shared and unshared. The significance of this fact for a pragmatic account of shifters is that *different deictic forms rely on different aspects of the indexical field.* Whether or not interactants share background knowledge of a referent is largely irrelevant to the usage of Presentatives, which require immediate sensory access. On the other hand, reference to an empirically remote place (say, 25 kilometers through the woods) requires proportionately more background knowledge. Given a sufficiently rich common knowledge of a place, even reference to it from a great distance can be accomplished with normally punctate, proximal forms. These facts can be explained naturally in terms of socially constituted modes of access to referents but are the undoing of any theory that claims that spatial proximity to the speaker is the key to deictic practice.

The main advantage of viewing indexical symmetry in the first way is that by lumping together many different aspects of context into the single dimension, it provides a unifying framework in which contexts can be compared. But a close description of deictic usage cannot consist solely of statements at this level of abstraction. The relational features of deictics selectively anchor to different dimensions of context. What kinds of symmetry are distinguished in a given language or category is an empirical question, just as it is an empirical question what relational values are encoded in the grammar. In general, an act of reference that relies on preestablished symmetric access to the object is what Silverstein (1976b) has called 'relatively presupposing', while one that introduces a new object into the common ground is relatively 'creative'. Discourse is clearly dynamic in these terms, insofar as new objects contribute to symmetry when they become mutually established.

While creative reference can transform indexical context, indexical context also constrains reference.[21] There is a simple proportion between the two which says that the greater the symmetry of the indexical ground, the greater the possibilities for individuated reference. This is equivalent to saying that the more information participants already share, the more precisely they can individuate referents. When they are face to face, engaged, mutually oriented, and share detailed background knowledge of referents, they can potentially mobilize any shifter in the language. Proper and successful reference can be based on the anticipation that the interlocutor will accurately identify the object (even a remote one), given only the relational description. The less they share, on the other hand, the fewer referential oppositions are available to individuate and the more difficult it is to succeed at deictic reference without further lexical description. This is summarized in (2).

(2)   Principle of relative symmetry
       The more symmetric the indexical ground (the more interactants already
       share at the time of utterance), the more deictic oppositions are avail-
       able for making reference (the greater the range of choice among distinct
       deictics).

This principle relates the state of interaction between coparticipants to the range of choices they have in selecting their terms of reference. It has further corollaries in the practices of deictic reference. One of these is that highly symmetric situations, where participants take for granted a common orientational schema, perceptual field, and background knowledge, can be treated in reference as if they were asymmetric. Interactants can take up different footings in relation to each other and to objects of reference, expanding or collapsing the distance between themselves and others through their choice of deictic forms. As we will see in chapter 9, the Exclusive locative *tol o?* 'out there' in Maya can be used to refer to the body space of an interlocutor just a couple of feet away. Such fore-grounded usage is consistent with the principle of indexical symmetry and demonstrates a basic fact about the deictic frame: the 'proximal' zone of talk is not just a place contiguous to interaction. Rather, it is a field of reference maximally accessible to the participants and hence maximally subdivisible by distinct deictic acts. To state it in more general terms, reference is possible only within a framework of coordinates that anchors it and serves as its origo. The more fully defined the origo, the greater the possibilities for individuated reference.

On the other hand, in cases where the interactive origo is relatively lean and participants cannot take for granted a symmetric ground, proportionately fewer possibilities are available to them for making reference. It is difficult for interlocutors who are in fact separated by spatial, experiential, or cognitive boundaries to use referring expressions that require a common ground in order to be interpretable. Thus the repertoire of semiotic forms (verbal, gestural) at speakers' disposal changes depending upon their relation to the field of ongoing communicative practice. In the absence of adequately symmetric conditions, deictic reference becomes impossible and lexical description is necessary. Since even nondeictics have indexical components, as Garfinkel, Searle, Putnam, and others have noted, the principle applies to all types of reference and not just to demonstrative use.[22]

It should be evident from the preceding discussion that the indexical origo of reference is neither a simple object nor a fixed point from which reference is computed. This raises a central issue in the description of linguistic practice, namely, how interactants jointly produce the indexical frameworks which function as the grounds for further acts of reference. To take a simple example of this, consider two speakers, A and B, engaged in a discussion about a third party, C. As talk progresses and the two exchange information about C, the symmetric ground of their interaction develops, opening up further possibilities for reference. Because they function in anaphora, textual cohesion, and the organization of information in discourse, deictics play a pivotal role in this process. Consider now what happens if A reports to B an interaction she had with C, using a combination of indirect speech and verbatim quote, as in "so there we are and C says to me 'Leave this right here, I'll be back for it'." In such a case, A's narration creates a story line and a textual frame (underscored), which in turn serves as the origo relative to which the quoted speech is interpreted. Note that the expression 'right here' in the quoted discourse refers not to A's current location but to the place of the originary utterance she is quoting. This is a very simple example of what I shall describe in chapter 5 as 'transposition'. As Jespersen observed, 'shifters' play a unique role in signaling transpositions among modes of discourse, or what might be termed 'voices' in text. When one considers that modes can be multiply embedded (a point emphasized in Goffman 1981), it becomes evident that the origo of reference not only changes over the course of talk but is a layered construct in which multiple participation frames may be interconnected. As soon as we recognize the interplay between demonstrative reference and textual organization, the relational character of the indexical ground stands out clearly. Different genres of discourse provide different possibilities for creating indexical frameworks and therefore different options for reference.[23]

2.2 REFERENCE AS A FEATURE OF THE SEMANTIC SYSTEM

To argue that reference in general, or deixis in particular, relies on a socially constituted frame of reference is not to argue that semantic meaning derives entirely from use. At one extreme, some scholars working within ethnomethodology have claimed that semantics as a conventional system is a misguided fiction that obscures the purely indexical character of meaning. Interactants negotiate everything, and orderliness in language is a product of the process, not some structure (Garfinkel 1967, [1962] 1972). Structural and transformational approaches to semantics in linguistics have traditionally adopted the opposite assumption, that expressions are used as they are precisely because they have relatively fixed meaning (e.g., Jakobson [1936] 1966; Katz 1971). Conceptual representations taken to underlie lexical items and sentences are a component part of a larger grammatical system and only secondarily belong to a conversational process. In its strongest form, such a semantics claims that a speaker's knowledge of her language is qualitatively distinct and isolable from her knowledge of the world (cf. Bolinger 1965). Cognitive grammar as presented by Langacker (1984: 172) starts from the still different, and radical claim that there is no division between semantics and pragmatics, between linguistic and extralinguistic knowledge. Rather, a single order of cognitive domains is posited as the 'base' in relation to which linguistic forms impose given figural images, which he calls 'profiles'.

The kind of semantics of understanding towards which this book is directed is distinct from all of the foregoing but has elements of each. The role of indexicality and situated practice was the topic of §2.1.3 and is irreducible in deixis.[24] The role of conventional linguistic meaning is undeniable when one looks at the grammar of deictic constructions and the lexical oppositions between the forms. Unlike much of the general lexicon, deictic forms fit into closed paradigmatic and contrast sets, what

Talmy (1983:227) called the "fine structure" of language. Their respective meanings are obviously determined relative to their linguistic oppositions, which implies a level of conventional structure apart from use. Still, the dimensions encoded in deictics have their source in the speech event, not the code as a purely conceptual object; participants, place, perceptual field, focus of attention, time, prior discourse are terms definable in a vocabulary of verbal interaction. In order to give anything approaching a comprehensive description of deixis, one must seek to combine properly linguistic meaning with situational meanings that arise in use.

This immediately raises three hard questions. First, how can one decide which aspects of situationally conveyed meaning are encoded in the language and which ones are due to the circumstances in which utterances are made? Second, what kinds of linguistic units (constructions and paradigms) make up the lexical and phrasal system of deixis? And third, how can these units be integrated with elements of the pragmatic frame into a schematic whole, corresponding to the figure-ground relation between the referent and the interactive context? In this section, I will summarize a set of guidelines for distinguishing conventional from occasional meaning (§2.2.1). Next, I will outline the construction types (§2.2.2) and paradigmatic relations (§2.2.3) found in Maya deixis. Finally, I will propose a prototype analysis, in which deictic categories are related to core fields of the speech event (§2.2.4).

2.2.1 Encoded vs. Conveyed Meaning

Grice's ([1957] 1971) idea of non-natural meaning, what a speaker intends that his addressee should recognize as his intention in making an utterance, was a first step towards defining a pragmatic approach to meaning. Linked to what Schutz would call the reciprocity of motives, this level of meaning occurs in interaction. Grice's later work developed a series of proposals regarding conversational practice, known as the theory of implicature (Grice 1967, 1975, 1978). One of the cornerstones of the theory is the distinction between the literal semantic content of sentences, what is said, and the situated meaning of utterances, what is conveyed. Conveyed meaning derives from literal meaning by the application of general principles of cooperative behavior, which Grice called the Cooperative Principle, and its associated 'maxims'.[25] In talk, the encoded meanings of linguistic forms are incremented by a pragmatic overlay consisting of 'implicatures'. In order to interpret or 'work out' the implicatures of an utterance, participants must have at their disposal (i) the literal encoded meaning of the forms uttered; (ii) the Cooperative Principle plus the maxims; (iii) the context of utterance, including shared background knowledge. While encoded meaning in this approach is determinate, constant across contexts, and undeniable in any single context, conversational implicatures are usually multiple and can be canceled by explicit denial or blocked by co-occurrent aspects of context.

The theory of implicatures can potentially simplify semantic description by helping to account for the variable meanings conveyed in talk while preserving a relatively constant and bounded semantics. This is highly desirable for a description of deixis, because of the necessity to integrate both kinds of information. Unfortunately, there are no unequivocal tests to distinguish encoded from merely conveyed features, but hypotheses in this work will be guided by five kinds of evidence.

(i) *Grammaticalization:* features of encoded meaning are, by definition, part of the language and therefore should correlate with facts of grammatical distribution, co-occurrence, and paraphrase. In the clearest cases, a feature will have obvious distributional consequences and a straightforward (set of) paraphrases.

(ii) *Consistency:* conventional meaning is rarely constant, such that all tokens of a type convey just the same one. Relatively unmarked forms expectably have a variety of uses. To be conventional, these uses must recur in a reasonably large number of examples. In the clearest cases, the candidate meaning also has analogues in other categories of the system, such as the correspondences between 'this' and 'here', 'that' and 'there', which suggest a single feature such as relative Immediacy. If an aspect of conveyed meaning is consistent neither across examples (instances) nor across categories, there is little use in claiming it is encoded.

(iii) *Cancelability:* nonencoded meanings are usually cancelable in one or more of the following ways. (a) the meaning can be overtly denied without resulting in a contradiction, as in Maya *tí?an té?el o?, má? in-wohe hač tú?uš yàan* 'It's over there, I don't know exactly where it is'. The underlined demonstrative phrase usually conveys that the speaker knows just where the referent is located, but the easy deniability of this aspect of meaning suggests that it does not belong to the language but to a set of contexts. (b) The meaning may be blocked by some alteration of the utterance form short of overt denial, as in *tí?an wá tú?uš té?el o?* 'it's somewhere over there'. The underlined indefinite expression blocks the inference that the speaker knows the precise location, just as the denial did above. (c) The exact same utterance form if produced under different circumstances fails to convey the meaning, as in *tí?an té?el o?* 'It's over there', said in frustration after unsuccessfully searching for a machete lost in the woods—it's over there somewhere, but I can't find it. Nothing in the utterance form itself signals the difference between this understanding and the precise localization a speaker achieves when (s)he uses the same form to point at the machete in clear view. Both uses are equally appropriate, and this demonstrates that precise knowledge of location is cancelable.[26]

(iv) *Elaboration:* phrases headed by deictics can be elaborated by lexical descriptions, as in *way tinwiknal e?* 'here in my place' and *le maák o?* 'that guy', in which the deictic particles (underlined) flank lexical descriptions, with which they are obligatorily coreferential. (The simple forms are *way e?* 'here' and *lel o?* 'that'). Lexically elaborated forms are adlocative, adnominal, and so forth, where the deictic modifies a description, whereas simple forms are prolocative, pronominal, and so forth, where it stands for the referent in the absence of other description. This provides a grammatical framework for an whole array of controlled co-occurrence tests in ad-X function. Furthermore, deictics differ in terms of their derivational and inflectional possibilities, especially person and number.

(v) *Calculability:* as pointed out in the literature (Grice 1967; Levinson 1983:117; Sadock 1978), conversational implicatures need to be worked out on the basis of inferences from particulars of context. Encoded meaning ought to be more or less immediately apparent without bringing into consideration too much information about any particular interaction. Given the form *way tinwiknal e?* 'here in my place', uttered in any referential context, one can deduce that the speaker is making reference to a spatial zone that (s)he inhabits, although one cannot determine whether this zone is his bodily space or his home (see §3.2). If in another case the same utterance form is used to convey the directive 'bring the machete here to me', this fact is understood only by relating the encoded meaning to other aspects of context. It requires calculation by inference and so is probably not part of the language.[27]

The thrust of these five guidelines is to help in determining what aspects of the overall conveyed meaning in an utterance are present because they are part of the language, and which are present because they are part of the social situation.[28] The division is mainly a matter of the relative consistency or constancy of association between form and meaning, not of the *kind* of information. An obviously situational feature such as the perceptibility of a referent or the eye contact between interlocutors could be encoded in a set of deictic forms, provided it fitted the criteria. It makes no difference whether or not such a feature has a clear impact on the truth of propositions (Fillmore 1985). The same goes for the lexical meanings of such things as particles, interjections, and derivational affixes which encode linguistic meaning of a systematic, but not always truth-functional, sort.

2.2.2 Syntagmatic Structure of Referring Expressions

It is obvious that statements about the encoded meaning of deictic expressions must be grounded in the analysis of the structure of those expressions. In describing the semantics of deixis in Maya, it is useful to distinguish a range of construction types, including adlexical combinations of deictics and nondeictic description, complex constructions containing n-tuples of deictics interpreted as mutually reinforcing or coreferential, pat expressions based on deictics, canonical forms, and individual morphemes. I will take these up briefly in the order presented.

The combination of deictic identification and lexical description, mentioned in §2.2.1, takes the general form $_X[ID_x$ lexical description $TD]$, where the Initial Deictic particle occurs in initial position in the constituent, and the Terminal Deictic particle occurs in final position.[29] ID particles represent specific grammatical categories, such as noun (N), locative adverb (Loc), manner adverb (Man), temporal adverb (Temp Adv), and ostensive evidential adverb (OSTEV). These category values are represented as subscripted x in the template, which shows that whatever the value of the ID, this will be the category of the entire phrase (x = X). Examples include expressions like the following.

(3)   le **maák** o ʔ
           'that guy'

(4)   héʔe **ʔin sukúʔun** o ʔ
           'there's my brother'

(5)   b'ey **yeéte k'ìin** a ʔ
           'like this by day'

(6)   to **nukuč k'aáš** o ʔ
           'out there in (the) high forest'

Deictics in Maya combine according to regular rules to yield a repertoire of constructions larger than what is apparent from the basic inventory. Sentences (not usually phrases) may contain between two and five (or so) particles, all of which mutually reinforce one another and are usually coreferential.[30] One of the main sources of such n-tuples is the set of focus constructions treated in §§10.2–10.3. Rather than attempt a general account of these at this point, I will summarize them in the following template:

(7) $_S[ID_1 \; X \; ID_2 \; ID_3 \; Y \; TD_1 \; TD_2]$

This template shows that up to three ID particles and two TDs can co-occur in a single sentence. The variables X and Y stand for lexical descriptions:

X must be non-null and usually contains a verb; *Y* may be null and cannot contain a verb. Some examples:

(8)   hé? **yan** hé?el o?o?
        'There it is right there.'

(9)   tí?-**an** té?el o?o?
        'It's right over there.'

(10)   tí?-**an** té? way **nàac̕'il** a?a?
        'It's right there near here.'

(11)   le **b'á?a** hé?el o?
        'This thing right there.'

In the case of nominal deictics, the template $_{NP}$[ID TD ID TD] occurs as well, even though this is extremely irregular from the perspective of the rules on combining other deictics.

(12)   le ti? e lo?
        'that one that' (or 'that's the one')

Although some of the constructions are more common in speech than others, there is little sense in which they are fixed phrases. Three regular properties of constructions are: (i) the relative linear order of IDs occurring in a single construction is governed by strict constraints that hold across all contexts; (ii) the grammatical category values of the IDs go a long way towards predicting the contexts in which they may occur; (iii) some constructions are more routine, more common, less noteworthy than others.

  In addition to the straightforward combination of deictics according to regular principles, there are numerous routine expressions. These are relatively transparent semantically and do not appear to be idioms in the narrow sense. Nonetheless, they are sufficiently frequent in talk to be automatic and considerably more common than other, equally grammatical constructions. They include:

(13)   ké b'ey a? ké tol o?
        'like this, over there'

(14)   kó?on way e?
        'Come here (to me).'

(15)   šen té?el o?
        'Go over there (beat it!).'

(16)   má? hé?el a?a?
        'Here it is of course' (lit. 'here it isn't').[31]

(17)   le wá ti ʔ
            'Is it the one?'

(18)   té ʔ way nàaȼ'il a ʔ
            'right there nearby here'

The expression cited in (13) is the standard way that Maya speakers make a 'dummy quote'. It is used roughly the way English 'this and that' is in a sentence like 'we talked about this and that', where it stands for some more extended discourse. The two parts of the Maya expression are introduced by the complementizer ké 'that' (Sp. que), an indicator of a tacit verb of speaking to which the demonstratives are object complements; cf. tuy áʔal ah ten ké b'ey aʔ ké tol oʔ 'he said to me that like this, that over there'.[32] Sentence (14) is no more correct as a summons that the nearly identical kóʔoten téʔel aʔ 'come right here'. Yet the way eʔ form is more commonly heard. Furthermore, the reduction of the imperative kóʔoten 'come (to me)' to kóʔon occurs only when it is in collocation with way eʔ, another indicator that the expression is routinized. Sentence (15) is a standard way of telling a child or other subordinate to leave wherever (s)he is and go elsewhere. The eventual goal is unspecified, and the force of the utterance is simply 'beat it'.

In (16) the ostensive evidential particle appears in combination with the negative particle. Rather than a true negative reading, this can only be interpreted as an emphatic positive presentation: 'there it is (obviously, can't you see it?)'. The use of negation to mark emphasis and increased speaker involvement is a general feature of the Maya language, and this is not a fixed or even noteworthy phrase. However, it appears to correspond to a speech act especially common in Maya conversation, that of pointing out or presenting a referent while conveying that one considers this object to be readily available to the addressee as well. Typically, it occurs in response to a question regarding the location of the object, and this is the context speakers cite when given the form and asked to gloss it. Example (17) is the most direct way of asking whether some referent currently available to the speaker and addressee is identical to some other referent already established as common knowledge. For instance, A tells B to go get his machete from a spot where several have been set. B takes one of the objects in hand and asks A if it is his, saying, 'is it the one?' This is the only instance in the language in which the question particle can be the sole nondeictic item intervening between an ID and a TD. Example (18) is as bulky as (17) is brief, with the combination of two locative deictics in immediate sequence. This is the only construction in which such a pairing occurs. The adverbial 'nearby' reinforces the conveyed meaning of the deictics, that the referent is somewhere close to the zone within which the interaction is taking place.

In each of these cases, the conveyed meanings I have cited fit well with the semantic values of the parts of the constructions. I am not proposing that they are idiomatic. What they are is routinized ways of saying what they say; they are impressionistically more typical than other, nearly equivalent expressions. Moreover, these six examples are intended to suggest the range of constructions that are routinized; they are not a representative sample of the total set. Other examples will emerge from describing the use of individual categories of forms.

The citation forms presented in table 1.1 appear to correspond to what speakers consider complete units. Most are composed of a pairing of ID with TD. As I noted then, these are neither the simplest forms attested in everyday speech nor the most specific and complex. Rather, like 'basic categories' in cognitive studies, they are the most general terms in the system that correspond to the structure of attributes in the perceived world (Rosch 1978:30; Lakoff 1987:31ff.). The relevant portion of the perceived world in this case is the actional frame of an utterance, particularly an act of deictic reference. It is commonplace to attest in discourse instances of *le, hé?, té?, way,* and most other ID particles without any accompanying TD. Lexical description, gestures, or available knowledge may suffice to identify a referent, and the TD is simply omitted. Similarly, at least four of the six TDs often occur without an accompanying ID, tacked onto a pronoun or lexical expression. They have the general effect of directing the reference into the indexical field of utterance. These facts notwithstanding, speakers cannot gloss an isolated Terminal Deictic if it is offered to them in the mention mode; they reject it as not Maya, or at least incomplete. Similarly, if one offers *hé?* or *way* to a speaker in requesting a definition, there is a good chance that the form will be rejected as unintelligible, incomplete, or not Maya. These facts indicate that the canonical forms correspond to some perceived sense of wholeness or communicative adequacy: they are the least a speaker can utter while still making an understandable utterance.

In order to see why the pairing of Initial and Terminal deictic is the most basic construction for most categories, it is necessary to examine the informational differences between the two sets. IDs encode the grammatical category feature of the form (N, Loc, Temp Adv, ...) and therefore determine the role of the referent in some larger proposition (argument, circumstance). They also encode relatively abstract distinctions between categories such as ostensive presentation (*hé?*), egocentric inclusive (*way*), and exclusive (*tol*), sociocentric (*té?*), and current

speech act participants as a whole category (*t-*). What the Terminal Deictics add to the semantics of the forms is a relatively subtle array of indexical values, including Asymmetric, new information (*-a?*); Symmetric,
preestablished information (*-o?*); Perceptible, but not in sight, which I
have labeled 'peripheral sensory' (*-b'e?*). The concept of relative Immediacy is encoded primarily in the TDs, although some IDs also imply a
spatial relation. The reason that canonical forms have two parts is that the
combination of categorial information from an ID with the indexical and
purely pragmatic information in the TD most closely fits the slots of the
Figure-Ground structure of deictic reference. The few ID particles that occur alone in canonical form are not used in referential contexts but have
other functions.

2.2.3 Lexical Sets and Oppositions

When one examines the inventory of forms in a deictic system according
to their grammatical categories and encoded features, the question arises
as to the structure of the paradigms themselves. The idea of a lexical paradigm is most closely associated with structural studies of lexical fields
and semantic oppositions (Lyons 1977:chaps. 8, 9; Fillmore 1985). Fillmore (1978:149–51, 1985:227ff.) cogently criticizes the tendency in
some field studies to concentrate exclusively on, and oversystematize, relations between words to the exclusion of relations between words and
the world. Furthermore, it is widely recognized that major portions of the
lexicon are not organized into paradigmatic oppositions, which limits the
application of the theory. These criticisms, however, do not alter the fact
that deictic systems **are** organized into oppositions within subsets, corresponding to dimensions in the speech event.

My overview of paradigmatic structure in deixis will concentrate mainly
on the issue of what kinds of relations are attested. Many scholars have
proposed that the relations between forms tend to be highly regular, setting up proportional series such as *here:there :: this:that :: now:then*.
While such series do occur in languages and can be supported with evidence, they may play a relatively limited role in the overall system. The
reason is that not all categories in any deictic system are constructed in
the same way. It is important to expect a variety of structures rather than a
single form that operates throughout the deictic system.

In what follows I will briefly describe and illustrate (i) privative oppositions in which one form is marked and the other not; (ii) an equipollent pair in which both forms are marked; (iii) a part-whole relation, in
which the semantic value of one form corresponds to a part of another;
(iv) phases in an ordered sequence, such as the temporal indexicals 'a

while ago', 'just', 'right now', 'in a moment', and 'later'; (v) a rank order among three features according to the degree of immediacy they represent; and (vi) a network of features organized by a small number of primitive relations. Finally, the question of the relative proportionality of contrasts and oppositions in different categories will be posed.

A privative opposition is one in which two elements differ by a single feature F, which is present in one member and absent in the other, $+F$ vs. $\emptyset F$. The positively marked pole is described as 'marked', and the $\emptyset$ pole as 'unmarked' for F. When Jakobson ([1939] 1966b) first proposed this framework for semantics, he observed that 'zero signs' are found in natural languages at three distinct levels: the superficial form of expressions, their signification (or what we would call 'semantics'), and the stylistic organization of discourse. It is primarily the middle of the three, the idea of semantic markedness, that concerns us here. Consider a pair of expressions such as *té'el a?* '(right) there' and *té'el o?* 'there', which differ only by the TD particles *a?* Immediate and *o?* Non-Immediate. If these make up a privative opposition, as my glosses suggest, then there should be evidence of this. Ideally, the marked member should have a more restricted grammatical distribution, because of its greater informational content, which limits the possibility of combination with other features. Thus, while the Non-Immediate deictic can be combined with the adverbs *nàa¢'* 'near' and *naáč* 'far', the Immediate one is rarely if ever used with 'far'. Further, only the Non-Immediate form is used routinely in non-referential contexts, where the speaker does not know or care the precise location (s)he is indicating. These will be called 'throwaway' uses in chapter 9: 'I heaved it out there (somewhere)', and 'Go there!' meaning 'beat it'. These differences in use reflect the positive specification of Immediacy in the marked pole, as opposed to its absence in the $\emptyset$ pole.

In attempting to apply markedness to a deictic system, it is important to bear in mind two basic assumptions of the theory. First, although privative relations appear on all three levels of semantics, superficial form, and discourse, there is no *necessary* correspondence between the three (Jakobson [1939] 1966b). A semantically marked feature could be indicated by a formally unmarked expression, and the zero pole of a semantic opposition could be expressed by a formally marked construction. It goes without saying that the stylistic markedness of linguistic expressions need not be identical to either their semantic specificity or their formal complexity. Therefore, correlations among the three levels need to be worked out rather than assumed.

Second, it is often stated that markedness theory is committed to the proposition that encoded meaning is invariant, so that all tokens of a given form have exactly the same meaning (e.g., Timberlake 1982). This is only partly true. Marking theory does posit an underlying level of meaning present in all instances of a form, which Jakobson called a *Grundbedeutung*. This is not unlike the idea that sentences have encoded meaning that remains constant across uses, even though situational meanings differ. But it also recognized in markedness that situational meanings arise and are part of the semantic description; Jakobson called them *Nebenbedeutungen* 'secondary meanings' and *Sonderbedeutungen* 'special meanings.' Furthermore, it is assumed that a single linguistic form can, and usually does, enter into several oppositions, implying that it bears several feature specifications. Marked status on one feature parameter does not assure marked status on another; the form 'men' may be marked for plural as opposed to the unmarked 'man', unmarked for gender as opposed to the marked 'woman', marked for *Homo sapiens* (or some such) as opposed to the unmarked 'primate'. Finally, it was recognized from the outset in marking theory that the unmarked member of an opposition tends to be used in a wider variety of contexts, with a wider range of functions than the marked pole. There is no claim that the unmarked form is semantically invariant at any level more specific than the absence of the feature for which it is unmarked. At the level of 'secondary' and 'special' uses, it is variety and not uniformity that is expected (cf. Friedrich 1974:9–22, 1985:185). As we shall see, the Maya deictics obviously enter into various oppositions, and virtually all show a range of distinct uses. This does not rule out a markedness account of at least some oppositions.

Whereas a **privative** relation opposes a positively marked pole, [+F], to an unmarked one, [Ø F], an **equipollent** relation opposes two positively marked poles, [+F] vs. [+Z].[33] An example is *way eʔ* 'here (Inclusive egocentric)' vs. *tol oʔ* 'out there (Exclusive egocentric).' Unlike the Immediate/Non-Immediate pair, this one shows no asymmetry in which one member can be used in a wider variety of contexts than the other. We find *way nàaȼ' eʔ* 'here nearby' and *to naáč oʔ* 'out there far away', but neither *way naáč eʔ* 'here far away', nor *to nàaȼ oʔ* 'out there nearby'. The Exclusive form naturally has 'throwaway' uses lacking in the Inclusive form, but the latter has several bodily centered uses lacking in the Exclusive form as well (see §9.2.1). The point is that the two are dichotomous in a way that the Immediate/Non-Immediate pair is not. If one were to assume that all oppositions are privative, the difference between the two pairs would be left unaccounted for.[34]

Privative oppositions are logically part-whole relations, in which the unmarked member includes the marked: the Ø form can be used in all of the semantic contexts of the +F form, in addition to others in which the +F form does not occur. In hierarchical terms, the Ø pole is superordinate to, and less specific than, the +F pole. But there is another sense of part-whole inclusion that applies to deictics. It is linked more to the geometry of the spaces to which they refer than to the range of linguistic uses they display. Being regional, the forms *way e?* 'here' and *tol o?* 'out there' tend strongly to refer to extended spaces that include within their scope the more restricted points referred to with *té?el a?* 'right there' and *té?el o?* 'there'. Similarly, the segment of time referred to by *b'ehelá?e?* 'today, nowadays' always includes the more restricted times of *saámeh* 'earlier in same day', *taánt e?* 'just (immediately prior in same day)', and several other temporal deictics. These inclusion relations cannot be captured in markedness terms, since the more inclusive forms are not used for the less inclusive ones. The referent of 'human body' includes the referent of 'thumb', but it does not follow from this that the two words form a privative opposition.

Another kind of relation, found especially in the temporal dimension of deictic systems, is that of phases ordered in a fixed sequence. 'Yesterday, today, tomorrow', form a sequence of days; 'a while ago', 'a moment ago', 'now', 'in a moment', 'later', and 'tonight', may in some languages (including Maya; cf. §1.2) be defined as a sequence of phases in the diurnal cycle. Further, the fixed sequence relation can be involved at least secondarily in spatial oppositions such as the 'forward path' use of 'here' (as in 'here we go') and the 'path already covered' use of 'there' (as in 'there is where we came from', cf. §9.2.2 for detailed discussion of Maya examples). Speaking more generally, the conceptual relation of successive points in a fixed sequence is one of the basic schemata in Maya spatiotemporal orientation. It is present not only in the deictic and non-deictic resources for spatial reference but also in the way actors construct and represent domestic and agricultural spacetime (see §8.4).

Rank-order relations are those in which several forms are ordered according to an established chain of precedence, such as the terms denoting ranks in a military system (Fillmore 1978:164). In such a relation, no two terms are on the same level, nor is any one usually used in place of another. The perceptual features Tactual, Visual, and Peripheral sensory (chapter 5) appear to exemplify a rank order. The chain of precedence is based on the relative immediacy and fullness of perceptual evidence corresponding to the feature, such that Tactual > Visual > Peripheral (Tact, Vis, Periph, where Peripheral is defined as nontactual, nonvisual perception; usually it is auditory, but it can be olfactory). Rank ordering can under certain circumstances be treated as a series of privative oppositions, so that highest rank correlates with the most marked, and the lowest with the least. The problem with this is that the upper and lower extremes in a ranking are not usually used to stand for the whole scale, and even very low-ranked terms can be highly specific semantically. This is the case with Peripheral sensory evidence in Maya deixis, which is perhaps the most highly marked term in the category (Hanks 1984a).

The kind of semantic structure that may correspond best to a deictic system as a whole is what Fillmore (1978:164) called the 'network'. A network is a system made up of a relatively small number of primitive relations, rather than any single one. For instance, in my account, Maya deictics are organized by a combination of **paradigmatic oppositions**, such as Immediate/Non-Immediate; relations of strict **inclusion**, such as 'a while ago' and 'today'; **sequential** relations, such as 'yesterday, today, and tomorrow'; **rank order** relations, such as the perceptual features; and some others that will be introduced in the course of detailed description.

The general problem raised by the variety of semantic structures in a single deictic system is the extent to which it is, in fact, a single sub-system in the language. Many linguists have observed the tendency for such terms to fit into regular, proportional oppositions, and this is so, to a degree.[35] But the key questions from a descriptive perspective are: which aspects of the system are proportional and to what degree of regularity? One goal of this work is to *demonstrate* the systematicity of Maya deixis, while making explicit numerous points at which the system breaks down into type- or token-specific features. Furthermore, the linguistic oppositions between features in the semantics of deixis are related to extra-linguistic schemata. They unavoidably link up with schematic knowledge which participants bring to the interactive situation and rely on in localizing referents. And they are also related to nonlinguistic schemata, such as bodily, domestic, and agricultural space. The kinds of homology and diagrammatic iconicity that unite the different categories in the language also unite categories to conceptual representations at play in other areas of social life.[36]

2.2.4 A Prototype Approach to Deixis

Where do we stand in the semantics of deixis? There is a close relation between linguistic meaning and language use, a basic premise of U semantics and virtually any level 2 or level 3 theory in Harman's terms. A central core of this relation is articulated in a Figure-Ground structure in which the figural element is the referential object and the ground is the indexical frame relative to which it is individuated. Indexical frames can be discussed and ordered in terms of their relative symmetry, and when this is done, they can be correlated with the kinds of identifying features for which they can serve as ground. Deictic expressions in referential context show several levels of formal complexity, from the single morpheme to combinations of five (and perhaps more) forms. The constructions can be summarized in terms of templates (the rules for which were alluded to but will be spelled out in chapter 10). The paradigmatic relations among opposing deictics are also various, including privative and equipollent marking oppositions, part-whole relations, successive relations, rank order, and networks. Obviously the idea of frames, from which we began, is yet another kind of organization. Can these various observations be integrated into a single descriptive account? And if so, of what sort?

I think at least part of an answer to these questions is to be found in the theory of semantic prototypes. Fillmore (1982) and Lakoff (1987:462ff.) have each proposed a prototype account of at least part of a deictic system, and I draw on their work in the following suggestions. Berlin and Kay's (1969) study of color categories demonstrated cross-linguistically one of the main ideas of prototype studies, that categories consist of both focal areas and boundaries, and moreover, that native speakers are more consistent in their judgments of focal values than boundary ones (13). Instead of envisioning semantic features that define necessary and sufficient conditions on proper referential objects, Berlin and Kay recognized that category membership is sometimes a gradient instead of all or none. Categories have focal, or 'core' referents, which are their 'best exemplars'. Furthermore, the boundaries between categories are not clean divisions, without volume, but fuzzy and relatively 'thick'. Beyond the best exemplars may be an entire range of uses of the category that are less than exemplary but nonetheless routine. In other words, the features defining the category are not necessary and sufficient to membership and not even all equally important.

The concept of core features permitted Berlin and Kay (1969) to lump together a broad range of potentially different dimensions into a single set of basic color categories that could be applied across languages. Among the dimensions they did not address were different qualities of light in relation to color, the limitations of Munsell chips (as an experimental tool), the different values attached to different colors in a given culture, object colors as opposed to luminous colors, and different kinds of category foci. Conklin (1973) points out that a description of color categories in languages ought to incorporate these elements. The analogous point for a descriptive framework incorporating 'basic deictic categories' is that highly abstract core features should be complemented by more specific

accounts of the interactional corollaries of use. The lumping that results
in relatively simple but denuded basic categories does not preclude a care-
ful splitting of the details of use and cultural context.

The concept of a 'basic category' belongs to a semantics oriented towards the language-external objects for which expressions stand. Rosch
(1978:30) observed that categories tend to become defined in terms of
instances that display the attributes most representative of the category as
a whole and least representative of items outside the category. This tends
to maximize the distinctions between 'best exemplars'. Basic-level categories are those that correspond to basic-level objects in the world. These
are defined at the most inclusive level at which there are attributes common to all instances. 'Chair' is a basic-level category, whereas 'furniture'
includes too many dissimilar objects, and 'halogen floor lamp' is too specific. In general, basic-level categories are overdetermined, since they are
reinforced by a number of other factors. One of these is the fact that the
objects to which they correspond are those with which speakers have the
most constant kinds of motor interactions (Rosch 1978:31–35). We can
see clearly in these features that the basic level is defined in terms of how
actors experience the world in which they act; and we see how the 'natural
discontinuities' and 'information-rich bundles' in the world become the
core objects of their categories. The same orientation is characteristic of
Berlin and Kay's (1969) use of color chips, Berlin's (1978) treatment of
Tzeltal Mayan numeral classifiers, and most other extensionally based
semantics.[37]

Nearly all prototype theorists have emphasized the central role of
actors' experience of the world in determining the semantic categories of
their language. Rosch (1978:40) pointed out that to speak of a prototype
is actually a misstatement or an abbreviation for a statement about judgments of typicality. Coleman and Kay (1981:30) determined the prototypical meaning of 'lie' by eliciting judgments and commentary from
native speakers on scenarios and hypothetical uses of the term. Fillmore's
(1985) emphasis on the role of 'interpretive frames' in U semantics can
also be seen as a natural outgrowth of the recognition that the situated
knowledge and expectations that speakers bring to their experience in the
world have a basic impact on the semantics of the language. This point
will become a major concern in §2.3, where we examine the role of native speaker common sense in reference.

A prototype approach to deixis can provide a means of incorporating
into the description several important points not well handled by more
formalist semantic theories based on necessary and sufficient features.

(i) **Variability.** Natural language deictics tend to be variable in the range of functions for which they are used. Lakoff (1984:13ff.) shows eleven subconstructions (particular uses) of deictic 'there', and we will see comparable numbers for the different Maya constructions in chapters 4, 5, and 9. By distinguishing core from extended uses, we can encompass the variability without forcing it into a single abstract meaning.

(ii) **Weighting.** The features or conditions making up a category are not all equally central; some have a higher 'cue validity' than others. One example of this is the difference between relational and characterizing features, as opposed to indexical, background features in referential deixis. The former, being more focal, tend to correspond to situational attributes with high cue validity, such as whether the interactants can touch, see, and merely recall the referent. Less salient but still differential are features of the relation between the two interactants; can they touch, see, hear each other?

(iii) **Actional context.** As Fillmore (1982:34) pointed out, prototypes may be linguistically realized by categories of which the best use is "one in which the speaker is appropriately engaged in the sort of activity in connection with which the category has been a special name." The linkage of deictic categories to actional wholes, such as presentative, directive, and singular definite reference, fits this manifestation of prototypes. Under this view then, the multifunctionality of deictic reference, its combination of indexical with relational and characterizing features and speech act force, is a natural corollary of the categories rather than a troublesome epiphenomenon of use.

(iv) **Native judgments.** Native speakers turn out to have well-formed and relatively extensive ideas about what constitutes typical deictic use, if one asks them. In these judgments, they rely systematically on knowledge derived from their background competencies as actors in their given culture. We will demonstrate this for Maya by working through the ethnographic foundation of this background knowledge and the ways in which it enters into the determination of reference in use. Elsewhere (Hanks 1983:part 3; In press), I have examined in detail the ways in which native ideas reify a set of typical uses while excluding or downplaying nontypical ones. This provides further evidence for which uses are the more central ones and which are extended. The reinsertion of the dimension of native concepts of language into semantic structure is one of the strongest features of this approach, which also serves to link it to recent developments in anthropological linguistics (Silverstein 1979, 1985; and see §2.3).

What kinds of features make up the semantic representation of a deictic construction? They include the following five.

(i) A feature indicating the **grammatical category** of the type. In

Maya, the Initial (ID) particles all bear a fixed feature which is invariantly in force whenever the type is instantiated: *hé?el-* OSTEV (ostensive evidential); *hé?el-* DMOD (modal auxiliary); *té?el-* DLOC (locative adverb); *tol-* DLOC; *way* DLOC; *le* DNOM (nominal); *b'ey* DMAN (manner adverb); *taánt-* DTEMP (temporal adverb); *t-* PART (participant). These features imply syntactic frames in which the particles can occur.

(ii) A feature indicating the core **communicative force** of the type, chosen from the set:[38] PRESENTATIVE (handing the referent over or acting it out); DIRECTIVE (pointing as a way of telling the addressee to look or focus attention on the referent); REFERENTIAL (identifying a referent uniquely, by whatever characterization); PHATIC (merely maintaining contact with addressee; not identifying any referent); EXPRESSIVE (expressing the speaker's felt certainty or intensity of involvement in the utterance).

(iii) Specification of the **referential structure** in its three components of (a) relational features, which I call R values; (b) indexical coordinates that serve as origo to the relation; and (c) characterizing features that designate properties of referents (such as Regional, Punctate, Human). The R values (a) of any deictic may be represented by a range of alternatives if the type displays a variety of uses in these terms. They include TACTUAL, VISUAL, PERIPHERAL SENSORY, DISCOURSE, INCLUSIVE, EXCLUSIVE, IMMEDIATE, NON-IMMEDIATE, as well as others to be presented below. These are semantic analogues of the modes of access through which participants individuate referents in the world-within-reach. The Indexical ground (b), as we saw above, actually consists of a fairly complex set of coordinates. Lumping them into the generalized dimension of relative symmetry, they can be treated as S (speaker), A (addressee), and SA (speaker and addressee). The first two are asymmetric and the third is symmetric.

(iv) **Bodily gestures** conventionally associated with the type, including the extending in the hand of presentatives, directed gaze and manual point with directives, the up-and-out flick of the wrist for EXCLUSIVE in Maya, and down-and-in of INCLUSIVE; such enactments as the Kuna pointed lip gesture (Sherzer 1973) and Maya body measures, insofar as they are associated with deictic types.

(v) Any **special constraints** on the distribution of the type relative to other expressions that cannot be motivated by the syntactic categories involved. Thus, for instance, presentative uses of OSTEV particles are subject to a range of restrictions on co-occurence in the same sentence with particles indicating speaker uncertainty, indefiniteness, interrogativity, and so forth (see chapter 5).

As the grammatical category features make explicit, deictic types are organized into subsets whose members all share the same grammatical feature. Thus, despite the differences of the four DLOC particles (*tíʔ*, *téʔel, way, tol*), they belong to a set whose common feature is DLOC; *héʔel* is the only OSTEV and *le* the only DNOM, but there are numerous DTEMPS. While the match between the linguistic categories of deixis and the coordinates of speech context is far from one-to-one, each major category of forms does correspond to a **core dimension.** A core dimension is the domain within the total deictic field that the formal category most finely subdivides. For example, the spatial location of a referent is something often relevant to a speaker's choice of deictic, but of all the forms in Maya language, it is the DLOCs which most finely subdivide the spatial domain, into an Inclusive/Exclusive opposition plus an Immediate/Non-Immediate one (see chapter 9). Space is the core dimension of the DLOCs. On the other hand, perceptual evidence of a referent is often relevant to deictic choice, but nowhere in the language is this domain more finely calibrated than in the OSTEVs, which distinguish Visual from Tactual from Peripheral sensory. The core dimension of the OSTEVs is Perception. Thus, **domains,** as used here, are elements of actional wholes in which deictic reference is performed, and **dimensions** are the semantic categories corresponding to domains. The core dimension of the DTEMPS is obviously relative Time, and that of the PART category is the Participant structure of the event. On the basis of observing everyday usage, one is led to posit at least seven deictic dimensions for Maya: Participants, Perception, Spatial, Temporal, Attention focus, Discourse, and Background knowledge. These correspond to domains of speech context that speakers attend to in selecting, as well as interpreting, a deictic.[39]

The accessibility relations (R values) of individual deictic types are taxonomically subordinate to the dimensions. Participant is subdivided by three values of person and two of number; Perception is subdivided by three values according to the sense engaged; Spatial is subdivided four ways, by Inclusive/Exclusive and Immediate/Non-Immediate, and so forth. Simplifying for heuristic purposes, the dimensions and R values can be summarized as in figure 2.1.

One major way in which Figure 2.1 is (over)simplified is that it presents the values as an unstructured list of alternatives within a dimension. We will see in chapters 4, 5, 6, and 9 that each dimension is structured slightly differently from the others, a point foreshadowed in §2.2.3 above. Equally egregious is the fact that this taxonomy is entirely unweighted, in the sense that it shows the inventory of R values without pairing them with any Indexical grounds. These are only the figural components in the referential structure.[40] In order to depict the basic Indexical grounds, we must introduce a further taxonomy, such as the one in figure 2.2.

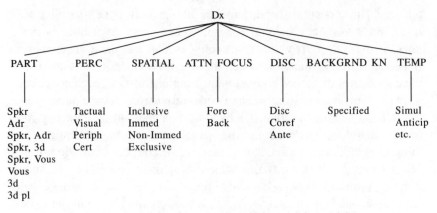

Fig. 2.1. Dimensions and values in the semantics of Maya deixis (partial).

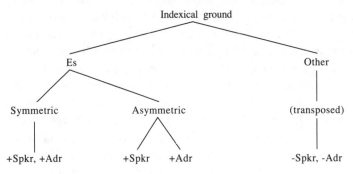

Fig. 2.2. Indexical grounds in Maya deixis.

Figure 2.2 shows that the different Indexical grounds significant in deictic use in Maya are divided into those based on the speech act participants (*ego, tu*) and those not based on current participants (other; [−*ego*, −*tu*]). Participant grounds are further divided into symmetric ([+*ego*, +*tu*]) and asymmetric ([+*ego*] or [+*tu*]). Non-Participant objects and narrated events serve as Indexical ground in a variety of transposed usages in Maya. For example, narrators may break into the events in their story, using the narrative frame as a ground—'Here we are walking through the woods'—or otherwise shifting voice in the discourse. Similarly, in quoted speech, deictic reference is grounded in some reported context. Ritual discourse in particular involves major transpositions, to be taken up in chapters 5, 7, and 8. In many genres, the current participants serve as the ground.

However, this leaves underspecified the correlations between Indexical grounds and R values, something the Figure-Ground structure forces us to consider. Are there regular pairings between the two, such that certain R values tend to be paired with a relatively more symmetric or asymmetric indexical frame? Suppose we listed the R values as a set of columns and listed the Indexical ground values as rows. The intersections would define cells, for which the sign (+) could indicate that the R value and I ground are paired in the semantics of some type, and emptiness could indicate that the pairing fails to occur. A form like *hé?el a?* 'here it is (presenting)' tends strongly to occur in contexts in which the speaker and the addressee are face-to-face, focused on the referent, and within actual reach of one another. This is equivalent to saying that the communicative force of Presentative, and the R value Tactual, tend to be paired with a highly symmetric Indexical ground (cf. §2.1.3). What would a whole system look like if laid out in terms of the combinations of R values with Indexical ground types, and how would systems compare? The Figure-Ground proposal inevitably forces one to examine the pairings of relational with indexical components. For heuristic purposes, we start from the simplest template of types, shown in figure 2.2, in which coparticipants occupy the origo directly. It should be borne in mind, however, that communicative practices routinely involve various kinds of decenterings and transpositions in which deictic categories play a key role. We will reconsider these questions in chapters 4, 6, and 10.

2.3 REFERENCE AS A COMMONSENSE CONSTRUCT

A major issue for the semantics of understanding is the source and form of knowledge that speakers bring to bear on the interpretation of utterances. What goes into an 'interpretive frame', and what can native speakers teach us about it? This is the third and final component in my approach to reference. Rosch's (1978) statement that the 'natural discontinuities' of objects in the world play a determining role in categorization can be misleading. It suggests that the structure of semantic categories in language may be reducible to a reflection of the structure of objects in the world.[41] Such a reduction fails to take account of the observed variability of languages and cultures and holds little promise for the study of deixis.[42] Sahlins ([1976] 1977) worked out a more productive synthesis, by drawing out the anthropological implications of Berlin and Kay's discoveries. He argued that perceptual structures, such as the *Urfarben* "are only the raw materials of cultural production, remaining latently available and incompletely realized until a meaningful content is attributed to the elements of the cultural set" (Sahlins 1977:177). Making the point more generally, the question What goes into a frame? cannot be answered by appealing to 'the natural discontinuities' of the world, because these are

the **resources** of cultural and linguistic production, not its determinants.
It is only when invested with meaning in a social context that these categories become constituents in communication. In chapter 3, I will argue
that bodily space, widely considered to be the 'natural bedrock' of deixis,
is itself a cultural construct. Insofar as it is meaningful, potentially
shared, and contributory to understanding, what goes into an interpretive
frame is therefore a social and cultural product.

2.3.1 Schematic and Local Knowledge

It is helpful to distinguish between two modes of knowledge that speakers
typically combine in understanding. **Schematic knowledge** is embodied
in prefabricated representations of objects and their relations. These objects are vastly many and include social spaces, individuals, and categories of events (Cicourel 1985:162; 1986:92). **Local knowledge** is that
which is produced as an "emergent element of the particular setting and
the way the participants project and revise their immediate comprehension over the course of an exchange" (Cicourel 1985:172). Thus, local
knowledge is necessarily diachronic in the sense that it is constantly changing, whereas schematized categories are more enduring. This is not to say
that they do not have a diachronic dimension, but rather that they change
at a different rate and according to different principles. The fact that interactants must combine the two kinds of knowledge in everyday talk is itself a source of change, leading to the creation and revision of schemata.

While the distinction between schematic and local knowledge is employed widely in cognitive studies (see Cicourel's 1985, 1986 synthesis),
it also fits directly into Schutz's treatment of the interactive process and
what he called the 'stock of knowledge'. In fact, one of the central components of Schutz's work was his study of the properties of social schemata as resources for interpretation and action. The stock of knowledge
was embodied, for Schutz (1970:74ff.), in preconstituted 'types', which
are routine patterns of experience and interaction through which actors
recognize objects, individuals, and events not as mere things but as instances of familiar categories. Confronted by a dog in the street, one usually sees a dog, not an arbitrary material form or swatch of color. Without
any local evidence, one can anticipate that it has teeth of a certain shape
and size range, a tail, and perhaps dewclaws. Recognition entails expectation. Furthermore, a knowledge of types is what makes it possible to
repeat an act of recognition or an act of expression. In absolute terms, no
two utterances, like no two dogs, are alike, but actors are commonsen-

sically certain that they can repeat themselves and repeatedly recognize objects in their world.

Schutz (1970:119ff.) saw the collection of types by which social actors know the world as a 'frame of reference'. This frame determines which facts and experiences actors treat as equivalent, and which ones as distinct. It transforms the utter uniqueness of experience into a repeatable event and serves as a schema for both interpretation and orientation. It determines in large measure what actors view as relevant to given experiences on the basis of their typical features. Part of the frame of reference is the assumption that in face-to-face relations, interlocutors' types are congruent and their perspectives at least partly reciprocal (cf. §2.1.3). Furthermore, actors typify themselves, situating and monitoring their own conduct and persona relative to the roles, categories, and routines that they apply to others and that they perceive others to apply to them.

Interacting with the schematic types that actors share is the local process of applying these types in understanding. Schutz observed that types are rectified and corroborated by supervening experience rather than being maintained as fixed structures. At any point in an overall communicative process, the knowledge taken for granted as already established between interactants is subject to revision.[43] Prototypes are a special instance of typification, and they are revisable in just the way Schutz has pointed out. In proposing to treat deixis in terms of such constructs, one commits oneself to describing the routine patterns of deictic practice, the schematic types which constitute the relevant 'frame of reference', and the ways speakers understand deixis itself as a typical part of the world.

In introducing this division among kinds of knowledge, it is appropriate to point out that for native actors, much of communication involves a practical mastery of activities that may not involve knowledge in the sense of cognitive representations and computations. Commonsense mastery of language depends on skill at the level of what Dreyfus and Dreyfus (1987:338) call "expertise." Expert native speakers produce and understand much of speech unreflectively, without evaluation of alternatives and without following rules as such. Instead, relying on extensive familiarity with situations and their outcomes, the expert simply does what is to be done in recognizable situations. Habituation, routine, and expertise are pervasive in linguistic practices and establish the baseline of automaticity that we associate with fluent native speech. Interacting with the conceptual level of referential structures is therefore the unreflective, more immediate level of embodied expertise. Typification as an ongoing social process has roots in both. We will return to habituation in chapter 4, when we explore participation frameworks in Maya that are semiotically complex but automatically intelligible to native speakers.

2.3.2 Native Metalanguage

For the reasons spelled out in the foregoing, a necessary component in the semantics of understanding is some account of what native speakers consider to be the most typical uses of their language.[44] Native metalinguistic commentary gives abundant evidence of the routine interactive frames in relation to which deictic functions must be understood. Speakers do associate deictics with coherent types of interactive frames. These consist of routine sequences of speech acts (interactive 'moves' in Goffman's sense) that typically unfold in the context of certain perceptual, kinesthetic, and locative-spatial coordinates. The 'typicality' of the frames lies in their being schematic rather than precise in detail, oriented toward the accomplishment of practical communicative tasks (like making an ostensive reference) rather than abstract descriptions, focused selectively on core features of the constructions rather than treating all features as equally important, and variable in application rather than determining necessary and sufficient conditions for proper usage.[45]

Native glosses of speech can provide an objective document of the information that speakers bring to bear on talk when they interpret it (Vološinov [1929] 1986: 112–25). In describing what they take to be the meanings of various expressions, they reveal the local standards of proper use. My research in Maya indicates that these standards consist of relatively complex actional wholes of which deictic constructions are a part. This is unsurprising given what we know of the structure of deixis, but the standards are nonetheless revealing because they engage the deictics with other, schematically represented coordinates in social context. The ethnographic foundation of indexical frames is, if not laid bare, then at least brought to the fore in a way not possible in routine practice (since the indexical component is usually the background, not the figural object of commentary).

Because speakers do not use language precisely as they say they do, their reports and commentaries give an imperfect, sometimes distorting picture of routine direct use. It is nearly always possible to show that the examples they come up with to describe their language are less than fully accurate for the phenomena they describe. Many details of form, context, and variation are overlooked. Consequently, if one were to view native commentaries as a corpus of meaning statements, they would be in need of extensive revision. By altering the indexical frames in which a single deictic form is illustrated, one can produce different conveyed meanings and cancel many of the components that speakers claim are present in their own examples. Insofar as their explanatory remarks are formulated in Maya, using other, nondeictic expressions, such as *nàa¢'* 'near', *naáč* 'far', and *-iknal* 'body space', they unavoidably introduce distortion— because these other terms have different extensions and conceptual structures from the deictics to which they are applied.[46] How can one propose to treat such flawed accounts as 'objective evidence'?

The value of native metalanguage as a social datum is not a function of its accuracy with respect to what it describes. It can only provide clues to the overall system of categories and uses. Rather, it is a documentary expression of what speakers *think* they (and others) do. It is in this sense that Vološinov ([1929] 1986) treated reported speech as a reflection of the 'social evaluation' of language. Dubbing the category 'linguistic ideology', Silverstein (1979:193) explained that "linguistic ideologies are any set of beliefs about language articulated by the users as a rationalization or justification of perceived language structure and use. If we compare such ideologies with what goes on under the name of 'scientific' statements about language, we might find that in certain areas the ideological beliefs do in fact match the scientific ones, though the two will, in general, be part of divergent larger systems of discourse and enterprise."

Native glosses therefore are 'objective', not because they are faithful to some factual record established apart from actors' common sense and ideological assumptions, but because they instantiate those assumptions.[47]

Native metalinguistic commentary has still other contributions to make to U semantics. These follow mainly from the fact that metalanguage is itself a type of linguistic usage. In talking about their own language in their own language, speakers must manage the distinction between use, mention, and quoted and direct discourse. As Jakobson ([1957] 1971) and Weinreich (1963) observed, it is a diacritic feature of natural languages that they can be used as their own metalanguages. Take the boldface portions of sentences '**that**'s not what I meant', 'don't speak to me **that way**', and 'this word "**here**" is a tricky one to define'. Although only the last sentence actually reproduces a linguistic form in the mention mode, all three show deictics used to refer to language, as the accompanying comments make plain. Reference to and comments on language are part of routine use, and metalanguage therefore falls within the scope of pragmatics even narrowly conceived (Levinson 1983:chap. 1; Morris 1971:47– 48; Silverstein 1979, 1985). What we stand to learn from the form of metalanguage is how speakers manage the communicative task of formulating intelligible statements that inevitably combine direct use, mention or quotation, reference to chunks of discourse or linguistic forms, and other modes as well (cf. Hanks In press).

As a commonsense or ideological construct, reference is therefore determined by the stock of social knowledge and common experiences that speakers bring to the speech event. The uniqueness and identifiability demanded in philosophical definitions of reference are secured by interpretive frames that are derived and sustained in a general process of 'typification'. In a sense, this is foreseen in the thesis that it is the expression in union with a context that secures uniqueness of reference. But by working through the encoded linguistic structures of deixis, the cognitive foundations of the categories in both local and schematic knowledge, and the social foundations and expressions of that knowledge, we trace out some of the consequences of this thesis. The result is a more explicit approach to reference as a social practice, in which language is articulated with its social and cultural context without reducing either to a reflection or epiphenomenon of the other.

2.4 Summary: Units and Levels of Referential Practice

In describing the approach to reference outlined in this chapter as 'relational', we pick up on a central theme of chapter 1. In place of a unitary egocentric view of deixis, in which the limits of the phenomenon are given in advance, I suggested that a more appropriate approach is one in which what we call deixis lies at the intersection of a set of relations. These include the articulations of linguistic form with actual utterance contexts, of conventional categories with real world particulars, of the speaking agent with other agents in a framework of participation, of linguistic components contributing to reference with ones contributing to other functions, of spatial with evidential domains of utterance context. The indexical foundation of deixis invites one to view it as a simple, direct anchor between language and the world. But we can see from the present chapter how misguided such a view would be. Limiting our discussion to ostensive reference as an act (§2.1), we find not a simple one-to-one mapping of word with thing but a specific relational structure in which objects of reference are individuated relative to indexical frameworks. This fundamental relativity has consequences for the entire description: the interplay between speech events and narrated frames motivates a wide range of other articulations in the semantics, actual practices, and commonsense understandings of deixis. One of these, which I dubbed the principle of relative symmetry, connects the interactive relation between coparticipants with the use conditions of referential forms.

Turning to deixis as a conventional system (§2.2), we worked towards a modified prototype framework in which contextual variation, functional plurality, and native speaker typification play a central role in defining semantic structure.

Finally (§2.3) the commonsense understanding of verbal reference by native speakers was adduced to offset a third order of facts, distinguishable from both the activity and the semantics of deixis. The commonsense understanding of deictic acts rests on interactions between schematic (or prefabricated) and local (or emergent) aspects of participant knowledge. Thus in understanding even simple cases of reference, as in 'Put it here (pointing)', interactants rely on their ability to synthesize already-established knowledge with new knowledge in the course of being produced. Moreover, speakers are able to comment on deictic usage in pointed and revealing metalinguistic glosses. These rest for their intelligibility on the semiotic mechanisms of metalanguage and on the practical mastery that native speakers possess and habitually sustain in their practices. Thus again we are faced with a relational interplay.

It is important to keep in mind that these three levels or moments in the overall makeup of ostensive reference do not line up in any simple, constant way. A description of actual usage will explain neither the structure of the language nor the indigenous understanding of it. None of the three is reducible to a precipitate or special case of the others, which is to say that they do not correspond neatly, nor do they stand in relations of taxonomic inclusion. Nor can we posit one or another domain as the derivational source of the others. This raises one of the central problems of this book, which can be summarized in a question: how can we move analytically between formal structures, actual speech events involving real agents, and the sociocultural contexts of which they are a part? My claim is that to do so requires a relational approach of the kind outlined here. Still very abstract, this schema will become more specific when we apply it to the description of referential practices in Maya.

In the following chapters, the analytic matrix will be extended considerably, and it is helpful at this point to look ahead to where we are going. Chapter 3 explores the sociocultural construction of the human body and its role in grounding deictic reference in Maya. This should be seen as an elaboration of the sociocentric foundation of reference, already introduced in §§1.2 and 2.1, as well as an attempt to give ethnographic backing to the idea of schematic knowledge by describing some of the organizing principles of body space and the domestic field among the Maya people with whom I have worked. The scale between symmetric and asymmetric interactive grounds, introduced in §2.1, is applied next (§3.4) to genres

of routine interaction around the homestead. The point is to show that the
indexical conditions on referential practices among coresidents are defined in part by their social relations. The language of relative symmetry
provides terms in which to explore the articulation between linguistic
structure, genres of discourse, and the social field. The specific consequences of social asymmetry for deictic reference are illustrated in the
final sections of the chapter.

Chapter 3 is organized into sections focused on what I will call 'fields'.
As used in this book, the term 'field' designates a social construct of intermediate size (larger than an interaction but smaller than a society), organized according to some identifiable principles and populated by some
identifiable set of agents. I will treat body space as a 'corporeal' field in
order to foreground its social character. This in turn is defined within the
'domestic field', in which social relations are regulated according to a native code of orderliness that links interactive patterns to social divisions
of rank, residence, and gender. The extended example of instrumental
speech in §3.5, in which deixis is shown to be highly sensitive to divisions in the corporeal and domestic fields, took place in the context of
agricultural labor. The main participants were a father and son who routinely work together, which grounds the example in the domestic field, as
well as in the overlapping field of agricultural production. In subsequent
chapters we will explore spatial and temporal embodiments of all of these
fields, as well as their symbolic articulations in what I will call the 'field
of ritual practice'.

There are important differences of scope and content in these various
fields, and in designating them with this term I do not wish to equate
them. My goal is rather to locate a set of problems in the relations between language and social space. In particular, a description of referential
practices must include some account of the social constraints on communication. This is especially obvious in the case of participant roles,
treated in chapters 4 and 5: As I will show, participation practices in
Maya interaction rest not only on a repertoire of social roles and interaction types but on limits as to who can occupy which roles. Certain forms
of interaction that would be semiotically possible in the language are socioculturally impossible because of the nature of the fields in which they
occur. Fields are characterized by an uneven distribution of knowledge
and ability among agents, differential rights of access to positions, routinization of field-specific genres of discourse, and limited grounds for
legitimating action (Bourdieu 1983). Certain fields, like the corporeal and
domestic ones, have quite well defined boundaries and mechanisms for
limiting access to outsiders (such as clothing, stone walls, and norms con-

straining entry). Others, like what I will call the deictic field, have more permeable, less clearly demarcated boundaries.

In Bourdieu's writings, fields (such as literary-artistic, educational, and sports) are characterized by competition and struggle over limited resources. In the present work, we are less concerned with these phenomena as such but share a focus on social asymmetries, differential access to communicative spaces and referents, the potential for innovation, and change. If the act of reference constitutes taking a position in the social world, as I have claimed, then verbal deixis can be described as a calculus of differential access to that world. This is what the relational structures mediate in linking referents to indexical grounds and therefore to ongoing interactions. In positing a corporeal or domestic field, we are not claiming that speakers follow a preestablished script but rather that certain social facts are given until further notice and are relevant to referential practices. Let us look more closely at the deictic field.

The **deictic field** is made up of the intersection of several **domains,** which we have called spatial, temporal, participant, discourse, attention focus, and background knowledge. These domains are in turn made up of varying numbers of more specific **modes of access.** For instance, the spatial domain of the Maya deictic field is made up of at least three modes of access, which we will call inclusion, exclusion, and relative immediacy (chap. 9). The perceptual domain is divisible into tactual, visual, and peripheral sensory access (chap. 6), while attention focus is divisible into foreground and background (which may be a scale; chap. 10). I call these modes of access because they designate relations linking objects and events in the social world with the communicative conditions in which these objects are referred to. Modes of access resemble intentional arcs in that they often lead from a conscious agent to an object, but they can also be more general than this. A relation like spatial immediacy can bind one zone to another in a publically recognizable way without being defined by any individual's subjective consciousness of it.

If the deictic field is made up of domains in turn made up of modes of access, then the linguistic system of deixis is made up of categories (or dimensions) in turn subdivided by features. The relational features that we call R values are basically semantic crystallizations of the modes of access, and the categories in which they are organized are the linguistic analogues of domains. The correspondence between elements at the levels of the linguistic system and the phenomenal context of activity is never perfect, as we pointed out above. In addition to domains, we need another term intermediate between the total deictic field and the specific modes of access of which it is ultimately composed. We will use the word 'zone' to designate any portion of the deictic field that is centered on a single participant or configuration of participants, distinguishing, for instance, the 'proximal zone' from the 'distal zone' and the 'speaker zone' from the 'addressee zone'. Notice that whereas a domain is characterized by a single class of modes of access (e.g., spatial), a zone includes various domains (e.g., spatial, temporal, perceptual) unified by a single degree of remove from ground (e.g., proximal). One of the formal corollaries of this distinction is the division in the Maya language between Initial Deictic particles, which differentiate domains, and Terminal Deictic particles, which differentiate zones of relative immediacy that cross-cut domains (chap. 10).

The three-way division between formal systems (linguistic, sociocultural), actual communicative practices, and sociocultural understandings of practice gives rise to one more set of distinctions that deserve mention here. In the course of analyzing person reference and participation in chapters 4 and 5, we will introduce a distinction between **frames, frameworks**, and **frame spaces.** Frames, as we have seen in this chapter, are generally defined as coherent schematizations of action and experience. As Brown and Yule (1983:239) put it, "a frame is characteristically a fixed representation of knowledge about the world." Under this definition, frames are schematic structures on the border between the semantic system of language and native typifications of practice. Like semantic structures, they have a conventionalized, relatively fixed aspect, but unlike them, they are not part of language as such. Like social understandings of practice, frames are based on metacommunicative schematizations, but unlike some schematizations, they are more or less well established in the local sociocultural context. For instance, in chapters 4 and 5 we will describe a range of participant frames in Maya, consisting of typical Speaker-Addressee-Referent relations, while chapter 6 analyzes perceptual-presentative frames and chapter 9 analyzes spatial ones. These frames function as pragmatic templates in which roles and categories are configured in standard (if not entirely fixed) ways. In chapter 5 we will introduce a distinction between simple, first-order frames and complex, second-order frames. As we will see, we need this in order to take account of differences in relative complexity. Demonstrative reference, we will show, always involves second-order frames, which are linked together by the relational structure of the expressions.

Not being confined to the linguistic system, the frame concept will play an important role in our description of spatial organization in the community under study. In chapters 7 and 8, we will propose an entire array of spatiotemporal frames that help organize spatial orientation, native understanding of the local geography, the layout of homesteads, agricultural practices (especially the swidden process), and ritual performances. Thus 'frame' will be used to denote a range of phenomena usually kept distinct in sociocultural description, including the conceptual structures embodied in demonstrative reference, cardinal directions and orientation, architectural floor plans, the layout and modes of labor on productive land, and the organization of ritual altars. The purpose of lumping these different phenomena under a single term is to emphasize the fundamental continuities between them. One of the central ethnographic results of this research is the demonstration that a limited number of frames with specific properties are recapitulated in all of these fields of practice among Maya agents. In order to show as clearly as possible the interpenetration of language and culture, we will work through the frames mobilized in different fields, exploring both homologies and transformations.

Whereas frames are schematic structures, frameworks are emergent formations that happen in the process of communication. Frameworks belong to the order of actual activity as it takes place. They are definitionally beyond the scope of both conventional codes (which can only define types and token replicas) and commonsense typifications (which, being schematizations, lack the emergence and actuality of frameworks). Frames are realized in frameworks, as semantic categories are realized in the production of reference. This realization involves replicating, combining, and alternating frames in potentially creative ways. While a frame is a standardized representation of roles, elements, and event types, the roles in a framework are all occupied by actual particulars. A frame is repeatable; a framework is not. For example, there is a standard type of participant frame in Maya address that I will call 'excluded addressee' (§5.2). The defining feature of this frame is that the speaker makes third-person reference to an actual copresent addressee. Eli reproduced the frame in the course of interacting with her husband MC and me in their kitchen on a specific occasion, thereby realizing it in an interactive framework. Frameworks virtually always involve negotiation, recipient design, and constant change as the social processes of which they are a part take place. They are defined at the token level of utterances, but they are not tokens of frame types, because they engage actual particulars and individuals, and because they are produced by interactions in which outcomes are not predictable.

With the notion of a frame space we move to the third movement of practice, in which native typifications are constituted, and fields are defined as spaces of positions and position takings. Goffman (1981) introduced the notion of a frame space in his study of radio talk, defining it as a set of potential footings available to an interactant but not currently realized. In other words, speakers make certain moves and take up certain positions in communicating, but they also chose not to make others that are nonetheless available to them. Identified with this residuum of virtual but not actual moves and footings, a frame space is smaller than a field but more inclusive than a framework. While any field subsumes many situations past, current, and future, a frame space is grounded in the present. As the framework of interaction changes, the possibilities open to participants change as well. In this book, the term frame space will be used to designate the union of an actual framework with other conditionally relevant but unrealized ones. In describing shamanic practice, for instance, we will speak of the special frame space of ritual performance, which includes what actually takes place in given events, along with the array of moves and frameworks that do not take place but could. Like frames, frame spaces may be more or less clearly bounded, depending on the case. One of the ways in which an account of communicative practice different from a standard pragmatic description is that it must address the socioculturally defined constraints on action without reducing them to preexistent rules. The concepts of field, frame space, and habituation (see chap. 5) serve this function.

The purpose of this section has been to summarize the analytic approach to referential practice in this book and to orient the reader to developments in subsequent chapters. The terms introduced here are not all relevant to all communicative practices, nor are they all clearly defined. They make up a frame of reference that will become specific only when we use it to analyze actual practices. This frame is a metacommunicative schema that will be completed in the framework of reference to particular examples. Its purpose is to facilitate analysis of communicative phenomena that stretch across traditional divisions between language and sociocultural context, linguistic and social theory, systems, and processes. Reference as we will treat it is a kind of articulation which engages all of these elements. The developments foreshadowed in this section go beyond the basic three-level approach of this chapter, but they fall within the conceptual frame space we have created. In chapter 3, we begin the ethnographic description upon which such developments unavoidably rest.

3   Foundations of Indexical Context:
Social Mediations of the Body

> *Le mot 'ici' appliqué à mon propre corps ne désigne pas une position*
> *déterminée par rapport à d'autres et . . . à des coordonnées exté-*
> *rieures, mais l'installation des premières coordonnées, l'ancrage du*
> *corps actif dans un objet.*
>   M. Merleau-Ponty, *Phénoménologie de la perception*

3.1 INTRODUCTION

In acts of deictic reference, speakers integrate schematic with local knowledge in the sense developed in the previous chapters. It is critical to an
understanding of deixis to recall that even very 'local' elements of context, such as a speaker's own corporeal experience and perceptual field,
are susceptible of schematization.[1] Various scholars have indeed argued
that the body is among the most fundamental zones of intersection between society and the biopsychological individual. In its materiality and
capacity for engagement, the body provides a series of natural oppositions, a 'raw material' in which collective categories and values are embodied (Comaroff 1985:7ff.; Turner 1980; Bourdieu [1972] 1977, 1980:
120ff.). Body space has a schematic structure, just does as the deictic
field, and it is related to other spatial schemata by processes of analogy,
homology, and transformation. Although deictics ground utterances in
the local interactive process, being indexicals, they are nonetheless conventional resources that fit into a larger stock of knowledge that Maya
speakers share prior to any instance of use. Even in acts of individuated
reference to the immediate 'egocentric' field of the speaker, these collective representations are available as public resources that speakers ex-
ploit. The role of the body in reference is therefore not limited to either
local or subjective aspects of speech. To see this, let us briefly consider
some different approaches to the notion of a schema.

   In most cognitive research, the term 'schema' (pl. schemata, adj. schematic) is used to designate a prefabricated conceptual structure that re-

mains relatively invariant throughout successive instantiations and that provides for holistic understanding of some portion of reality. Agar and Hobbs (1985:415), for instance, summarize the concept as developed in artificial intelligence and psychology as "simply a convenient term to characterize some related inferences." What we are calling frames here are schematic constructs insofar as they organize inferences and have relatively constant structure. In a recent book, however, Mark Johnson has proposed a different approach to schemata, in which they are non-propositional structures that connect concepts with percepts. Drawing on Kant's treatment of the imagination, Johnson sees these structures at play in organizing experience and comprehension in general. While they are also general in the sense of containing terms common to many experiences, schemata "emerge as meaningful structures for us at the level of our bodily movements through space, our manipulation of objects and our perceptual interactions" (Johnson 1987:29). That is, the relative abstractness of these structures is offset by the fact that they are part of our most concrete engagements with the world. This makes them dynamic rather than static (29) and becomes the basis of Johnson's discussion of understanding, imagination, and embodiment in a later chapter (Johnson 1987:173–93). Meaning and rationality, he says, are both embodied, to the extent that they are linked to image schemata and their extentions (190).

If Johnson's approach to schemata and embodiment developed out of his reading of Kant, it also derives from a reading of phenomenology, which he acknowledges but does not discuss explicitly. Merleau-Ponty ([1945] 1967) proposed that a fundamental part of our experience in the world is rooted in what he called our *schéma corporel*. His definition of this key concept differs from both cognitive notions of schemata and the human body, and from Johnson's appeal to embodiment, but it bears interesting relations to them. Since the work cited by Merleau-Ponty also plays a central role in Bourdieu's ([1972] 1977) early outline of a theory of practice, it is worth working through at least parts of it in some detail. Furthermore, when we reconsider modes of embodiment in relation to referential practice, Merleau-Ponty's approach will emerge as a powerful (antithetical) complement to the cognitive one and will provide a vocabulary for talking about aspects of deictic practice that go beyond mental representations.

It is important to appreciate from the outset that Merleau-Ponty's framework for the body was developed as a critique and an alternative to what he called 'intellectualist' models. Most cognitive explanations of understanding fit this label insofar as they invoke mental representations and processes of inference (however automatized) as their basic terms. Merleau-Ponty used the idea of the *schéma corporel* as an alternative to mental representations, a way of asserting that there is knowledge **in** the body. Rather than a fixed data structure or even a component of the 'imagination' (in Johnson's sense), the *schéma corporel* is the concrete, always changing self-awareness that actors have of their own bodily position in space. Merleau-Ponty phrases this reflexive component as "une prise de conscience de sa propre position," an intersensorial unity always grounded in the immediate experiential field of the actor. Rather than fixing the body in a set of inert categories then, the *schéma corporel* is dynamic, as is the body in motion. The key issue of generality is treated in this phenomenological framework not in terms of an abstraction away from experience but as a transposable concreteness (165): the *schéma* includes not just one's actual position but the sense of infinitely many other positions that are possible but not actually occupied. For instance, an actor sitting with legs crossed in a room has a preconceptual apprehension of his or her own placement but also a sense of the unquestioned possibility of changing position, shifting in the chair, standing and crossing the room, and so forth. As Merleau-Ponty put it, "le sujet normal a son corps non seulement comme système ouvert d'une infinité de positions équivalentes dans d'autres orientations. Ce que nous avons appelé le schéma corporel est justement ce système d'équivalences, cette invariant immédiatement donné par lequel les différentes tâches motrices sont instantanément transposables" ([1945] 1967:165). Both the actuality and the potentiality of spatial positioning, the *schéma* generalizes experience, not by abstracting concepts, but by transposing actual postures. (Transposability becomes a key feature of the habitus for Bourdieu.)

For Merleau-Ponty, the *schéma corporel* encompasses all body parts, unifying them into a single whole. This whole plays a dual role in spatial orientation. On the one hand, it is an active posture engaging the present task, putting the body itself in the world, "leaning towards" it to engage in a focused way. On the other hand, it is a ground, or to use the phenomenological term, a 'horizon', relative to which other objects and spatial relations are grasped ([1945] 1967:117). Like other theorists in the phenomenological tradition, Merleau-Ponty sought to incorporate aspects of Gestalt psychology, and the duality of the body is partly due to its role as both figure and ground in Gestalt structures. This would suggest that in deixis, which we know to incorporate a referential figure on an indexical ground, the body plays both roles as well (I argue this in chapter 9 below).

What can we derive from these different approaches to the role of the body in understanding? It seems obvious that referential practices, and particularly those involving deixis, put in play prefabricated cognitive schemata. The general relational structure of deixis, the categories of R values, pragmatic features, types of indexical grounds, and their standard combinations are all schematic resources for thinking and acting with language. The human body is part of this schematic order insofar as its perceptual, conceptual, and motor engagements are the basis on which structures are produced. The spatial schemata illustrated in chapter 9, for instance, presuppose the human body and provide terms in which to refer directly to its subspaces and orientation in the current surround. Deictic usage organizes inferences and contextualization processes. At the same time, preconceptual schemata like those proposed by Merleau-Ponty, and later by Johnson, are involved when speakers actually implement structures while communicating. That is, the actual indexical grounding of a deictic utterance and the individuation of a real particular in the role of referent. Here the duality and dynamism of the corporal schema interlocks with the structure of reference: the body is engaged minimally as ground or horizon for referring elsewhere and maximally as both ground and itself (or its parts) the figural referent. The intersensorial unity of the corporal schema is also in evidence in deixis, for as we will see in chapter 6, perceptual and cognitive orientations receive the same dual engagement as does the spatial position of the body. In some cases, they are indexed as the ground from which objects are denoted, and in others they serve as both indexical ground and the figural referential objects themselves.

But even this combined approach to the corporeality of reference is incomplete insofar as it leaves out the intersubjective basis of the *schéma corporel* and also of the prefabricated schematic categories of the linguistic system. Speakers do not participate in communication as neatly bounded subjects but rather as parts of interactive frameworks, temporary occupants of relationally defined roles. Maya language encodes this sociocentrism in distinctions such as the relative asymmetry of all *-a$^?$* deictics as opposed to the *-o$^?$* forms, and the egocentricity of *way e$^?$* 'here' and *tol o$^?$* 'there', as opposed to the sociocentricity of *té$^?$* 'there' (chapter 9). The interactive foundation of body space is a point on which both cognitive and phenomenological approaches are prone to break down. In arguing that the body is a ground of reference, one slips quickly into the assumption that the intersensorial unity in question belongs to just one person. In fact, as we will see in detail, the communicative process to which deictic reference is 'posturally' adapted belongs to interactive frameworks in the first instance, and only secondarily to the individuals who occupy their subportions (chapters 4 and 5).

Thus we must look beyond the corporal schema as previously constituted and bring corporeality to the next level of the social space occupied by coparticipating parties to communication. The boundaries of corporeality, the limits on who can occupy what positions of social formations, the varieties of reciprocity (and their breakdowns) are all factors that lead us to posit a larger unit for the body, which we can call the **corporeal field.** Much of the present chapter is directed towards showing with ethnographic details how the *schéma corporel* of individual actors is subsumed and generalized through social relationships to encompass various interactive formations and processes. Section 3.2 sketches the cultural definition of the living body in Maya, including its physical basis, actional orientation, and distinctive space. If there is a genuinely egocentric moment in deictic practice, it is linked to this space.

Section 3.3 then places individual actors in the context of social relations around the homestead. The objective is to make it clear why we must look beyond the individual in order to account for regularities of referential speech. The marked status asymmetries among household members and their clear impact on language use are the themes of this discussion, which will lay the groundwork for the subsequent analysis of deictic space. The next section (§3.4) briefly describes a set of interactive genres that illustrate the consequences of social relations for conversational practice in Maya. The pragmatic conditions on who can engage in these genres, with whom, and under what conditions, are part of the larger set of social conventions governing proper interaction among Maya. These in turn are reflected in the relative symmetry and asymmetry of the indexical ground of demonstrative reference, as outlined in chapter 2. Thus the idea of indexical symmetry, which may appear abstract or arbitrary in isolation, is a basis for relating aspects of utterance context with the differential rights and obligations of social actors engaging in the communicative process.

The final section returns to the question of how deixis is **embodied** in communication, and on the other hand, how communicative processes are embodied in deixis. We will discuss an extended example taken from recorded interactions in Maya. These show the interplay of many of the ethnographic phenomena described in the preceding sections of this chapter. More importantly, the examples will show how *schémas corporels* are produced in social situations according to the changing relevancies and positionings of the actors. The quasi-postural orientations in which Maya speakers engage during conversation derive, not from the order of prefabricated schematic concepts, nor from the locally variable *schéma corporel,* neither of which can account for the interactive adjustments

inherent to ongoing practice. Rather, they derive from the interplay between these factors along with the (superindividual) corporeal field and
the larger social field in which the interaction takes place.

The generalization of the corporeal schema into a socially based field is
part of another kind of generalization, one that involves the transposition
of the indexical ground of reference from the body to more abstract aspects of communicative context. Thus deixis can be grounded on previous discourse—as is clear in anaphoric uses—on fictional characters
(whose corporeality can only be projected through memory or fantasy), or
on aspects of utterance frameworks other than the body schemata. This
brings us to a final point of broad significance to the study of referential
practice, namely, the distinction between corporeality on the one hand
and the more general phenomenon of embodiment on the other. Referential categories and practices can be embodied in aspects of activities
that are not traceable to the body, just as the schematic structures involved
in reference can be realized in aspects of sociocultural reality other than
language. For instance, in the later chapters of this book, I will show that
the schemata involved in deictic reference and in spatial descriptions in
Maya are also embodied in such varied media as domestic floor plans, the
principles according to which agricultural fields are bounded off, and the
layout of shamanic altars. Disparate though these may appear, they are
fundamentally related in Maya culture and will serve to make the general
point that, as Panofsky (1976) argued, visual and discursive production
may be guided by a common set of controlling principles played out as
mental (and bodily) habits.

3.2 CULTURE IN THE CORPOREAL FIELD

3.2.1 Materiality of the Body

The simplest representation of the human body in its physical aspect is the
one used by shamans in ritual discourse.[2] The body is made up of the
same elements as is the rest of the material world: a person's *wiínklil*
'body' is his or her *lú?um* 'earth'. One's breath and animacy are one's
-iík 'wind'—also related to *yiík'al* 'force, heat of a fire, momentum', and
yiík'el 'bees (of a hive), ants (swarming in the earth)'.[3] Like the earth and
all animate objects on it, the human body has a *k'iinil* 'heat' of its own,
evident in the opening and closing of pores, the passing of sweat, fever,
anger, the coolness of relaxation, the chill of numbness, and numerous
other bodily processes. This heat derives ultimately from the sun and
must be held in a relatively delicate balance in order to safeguard the
well-being of the individual. Through the double action of heat and the
movement caused by the body's wind, the water of one's earth is trans-

formed into *k'íik'el* 'blood'. These elemental relations are not widely appreciated by nonspecialist Maya adults, although they are an important part of shamanic practices and descriptions. Most Maya people regularly attend to their corollaries: the balance of hot and cold is a ubiquitous concern in everyday life, as is the breath, the effect of wind on the individual, the flow of the blood, and the need for water. In the cures and other ritual discourse performed by shamans, these elements receive systematic representation and function as metonyms of the entire person. For instance, in the *tiíč'k'aák* 'divination', a diagnostic procedure, the divining crystals (*saástuún*) provide the shaman with a representation of the patient's earth, showing the location of any abnormal winds (Hanks 1984b,c). This is precisely the same mechanism that applies when the crystals are used to examine the 'earth' of a homestead, thereby treating the body and the home as equivalent (cf. chap. 7 below).[4] In the *saántiguar* prayer, in which an individual is blessed, and the *paá? ?iík'* 'drop wind' prayer, in which ill winds are exorcised, the earth of the person is presented, swept clean, and cooled (Hanks 1984c). The derivation of blood from water and the localization of distinct winds in different regions of the body are part of a larger system of specialized knowledge of body parts and processes. Shamans possess this knowledge as part of their technical specialization in health care for individuals, social groups, and their environment. It informs their schematic representations of the body, as well as their momentary orientations and understandings of particular bodies.

3.2.2 Animacy and Will

Beyond their bare material elements, human actors have two basic attributes that link them with other higher animates and that make it possible for them to engage in the world in a directed manner. These are the *-oól*, which covers roughly the will and the capacity for involvement and sensate experience, and the *-iík'* 'wind', understood in this context as 'awareness'. The term *-oól* also applies in standard usage to the heart of a tree, the sprouting center of a palm tree or plant, and the loaded ammunition in a rifle. It is inalienably possessed and when possessed by a human may be modified by any of a variety of adjectives including *kí?imak* 'happy', *siís* 'cold', *čokow* 'hot', *há?ak* 'surprised', *naáy* 'becalmed', and *toh* 'straight (happy)'. The *-oól* can also be the object of transitive predications, such as *kušulik inwoól* 'it finishes my *-oól* (overwhelms me)', *kubèetik inwoól* '(s)he does my *-oól* (kids me)'. Other derivations include *kinwok'oh?oó(l)tik* 'I beg (lit., weep *-oól-it*)', *kinwoó(l)tik* 'I want, wish', *yoólilil* 'on purpose, intentionally', *yah tinwoól* 'it pains me, I'm sorry', and *má? tuyoól yàan i?* '(s)he's not in his/her *-oól* (out of control, drunk or mad)'. The linkage between this aspect of the body and the actor's ability to formulate intentional action is a basic fact in Maya common sense, and references to the -oól are very common in daily discourse. At least one use of the term -iík' indicates that it too may stand for an individual's oriented awareness in his current context. When a person who is daydreaming or obliviously misperforming some task is called to attention by a superior, this is described as tuk'á?asah yiík' 'he snapped him out of it, got his attention (lit., reminded his wind)'. In most other contexts, the capacity for directed attention is derived from the -oól and associated most directly with focused gaze, to which we now turn.

3.2.3 Perceptual Field and Its Valuation

It is likely that, as Bühler (1982:126ff.) suggested, the senses of sight, hearing, and touch have a universal role in the micro-organization of social activities. Surely, normal communication requires the ability to perceive and be perceived. Yet this universal fact tells us nothing about how perceptual categories are mobilized, invested with significance, or how they are related to other forms of knowledge in human cultures and their communicative systems (Sahlins [1976] 1977). In Maya, there are two basic verbs of perceiving, ?ilik 'to see (it)' and ?ú?uyik 'to sense (it) (with any faculty other than sight)'. Both of these verbs are inherently transitive, that is, each implies an object. Although both may undergo passivization demoting the perceiver to a peripheral status 'It is seen (by me)', neither undergoes object demotion. There are no middle voice (objectless) forms for these verbs, although the middle voice is common elsewhere in the Maya verbal system (see Bricker 1978). In the case of ?ú?uyik 'to sense', the mode of the perception depends entirely upon the object it takes.

Both of these verbs are associated with more than mere perception of objects. As in European languages, 'seeing' in Maya is a typical metaphor for understanding, and speakers commonly ask their interlocutors if they 'see' their point. An infant who shows quickness and awareness is said to have saási yič 'light (in) his or her eye'. 'See' in Maya also functions as a routine device for maintaining contact with an addressee. In this phatic function, the utterance tawilik ↑ 'Do you see? (get it?)' is very frequent in conversation and is subject to idiosyncratic phonological reduction, down to talik, taik (see Hanks 1983:116ff.). To 'sense', on the other hand, is often understood to mean 'to pay willful attention to'. Checking on an addressee's attentiveness, speakers ask tawú?uyik ↑ 'Do you hear (it)?' This form does not collapse phonologically the way the corresponding one with 'see' does, and it is (impressionistically) less frequent in conversation. This is perhaps because of the overtone of directivity often conveyed by the question, as in English 'Do you hear?' 'Are you listening to me?' when used to convey an order to pay attention. The utterance is power coded and therefore most likely to occur in asymmetric contexts where the speaker has the right to issue directives to the addressee (see §3.2.5 below). Parents scolding a child or friends calming down an angry or drunk companion might punctuate their speech with this question. The idea of paying aural attention to directive language without necessarily understanding it is aptly reflected in the Maya expression for 'attending mass', ʔúʔuyik mìisa 'to hear mass'. Moreover, a person said to ʔúʔuyik t'àan 'hear speech' is understood to be reasonable, obedient, and respectful, while one who doesn't hear speech, máʔa tuyúʔub'ik t'àan, is disobedient, rebellious, drunk, demented, in a rage, or otherwise intractable.[5] Thus the two basic verbs of perception also code understanding, the ability to 'see' a situation, and attentive reasonableness, the ability to 'hear, listen to it'.[6]

There is another, less familiar association with vision in Maya, which foregrounds the agentive quality of gaze as a willful act. People and certain domestic animals are susceptible of conveying the 'heat' in their own body to the body of an infant merely by gazing on the infant. This is particularly true of adult men sweating from physical labor, men or women shortly after sexual relations, and women menstruating, all of whom pose a real danger to any infant under about a year old. This phenomenon is known among the Maya as ojo 'eye', a familiar concept in Mesoamerican cultures where the hot-cold syndrome is found (Logan 1977; see Villa Rojas [1945] 1978:386ff. and Hanks 1984c:134 for a fuller description of the Maya case). The illness results in diarrhea and possible dehydration of the child. It can be diagnosed by a shaman using crystals, who can see the excess heat in the infant's body and make hypotheses (on the basis of what he sees in the crystals) as to who gave the child the eye. This latter bit of information is crucial, because the fastest cure is to find the adult who caused the illness, and have that person hold and touch the infant. The touching restores the child's own temperate body state, which calms the intestines. These things are known as a matter of common sense by adults, particularly mothers, and they motivate other patterns of behavior, such as covering infants with a mantle whenever they are in the presence of outsiders, to keep them out of sight.[7] Interestingly, while making visual contact is thus seen as a potentially effective act, aural contact is not. There are no objects or individuals that one can affect by listening to them, however fixedly and in whatever state of being the listener. An actor can č'ehšikintik 'cock one's ear (listening attentively)' as well as (s)he can stare, but the former has no recognized effect on the object, whereas the latter does. In prayer, shamans ask God to *sutk awič apaktikó ʔon* 'turn your gaze to look on us', while the expression *paktik santo* 'looking at (a) saint' is an often heard oath of honesty (F.137.A.330). In both instances, directed gaze constitutes an effective bond between seer and object.[8] The term for gaze, *paktik* (verb) can be further modified to reflect anger, as in *šȼ'eépaktik* 'to look angrily at from the side', *šleé ʔpaktik* 'glare fixedly, angrily at', and *nunulpaktik* 'look up and down, side to side at (on the point of blows)'. One male speaker volunteered the revealing (if macho) hyperbole *tinšaáhšakč'iíntik yeétel impàakat* 'I threw him down (to the ground) with my look' (BB.4.111).[9]

3.2.4 Bodily Orientation

The orientations and actional capacities of individuals, implicit in their physical states and processes, are given a more directly spatial representation in the ideas of *taánil/paàčil* 'front/back', *šnó ʔoh/šȼ'iík* 'right/left', and *yoók'ol/yàanal* 'up/down'. When applied to the human body (*schéma corporel*), the first axis is grounded in the visual field and normal forward locomotion of actors (see interesting discussions of body orientation in Bourdieu [1972] 1977; Bühler 1982:102ff.; Evans 1982:154ff.; Hallowell 1955; Talmy 1983). *taán* 'front' and *pàač* 'back' are noun roots that can also be possessed, as in *tintaán* 'to my front, in front of me', and *timpàač* 'to my back, in back of me'. Similarly, 'right' and 'left' can be possessed, as in *tinšnó ʔoh* 'to my right' and *tinšȼ'iík* 'to my left'. The forms I have cited as 'up' and 'down' are actually invariably possessed relational nouns that could equally well be glossed 'over, atop' and 'under, below'. When the possessor is a human, they indicate the space above and below the person in the normal upright orientation—for a person lying face down on the ground, 'over' is to his back and under to his front. The center is not merely the body, then, but the body as it normally engages in movement and action (just as Merleau-Ponty's discussion of the phenomenal body would lead us to expect).

The spatial coordinates of bodily orientation also imply moral evaluations, and there is a strong association between up, front, and to the right as morally positive, and down, back, and to the left as morally negative. The vertical dimension is most systematically encoded in the cosmological premises and discourse forms of Maya shamans, where higher always implies more powerful and beneficent (Hanks 1984c). It is also a matter of common sense, however, appreciated by nonspecialists and reflected in daily expressions, such as *yàanal k'áaš* 'under the (wild and dangerous) woods', *yàanal ha ʔ* 'under water (describes an 'underhanded' decep-

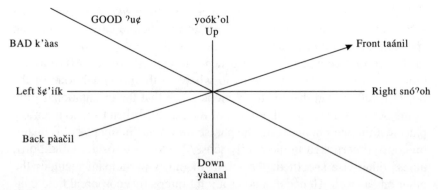

Fig. 3.1. Coordinates of body space.

tion)'. 'Front' and 'back' are, if anything, even more strongly associated with good and bad. Things from behind are dangerous, hidden, oppressing, while things in front are more likely to be benevolent, honest, and in clear view. The left hand is literally the 'angry' or 'sinister' one, being derived from the root ¢'iík 'angry, vicious' (as in swarming wasps and raging bulls). These aspects of corporeal orientation can be schematized as in figure 3.1.

3.2.5 *Iknal* as a Corporeal Field

In addition to the spatial coordinates and orientations described in the foregoing, there is one more concept that figures centrally in Maya speakers' commonsense grasp of bodily space.[10] This is the *-iknal* 'place', an inalienably possessed noun stem which denotes the proximal region around the object or individual functioning as possessor. When the possessor is human, the phrase conveys roughly 'in the company of X', or 'close to, alongside, with X'. It fits into a series of locational noun stems denoting the various social and personal spaces of an actor. These include one's *-otoč* 'house, abode' (inalienably possessed), *nah* 'house, fields, proximal region of', *kahtalil* 'homestead, residential compound', and the actor's several habitual workplaces, such as one's *soólar* 'yard, orchard', *paárseláa* '(irrigated) field', and *kòol* '(unirrigated) plot (*milpa*)' (see §7.2). On one common reading, an individual's *-iknal* is equivalent to his or her *nah,* that is, the home or habitual place (BB.3.54; 12.B.630). Similarly, *kó?oš tinwiknal* 'Let's go to my place' is a routine way of inviting an addressee to come to visit one's home.

There is a second interpretation of *-iknal* in which it is not a fixed place that is owned the way a house is owned but a mobile field of action related to an agent the way one's shadow or perceptual field is. This is the sense

linked to the bodily activity of a speaker. Although *-iknal* is usually possessed by a human noun, this need not always be the case, and one can
speak of the *-iknal* of an animal, a tree, a well, or even a moving vehicle
(as Man observed when discussing the term with me [BB.3.54]). Furthermore, the expression is vague as to where in the proximal zone of the
object it refers, and there is no obvious sense that the orientational front
of the object is a privileged referent of its 'place'. When used to refer to a
place within one's homestead, the phrase *tinwiknal* 'in my place' is unambiguously interpreted in the bodily sense. Under face-to-face conditions,
unless otherwise specified, the *-iknal* of either participant includes the
other one as well. Hence it denotes a joint interactive corporeal field containing reciprocal perspectives rather than an individual *schéma corporel*.
When interactants are separated, and the current framework is relatively
asymmetric, then the *-iknal* of a participant is typically egocentric, depending upon the perspective adopted. I have also attested uses of what
appears to be a metaphorical extension from the bodily sense of the term,
in which a speaker's *-iknal* was his habitual way of thinking or doing
things.

The regional scope of one's *-iknal* 'place' is variable, as is the degree
of remove at which speakers locate objects in vertical, horizontal, or lateral relation to themselves. Compared to the deictic *way e?* 'here', which
is routinely used to refer to the entire homestead or work site, *-iknal* is
interpreted more narrowly to denote the inner space of a single structure,
such as the sleeping house (see §7.2). This inner space can be encompassed in a single visual field and is in practical reach of any adult within
it. As Vic reasoned while discussing the meaning of the term *-iknal*, even
if people standing inside a house are not mutually oriented, they are considered to be in a single *-iknal* so long as they are able to *hear* a single
conversation (12.B.630). Bearing in mind the relation to perception, socially defined spatial boundaries, and shared body space, we can schematically represent the *-iknal* in figure 3.1 by adding a shaded zone around
the point of intersection of the three orientational dimensions, as in figure 3.2. The shading should be understood to be situationally variable,
according to the relative extent of the corporeal field in given contexts.

3.2.6 Corporeal Field and Centered Reference

There is a cliché in Maya which says that every person is a different
world. People invoke this often when rationalizing perceived differences
in character between individuals or misinterpretations of others' intentions. The thrust of the remark is that there are sharp limits on the degree
to which one can know another person and share in his or her feelings.

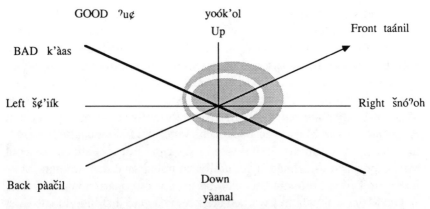

Fig. 3.2. Coordinates of body space with *ʔiknal* (variable scope).

People interact on the basis of common assumptions and shared codes of proper conduct, summarized in the idea of *legalidad* 'legality, propriety', yet they are keenly aware that actors harbor hidden agendas, and that each person 'follows a different road'. The components of a person which most individuate him or her are the *tùukul* 'thought' and *náʔat* 'understanding'. Not only do people think differently, in ways knowable only through inference, but it is with their thought that they formulate plans, worry about things outside their current circumstances (the Maya equivalent for 'worry' is *sèentuklik* 'think intensely') and 'travel' through time and space without moving their body. Interlocutors can not reasonably assume that they know each other's true agendas, or that they are really on the footings they appear to be on. These points were explained to me by three senior men on different occasions and are consistent with my own observations of how Maya people reason about persons, their motivations, and responsibilities. The people represented in this study are thus cognizant of the complexity of an individual's relation to his or her immediate actional context, and they are rarely inclined, in my experience, to take a person's representations at face value.

The physical existence of the body links it inextricably to the larger natural world through shared elements and processes of change in state, notably in terms of 'heat', 'wind', and 'dryness'. Individuals are taken to have different relative capacities for involvement, according to the states of their *-oól*, and their perceptual apparatus determines a unique field of sensate experience. Their ability to comment on their sensate experiences, which Maya speakers routinely do in the course of expressing opinions of most kinds (see §3.2.2 above), rests on the kind of reflexive *prise de conscience* that was fundamental to the *schéma corporel* as Merleau-Ponty defined it. Perception is closely related to the interpretation of sensory and other data, as well as the ability to participate reasonably in social interaction. The body defines an oriented egocentric space with an up, down, front, back, right, and left, in which the first term of each pair is morally superior to the second. This central place, at the intersection of the three axes, is also described as the *-iknal* 'bodily space'. The entire cultural construction of the body, which I have likened to Merleau-Ponty's *schéma corporel,* gives substantive content to the idea of 'egocentricity' in Maya, because it constitutes the individual body in motion that we posit in the central role of speaker. But it is already evident that body space so defined is culturally saturated, and that through social interaction, it is routinely occupied by groups of coparticipating agents.

The Maya with whom I worked are keenly aware that individuals exist within networks of social relations, that they share knowledge, experience, and goals, that they are constrained by a common sense of acceptable behavior, and that they live out comparable life courses. The ideological commitment to the uniqueness of individuals holds only within a presupposed frame of social reference. This social frame unavoidably impinges on our understanding of verbal deixis, because it provides a basic set of common referents that speakers know they share as a matter of course. By situating the individual actor within a series of social relations, we prepare the ground for situating egocentric reference within the encompassing social field in which it occurs. In chapters 4 and 5, the linguistic basis of this interpretation will be spelled out. As a preliminary indication of what is at stake, consider the category *-iknal*.

A person's *-iknal* 'place' corresponds quite closely, on one reading, to his or her 'egocentric space' as discussed by Evans (1982); the immediate sphere of bodily activity, at the center of the vertical, horizontal, and lateral axes of space. Unlike paradigmatic egocentric space, the Maya *-iknal* may be possessed by inanimates (meaning 'around, near x') or by more than one interactant—one can speak of 'our *-iknal*' in a way that it would not make sense to speak of 'our egocentric space'. Furthermore, the *-iknal* may be interpreted as referring to an individual's home, not his or her present perceptual-actional context. In both of these ways, an individual, apparently egocentric place may be grounded in the social relations built upon coparticipation in the shared here and coresidence in the shared homestead.

The play between genuinely egocentric and sociocentric dimensions of context also emerges in deictic use. There is a categorial distinction between the two kinds of space in the locative adverbial roots (see chap. 9), a fact which demonstrates the necessity of including the distinction in the universal repertoire of deictic oppositions. In the terminal deictics (the enclitic forms on the horizontal axis in table 1.1), the play between ego and sociocentric frames shows up in the opposition between -*a*? and -*o*? terminals. The former indicate referents immediate to the speaker or newly introduced, and the latter indicate referents farther off or already known by both interactants. Thus -*a*? marks asymmetrically available referents, such as parts of the speaker's own body, and -*o*? marks the common ground of shared knowledge. As Maya speakers can readily report, however, the asymmetric -*a*? forms are most properly used when the two interactants are already in a face-to-face relation, so that the addressee can perceive the precisely indicated referent. Thus the asymmetry is a limited one which presupposes reciprocity of perspectives (see also §§1.2, 8.3, and chap. 10). The -*o*? forms, on the other hand, tend to be the ones mobilized when interactants are conversing over a distance or are separated by other physical or social boundaries.

This pattern of use has the consequence that egocentric space becomes an object of individuated reference in Maya speech just when there is a face-to-face relation already established between participants. Even though speakers talk over various kinds of remove, they make referential divisions in their immediate zone pretty much only when their addressee is close at hand. Thus, egocentricity comes into play in indexical reference under sociocentrically defined conditions.

3.3 THE SOLAR UNIT: SOCIAL RELATIONS IN THE HOMESTEAD

Comaroff and Roberts (1981) show that the Tswana conception of the house "embodies both a set of primary social values and elementary structural forms, along with the principles of their reproduction and elaboration" (49). This native conception is the point of origin of the value oppositions and structural elements contained in what Comaroff and Roberts call the constitutive order, to which they oppose the lived-in (experienced) universe (68). My claim here is different but related: the Maya household as a social organization embodies principles of segmentation, reciprocity, and asymmetry that are the basis of communicative patterns, particularly those which involve reference to or interaction in domestic space. In other words, the divisions and relations between coresident social groups are played out in spatial (and temporal) boundaries around the household, which in turn condition speakers' referential and other communicative practices. Alongside body space, domestic space is one of the core sources of schematic knowledge engaged in the conventional structure and use of deixis, a claim taken up in detail in chapter 7 (cf. Friedrich [1964, 1970] 1979).

The basic residential unit in contemporary Yucatán is the *solar* 'yard,

homestead', also commonly called *kahtalil* 'homestead' when it is located in a rural area. Residence units range in size from a single nuclear
family, parents and children, to three, or rarely four, nuclear families
related by descent through the males. Up to four generations may be represented in a single extended household, although two to three are apparently more common. As Villa Rojas ([1945] 1978:236) showed for east
central Quintana Roo, Redfield and Villa Rojas ([1934] 1962:90) for
Chan Kom, and Thompson (1974:27 ff.) for Ticul, contemporary households in Oxkutzcab are of several types, whose variation is partly accounted for by the developmental cycle of the family. Following Fortes
(1958), Thompson proposes four phases in a single 'temporal pattern':
establishment of the autonomous household of a single family with a
child; expansion, as the elder sons marry, bringing wives into the home
and producing children; dispersion, as daughters marry out and elder sons
gain financial independence, allowing them to move out and establish
their own homes; and replacement, when the founding couple die and are
replaced as heads of household by the remaining son and family. While
far from invariant, this cyclic pattern sheds light on the homes with which
we shall be concerned in this discussion.

One aspect of households that the developmental perspective clarifies
is the obvious fact that they change over time. In 1977, for instance, DP
and DA resided in a single *kahtalil* with their two youngest sons, both of
whom were married, with one and two children, respectively. By 1985,
the two sons had six children apiece and resided together in a single *kahtalil*, with DP and DA, the founding pair, now living in their own household nearby but not adjoining the sons. DP (the male head of the family)
explained this move by saying that with twelve children around, there was
no peace and quiet (an understatement to say the least). Similarly, in
1978, DC, a senior male whose estranged wife resides in Mérida, lived in
a single *solar* in Oxkutzcab along with a seventeen-year-old unmarried
son, whereas in 1985, the same *solar,* with additional house structures, is
home to DC and all three of his sons, two of whom are married, with four
children and one child, respectively. In terms of phases, the case of DP
and DA appears to illustrate expansion, dispersion, and ultimate replacement of the senior couple by their eldest son as head of household. (Although replacement was motivated by expansion, not by death of the
senior couple.) DC's home was in a state of dispersion in 1978 and was
greatly expanded in following years, indicating that the order of phases is
not invariant. Is and his wife, another Oxkutzcabeño couple, live in the
(urban) *solar* they established shortly after marriage, sharing it today
with their two sons, of whom the eldest is married with two children.

Their original purchase of the house was explained to me as a necessity, because there was no room in the house of Is's father when they got married (BB.4.115). At the time, Is's younger brother was residing with his parents in the paternal *solar,* along with his wife and children, making it a three-generational homestead in the process of dispersing. Balim and Chio, two other adult men, currently reside in their own households with their wives and unmarried children, putting them at the early stages of expansion. Chio, whose oldest son is ten years old, is distinctly oriented toward this expansion and has recently acquired two plots of land adjacent to his own. He explained the acquisition as a way of preparing a place of residence for his son with his eventual wife. (The *solar* in which they currently reside is judged too small.)

Land is inherited through the male line, passing from father to son, and the *solar* is, under ideal circumstances, a sign of the persistence of the patriline. Chio's acquisition of lands for eventual transferal to his son is a common strategy, also employed by DP, who between the mid 1970s and 1985 systematically acquired rights over four plots of rural land, totaling approximately fifty mecates (a measure of surface area 20 by 20 meters), which he distributed among his three adult sons. These lands include mature fruit orchards and make up a considerable domain of family production as well as residence. On the other hand, DC's current situation illustrates the pitfalls of not acquiring land for one's sons, since his urban *solar* is his only land, measuring just three mecates. For lack of productive land, his two eldest sons have been forced to seek nonagricultural work as masons, tailors, and day laborers. Moreover, since the strip of the family plot belonging to DC proper will be passed on to his youngest son when he dies, the three brothers will be forced to live within the walls of a single *solar.* This prospect is disturbing to the two elder brothers and their wives, since the youngest is perceived to be dishonest and *k'asá?an* 'rotten' (BB.4.67).[11]

3.3.1 Residence Patterns: *?ilib'¢il, há?ankab'¢il*

From the perspective of the residence choices of newly formed married pairs, the Maya conventionally distinguish between two formations: (i) transitory uxorilocal residence, called *há?ankab'¢il,* from *há?an* 'daughter's husband', in which the son-in-law resides temporarily with the parents of his wife; (ii) enduring patrilocal residence, called *?ilib'¢il,* from *?ilib'* 'son's wife', in which the wife resides in the home of her husband's parents. Villa Rojas ([1945] 1978:238) documents that the former pattern was quite common in Quintana Roo, but it appears relatively rare in Oxkutzcab, as it was in Chan Kom (Redfield and Villa Rojas [1934] 1962:91

cite just 1 case out of 45 households). Among current Oxkutzcabeños, the son-in-law who resides with his wife's parents is considered either very docile, for submitting to the will of his parents-in-law, or in an unfortunate position (BB.4.58). DC recounted the problems he had had during his own period of *háʔankab'ҫil*, necessitated by the death of his own father: he had worked happily in the fields of his father-in-law "as a beloved son," but came into irreconcilable conflict with his mother-in-law, who persisted in undermining his authority over his wife. According to DC, the conflict ultimately caused the death of his wife, his first of three (F.140.B–142.B, recorded 2/2/87). Among the ten or so households with which I am familiar, there are no instances of uxorilocal residence, but eight include, or anticipate, patrilocal residence. Depending upon the number of sons in the family and how narrowly one defines the *solar* unit, such households may include between one and three or even four women brought in by marriage. In such cases, the husband's patrilocal household becomes the primary one with which the woman identifies. She thereby enters into a relation of subordination to the parents-in-law and ranking relative to coresident sisters-in-law. Ranking is apparently in terms of the birth order of their husbands, although in the cases with which I am familiar, this coincides with the relative age of the women.

While uxorilocal residence is apparently short-lived, patrilocal residence tends to persist, subject to independent processes of dispersion, because the residential *solar* itself is inherited through the male line. In being incorporated, the new bride is subjected to the evaluation of the more senior members of her husband's household, and not all cases run as smoothly as the ideal. One woman told of having been rejected by her husband's mother, who ended up accusing her of witchcraft and infidelity, both of which she denied. She was forced to live with her own mother and to make her cooking fire in her mother's kitchen, so as to avoid the other sister-in-law residing in the husband's household. She eventually came to blows with her husband, who sided with his coresidents, and they split up, leaving her to raise six children alone (F.147.A.020). This example points up the potential stresses on the daughter-in-law who is incorporated into the *solar* of the husband, even though it is the inverse case, where the son-in-law is incorporated into the wife's parents' household, that is considered the most fraught with difficulty.

3.3.2 Head of Household

Every *solar* unit has a head in the person of the senior resident, usually male, who is recognized as the highest authority in decisions affecting the household, whose name is used to refer to the entire collection of residents and to whom the *solar* belongs legally. Typically, the head of household is the eldest man, although in some cases it is a widowed or divorced female. In female speech, it is usually the wife of the senior male who is referred to as the head of household. The practice of using the name of the head of household to refer to the whole group can be seen in examples such as the following.

Coming from Mérida to Oxkutzcab after having been away for a year, I met up with the father of DP's coresident daughter-in-law. I asked him, *kuš tuún DP, biš anih* 'What about DP, how is he?' intending to refer to DP himself. The man responded by describing the household members one by one, taking DP as a metonym of the whole group of which he was head (BB.4.53). Maya speakers commonly use the expression *letió?ob don Hulano* 'them Mr. So-and-so' to refer to the members of So-and-so's household. The phrase combines plural marking on the pronoun with the apparently singular personal title. This combination would be ungrammatical if the proper name were not interpretable as referring to a plurality of referents, since the pronoun and name are automatically coreferential in this construction. On the other hand, Toni refers to the household of her father as *nal inmàamah* 'my mother's place', and Pilar refers to the home of her parents-in-law as *nal inswèegra* 'my mother-in-law's place'. These usages are typical of the indexical pattern according to which women refer to households by way of the senior woman.

While 'head' of household is defined by seniority and ownership, individuals actually exercise different degrees of authority around the house. DP and DA (senior husband and wife) take a very active role in supervising the daily conduct of their two youngest sons, both of whom are over thirty, with wives and six children apiece. The sons reside in a *solar* given them by DP, and his exercise of authority includes often daily walks through the house and kitchen of the sons, barking orders and little criticisms at the residents. DA follows a similar pattern in relation to her daughters-in-law, who are made to toe the line. DC, on the other hand, heads a household of three sons, two daughters-in-law, and five grandchildren, but does so with very little display of authority and an almost deferential avoidance of interfering. While DP and DA peruse the domestic space with impunity, DC gently enters his son's homes only when beckoned or expected and expresses opinions about their actions, rather than telling them what to do. It is the sons, and not the father in this home, who set the tenor of daily life, even though they respect and defer to the father without protest when he does speak.

Is's place is another illustration of the same point, that heads of household may wield less than absolute authority. When I was discussing family history with him on February 2, 1987, he explained to me that he had forbidden his daughter to wear short pants outside the homestead, a practice he finds immodest, even though it is encouraged by grammar school teachers. Inside the *solar,* it was acceptable. Furthermore, he had told his coresident son to tell his wife and their children the same thing. So long as the wife and children are in the son's house (within the same walled *solar*), the son is charged with seeing to it that they dress properly, but when they pass through Is's house, *he* is the authority and can impose his will. Since his house is located directly in front of the main entrance to the *solar,* virtually everyone who enters or leaves comes under his gaze. This notwithstanding, he observed with a smile that when he is not there, for instance, when he stays at his *milpa* for several days at a time, the women don't follow his rules (BB.4.117). Were he to exercise the kind of force that DP does in his home, he would probably have told his daughter-in-law directly how to dress instead of telling his son to tell her.

3.3.3 Coresidents: Affinal and Consanguineal

Pulling together these observations on *solar* units, we can summarize the typical sets of coresidents as including the boxed portions of figures 3.3 and 3.4, the former showing consanguines and the latter affines. While all coresidents are normatively solidary, there is a special link between first-degree consanguines, particularly brothers and parent-offspring pairs. Offsetting this is the potential for competition and estrangement between brothers as they begin to inherit property.[12] DP's three sons appear to show a standard pattern, according to which juniors defer to seniors, and all stick together in relation to outsiders, yet they are indirectly critical of one another and less than totally trusting. For instance, MC once explained that if a man's brother were allowed to simply enter his home in his absence, the brother would surely seduce his wife, a morally repugnant but apparently plausible possibility. Thus brothers are individuals with whom one must be vigilant. DC's elder sons, as mentioned above, feel the bond of fraternal affection for their younger brother yet assert that he is a good-for-nothing whose presence in their household is a direct threat to the upbringing of their children.

Coresident affines, on the other hand, beyond the nuclear marriage pair, seem typically to have ambiguous relations. In particular, the relation between daughter-in-law and mother-in-law is prone to stress, while those between daughter-in-law and father-in-law, and wife and husband's brother, are based on avoidance. A daughter-in-law addresses her husband's parents (especially the father) rarely and only for specific purposes. While the mother may work daily with the daughter-in-law and

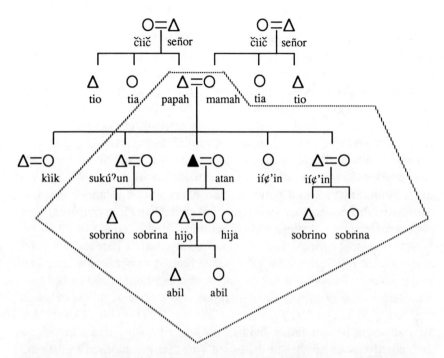

Fig 3.3. Solar coresidents: consanguineal. Enclosed portion of figure indicates typical coresidents in a single extended household.

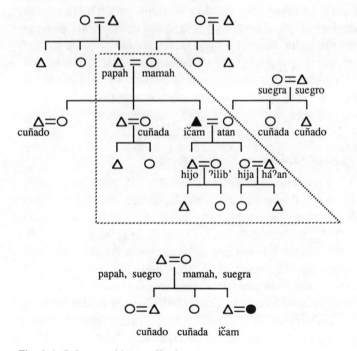

Fig. 3.4. Solar coresidents: affinal.

develop obvious solidarity with her (like DA with Pilar, the wife of her son; they frequently work together and share a single kitchen), the father tends to address her only for the purpose of directing her behavior, and even then usually through her husband. Brothers, in my experience, almost never address or even acknowledge the presence of their brother's wife. Sisters-in-law are in a relatively symmetrical relation and may develop mutual affinity, but are ranked according to the relative age of their husbands and the length of time in the household. Thus, the primary affinal relations in the household are potentially troublesome and expected stress points in the social network. Secondary affinal relations, such as wife to husband's brother's children, or to husband's grandparent, are more variable and not subject to conventional avoidance.

Noncoresident affines, and in particular the wife's parents, are relatively distant relations whose presence is limited to periodic visits. One young wife explained that her parents had come to visit her in her husband's home just two times in the two years of her marriage, even though they reside in Tekax, less than twenty minutes away by bus. Despite her deep affection for her father, he had not visited during that period, and she actually assumed that he had died and that her mother was hiding this fact from her to shield her from grief (F.137.A.210, 240). Another woman, a mother of six married for seven years, had not visited her parents for over a year, although they resided in Mani, just ten kilometers from Oxkutzcab. Her husband drives a truck which could easily provide transportation for visits, but they rarely go, except for the periodic *wàahil kòol* 'bread of (the) *milpa*' thanksgiving ceremony, at which the extended family and friends gather en masse (cf. chap. 8 below). Typically, among these people, the relation between a woman and her parents is very diminished after marriage, and that between man and his parents-in-law remains civil and somewhat distant.

3.3.4 Relation Terms for Household Members

Figures 3.3 and 3.4 are labeled with the standard Maya terms used to describe kinsmen, most of which agree with the usage reported in other ethnographic descriptions (Redfield 1941:chap. 8; Redfield and Villa Rojas [1934] 1962:93; Thompson 1974:31; Villa Rojas [1945] 1978:245). In the brief glosses in table 3.1, the first column shows the canonical referential form which would appear in the possessive frame [*ʔin-____*] 'my X'; unless otherwise indicated, the forms are inalienably possessed, meaning that nonpossessed tokens in referential function receive special marking (to be described presently). The second column shows the 'vocative' form used in addressing the individual. The main formal difference

TABLE **3.1** Relation Terms for Household Members

Referential	Vocative	Gloss
màamah	mámih	mother
papah, tàata	pápah	father
yùum	yuúm	father (esp. gods)
ʔìihoh, ʔìihah, pàal	ʔíihoh, ʔíihah, paál	son, daughter
čìič	čičiʔ	grandmother, either side
señor	señór	grandfather, either side
káʔaseñor	?	great grandfather, either side
àab'il[a]	paál	grandchild
káʔaʔàab'il	paál (?)	great grandchild
sukúʔun	sukúʔun	elder brother
kìik	kiík	elder sister
ʔiíʢ'in	ʔiíʢ'in	younger sibling (either sex)
tìiyo	tío	uncle (FBr, MBr, FSiHu, MSiHu)
tìiya	tía	aunt (FSi, MSi, MBrWi, FBrWi)
sóobrinóoh	sobríinoh	BrSo, SiSo, HuBrSo, WiBrSo, HuSiSo, (WiSiSo)[b]
sóobrináah	sobríinah	BrDa, SiDa, HuBrDa, WiBrDa, HuSiDa, WiSiDa
atan[a]	—[b]	wife
ičam[a]	—[b]	husband
swèegroh	swéegroh	husband's or wife's father
swèegrah	sweégrah	husband's or wife's mother
háʔaŋ	—[b]	daughter's husband
ilib'	—[b]	son's wife
kunyàadoh	kunyádoh	WiBr, SiHu
kunyàadah	kunyádah	BrWi, HuBrWi

[a] Absence of initial glottal stop / ʔ/ following possessive pronoun; presence of glottal stop in *ʔìiho* indicates 'hard' glottal, co-occurs with preconsonantal pronouns (chapter 4).
[b] Unattested.

between referential and vocative variants is the tendency towards high pitch on the final syllable or rising final contour in vocatives. These are only the most standard terms, and their actual use is subject to various pragmatic conventions which we will not treat here.

In addition to these expressions, there are numerous common phrases that may occur possessed or nonpossessed, especially for spouses: *šnoh wiínik* 'wife (lit., fem. great human)', *šnuk ťuúl* 'wife (lit., fem. great rabbit)', *šbyèeyhah* 'wife (lit., fem. old lady)', *faámilyáah* 'wife', *byèeyhoh* 'husband (lit., old man)'.

When used in the nonpossessed form to make reference, certain inalienably possessed relation terms are marked by the suffix *-ʢil*. These include mainly the first-order consanguineal terms for mother, father, all siblings, husband, and wife, as well as daughter-in-law and son-in-law.

Recall that the terms for in-law residence also contain the suffix, *há?-anka?-¢il* and *ili?-¢il*. Cf. *màama-¢il* '(a) mother', *tàata-¢il* '(a) father', *sukú?un-¢il* '(an) elder brother', *?ìi'in-¢il* '(a) younger sibling', *laák'-¢il* 'siblings', etc. The same suffix is used with the nonpossessed stem *yùun-¢il* 'owner, lord', but with the specialized meaning 'Lord (God)'. While possessed *?u-yùum-il* is commonly used to refer to a human owner of property, the *-¢il* form is restricted to spiritual lords and appears to convey a deferential, loving regard for the referent.

3.3.5 Rank and Seniority around the House

There are quite distinct status asymmetries among the members of a Maya household in terms of which individuals pay and receive deference. While the signs of deference in action are complex and often subtle, the principles of status assignment are evidently simple: elder is superior to younger, and male is superior to female. It is unclear to me whether generational precedence overrides age in cases such as an uncle younger than his nephew, and it is also unclear whether the relative age of brothers determines the relative rank of their wives or whether it is the age or length of time in the household that determines it. In the households under study, these dimensions coincided. Among brothers, age ranking is especially significant, with the younger normatively being obedient to the elder and avoiding all criticism of him. The strength of this bond is evident in the reticence of men to criticize their elder brother, their expected submission to his criticism, and their recognition that he has greater rights over collective undertakings than they do. A pointed example of this occurred on February 4, 1987, as I was making a floor plan of DC's *solar,* discussing the water tank in the yard with Lol, the younger brother of Man. The two brothers had built the water tank together, a rectangular concrete box approximately 3 by 2.5 meters on the sides by 1.5 meters high. The tank lies partly on Lol's land and partly on Man's, and the water is shared property, just as the water from the hose at the front of the yard and the electricity are shared. But Lol explained that actually, since Man was his elder brother, the water tank was built more on his land than on Lol's. Even though the water seeks its own level and is used in common, the *sukú?un¢il* gets a sign of respect, *?ump'eéh respèetoh* (BB.4.62). Similarly, the precedence of male over female is reflected vividly in the expected submissiveness of wives to the will of their husbands, the acceptability of occasional wife beatings, and the expectation that husbands will circulate freely in the community, but wives will be either in their own home or out on an errand sanctioned by their husbands (cf. §3.3.6 below). In elder sister–younger brother relations, it is uncertain to me which is considered superordinate, since it is their solidarity which is emphasized. In all asymmetric interactions, paying respect in word and attitude is called *¢iík,* as in *k-in-¢iík-ik ?impapah* 'I pay respect to my father'. This mode of speech is described briefly in §3.4.

3.3.6 Social Zones of the *Solar*

As a social space, the *solar* is bounded off from the outside world and internally divided into areas corresponding to each of the nuclear families residing within it. In chapter 7, the fine-grained subdivisions of the household are discussed, while here I wish to make the more basic point that the social organization of residents is a fundamental part of domestic space. This has consequences for how speakers conduct themselves verbally around the house, as well as how they make reference to its subdivisions. To begin with, there are binding rules on how nonresidents enter a Maya homestead. They announce their presence at the outer entrance, by knocking on the door if it is within reach of the street and by calling out if it is not. According to native testimony and my own observations, it is considered rude and *sub'¢il* 'shameful' to cross the outer threshold until told to by an adult resident (F.137.B.046), preferably the most senior individual present at the time. In urban households, where the front door of the main house is often right at the street entrance to the yard, women frequently place their sewing machines to the side of the front door, giving them a view of all who pass by, as well as those who enter. Visitors who enter are usually received in the main house, or at or just inside the front gate. For example, on February 2, 1987, I visited Is, whom I had known as an acquaintance for ten years. When I arrived at the door, his wife was sitting at her sewing machine in the doorway and invited me in, saying *?òoken don Wiíl!* 'Come in Don Will'. She offered me a chair directly in front of her machine and continued sewing as we talked. One of the children came through the house, and she told him to go tell Is that I was here. About fifteen minutes later, he showed up (BB.4.114). If, on the other hand, a group of strangers comes to the gate of the house, only one will properly enter, and the rest will wait outside.

When entering a multifamily *solar,* an adult of one family usually does not invite a visitor to enter the space of another, unless the visitor already has a privileged relation to the members of the house. In DC's *solar,* the practice is different, because DC is a *hmèen* 'shaman', who receives patients in his home on a regular basis. Patients, called *?ú?ulab'* 'arrivers', routinely enter his yard and approach his front door (set back approximately thirty feet) *as they announce themselves,* rather than calling out and waiting for his response. All members of the household except the

youngest children habitually respond, telling the patients to enter. A typical scenario occurred when one woman called out *tàal téelóo* 'Coming in
theeere!' while tentatively entering the yard from the street. Margot, the
senior daughter-in-law, responded by leaning outside the door of her
kitchen, some fifty feet away, shouting *ʔòok en iʔiʔ* 'Go on in there!' the
standard response. DC's front door was closed and he was nowhere in
sight as the woman opened the door and slowly entered the house. She
called out once again, using the same expression, but after entering, causing Margot to chuckle, since the 'there' in the greeting is appropriate
when uttered from the gate, whereas the woman was already inside
(BB.4.66, 82).

Except in cases like the foregoing, where the home of one *solar* member is a place of regular transaction with outsiders, it is the head of the
immediate family—the husband or wife—who may bid one to enter.
While there are virtually never walls or fences dividing the inner space of
the *solar,* there are very sharply defined areas corresponding to the property lines of the males.[13] After the early years of marriage, each adult son
is owner of his own section, and household members attend respectfully
to the divisions. In DC's household, the total area is divided into three
strips, belonging to him and each of his two oldest sons. Similarly, DP's
solar is divided into four areas corresponding to him and his three sons
(see §7.2). Chio's yard is divided in half between him and his older
brother; even though the latter does not reside there, the land is his by
inheritance and remains untouched by Chio. These divisions are not always apparent to outsiders, because they are marked only by inconspicu-
ous boundary stones or sight lines between physical features, but they
constitute real boundaries which constrain the circulation of actors in
daily life.

The most immediate sign of the divisions is the fact that each marriage
unit has its own *nah* 'house' where members sleep and store valuables,
including the family *sàanto* shrine, hammocks, rifles, clothing, and important documents. As will be shown in detail in the floor plans of chapter
7, traditional Maya kitchens are in separate thatch structures, set within
the yard behind the main houses. While one resident daughter-in-law may
share the kitchen of the senior woman, relatively independent wives usually have their own kitchens, and this is the center of their personal domains.[14] The grouping of main house plus kitchen is the basic residential
structure of the marriage unit within the *solar* (see chap. 7 for details).

The divisions between component homes in the household are evident
in the paths taken by visitors. In DC's *solar,* each of his sons has his own
entrance way, and visitors to one house do not cross through the yard of

another, even when this is the most direct route to their destination. At about 9:00 A.M. on January 30, 1987, a *mestiza* (woman dressed in traditional huipil) appeared at the gate of DC's house and addressed Margot, the wife of Man. She had come to be fitted for an article of clothing that Lol was going to sew. As she came through DC's entrance to the yard, assuming she had arrived, Margot informed her that Lol's place was next door, saying:

(1)   má² way e² → té² t-u-laá² um p'eé nah o²
            'Not here, there at the other house.'

Although they are all within the same walled *solar,* the order of houses is (south to north) DC (head), Man (elder son), then Lol (younger son), side by side facing the street, such that the woman would have to walk through Man's courtyard to get from DC's house to Lol's. When Margot responded to her, the woman laughed, saying she didn't even know which door to enter by. Rather than continue through the yard, however, she re-exited from the homestead and walked down to Lol's door by way of the street. I later told Lol of the incident, and he said the woman had responded in the natural way, since one does not just walk through someone else's yard (BB.4.20; F.137.B.015).

The internal divisions of domestic space constrain residents as well as outsiders. Physically mature males do not enter the kitchen of their brother's wife, nor of their aunt, without being invited by the brother or uncle. The motivation for this is the deep symbolic link between the *k'oób'en* 'kitchen' and the woman who tends the *k'oób'en* 'cooking fire' from which the structure gets its name (see discussion of gender, §3.2.6). Nor does one enter the *nah* 'house' of another without invitation, since, as they say, someone might be dressing or bathing, and to enter would violate their privacy (BB.4.107). Women too are responsive to these constraints and generally remain outside others' living quarters, conversing with one another while working in the courtyard area. Children under about the age of twelve play and squall throughout the *solar,* crossing boundaries freely. In some cases though, such as DP's extended *solar,* different family units may have their own dogs, who stake out the family turf and constitute a very real impediment to perambulation, even for children (and turkeys and piglets).

The independence of marriage units within a single *solar* is based also on their relative economic independence from one another. In all of the households under study, the land is officially divided into parcels owned by the individual men, and the men work their own fields, orchards, or in other occupations apart from their siblings. They harvest separately and keep separate the money derived from selling produce at market. Domestic animals such as bulls, pigs, turkeys, chickens, pigeons, and goats are owned by individuals or married couples. Firewood, food, medicine, and miscellaneous household commodities are acquired and consumed by individual marriage units. To my knowledge, no tasks around the household are rotated among residents of different nuclear families; each family cares for its own parcel and its own affairs. Although there is much cooperation and an ethos of solidarity among coresident families, in virtually all joint undertakings, the separate contributions of the individual families are reckoned.

The separation between families in the *solar* is played out in myriad ways in the daily interactions of residents. As a temporary resident of DC's place for five weeks during 1987, I was able to observe in some detail how extended family members attended to their location and movement within the household, as well as to mine. Eating together is an important form of sociality in Maya culture, and I found that each brother and his wife wanted me, as honored guest, to eat in *their* kitchen, as reflected in the following extract from my field notes from January 29: [15]

> Sitting in the eating area (5) of Lol and Fi's place. Fi is ironing a shirt on the table next to me, while Lol and his friend play guitar and sing in the adjoining room (6). Fi has just served me coffee and sweet rolls for evening *uk'ul* 'supper (lit., 'drink', used for both morning and evening meal). She knows that I am waiting to have supper at Margot's table, but insists I have some there too. . . . Shortly later, Margot calls me next door to her table for supper. She poked her head into Lol's eating area (5), without entering. Shortly later, when I was sitting at Margot's table (1) over supper with DC, Fi appeared at the back door, and watched us without saying anything, nor entering. (BB.4.19)

In subsequent discussion, Fi assured me that she never cooks at the oven of Margot, and that even though the *solar* is one big family without any divisions, each family still has its own *-otoč* 'house'(F.137.A.529). That evening, the entire group ate together at the table of Man and Margot in celebration of my return. Fi breastfed her several-month-old infant at the table, but whereas she does this without covering her breast or the child when in her own home (even in my presence), here, in the company of coresidents, she covered herself, as she would were she 'outside' (BB.4.47). In interactions with these families, as well as with DP's and a number of others, another fact became clear: when a guest, such as I, visits one home in the *solar,* this is not equivalent to visiting the entire *solar.* During my residence with DC as well as with DP, I was expected to visit the coresident families periodically in their own domains, to eat, wash up, or just converse in *their* house. Because women spend most of their time working in their own home and rarely go visiting without a recognized goal, a sleep-in visitor at a coresident house can go for days or weeks and hardly ever see the woman of the adjoining house. Particularly with third-level coresidents, who are on the other side of an objective divide, one might never lay eyes on the woman of the next house, especially if she is of childbearing age.

Despite their basic distinctness, marriage units cooperate and collaborate, overlaying their given social and sociospatial relations with bonds of joint interest and mutual regard. DC, Man, and Lol share the cost as well as consumption of electricity and municipal water in the household. They freely share tools such as machete, pick ax, chisel, hoe, hose, and knife (BB.4.28), although specialized tools like rifles, sewing machines, DC's divining crystals, and stereo recorders are not borrowed (cf. Villa Rojas [1945] 1978:241). They jointly construct various domestic structures like houses, kitchens, walls, and water tanks. Despite assertions to the contrary, Fi and Margot, like the sisters-in-law at DP's house, do occasionally cook for or with one another (F.137.B.160). For instance, on January 30, the entire group ate at Margot's table, but it was Fi who prepared the food at her fire next door (BB.4.26). As the single head of household, DC heats water for bathing on Margot's cooking fire and eats at her table daily (BB.4.86). While the two adult women currently wash laundry and dishes separately, in the past they shared a single *bateya* 'washing basin'. In DP's extended family, an analogous range of generalizations obtains, with the addition that the men coordinate their efforts to obtain irrigation water from the municipio and to transport produce from their fields to the market, some twelve kilometers away by paved road.

It is convenient to view residence patterns around Oxkutzcab in terms of three concentric circles. The first is the individual marriage pair with their offspring and possessions, the second the union of coresidents within a single walled *solar,* and the third the union of adjoining or adjacent *solars* of agnatic kinsmen. The first level marks the individual's 'core' home, his enduring *-iknal* 'place'. This is where he is when he is home, or as the Maya say it, *kulá?an* 'seated'. At the second level of inclusion, coresidents of the *solar* share utilities and typically undertake certain collaborative projects together, such as building or repairing the wall around the household. They usually share a single courtyard through which members routinely pass, even if the living structures are not all oriented the same way to it. Some households at this level are more tightly integrated than others, but the ideal model is one of solidarity. This is the level of household corresponding to the beneficiary of the traditional Maya purification ceremony called *heéȼ lú?um* 'fixing earth' (see chap. 7). The *solar*, as defined by the walled (or otherwise marked) perimeter, sets the limits of the space purified in the ceremony, and the residents of that space are the ones who pay for and benefit from it. The third level of inclusion is the most tenuous, since it encompasses both adjoining *solars* separated by a marked boundary and adjacent ones separated by up to hundreds of meters and perhaps several nonkin neighbors. What links the third-level set together is the bond of agnation between the heads of household. This usually implies solidarity and a common biography in which one or another of the households was the one from which all the brothers came.[16] Furthermore, it implies a ranking of the households by the age and generation of the heads, although it is unclear what role such ranking has in their relations. In DC's case, his current *solar* (second level) was in the possession of his parents when he was a boy. It was part of the same great tract of land that included his current yard, along with that of four neighboring *solars*. All but one of them has been sold off, and today, only the *solar* to the east belongs to an agnate, DC's older sister. Is's father and brother live in a *solar* around the corner from him, and they make a third-level group who collaborate and spend time together despite their physical separation. In acquiring plots of land around his neighborhood for eventual habitation by his son, Chio is in the process of building a third-level homestead out of his currently second-level one.

The density and affective quality of daily contact among third-level coresidents varies considerably, depending upon the individuals and their social relations. DC's sister, for instance, stops by to visit her brother's home several times each week, and DC is apparently always aware of her state of mind. Her two sons, who coreside with her in her *solar*, freely walk through DC's yard from their own yard behind it and greet their *primos* 'cousins' at their own back doors. Yet there is a mixture of estrangement in their relations, since the elder sister is considered delusional, only occasionally coherent (having been struck in her childhood by the wind of locusts), and the sons are considered violent and irresponsible. Milo is a third-level coresident with his younger brothers MC and VC, but they almost never set foot in his house and there are some mixed feelings between them and him.

3.3.7 Gender and the Division of Labor

There is a strict division between male and female activities around the home, with corollaries in the way adult men and women inhabit their living space. Some of the terms of this distinction have been mentioned in the foregoing, including the tendency of women to stay around their own home and their responsibility for food preparation and presentation and washing. Much of what I have been able to observe in Oxkutzcab fits in with or extends Redfield and Villa Rojas's ([1934] 1962:68) concise summary of division between the sexes in Chan Kom. Men do all major agricultural labor, both in the traditional *milpa* '(unirrigated) corn/bean/ squash field' and in the mechanically irrigated orchards and leveled fields cultivated for commercial production. This includes selecting the plot, clearing and burning the forest, plowing or hoeing, planting, weeding, spraying, irrigating, tree splicing (*ingiertos*), and harvesting (see chap. 8). Women occasionally get involved in harvesting in the orchards, where citrus, mango, avocado, and achiote (*k'ušub'*) trees are a main source of production, but their participation in other phases is nearly nil. On the other hand, women typically take produce to the market to sell and do much of the family shopping as well. At different times of the year and of their careers, men work as *naáhal* day laborers, particularly masons, mason's helpers, truck drivers, hired agricultural hands, pickers, and forest clearers. While women bring in sometimes very considerable income sewing or doing laundry, these tasks tend to be performed in their own homes and are not described as *naáhal*. Men typically work outside the residential *solar*, often in groups, in the open hot sun, performing heavy labor punctuated by periods of rest, such as the mid-morning *k'eyem* 'pozole' break, or cigarette breaks. Women work alone, around the house, ideally in the shade, at relatively lighter tasks from which they seemingly never rest. The building and repairing of domestic structures, including the house, kitchen, bird coop, pigsty, corral, wall, and fence and the laying of *šú'uk'* 'boundary stones' are all exclusively male activities. Only men bear arms for hunting, and only they participate in the offering of maize and meat to Maya *yunȼiló'ob'* 'lords' in the rain, thanksgiving, and purification rites (although it is the women who prepare the offertory food). Men, but not women, operate moving vehicles, bicycles, tricycles, and trucks, while women ride, usually on the back. At mealtime, women serve men but do not typically join them in eating. Men eat at a table, usually removed from the heat of the kitchen fire, while women remain within reach of the fire (cf. Nash [1971] 1975:293–96).

When a man is heathily engaged in work, he is said to be *čokow* 'hot', that is, forceful, potent, and invigorated by the heat of the sun. The sun hardens a man's body as he works, making him *maásisóoh* 'hard'. A woman when healthy is relatively cooler, and indeed, the description *čokow* usually implies sexual promiscuity when applied to females, espe-

cially *čokow pòol šč'uúp* 'hotheaded girl, slut'. When pregnant or menstruating, women are relatively 'hotter', and are said to be *k'ohá?an*
'sick'. Women work in the shade and are typified as *suave* 'soft', *?o?olkil*
'baby soft', *kukutkil* 'attractively chubby', and *k'àab'(il)* 'juicy'. Elderly
women are said to *tiíhil* 'to dry', to be *tikin* 'dry'. When working in the
orchards or extracting *sahkab'* 'calcified earth' from pits, men climb up
trees and go underground, just as they walk *yàanal k'aáš* 'under forest'
when hunting or going to their *milpa*. Women apparently never climb
trees, rarely enter *sahkab'* pits, and do not walk in the forest unaccompanied. These various associations can be summarized by saying that
women are linked to the earth's surface, which is, at its best, cool, moist,
fecund, the ground in which plants grow. This might also explain the
well-known fact that Maya women are much more prone to walk barefoot
than men, and that the *k'oób'en* kitchen, a basically female space, is almost never given a concrete or tile floor even in modernizing households.
Maya women stay on the ground.

Other specifically female tasks around the household include the management of domestic water—getting it from the well, storing it, heating it
for bathing, washing with it, and watering domestic gardens, flowers, and
animals. Women feed the dogs, pigs, and poultry, and occasionally tend
the bulls, although this is seen as a properly male task.[17] They sweep,
straighten, and weed around the home and courtyard, sew and iron domestic clothes, and care for the children. They maintain the flowers and
candle in front of the family *sàantoh* 'saint shrine', as well as the domestic cooking fire (a smoky, onerous job). Insofar as the men build the domestic enclosures in which women spend most of their productive time,
they can be said to be in an encompassing relation to them, perhaps the
best symbol of which is the *k'oób'en* kitchen encompassed by the *solar*
walls and houses. Like the woman of which it is a metonym, the kitchen
is private, wet (water is stored here), the locus of domestic fire and food.
The man's *k'an če?* 'stool' on which he sits when eating is located in the
kitchen, just as the placenta that nourishes an unborn child, also called
the *k'an če?*, is located in the woman's *hobon* 'belly'. Eli, a thirty-year-
old mother of six, mobilized these associations when she said, recounting
her husband's sexual infidelities, *?oól impuúl uk'an če?* 'I almost tossed
out his stool', meaning, 'I almost kicked him out of the house for good'.[18]

3.3.8 Beyond the Household

This book is based on an in-depth investigation of communicative practices among a small group of people in the municipio of Oxkutzcab, and
my ethnographic descriptions have accordingly focused on the details of

the households to which these people belong. Still, it would be misleading to stop the description at the household level without at least indicating some of the mechanisms by which households are integrated into the
surrounding community. Here I will briefly indicate some that I have not
investigated in depth but which would surely deserve more treatment in a
fuller study of communicative practices. Perhaps the most obvious is the
large commercial market in Oxkutzcab, where local farmers sell their
produce, especially fruits, by the truckload to merchants from all over the
Yucatán peninsula and beyond. The market is also the central shopping
area and a convenient place to eat lunch, wait for transportation to or from
all points, conduct any municipal business (the *palacio municipal* is just
across the street), or go to the doctor. Through the market, people regularly come into contact with new acquaintances and groups of actors from
far beyond their own area of residence. Furthermore, they do so under
conditions of unequal distribution of the wealth that flows through the
market, a fact which establishes a whole order of socioeconomic asymmetry that has an important impact on people's communicative practices.

Linked to the market economy, many Oxkutzcabeños engage in wage
labor in the agricultural sector (felling, weeding, picking), in masonry,
fence making, transportation, and other occupations. Some of this is
seasonal, fitting into the interstices of the growing year (see chap. 8).
Women routinely travel to market either in Oxkutzcab or as far off as
Mérida, trading en route or bringing produce to trade in the markets.
These occupations further extend the network of contacts and interlocutors sustained by typical adults, both men and women. Similarly, the
network of roads and transportation that supports the regional economy
cross-cuts the local divisions of household and town, linking people between towns. For instance, MC drives a truck between Oxkutzcab and the
Cooperativa area as a full-time occupation. This brings him into repeated
contact with households all around the area and as far off as Mérida,
Chetumal, and Ciudad del Carmen. Similarly, most people have immediate relatives (siblings, parents, offspring) living in neighboring towns,
such as Mani, Yotholim, or Tekax. On the whole, people's social networks are frequently quite far-flung and are mediated by economic, kin-
based, or other social ties.

Also impinging on the local sphere of the household is the all-important
ejido system of land distribution, in which members are divided into sections according to the locations of their agricultural fields. *Ejido* meetings
and elections bring together large numbers of people whose lands are adjacent and who draw irrigation water from the same section of the municipal water system. The latter consists in a network of numbered electric

pump houses which draw water for agricultural and household uses (flood irrigation in the orchards and shallow canal irrigation in the vegetable fields). Members of the same *unidad* 'section', called *socios,* often meet informally during breaks from work or while walking to or from their fields. Sitting in the shade, they discuss current plans or just shoot the breeze, developing sometimes long-term friendships, alliances, or antipathies. The sectional groups are also the primary beneficiaries of the *č'aá čaák* 'rain ceremonies' performed in late July and August.

These and other links between individuals and the larger social world must serve as an underexplored background for the focal communicative practices on which this study is based. In chapters 7 and 8, where we describe the geographical and regional context of the research, we will return briefly to them, although mainly for the purpose of grounding a discussion whose theme lies elsewhere.

3.4 SYMMETRIC AND ASYMMETRIC INTERACTIONS AROUND THE HOMESTEAD

Given the foregoing, it will be clear that many of the interactions that take place (and some that don't) around the homestead are based on age, gender, or residence unit asymmetries between participants. In this section, I will sketch (i) the place of etiquette in domestic interactions, (ii) the concept of social symmetry as applied to verbal interaction in Maya, and (iii) an outline of some speech genres commonly used around the extended *solar.*

3.4.1 Orderliness in the Household

While Maya speakers highly value humor, affection, and spontaneity in speech, they are keenly aware that language use is governed by rules of propriety to which individuals should and must submit. The sense of propriety, called variously *legalidad* 'legality, properness', *cortiedad* 'courtesy', *respeto* 'respect', that which is *hač tubèel* 'right, correct', as opposed to *má? patali?* 'no good', *helá?an* 'weird, off, strange, bad', permeates adult interaction around Maya households. Speakers defer to their status superiors, agreeing with, or at least not challenging, their assertions, following their directives if reasonable, addressing them only with certain titles or sometimes not at all. The impunity with which DP circulates in the domestic spaces of his sons is of a piece with his habit of telling them what to do and criticizing them when he deems it appropriate. The avoidance by men of their brothers' wives is constituted in part by their almost never speaking to one another. In short, talk around the house is part of the social organization of daily life, and it is governed

by a linguistic etiquette focused primarily on who and where the participants are.

The orderliness of domestic interactions gives them a generic typicality
according to which they are intelligible and repeatable.[19] DC's son Lol
explained how the members of their household always show respect for
one another, saying *diàarios tó?on e? → yàan kçiík ih* 'daily, we, we pay
our respects (to one another)' (F.137.B.543). He went on to detail who
can speak to whom and in what terms and then summarized with an affirmation of 'the system': *b'èy usistema k máan tó?on o?* 'that's how the
system is that we go by' (BB.4.12). Margot, the wife of Lol's brother and
hence his most distant *solar* mate, independently recapitulated nearly the
same system in describing her own language use. In fact, the three homes
sharing the *solar* are in many ways idiosyncratic, which makes this perceived regularity stand out. DC, a shaman, has a pet skunk living in his
house and receives visitors at all hours. Man and Margot, with four children and a pet parrot named *Puto corrito* 'Nonstop faggot' (in imitation
of his most common vocalization), see themselves as in a 'struggle to im-
prove their lives' with education, cinder blocks, and Western health care.
Lol and Fi, with their first infant, work together sewing clothing for cus-
tomers, sing frequently together around the house as he plays accordion
or guitar, and even sing with his male friend, a practice Man finds scan-
dalous. An insomniac, Lol commonly plays the guitar and sings throughout much of the night. These idiosyncratic differences, which could be
elaborated considerably, make even more salient the orderliness in relations among coresidents. Though less prone to discuss their own interactions, the adult members of DP's extended household are also scrupulous
in their spoken treatment of one another and often invoke the idea of
properness in discussing peoples' conduct. Hence the schematic codes of
conduct and divisions among actors are embodied in the frame spaces in
which they communicate (actual and potential; see §2.4) and inevitably
have an impact on the actual frameworks they produce in their interactions as well.

3.4.2 Symmetry and Asymmetry

Patterns of interaction among coresidents, like the spatial arrangement of
domestic zones and structures, presuppose and help to constitute social
relations around the household. Residents interact in accordance with
their asymmetric status, gender, and immediate place of residence.[20]
While there are no pronominal distinctions in Maya analogous to the indexical values of *tu/vous* in European languages, a kind of 'asymmetric
power pragmatic' is discernible nonetheless (cf. Brown and Gillman

[1960] 1972; Errington 1988; Friedrich 1966, and Silverstein 1976b). Markedly asymmetric, nonreciprocal, interactive genres include *k'èey, laánk'èey* 'bawl out, criticize sharply', and *tusik b'èel* 'order around', which superiors address to inferiors. *ȼiík* 'pay respect to' and *ʔúʔuyik t'àan* 'obey' are often nonreciprocal, indexing inferior to superior, though not always. In addition to asymmetric genres, there are relatively symmetric ones, in which the structurally based status differences between participants are less salient or not in play; *ȼikbal* 'converse, conversation', and *baášal t'àan* 'play talk, joking' are two examples. Finally, there are other, more specialized ways of talking that may occur around the household and that are focused on the expression or elicitation of emotion: *pòoč'i* 'to insult', *kikit'àan* 'sweet talk'.

These ways of speaking embody the play between symmetry and asymmetry among interactants and provide a bridge between the social-structural basis of participant relations and the linguistic forms of speech. As a set, they are less diverse than the Kuna linguistic varieties and languages described by Sherzer (1983), and all fall squarely within everyday Maya, as opposed to ritual speech (see chaps. 7, 8 below). Whereas the Kuna varieties are ordered in Sherzer's description (chap. 2) by relative formality, my overview of everyday Maya will be ordered in terms of the participant relations indexed by use of the genres. Like Sherzer, I rely on a notion of genre which combines formal features of message tokens along with aspects of the interactive field in which they are produced.[21] The description is illustrative rather than comprehensive. My purpose is to lay the groundwork for an account of demonstrative reference and address as verbal practices unavoidably linked to the play between participant symmetry and asymmetry. Accordingly, the discussion proceeds from asymmetric to symmetric genres, followed by an extended example of deictic reference in task-oriented speech at a work site.

3.4.3 Asymmetric Genres

Perhaps the most obvious example of asymmetric address is *k'eyik* 'bawl out' and *laánk'eyik,* its more intense counterpart. One of Eli's children is playing with food on the table as she tries to set it. Exasperated, she says loudly *tiít abaá téʔeloʔ ʔiího→* 'Beat it out of there, son! (lit., stretch yourself there, son)'. This is a mild case of *k'èey* speech in which the speaker verbally 'shoves' the addressee to alter his behavior, clearly asserting her authority but not sustaining a confrontation. A more dramatic example occurred in DC's house, where the youngest brother Victor at one point stole some cassettes from my suitcase, which was stored in the elder brother's home. The senior men of the household, his father and two brothers, dragged him physically into his father's home, where they stood around him and told him to admit to his deed and return the cassettes. He stood mute, eyes downcast, as they *laánk'eyah, k'eék'eyah* 'blasted him verbally' in the overfast, tonally flat, falling final intonation contour of this genre,

(2)   ↓–   –↓
                »–   –»
        tú?uš t-a-¢'aá le báal o?→ k'ub e bá?al o? ↓
        'Where'd you put the stuff? Hand over the stuff!' (BB.4.32)

This continued for nearly half an hour, during which Victor persisted in denying culpability, while his brothers raged that he was mocking them, *kaburlartikó?on* 'you're making fun of us', that they would give him a beating, that they had taken note of his behavior, and that it was no damn good. He finally admitted his action and told how and when he had done it, but not before taking a verbal beating that included questioning his legitimacy as the son of DC.

The most typical, if not the only, kind of speech addressed to domestic animals is *k'èey*, the directives used to shoo them away. There are different styles for different kinds of animals. Dogs, and only dogs, conventionally get the drawn-out bilabial ingressive sound made by pursing the lips and making a maximally loud and abrupt 'kissing' noise, typically followed by the utterance *bikíh* 'No!' delivered overloud with extra stress on the final syllable. Chickens and turkeys get the repeating voiceless fricative sound *č+č+č+č+!* with breathy offset for each segment, or the continuous, voiceless *hwúúušššš!* repeated several times. If the animals do not respond, a stick or projectile usually follows, an especially clear instance of the power asymmetry of the speech genre.

A milder form of directing an addressee is what is described as *tusik b'èel* 'order road'. While *k'èey* implies a sharp or even furious delivery style, *tusik b'èel* refers mainly to the fact that the speaker is telling the addressee what to do. This can be done with attenuated requests (soft, overhigh pitch), instructions, or blunt directives, depending on the case. Adults describe it as a parental duty that a mother 'order' her daughter, and a father his son, in order to teach them how to work properly. DP sits in the kitchen of his son's wife and corrects her every move, 'Don't do it like that, do it this way'. Leaving, he sees a piece of smoldering firewood by the kitchen door and barks from outside *má a na¢' e bá?a tée hòol na a?* 'Don't leave this thing here by the entrance!' (BB.5.5). His utterances are all instances of *tusik b'èel,* which he sees as his right and responsibility towards his son's wife. On February 2, as DC was having supper at the table of Margot, a young, unmarried man arrived at the back door to request a *saántiguar* treatment. He is a regular patient of DC's who commonly joins the family in conversation inside the house, and his unannounced appearance at the back door was treated as routine. Margot exercised her authority as senior woman of the house and told him tersely:

(3)   šén tol o`→ taán uyuk'ul, šeén to ič nah o`
            'Go over there. He's having supper. Go over to the (other) house.'
            (BB.4.129)

The inverse of criticizing and ordering around is the respectful, deferential footing speakers adopt when engaged in *¢iíkil* 'pay respect' speech. This is evident when members of DC's household greet each other with their most proper address forms, *bweénos diías papah* 'Good morning, father,' from son or son's wife to father; *bweénos días don Wiíl* 'Good evening, Don William' from child to father's *compadre* (cogodparent). Similarly, when a wife falls silent in a conversation joined by her husband, in effect giving him the floor, or a son assents to his father's statement even though he secretly disagrees with it, or a visitor addresses a resident from a respectful distance, these are acts of verbal respect. Just before lunch, Margot, who is my *comadre* 'cogodparent', a relation of reciprocal respect, called me to the table from the doorway of the room I was working in, leaning forward, smiling, almost whispering:

(4)   Margot: čõmpádre→ kó`ot en hañǎ
                    'Compadre, come eat.'

            WH: kuš tuún DC?
                'What about DC?' I asked.

            Margot: ¢'úb'in t'ambi.
                    'He's been called.' (BB.4.120)

Margot's demeanor and delivery style, as well as the fact that DC, the head of the household, had already been called to eat, showed her desire to 'pay respect'.

It is worth reiterating that this kind of speech, like the others, encompasses a range of utterance types and consists mainly in a footing that speakers adopt in talk, not a specific set of utterances or a kind of language as such. Being a sign of consideration, *¢iík* is also considered a proper mode of approaching strangers or reciprocating their address. Thus, while often a sign of nonreciprocal deference in an asymmetric relation, such as son to father, it may also be exchanged reciprocally as a sign of mutual respect.

To 'hear speech' in Maya, *ʔúʔuyik t'àan,* is to be reasonable, tractable, and above all, mindful of the rules set down by higher authorities. Around the house, subordinates who are ordered by their elders or spouses are expected to follow directions. An individual who proposes to do something likely to lead to trouble is expected to respond to a reasoned plea, even if it comes from someone structurally subordinate to him, such as a son or younger brother. These are cases of 'hearing speech'. It is the opposite when one is a *terko* 'pigheaded, stubborn' (cf. *terkiedad* 'pigheadedness') or *rebelde* 'rebellious', in which case words and rules go unheeded. Like signs of respect, *ʔúʔuyik t'àan* is in the clearest cases a nonreciprocal attentiveness one speaker pays to another, but it may also be seen as reciprocal when used to describe the general reasonableness of people who follow the guidelines of *legalidad* 'legality'.

3.4.4 Symmetric Genres

It would be wrong to suggest that Maya speakers constantly attend to their differences of status and experience in their everyday speech. There are strong bonds of affection, friendship, solidarity, and common experience that link interactants and put them on a relatively symmetric, reciprocal footing. There is an explicit sense among Maya speakers that both parties to an interaction should contribute to it, that to fail to contribute or to prevent an interlocutor from doing so is to violate the norms of sociability. Among the prototypically symmetrical genres of interaction, *¢ikbal* 'conversation, discussion, narrative' and *baášal t'àan* 'play speech, joking' are good exemplars. These are activities one engages in when visiting, sitting together over food or drink, when men smoke a cigarette together during a work break or just hang out together over coffee in the market, when women talk across the courtyard from their respective washbasins, and in the back of a truck when people are on their way to do errands. One is typically received in a Maya house with an invitation to *ʔòoken, héʔe b'áʔal akutal aʔ, kóʔoš ¢ikbal* 'enter, here's something to sit on, let's converse', and people report, as well as evaluate, such exchanges as *ha¢'u¢* 'beautiful' or *maʔ ha¢'u¢ iʔ* 'not beautiful' *¢ikbal.* The former is a source of *kíʔimak ʔóolal* 'happiness', *toh ʔóolal* 'contentedness', whereas the unwillingness to engage on this footing is a sign of estrangement or aloofness. Discussing an exchange I had had with another speaker, in which my interlocutor responded to my utterance by repeating it in slightly altered form, Man and Margot nicely illustrated the expectation of joint engagement as it applies to *¢ikbal.* I wondered if the other speaker was correcting me in altering my utterance or just agreeing with me by reaffirming it in slightly different form. They explained that she had been agreeing but naturally did not want to repeat my words verbatim, since to do so would give the appearance that I was talking to myself. There must be *cambios* 'changes' in the talk. Man went on:

(5)   tumèen   kinnuúkik   teč le hé?eš tawá?alil e? ↑   yan atuklik
        'because (if) I answer you just as   you've said it,   you'll think

        tinhùun kint'àan.   Wá kuyú?ub'al le t'àan mèen ulaák'
        all alone I'm talking. If   that talk was heard by another

        maák e?, yàan   utuklik e? tèen pašik ↑   tèen   ?òok'ostik
        person, he'd think   I'm the one playing (the tune),   (and) I'm the
        one dancing to it (too).

        k'abeét uhoók'ol ušeét'e
        His (the other person's) part has to come out too.' (BB.4.108)

In order to have a conversation that is *tuúlis* 'whole', there must be two different parts, each speaker contributing his own distinct part.

Maya speakers are known for their verbal humor, which includes a large repertoire of preexistent jokes and humorous stories, spontaneous puns, innuendo, hyperbole, caricature, and deception. Much of the spontaneous joking that punctuates conversation focuses thematically on sexual relations, slight misunderstandings of ambiguous circumstances, and incompetence imputed to the addressee or someone else. The speaker that has one over on the other is said to *mèentik uyoól* 'kid him, do (act on) his will' (see §3.2). While joking is apparently most intense among gatherings of men, it is also common between men and women, although not among coresident mixed pairs. It is considered inappropriate to engage in blatantly sexual humor or vulgar cursing in the presence of women, particularly senior ones, and 'play speech' in its most elaborate forms tends (in my experience) to occur away from the residential portion of the *solar,* where the women and children are. This is not to say that there is no passing humor around the house, but that the range of devices used is restricted and the jokes understated. This may be because most of spontaneous 'play speech' is a reciprocal activity in which each participant tries to entrap the other, twisting his or her words for humorous effect. There are sufficiently binding constraints around the household on who can address whom and how that such reciprocity is ruled out in most situations.

Two of DS's daughters-in-law, coresidents, were eating tacos in the market when I came upon them and stopped to *¢ikbal* 'converse'. We had known each other for several years, although not well. One of them offered me a plate of food, saying with a grin *héʔelaʔ wiíl, héʔel awóʔoč a?* 'Here it is Will, here's your food,' at which the other burst into laughter. The implication of her utterance, including the grin, presentative gesture, and reference to feeding, was that she was mock offering her own body (not a provocative act in this context). JC, a man in his mid seventies, is locally famous for his relentless *baášal t'àan* and his willingness to turn conversation with almost anyone into a string of double entendres, such as when he is greeted *ʔoóla wiínik b'iš awanil?* 'Hi man, how are you?' to which his response was for a time *laáyli walakbal eʔ* 'Still standing (erect).'

Men frequently exchange *baášal t'àan* in the brief greetings they trade outside the house when passing in the streets. A routine exchange might go as follows: AB, an adult man, is walking towards the market early in the morning when he sees TG, a familiar, passing on a bicycle. The exchange takes place as TG passes, without slowing:

(6)   AB: heéy TG! hábisken eʔ
        'Hey TG, will you take me along?' (= can you take my whole penis?)

        TG: héʔeleʔ naáken iʔ
        'Sure, get up (on the back of the bike)' (= sure, just try and jump on me).

        AB: hátáʔakeneʔ
        'You'll shit on me.' (10/22/80)

Assume AB is carrying a load of firewood or produce on his back with a tumpline. TG shouts in passing:

(7)   TG: maáreh, ʔal akùuč
        'Maria! your load is heavy (= your genitals are big).'

        AB: héʔelaʔ
        'Here it is (come and get it).'

        or AB': héʔeš sùuk abisik teč eʔ
        'Like you're used to taking on (= you like men with big genitals).'

        or AB": máʔ sùuk imbisik ten iʔ→màas sùuk ašbáʔal
        'I'm not used to taking it, (but) your girlfriend is (= I'm sleeping with your girlfriend).' (10/22/80)

Such play turns partly on the existence of a set of words and phrases that male speakers know have potentially double meanings, including *bisik* 'to take (be sexually penetrated)', *kučik* 'carry (be sexually penetrated)', *kùuč* 'load, genitals', *siʔ* 'firewood (erect penis)', *kàab'* 'honey (semen)', *kèeso* 'cheese (female genitalia)', *čiwoól* 'tarantula (vagina)'. When these terms, and many more, occur in speech, speakers have the option of turning them towards their secondary meanings or taking them at 'face' or 'literal' value. Thus, 'play speech' is above all a response mode that consists in responding to the humorous potential of the interlocutor's most recent utterance. Under its effects, discourse interpretation stays open to a whole universe of possible meanings that competent participants recognize but never state. VI once explained that this opening up is the essence of *baášal t'àan,* but that it can be dangerous if one speaker takes offense (F.63. October 22, 1980). The speech *kusatik ubaáh* 'loses itself, gets lost' in ambiguity and unstated interpretive possibilities. More than a list of words with double meanings, play turns on the willingness to hear whatever is said for its humorous potential. This is surely one of the reasons that speakers find it very difficult to talk about *baášal t'àan* in the abstract, since it is an interactive genre that presupposes chains of utterances by different speakers.

In VI's explanation, he cited examples of opening utterances, intended to initiate playful interaction between men working together. His examples aptly illustrate the trope of equating two referents as a way of indexing a set of unstated corollaries. Seeing his co-worker's wife walking towards the market, a man says to him, *hé? kimbin o?* 'there I go', pointing to the woman. *tú?uš yaneč* 'Where are you?', the other responds. *hé? kimbin hmàan o?* 'there I go shopping', the first counters. At this point, the talk can proceed in the direction of play or of insults designed to provoke. The initial speaker has conveyed either that he is the addressee's wife, implying that the addressee prefers men to women, or that he is off following her for sexual favors. Alternatively, the first speaker could say, pointing to a dog, *hé?eleč o?* 'there you are', equating the addressee with an animal considered vile. In response, *hé?el a? pèek'* 'here it is. Dog!' making reference to his own body (or body part) and calling the addressee 'Dog'. This freewheeling reference to spouses and body parts is the antithesis of the highly respectful avoidance relations that men typically maintain with respect to the wives of their friends. Right after offering the above examples of openers, VI went on to explain that he had never set foot in the house of his best friend and co-worker Tigre, nor would he even so much as make reference to the existence of his wife. These avoidances are powerful constraints on speech, gaze, and spatial movement that are inverted in both play and insult.

Beyond 'play speech' proper, practical jokes that play on people's fear or ignorance are a favorite form of entertainment, even around the house.

Man and Lol recounted with glee how they used to play tricks on their father when they were boys. Once they rigged up a string to DC's large *sàanto* crucifix, which stays on his altar, in front of which he performs most cures and all divination. They tied it so that while he was performing the *saántiguar,* with the patient looking intently upon the crucifix (as DC instructs them to do), they could make it wobble back and forth. Laughing hilariously, they told of how they had frightened an old woman who took it to be a sign of DC's tremendous power. Another time they set up loudspeakers under DC's altar and in the roof and used a borrowed microphone to confuse a patient who was sitting alone waiting for DC to return; they talked to her as if from out of the *santo.* A young man who visits DC often was startled the first time he saw me in the house and asked if I spoke Maya and who I was. Man and Lol spontaneously cooked up the story that I was DC's lost brother and that I had simply appeared one day out in the back yard. They strung him along for some time with this story, much to their enjoyment.

There is a traditional Maya story about a boy whose father died and for whom a vigil was kept in the family house (as is the practice). Known to be flippant, the boy was told by his mother to simply stand watch over the body, which was laid out on the table in its white mantle of death, and not say a word, while the others prepared for the ceremony. A mouse that lived in the roof, it turns out, came down and ran across the table; the boy tried to swat it, knocking over the candle, which set the mantle on fire, which in turn burned the body to a crisp. The boy never called for help, because he took literally his instructions to be quiet. This story, which many people find hilarious, combines the elements of unforeseen misfortune, communicative incompetence based on literal understanding, and a mechanical string of consequences. One of the most salient contexts in which I have heard the story recounted, with laughter, was in front of an actual corpse during a real life and death *velorio* 'vigil' at which some people were wailing, others sitting quietly, and others chuckling at the thought of a mouse setting fire to the *ʔánimáas* 'dead person' (BB.4.140). DC was once listening to a long tale of misfortune told by a man who had come to him for advice. It appears that he and his brother had both had sexual relations with the same woman, who was now pregnant, and the man was gravely concerned to know whose responsibility the child was. He was quite upset and took the better part of an hour telling his story in detail. DC found it so humorous—so awry and ill conceived—that he laughed throughout much of the story, before telling the man that the responsibility was *his*.

3.5 INSTRUMENTAL SPEECH

It is appropriate to conclude this brief summary of everyday speech genres with an example of what we can heuristically call 'instrumental speech', although there is no such label in Maya (cf. Lyons 1977:826; Turner 1967:32ff.). I have in mind the task-oriented exchanges that take place between people working together—masons building a wall, women at work in the courtyard, men clearing trees together or digging canals in a field. The special interest of such talk for a study of indexical reference is obviously the relatively high proportion of deictic references, directives, and presentatives it contains by virtue of its focus on collaborative engagement. The interplay between preexistent status asymmetries between participants and the momentary footings they adopt in talk is especially clear in contexts in which the instrumental function is dominant.

Coresident males typically collaborate in at least some labor, like moving produce to market by truck, repairs around the household, and irrigating, provided their orchards or fields are contiguous. Ideally, senior fathers of adult men work and become partners with one of their sons, as is the case of DP and VC, who share a *parsela* and work jointly in DP's orchard, and Is and his father, who have made *milpa* together for the past twenty years. VI and his younger brother Gwal have worked side by side as masons for several years, and Man and Lol have worked together as masons, tailors, and on home improvements, as well. In the *heéȼ lú?um* 'fix earth' and *wàahil kòol* 'loaves of the field' ceremonies, of which the beneficiary is the total (second level) *solar* unit, the adult men collaborate in the preparation and execution of the ceremony, while the women jointly cook the meat, all under the close supervision of the shaman.

DP, VC, and I are working together hoeing out a canal along the back boundary of DP's *solar* (see fig. 3.5). Sitting on the edge of the canal, as I loosen the earth with a pick and VC hoes it open, DP tells me that he plans to plant a row of pepper bushes along each bank:

(8)   ti⁷ **e** kàanal k-**im**-b'èetik **a**⁷ → káʔa p'eé sùurko kén u-b'i seh →
           'In this ditch I'm making,   two rows will it take,

           ump'é **té⁷el a** →   **ump'eé tée bey a**⁷ →
           one right here (pointing),   one like this here (pointing).

           káʔa ȼol pak'aál kén **in**-ȼ'aáeh
           Two rows of plants will I put (there).' (2/18/87; BB.5.30)

DP's first person singular reference to what **he** was doing, when actually he was sitting watching us work, was a clear instantiation of his rank as the head, not only of the current undertaking, but of the household in which we all resided and the *solar* in which we were working. Regardless of who wields the hoe, it is DP who is making a ditch to plant peppers.

To make reference to the different banks of the ditch, DP has selected Immediate deictic forms ending in the -*aʔ* terminal particle (boldface). Given our shared spatial context and the fact that all three of us were already engaged in the task, the Non-Immediate form *téʔeloʔ* 'there' would have been an equally proper choice of word. The use of either deictic presupposes the shared perceptual, spatial, and actional frame in which we were all located at the time. However, the act of defining the rows by pointing them out with this form is an **asymmetric segmentation**, which presents them as new information not already shared among the interactants. In fact, it was new to me, the addressee, although surely not to VC, also a ratified hearer. In the framework of its utterance, DP's reference to the anticipated rows of vegetables (in a place currently overgrown with weeds) produces a spatial division that will subsequently be part of the joint corporeal field of our labor. By choosing the Immediate, asymmetric deictic, DP puts himself in the role of defining his referents as his own, not as joint 'givens'. This way of aligning himself in relation to his referents is parallel to his use of the first person singular pronoun (boldface) to describe himself as the one doing things; both phrasings put him in the role of defining the agenda. VC, a respectful son, would no more make such a unilateral assertion in his father's presence than he would attempt to order him around. That is, though less obvious than some highly marked speech genres, the asymmetries of indexical reference also connect with the asymmetries of social status.

Shortly afterwards, VC was bent over working on the canal with the pickax, when DP told him to dig out a *poseta* 'basin' in which to plant a bush. DP was standing almost directly over VC, within a meter of both him and the pocket of earth where the hole was to be dug (a circular basin about 1 meter across). As he spoke, he pointed to the west side of the ground and told VC to dig it out a little more (map BB.5.32):

(9)   **tían tée** čik'in **oʔ** →
          'There's where it is there on the west.' (2/18/87; BB.5.30)

Why has DP switched from the Immediate to the Non-Immediate locative deictic, even though the place he is referring to is less than a step away from him? He is still giving orders asymmetrically, by hovering over VC and telling him where to dig. VC was the one digging the *poseta* in his own most immediate activity field, but this was true of the previous utterance too. A clue to the difference is the utterance fraction *tían* 'there's where it is'. This is an anaphoric device indexing prior mention to the referent, indicating that both DP and VC are attuned to the location of the *poseta*, probably because they have talked about it before (although not in the immediately preceding talk and not in my presence).[22] Hence, DP has shifted his own *schéma corporel* from a focus on himself and his future projects (8) to the reciprocal zone of common knowledge established in previous discussion or shared awareness (9). Furthermore, while DP is the head of the *solar* and the primary authority in the plan to plant pepper bushes in the first place, it is VC who will perform the specific task of digging the *poseta*. What the choice of Non-Immediate deictic does here is put the referent in VC's activity space while indexing the **shared** background knowledge that he and DP have of the arrangement of the ditch. Despite the recognized status asymmetries between the two, this usage is a relatively **symmetric** one, because it relies on what the interactants share.

Another typically symmetrical usage followed shortly after, when DP judged that the job was done, looking at the site and saying:

(10)   **hé?el o?** ¢'oká?an **bey o?**
         'There it is, it's finished as is.' (BB.5.31)

This utterance is a standard way of bringing an activity to a close by summarizing it in a single deictic reference. Because the activity being summarized was a joint effort undertaken prior to the moment of utterance rather than a one-man performance anticipated in the future, the appropriate deictics are the relatively more symmetric, Non-Immediate -*o?* forms. (English is the same: one usually says 'There, that's that' to finish an activity, but something like 'Here goes, this is it' to begin.)

Moments later, DP was standing on the bank of a ditch connecting with the one we had just prepared, while VC was standing on the other side, opposite and several meters behind him (see fig. 3.5). DP had just told VC of his plans to open up the second ditch, running parallel to the eastern portion of the one we had already done. It was an overgrown section of ground where there had been an irrigation ditch in the past. Directing his gaze and pointing at the overgrown ditch in his foreground, with his back to VC on the other side, he says:

(11)   **hé? le** kánal tuún k-**inw**-áaik teč **a?**
         'Here's the ditch I'm telling you about.' (BB.5.31)

In this utterance, DP switches back to the **asymmetric** stance of characterizing the ditch entirely from his own perspective rather than including

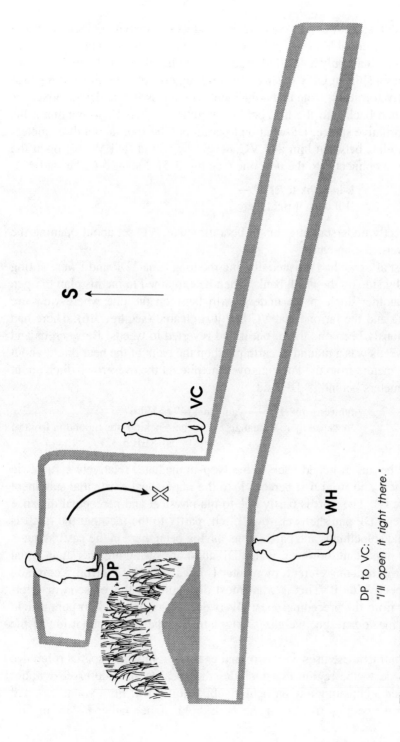

DP to VC:
"I'll open it right there."

Fig. 3.5. Irrigation ditch: 'I'll open it right there.'

his addressee, VC. He once again produces a spatial segmentation not already accessible to VC and me: in fact, there was no canal in the place he pointed at, only a patch of ground where he anticipated one. This constitutes a shift in DP's *schéma corporel*, again isolating him and his prospective projects. Note that coincident with the switch in deictic adverb is a switch back into the first person singular subject 'I'. Maintaining his authoritative stance, DP went on to point out the spot, about three meters from him, between him and VC, where he would (tell VC to) open the ditch to connect it to the new one (see fig. 3.5). Facing VC, he said:

(12)   **k-in**-he²ik **té²el a²** →
            'I'll open it right there.'

Correctly understanding this to be a directive, VC set about opening the not-yet-existing canal.

Just after we had finished digging the long canal, DP and I were sitting side by side on the north bank, when he explained to me his plan to open yet another ditch in the undergrowth between the one where we were sitting and the far one that VC had just cleared (see fig. 3.6). There had previously been one there, but it had reverted to weeds. Between us and the weeds was a mound of earth piled on the bank of the near ditch, about three meters from us. Pointing over the pile, at the overgrown ditch about two meters behind it, DP said:

(13)   tumèen   **té²el o²** → yan cánal **té²** pàačil **o²**
            'because there's a canal   there behind (the mound in front of
                                            us)' (BB.5.32)

Here he has switched back to the Non-Immediate, relatively symmetric deictics, and from first person 'I' to the impersonal existential statement 'there is'. The shift is partly due to the physical and perceptual distance between DP and the overgrown ditch, partly to the fact that the ditch is behind something, and partly to its having been there in the past. What is most important, however, is that DP and I are sitting together at an equal remove from the referent, momentarily engaged in *¢ikbal* from a common perspective on it. This is what most distinguishes this episode of reference from the preceding ones: DP is occupying a shared corporeal field with me, our respective gazes originating in the same subportion of the space.

Contrast these uses with two final examples, in which spatial reference is made to the region that includes the speaker and addressee without further segmenting any particular subportions of it. Fi, a young married woman residing *²ilib'¢il* in the household of her father-in-law in Ox-

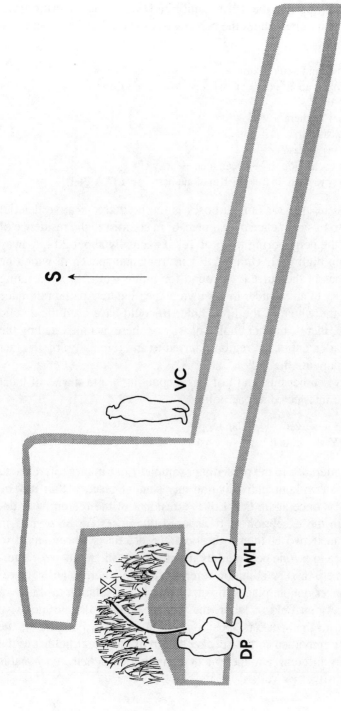

DP to WH:
'There's a ditch back there.'

Fig. 3.6. Irrigation ditch: 'There's a ditch back there.'

kutzcab, was telling me about her family in Tekax, a neighboring town (see fig. 7.4). I inquired about the residences of her elder sisters, and she responded as in (14):

(14)   WH: kuš tuún akìik ó'ob' →   tú'uš yàan ↓
           'What about your elder sisters? Where are they?
       Fi: tían o
           'They're there.'
       WH: tek'aš ↑
           '(In) Tekax?'
       Fi: tían tek'ašó'ob' e' → čeén tèen → **way e'**
           'They're there in Tekax. I'm alone here.' (F.137.A.263)

The key word in (14) for our purposes is the boldface locative deictic, which refers to Fi's residence in Oxkutzcab, in contrast to the residence of her sisters in the neighboring town of Tekax (actually about 20 km away along the main highway). Unlike DP's instrumental speech in which he marks out areas in the current surround for future work, Fi is narrating personal history to an outsider in her own home, and her spatial reference encompasses the whole of the household. Fi could have used the deictic *té'el a'* 'here, there', but her choice of *way e'* 'here' is motivated by the relatively great extent of the region referred to and (crucially) by the fact that she is occupying the region.

Similarly, when her husband Lol was recounting to me stories of local corruption, he interjected at one point:

(15)   sí le **way** a' → paklan tòop
           'Yeah, around here, (everyone) screws each other.' (BB.4.12)

Just like Fi's utterance in the preceding example, Lol's makes reference to the local region without individuating any smaller place within it. The crucial factor is once again that Lol is a resident of the region he is describing. With the exception of transposed utterances (to be treated in depth in the next two chapters) the boldface deictic is *always* used to make reference to a zone occupied by the speaker at the moment of utterance; the home is a very common referent. Hence whereas DP's instrumental utterances denote places distinct from, but in relation to, his own position in the joint field of labor, these two examples denote inclusive zones relative to the speakers' position within them. In both cases, the references are embodied in the speaker's current corporeal field, but the embodiment is different, and the role of the individual *schéma corporel* is accordingly distinct as well.

What then is the relation between the kinds of interactive alignments indexed in highly marked speech genres such as *k'èey* 'bawl out' and *tusik b'èel* 'order around', on the one hand, and the microalignments in evidence in routine acts of reference, on the other? They are at least partly governed by the same set of preexistent social relations, according to which a head of household can unilaterally speak down to, in front of, or behind any subordinate member, asserting in his or her own first person the authoritative word on what is going on and how it is to go. In an important sense, the asymmetry of telling a co-worker 'I am doing this right here' to describe the project in which both are jointly engaged is the same as the asymmetry of telling that person what to do. In the scenarios presented, DP's structural position as head of the household gives him the authority to adopt both an **asymmetric**, authoritative footing and a **symmetric**, solidary footing, according to his own communicative purposes. Like different physical postures, these footings embody dispositions to act in different ways. The former indexes the nonshared, new, or 'egocentric' status of the referent as belonging to the speaker alone, and the latter indexes its shared, given, or 'sociocentric' status. The former often involves the production of divisions that will subsequently be schematic, while the latter builds on already schematized divisions. By the same authority, DP routinely shifts between a solidary style of *¢ikbal* 'conversation', drawing on shared experiences and inclusive humor, and a power-laden style of giving orders and defining agendas.

This indicates a further element of the speech genres sketched here, which is worth emphasizing. In the course of about forty-five minutes around the work site, DP changed his indexical alignment many times; just four of them were presented above. Similarly, he could easily switch between *¢ikbal* 'conversation', *baášal t'àan* 'play', *k'èey* 'bawling out', and *tusik b'èel* 'ordering around' as many times over the same period. These conversational genres should be thought of as consisting of speech styles along with footing alignments that speakers combine and play off one another in sometimes rapid sequence. The changing symmetries and asymmetries of the framework of reference display the same quick mutability.

3.6 EMBODIMENT OF REFERENCE

What do these examples and ethnographic facts tell us about the general phenomenon of embodiment in language, and especially in referential practices? In the passage quoted at the outset of this chapter, Merleau-

Ponty asserts that when a speaker uses the word 'here' in reference to his or her own body, something special takes place: the body is not individuated relative to any exterior coordinates but is actually "anchored in an object." This anchoring is the original establishment of spatial coordinates according to the phenomenologist, the means by which an actor takes up a position in the world. Recalling examples like (14–15), one has a sense that Merleau-Ponty was on to something basic, but that his statement is only partly true. Fi and Lol both make reference to zones whose distinctive feature is that they are actually occupied by the speaker at the moment of utterance. The two install themselves in this zone in the very act of making reference to it. DP also takes up a position forcefully in the utterances cited, yet he never makes reference to his own body. Instead, he indexes his corporeal field as a ground, of which VC and I were also occupants, and denotes bounded places in relation to it. While DP does not put his body in the canal when he makes reference to it, he nonetheless inevitably takes up a position relative to it and to his interlocutors. Just like the gaze that inhabits its object in Merleau-Ponty's opening remarks on the body ([1945] 1967:81ff.), indexical reference is a way of inhabiting the world and DP, Fi, and Lol all engage in it.

The first point then is that embodiment takes place not only when the body is the focal object referred to but, more pervasively, when the body belongs to the ground from which reference takes place. The relational structure inherent in indexical reference articulates both focal and backgrounded positions.

The second point has to do with the role of the individual speaker as owner of the *schéma corporel* that is the basis of embodiment. Here Merleau-Ponty's focus on the individual led him to overemphasize the isolability of the acting subject. In referential practices it is rarely the speaker as a single individual who makes up the ground. Recall DP's shifts in footing as he issued directives and predictions in his role as the head of the household. It is true that he focalized himself through first person singular reference and asymmetric locative deictics. Yet it was constantly relevant to his word choice that we were all working in the immediate area, that VC and I could see his referents once he pointed them out, that certain kinds of discussions had already taken place and were accessible by memory. The social mediation of reference is the necessary horizon without which subjects could not individuate themselves or the objects to which they have access. Fi (14) and Lol (15) necessarily take up a position in their home by the terms of their reference, yet they do so in relation to other places being discussed and to me, their addressee.

Merleau-Ponty goes too far when he asserts that the body is the original anchor, which is not itself anchored in an "external" world.[23]

Study of referential practices leads to the conclusion that the two kinds of anchoring are two faces of the same process. The origo is not an individual *schéma corporel* but a corporeal field occupied by two or more coparticipating interactants. This means that the intersensorial unity that is basic to the phenomenological schema must be embedded in an 'interperspectival' unity in order to serve as the ground of communication. Given the importance of talk in forming experience, it is unsurprising that the Maya term *-iknal* 'bodily space' is used to refer to both the intersensorial unity of a single speaker and the interperspectival unity of a corporeal field that includes others too (via coresidence in the homestead or coparticipation in the act of reference). Embodiment, even when it crucially involves the human body, cannot be treated from the perspective of an isolated speaker.

Discourse practices, such as the ones I have loosely called genres in this chapter, can also embody meaning and social relations. Here we refer to aspects of the sociocultural frame of reference that go beyond bodies in motion to include principles of rank and proper etiquette in domestic interactions, kinship relations, and divisions of labor by gender and age (§§3.3–3.4). These constitute **schematic** dimensions in the domestic field that cooperate with body space in grounding reference. Power-laden interactive genres such as scolding, bawling out, and ordering around (superiors to inferiors) and respecting and obeying (inferiors to superiors) embody social differences as part of their conditions of use. Play speech, particularly in its fast and dirty forms, is a relatively symmetrical genre of exchange, typically reciprocated among men away from the primary residential area of the *solar*. Task-oriented reference and description shows further, more subtle linguistic reflexes of social asymmetries. While not as obviously charged as some other genres, routine acts of reference are unavoidably caught up in the broader social field too. This is evident in the terms speakers select to identify referents, as well as the alignments they take up relative to their interlocutors.

Deictics, pronouns, and indexical referential expressions are among the fundamental referring items in all natural languages, while at the same time they conventionally index the interactants' egocentric, altercentric, or sociocentric footings. By combining in a single act the background frame of reference, along with the ongoing framework of coparticipation, deictic practice embodies individual *schémas corporels,* the interactive corporeal field, and the schematic structure of sociocultural context into a unified whole. Neither egocentric nor concrete, this enactment, which we can call 'embodied reference', has little to do with the apparent self-evidence of pointing to the ground one stands on. In chapters 4 and 5 we will explore person reference in conversation, building on the corporeal field but exploring its transposability in much more detail.

DC in his yard

All photos by William F. Hanks

DC making a point

DP resting in his hammock

Doña Toni

VI after work

Margot in her kitchen

DA in her kitchen

Eli in her kitchen

Couples: DP and DA   Couples: MC and Eli

Couples: VC and Pilar

Couples: Man and Margot

Pilar and daughter in courtyard

Leti with her mother, Margot

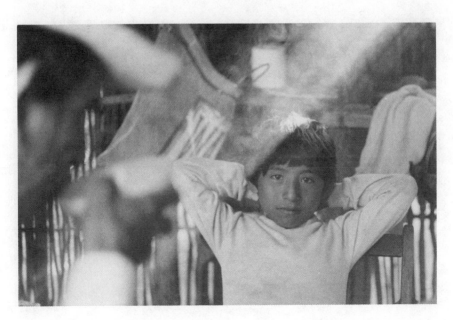

Man's youngest son, Gordi

Eli's kitchen and wash area (viewed from courtyard).

DC's altar: saints, music and medicine

DC's office (viewed from behind)

II Person, Participation, and Perception

4 Participants and Persons

4.1 INTRODUCTION

The person categories associated with pronouns provide a natural starting point in the description of deixis as a linguistic system. Not only do pronouns have the same relational structure as other shifters, but in many instances of use, they denote participants, whose corporeal field is central in defining the framework of reference. In speech, the participants and their relations are available as an immediate horizon relative to which spaces, objects, events, and other actors can be identified. Moreover, when a speaker uses the form 'I' to denote himself or herself, or 'you' to denote an addressee, one senses something greater than mere reference, Indeed, these uses often have the originating effect of establishing a co-engagement between participants, generally considered a requisite for communication. Like the self-centered use of 'here' that for Merleau-Ponty marks the original placement of the subject in the world, the standard uses of some pronouns appear to mark the same direct anchoring of the participants in the world.

The affinity between corporeality in spatial deixis and self-reference in participant deixis is not accidental. The participants in talk are the occupants of the corporeal field itself, the source points of the intersecting perspectives that it entails, the ones who have the reflexive *prise de conscience* that distinguishes coengagement from mere contiguity. In making reference to themselves, they project themselves and their perceptual, cognitive, and affective engagements from the actual face-to-face situation onto the plane of discourse; they project themselves from the current context into a narrated one (the event line in which the referent of 'I' was, is, or will be a player). In this projection, a participant's engagement in the overall phenomenal context of speech shifts from the background horizon of reference to the figural object of reference.

Pronouns are the main linguistic resources through which actors manage this shift in their own standing relative to the framework of reference.

By binding the indexical and referential planes of participant engagement, these forms establish a relatively simple set of correspondences between narrated frames and actual frameworks. No matter how long a story goes on, how deep the narrative embedding of persons in it, how subtle the actual relation between the corporeal interactants, and what they are talking about, pronouns automatically signal their footings with respect to events narrated.[1] This footing is in turn part of the overall posture of the actors that is embodied in their phenomenal field.[2]

This chapter explores the basic categories of person encoded in Maya participant deictics, relating these to the semantic structures of deictic reference, on the one hand, and to routine patterns of language use around Oxkutzcab, on the other. In chapter 5, more complicated, nonbasic uses of pronouns will be examined, where the ground of reference is transposed from the corporeal field, and the denotata of participant deictics are not in fact the current interactants. In order to describe pronouns adequately, we will need to introduce a couple of new distinctions among aspects of the framework of reference. These will be based on the same divisions between schematic resources, embodied practices, and sociocultural fields that have organized the discussion so far (cf. §2.4) and that will organize the subsequent treatment of spatial orientations as well (chaps. 7–10). We begin with a brief summary of ideas already introduced that will play a significant role in this and the next chapter.

4.1.1 Where We Stand So Far

Chapter 2 presented a relational approach to demonstrative reference that was based on a combination of three perspectives, namely, communicative practices, semantic systems in language, and native speaker commonsense reasoning about language. With respect to the first of these, it was suggested that acts of demonstrative reference are based upon a relational structure linking linguistic forms to **two** objects, a focal referent (the object talked about) and a backgrounded indexical origo (the speech event context relative to which the referent is identified). Shifters, including demonstratives and pronouns, were described as linguistic forms whose conventional meanings specify the relation R between the indexical ground i and the referent x. If this formulation is valid, it should be possible to describe pronouns in terms of the participant relations R they stand for, paired with the indexical grounds i relative to which the relations are applied in address and reference to persons x.

In terms of the semantics of demonstratives, it was suggested that the encoded meanings of such forms are best characterized in terms of a prototype semantics which recognizes a range of linguistic constructions along with the kinds of actional frames in which they are deployed. The concept of a frame provides a basis for relating participant configurations, such as speaker-addressee (Spkr-Adr), to spatial and temporal dimensions of speech context. On the one hand, participant relations and spatial and temporal structures are merely special cases of the frame concept, in that they are each made up of terms "motivated by, founded on and co-structured with . . . coherent schematizations of experience" (Fillmore 1985:223). On the other hand, these distinct kinds of frames are combined in the actional wholes of speech, which means that they relate to one another as constituent parts of the interactive process. Thus it should be possible to show specific and concrete relations between pronouns, whose core dimension (see §2.2.4) is the participant frame, and demonstratives whose core dimensions are perception, space, and time.

Chapter 2 also introduced the concept of relative **symmetry** in the relation between participants, defining this in terms of the degree to which interactants share a common attentional, perceptual, spatial, verbal, and cognitive framework in which to identify objects of reference and address. If principles stated in terms of symmetry really do govern demonstrative usage, then they should be in force in pronoun use and other resources for participant individuation as well. Finally, chapter 2 introduced the idea of schematic knowledge which native interactants possess as a matter of common sense and which contributes significantly both to the semantic structures of their language and to their typical modes of verbal practice. In chapter 5, we shall examine how participant frames are established and transformed in reported speech and metalinguistic commentary in Maya.

Chapter 3 provided a basic ethnographic sketch of the Maya construction of the human body, aspects of the social relations among coresidents in domestic units, and some of the canons of orderliness that govern everyday verbal interaction. Five points made in that description will weigh heavily in this chapter and the next.

(i) The grounding of much of the referential process in the corporeal awareness, orientation, and space of interactants has a determining impact on participation frameworks, anchoring them to the current phenomenal field.

(ii) The placement of actors in culturally constituted corporeal fields, overlain by highly organized domestic and work arrangements, has the consequence that persons occupy only certain positions in participant frameworks. That is, the mapping between social actors and participant roles is by no means free. Rather, as Bourdieu put it, interaction takes place in a **field of positions** (of which the corporeal and domestic fields are a part), and the objective possibilities of reference, self-description, address, and self-actualization in speech are constrained. It is simply not possible for VC to take up an authoritative or directive stance relative to his father, nor for him to quote his father's speech for the purpose of mockery, nor for a wife to make such utterances relative to her husband. For an account of participation frameworks, this implies that analysis should be directed towards socially meaningful actual practices and build up a description of the kinds of participation frameworks they sustain (see Irvine 1987).

(iii) There is a significant relation between symmetry in participant relations, on the one hand, and genres of speech, on the other. Genres carry with them participant configurations in the form of schematic frames, such as the prefabricated types of participation involving commander and respondent, joker, target, and audience, deliverer and object of *k'èey* 'bawling out'. Certain genres require a high degree of symmetry or asymmetry among coengaged actors. Thus a description of participant categories in language must take account of the generic contexts in which they are realized, as well as the interactive frameworks they help sustain in practice. The sketch of orderliness in domestic interactions in chapter 3 illustrated this point, and chapter 5 will explore it further.

(iv) The bond between participant reference and corporeality from which we started this chapter helps to anchor all reference in the phenomenal field in which it is produced. It is natural for the body to be in play when we are dealing with the representation of the speaking self, and few if any verbal forms have the appearance of directness and egocentricity that accrues to 'I'. But even corporeality became an intersubjective fact upon closer examination; the self-reflexive posture that is the individual *schéma corporel* takes shape in relation to a corporeal field occupied by all coparticipants (and perhaps bystanders). In analogous fashion, we will see by means of examples of attested pronoun use in Maya that the participant configurations that ground reference are themselves embodied in social relationships and are susceptible of various forms of transposition. The embodiment of deixis in practice goes beyond corporeality to include narrated, recalled, inferable, or just imaginable contexts that serve as ground for further reference.

(v) Finally, the discussion of task-oriented speech at a work site in §3.5 argued that demonstrative reference is a socially loaded act, insofar as it entails the speaker's taking up a certain orientation relative to his or her interlocutor and to the referent. DP, the authoritative *nohoč maák* 'great person', speaks for his sons and appropriates the objects of his reference by identifying them from his own perspective rather than a shared

perspective. The figure-ground structure of shifters and their respon-
siveness to relations among interactants guarantee them a role in the constitution of participant frameworks in speech.

4.1.2 Participant Frames and Demonstrative Reference

In order to appreciate the role of participant frames in reference, it is
helpful to recall the distinction between frames and frameworks. As we
have seen (§§2.4, 3.2) the former are relatively stable, prefabricated,
schematic constructs based on actional or conceptual wholes. While not
part of language in the codified way that grammatical structure is, frames
are nonetheless conventionalized forms that attach closely to semantic
structure. Frameworks are emergent (continuously changing, nonrepeat-
able), 'local' configurations that are produced interactively in talk and
that are the primary objects schematized in frames. Frames are 'incomplete' in the sense that they are simplified, hence partial, representations,
whereas frameworks are incomplete in the different sense that they are
continuously changing, hence temporary states of affairs. Frames are the
stereotypical resources used to generate frameworks. Frameworks include
the receding horizon of what Garfinkel called the "etc. clause"—the in-
exhaustible details that would have to spelled out to explain the framework completely but that can never be fully specified (because each new
specification introduces more incompleteness).[3]

In spatial, temporal, and object reference (nonparticipant), the current
participant framework functions as the origin point of perspectives. That
is, the ongoing 'we' of coparticipation is the **indexical zero point** relative to which 'here', 'now', and 'this' are defined, and proximity, remoteness, and accessibility are computed. In address and reference to persons,
on the other hand, participation frameworks and their component parts
are categorized in **focal relational features**, such as Spkr, Adr, Non-
Participant. It is through these features (or some more finely honed version of them) that individuals occupying participant roles are identified as
objects of reference and address. Participation frames make up the 'core
dimension' of pronouns, just as spatial frames are the core dimension of
the Locative deictics (DLOCS; chapters 9–10), and perceptual frames are
the core dimension of Ostensive evidentials (chap. 6).

In reported speech, described in chapter 5, the dependence of demonstrative reference upon participation frameworks is especially evident.
When a speaker indicates that in his or her current utterance (s)he is
reproducing the speech of some other speaker under different circumstances, the identification of objects of reference and address in the reproduced discourse is performed, not relative to the current corporeal

field, but relative to the (projected) field of the reported speaker. Quotation, mention, and report are kinds of footing in Goffman's terms, consisting in the transposition, suspension, or alteration of the participant ground relative to which referents are located. All of these factors reflect the centrality of participation frameworks in the process of demonstrative reference in interaction.

The inverse case holds as well, namely, demonstrative individuation can be shown to be a central part of the establishment and maintenance of participation frameworks in talk. This is a theme that will emerge over the course of subsequent chapters, in which we examine the referential process in detail. For present purposes, the evidence that demonstrative use partly regulates participant frameworks and the schematic frames they involve can be illustrated in each of first, second, and third person identification. Perhaps the most obvious instances of this are cases of self-presentation through first person reference: 'I am so-and-so', 'Here I am', 'I'll take that one', 'I was walking down the street', 'Give it to me', 'They'll see me', and so forth. In such utterances, the speaker makes reference to himself as object of 'I' (or 'me'), and describes himself in the terms of the sentence. To borrow Goffman's phrasing, the speaker projects himself as a 'figure', a protagonist in a scene, story, "someone after all who belongs to the world spoken about, not the world in which the speaking occurs" (Goffman [1979] 1983:147).[4] What Goffman noticed here is that the individual acting as speaker, the one who performs the current act of reference, constitutes himself or herself as an object of description, as well as an actor engaged in executing a speech act. Of the two, it is the described narrative figure, for Goffman, that predominates in speech. The corporeal utterer, which he calls the 'animator', is always a step removed, veiled in one or another self-display. What this means in the present terms is that the participant footings of individuals in interaction cannot be accurately formulated without attending to the ways they describe themselves. To put this in the notation used in the ethnography of speaking (adapted from Jakobson 1957, 1960), participant categories and incumbencies in the speech event (E^s) cannot be analyzed apart from the narrated event (E^n), since the latter partly determines the former. Consider a couple of Maya examples.

DC, a shaman who pays close attention to his dreams, remarked one day that through dreaming he travels and learns but sometimes finds it difficult to recall his dreams after awakening. He explained:

(1)   tak tuȼ'uú? e lú?umó?ob' o? → k-**in**-maán lobal i? → pero le
            'Even though deep into the lands (places) I travel,   yet these

b'á?al o? ↑ kupuúçu **ten**
things,   they (still) escape **from me.**' (BB.4.120)

He then went on to tell me the story of a powerful dream in which he
was taken prisoner, brought to an open plaza, and bound to a tree, where
he was about to be devoured by a jaguar that was set loose upon him.
The place was brimming with people watching as his abductors came to
take him.

(2)   Entonses, ká t-**inw**-il e? ↑ hač toóh ti **ten** b'ey a?
        'So then I saw,   right straight at me like this

        ká h tàal č'ab'il-**en**,   káb'isá?ab'-**en**
        then they came to get me, and I was taken away.'

Brought to the plaza and tied to the tree, he found himself right next to
a young girl, also tied up. The jaguar bounded towards them, and he
sighed:

(3)   há?alib'e? kí?ičkelem hahal dios, way k-**in**-ç'ó?okol e?
        'That's all Beautiful True God,   here I come to an end.'

But the cat was fixed on the girl, not on DC, and he was able to extricate
himself and fend off the beast.

(4)   má? **tèen** tupakt-**en** i? sinon le šč'uúpal o?
        'Not me was he staring at, but rather the girl.' (BB.4.121)

The question is whether these nine instances of the first person singular
(in bold) are actually coreferential and whether the embedding of successive narrated figures has any bearing on the actual speaker of the story,
the DC sitting before me at the time. In response to the latter, it is clear
that DC is adopting different footings, since he considers dream travel to
be an activity in which a special part of the self engages, not the whole
phenomenal subject. Hence, *he* posits a distinction between the individual in the dream and the one currently occupying his *schéma corporel!*
Notwithstanding the difference between them, the dream traveler is part
of the current self, and his experiences are formative of this self. This
entire dream was in fact interpreted by DC as an explanation of events
that had actually occurred to him earlier and that accounted for aspects of
his current life situation. Less dramatic but consistent examples arise
whenever speakers describe actions undertaken by them under previous,
anticipated, or merely hypothetical circumstances. And the same applies
to present tense predications in which one describes oneself as currently
engaged in a project, such as: *kimbin h k'iíwik* 'I'm going (to the) mar-

ket', *taán tuún in ¢'ó'oksik le b'á'al a'* 'So I'm finishing this thing off', and *b'ey kimb'èetik a'* 'this is how I do it (showing)'. The description projects a certain figure of the uttering self, and therefore the contours of the E^n help constitute the E^s.

These observations obtain equally well in the case of second person reference and address. Addressees enter into interaction, not merely as corporeal subjects perceiving the utterance act, but as agents portrayed in certain terms: 'you are the son of Ponso and brother of Manuel', 'I saw you yesterday', 'tomorrow you and I will work together', 'take that with you', and so forth. Just as the speaker who utters a 'response cry' (Goffman 1983) presents the figure of a person in possession of himself or herself, so the addressee singled out by a vocative 'Hey you!' 'Good day, Madam', or 'Excuse me, Sir', is also given a certain treatment.

The role of nonparticipant (third person) reference in establishing participant frameworks is less obvious but not less important. Because of its figure-ground relational structure, all demonstrative reference entails a self-orientation on the part of the individual performing the act, what Merleau-Ponty called the *prise de conscience*. Demonstratives and other shifters provide the terms not only of reference to self but of reference relative to self, and self relative to others as well. An utterance like 'I am over here', enacts an alignment by individuating the Spkr as referential object. But when a person asserts 'That's the one over there', (s)he also takes up a certain footing relative to the situation of utterance. In both cases the utterer is engaged in a referential enactment—in one case as a referent and in the other as an indexical ground.

One thing we can learn from this is that participant construction in discourse, like embodiment in general, proceeds on at least two levels at once, the focal level of address and reference to participants and the backgrounded level of reference relative to participants. The relation between interactants, their respective locations, the spatial and perceptual domains of the speaker, and the temporal frame of reference are all part of a Spkr's taking up a position and orientation in the current participant framework. The fact that demonstratives are typically associated with bodily gestures such as pointing, showing, and handing over the referent is further evidence of the same thing. The speaker manages her own corporeal orientation while also directing that of the addressee, constantly placing herself in the social world in the very act of making reference to it. Participation frameworks inevitably reflect the same duality; they are both the outcome (product) and the indexical source of reference.

4.1.3 Participant Frameworks

Goffman ([1979] 1983) came to the concept of a participation framework by way of examining the general problem of 'footing' in speech. By footing he meant the "alignment, set, projected self" of a speaker, his relation to his current words.[5] A shift from direct to quoted discourse, the use of an evidential particle to indicate that the speaker is certain or uncertain of the truth of his statements, or that he is speaking from hearsay, or play acting, are all ways of regulating footing, and Goffman saw such shifts as ubiquitous in conversation. He took them as evidence that participation frameworks require for their description a more finely honed set of participant roles and relations than the traditional 'Speaker-Hearer' or 'Speaker-Addressee'. In our terms, Goffman argued that the complexities of actual participation frameworks require for their proper description a set of schematic frames finer than those provided by the traditional dyadic roles.

Considering first the role of hearer, Goffman distinguished ratified participants from overhearers, the former being members of the interaction relation proper and the latter being peripheral (such as bystanders) (Goffman [1979] 1983:131). In speech directed to a group, he distinguished cases in which one individual is addressee and the rest of the group are overhearers or witnesses from cases in which the entire group is addressed as an aggregate.

Given these categories of participation, Goffman went on to categorize interactions according to the participants engaging in them: 'dominating communication' is the focal engagement between ratified participants, while 'subordinate' is nonfocal, possibly surreptitious (in which case it becomes 'collusion'). Subordinated exchange between a subset of ratified participants is 'byplay', while that between one or more ratified participants and at least one bystander is 'cross-play' (since it 'crosses' the boundaries of the dominant). 'Sideplay' consists of the hushed talk between bystanders. Once we recognize a category of bystander, therefore (regardless of what we call it), the traditional dyad is breached, and the possibilities for simultaneous ongoing interactions multiply (see also C. Goodwin 1981, 1984; M. H. Goodwin 1982, In press). For more complex stage productions, such as a public ritual event in Maya, the audience can participate in the production in other ways, for instance, by displaying a certain level of involvement in the ritual offering and a benevolent regard for their fellow humans.

Apart from what he called the "participation framework," Goffman described the "production format," by which he deconstituted the role of speaker. The actual phonator or "animator" of the utterance corresponds to the actual recipient, both of these roles being linked to the production and reception of sound. The "author" is (s)he who has selected the words and sentiments expressed in the utterance, and the "principal" is the original source whose position is established and who bears ultimate responsibility for the expression. Thus, an individual can recite (animate) a speech authored by a speech writer, whose ultimate principal is a higher authority (as in a vice president delivering a speech in which (s)he represents the positions of the president). Similarly, a speaker can quote a prior utterance by himself in which he was repeating what had been said by some third party.

In order to keep these embeddings straight, Goffman (and later Levinson 1987) observed, we need to distinguish at least the roles that he laid out. From the perspective of speech act participants, the challenge is to signal and monitor footing shifts, so that multiple embeddings will remain intelligible, despite their considerable complexity and changeability.

Levinson (1987) developed several aspects of Goffman's approach to footing. The first of these is the decomposition of roles into features, including participant, transmitter (cf. animator), motive (cf. principal), addressee (individual identified by second person pronoun, vocative, gaze, or gesture), recipient (reciprocal of principal) and channel link (an individual capable of receiving a message) (172). Levinson's proposal is to begin from a relatively simple set of 'basic level' categories (see below), from which a set of derived categories can be obtained by Boolean operations. The ultimate goal would be to decompose the basic level categories into component features and derive further categories from these rather than directly from the basic level terms. The evidence used to justify proposed distinctions would consist of a demonstration that in some language under some circumstances, the candidate distinction is systematically attended to by interactants or encoded in linguistic forms (164); from this it would follow that a universal inventory of participant categories must have access to the distinction in question, even though in some (or perhaps many) languages, it is not operative. The major comparative question in such an approach is why so many languages have grammaticalized the distinction between speaker and addressee, if these two are merely a simplified version of the available roles.

A second development of Levinson is his conscientious use of the distinction between participant roles, on the one hand, and incumbents of the roles on the other. C. Goodwin (1981, 1987) and M. H. Goodwin (In press) have shown that a single participant role may have multiple simultaneous incumbents, and that a single individual may be incumbent to several roles simultaneously in talk. Furthermore, the production of utterances, directed gaze, and bodily posture are used together to manage interactants' changing engagements in conversation (see esp. C. Goodwin 1981: chap. 3). These facts indicate that processes of role claiming and assignment—attaching individuals to participant roles such as Spkr, Adr—are subject to negotiation and even dispute in interaction. As Goffman often pointed out, interactants sustain multiple engagements at the same time or in brief sequence, at varying levels of intensity. Taken together with a more delicate inventory of schematic roles, this fact considerably increases the complexity of participant footing in talk. The superficial simplicity of a pronoun system such as the one in Maya (see §4.2) actually belies a quite complex set of interpretive procedures that one must go through (or otherwise fulfill) in order to identify the actual referent of a token pronoun in context.

At what level of analysis into components do we find the proper units in which to explain the attested role configurations, and how can speakers keep it all straight in everyday interaction?

Before addressing these questions, there is a further source of complexity in demonstrative reference which I must make explicit. It is obvious that interactants coordinate gaze, gesture, posture, and word in the course of making demonstrative reference, but how do they do it? Speakers' actions in these modes do not necessarily all stand for the same objects and may even serve to pick out different objects. For instance, one can easily make verbal reference to a spot 'right there on the table', while facing an addressee, looking at her (away from the table), and pointing vaguely at the region of the table. In English, as Goodwin (1981) showed in great detail, gaze and bodily posture are used not only to identify referential objects but to manage the mutual orientation of interactants as well. This duality is also present in Maya interaction. Considering the different signaling modes involved, we could say that the objects can never be truly identical but are at best coincident. One points at something visible, faces something with a determinate location, makes verbal reference to something identifiable, and these different relations define different semiotic objects. In a given event, the objects (including participants) individuated in these distinct signaling modes may bear relations such as inclusion, overlap, or immediate proximity to one another, rather than coincidence. Thus, 'right there' can be reinforced with a vague toss of the arm towards the general region within which the specific point of reference is to be found. In many instances, the different modes are reinforcing only at the higher level of the speech act as an interactive whole, since gaze and posture may fix the contact of speaker to addressee, while a manual point simultaneously individuates the referent. These factors are all linked to the phenomenal copresence of actual interactants and therefore pertain centrally to the animator-receiver relations in the participation framework. Apparently not even the physical copresence of actors can be assumed to be simple and merely concrete, something made particularly obvious in the works of C. and M. H. Goodwin.

If the production of referential frameworks involves so many complicating factors, how are frames, their schematic counterparts, produced? How do we move analytically from the field of practice to the system of schematic resources used in practice? How do native actors produce schemata in the course of communicating? Part of the answer to these questions lies in the language as a repository of conventional categories whose use in discourse instantiates and potentially alters preexisting schemata. Person categories are different from participant roles, but they are always linked to these roles through reference or indexicality. Hence the use of these deictics tends to sustain an inventory of participant frames by focalizing them, engaging them as ground for further reference, or both. A particularly important instance of this is metalinguistic discourse, in which interactants describe and comment directly on aspects of participant frameworks. In my discussions with them, Maya speakers displayed the ability to comment lucidly on the interactive conditions and consequences of utterances, drawing on prefabricated schemata and creating new ones through reference and description. We will explore this in chapter 5.

Socially recognized genres of discourse also tend to sustain participant frames by encompassing them in larger schematic structures. Recall, for example, the verbal style, lexicon of sexual equivalences, and indexical symmetry characteristic of *baášal t'àan* 'play speech' or the combination of asymmetry, directivity, and confrontational posture of *k'eéy* 'bawling out' (§3.4). Such genres incorporate typical participant relations as schematized aspects, thereby making them expectable, repeatable, automatically inferable. Thus, when a speaker reports an exchange as an instance of play speech or bawling out, a native interlocutor can immediately infer that the participants in the exchange occupied certain positions relative to each other, partly based on other features of their respective social identities, such as age, gender, and so forth. Both genre labels as descriptive expressions and the categories of actual practice they stand for contribute to the production and maintenance of participant frames.

There is a third factor in the production of schemata that is more general than either language structure or discourse genres (but is related to both). This is the factor of habituation. Social actors tend to act in habitual ways, and this in turn tends to stabilize practices, making them repeatable and therefore expectable and available for use. The process applies equally well to features of communicative interaction that speakers are aware of and talk about as to features they may never even notice.

4.1.3.1 *Habituation and Basic Level Participant Frames*

It would be easier to understand the fluency with which interactants seem to manage participant frameworks and locate themselves relative to them if it could be shown that some mechanisms exist that simplify their task. Perhaps the analytic decomposition of participant roles into more fine-grained features bears little or no relation to the practical tasks of language users attempting to make and interpret reference. In his early discussion of language as a tool of classification, Boas ([1911] 1966:20–21) observed that human thought proceeds by categorizing the infinity of objectively diverse experiences into representations of a limited number of categories. He concluded that "the infinitely large number of ideas has been reduced by classification to a lesser number, which by constant use have established firm associations, and which can be used automatically." In the absence of this reduction, according to Boas, language would require an infinite number of sound vehicles in order to express constantly shifting experiences. It is possible that the apparent complexity of participation frameworks from a cross-linguistic perspective is greatly simplified in any language. The total set of possibilities is reduced by classification to a limited set of schemata that are used habitually.

Whorf (1941) significantly developed the Boasian insight that language is a medium of habituation, bringing to it Sapir's attention to the 'self-contained system' of classifications in language (Lucy 1985). Whereas Boas examined most closely grammatical categories rather than syntactic constructions or utterance types, Whorf's analyses encompass whole 'patterns of speaking' definable only at the level of phrasal syntax and standard usage (see, for instance, his analysis of number categories). Following Sapir ([1931] 1949), Whorf saw standard linguistic patterns as providing structures that are formed in relation to certain objective realities and subsequently extended through analogy to other, objectively dissimilar experiences. For participation frameworks, the analogous case would be that participant categories in language are formed in relation to certain corporeal relations (e.g., animator-Spkr–recipient-Adr), and only then extended by analogy to other, less-transparent cases.

The habituation and automaticity of much of language use was also noted by the Prague School linguists and used by Havránek ([1932] 1964) as the basis of the functional dimension of foregrounding versus automaticity. Automatized linguistic expressions are those which are typical, expected, routine, and therefore immediately interpretable. Foregrounded uses, on the contrary, are relatively unexpected, atypical, and may require special interpretation. The distinction can be applied to linguistic forms or to the conveyed meanings of forms (a routine form can be used in the foregrounded way). Whereas for Boas, conceptual and linguistic categories buffer speakers from the actual unrepeatability of experience, for the Pragueans, relative automaticity and foregrounding is a dimension applicable to both a verbal form and its use. Furthermore, the tension between the two is taken to be a feature of all language use, except for certain socially specific functional dialects, where automaticity is maximized (what Havránek calls 'scientific'). Coming from this line of thought, it would be expected that participation frameworks, whatever their potential complexities, are to a large degree automatized in any culture, and that foregrounded departures from the routine patterns are both possible and purposeful.

The automatization of practice produces schematic knowledge (of the sort described in cognitive research) but also has a corporeal dimension. Quite apart from what actors know about talk or how they form mental representations of it, their habitual postures and orientations make up a schematic background that is in play whenever they engage in talk. Merleau-Ponty argued that knowledge resides in the body itself rather than in constructs of the mind. He used the notion of habit as a ground for the repeatability of experience and body engagements, a way of denying mental representations. From our perspective, it can be seen as a ground for producing both mental representations and (preconceptual) 'corporeal knowledge'.

Interpretive sociologists have long focused on 'typification' in social life (see §2.3.2 above), the process whereby actors represent (and therefore understand) themselves and their world through routine patterns of experience and interaction. Schutz ([1932] 1967:163ff.; 1970:part 2; 1973:7–27) saw typification as a fundamental feature of the commonsense construction of experience, a prerequisite of intersubjectivity. Garfinkel ([1962] 1972) followed Schutz in focusing on the routinization, repeatability, and accountability of experiences, all of which rely on the basic idea that social practice is structured in typical ways. One of the conclusions that Garfinkel drew from this was what he called the 'specific vagueness' of most of what gets said in everyday interaction, the fact that speakers never make plain precisely what they mean but rather rely on background expectancies to fill in where their overt expressions leave off ([1962] 1972:15).[6] This 'etc. clause' and the more general phenomenon of typification obtain in the case of participant categories: they imply that the analytic complexity of footing and participant categories is probably *not* a feature of everyday practice but rather of the mode of analysis in which social scientists examine practice. However we resolve the analytic issues raised by Goffman, the *practical* problem of interpreting the reference of 'I' or 'you' in context may be radically simpler for a native speaker than for an external observer. The native speaker operates within a socially constituted 'frame of reference', to use Schutz's expression, which narrows the interpretive possibilities to a manageable range.

In a prototype approach to demonstratives, further mechanisms are available to explain the simplification of practice in the form of basic level categorizations and prototypical category members. Together, these reduce the astronomical number of logically possible participant frames (if the categories combined freely and incumbency were unconstrained) to a smaller number of interpretive possibilities. Levinson (1987:175) suggests the existence of basic level participant frames but does not follow it up beyond saying that pronouns are structured in accordance with canonical situations of utterance (183). I think a stronger case can be made on this point, building on the aforementioned precedents.

'Basic level' categories as used by Rosch (1978), Coleman and Kay (1981), Lakoff (1987:46–47), and other cognitive theorists, are part of the cognitive organization of taxonomies (see also §2.2.4 above). A taxonomy can be defined as a taxonomic structure plus a set of terms, where the former consists of a hierarchy of inclusion relations among sets and the latter of a set of labels standing for taxa (see also Lounsbury [1964] 1969:205ff.). The highest level in the taxonomic structure is the 'unique beginner', commonly labeled 0, and the subordinate (included) levels below it number 1 through *n*, according to their number. Sets subordinated to a common taxon are said to *contrast*. The basic level in such a structure is neither the most inclusive unique beginner nor the most specific (included, subordinated) term, but rather an intermediate level of inclusiveness somewhere between the two. Rosch (1978:28ff.) determined the basic level from two principles of cognitive organization: that (i) the task of category systems is to "provide maximum information with the least cognitive effort," and (ii) "the perceived world comes as structured information rather than as arbitrary or unpredictable attributes." These two principles jointly imply that not all levels of categorization in a taxonomy are equally effective. Rather, "the most basic level will be the most inclusive (abstract) level at which the categories can mirror the structure of attributes in the perceived world" (29).

It is important at this point to keep in mind that Rosch is describing the relation between categories and the world *as perceived*, not the world as it might be said to *be* apart from any perceiver. Elsewhere it is clear that she also considers the way people interact with the world to partly determine their categories (1978:33–34). This line of reasoning therefore need not assume immaculate perception but can build on perception mediated by sociocultural values and practices. In this light, Rosch's remarks can be seen to extend productively the idea of routinization and habituation as developed in the aforementioned works. It is precisely through routine patterns of experience that the world is perceived and that the basic level is grounded. As Rosch says, basic level objects are the ones actors have the most constant kinds of motor interactions with, the ones with the most similar shapes, and the ones on which speakers can most readily comment (see also Lakoff 1987:46). On this point, cognitive research joins Merleau-Ponty in grounding meaning in habitual 'motricity'.

The first step in defining basic level participant categories is to separate the categories (roles) themselves from the various terms and expressions in language which stand for them. A long literature on systems of address, including Brown and Gillman ([1960] 1972), Errington (1988), Friedrich (1966), Silverstein (1976b), and Ervin-Tripp (1972, 1976), along with the previously described research on participation frameworks, provides a solid basis for this first distinction. The most inclusive term of the field I call 'participant frame', and the sets subordinated to it might include: (ratified participants vs. nonratified participants), (producers vs. receivers), (addressee vs. other), (animator vs. author vs. principal), (message bearer vs. ultimate target) and (perhaps) (bystander [copresent unratified] vs. overhearer [noncopresent unratified]).

The second step is to determine the level of inclusiveness at which 'basic' categories are found, in the intermediate levels between the most abstract (underdifferentiated) and the most specific (overdifferentiated). The basic level should be the one at which the categories correspond most closely to the way interactants perceive participant frameworks, the highest level at which member categories have similarly perceived overall shapes, the highest level at which a single mental image can reflect the entire category, the level with the most commonly used labels for category members, and the level at which terms are used in neutral contexts and at which most of our knowledge is organized (Lakoff 1987:46–47). For participant frames, the categories that display these characteristics are not finely distinguished features such as those developed by Levinson (1987:172) but grosser, more inclusive categories like Goffman's, or even very abstract ones, including all kinds of 'speakers' and 'addressees'.

Interactants routinely make several **default assumptions** about face-to-face contexts which further reinforce the tendency to categorize at an intermediate level of inclusiveness.[7] (i) Unless it is indicated or already otherwise known, it is assumed that the person who produces an utterance is the source of the proposition stated, the one who chooses the words, and the one whose position is expressed. That is, it is assumed that animator, author, and principal are identical. When this is so, no production category more specific than 'speaker' need be managed. (ii) If gaze, posture, gesture, and utterance all figure in a communicative act, then either they are reinforcing or they focus on complementary components of the frame (e.g., animator-receiver contact vs. participants-referent access). Speakers do not routinely direct their interlocutor's attention to several contrasting objects at once. (iii) Until further notice, the addressee to whom sound is directed is the target of the utterance, in which case 'addressee' and (untargeted) 'overhearer' may be adequate categories of reception. (iv) Symmetry and asymmetry of access as defined in this book are computed only relative to individuals occupying roles *in the same participant frame*. Therefore, if an utterer is speaking for himself in performing an act of demonstrative reference (according to assumption (i)), then it is his copresent interlocutor who must be able to identify the referent and not some other ultimate target (within earshot or not). While subcategories of producers and receivers can be embedded in an utterance and clearly do vary across utterances, they do not vary independently of one another. These constraints can all be overridden under proper circumstances, but their routine effect is to reinforce the tendency of interactants to ground reference and address in the current corporeal sphere.

A final factor serving to simplify the management of participant frames in interaction is the figure-ground structure of demonstrative reference and address. Even if a relatively complex configuration of indexical categories is in play at any point in talk, cross-linking participants, places, and objects, not all factors are of equal salience. Only certain portions of the total frame are focal over any stretch of talk, with the others backgrounded. For example, an utterance like 'it's right over there' can be equivocal as to precisely whom it is addressed to, on what authority, and for whose ultimate reception, while still focusing quite directly on its referent. To use Garfinkel's expression, an 'etc. clause' (vagueness, multiplicity) in the indexical ground of reference does not preclude precise individuation (specificity) of a referential focus. A figure-ground structure can incorporate both in a single, elegantly simple form.[8]

In order to describe participant frames in relation to verbal interaction, therefore, the appropriate categories are likely to be fairly gross and are made referentially precise only when paired with actual indexical grounds.

Categories such as Spkr, Adr, and Other, which conflate finer distinctions like [animator, author, principal], may be not only feasible but also more relevant than any very delicately distinguished 'etic' framework. Habituation, routinization, default assumptions, and basic level effects all reinforce an intermediate level of participant category, contributing to the overdetermination of categories like 'corporeal Spkr', the animator-author-principal. We need to take into account that participant frames are constituted at two levels, as referential objects and as indexical grounds relative to which reference is calculated. The duality precludes any description that merely conjoins categories without taking into account their different relations to the whole. Furthermore, habituation and routinization are social facts, and this has implications for how we derive participant categories. An etic grid derived by juxtaposing examples from different languages (in the manner discussed by Levinson 1987) can make a valid contribution to the study of linguistic forms but does not provide an adequate framework for the description of practices.

In the remainder of this chapter, I will describe Maya pronouns as a linguistic subsystem of deixis, incorporating a set of basic level person categories deployed in routine ways in Maya conversation. Chapter 5 describes an array of more elaborate participant frameworks in Maya culture, in terms of their social organization, constraints on incumbency, and emergence in the course of interaction.

4.2 PERSON IN MAYA

A full description of the role of participant frames in interaction must include an account of the linguistic resources for person reference.[9] It is helpful to distinguish at least four types of verbal expressions routinely used to identify participants: pronouns, names, descriptive epithets (including relational forms such as kinship terms), and interjections used to establish and maintain contact. Among these, pronouns have a special status because of their figure-ground semantic structure, just as demonstrative adverbs have a special status among resources for spatial reference (see chap. 9). Furthermore, pronouns are systematically related to other demonstratives by shared morphemes and parallel composition in many languages, including Maya. Relational (R) values for Maya pronouns can be described with a fairly simple inventory of basic level categories, including Spkr, Adr; Inclusive and Non-Participant (or perhaps [-Spkr, -Adr]); each of which must in any instance be interpreted relative to an indexical ground in the familiar $R(x,i)$ relation. Number, at least in the third person, is a distinct category, describable in terms of one-place predicates such as $Sing(x)$, $Plur(x)$ (but see Benveniste [1956] 1966a;

Levinson 1983:69, Silverstein 1976a). Similarly, case and gender, to the extent that they are present in a language, are distinct from the relational values indicating role.

Implicit in these remarks is the claim that reference and address, while obviously distinct modes of speech, are nonetheless equivalent in terms of identifying individuals—referents on the one hand, addressees on the other. It is true that address forms have special uses not usually available for referential expressions, such as initiating a participation or summoning an addressee (Levinson 1983:70–71; Zwicky 1974). However, even initiating address, which is highly focal, could be said to be merely a special case of address, analogous to highly focal, relatively creative instances of reference (Silverstein 1976b). In Maya, both pronouns of address and referential demonstratives may occur in foregrounded constructions in which two shifter tokens in the same sentence are coreferential, as in *teč k a b'in* 'You you go (you're the one who goes)' and *té? k a b'in té?ela?* 'Right there you go right there (right there's where you go).' As I will try to show, there are further underlying connections between pronominal morphemes and the referential demonstratives. In particular, there is a prefixal series of pronouns which display parallels to Initial Deictic (ID) bases, and a suffixal series of pronouns that parallels the Terminal Deictic (TD) enclitics. The thrust of these remarks is that the address forms are functionally and formally related to referential demonstratives, a fact underemphasized in classical accounts of pronouns which focus on the uniqueness of first and second person forms and attempt to derive entire demonstrative systems out of this dyad.

From a comparative perspective, modern Maya pronouns are quite simple. There are three main series, two affixal and one independent lexical. The affixal series consists of a set of prefixes and a set of suffixes that attach to nouns (or nominal modifiers), verbs, auxiliary elements, adjectives, and with restrictions, to particles. There is also a lexical series composed of the pronominal suffixes attached to the particle *t(i?)*. Hence, *?in-, -en, t-en* 'I, me'; *?a-, -eč, t-eč* 'you'; and so forth as in table 4.1.

As table 4.1 shows, all three series distinguish three persons, Spkr, Adr, and Other (which summarizes non-Spkr, non-Adr 'third person'), and two number values, singular and plural. There are no features of gender, shape, noun class, animacy, or humanness, or any other inherent features of the referents to which the forms are applied; there are no distinctions of deference encoded in the forms or in the patterns of second person usage.

In all three paradigms, there is a first person plural Inclusive form, derived by combining the first plural prefix with the second plural suffix. It

TABLE **4.1** Maya Pronouns: Basic Series

		Prefixal[a]		Suffixal[b]		Lexical[c]
Spkr	ʔin-	k-		-en	-óʔon	t-en	t-óʔon
		k- . . . -éʔeš			-óʔon-éʔeš		t-óʔon-éʔeš
Adr	ʔa-	ʔa- . . . -éʔeš		-eč	-éʔeš	t-eč	t-éʔeš
Other	ʔu-	ʔu- . . . -óʔob'		-∅	-óʔob'	le ti ʔ	le tiʔ-óʔob', le óʔob' ti ʔ

[a]Cross-index or refer to possessor of N, subject of V_i and V_t in the incompletive aspect.

[b]Cross-index or refer to object of V_t, subject of V_i (nonincompletive), subject of Equational.

[c]First and second person unmarked for case; third person subject or object of V_t, subject of V_i or equational, possessor only (nondative, benefactive, locative).

is used only in addressing a plurality of interlocutors, and there is no explicitly Inclusive form for use with a singulary addressee. In the prefixal series, there is a noteworthy asymmetry in plural formation, with the Spkr category indicated by a single morpheme, but the Adr and Other categories formed by combining the would-be singular prefix with the corresponding plural suffix. These forms attach to the beginning and end of a word or phrase to make discontinuous pairs. The affixal series may function syntactically as agreement markers, cross-indexing a NP in the same sentence, or as pronouns unaccompanied by any NP in the same sentence, as shown in examples (5–10).

(5)   k-u-b'in   le   maák oʔ
        Inc-Pro3-Vb   that man
        'That man goes.'

(6)   k-u-b'in
        Inc-Pro3-Vb
        '(S)he goes.'

(7)   k-u-b'in-óʔob'   (le maák-óʔob'oʔ)
        Inc-Pro3-Vb-pl   (those men)
        'They go', or 'Those men go.'

(8)   k-a-b'in   tèeč
        Inc-Pro2-Vb   Pro2
        'You go.'

(9)   k-a-b'in
        Inc-Pro2-Vb
        'You go.'

(10)   k-a-b'in-éʔeš
        Inc-Pro2-Vb-pl
        'You (plural) go.'

The mechanisms of morphological and syntactic case marking in Mayan languages have received a great deal of attention in the literature, and the present remarks are intended only to orient the reader to the forms.[10] The prefixal series, commonly called the 'A set' by Mayanist linguists, mark possessor when prefixed to a noun or NP, transitive subject when prefixed to a transitive verb, and intransitive subject when prefixed to an intransitive verb in the incompletive (nonpast) aspect. The suffixal series mark equational when attached to a noun, NP, or stative verb and show a split in their valence when attached to active verbs: in the incompletive aspect suffixes mark only object of transitive (or pluralization of subject in the discontinuous pairings described above); in the past, perfect, and optative paradigms, they mark subject of intransitive, as well as object of transitive. Thus there is a split is as shown in (11) below.

(11)   Case values of Maya pronouns: Prefixal and suffixal

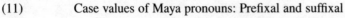

Incompletive   non-Incompletive

A stands for transitive subject, S for intransitive subject, and O for transitive object (see DuBois 1987:808 and references cited therein). It is standard to describe the kind of alignment shown in the Incompletive aspect in Maya as Nominative-Accusative, and that in the non-Incompletive paradigms as Ergative-Absolutive (see references in note 10). Examples 12–17 illustrate the first person forms.

(12)   k-**inw**-oksik-Ø
            Inc-Pro1-V_t-Pro3
            'I put it in.'

(13)   k-**inw**-okol
            Inc-Pro1-Vb
            'I enter.'

(14)   k-uy-oksik-**en**
            Inc-Pro3-V_t-Pro1
            'He puts me in (causes me to enter).'

(15)   t-**inw**-oksah-Ø
            Pst-Pro1-V_t-Pro3
            'I put it in (past).'

(16)   ʔok-**en**
             Vb-Pro1
             'I entered.'

(17)   t-uy-oksah-**en**
             Pst-Pro3-V$_t$-Pro1
             'He put me in (past) (caused me to enter).'

The independent lexical pronouns are formed transparently from the
suffixal series attached to the relational particle *ti*ʔ 'to, for, from, at,
of (possessor)'. This particle is a proclitic that regularly occurs in two
shapes, as an independent lexical item (18), and as a phonologically reduced form which attaches to the following vowel-initial word (19), or to
which a suffix is attached (20).

(18)   ¢'aáh   **ti**ʔ ʔin-sukúʔun
             Vb-Imper Rel Pro1-N
             'Give (it) to my brother.'

(19)   ¢'aáh   t-in-sukúʔun
             Vb-Imper   Rel-Pro1-N
             'Give (it) to my brother.'

(20)   ¢'aáh   t-en
             Vb-Imper   Rel-Pro1
             'Give (it) to me.'

Notice in table 4.1 in the Non-Participant category, that instead of the
expected lexical form *ti*ʔ-Ø we find the composition *le ti*ʔ 'he, she, it, the
one', in which the define article *le* precedes the relational particle. The
bare form *ti*ʔ-Ø does occur, but with the reading 'to, from, for, of him,
her, the one'. As such, it is part of another paradigm of lexical pronouns,
the 'dative' series, shown in table 4.2.

TABLE **4.2** Maya Lexical Pronouns: Dative and Possessive

	Dative[a]		Possessive[b]	
	Sg	Pl	Sg	Pl
Spkr	(tiʔ)t-en	(tiʔ)t-óʔon	ʔin-tiʔ-al	k-tiʔ-al
		(tiʔ)t-óʔon-éʔeš		k-tiʔ-al-éʔeš
Adr	(tiʔ)t-eč	(tiʔ)t-éʔeš	ʔa-tiʔ-al	ʔa-tiʔ-al-éʔeš
Other	tiʔ(le tiʔ)	tiʔ(le tiʔ-óʔob')	ʔu-tiʔ-al	ʔu-tiʔ-al-óʔob'

[a]Dative, possessive, benefactor, source, goal, location; 'to, for, from, of, at me,' etc.

[b]Possessive (predicative unless subordinated), benefactive, purposive (third person only); '(is)
mine, (is) for me,' etc.

The dative series of pronouns are those that occur in syntactic constructions in which the relational particle is required to indicate that the referent of the pronoun is in a case relation other than S, A, or O. The relation
may be dative (as in 'give to, say to'), possessive (as in 'there are brothers
to him', meaning 'he has brothers'), benefactive (for him), source (from
him), goal (to, towards him), or locative (at, by it). The main peculiarity
of the series is the split between first and second persons, on the one
hand, and third person on the other: the former contain the relational particle in initial position in their own lexical structure, and the independent
particle may be used (*ti⁷ t-en* 'to me') or omitted (*t-en* 'me, to me') without relevant difference in meaning. In the non-Participant category, the
definite article is initial in the pronoun construction, and this precludes a
dative reading (no NP of the form *le X* can be used as a dative unless
accompanied by *ti⁷*). Hence, the particle must be added, yielding *ti⁷ le-ti⁷*
'to the one (etc.)'. In accordance with the general convention that NPs
whose reference is retrievable from context may be omitted in speech, the
lexical pronoun may then be omitted from this phrase, leaving *ti⁷-Ø* 'to
the one (etc.)', which could be a reduction of *ti⁷ le-ti⁷*, *ti⁷ le maák o⁷* 'to
(etc.) the man', or any other NP introduced by the relational particle.

On the other hand, the first and second person dative forms may also be
reduced, but when they are, what is elided is the *ti⁷* particle rather than
the pronoun, since this particle is initial in the pronoun in any case. Thus
examples like (21–23) are common.

(21)   . . . yàan bá⁷aš   ink'aát inwú⁷uyik **teč** a⁷
              '. . . there's something I want to hear from you here' (BB.4.68–73)

(22)   le kán tàak le ti⁷ kinwáaik ti⁷ ká ukašt **ten** si⁷
              'When he comes I'll tell him   to go find me firewood.' (BB 5.38)

(23)   hé⁷ le cánal tuún kinwáaik **teč** a⁷
              'Here's the canal I'm telling you about.' (BB.5.31)

To the right of the lexical series in table 4.2 are the possessive pronouns, corresponding to English 'mine, yours, hers, etc.' These are transparently composed of the same relational particle *ti⁷* plus the suffix *-al*, to
form an inalienably possessed relational noun. The construction has several distinct grammatical functions: (i) without further modification, the
first and second person forms function as predicative elements glossable
as 'it is mine, it is for me, it is yours, it is for you (etc.)'; (ii) with flanking
demonstratives, the same forms are referential: 'mine, the one for me,
yours, the one for you (etc.)', depending on the grammatical context.
(iii) In addition to these functions, the third person form is also used as a
complementizer, *⁷u₁-ti⁷-al S₁* 'in order that S', where the third person

possessive pronoun cross-indexes the S (just as it would normally co-reference a possessor, *ʔu₁-tiʔ-al hwàan₁* 'It's Juan's'). This is typical of the relatively less marked Non-Participant form. Unlike the dative series from which they are derived, these forms are not used to code location, goal, or source, a restriction consistent with their derived status.

4.2.1 Bound Forms

The prefixal series actually occur in two variants, preconsonantal forms, which are shown in table 4.1, and prevocalic forms, shown below.[11]

> inw-
> aw-
> uy-, y-

The first person plural prefix does not undergo glide insertion. These prefixes attach directly to a noun or verb base in many cases, as in *ʔin-sukúʔun* 'my elder brother', *ʔinw-iíȼ'in* 'my younger sibling', *ʔinw-ohel* 'I know (it)', *ʔin-k'ahoól* 'I know (am familiar with)'. Whenever there are modifiers (quantifiers, adjectives) preceding the noun, or infixes preceding the verb, the prefixal pronoun precedes these as well. In NPs, the only element that precedes a pronominal prefix is the article.

(24)   le   ʔin- káʔa tuúl mehen t'uúl
        DNOM Pro1 Quant NC Adj   N
        'These my two little rabbits.'

(25)   t-**u**-hač   laáh bisah-Ø
        Pst-Pro3-Intrs Total Vb-Pro3
        'He really took it all (away).'

In the verb complex, the pronominal prefix, marking A or S, may be separated from the verb by a small number of particles such as the two in (25); it is itself preceded by any verbal auxiliaries, such as the past tense *t-*, aspectual elements, verbal negation, and the interrogative particle.

The third person prefix has grammatical functions unlike those of the first and second, including its use in a number of relational expressions, *ʔu-màasil* 'more (of it)', *ʔu-laák* 'another (of it)', and the superlative of adjectives, *ʔu-màas máʔalob'-il* 'the best (lit., its most good)'. Prefixed to a deadjectival noun, it functions as a general marker of definiteness: *ʔu-máʔalob'-il* 'the good part (lit., its goodness)', *ʔu-čak-il* 'the red part (lit., its redness; idiomatic 'the hard part')'. Prefixed to a verbal auxiliary, it cross-indexes a clause, *k-u-ȼ'óʔok-ol in-meyah* '(when) I finish working (lit., it₁ finishes [I work]₁)'. These facts are again consistent with the special status of third person as a grammatical device.

The suffixal pronouns, regardless of grammatical function, follow all suffixes to the noun or verb and mark the final boundary of the word. The third person (Non-Participant) singular category is indicated by formal Ø, as opposed to the plural *-óʔob'*, and is also semantically unmarked with respect to it: *-óʔob'* is commonly omitted even when a plural reading is required, as in (26).

(26) k-u-b'in   káʔa-tuúl   maák
      Inc-Pro3-Vb Quant-NC   N
      'Two men are going.'

The nonplural form Ø can therefore stand for either pole of the plural/ nonplural opposition, whereas the more marked plural form *-óʔob'* indicates unambiguously plural. This suffix is also the general plural marker in Maya, as in *yáʔab' maák-óʔob'* 'many people' and *ʔin-nuúkul-óʔob'* 'my tools'. This fact adds yet another grammatical function to the form, which may signal: (i) plurality of the third person possessor, A or S, when coupled with a prefixal pronoun, as in *u-sukúʔun-óʔob'* 'his elder brothers', *k-uy-ilik-óʔob'* 'they see them (or him)'; (ii) plurality of an O or S (non-Incompletive or equational), as in *k-uy-ilik-óʔob'* 'he sees them, they see them', *ʔin-sukúʔun-óʔob'* 'they are my elder brothers'. Thus, as these examples illustrate, combinations of prefixal pronouns with the third person plural occur freely where the two have distinct referents and grammatical functions. Since there is no lexical copula 'to be (equational)' in Maya, any noun or NP can be used as a nominal sentence: *ʔin-sukúʔun-Ø* 'he is (or they are) my brother(s)', *ʔin-sukúʔun-óʔob'* 'They are my brothers'. As a consequence of these facts, an NP flanked by third person prefix and suffix is multiply ambiguous until placed in context: *ʔu-sukúʔun-óʔob'* 'they are his brothers', 'he is their brother', 'they are their brothers', 'his brothers', 'their brother', 'their brothers'.[12]

A single nominal or verbal base may have more than one suffix pronoun attached to it, although never more than two, and never two non-null forms of the same person category. Thus, *-Ø-óʔob'*, *-en-éʔeš*, *-eč-óʔob'*, *-Ø-éʔeš*, etc., occur in examples like (27–29), but *-óʔob'-óʔob'*, *-éʔeš-éʔeš*, *eč--éʔeš*, *-en-óʔon*, and *-óʔon-óʔon* do not.

(27)

	-Ø-óʔob'	'They see him.'
	-en-óʔob'	'They see me.'
k-uy-ilik	-óʔon-óʔob'	'They see us.'
	-eč-óʔob'	'They see you (sg).'
	-éʔeš-óʔob'	'They see you (pl).'
	-óʔob'	'They see them.'

(28)

k-aw-ilik

-en-é?eš	'You (pl) see me.'
-ó?on-é?eš	'You (pl) see us.'
-é?eš-ó?ob'	'You (pl) see them.'
-é?eš-∅	'You (pl) see it.'

(29)

?a-sukú?un

-en-é?eš	'I am your (pl) elder brother.'
-ó?on-é?eš	'We are your (pl) elder brothers.'
-é?eš-ó?ob'	'They are your (pl) elder brothers.'

It should be possible in theory to form constructions with three suffixal pronouns, as in *k-uy-ilik-ó?on-é?eš-ó?ob'* 'they see us (Inclusive plural Adr)', but I have never attested such a form and therefore posit the constraint that maximally two suffixes may occur. It can be seen from these examples that when nonidentical forms co-occur, they always follow the superficial order Spkr > Adr > Other. This is clearly motivated by the hierarchical order of the participant roles which they encode, and is consistent with other grammatical facts in a number of languages (Silverstein 1976a; DuBois 1987).

4.2.2 Lexical Forms

The independent lexical pronouns have a number of noteworthy characteristics. The basic series shown in table 4.1 refer to participants and nonparticipants in core case roles (A, S, and O). In the first and second person categories, but not in the third, these are also used for dative, benefactive, and locative relations, making them the least constrained grammatically of all forms in all five series (affixal and lexical). Since the affixal series mark person in the verb and predicative noun, and independent lexical NPs are not required to form a complete sentence, the independent lexical pronouns are almost never obligatory in order to establish reference. They are optional from a grammatical perspective. The two cases in which independent pronouns are necessary in order to identify referents are the first and second person forms when in dative function, as in (30).

(30)   t-u-ȼ'aáh-∅   **t-en**   le   b'á?al o?
        Pst-Pro3-Vb-Pro3 IndPro1 DNOM N   TD
        'He gave (to) me that thing.'

In sentences like this, the independent pronoun is the only place where first person is marked. It cannot be promoted to suffixal position on the Vb, since this is reserved for the transitive object (that thing), which is cross-indexed by the suffix -∅. By contrast, the same sentence with a third person dative would not have the *le ti?* of the pronominal series in place of *t-en*, but rather *ti-Ø* from the dative series, where the only indication of person is the absence of any marking at all.

The Non-Participant (third person) is composed out of the same *ti?* particle preceded by the nominal deictic (DNOM) ID *le*. This morpheme is the only ID base in the DNOMs, on which the definite article *le*, the immediate demonstrative *le-la?* 'this', and Non-Immediate *le-lo?* 'that' are all founded. Its presence in both pronominal and demonstrative subsystems reflects a basic connection between the two. In fact, the form *le ti?* belongs equally to both subsystems. It encodes uniqueness and specificity of reference to a nonparticipant object without any indication as to its relative immediacy to the indexical ground, humanness, animacy, or any other relational or inherent features. It can be glossed simply as 'the one (we both know)'. The convergence of the two subsystems is shown in figure 4.1.

Unlike the other DNOMs, *le ti?* shows a distinctive plural formation, since in the other forms the plural morpheme attaches to the ID base *le*, whereas with *le ti?* it attaches to the *ti?*. This suggests that the bond between *le* and *ti?* is different from that between *le(l)-* and the TDS-*a?* and -*o?*. There is what appears to be an analogical formation occasionally attested in which the plural of *le ti?* appears as *le-ó?ob'ti?*, although this is less common. The layout of figure 4.1 suggests a further correspondence between Immediate demonstratives and first person pronouns, and Non-Immediate demonstratives and second person forms. This is borne out by further evidence from the use of demonstratives which cannot be spelled out here but will be summarized in chapter 10 (see also Hanks 1983, 1984a).

Another difference between the first and second person forms and the nonparticipant form stems from their relation to the possessive series in

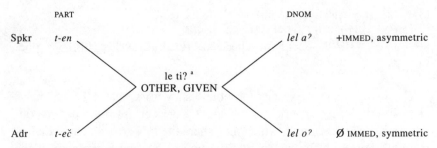

ªGIVEN summarizes Anaphoric, Background Knowledge, identifiability without immediacy (Hanks 1983:chap. 5).

Fig. 4.1. *Leti?* at the juncture of PART and DNOM series.

table 4.2. Consider first the alternative ways of formulating possession in Maya. The sentences in (31–32) all assert the possessive relation, with the possessor identified by a shifter. The first two sets show dative constructions in which the horse is said to exist 'to, for, of (etc.)' some individual. While the Spkr and Adr forms may precede the possessum (31), the nonparticipant forms automatically follow it (32). In (32), note that while plain *ti?-Ø* may occur, plain *le ti?* 'the one' cannot. This is because a dative form is required.

(31)

$$
\text{yàan} \left\{ \begin{array}{l} \text{t-en} \\ \text{t-eč} \\ \text{t-ó?on} \\ \text{t-é?eš} \\ \text{*ti (le ti?)} \end{array} \right\} \text{¢iímin}
$$

'I, you (etc.) have (a) horse(s).'
(lit., '[there] exists to me,
to you, etc., horse[s]')

(32)

$$
\text{yàan ¢iímin} \left\{ \begin{array}{l} \text{ti?-Ø} \\ \text{ti?-ó?ob'} \\ \text{ti? leti?} \\ \text{ti? lelo?} \end{array} \right\}
$$

'He has, they have (a) horse(s).'

Corresponding to these dative constructions are equally standard sentences in which the possessor is encoded in a prefixal pronoun attached to the possessum (33–34). Here the difference between first/second and third person forms is less evident. Example (34) shows the morpheme breakdown of these examples.

(33)

$$
\text{yàan} \left\{ \begin{array}{l} \text{?in-} \\ \text{?a-} \quad \text{¢iímin} \\ \text{k-} \\ \text{?a-} \dots \quad \text{-é?eš} \end{array} \right.
$$

'I, you (etc.) have (a) horse(s).'
(lit. '(there) exists my, your (etc.)
horse(s).')

(34)   y-àan   ?u-¢iímin-(ó?ob')(le ti?, lelo?)
        Pro3-Vb Pro3-N-(pl)   (DNOM)
        'He (the one) has (a) horse(s).' (lit. '(there) exists his horse [the,
        that one]')

The independent possessive pronouns shown in table 4.2, which we can call the *?in-ti?-al* series, are evidently derived from the dative construction in (31–32), with which they share the *ti?* particle. The transformation involves three changes: (i) the lexical Vb and possessum of the dative construction are deleted; (ii) the suffix-*al* is attached to the *ti?* base (obligatory after (i)); (iii) the semantic possessor is promoted from dative to possessive coding. The output, *?in-ti?-al,* can be modified by demonstratives, *le ʔin-tiʔ-al oʔ* 'that one mine', and if it is, it may function as a core NP in a clause: *¢'aáh t-en le ʔin-tiʔ-al oʔ* 'Give me mine there'. If left unmodified by demonstratives, the *ʔin-tiʔ-al* series function as predicative elements rather than referential nouns, as in the sentences, *ʔin-tiʔal-Ø* 'it is mine, it is for me', *ʔin-tiʔal-eč* 'you are mine, you are for me', *ʔa-tiʔal-éʔeš-óʔob'* 'they are yours, they are for you (pl)', *ʔa-tiʔal-óʔon-éʔeš* 'we are yours, we are for you', *a-tiʔal-éʔeš-óʔob' le ¢iímin oʔ* 'those horses are yours (pl)'. Note that they take suffixal pronominal marking, appropriate for equational sentences, and that the suffixes obey the familiar $1 > 2 > 3$ order. When accompanied by a full NP, as in the final example cited, the NP follows the predicative element, just as we would expect.

The discrepancy between first and second person and third person forms that is evident in examples (31–32) also shows up in the alternations in (35–36). Here we see that in the participant categories, possessive nominalizations alternate with standard pronouns flanked by demonstratives; or to state it the other way around, standard pronouns, when modified by demonstratives, can be used as possessives.[13] There is no similar alternation in the third person.

(35) le ʔin-tiʔal aʔ ~   le ten aʔ   'this one mine'
      le ʔa-tiʔal aʔ ~   le teč aʔ   'this one yours (sg)'
      le k-tiʔal aʔ ~   le tóʔon aʔ 'this one ours'
      le ʔa-tiʔaléʔeš aʔ ~ le téʔeš aʔ 'this one yours (pl)'

(36)
      le ʔu-tiʔal aʔ ~ ⎧ *le le tiʔ aʔ
                        ⎪ *le tiʔ aʔ
                        ⎨ *le tiʔ le tiʔ aʔ   'this one his, hers'
                        ⎪ *le tiʔ Ø aʔ
                        ⎩

The forms shown in the middle column of (35) are rarely attested and came to my attention only once in spontaneous talk. Man was describing to me and his wife how Turkish merchants in Mérida had been hurt by the policies of a recent governor. Their sales dropped because of the taxation of imports, and in response they went to the governor and complained. Man quoted their complaint as in (37).

(37) le   tóʔon   aʔ → máʔ t-u-máʔana → k-ih   le   tùurkos
      DNOM   IndPro1 TD   Neg Aux-Pro3-Vb Quot-Trm DNOM N
      ' "Ours, it doesn't sell," say the Turks.' (BB.4.160–1)

When I heard this utterance, I asked Man about the leftmost pronoun, and he glossed it as *le k-tiʔal aʔ* 'this ours', the standard form. Surprised, I asked him whether one could equally well say the remaining forms in

(35), and he affirmed that people do say them. He failed to cite any third person form, and when I offered the ones in (36), he rejected them straight-away as impossible. Uncommon though these alternations apparently are, they indicate both the difference of the third person category and the rela-tively more marked status of the possessive pronouns relative to the basic series. The latter may be used in place of the former, but the inverse does not hold, since one never finds *le ?in-ti?al o?* in place of *t-en* for person reference in the core grammatical cases.

If these analyses are correct, then the three series of lexical (or perhaps 'phrasal') participant shifters are straightforwardly interrelated. The stan-dard *t-en* series is the most basic of the three. The dative *ti? t-en* series can be derived by addition of the particle *ti?*, conditioned by its grammati-cal role in the sentence. Both standard and dative series are referential and function grammatically as NPs. The dative phrases are the source of the possessive derivations, which are predicative rather than merely refer-ential (not 'mine', but '(it) is mine'). In all three series, there is a split between Spkr, Adr forms and the nonparticipant third person, apparently because the latter is actually a DNOM and not a true PART category.

4.2.3 Person Categories in Use

This section will illustrate basic patterns of referential use of Maya pro-nouns, proceeding through the categories from Spkr to Adr to non-participant. In chapter 5, relatively complex participant frames will be discussed in relation to their social settings and the linguistic resources with which they are managed. Here the objective is to present attested examples of routine pronoun use, focusing on what these indicate about the conventional person categories in the language.

4.2.3.1 *Spkr*

The Spkr (speaker) category, as used here, includes first person singular and plural. In Maya, there are three distinct constructions for first person plural: (i) the simple form, which is semantically unmarked for inclusion or exclusion of Adr (addressee); (ii) the overtly marked Inclusive form, which in Maya is restricted to inclusion of a Plural Adr; and (iii) 'third person Included', which includes the Spkr with some other nonpartici-pant, usually excluding the current Adr. Of these three, the first is formed with a single morpheme, *-ó?on,* the second is formed by the combination of first and second person plural morphemes, *-ó?on-é?eš,* and the third is formed periphrastically by the first person plural *-ó?on* plus the phrasal description of accompaniment, *-ó?on yeétel X* 'us with X (= myself and X)'. The common features of the three are that they all include the speaker among the classes of participant to which they refer, and they all include at least one other beyond the speaker (hence 'plural'). At the basic level (making the default assumptions discussed in §4.1.3 above), Spkr pronouns signal that the individual or group referred to is identical to or includes the one performing the act of reference. Hence, when a Maya speaker says, *h b'in-ó?on yeétel leti?* 'I went with him (lit. we went with him)', (s)he refers to himself or herself, projecting a figure in the terms discussed by Goffman (see above). If any intervening frames are in play, through quotation or transposition of the indexical ground in narrative or conversation, then the current utterer need not necessarily be the individual referred to, as in 'Miguel said "Give it to me"', where 'to me' refers not to the current utterer but to the one named Miguel.

In other examples of embedded quotation, a speaker can quote himself, producing successive tokens of 'I' that are apparently coreferential. Still, as Goffman observed, these 'I's' project figures of the Spkr, which may not be strictly coreferential. 'I said "I told them 'I am the one who did it.'"' In this utterance, the first token of the first person pronoun (I said) presumably refers to the individual who performed the earlier act of saying. The medial pronoun (I told) refers to the individual who had previously performed the act of telling. Finally, the last token of 'I' refers to the individual identifying himself as the agent of some still earlier action. We naturally assume that all three individuals are one and the same person, who remains identical across scenarios, but it is easy enough to see that this can be questioned. There may be a long time lapse between the three events, so that the act of telling occurred ten years earlier and the 'I am the one who did it' utterance ten years earlier still, when 'I' was dreaming, adolescent, or otherwise not what 'I' is today.

We can summarize the reference of the Spkr pronouns roughly by saying that they are used to refer to any one of three objects: (i) The current animator of the act of reference, the 'bodily Spkr', alone or aggregated with others, copresent or not. In this case, the statement uttered characterizes the current Spkr as a figure of reference and description, a participant in some narrated event(s). (ii) The same individual (or a group including the same individual) identified as subject of an immediately superordinate verb of communication, as in '{I, you, he} said "{I, we} won't do it."' Note, in examples such as these, that whatever pronoun is selected in the first clause, it is invariantly coreferential with the 'I' in the quoted speech. If the quoted speech has a plural form, its reference overlaps with, but need not be identical with, that of the superordinate pronoun. This quasi-anaphoric function of Spkr forms will be further discussed in chapter 5. (iii) The individual or group referred to is a projected figure performing an utterance in the next embedding indexical frame, as in (ii), but no overt linguistic forms signal the transposition. In the absence of a reported speech formula, an intervening frame may be retrievable from prior talk or otherwise given in the speech context. For instance, a woman holding her three-week-old infant, squirming after having its face washed, can say to it 'Oh mommy, I don't like it when you wipe my face off!' speaking for the infant with no linguistic keying of the transposition.

The three interpretations of Spkr pronouns (I, we) can be unified in the generalization that this pronoun, like the others, is interpreted relative to an actual indexical ground, which may be the phenomenal sphere of the current bodily speaker and addressee, a different phenomenal sphere described in reported speech, or some fantasized utterance event projected by the utterer's words taken in their context. Regardless of these differences, what the Spkr forms signal, in opposition to the non-Spkr forms, is a relation of identity: the one performing the utterance (whoever that is) is the one referred to.

Examples of simple self-reference in Maya conversation are not hard to come by. Sitting in Lol's house, I asked him how many rooms it had, and he responded that both his and his brother's house, which share a wall, have three rooms apiece.

(38)   way e? ?oóš p'ée kwàarto → ?oóš p'é kwàarto **ten i?** →
            'Here, three rooms.   Three rooms of mine (to me),

            ?oóš p'ée tinsukú?un o?
            (and) three of my older brother's.' (F.137.A.465)

The pronoun form is from the dative series, signaling possession. It refers to Lol, the actual utterer. It is worth noting that my question, to which Lol was responding, was simply, 'How many rooms are there here'. He could have answered merely, 'There are three here', or 'We have three and they have three'. Instead, he links the rooms both to our current 'here' and to himself as owner. It is consistent with rules of property ownership in Maya homes that he single out himself and his brother as the owners rather than their respective families as wholes.

Riding along the highway in the back of a cargo truck heading for Yaaxhom, Bertim and a friend were conversing intermittently. Reaching a heavily populated stretch of road, the truck made several stops to let off women and children who were returning from Oxkutzcab, and the two men fell naturally into helping the women disembark, unloading their crates and purchases for them. After a few stops, the truck reached an intersection and stopped again, this time for Bertim's interlocutor. Getting down, he said to Bertim (and for my ears),

(39)   pwes way **ten e**⁷ →
                 'Well, here ('s where) I (get off).' (BB.5.4)

Were there any possible question as to the referent of *t-en* 'I' in this utterance, the pairing of the form with the DLOC 'here' and the ongoing act
of disembarking from the truck unambiguously anchor it to the bodily
speaker.

Pilar was still mourning the death of her mother two weeks after the
event when she discussed her family with me in the courtyard of her
home. She had performed the *⁷u trèes diàas* 'three days' (prayers)' for
the deceased here in her home instead of in the home of her father, because her parents and siblings had all converted to Protestantism. Opposing her practice to theirs, she said

(40)   **ten e**⁷ → t-**im**-bèet um p'eé uresar way e⁷ →
                 Me,   I did   a recitation   here

                 . . . **in**-laák' ó⁷ → miš
                 . . . my siblings,   not

                 untuúl b'èet i⁷   tumèen té⁷e kub'in o⁷
                 one of them did any because they all go there.' (BB.5.27)

The first person pronouns in this utterance project a figure through which
Pilar presents herself in contrast to the others, along with the corresponding contrast between her 'here' (our current location) and the 'there' of
the others (the unmentioned but retrievable 'templos' in which the Protes-
tants are known to practice).[14]

Lol was explaining how he and his brother had raised the funds necessary to construct their cinder-block houses by selling off some of their
possessions. He had sold a stereo, and his brother Man had sold a sewing
machine.

(41)   ⁷**in**-sukú⁷un e⁷   tukonah ti e maestro   tàal way a⁷a →
                 'My elder brother, he sold (it) to this teacher who comes around
                                                                             here,

                 tukon   um p'eé ti e màakiná o⁷ →
                 He sold one of the machines.

                 ten e⁷ t-**in**-konah ti **in**-besìino yàan té⁷el a⁷ →
                 Me,   I sold to the neighbor   right there,' (across the street)

                 le ⁷estèerio kupàaš   té⁷el o⁷ →
                 'the stereo that plays over there.' (across the street)
                                                        (F.137.A.435)

Just as Pilar had contrasted herself to her siblings and parents, Lol contrasts himself in this utterance to his brother. As in preceding examples, the contrast in person is reinforced by a parallel contrast in space: the older brother sold to the teacher who comes *way* 'around here', whereas he sold to his neighbor *téʔel aʔ* 'right there' across the street.

In these examples, the fit between utterer, or 'animator', and the referent of the pronoun is the basic one: the individual before me is the same as the one being described. To the extent that they are past tense predications, of course, the 'I' referred to and described may differ nontrivially from the current speaker. Following Goffman's reasoning, we could say that all first person usage projects a figure, and whether that figure is described in the past or in the very present does not alter the more basic fact that a self-attribution is being made. DC, a shaman with about thirty-five years' practice, is committed to living on the edge of poverty, preferring to let God and the spirits bring him his daily needs. He describes himself in just these terms.

(42)   DC: **ten** uheét meèn šuluʔ ʔoóȼil **en**
              'Me, I'm wicked   poor.' (BB.4.9)

In utterances like this one, it is clear that the speaker is creating his own image through description. Other examples also project a self-image but may be explicitly keyed as fantasy, as in (43). MC and I were discussing ways of responding to a question, when he observed that a response I offered was odd.

(43)   wá kuyúʔub' al le t'àan mèen ulaák'   maák eʔ,
             'If that talk was heard by   another person,

             yàan utuklik eʔ **tèen** pašik ↑ **tèen** ʔòok'ostik.
             he'd think I'm the one playing (the music), and I'm the one
             dancing (too)!' (BB.4.108)

This expression conveys that the individual is 'dancing to his own drum', talking to himself or otherwise oblivious to his interlocutor. Here the first person morphemes could be said to refer to MC, the current utterer, but what they say about him is counterfactual, since he would not make the utterance in the first place. He doesn't dance to his own song. Furthermore, what the expression reports is the hypothetical thought of a hypothetical person, making it twice (or perhaps three times) removed from actual reality. Similarly, in DC's descriptions of his travel during dreams (1–4), we must wonder whether the referent of his first person singular pronouns is identical to his current self in speech. Complicating factors notwithstanding, even these examples are taken automatically to project a figure of the very individual speaking. MC wouldn't make the ill-formed utterance, and a part of DC really was attacked by the jaguar, even if in the other realm of a dream. Both present their speakers as certain types of characters. Such self-presentation is ubiquitous in Maya speech and is motivated partly by commonsense premises such as the uniqueness of the individual (see §3.2). In my experience, Maya adults show little reticence to talk about themselves.

When we move from singular to plural in the Spkr forms, questions arise as to the scope and composition of the group referred to. I pointed out above that three first person plural forms are distinguished: a general plural, an inclusive plural, and an exclusive plural, both of the latter morphologically complex. The simple form is the least specific and is used in reference to groups including the Spkr with Adr (with or without others), or the Spkr with some other. Whether or not Adr is included, there is important contextual variation in the matter of which group of others is included with the Spkr. In the course of a single conversation, a Spkr might use the simple first person plural in reference to the ongoing 'we' of himself with his Adr, the primary 'we' of himself with spouse and children, the next level of himself with coresident affines, with his co-workers, himself as representative of 'we of Yucatán' as distinct from the North American 'you' of a visitor. Which particular 'we' is in play may be explicitly described in the sentence, recoverable from immediately adjacent talk or background knowledge, or left unclear. This same variability will be shown to arise in the scope of 'here', since different 'we's' correspond to different 'here's', variously embodied in spatial divisions and practices.

Coming to a point of closure in his description of how difficult life is nowadays, DP asserted that the history he had sketched out was what caused the ills of contemporary life.

(44)   sí le ti e topmail ó?on o? →
            'Yeah, that's what's shafted us today.' (BB.5.22)

The pronominal reference includes him in a much larger group, encompassing all Maya, or all campesinos. On a separate occasion, DC was describing local Oxkutzcabeño ways of doing things and summarized by saying:

(45)   le k-ná?atik tó?on a?
            'This is what we understand.' (BB.4.66)

One week earlier, Lol was speaking to me of life around Oxkutzcab and his own household, when DC, also participating, interjected for my benefit:

(46)   laáh b'ey e bìida **tó'on** way o'
         'All that's how the life (is) for us (around) here.' (BB.4.12)

These last two examples quite clearly exclude me (the Adr) from the group referred to, since they occurred in discourse in which DC and Lol were describing their life to me. The contrast between my being a North American and their being Maya from Oxkutzcab was always available (although not always in play). Sentence (46) once again links the referent of 'we' to the referent of 'here', reinforcing the place in which the life being described is lived.[15]

In the course of describing their homesteads to me, speakers commonly made first person reference to the social groups to which they belonged by kinship and coresidence. Lol, for instance, spelled out maxims of etiquette observed by him and his coresident kin (wife and children, elder brother with family, father), and then summarized saying:

(47)   b'èy usistema **k**-máan **tó'on** o'
         'That's the system by which we go.' (BB.4.12)

In the course of his description, he made it clear that not every household runs the way theirs does, and the referent of the Spkr pronouns was Lol's own coresidents, a group which also excludes me, his Adr. There is always available a distinction between coresidents and others beyond the perimetral wall of the homestead. In other examples, the 'we' of coworking brothers or of the single marriage unit can also be the object of reference.

In all of these cases, the first person plural automatically projects a figure by lumping the current Spkr into a social group, the 'we' referred to. The variation in the scope of the 'we' is an unavoidable consequence of any individual's belonging to many distinct aggregates at a single time. From the viewpoint of deixis, it is the same variability in scope that we see in different uses of 'here' and 'there'.

The first person inclusive in Maya is signaled by combining the first person plural with the second person plural pronouns, in one of two ways: k-. . . . -é'eš, or . . . -ó'on-é'eš. Observe that in both of these, the first person form precedes the second person form, and both must be plural. None of *'a-. . .-ó'on, *'in-. . .é'eš, *-é'eš-ó'on, *-en-é'eš is attested (in the inclusive reading), and the attested forms are used only, so far as I know, in addressing or making reference to groups. A straightforward referential usage arose, for instance, when Margot corrected an utterance I made. She had pre-

pared a pan of scrambled eggs for breakfast and brought it into the house for me
to eat at the table. I remarked that she had made quite a lot but that it was for the
whole family, saying:

(48)   WH   pero lel o⁷ tak atí⁷alé⁷eš
              'But that's for even you all (too).'

        Mgt   **k-ti al-é⁷eš** keč,   tumèen **tó⁷on yete teč**
              ' "It's for us all" you should say, because (it's) us with you.'
                                              (BB.4.77)

Margot rejected as inappropriate my second person plural formulation, in
which I took it for granted that I would eat with them, and tried to focus
on the fact that the eggs were for them too. Note that immediately following her correction of my utterance, she glossed the correct form 'us with
you', which is in fact a proper description of the group referred to. Although I will not discuss the problems associated with reported speech
here, it is noteworthy that Margot's first utterance is an instance of quotation for the purpose of putting words into an interlocutor's mouth (in this
case, mine), whereas the gloss she gives thereafter is direct speech. As a
result of this shift in footing, the because clause is actually *not* a straightforward gloss of the preceding; Inclusive first person plural does not mean
'us with you (sg)', but rather 'me (or us) with you (pl)'. Taking into account the transposition, the gloss is accurate.

   In social contexts in which a single speaker is addressing a group, as
when a boss on a work site addresses his workers, or a politician addresses a crowd of potential constituents, the first person Inclusive is used
for the rhetorical effect of including the group while maintaining the Spkr
and his or her audience in a single aggregate. DC was bringing to a close
a clinical episode in which he had performed a divination for two women,
and he explained to them how they collectively would have to handle the
problem, according to what he had learned in his divining crystals. Coming to a close, he reinforced his advice to them:

(49)   b'ey k'ab'eét **k-mèeŋk-é⁷eš** o⁷
            'That's how we (Incl) must do it.' (BB.4.9)

On a separate occasion, recounting to me how he had addressed a large
group of men at a gathering, he reported having exhorted them at several
points during his speech:

(50)   bey ⁷anil-ó⁷**on-é⁷eš** a⁷
            'This is the way we are (Incl)!' (BB.4.12)

One of the most vivid examples of the Incl occurred when DC was re-counting to me a trip he and his two sons had taken to Michoacan, Mex-ico, in order to cure a man of a dreaded illness. They were all impressed with the speed of the bus they took and the way it careened along the highway, even through a great tunnel in the side of a mountain. At one point when he was sure they were about to veer off the road, he cried out to his sons, both next to him in the bus:

(51)   ¢'oká²an **t-ó²on-é²eš i²**   pàalal-é²eš!
         Vb-stv   Pro Dat-1pl-2pl Loc N-2pl
         'We're done for, kids!' (BB.4.100)

This utterance is interesting for several reasons. The fact of its being a case of an embedded quotation will not be taken up here. However, it shows an Incl form from the dative series, along with the locative particle *i²* indicating the current location of the Spkr at the time of the utterance, plus a vocative N. In each of these examples, the participants referred to are the current utterer (within the quoted frame) and the current address-ees (also relative to the quoted frame).

The most commonly attested Incl form (speaking impressionistically) is the hortative use of the verb 'to go', what in English is rendered as 'Let's (go) do x'. The verb 'to go' is suppletive in Maya, and the impera-tive is signaled by the forms *kó²oš* and *k-ó²on-é²eš* 'let's go'. The former is unmarked for plurality of Adr and may be used in addressing either an individual or a group, while the latter is specifically plural Adr. Both may be used for actual physical displacement, 'let's go', or for undertaking an activity which need not involve any movement, as in *kó²oš ¢ikbal* 'let's converse'. On the other hand, *k-ó²o-t-en*, *k-ó²o-t-en-é²eš*, and *k-ó²on* are all used for the summons 'come here (to me)'. The first is used in addressing an individual or a group, the second in addressing a group, and the third is unspecified for number of Adr (but restricted to non-S-final position).

The final variant of the first person is what I have called the 'third per-son Included', because this form explicitly includes some nonparticipant along with the Spkr. The construction is We . . . with X, meaning what in English would be phrased I . . . with X, that is, the Spkr accompanied by some other X. In order to say 'I went with Manuel', one would nor-mally say the translational equivalent of 'we went with Manuel', as in *h b'in-ó²on yeétel manwel*. The chief peculiarity of this construction is that the Spkr pronoun is marked Plur rather than Sing, even though there is only a single copresent incumbent of the Spkr category. The plurality im-plies that number in the first person pronoun is assigned at the level of the

whole clause and therefore includes the aggregate of the grammatical subject with the accompanying third person. The construction usually excludes the current Adr, as far as I know, but I believe it can also be made
to include a plural Adr, as in *t-ó?on-é?eš yeétel manwel* 'us (you all and
me) with Manuel'. Unfortunately, I lack data on this form. In any case,
this periphrastic construction allows specification of the third parties by
introducing them in an accompanying (comitative) role.[16]

4.2.3.2 *Adr*

The feature Adr (addressee) stands for the current interlocutor to whom
the speaker is directing his or her speech. Making the standard assumptions (§4.1.3 above), this individual typically shares a perceptual field
with the speaker (minimally auditory or visual, maximally tactual). Like
the Spkr forms, the Adr forms encode an equivalence between the referent and a component of the indexical ground; the individual or group individuated by 'you' in a given case is identical to, or includes, or overlaps
with the copresent addressee(s) to whom the utterance is directed. The
Maya forms are simple: *?a-, -eč* for singular and *(?a- . . . .)-é?eš* for plural
(holding aside the first person Incl, which of course also bears the feature
Adr). Third person forms are not used in Maya for address or reference to
addressee, and the number of Adr is evidently assigned on the basis of
quantity, not deference. Plural forms are not used in respectful address or
any time when a single individual occupies the Adr role.

The indexical ground of the Adr category is transposable in the same
way as is that of other shifters. When Adr forms are embedded in quoted,
hypothetical, or otherwise 'keyed' speech, the identity between referent
and current addressee may break down. We can summarize three alternative interpretations (cf. §4.2.3.1): (i) The current receiver of the act of
reference, the 'bodily Adr', alone or aggregated with others, visually
copresent or not. The Adr is the one who is both 'channel linked' (to borrow Levinson's [1987] term) and the intended recipient of the utterance
(in contact, in Jakobson's [1960] term). The Adr is projected as a figure
through the terms of address and description, just as is the Spkr through
terms of self-presentation. (ii) The same individual (or a group including
the same individual) coded as the dative of an immediately superordinate
verb of communication, as in 'He said to {me, you, her} "You cannot
go."' The Adr form in the quoted segment of this example is automatically interpreted as coreferential, or overlapping in reference, with the
pronoun in the dative relation in the embedding clause. (iii) The individual or group referred to is a projected figure receiving an utterance in

some indexical frame other than the actual one, but there is no overt linguistic signal of the transposition. The intervening frame is retrievable
from prior talk or otherwise given in the speech context, as in a mother
saying to her infant, "Aw, mommy! That hurts!" projecting herself as
Adr in a fictive event.

The singular Adr forms refer uniquely to the one individual to whom
the utterance is directed, individuating him or her apart from all others.
The others include the Spkr, other copresent individuals recently or shortly
to be addressed, or other third persons in a nonparticipatory role (in the
current indexical frame, embeddings and transpositions taken into account). Pilar contrasted me to herself and her husband VC when she explained that the day before I arrived at their home, they had come back
from a trip to Mérida, seeking medical care.

(52)   hóolhéak ʔúʔ-uk-óʔon hoʔ → ká   ʔúʔul-eč   teč →
         DTEMP   Vb-Opt-Pro1 N   Comp Vb-Pst-Pro2 Pro2
         'Yesterday we had arrived (from) Mérida when you arrived yourself.' (BB.5.27)

The initial DTEMP in (52) is the form usually used to make reference to
'yesterday', the day before 'today'. Here it has been transposed and refers
instead to the day before the day of my arrival, both of them in the past
relative to the day of utterance. The contrast between the two events of
arriving is coded in the construction [DTEMP Vb1-Opt . . . Comp Vb2-
Pst], in which the temporal reference of the first (subordinate) clause is
computed relative to that of the second (subordinating) clause. This provides a grammatical frame within which the person inflections are brought
into contrast as well, [-óʔon . . . -eč teč]. The independent second person
in final position is redundant from a purely referential perspective, since
the suffixal pronoun makes the reference unambiguous. Its presence is motivated rather by the contrastive frame, which it reinforces, foregrounding
the reference to Adr. It is also noteworthy that starting at the Vb, the two
clauses are phonologically parallel: they have the same number of syllables, and each contains the same vowel in ultimate and penultimate
positions. This lends an acoustic balance to the contrast that would be
lacking if the independent Pro2 were absent.

Shortly after I arrived in his home after an absence of a year and a half,
DC summoned me gravely to conversation, saying:

(53)   kóʔoš ȼikbal, čeén ȼikbal,
         'Let's talk,   just talk,

         tumèen yàan báʔaš in kʼaát inw úʔuy ik teč aʔ
         because there's something I want to hear from you.' (BB.4.68–73)

This utterance initiated a conversation that lasted several hours, in which DC asked me point-blank why I had returned and whether I intended to continue studying shamanic practice with him. The independent Adr form functions as a dative source in its clause, and so it is motivated on purely grammatical grounds and is not contrastive like the previous example. Still, a sharp contrast is established in this utterance by the way it isolates its addressee (myself) from its speaker and initiates a discourse in which the addressee was asked to explain and justify his position. Although we had worked together for six years at the time, this utterance presupposed no joint 'we' more enduring than the conversation we were embarking on. In fact, it was my relation to our joint engagement that I was pressed to justify, and the ensuing discussion brought the whole relation into question.

Lol recounted the story of how he and his elder brother Man had planned to build their new homes together, one 'part' for each:

(54)   . . . péro ¢'óok ktuklik e⁷   lel a⁷ → ump'eé pàarte teč i⁷
            . . . 'but we had (already) thought, "this (plan), (there's) one part
            for you,

            ump'eé pàarte ten i⁷ →
            one part for me."' (F.137.A.435)

As in many examples, there is a transposition here from the current frame of my conversation with Lol to a projected narrative frame in which he and his brother had said, one to the other, "one part for you and one for me." Within this embedded frame, the two pronouns contrast the individuals and foreground the fact that to each corresponds a separate part of the place. The contrast and evenness of distribution is further foregrounded by the identical lexical and syntactic frames in which the pronouns occur.[17]

DC told of how an old man, approaching death, divides up his wealth among his sons, saying as he does so:

(55)   hé⁷ teč a⁷ → hé⁷ teč a⁷ → hé⁷ teč a⁷ →
            'Here's for you. Here's for you. Here's for you.' (BB.4.50)

Similar to the preceding example, this one individuates single addressees by juxtaposing them in grammatically and lexically parallel constructions. While Lol's scenario portrays two brothers in a Spkr-Adr dyad, DC's portrays a father and his three sons in a slightly more complex participant framework, Spkr-Adr$_1$-Audience (ratified hearer). Each son participates in both Adr and Audience roles in sequence.

One of the noteworthy features of second person pronouns in Maya is their use in negative constructions, as in *má⁷a t-eč* 'No (as one-word utterance), not (general negative marker)' and *miš t-eč* 'neither, not even'.

We know that the morphemes involved are in fact the pronouns, because
(i) both *máʔ a* and *miš* occur elsewhere with their expected negative
meanings, and both govern phrase final *iʔ* of negation; (ii) under the
proper circumstances, the person suffix may be omitted or pluralized,
-éʔeš, if the utterance is addressed to a plurality of interlocutors; (iii) the
t-eč element is separated from the negative under the proper circumstances, just as would be expected if it were the independent pronoun. So
in response to a question, one might get *máʔ ʔinw ohe teč iʔ* 'I don't
know (you).' The precise nuance of this sentence, as opposed to the corresponding one lacking the independent pronoun, is not clear to me.
Often the full form *máʔa teč* conveys a definitive, slightly emphatic 'no',
commonly ending in a falling contour, as in *máʔa teč ↓ máʔ timb'in
umpuliʔ iʔ* 'No. I'm not going once and for all'. Or the response *máʔ
tuún teč* 'No way' (BB.4.94) as a firm rejection of one's suggestion.

In other cases, an Adr form combined with the negative can convey a
palpable focus on the separation between the speaker and his or her addressees. MC, VC, and Milo are brothers, in ascending order of age. MC
drives the family truck as his primary occupation, while VC and Milo
work their fields and orchards. All three have orchards, which adjoin one
another. One evening Milo, his son Sil, and MC were discussing their
plans to irrigate; VC was absent but had evidently discussed the matter
with Milo during the day. Milo asked MC about a detail in the plan, and
MC responded:

(56)   máʔ inwohe **téʔeš** iʔ →
            Neg Pro1 Vb Pro2pl Trm
            'I don't know (you all).' (BB.5.37)

Although I would be hard-pressed to give evidence of it, MC's utterance
seemed to have an edge of defensiveness in this context. It conveyed that
MC wasn't the one who would know the details of the plan, since they all
had obviously discussed it during the day when he was absent. The asymmetry in their background knowledge on this point divides MC from the
others—he is the only one who drives the truck and is separated from all of
them all day. This, I suggest, is what motivates the presence of the pronoun
in his utterance, and its effect is to exclude himself from the group.

Narrators may use negatives expanded by Adr forms to project emphasis and increase the contact between themselves and their interlocutor. DP
told me the story of a man who had come to Oxkutzcab long ago, a man
who displayed great ability as a curer and great generosity. He was a
stranger when he came, and he never took a wife. He never even left his
house to go out to market or to the park. This last, DP said:

(57)   **miš teč** uhoók'o k'iíwik →
       Neither did he go out to (the) market,

       miš teč uhoók'o pàarkée →
       nor did he go to the park.

       čen tuyotoč yàan
       Just at home he was.' (BB.5.22)

Note first in this example that the Adr forms do not refer to any individual with a role in the proposition.[18] DP is not saying that I did not go to the park, but that his narrative character did not. Accordingly, the verbs are in the third person. The Adr pronouns function rather to foreground the negative and the contact between DP and his addressee. The two conjuncts are exactly parallel syntactically and are identical except for the final Ns, market and park. Together these two summarize the town center where men go to drink coffee, play dominos, and exchange gossip. The last line restates the theme in a different form.[19] By not going to these places, the man rejected the normal sociality of town life, one of DP's main themes. When he eventually did begin to go out, see women, and ultimately take a wife, he lost his ability to cure.

4.2.3.3 *Non-Participant*

The nonparticipant forms signal that the referent is neither the current animator nor the current receiver, but some third party(s). Whereas the Spkr and Adr forms encode that the referent they identify is *identical* to some participant in the current indexical field of interaction, the nonparticipant forms signal a *disjunction* between coparticipants and the referent(s). For heuristic purposes, we can assign this category the feature Other, meaning non-Spkr, non-Adr. In the context of quoted speech, the indexical field of coparticipation need not be the current one but can be some other, as in '{I, you, he} told {me, you, him} "**He** won't do it."' In this case, the Other form (boldface) in the embedded quotation is obligatorily non-coreferential with either of the preceding pronouns in the superordinate clause. The report frame (underlined), and not the actual current framework, establishes the indexical coordinates relative to which the embedded pronoun is interpreted. Note that if it were 'He told me "He won't do it,"' then the current addressee could in fact be the referent of the quoted 'he'—I tell MC that VC told me that MC wouldn't do something. On the other hand, the referent of quoted 'he' could *not* have been a coparticipant in the originary event being reported. That therefore is the frame relative to which the pronoun is interpreted. Speakers also can project fictional nonparticipants by transposition without supplying an explicit metalinguistic frame to show it. A mother puts words in her infant's mouth, 'That hurts!' 'This is yucky!' 'He's funny!' identifying referents (perhaps a copresent adult, or her own activities as she attends to the child) from the child's perspective. This capacity to project transposed, fictional, or narrated indexical frames is basic to communication; it is a design feature of shifters.

What appears to be distinctive of the Other forms in Maya is that they signal that the referent and the relevant indexical frame of coparticipation are disjunct. This does not mean that an individual identified with a form encoding Other cannot in fact be corporeally copresent, part of an audience, or even an intermittent coparticipant in the interaction. It means rather that during the current utterance event, during which the indexical frame is held constant, the individual occupies neither Spkr nor Adr roles.[20] This disjunction, of course, raises the further question of how coparticipants can identify the referent, since it need not even be copresent, and since the third person forms encode no descriptive features (gender, humanness, animacy, etc.) whatsoever. The answer is that in routine practice, the referents of Other pronouns are identifiable on the basis of shared background knowledge or discourse antecedents, or they may be further described in the sentence.[21]

Many examples of the Other pronouns *le ti?*, *le ti?-ó?ob'* 'the one, the ones' are coreferential with a preceding expression in the discourse. Man was recounting the voyage he and his brother and father had taken to Michoacan when he came to the description of a great hill down which the train ran, gaining speed as it went, to then ascend the next hill coming up.

(58)   le yiík'al uyeénl o?, **le ti?** mèentik ukrusàar e suúbidá o?
            'The momentum of its descent, that's what made it cross over the
            next rise.' (BB.4.100–101)

In this utterance, the boldface pronoun is interpreted as coreferential with the immediately preceding NP, flanked by the demonstratives *le . . . o?*. It functions, grammatically as a transitive subject focus, and for this reason the verb with which it is associated lacks any prefixal pronoun (we would otherwise expect *?u-mèentik* 'it makes, causes [it]'). Similarly, Lol returned from the market one afternoon and showed me the purchases he had made, coming to a close with:

(59)   hé?el o? → **le ti?** binen inman a?
            'That's it, this is what I went to buy.' (BB.4.31)

Here the pronoun codes the object of the embedded transitive verb 'buy' and is coreferential with the preceding OSTEV deictic. I have glossed these as cleft structures in English, because they are predicative: not 'the one I went to buy', but 'it is the one I went to buy'.

Margot and I worked through a fairly long questionnaire on word order in Maya, and I asked her after a while whether she found it tedious. She looked upon the questionnaire and responded:

(60)   má? šàan inwú?uyik lel o? → tumèen **le ti**?ili kint'aŋk o?
         'I don't find that long (boring), because it's what I always
         speak.' (BB.4.135)

In the *because* clause, the independent pronoun is coreferential with the preceding demonstrative (*lel o?*), and they both identify the questionnaire and its object.[22]

In some cases, the preceding expressions to which an Other pronoun is linked do not themselves make reference to a specific individual. Man was explaining to me some standard Maya expressions for telling an interlocutor to beat it (get lost), when I noted that several contained the DLOC *té?el o?* 'there', for instance, *šen té?el o?* 'Go there, go away, take a hike'. This puzzled me, because the DLOC did not seem to refer to any particular place (see §9.2.2.2: 'throwaway' uses). When I asked Man where the Adr would go in response, he said only *le ti?* 'the one', meaning the Adr, would know (61). The force of the utterance is to send the person anywhere away from the Spkr, and it makes no difference where (s)he goes. But it also makes no difference who the person is. The pronominal reference is only hypothetical, and there is no individual uniquely identified as referent outside the current discourse. Whosoever fits the scenario can be the one.[23]

(61)   čeén **le ti** yohe tú?uš kubin
         'Only he (the one told off) knows where he'll go.' (BB.4.107)

The form *le ti?* is unique among the pronouns for its association with a specific set of individuals, what we might call the 'primary others' of the Spkr. These are the other actors with whom one has fundamental and routinely active relations, starting with one's spouse, but including a sibling co-worker or a spirit guardian, for instance. The unique status of these as always available for reference is reflected in the fact that *le ti?* is used without further description, without any antecedent in the preceding talk to refer to one's spouse. Unlike English speakers, Maya speakers rarely use proper names in referring to their spouses; pronouns and other relation terms are more common. Lol, his wife Fi, and I were discussing domestic arrangements between the coresident families in his household (see §3.3), and we came to the question of the purchase and preparation of food. We had eaten as a group that afternoon, and I asked who had prepared the food. He responded simply:

(62)   ´Lol   tubèetah **le ti**ʔ téʔel oʔ
              'The one made it there.'

      WH   b'iš téʔel oʔ →
              'What do you mean "there"?'

      Lol   **le ti**ʔ b'èet tée → h té way bey aʔ ↓
              'The one made it there, right here by here.' (F.137.B.160)

We were sitting in the eating room of Lol's house (room 5 in fig. 7.8) at the time, and the referent of the DLOC expressions was Fi's oven, just outside the door behind us. What is noteworthy here is that we were discussing the entire household at the time, and the referent of the first *le ti*ʔ could have been the wife or daughter of Lol's brother Man, whose cooking area is also just outside in the courtyard. In fact, if Man had made exactly the same utterances in the same context, they would have referred automatically to his own wife and her oven. The key point is that of all the theoretically possible referents, the spouse is the preferred one for *le ti*ʔ. Later in the same conversation, Fi commented on the authority of the men in household, referring to Lol (still sitting with us) as merely *le ti*ʔ, a practice I found initially confusing (F.137.B.230).

Sitting by the fire with my comadre Eli at dusk in area I of their household (see fig. 7.6), we talked as she prepared me a cup of coffee. The children were outside feeding the bull by candlelight, and her husband MC was not due home for another hour and a half. Our talk was intermittent and interrupted by her addressing the children. Handing me the cup of hot water, she remarked matter-of-factly:

(63)   sùuk uyuk'ik kàafe šan **le ti**ʔ
              'He habitually drinks coffee too.' (BB.5.66)

There had been no prior mention of MC, but he is always available.

In each of these examples, it could be relevant that the referents—Lol, Fi, and MC—are also well known to me, that the conversations took place in their own homes, and that my interlocutors could take these things for granted. But the *le ti*ʔ of primary others also occurs in contexts in which there is significant asymmetry in the knowledge of interactants, and the other is not currently present. When commenting on his familiar spirits, outside the frame of ritual performance, DC makes reference to them simply as *le ti*ʔ-*óʔob'* 'the ones'. He takes it for granted that his interlocutors have only a vague notion of who he means, since a knowledge of the spirits is itself a precious and highly specialized acquisition that few gain. Although I do not have any recorded examples, I am fairly sure that *le ti*ˀ may also be used in reference to a spouse whom the interlocutor has never met or may not even know of.

Of course in many instances of *le ti*ˀ, the referent is some individual or object distinct from one's significant others and not already under discussion. In these cases, the issue of successful identification arises, and speakers need to increment the description in order to help the Adr get the reference. One interesting form of incrementing the informational content of *le ti*ˀ is by combining it with a DNOM, such as *leti*ˀ *el a*ˀ, *leti*ˀ *el o*ˀ 'this one here, this is the one', 'that one there, that's the one'.[24] As the glosses indicate, these forms are grammatically ambiguous (taken in isolation): they may be either a single referential NP composed of four deictic particles or a nominal sentence predicating equivalence between two objects. If pluralized, the plural morpheme may suffix to either the first or the second element, *le ti*ˀ-*ó*ˀ*ob' el o*ˀ, *le ti*ˀ *el-ó*ˀ*ob' o*ˀ 'Those ones, those are the ones'. A good example arose when Tigre was describing his brother to me (whom I did not know) and showed me two pictures of groups of people. Pointing out his brother in each photo, he said:

(64)   le ti? el a?, le ti? el a?
              'He's this one.' 'He's this one (too).' (pointing in the different
              photos)

If Tigre had had only a single picture and wanted to say 'this is him', he could utter either half of his utterance and it would stand as a full predication. In this example, it would be possible to gloss it simply as 'This one is this one', if we take the two halves to be single NPs equated.

Sitting in a Ford station wagon taxi, about to leave from Mérida for Oxkutzcab after a year's absence, I recognized the two people who got in beside me. They were the parents of Pilar from Cooperativa. The woman was obviously distressed, pallid, and shaky, and her husband, sitting between her and me, was sad and subdued. I greeted him, and he smiled, addressed me by name, and told me without further introduction,

(65)   ?umàma pìilar **leti el a**?
              'The mother of Pilar (is) this one. This is Pilar's mother.' (motion-
              ing) (BB.4.8)

Here the incremented pronoun functions as an NP, cross-indexed by the possessive *?u* prefix on *màama*. The presence of *le ti*ˀ may reflect the fact that the woman is his wife, but the *a*ˀ terminal is motivated by the facts of her physical immediacy and new introduction into the conversation.

In other cases, the incrementation of *le ti*ˀ may involve lexical description, as in *le ti? e maák* 'that person, that's the person', and *le ti? ?in sukú?un* 'that one my brother, that's my brother'. In these cases, the lexical N must be preceded by the definite article, as in the first example, or possessed, as in the second; phrases such as **le ti? maáskab'* 'the one machete', lacking an article or possessive pronoun, are ungrammatical. Furthermore, the sequential order of the pronoun relative to the description is invariantly [*leti? NP*], whether the NP is a DNOM (65), an Art + N, or a possessed N. Thus, none of the following occurs:

(66)   *le maák **leti**? b'èeteh
          'That person (is the one who) did it.'

(67)   *le **leti**? yàan ab'isik o?
          'The one the one you'll bring.'

(68)   *le **leti**? o?
          'That person.'

Nor may the incrementing description be separated from the *le ti?* by any intervening lexical items; the two form a continuous unit.

Just as NPs and demonstratives can be variously elaborated in other contexts, so too they can be expanded in these constructions. The order of elements is always *le ti? e NP(S)*, with the NP following the Art or possessive, and the terminal deictic (if there is one) in final position. Thus, <u>*le ti e má? inw oh el o?*</u> is a standard way of saying 'That's right what I don't know' (BB.4.75), and <u>*le ti? e diplòomá o?*</u> 'It's that very diploma' (BB.4.120–24), assuming the normal anaphoric availability of the referent. Similarly, the pronoun may be even further incremented by combining it with the OSTEV deictics, to yield *leti e hé? . . . o?* 'It's that (one) right there, that's the one', as in:

(69)   **leti e hé**? kin¢áa teč o?, **leti** kintó?ok o?
          'This one I'm giving you is the one I'm wrapping.' (BB.4.9)

DC made this utterance while wrapping up medicine he was dispensing to a patient. My notes are inadequate to determine what he had said just before the utterance, but it clearly shows that deictics other than the nominal demonstratives can be used to increment the pronoun. This is consistent with my other observations.[25]

4.2.4 Evidence of Hierarchy Among Participant Categories

Benveniste ([1956] 1966a, [1958] 1966b, [1965] 1974) argued that so-called third person (nonparticipant) pronouns are fundamentally distinct from first and second persons, since they belong to the syntax of language and not to discourse production. He saw discourse as "les actes discrets et chaque fois uniques par lesquels la langue est actualisée en parole par un locuteur," and assigned the Spkr and Adr forms to this domain. Since he proposed them, his analyses have been revised and expanded in the light of greater comparative evidence and more thorough investigation of the way person systems in language work (Errington 1988; Friedrich 1966; Silverstein 1976a, b). In the Maya language, the proposed split between third person (Other, Non-Part) and first (Spkr) and second (Adr) is relatively well borne out, and there are numerous points of contrast. But it is crucial to keep in mind that this difference rests on a foundation of commonality that unites pronouns with other shifters (a point made forcefully by Silverstein [1976b]).

By way of summary, I will draw together the evidence for the dichotomies between Spkr, Adr, and Other categories in the Maya pronouns. I have tried to show not only that these categories are encoded in the language but also that they have certain consequences for grammatical form. The dichotomy between Spkr/Adr forms and Other forms corresponds to three noteworthy grammatical facts: (i) number is structured differently in each of the categories; (ii) in the lexical series, the third person has a quite different range of uses than the other two; and (iii) in all five paradigms, third person forms have specialized grammatical uses that set them apart from the others.

In the suffixal series, there is an obvious asymmetry between first/second and third person forms: third person singular is signaled by formal $\emptyset$, the only one in the paradigm. Moreover, this $\emptyset$ also corresponds to the unmarked pole of a privative opposition at the level of semantics, since it may be used to stand for either singular or plural. The plural morpheme -ó?ob' is more marked (hence, specific), because it invariantly signals plural. Thus, number is structured $[+, \emptyset \text{ Plural}]$ in the Other category. In the Spkr and Adr categories, distinct non-null morphemes indicate both singular and plural, and there is no pattern of usage whereby the singular forms are used for reference or address to pluralities.[26] Furthermore, the third person plural morpheme is the general plural marker in Maya, whereas the Spkr and Adr forms are specialized and refer only to aggregates participating in the speech event.

With regard to number, the Spkr forms are also unique in that there are three distinct plural constructions, the general first person plural, the Inclusive of plural Adr, and the 'third person Included' plural. Of the three, the first is clearly the least marked both formally (monomorphemic as opposed to derived) and semantically (nonspecific as opposed to specific). It is used to refer to: Spkr + Other(s), Spkr + Adr(s), Spkr + Adr(s) + Other(s), whether the Spkr is himself singular or part of a copresent col-

TABLE **4.3** A Referential Hierarchy in the
                Plural Pronouns

	Spkr	Adr	Other
k-, -ó^ʔon	+	+	+
-é^ʔeš	−	+	+
-ó^ʔob'	−	−	+

lectivity. The Inclusive of plural Adr form is derived by combining Spkr with Adr suffixes directly and is used only with a plural Adr. On the other hand, the third person Included is formed periphrastically, with the Spkr-Pl affix attaching to the verb and the third person coded in a separate phrase, 'with, and X'. This form is used to refer to Spkr(s) + Other(s), usually excluding Adr(s) (although more data are needed on this point).

The Plural Adr form, -é^ʔeš, is used to refer to a singulary Adr plus Other(s) or to a collectivity of copresent Adrs. In all cases, the group excludes the Spkr. The third person Plural may refer indifferently to copresent Others, to a single copresent Other plus one or more noncopresent Others, or to noncopresent Others. Both Spkr and Adr are invariably excluded from the group.

These facts are indicative of a referential hierarchy among the suffixes, in which first person plural is the most inclusive form (potentially including Spkr, Adr, Other), second person plural is next (potentially including Adr and Other), and third person is the least inclusive.

What this hierarchy represents are the inclusion relations among the sets of actors to whom the pronouns are used to refer. It can be read as follows: -ó^ʔon can be used to refer to an aggregate including the current speaker along with the current addressee and some third person; -é^ʔeš can be used to refer to an aggregate including the current addressee along with some other, but excluding the speaker, and -ó^ʔob' can be used to refer to Others, excluding both current speaker and addressee. The hierarchy is parallel to the one which governs the superficial order of suffixes when they co-occur in a phrase, Spkr > Adr > Other. The two are nonetheless distinct, because the latter governs both singular and plural rather than only plural, and it determines not the denotational extension of the forms when uttered but their superficial linear order in grammatical structure.

In the lexical series, the third person forms *le ti^ʔ, le ti^ʔ-ó^ʔob'* 'the one(s)', have formal as well as semantic peculiarities. They are derived from the *ti^ʔ* base by addition of the definite article, making them structurally parallel to demonstratives, *lela^ʔ, lelo^ʔ*. They also combine with the demonstratives in incremented constructions, as in *le ti^ʔ-ó^ʔob' e l o^ʔ*

'those ones'. To my knowledge, there are no corresponding forms *ten el o?* 'that me', *teč el o?* 'that you', etc., nor can these be repaired as *le ten a?*, *le teč o?*, etc. It is true that the last two constructions do occur, but they do not correspond to the incremented third persons; *le ten a?* abbreviates the possessive relation and means 'mine, my ones here', not 'this me (as opposed to some other me)'. In fact, this abbreviated phrasing of the possessive is another point of distinction between the persons, since only the first and second person categories participate in the alternation; *le ?in-ti?al a?* ~ *le ten a?* 'mine (this one of mine)', but not *le ?u-ti?-al o?* ~ **le le ti? o?* 'his (that one of his)'. Finally, the third person forms are semantically distinct because they are used to refer to nonparticipants irrespective of humanness, animacy, or discreteness, whereas the participant forms are restricted to human or spirit interlocutors (perhaps some familiar animals are addressed occasionally in the second person, though different patterns usually apply; see §5.2). The third person forms are the only ones strongly associated with a particular class of referent, which I have called 'primary others'. Neither first nor second person forms are associated with particular individuals.

In every paradigm, the third person forms have grammatical functions external to the participant subsystem, a fact which bears out Benveniste's prediction. The bound forms are used to cross-index grammatical constituents in various constructions, such as [Pro3-Aux [Vb]]$_{VC}$ for a verb complex with an auxiliary, [Pro3-N [NP]]$_{NP}$ for possessive phrases, [Pro3-RN] for relational nouns (in front of, behind, alongside, for, etc.), and complementizers, with the pronoun cross-indexing an S. In all of these structures, the Pro3 form is endophoric, cross-referencing a chunk of discourse rather than making reference to an individual beyond it. The plural suffix in the third person is identical to the plural marker for all nouns, thus conflating number with the nonparticipant category. The lexical form *le ti?* is used as a clefting device in discourse, as in *leti? e meyah kimb'èetik o?* 'It's that work I do, that's the work I do'. In the possessive series, the third person singular functions as a complementizer, *?u-ti?al* '(is) his/hers, for him/her, in order to S'. Thus in each case, the Other form is mobilized in the grammar to signal some aspects of syntactic organization apart from reference to persons.

4.3 CONCLUSION

First and second person pronouns are hierarchically superordinate to nonparticipant pronouns and demonstratives, and this is evident in both the structure and the use of the Maya forms. This fact notwithstanding, there are fundamental relations between the participant forms and the others, as

I argued at the outset of this chapter. The fact that *le tiʔ* 'the one' participates in both pronoun and demonstrative paradigms is one indicator of
this, and others will emerge in subsequent chapters when we examine Ostensive evidential (OSTEV) and Locative (DLOC) adverbs. Here I want to
underline two aspects of the relation between Spkr/Adr forms and DLOCs.
The first is the fact that they are combined in interesting ways in utterances. In seven examples in the foregoing, a speaker coupled person reference with spatial reference in the same clause (38, 39, 40, 41, 46, 55,
62). The pairing of the two categories is a rhetorically effective way of
drawing a distinction between a coparticipant and some other individual
by attaching them to different spaces. In fact, it will come as little surprise in chapter 9 when we see that there are semantic affinities between
participants' corporeal fields and the different spatial deictic zones of the
speech event.

The second relation of note links the plural pronouns and the DLOCs in
terms of their referential scope: the various 'we's' to which an actor belongs corresponds to different 'here's', that of first-order coresident kin,
comembers of a second-level homestead, co-workers in a field, neighbors, etc. (see chap. 3). Just as *-óʔon* can refer to an aggregate including
the Spkr with or without the Adr, with or without some Other (so long as
the sum is more than one), so too *way eʔ, téʔel aʔ* 'here' can refer to a
zone including the Spkr with or without the Adr, with or without some
Other. The second person *-éʔeš* invariably excludes the Spkr but may or
may not include some Other, just as *téʔel oʔ, tol oʔ* 'there, out there'
usually exclude the Spkr's zone (see §9.2). In the foregoing, examples
(46–48) showed variable scope of 'we', parallel to 'here'.

These two kinds of relation pertain to the referential functions of the
pronouns and deictics and how they are computed relative to indexical
grounds. It is appropriate in concluding this chapter to summarize what I
take to be the R values of the Maya pronouns, based on the foregoing
description. We can call the entire set of first, second, and third person
relations 'participant categories'.[27] The highest-level split comes between
the core participants and the Other forms, as was shown in the summary
to §4.2.4. In the Other category, we need only distinguish [+Plural] from
[∅Plural]. Were we to include the DNOM demonstratives in the series, the
Other category would be subdividable into Immediate vs. Non-Immediate,
analogous to Spkr vs. Adr (Hanks 1983:chap. 5). The reason for not
doing so is that these forms clearly make up a grammatically distinct subsystem whose referential focus is not the participants but objects localized
relative to participants. When I describe more elaborate participation
frames in chapter 5, it will become necessary to make further distinctions

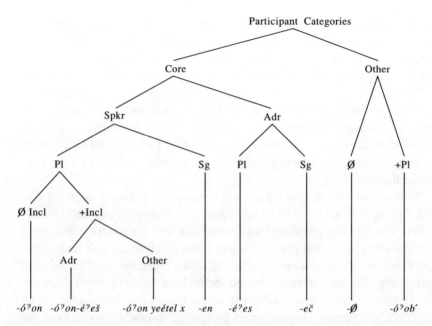

Fig. 4.2. Taxonomy of participant categories of Maya pronouns.

in the Other category to describe kinds of audience, although no evidence of this has been presented so far, and the distinction is nowhere encoded in the grammar. The category of Core Participants subdivides into Spkr and Adr, these being the basic level terms for the producer and receiver of the utterance. Both are further subdivided into Singular vs. Plural. The [Spkr, Plur] category is further subdivided into an unmarked term and two explicitly Inclusive terms, Inclusive of [Adr, Plur], or Inclusive of [Other]. These relations are shown in figure 4.2.

Figure 4.2 shows graphically the asymmetry between the participant categories: the Spkr categories have the most taxonomic depth, contrasting number, presence or absence of Inclusion, and participant category of the included one(s). Furthermore, the terminal forms at the bottom are arrayed in a hierarchical fashion, recapitulating the order of table 4.3: the referent of -ó?on can include participants fitting all descriptions to the right of it; the referent of -é?eš can include participants fitting all descriptions to the right of it but none of those to its left. Third person -ó?ob' is just Other and never includes within its reference the current Spkr or Adr. The most inclusive form in terms of reference is the one with the richest formal subdivision.

In the descriptive framework of this book, the categories in figure 4.2 are R values, that is, relational predicates that link a referential object to an indexical ground. In terms of identifying referents, the pronouns function in basically the same way as do other shifters, through the Figure-Ground pairing. This implies that in order to compute the reference of any of these terms, we must ground it to an indexical field. The remarks in §4.2.3 on the alternative interpretations of the pronouns illustrated the necessity of indexical grounding. A different individual is identified according to whether the form is computed relative to the current corporeal field ('I' = animator), as quoted speech relative to a narrated field ('I' = narrated figure), or as fantasy relative to a hypothetical field ('I' = projected figure).

What is most important for the conventional R values in figure 4.2 is that they remain more or less constant across transpositions and embeddings. The fact that speakers can transpose a first person form in quotation does not mean that the distinction between animator and author has any place in the conventional categories of the language. Rather, this is a fact of use. The only R value needed for such an example is Spkr, signaling identity of referent and utterer. If we fail to make this distinction, then the candidate participant categories proliferate drastically to account for different sorts of multiple embeddings and transpositions that arise only when the categories are configured into frames and frameworks.

To see the difference between the three levels, contrast the paradigm in figure 4.2 with a simple participation frame consisting of a corporeal speaker addressing a corporeal addressee in reference to their current here. Assume the speaker says, *kó?oš té?el a?* 'let's go there (this way)', while pointing out the direction in which the two will proceed on foot (a routine utterance in Maya; see chap. 9). In figure 4.2, categories of person encoded in the Maya language are displayed in a taxonomic hierarchy which relates them to each other by opposing them but does not relate them to each other or to other demonstrative elements by combining them nor to the indexical grounds with which they must be paired in order to make reference to actual participants. In the syntagmatic context of a frame, these other factors do come into play. The first person plural inflection combines with the sociocentric Immediate category of the DLOC to project a participant frame something like the following:[28]

Spkr$_{corp}$ leads Adr$_{corp}$ on a trajectory away from the current locus

In the simple phenomenal framework we have set up, we have assumed that the two are on foot and can further assume that it is DC speaking to Man walking slightly ahead of him, traversing a section of woods on the way to a homestead where DC will perform a rain ceremony and Man will assist him. These further assumptions pertain to the 'local' framework of utterance, the sociocultural particulars occupying the frame in a unique case. They do not belong to the schematic frame(s) instantiated, and surely not to the linguistic categories whose use calls up the frames. Similarly, if we assume that the utterance is actually issued in quotation, as DC recounts to me what he said to Man the day before (while they were traversing, etc.), then there is an indexical transposition. While quotation may correspond to a schematic frame type (see chapter 5), this instance of it occurs in the phenomenal framework we have assumed. Indexical transposition does not belong to the linguistic categories of person but to the frames and frameworks in which they are used.

In chapter 5, we will examine some routine participant frames in relation to the social situations in which they arise in Maya culture. In a figure-ground approach such as the one proposed here, we can take transpositions into account systematically without confusing them with the relational values themselves. If we fail to distinguish the referential figure from the indexical ground, on the other hand, the result is not only an erroneous, flattened view of the referential structure but a proliferation of interactive relations masquerading as grammatical ones. The routinization and default assumptions discussed in §4.1.3 overdetermine the fixing of the indexical ground in the corporeal field of the animator and receiver. This can be overridden easily, of course, but when it is, there is usually an overt indicator, and the relational structure of deictics insures a chain of links between the corporeal field and others to which reference is transposed. The notion of the basic level links participant categories into schematic frames, which are in turn produced in routine interactive frameworks. As we will see, a **framework** may consist of a combination of basic categories and nonbasic incumbencies (see cases of reference in §5.2).

5   Complex Participation Frames in Social Context

5.1 INTRODUCTION

We ended chapter 4 with the three-way distinction between participant **categories** as paradigmatically defined, participant **frames** as schematic configurations of categories corresponding to actional wholes, and interactive **frameworks**, which are the actual ongoing processes in which frames are used by real actors for real communicative purposes. We suggested that communicative practices, as they unfold in frameworks, tend to produce schematic frames, because of the regularities of linguistic categories and the resources they provide for metalinguistic regimentation, discourse genres, and the tendency of actors to interact in habitual ways. We examined the linguistic forms of participant reference and what appear to be basic level participant frames in Maya.

This chapter moves beyond basic level participant frames (henceforth P frames) to explore more complicated kinds of participation, such as reported speech, transposed demonstrative reference, ways of highlighting or excluding a copresent participant, and the constrained participations of ritual performance. These communicative contexts have in common that the P frames they entail are in some way elaborated: the normal identity relation between corporeally engaged individuals, on the one hand, and the Spkr, Adr roles encoded in their speech, on the other, may fail to obtain. Reported speech works this way, insofar as the Spkr performing the report is distinct from the (narrated) Spkr whose speech is reported. Alternatively, an actual copresent Adr can be referred to in the third person and thereby excluded from the frame projected by the utterance. This occurs in Maya, particularly in speech directed at domestic dogs. In Maya shamanic ritual, the constraints on participant involvement are severe, with the effect that the P frames typical of ritual events are highly specialized and include roles and occupancies not often operative in everyday interaction.

5.1.1 Complex P Frames

Nonbasic P frames pose an important descriptive problem for the pragmatics of deixis. At least two alternative strategies are available to describe
them: (i) increase the inventory of available participant roles, for instance, by way of a feature analysis such as that suggested by Levinson
(1987); or (ii) derive the complexity from the embedding of multiple
frames, each of which is in itself relatively simple.[1] The first alternative
risks multiplying the inventory of roles, perhaps indefinitely. The second
alternative gets by on a simpler inventory of P roles but requires a set of
principles for the amalgamation of simple P frames into complex ones.
Rather than posit [Animator [Author, Principal]] categories to describe
quotation, one could posit just a single role Spkr instantiated twice [Spkr1
[Spkr2]]. The two approaches are, of course, not mutually exclusive, as
Goffman's work demonstrates.

In this book, the second approach is emphasized for several reasons. It
fits naturally with the description of demonstrative reference in terms of a
referential figure set off from an indexical ground. This is a plus, because
complex frames arise in the other categories of deixis as well, and we find
spatial, temporal, and other kinds of transpositions to go along with participant ones. Take the case of locatives, like 'here'. Do we need to posit
a new spatial R value in English to account for its reference in an utterance like the following? 'I recall that she was very upset and told me they
had said to her "Stay right here until we get back." But she hadn't waited
after all'. Just as the referent of the final 'we' exists only at several steps
remove from the corporeal field of utterance, so the referent of 'here' is at
the same remove. Embeddings and transpositions of the P frame in no
way alter or multiply the inventory of figural R values (of which participant categories are a subset). Instead, they arise out of displacements of
the indexical ground from its normal (basic level) locus in the corporeal
field. In the R(x,i) relational structure, we have already available a way
of talking about complex frames without increasing the number of basic
categories.

A second reason for preferring the embedding solution is that it makes
more productive use of the difference between P roles, P frames (**configurations** of roles), and P frameworks (**occupied** configurations of frames).
We can derive the complexity of at least some P frames, not from an expanded inventory of roles available in a community, but from the social
standards of role incumbency and assignment. These apply in the first instance to frameworks, constraining and regimenting what real actors do in

the course of communicating. However, modes or features of role incumbency can be habituated and conventionalized in schematic frames too. Thus we can speak of a frame consisting of a configuration of roles occupied in a typical way. C. Goodwin (1981) and Levinson (1987) are undoubtedly right in emphasizing that P roles must be distinguished from incumbencies. The parallel distinction applies also to demonstrative reference, separating the referential categories of deixis, the R values, from the realization of those values in indexical frameworks, the i in $R(x,i)$. However, just like referents, indexical grounds can be typified and schematized into standard frames, and this means that types of incumbency can be part of P frames, as well as part of frameworks. By exploring frame embedding and displaced incumbency as sources of frame complexity, we can simplify the description considerably.

In his discussion of footing, Goffman (1981:128ff.) described interactive "frames" as sets of social relations between actors, their situational alignments to one another, to their speech, and to the larger engagement.[2] Frames of interpretation define 'what is going on' in social situations and are built up in accordance with "principles of organization which govern events" (Goffman 1974:40). Two characteristics of frames in this sense stand out: (i) the fact that they are multiply combined and superimposed in talk (through what Goffman called 'embedding'); and (ii) the fact that speakers shift their footing among them with great ease, signaling their current incumbency with 'kèys'. 'Keys' are signs (not necessarily linguistic) that indicate a speaker's alignment in relation to the current interaction, such as a wink signaling irony, a shift in accent signaling intimacy or anger, a shift from *tu* to *vous* pronoun forms signaling estrangement, or a shift into controlled breath groups signaling the onset of prayer (Hanks 1984c).

5.1.2 Fields, Frame Spaces, and Genres

Whereas a **framework** is an actional whole sustained in the course of practice, a sociocultural **field** is what organizes the possibilities for producing frameworks (see §2.4).[3] Fields regulate agents' access to frames by determining the principles of legitimation according to which given forms of engagement are possible, probable, impossible, defensible, 'accountable' (Garfinkel [1962] 1972), negatively or positively valued. In Bourdieu's (1983) terms, a field, such as the literary-artistic, scientific, or academic fields in contemporary France, is a space of positions and position takings (*prises de position*) that presents itself to each agent as a range of possibilities, or a 'space of possibles' (344).[4] From the perspective of an agent, a field is defined by the relation between the chances of access to positions and the dispositions or orientations of each agent relative to them. Fields are historically derived and differ from one another in several important respects: (i) relative autonomy or subordination with respect to each other (Bourdieu 1983:319ff.); (ii) the character of the boundaries distinguishing the field and the mechanisms used to regulate access to it; (iii) the degree to which the field is institutionalized and recognized by actors in the society; (iv) the possibly cross-cutting principles of legitimation governing action in the field (1983:331); (v) the rhythm and sequencing of action in the field and the overall rate at which it changes; and (vi) the objective distribution of capital (symbolic as well as economic) among positions in the field.

There is a strong affinity between social fields in the foregoing sense and what Goffman called a "frame space." According to Goffman, a frame space designates the set of possible but not currently realized footings available to interactants at any point in talk (see §5.2.1). Within any frame space, interactants actually take up various footings in their utterances, while leaving others as unrealized but relevant alternatives. A 'space of possibilities' in Goffman's sense is defined within a field of action in Bourdieu's sense, the joint result being to overdetermine (guide, constrain, govern) the kinds of P frames produced.[5] Individual agents have at their disposal certain participants, in which their own likely roles are to some extent limited. A storyteller has great latitude in the kinds of frames (s)he projects in the description, but the actual indexical frame of the telling still constrains the footings (s)he adopts relative to his or her audience (§5.2.2). A speaker teaching her language to a foreigner may produce indefinitely many hypothetical frames for illustration, but she does so within the frame space of the pedagogical interaction itself (§5.2.3). In performing a ritual discourse, a shaman creates a precise diagrammatic icon of the cosmos, which by transposition alters the current context of production. But this process is defined in the field of shamanic practice and anchored in the special frame space of performance (§5.3). In each case, the local production of relatively complex P frameworks takes place within a particular space of possibilities, which may be defined relative to one or more fields. Relations around the homestead, for instance, can be seen to constitute a domestic field in which coresidents are the participants, while shamanic practice is clearly a specialized field with numerous boundary mechanisms. To each corresponds a frame space within which actors' engagements occur.

A description of frame spaces can be made more precise in turn by reference to the notion of **discourse genres**. Genres, viewed as socially constituted types of verbal practice, help define the range of possible footings a speaker has access to at any given point in an interaction (cf. §3.4). For example, in telling a certain kind of story, it is expectable that the teller will use certain footings, whereas others are unlikely or out of the question. The P frames produced and sustained in ritual events must be investigated relative to their respective performance genres, since not all types work the same way. As we will see, some features are common to shamanic prayer in general, some are specific to curing events, and others are specific to divination.

The necessity of moving beyond frames to some more comprehensive unit(s) such as the field or the frame space is evident when one considers that speakers and addressees in society do not all have equal access to participation frames. Not everyone can play every position he wishes. Rather, the mapping between agents and participant roles is quite constrained and may be subject to dispute, competition, negotiation, boundary mechanisms, and conventions of taking up or vacating frames. Certain P frames themselves arise only under restricted circumstances, such as the carefully bounded engagement between a shaman and his spirit addressee, or the 'imperial' first person singular of a head of household speaking for an entire collectivity. These simple but basic facts are not accounted for in a description of categories, or even frames, as defined here, because they derive from the social system beyond the immediate frame. The relation between an ongoing participation framework and the larger social system is mediated by what will be called the **frame space**.

The focus of this chapter on complex frames leads naturally to the relation between P frames, frameworks, and the encompassing social frame spaces in which they arise. Agents' rights of access to P frames—their possibilities for incumbency in frameworks—are governed by the social field in which the interaction is taking place. The field has among its conditions the production of discourse fitting certain genres. Genres define the range of possible frame types with which they are compatible, otherwise known as the frame space. This, in turn, is the background or horizon from which actual frameworks are constructed. Frames, the schematized resources combined in frameworks, are generated partly from the immanent regularities of practice and partly through the reproduction of socially recognized genres.

5.2 DECENTERED PARTICIPANT FRAMES

This section will present a range of nonbasic P frames in Maya, focusing on the embedding and combination of participation roles as a source of frame complexity. This focus leads me to posit a relation between a variety of phenomena usually treated as distinct. These include explicit quotation (direct discourse), indirect report, 'transposition' of deictic categories (Bühler 1982:210ff.), certain kinds of highly creative reference, and the subtle shifts in perspective that can be seen to underlie much of deictic reference in connected discourse. These phenomena have in common that they rest on displacement or alteration of the indexical ground of utterances. In the clearest cases, the i ground of demonstrative reference is transposed from the current corporeal sphere of utterance and projected into some other sphere. This necessarily alters the referential interpretation of most shifters, although obviously it need not alter the conventional relational values of the forms. An 'I' in quoted speech could well *refer* to the corporeal Adr, as in 'You said, "I don't want any",,' but 'I' never *means* Adr for linguistic purposes. In less clear cases, an utterance may project a P frame only subtly different from the actual one. Imagine a speaker who hollers to her interlocutor, 'It's right here on the left', where the underlined terms are to be interpreted from the perspective of Adr, not the Spkr. The shift in perspective is a transposition, or what Lyons (1977: 578–79) called a "deictic projection". All of these examples involve what I will call 'decentered' reference.

Shifters (pronouns, demonstratives, tense) are the prototypical exemplars of interactively 'centered' referential categories, in that they identify referential objects relative to indexical grounds. The term 'decentered' will be used narrowly to describe certain uses of centered linguistic categories.[6] These uses, individual tokens and classes of them, have in common that the indexical ground of reference has been decentered from the actual phenomenal context of speech. If a deictic category is normally egocentric, picking a referent relative to the Spkr, then it is decentered whenever it is used so as to index, not the current utterer, but rather: (i) his or her interlocutor; (ii) some narrative personage identified in adjacent discourse; (iii) some other speaker, possibly himself or herself under different circumstances; (iv) any other non-ego-inclusive ground independently signaled or reconstructible in the utterance context.

This way of formulating 'decentering' has two consequences. First, it requires that one specify the 'normal' ground of the category, in order to identify pragmatic departures from it. If a language had a spatial deictic category prototypically grounded on the Adr, meaning something like 'there (where you are)', then that category would be decentered if used from the perspective of the Spkr or anyone other than the Adr. Decentered uses are pragmatically foregrounded in that they depart from the normal, automatic patterns of reference; like all cases of foregrounding, the marked, nonautomatic use can be identified only in relation to the unmarked, automatic one. Second, virtually every case of decentering involves a recentering. Shifter categories do not lose their indexical component, nor is it neutralized, canceled, or filtered out in decentered usage. The closest we come to this is the 'mention' mode, in which the linguistic form is held up for comment rather than being used for reference at all (cf. Hanks In press).[7] In unattributed mention, such as ' "here" is a four-letter word', the deictic presumably projects no indexical ground, just as it picks no referent. In all referential uses, however, whether decentered or not, a ground is in play. When a mother projects speech into the mouth of an infant, 'Oh mommy, I like this!' while feeding her, there is actually a recentering: the tokens 'I' and 'this', usually used from the perspective of the corporeal Spkr, have been displaced onto the infant. Hence the Spkr becomes 'mommy' and the addressee 'I'.

Centering involves the ways in which utterances project P frames in their backgrounded indexical components. The distinction between the referential focus and the indexical ground elements in deixis provides a simple but powerful way of describing decentered uses of the forms. As suggested above, in many cases, we can say straightforwardly that the i ground has been shifted away from its normal anchor in the corporeal sphere, and therefore the R value is to be computed relative to some new, decentered ground. This describes the shifts in the preceding example of transposition. It is important to remember, however, that the implementation of referential values of demonstratives and pronouns can also alter the indexical ground of an utterance. An initiating 'you' can be said to create a phenomenal, indexical relation between the utterer and the addressee by way of referring to the Adr.

In Goffman's terms, the referential figures projected by demonstrative use include and can transform participant configurations in the actual utterance framework (see §4.1.1). This means that a sudden change in the indexical ground can result from relatively creative acts of reference and not only from wholesale displacements of the ground, such as quotation. Still more attenuated instances of shifts in the indexical framework can be seen over the course of much connected speech. In chapter 9, for instance, I will show how speakers shifted their spatial and participant frames in the course of recounting the history of their homes. Analogous processes are at work in much of narrative, where a teller portrays and transforms his or her relation to events in the story, as well as to the interlocutor(s). Footing shifts are instances of decentering insofar as they alter the immediate indexical ground by shifting it or embedding others within it, or it within others.

5.2.1 Frames, Simple and Complex

'Embedding' is one of the three central themes that Goffman announces in *Forms of Talk* (1981:3), and it is relevant to the problem of decentering. Goffman uses the term initially in reference to reported speech, in which the current utterer is distinct from the 'subject' of the utterance. But subsequently, he grounds the notion in the fact that speakers project **figures** of themselves through talk (cf. §4.1.2) and can 'displace' time and place by representing their own past (or fantasized) utterances or thoughts (1981:147–49). This then leads to the existence of multiple embeddings, as in the example, '[To the best of my recollection, I think that [I said [I once lived that sort of life]]]', where each bracket marks a deeper embedding. The idea is that within a single phenomenal utterance, several utterances can be animated. In storytelling commonly, narrators are "likely to break narrative frame at strategic junctures: to recap for new listeners; to provide . . . encouragement to listeners to wait for the punch line, . . . or to backtrack a correction for any felt failure" (1981:153). Thus, embedding need not involve reported speech, but it always involves at least two footings, along with their respective associated figures. Stated in present terms, a single phenomenal framework can include multiple frames among which speakers can shift their indexical ground (footing), sometimes maintaining more than one ground at a time (as in quotation or other transpositions). Goffman (1981:153) went so far as to observe that not only utterances but even interactional arrangements can be embedded. Entire P frameworks, including their spatial and temporal dimensions, can be schematized in the form of frames and transposed from one indexical context to another.

The referential projections that produce embeddings in Goffman's terms, and the indexical displacements that produce decenterings in ours, are both ways of abstracting away from the corporeal field of speech. As we saw in chapters 3 and 4, corporeality is basic in referential practice, but it is not invariant, nor can it be equated with the physical body in any of its capacities. The phenomenal frameworks in which embodied reference takes place usually arise in corporeal fields but typically involve frames of reference other than corporeality as well. The problem is to determine what role the bodily ground of participant engagement plays in relation to other, coarticulated grounds. In this chapter I will show that the referential interpretation of shifters automatically provides a set of links binding nonbodily frames in discourse back to the ground of copresence between animators and receivers. The deictic mechanisms that engage the body in referential practice simultaneously provide the means for disengaging it, or at least masking its presence beneath layers of discourse. Phenomenal frameworks are embodied in their entirety but are bodily only in some parts.

Although he does not develop it systematically, Goffman was clearly awake to the question of how multiple frames fit together into a single whole. He drew together the different footing possibilities to which a speaker has access, in conjunction with the participation statuses (s)he could enjoy, into what he called a frame space. "When the individual speaks, he avails himself of certain options and foregoes others, operating within a frame space, but with any moment's footing uses only some of this space" (1981:230). The notion of frame space as used in this book developed from Goffman's usage. Note that whereas a framework is the actual engagement sustained by interactants, a frame space encompasses this actuality in the horizon of possibilities unrealized. The framework provides the primary indexical ground(s) of reference, but is itself grounded in a frame space. This suggests a two-layered indexical ground: the inherently local one(s) in the framework and the further backgrounded one of the space of possibilities (see §10.4). Frame spaces are 'normatively allocated' and imply limits beyond which a speaker is in violation, such as when a person self-intrusively comments on his own performance during it. Recall that the idea of a limited range of possible frames to which an agent has access is analogous to what we are calling a 'field', in that both regulate frame production (albeit in different ways; cf. §5.1.2).

In asking how social situations constrain the footings adopted by speakers, Goffman draws on his long-term interest in the phenomenon of interactive involvement, while simultaneously positing the new social formation 'frame space'. Unfortunately, his discussion tends to treat the former as a matter of the engagement of the individual in his or her utterance, a 'production format' defined independently of the addressee and other coparticipants. This is consistent with his separate descriptions of production and reception formats and with the definition of a frame space as that which an individual occupies. But an interactive frame space would necessarily include more than individuals, and it is unlikely that the positions available to the coparticipants could be treated as independent of each other. What Goffman fails to suggest, but the study of deixis make clear, is that the **interperspectival** space consisting of that which is mutual, reciprocal, or distributed among coparticipants is also part of the frame space. It is within this total range of possibilities that action is centered, and that decenterings take place.

We can presume that Goffman's descriptions of complex events like lectures and radio talk productions are meant to illustrate general phenomena at play in everyday talk too. Frame spaces and their attendant constraints are part of all interaction and include not only the current state of talk but the range of possible configurations of coengagement available at any point. It becomes obvious from Goffman's discussion that even the simplest frame spaces are actually quite complex and socially regulated. Hence, we would expect that the social identities of agents and the fields within which interaction occurs would both affect the frame configurations projected in talk. Centering and decentering of indexical categories are inevitably part of the social process of generating frameworks in social spaces; the center shifts as interactants displace their assumed zero point to different oriented subspaces within the frame space.

The social present of an act of reference, the 'now' in which practice occurs, is therefore a layered construction which includes at least the following four factors: (i) the corporeal arrangement of interactants relative to each other and to the social field; (ii) the participant frames projected by the referential and descriptive values of the utterance (which may or may not coincide with the corporeal frame); (iii) participants' indexical footings in the emergent framework; (iv) some array of possible but non-actual arrangements that serves as a horizon against which the act takes place (and without which the here-now of the utterance would lose its distinctness).

In order to better describe the schematic constructs corresponding to this composite context, it is helpful to distinguish among types of frame. Two obvious dimensions of contrast are degree of compositionality and degree of typicality. With respect to the latter, we have introduced and will return in detail to the distinction between basic level deictic acts and decentered ones. With respect to compositionality, we need minimally to differentiate what I call 'simple' from 'complex' frames, where complex frames are based on a combination of two or more simple ones. For example, the corporeal field of interaction corresponds to a simple frame, which includes the physical arrangement of coparticipants and figural referents, their relative contiguity, perceptibility, attention focus, and bodily postures.[8] If A and B are face-to-face, talking about some referent *x,* say an irrigation canal off to their side, then the actual corporeal relation between A, B, and the canal corresponds to a simple frame, available to A and B as a resource for reference. In many daily situations, the corporeal arrangements of participants and referents are routinized, typical, deeply familiar to them. In describing corporeality as a frame, it is this familiarity that we focus on. At the same time, it is clear that corporeal relations are emergent and that the schematic quality of the present is in tension with its emergent quality.

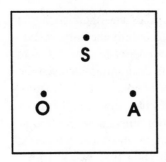

Fig. 5.1. Simple participation frame.

Another example of a simple frame is the referential-descriptive event projected in an utterance like 'it is here'. Through the R values of the pronoun and the deictic, the tense and the semantics of the verb 'be', this sentence predicates a locative relation between an object and a space, within some time frame (assuming it is not a generic proposition). Similarly, 'the book is on the table', 'I dived in the lake', 'we'll arrive in a minute', all project states of affairs through their referential-descriptive content, through what they say about the world, and these can be schematized in frames. Since our focus is on participation frames, as opposed to other kinds, we will simplify still further, using the role values corresponding to participant deictics, as in figure 5.1.

The referential frame and the corporeal frame are distinct; what a speaker says about the world is different from the situation in which (s)he says it. For our purposes, we will treat these two as separate simple frames, whose relevant schematic structure is approximately as in figure 5.1. We may need to add more components or differentiate relations among elements in a simple frame, but this will suffice for present purposes. As a corollary of the default assumptions outlined in chapter 4 and the special relation between deixis and the body, the corporeal frame of interaction is privileged among simple frames. No one needs to comment on the bodily engagements sustained during interaction in order for them to be available to the parties and relevant to communicative practice. The pervasiveness of deixis in speech is evidence that speakers attend to corporeality, even in formulating reference to other things. (Gesture, gaze, and alignment provide further evidence; cf. research by C. and M. H. Goodwin.)

The act of reference always involves a complex frame as we have defined it: the corporeal one in which the act occurs serves as an indexical ground from which the referential frame is projected. It is immediately evident that reported speech involves a complex frame, since the reported speaker is embedded within the discourse of the corporeal frame, and the quoted speech attributed to him projects yet a third frame. In §5.2.2 we will examine attested instances of quoted speech in Maya that involve four or more frames at once. Similarly, I will argue that transpositions require complex schemata involving three or more component frames. Centering as treated here presupposes for its definition a complex frame, and recentering therefore does too. Based on the minimal case, a complex frame can be described by the diagram in figure 5.2 (or some elaboration of it for cases of three or more frames in the discourse).

The question naturally arises of how component frames in a complex hang together. How are they related to each other, and how do we know? In the case of deictic reference, the relational values of the forms are what mediates between the two frames. By way of features such as Spkr, Adr, Immed, and Anaphoric, the pronouns, demonstratives, and deictic adverbs precisely specify contours of the referential-descriptive (narrated) frame relative to the ongoing one in which the discourse is produced. We can represent this as in figure 5.3, where the relational value is an arc from ground to figure. There are undoubtedly other mechanisms that serve to bind constituent parts of complex frames, just as there are other forms of indexicality apart from the ground of deictic reference and other modes of description beyond R values. But for describing indexical reference, figure 5.3 provides a relatively straightforward notation that we can make more precise in the course of applying it to actual examples. Moreover, this mechanism is operative in both individual acts of reference and the production of text in longer discourses.

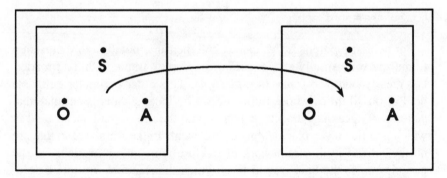

Fig. 5.2. Complex participation frame.

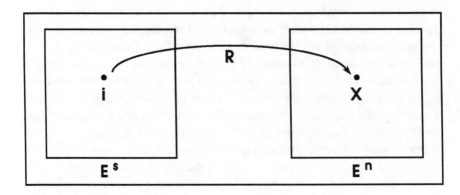

R is the relational feature of the shifter.
i is the indexical ground (in the current speech event frame).
X is the referential object (in the narrated event frame).

Fig. 5.3. Relational structure of deixis as a complex frame.

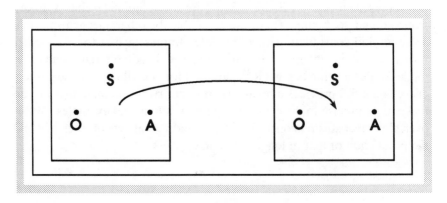

Fig. 5.4. Frame space.

For heuristic purposes, we can extend the same notation to represent a frame space by simply encompassing a complex frame within a broader, less clearly bounded frame (see fig. 5.4). This outer perimeter defines a field of possibilities whose limits are set by local standards and habitual patterns of speaking, discourse genres, and the preexistent social field in which practice takes place. Objects and events in the frame space that are not actualized in the framework of talk are nonetheless available to the participants as the background from which their actions are intelligible. When we describe patterns of referential practice around the Maya homestead or in the context of ritual performance, we are building up a frame space in which any particular instance can be understood. Many aspects of frame spaces, though probably not all, can be brought into referential focus in talk, and when they are, they enter into the schematic frames of discourse.

5.2.2 Varieties of Decentered P Frames

By arguing that reported speech, deictic transpositions, and certain kinds of creative reference are all instances of decentering, I do not wish to suggest that they are equivalent. We can distinguish a range of decentering types, which differ from one another at least in terms of the manner and relative explicitness of their formal keying and in their pragmatic corollaries. While no modern linguistic accounts have attempted to link these different pragmatic phenomena, to my knowledge, both Bühler ([1932] 1967:219) and Jespersen ([1924] 1965:290) suggested that deictic transposition, or 'shifting' in Jespersen's terms, is closely related to reported speech. The reason is evidently that both of these linguists characterized reported speech partly by way of its effect on the interpretation of pronouns and demonstratives. The effect is indeed analogous to transposition in direct (nonreported) speech, since the ground relative to which referents are identified is **recentered** in both cases. The recentering takes place within a complex frame in which the zero point is transposed from the corporeal frame to the represented one.

Furthermore, Jespersen saw a stylistic relation between canonical transposition and direct quotation. He described them as "an outcome of the same psychological state with its vivid imagination of the past that calls forth the 'dramatic present tense'. Hence, we often find that tense employed in the inserted 'says he, say(s) I' instead of 'said'" ([1924] 1965: 290). The 'dramatic present tense' here is a classic instance of transposition, in which the narrator projects himself or herself into the narrated frame. Beyond the structural similarity of projecting an indexical ground distinct from the actual corporeal one, decenterings have in common the stylistic effect of vividness.

5.2.2.1 Canonical Quotation

In this section, the main focus will be on quotation as a kind of indexical transposition rather than on the logical structure and derivation of quoted and indirect discourse (cf. Partee 1973; Platts 1979:chap. 5; Banfield 1982:chap. 1). Jespersen ([1924] 1965:290) distinguished the two kinds of report by saying that in direct quotation, one purports to reproduce the exact words of an original speaker or writer (de dicto interpretation), whereas in indirect quotation, "one adapts the words according to the circumstances in which they are now quoted" (de re interpretation). Quotation reproduces an approximation of the original utterance, whereas indirect discourse produces a rough paraphrase of it. Thus, when Man says in the course of a story, *kuš tuún le tó?on a? kih e tùurkos* ' "And what about ours?" say the Turks', he produces the direct quote within the frame projected by 'say the Turks'. Supposedly the question actually reproduces the utterance of the Turks, whereas an indirect paraphrase might go something like, *le tùurkos k'aátik b'á?aš kúŋ ?učul ti le utí?aló?ob'* 'the Turks ask what'll happen with theirs'. Thus direct quotation is formally closer to an original saying, whereas indirect discourse is more tenuously linked.

For the purposes of this discussion, direct quotation will be treated as decentered, meaning that the indexical ground is displaced from the current corporeal frame of the Spkr making the quote. It should be noted that if one takes as starting point the original utterance in its phenomenal field, then the inverse holds: direct quotation is described precisely as nondecentered, since none of the indexicals have been transposed into the current frame of the report. This is the perspective Jespersen ([1924] 1965: 292) adopts, for instance, when he says that in indirect discourse, person, tense, and mood are 'shifted'. My reasons for starting from the perspective of the quotation and not from what is quoted include the following: (i) Speakers 'quote' imagined, fictitious, and otherwise nonexistent speech events, making it difficult to consistently adopt the quoted frame as primary. (ii) It is not always clear what direct utterance corresponds to a stretch of indirect discourse, which can be a relatively loose 'paraphrase' (cf. Banfield 1982:26–27 on nonderivability of indirect discourse from direct discourse in syntactic terms). Hence, to start from an original utterance is to lose the comparability of the two forms of report. (iii) Frame embedding occurs in the quote, not in the initial utterance that will be quoted subsequently.[9] (iv) Quotation is a kind of usage occurring in a phenomenal field, which we will therefore examine as such.

The formal marking of quoted speech in Maya consists primarily of (i) the framing devices corresponding to verbs of communication; (ii) the manipulation of shifter categories to project the indexical frame of the quoted event; and (iii) the use of interjections, interrogative and imperative modes, and expressive particles which cannot be neatly paraphrased or are excluded from indirect report (cf. Banfield 1982:28; Jespersen [1924] 1965:292).[10]

Framing keys corresponding to verbs of communication in Maya include verbal expressions and particles. The only form reserved for direct quotation is the particle *k-*, which obligatorily follows the quoted discourse and takes suffixal person marking for a quoted subject. This form is used in re-presenting both speech and gestures (antecedent to the report or fantasized). Lucy (In press) has shown the form to be grammatically intermediate between a verbal element and a particle. Like a verb of saying, it inflects for a communicating subject and can take a dative complement, as in:

(1)   yàan im-bin   {k-ih, k-uy-á?alik}   t-en
        Aux Pro1-Vb {Quot-Trm, Aux-Pro3-Vb} Dat-Pro1
        ' "I've gotta go," he said to me.'

Unlike standard verbs, however, the particle cannot bear tense, aspect, or mode marking, cannot be questioned, negated, or adverbially modified in any way to describe the utterance it reports. The fact that it must follow the quote also makes it unlike a verb, since verbs of speaking can either follow or precede the report in Maya.

(2)   a. kuyá?alik t-en (bey a?) yàan im-bin

        b. *kih t-en (bey a?) yàan im-bin
           'He says to me (this): "I've gotta go." '

In general, there are fewer verbs of speaking in Maya than in English, and they are used less frequently. The performative usage, 'I (hereby) tell/ask/request (etc.) (to you) that S' is particularly rare, even making the necessary adjustments for tense and adverbial modification. The one notable exception to this generalization is ritual speech, in which metalinguistic verbs are used very frequently to perform specific illocutionary acts (see §5.3). The most common forms are -á?alik 'to say it', and t'àan 'to speak, address (subject = a person), to mean (subject = a sign), language'. The transitive form t'anik 'to speak it' may take a language, a linguistic expression, or a message as object, as in kut'anik màaya 'he speaks Maya', or an individual, as in kut'anikeč 'he addresses you'. Both verbs can be used to key either direct or indirect discourse.

The transposition of shifter categories is a second major resource for signaling quotation. Rather than occurring external to the quoted discourse and framing it, as verbs of communication do, transposed, 'shifted' shifters signal that the strip of discourse of which they are a part is itself quoted. Hence, the shifters in the boldface portion of the following example are transposed to signal quotation.

(3)   **way   k-in-kutal e?   k-ih**
        DLOC   Aux-Apro-Vb Trm Quot-Trm
        here I sit he says
        ' "I'll sit here," he says.'

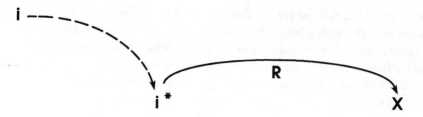

Fig. 5.5. Transposition of the indexical ground. The referent (X) is identified relative to a new indexical ground (i*).

In this example, the quotative particle following the boldface discourse works together with the transposed shifters within the quote to key its special status. 'Here' and 'I' refer not to the location of the actual utterance but to the projected location within which the original utterance took place. In normal nontransposed usage, the DLOC *way e?* is used to refer to the region including the corporeal speaker, abbreviated INCL (x,i) where *x* is the referent and *i* the indexical ground. In the quotation, on the other hand, the indexical ground has been transposed so that what is included in the region referred to is not the phenomenal framework *i* but some other frame *i**. schematically, this decentering can be represented as in figure 5.5. The interpretation of the person reference to 'I' in the quoted discourse would work the same way: it makes reference to an individual occupying the role Spkr in the projected indexical frame, *i**, not in the actual corporeal one, *i*. Consequently, the referent of 'I' in the quote is necessarily distinct from the actual speaker doing the quoting.

Viewed in relation to frame embedding, shifters provide a powerful reference-tracking device. In any anaphoric usage, they maintain sameness of reference over a stretch of discourse and so contribute directly to cohesion in the narrative frame of text (Halliday and Hasan 1976; Halliday 1985; Foley and Van Valin 1984). More significant for our present purposes, however, is the way that shifters contribute to reference tracking *across different frames*. In routine direct reference and description, they relate the projected frame to the actual current one, as shown in figure 5.3. In transposed usages, they relate the projected referent to a projected indexical frame, as shown in figure 5.5. And when transposed and nontransposed usages are combined in an utterance, the shifters track reference across the embeddings. Consider the simple paradigm in table 5.1. In the paradigm in table 5.1, the pronoun occurring in position 1 is within the quoted discourse and is therefore transposed relative to the corporeal frame, whereas the forms in positions 2 and 3 are nontransposed. Thus

TABLE **5.1** Pronouns in Reported Speech

Position 1	2	3	1	2	3
	k-en	*t-eč*		I said to	him
	ken	*ti ʔ-Ø*		I said to	you
	keč	*ten*		you said to	me
'hé ʔ im b'in e ʔ',	*keč*	*ti ʔ-Ø*	'I'll go',	you said to	him
	kih	*ten*		he said to	me
	kih	*teč*		he said to	you
	kih	*ti ʔ-Ø*		he said to	him
	ken	*teč*		I said to	him
	ken	*ti ʔ-Ø*		I said to	you
	keč	*ten*		you said to	me
'hé ʔ a b'in e ʔ',	*keč*	*ti ʔ-Ø*	'You'll go',	you said to	him
	kih	*ten*		he said to	me
	kih	*teč*		he said to	you
	kih	*ti ʔ-Ø*		he said to	him
	ken	*teč*		I said to	you
	ken	*ti ʔ-Ø*		I said to	him
	keč	*ten*		you said to	me
'hé ʔ u b'in e ʔ',	*keč*	*ti ʔ-Ø*	'He'll go',	you said to	him
	kih	*ten*		he said to	me
	kih	*teč*		he said to	you
	kih	*ti ʔ-Ø*		he said to	him

if A says to B, ' "**I**'ll go," **you** said to **me**', then the forms 'you' and 'me' are directly interpreted as referring to A and B, respectively, whereas the 'I' cannot be interpreted directly as the current Speaker. It refers to B, not to A.

These examples consist of complex frames in which three simple frames are related to one another: (i) the corporeal speech event frame, *Es,* in the role of indexical ground; (ii) the projected speech frame described by the quotative particle with addressee in dative case, *Esn;* and (iii) the projected event of going predicated by the quoted utterance, *En.*[11] The relations among the three are represented schematically in figure 5.6.

The speech event projected by the phrase 'you said to me' (etc.) is intermediate between the indexical frame (*Es*) and the narrated event predicated by 'I'll go' (*En*).[12] It functions simultaneously as the object of reference and description relative to the corporeal frame, and as the transposed indexical ground relative to the narrated event of going. Because of this, there is necessarily an interdependence between the interpretation of the pronoun in the quoted speech (position 1) and the pronouns in the

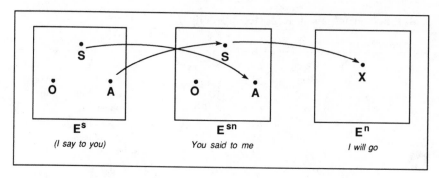

Fig. 5.6. Quoted speech frames.

quoting speech (positions 2, 3) in table 5.1. The general rules stated in terms of the positions in table 5.1 are:

(4)   a. If the quoted pronoun in position 1 is the Spkr form, then it is always coreferential with the pronoun in position 2, which refers to the subject (Spkr) of the verb of speaking (Spkr = Spkr).

        b. If the quoted pronoun in position 1 is the Adr form, then it is always coreferential with the pronoun in position 3, which refers to the indirect object (Adr) of the verb of speaking (Adr = Adr).

        c. If the quoted pronoun in position 1 is the Other form, then it is never coreferential with either pronoun in position 2 or 3 (Other = Other).

Thus, from ' "You'll go," you said to me' we derive by rule (ii) the equivalence, 'you' = me. From ' "I'll go," he said to you', we derive by rule 1 the equivalence 'I' = he; and from ' "He won't go," he said to me', we get, by rule 3, 'he' = he.

If we take a more complicated example, in which more than three frames are in play, the rules for reference tracking remain constant.

(5)   k-**inw**-áʔalik tiʔ-Ø ká šíʔik-Ø keč tiʔ   -Ø
              ' "I tell   him Ø to go"   you say to him.'
              1   2   3   4   5

Sentence (5) is a fictitious sentence that could be appropriately used in Maya to advise an interlocutor regarding what (s)he should say to some third party. There are at least four frames in play in the example: (i) The actual context of utterance *Es,* A talking to B, which functions as the indexical ground for the pronouns in positions 4 and 5. (ii) The speech event *Esn* projected by the sentence in which 4 and 5 are subject and indirect object, respectively, in which B addresses C, saying to him, 'I tell him to go'. (iii) The second speech event *Esn** projected by the embedded verb of speaking to which the pronouns in positions 1 and 2 are argu-

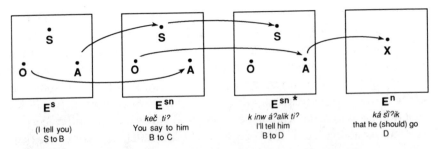

Fig. 5.7. Complex frame: 'I'll tell him that he should go', you say to him.

ments. In this frame, B told D to go. (iv) The narrated event *En* projected by the complement 'he should go', in which D goes. The relation between frames is diagramed in figure 5.7.

What figure 5.7 shows is a chain of relations from the actual corporeal ground in which (5) is uttered through the narrated frame in which some third party (D) goes somewhere. Each speech event frame (indicated by lowercase *s* in notation) functions as the indexical ground relative to which a represented event (indicated by the presence of lowercase *n* for 'narrated', following standard usage) is projected. Thus the frame labeled *Es* serves as the indexical ground relative to which *Esn* is projected, *Esn* in turn serves as the indexical ground relative to which *Esn** is projected and *Esn** is the indexical ground relative to which the event of going is projected. Thus, each of the *Esn* frames has a dual status, as both the projected object of reference and the indexical frame relative to which a further reference is grounded.

The correspondences between these four event frames are subject to the same rules as noted above, which can be restated in general terms as:

(6)   a. If a quoted pronoun is first person, it refers to the speaker in the indexical frame of utterance.

       b. If a quoted pronoun is in second person, it refers to the addressee in the indexical frame of utterance.

       c. If a quoted pronoun is in the third person, it refers to some individual distinct from both speaker and addressee in the indexical frame of utterance.

These three statements account for the interpretation of the pronouns in (5). The Spkr form 'I' in position 1 refers to the individual occupying the speaker role in the quoted frame (by rule a). The Adr form 'you' in position 4 refers to the addressee in the actual indexical frame (by rule b). The two are therefore coreferential, since 'you say' projects the current addressee as speaker in a new utterance frame, and 'I'll tell' issues from that new frame, with the current addressee acting as its speaker. The third person, Other forms in position 2, 3, 5 each refer to a nonparticipant relative to an indexical ground: 'him' in (5) refers to someone other than the coparticipants in the current exchange *Es;* 'him' in 2 refers to someone other than the coparticipants in the *Esn* in which it is uttered. It follows that the forms in 5 and 2 are noncoreferential, since the former projects its referent as addressee in the speech event *Esn* which serves as indexical context for the utterance 'I told him that he should go'. From position 2 to 3, there is no shift in indexical frame, and the two are therefore coreferential, making 3 noncoreferential with position 5.

Working through the correspondences between frames in example (5) makes the interpretation appear quite complex. This appearance is due not to the operation of new principles but to the iterative application of already available ones. The so called 'rules' in (6) are no more than a restatement of the relational R values of the pronouns (see §4.3.1). What (6) says is that the shifters embedded in quotation are interpreted in exactly the same fashion as shifters issuing directly from a current speaker: a referential frame is projected relative to an indexical one. What is special about table 5.1 and example (5) is that more than one indexical frame is in play. Reported speech formulas like 'you say to him' project in their descriptive-referential mode a speech event frame, *Esn,* which can then serve as indexical ground for further referential projections. Because they always articulate indexical with referential frames, shifters provide a natural mechanism for tracking referents across embeddings. The rules for interpretation are the familiar ones of direct speech, just as the roles for participation are the familiar ones from basic level corporeal frames.

Quoted speech is used in Maya conversation for a variety of communicative ends. For example, when a speaker corrects the speech of his interlocutor (s)he may do so by issuing in quotation the correct form. This is what happened in the exchange in example (48) in chapter 4, reproduced here as (7).

(7)   WH: pero lel oʔ tak atíʔaléʔeš
              'But that's for even you all.'

        Mgt: kti aléʔeš **keč**, tumèen tóʔon yete teč
              ' "It's for us all" you (should) say, because (it's) us with you.'
              (BB.4.77)

Margot has used the quotative particle (in boldface) in order to issue in keyed speech an utterance that I ought to say. She puts words in my mouth by attributing to me an utterance I never said (but should have).

This illustrates a very common usage in Maya interaction, whereby a speaker projects words into the mouth of an interlocutor. In banter among solidary interactants, usually of the same sex, quotation is used to poke fun at an addressee, portraying him or her as the speaker of a ludicrous or self-demeaning utterance.

Speakers routinely 'quote' utterances that never occurred and perhaps never will occur as direct speech. The quotative particle and the verbs of communication are used to key the frame embedding, regardless of the existence or nonexistence of the original utterance. Given this, it is not surprising that the devices keying reported speech may be further modified to make clear the modal status of the quoted discourse. In particular, the evidential particle *b'in* indexing hearsay and knowledge derived from custom and the particle *wal e²* indexing that the proposition in which it occurs is merely probable rather than actual can both be used in combination with *k*-quotatives.

(8)   yàan in-tàal   **k-ih**   b'in
        Aux Pro1 Vb   Quot-Trm   Prt
        ' "I will come" he says (so I hear).'

(9)   yàan **b'in** u-tàal
        Aux Prt Pro3 Vb
        'He is to come (so I hear).'

(10)   ká²aná²an-en k-ih   **wal e²**
        Adj-Pro1   Quot-Trm Prt
        ' "I am tired" he says probably.'

The hearsay particle usually occurs immediately after the verbal auxiliary, provided it is an independent word, but may occur alternatively in S-final position, as in *hé² bin usùut uyaánteč e²*, *hé² usùut uyaánteč bin e²* 'He'll return to help you (so I hear).' *wal e²* usually occurs in S-final position, but may occur S-medial following a major predicative element: *hé² usùut uyaánteč wal e²*, *hé² wal usùut uyaánteč e²* 'He'll probably return to help you.' To my knowledge, the two particles are not combined in a single utterance.

When used alone, the hearsay particle in (8–9) does not presuppose any antecedent speech event. The speaker of (9) may have learned that the subject was to go somewhere by being told this, by overhearing, or simply because it is common knowledge. In any case, the form of the utterance marked by this particle is not attributed to any speaker other than the current one. Unlike *k-ih*, *b'in* does not project a new indexical frame, and any shifters accompanying it are interpreted relative to the current frame (corporeal or projected, depending on the case). Also unlike the quotative, *b'in* cannot be inflected for person, nor can it be accompanied by a dative phrase encoding an addressee. Rather than projecting a separate event of speaking, it qualifies the evidential status of what is currently being said. In (8), it qualifies as merely hearsay the speech event projected by the quotative. The parallel phrases *k-u-t'àan b'in* 'he says (it is said)' and *kuyá?alik b'in* 'he says (it is said)' are also attested.

When either the hearsay or the probability particle modifies a verb of speaking or a quotative, it always follows it, as it does in the examples. However, examples such as (11–13) are also attested.

(11)   yàan **b'in** in-tàal   **k-ih**
         Aux Prt Pro1 Vb Quot-Trm
         ' "I will come (so I hear)" he says.'

(12)   ká?aná?an-eč **wal e?** **k-ih**
         Adj-Pro2   Prt   Quot-Trm
         ' "You are tired probably" he says.'

(13)   yàan **b'in** in-tàal   **k-ih**   wal e?
         Aux Prt Pro1 Vb Quot-Trm Prt
         ' "I will come (so I hear)" he probably says.'

In (11–12), the evidentials are part of the original utterance attributed to the subject of the quotative 'he'. That is, they qualify the indexical frame projected as the referent of 'he says'. In figure 5.8, the evidentials index the frame labeled *Esn,* whereas the pronominal suffix on the quotative particle indexes the current *Es.* In (13), the original utterance in *Esn* is qualified as hearsay, as it is in (11), but the current frame in which the quote is described is also qualified as probable. Hence, *b'in* indexes hearsay status in *Esn,* while *wal e?* indexes probability in *Es.*

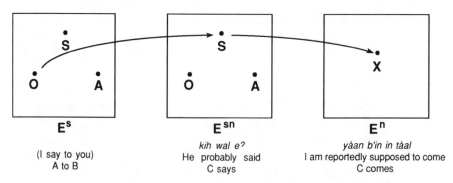

Fig. 5.8. Complex frame: He probably said, 'I'm reportedly supposed to come'.

Canonical quotation, in which a clause describing the original speech event marks off the quoted discourse, is something of a special case. As we have seen, the reported speech event is referred to and described in a report formula, such as 'he says to you'. This object of reference then serves as the indexical frame which grounds the quoted utterance. But projected speech does not always work this way, and Maya speakers, like English speakers, can issue a transposed quote without saying that they are doing so. A shift in voice quality, phrasing, or bodily posture can index that the discourse being produced is to be interpreted as the speech of someone other than the current speaker. These are standard instances of keying in Goffman's sense, where the key accomplishes through indexical decentering what the reported speech device accomplishes through description—it projects a new indexical frame for the discourse. Consider example (14):

(14)   wá k-a-k'aát   ten   e²→ kuš tuún pàablo tú²uš yàan→
            Q Aux-Pro2-Vb IndPro1 TD   Prt Prt N   Adv Vb
            'If you ask(ed) me, "What about Pablo, where is he?"

            tí²-an-ó²ob' té²   t-y-otoč a²
            DLOC-Vb-pl DLOC Prep-Pro3-N-TD
            "They're right there at their house."' (F.1.A)

This utterance was produced by DP in the course of explaining to me the meaning of the expression 'he's right there'. In the first line of text, DP projects the hypothetical speech event as an object of description with the introduction, 'if you ask(ed) me'. This hypothetical frame serves as the indexical ground for the subsequent sentences. The next utterance, in double quotes in the gloss, is the hypothetical question, which I am supposed to direct to DP about Pablo.[13] But in the boldface material, there has been an unsignaled transposition: this stretch of talk is DP's hypothetical response to my question. Hence, the indexical frame on which the utterance is grounded has DP in the Spkr role and me in Adr role. As stated, the hypothetical response contains no first person reference, but had the response been *má² inwòohl i²* 'I don't know', the Spkr pronoun 'I' would be taken to refer to DP, not to me. DP could as well have made this explicit by describing his response overtly, saying: 'I would answer you, "There they are right there."' In the latter form, the indexical coordinates are filled in with the description 'I would answer you', whereas in the example as DP produced it, these coordinates must be reconstructed. There are no semantic elements in the discourse in its present form that refer to or describe the indexical context of DP's response. Given the

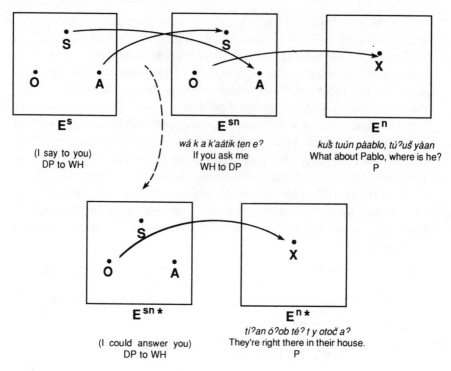

Fig. 5.9. Complex frame: If you asked me, 'What about Pablo, where is he?' they are in their house.

hypothetical question and a shift in intonation, we can reconstruct the indexical frame, but it is nowhere said. This is shown schematically in figure 5.9.

In figure 5.9, the first frame, labeled *Es,* corresponds to the actual interactive context in which DP addressed the utterance to me. He is speaker, I am addressee, and we are sitting face-to-face in my house. The second frame, labeled *Esn,* is the hypothetical speech event projected by the clause 'if you say to me'. I, actual Adr, am projected as Spkr in the event, and DP, actual Spkr, is projected as Adr. The question regarding Pablo treats him as a third person, Other relative to the hypothetical frame (just as, in fact, my real neighbor Pablo was an Other relative to the actual frame). It projects an *En* in which the character Pablo is located somewhere. But starting at 'There they are in their house right there', a descriptive statement is asserted from an undescribed indexical frame, labeled *Esn** in the figure. In *Esn** DP occupies the role of Spkr and I the role of Adr. The dotted arrow indicates the transposition. DP's hypothetical response in turn projects a second *En* in which Pablo is 'right there' relative to *Esn**.

DP's unstated shift from the indexical frame in which I am speaker addressing a question to him to one in which he is addressing a response to me is intermediate between canonical quotation and deictic transposition as Bühler ([1934] 1967) described it (see §5.2.2.2). As in quotation, DP displaced or 'decentered' the indexical ground relative to which a strip of discourse is to be interpreted. Given this, it is possible to paraphrase his hypothetical response with a fuller version in which he says '**I would answer you**, "There they are . . ."' or some such.[14] However, this paraphrase should not obscure the fact that DP actually did not describe his frame as does the boldface clause. He merely keyed a shift in footing by changing intonation and issuing an assertion immediately after the hypothetical question. The reading on which it is a response uttered by the one to whom the question is addressed is overdetermined by its sequential position and intonation, but it is nowhere stated.

This suggests that there are at least two distinct mechanisms whereby an embedded participation frame is projected: (i) it may be described and referred to, as in the canonical metalinguistic report 'X told Y'; or (ii) it may be indexed, that is, reconstructible on the basis of co-occurrent aspects of the utterance for which it serves as ground. In the first case, the indexical frame starts out as an object of reference, which is then the ground relative to which further narrated frames are projected. In the second case, the indexical frame is simply assumed. The difference is reflected in the schemata in the use of a dotted arc for unstated transposition and a solid arc for referential projections. The solid arcs all start from some point in an indexical frame and lead to some point in a projected frame, tracing the correspondence.

5.2.2.2 *Transposition*

Bühler's ([1934] 1967:210ff.) classic discussion of transposition comes in the course of describing what he called *Deixis an Phantasm*, the use of deictic categories for reference to objects available only from memory or in fantasy. He distinguished three kinds of transposition, which have in common that in every case, a speaker displaces his speech in such a way as to ground it in a set of coordinates other than the actual corporeal field. The first kind (i) Bühler described as "Mohammed goes to the mountain," wherein the speaker projects himself into the narrative frame, describing as immediate objects and events that are in fact located in a distant time or space. For example, sitting with a friend over coffee, a speaker says, 'I'm standing at the edge of the forest, alone. Suddenly I hear this crash . . . .' The shifters in the utterance project the speaker into the immediate perceptible surround of the narrated event.

(ii) The second was 'the mountain comes to Muhammad', wherein the speaker describes objectively distant objects as if they were close at hand. Here the speaker remains grounded in his or her own current phenomenal sphere but draws into the sphere objects of reference that would normally be considered outside of it. Describing an event that occurred far off in time or space, the speaker says 'He's stretched out like this (showing), with his arms wrapped around the animal.' These utterances use the immediate frame of the telling as a scene on which to present the narrated event.

(iii) The third type of transposition recognized by Bühler was cases in which neither the speaker nor the referent is drawn to the place of the other, but the speaker describes the referent as though he could point to it right before himself, when in fact he cannot. Sitting in the lowlands, A says to B, *té? kin meyah té? pú?uk a?* 'I work **right here** in the Puuk (high ground)'—when in fact the work site in the Puuk where he labors is fifteen kilometers away from his current location.[15] One would normally expect, '**there** in the hills', but A has taken a larger than expected spatial 'here' as his indexical frame, and relative to this frame, the work site is appropriately characterizable as 'immediate'.

All three of Bühler's cases involve the relation between the speaker and the object of reference. His third type is related to the second, with the difference that the speaker in case (iii) does not expand his current indexical frame but rather projects the referent right into its core (the immediate perceptual/ostensive zone). Unlike the first case, the third draws the referent into copresence with both interlocutors at the place of speech rather than projecting the speaker on a solitary 'journey to the mountain'. Using the heuristic of schemata, these three can be represented as in figure 5.10.

The first schema in figure 5.10 shows the transposition of the speaker from his or her corporeal frame into the narrated one in which (s)he is face-to-face with the object (labeled O for Other). For example, there is a traditional Maya narrative about a deer charm with which hunters attract deer in the forest. DC had spent some years hunting when he acquired one and went on to become very successful. Eventually, the deer reclaimed the charm, as is customary, in a dramatic confrontation between DC and an entire herd of deer in the forest. He was fighting (literally hand to hoof) with one he had just wounded, in order to finish it off, when he was surrounded by the others. So many, in fact, that he was forced to climb up the nearest tree. It was a moment of great tension in the narrative because

Type 1. Speaker goes to the referent

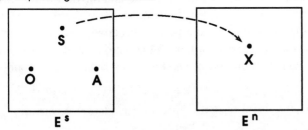

Type 2. Object of reference is made present

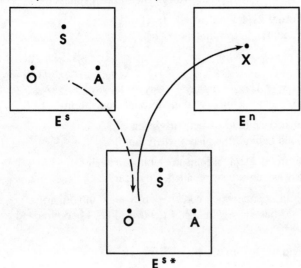

Type 3. Speech frame is expanded to include referent

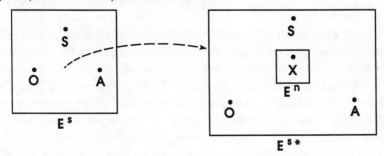

Fig. 5.10. Bühler's three transposition types.

in the scramble, he had left his rifle on the ground and the deer were closing in, snorting and pounding the earth. Among them were two large
bucks, one of which had a wasp nest on its head between its antlers and
the other of which bore a crucifix with a lifelike Christ on it. The wasps
were swarming as the two approached, and DC was terrified. He recounts:

(15)   1. . . . mariah santiísima ↓ ʔiči tiʔ báʔatéʔe b'ey yeéte le b'áʔal čeʔ
              'Holy Mary!   In the throes of battle like that with the
                                                      animal,

        2. inčáačmah yòok **b'ey a**ʔ →   káa h tinwúʔuyah ⌣→
           I wrenched its leg like this (showing). Then I hear, (pause)

        3. **héʔ tuún kutàal keéhóʔob' o**ʔ ↓ té?el oʔ →
           Here come deer (right towards me)! There!

              β-   -β
              ˇ-   -ˇ
        4. láay → lay lay → láay → lay lay → láay → lay lay →
           (sound of deer approaching, walking through vegetation)

        5. péroh → tubak'pàač tuún → le túʔuš yanen eʔ ↑
           But, all around behind (the place) where I am!

        6. ¢'óʔok tuún uroódyàartáʔal impàač → tumèen keéh
           So my back was entirely surrounded,   by deer!

        7. káa tinwilah inčááčmah yòok e kéeh → b'ey →   intriíŋkarma
           Then I saw—I had seized the leg of the deer, like, I had wrapped
              him up.

        8. pekliken yéete téʔ lúʔum oʔ ↓
           I was lying down with him there on the ground.

        9. **péeroh héʔ kutàah keéh téʔel o**ʔ
           But here come the deer over there!' (F.82.A.1.204 ff.)[16]

DC is an accomplished storyteller, and he conveyed the dramatic tension of his situation by a series of transpositions. In line (15.2), there is
what I take to be a transposition of type (ii), where DC demonstrates the
way he grabbed the deer's leg, presencing the event for me to witness. In
this gesture, he uses the corporeal field as a stage on which to project the
narrated event (*En*), and the deictic adverb (underlined) makes the fight
present by referring to its reenactment in his ongoing movement.[17] The
following sentence describes the *En* from the centered perspective of the
current frame and projects a past event of hearing. Instead of telling us
what he heard, however, the next line (15.3) reproduces his incredulous
utterance at the time of the *En*. Although it contains no reported speech
formula to identify it as such, the utterance is transposed, and the deic-

tics, *hé?* . . . *o?* 'There it is' and *té?el o?* 'there' index the visual and spatial field of his encounter with the deer (*Esn**), not his current field as he is talking with me (*Es*). In a move inverse to the one in line (15.2), he has projected himself into the narrative frame, an instance of the type (i) transposition.

Line (15.4) continues within the *Esn**, reproducing the sounds of the deer approaching—the sounds he heard—instead of describing them for me. His voicing of the sounds is the equivalent of quoting the deer's approach through the bush, using transposed speech whose ground is the *En* in which the deer are a perceptible reality. Line (15.5) shows that this is a transposition of type (i) and not of type (ii), because it describes DC being surrounded with no implication that we are currently surrounded or should imagine ourselves to be. Lines (15.6–15.8) flesh out the description of the *En* and DC's battle with the deer. This then serves as indexical context for the transposed speech in the last line. Once again, DC is animating an utterance whose indexical ground is in the narrated event (type (i) transposition), since he was not claiming that deer were approaching us as he told the story. In fact, as a foreigner and nonhunter, I would never find myself in such a confrontation, which occurs only to hunters with a deer stone and only when they are alone.

Examples of Bühler's third type of transposition are common in conversational Maya. The current corporeal frame may be expanded so as to permit description of objectively distant objects as though they were close at hand. This process abstracts from actual perceptibility to virtual perceptibility, rolling back the limits of the current framework into the background frame space. Talking in Oxkutzcab, I asked a man, *tú?uš atàal* 'where do you come from?' and he responded *té? teritòoorió a?* 'right here in the territory (of Quintana Roo).' Given that Quintana Roo is a couple of hours from Oxkutzcab by bus, one would have expected the man to say *té?el o?* rather than *té?el a?*.[18] Similarly, addressing AB's wife at the front gate to his home, I asked if he was home. The woman responded *čeén té? kumeyah té? kaáretèera a?* 'He's (out) working right here at the highway.' The choice of a proximal deictic to make reference to a place a couple of kilometers away serves to deemphasize the distance, drawing the place referred to into the proximal field. In the case of the regional deictic *way e?* 'here', the standard uses include the full array from 'here' in the immediate bodily area of the speaker to 'here' on the earth. This range of variable extent permits speakers to achieve effects like type (iii) transposition by expanding their assumed 'here'. In Yucatán, the loose meaning of *ahora* 'now' and especially of *ahorita* 'right away' and their Maya paraphrases (*b'e?òora, b'e?òoritas*) is well known.

Told that something will occur *b'e?òora* 'now', one knows only that it may occur soon. The assumed scope of the temporal present may be as narrow as minutes or as broad as hours. Routine examples like these make it clear that type (iii) transposition is common, a point developed in detail in chapter 9.

Transposition is related to quotation in that both involve the decentering of the indexical ground of shifter categories from its normal locus in the corporeal frame of speech to some other frame. In canonical quotation, this other frame is a speech event, projected as an object of description (*Esn*) in a metalinguistic sentence such as 'he asked me'. The moment of decentering, however, is the quotation of the original utterance, not the uttering of the metalinguistic key. The quote takes the *Esn* frame as its indexical ground and makes reference relative to it rather than directly describing it. Thus in ' "I went to see you" **she said to me**,' 'I' indexes the reported *Esn* projected by the boldface sentence. We know this because it refers to the individual occupying the Spkr role in the reported event, therefore the same one referred to as 'she' (Other) in the nonquoted discourse. It is only because they index different grounds that 'I' and 'she' can be coreferential; when the two are grounded in a single indexical frame, as they are in the boldface sentence, their contrasting relational (R) values assure that they will be noncoreferential.

Some cases of quotation are not signaled by metalinguistic report, even though the shifters are decentered. This is the case with DP's example scenario in which I ask him where Pablo is and he responds, 'he's right here'. He nowhere tells me that this last utterance is a response from himself to my question in the hypothetical frame. Rather, with a slight change in intonation, he makes the leap from animating one character to animating another. The importance of this example is that it shows that even in relatively clear cases of quotation, there need not always be a metalinguistic phrase to project the new *Es* frame as an object of reference and description. Speakers can transpose into a new frame the way they change posture, without explanation, knowing their interlocutor will be able to follow or reconstruct the shift. These cases are much like transposition in direct speech, in which the speaker shifts from his own to his interlocutor's perspective, using the Adr or some other available orientation point as indexical ground, without announcing the fact. A is facing B and asks him to get the bowl 'on the left' meaning left relative to B's *schéma corporel*.

What Bühler called 'transposition' is entirely tied to the relation between speaker and referent, without regard to the inversion in perspectives between speaker and addressee. Still, his three types obviously involve the projection of a new speech event frame distinct from the actual one—the speaker steps into the narrative world, brings the narrative world into the present frame, or expands the present frame to include some referent. In each case, the transposed speech indexes the *projected* frame the way quoted speech indexes the reported event of speaking (*Esn*). When a mother says to an infant while bathing it, 'Oooh, I like that, mommy!' there is a transposition, not a quotation. For the purpose of identifying the referent of 'I', however, the indexical frame is displaced just as it would be were the utterance an attributed quote. Furthermore, in the preceding examples of standard transposition in narrative, the storyteller establishes an *En* frame through description—I was stretched out, locked in battle with the deer, etc.—which then becomes the indexical context for an utterance, 'Here come the deer!' There is no quote, and DC may never have said 'here come the deer', but a narrated frame is projected by description and used as an indexical ground. It is this projection and its use as an indexical ground relative to which embedded shifters are interpreted that marks it as a case of decentering.

Therefore we can both distinguish and relate canonical quotation to canonical transposition. A distinction is necessary between decenterings in which the new indexical context is projected as an object of reference and ones in which it is indexed without any description. Both kinds of decentering occur with both quotation and transposition. 'He said' and other metalinguistic formulas project a speech event frame, an indexical ground for a quoted utterance. Similarly, the kinds of scene-setting description illustrated in example (15) set up a frame for speech, among other things. This kind of projection is shown in the schemata by the solid line arrow. Other cases of quotation and transposition come without descriptive labels, and an interpreter must simply posit a new frame from which to interpret the utterance. These are shown with the broken-line arrow. Among the referential projections, the most obvious difference between quote and transposition is that in the former, what is projected is a narrated speech event (*Esn*), whereas in the latter, it is merely a narrated event (*En*). It is more difficult to distinguish between speech projected from the mouth of an addressee or fictional character (unannounced quote) than speech indexing the perspective of an addressee or other (unannounced transposition).

5.2.2.3 *Creative Reference*

In this section, I will outline two kinds of relatively creative demonstrative reference commonly attested in Maya conversation, which we can call anticipatory and displaced reference. Anticipatory demonstrative reference consists in the use of present, presentative, or other inherently immediate deictics in reference to objects (individuals, events, places) that are not actually accessible in the corporeal field but will be so in the immediate future. A paradigm example is the following.

(16)   b'e'òora kintàal   a' → má' tinšantal → **hé'**   **kintàal**   **o'**
         now   I return TD   Neg I delay   OSTEV Aux-Pro1-Vb TD
         'I'll be right back. I won't be long. Here I come.' (BB.2.26)

This utterance was produced by MC, addressed to me in his house. He was about to run out briefly for an errand but wanted me to wait for him to return. The first two sentences describe his imminent return, but it is the boldface sentence which breaks through into creative reference. It literally presents MC's return as though it were visually perceivable already, when in fact he had not yet departed. This usage can be analyzed as a standard case of anticipatory reference, parallel to the anticipatory uses of *lel a'* 'this', *b'ey a'* 'like this', and *té'el a'* 'here' (in this direction; cf. §9.2.2.1). The trouble with this is that other anticipatory uses are consistently associated with the *a'* forms, whereas MC has uttered an *o'* form. Had he wished to, he could have said *hé'e kintàal a'*. This is a standard way of saying 'here I come', provided the speaker is on his way or just about to be. In terms of transposition types, what MC has done is project a narrative frame (*En*) consisting of his return to the location of utterance, as if it were currently visible in that location. Insofar as his utterance is genuinely anticipatory, it appears plausible to treat it as a type (iii) transposition, in which the frame of actual perceptible reality is expanded to include the near future (see fig. 5.10). The inverse occurs in cases like:

(17)   A: tú'uš yàan le maák o'
            'Where is the guy?'
         B: má' hé'   h   b'in o'
            Neg OSTEV Pst Vb TD
            'There he went (just).'

In (17) the presentative is used in collocation with the past tense to make reference to an event of going which is in the immediate past relative to the moment of utterance. The man is already gone, and what the utterance conveys is that his leaving was recent and was witnessed by the speaker. As in anticipatory reference, the temporal and perceptible limits of the present have been expanded to include nonactual aspects of the frame space. Thus the third schema in figure 5.10 applies to both cases.

Another kind of creative reference occurs with some frequency in Maya conversation, in which the speaker refers to himself or his addressee as if (s)he were actually elsewhere. This is like the anticipatory examples in that it projects a coparticipant into another frame, but in this case, there is no sense in which the projected frame is about to be, or was recently, factual. Looking at a squashed fruit, A says to B, *hé?el eč o?* 'There you are (that's you).' Verbally presenting B while visually fixing on the rotten fruit, A simultaneously projects two frames, a corporeal one in which the fruit is presented (as presentatum of *hé?el-o?*) and a referential one in which the Adr is equated with the fruit (as referent of *hé?el-eč-o?* 'you'). B responds by tossing back the insult, *tèeč wal e?* 'better you' (F.19.B.010ff.). Looking at a passing woman, one young man says to another, *hé? kimb'in o?* 'there I go', conveying that the woman is sexually attractive to him. In these cases, it is counterintuitive to claim that the speaker is anticipating a state of affairs in which the equation asserted will be accurate. Rather, in the utterance the speaker projects himself or his interlocutor into a fantasized frame in which it is accurate. This fantasized frame is not a new speech event, as in quotation from fantasy, but just a new situation or engagement for one of the interlocutors. What is peculiar about such examples is that the narrated event is presented as though it were actually right before the eyes of the interactants, when it is in fact contradictory to their situation. Since there is no evidence of an expansion of the perceptual field of the present, these cases are better treated as projections of a coparticipant into the narrative world corresponding to the description. In this sense, they are most similar to Bühler's transposition of type (i), where a participant is projected to the frame of reference.

5.2.2.4 *Excluded Addressee*

Another kind of decentering in Maya turns on what could be called 'excluded addressee'. This arises canonically in contexts in which three or more agents are engaged and one party is spoken to, or about, in the third person (nonparticipant) category. Addressing one interlocutor, the Spkr comments on the other copresent party as if (s)he were not a coparticipant. Imagine that Sil, Manuel, and Felis are talking. Sil asks Manuel what he plans to do, and Manuel explains. Sil then replies by commenting to Felis, in full presence of Manuel,

(18)   čiŋgon e   maák a?
              slick   this guy
              'This guy's slick.'

Sil's utterance conveys a positive evaluation of Manuel in familiar terms that index their rough status symmetry. It refers to Manuel as a nonparticipant by describing him in the third person. He is obviously not a canonical Adr, even though he is copresent and participating. Yet he is not merely a copresent third person or audience, since what he is party to is a statement made in response to him, about him, and which he is meant to hear.

In order to describe such usage, we could posit a new category of participant, such as Excluded Adr, or we could posit a frame embedding. Under the latter analysis, Man is a nonparticipant in the frame projected by the description, just as the third person linguistic forms indicate. At the same time, he is a fully ratified coparticipant in the immediately prior speech and in the current phenomenal frame of Sil's utterance. If he feels so moved, he can respond just like other addressees. This engagement of the third person addressee is also evident in other examples, where such a decentered reference is used to kick off *baášal t'àan* 'play speech'.

(19)   topá'an e   ší'ipal o' mátik múk'ahoóltik   utàata
           screwed that boy   'cuz Neg he recognize his father
           'That kid's screwed; he doesn't even recognize his own father.'

The utterance in (19) was addressed to me by a young man in reference to another man who was working with him, right at his side.[19] The two were already engaged in a larger group interaction when I appeared. The force of the utterance is to challenge the man referred to to exchange humorous insults with the speaker; it conveys 'I sleep with his mother (therefore I am his father), and he doesn't even know it.'

The use of relation terms for roundabout and usually ribald reference to addressee is apparently a widespread pattern in Maya (Bricker 1970). What is special about this example is the third person formulation of the copresent man as *le ší'ipal o'* 'that kid', a nonparticipant. This reference is grounded in an indexical frame from which the man is present only as a nonparticipant, and yet at the same time he is actually being addressed in the phenomenal frame. The utterance presupposes that the target will attend to it and seeks to engage him further. If we view this as an embedding in Goffman's sense, a decentering in current terms, it would appear to correspond to figure 5.11. In this figure, the narrated state of affairs is described from the perspective of a speech event frame in which the corporeal addressee figures as a nonparticipant. Hence, the broken arrow projects an actual addressee into the Other category, and the solid arrow then describes this same individual in the third person.

Under this analysis, the participant roles in such examples are no more complex than the three categories of person. It is the mapping between individuals and roles that is complicated by the fact that a single individual is treated as both inside and outside the frame of coparticipation. The pe-

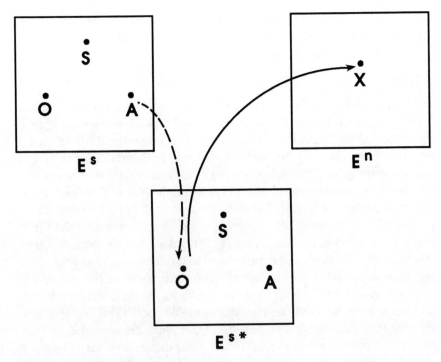

Fig. 5.11. Excluded addressee.

culiarity of such uses is not in the participant categories themselves but in the relation between categories and occupants. This analysis is consistent with what Irvine (1987:10) calls 'clashing structures', a type of implicated dialogue, in which the P frame projected in an utterance fails to coincide with the corporeal frame of production or with other implicated ones.

A similar exclusionary embedding is typical of speech directed at dogs, which is always, in my experience, cast in the third person. When a dog is slinking into the kitchen hut, for instance, and a household member undertakes to shoo it away, a typical utterance form is *bikih!* 'Let it not be the case!' (loud and breathy voiced with stress on second syllable), or *tú?un kub'in e pèek' o?* 'Where's that dog going?' Both are spoken forcefully at the dog, possibly accompanied by a projectile, and are meant to get an instantaneous response. The projectile is a fair indicator of the aggressive character of the act, which confronts the target with two contradictory indexical frames, one actual and reinforced by the hurled object and the other transposed, constituted by the verbal utterance. This is another case of transposition: the description projects an indexical frame from which the dog is excluded, while the corporeal orientation of the utterance as an act projects the dog as Adr. The dog, of course, only has access to the corporeal frame.

5.2.2.5 *The Constantly Shifting Indexical Ground*

In examples like the foregoing, it is fairly clear that a decentering has taken place, and the line between transposed and nontransposed speech seems neat. The heuristic schemata used to diagram the different transpositions force one to distinguish cleanly among them and imply that in any utterance there either are or are not cases of any type. But recall that the concept of decentering is tied inevitably to the idea of a normal, automatic, nondecentered usage, in which the indexical ground is right where it should be, so to speak. We recognize cases of decentering by their failure to correspond to the normal cases. It is relevant to the plausibility of this view that speakers make basic-level assumptions and routinize their indexical usage so as to privilege the corporeal frame as the one that is available until further notice. This is significant, since it weights the actual frame more heavily than the other possible ones. (This is implicit in the schemata from the fact that all start from some *Es*, regardless of how they differ in their projection of others.) No matter how far removed a projected speech frame is from the actual circumstances of its production, there is a chain of indexical-referential correspondences leading back to the corporeal participant frame. Were this not the case, and were interactants not able continually to reestablish ground in their corporeal fields, it would become necessary to sustain the common grounding of reference through extensive description. Even detailed description fails ultimately to identify individuals unless it is joined to a body of background knowledge, and interactants must share both the adequate knowledge and a reasonably common appreciation of where they stand relative to it.[20] Lacking this common grounding, coparticipants can fall 'out of alignment', and it becomes uncertain whether at any point, 'it is "now" now', 'we are "here" here', ' "you" is you', or ' "I" is me'.

On the other hand, the bodily grounding of reference does not really fix the center, as the examples show. Within the phenomenal frame are the coparticipants and their respective fields of perceptual, spatial, and conceptual access. The fact that speakers can shift from their own to an addressee's perspective, as in 'it's on the right', meaning 'on your right, my left', is indicative of a basic property of phenomenal interactive frames: taken simply as first-order constructs, they are already complex and include perspectively oriented subspaces (corresponding to the different interactants). In fact, the clean statement of transposition provided by

Bühler is made possible partly by the simplifying assumption that the normal ground of deixis is the subjective sphere of the speaker. When we reject the assumption of speaker-centricity, as we do here, it becomes subtle and difficult to say what the 'normal' center is for any shifter. And without this statement, it is impossible to recognize at least some cases of 'decentering'. In subsequent chapters, I will show how the indexical center of demonstrative reference shifts constantly in the course of routine interaction. Not only does it pass back and forth between interactants, as in the Ping-Pong ball model of speech, but interactants themselves repeatedly shift their perspective from their own to a common one that they share with an interlocutor, to the interlocutor's, to that of the personages they are talking about, and so forth. Decentering is not an occasional curiosity but a basic part of interactive practices, and this once again affirms the necessity of detaching embodiment from corporeality: body engagement is a resource for indexing transposition, but it is not the constant ground it is for prototypical nontransposed corporeal usage.

5.2.3 Metalanguage and Centering

When native speakers discuss the meaning or use of shifters in their own language, they produce a wealth of evidence regarding processes of centering. On the one hand, they use their linguistic resources to construct coherent discourse in which there are many transpositions, putting the language to work directly to manage multiple frames. Metalinguistic discourse in Maya illustrates the use of quotation, report formulas, paralinguistic signals of footing shifts, the keying of hypothetical as opposed to 'real' discourse, the integration of reported speech as a topic for commentary, and the use of shifters to refer to shifters—as in 'the "that" there in that utterance is unclear. It would be better to say "this".' (Hanks 1983:chap. 7; In press). Thus, speech focused on explaining speech is a part of direct verbal practice.

At the same time, what speakers say about their language reflects local standards of usage according to which they interpret and evaluate speech. In this perspective, metalanguage is a step removed from direct practice, being **about** it rather than **part of** it (cf. §2.3 above). There is no question that native common sense and ideological representations of language are 'distorting' when compared to what people actually do with speech (Silverstein 1979). But this fact in no way alters the value of their statements as a reflection of how they typify language. In particular, what people say about expressions containing demonstratives may reveal how they perceive the indexical frames in which the forms are used. This would have obvious relevance to a description of the corporeal frame, since it would help to indicate the sorts of factors that native speakers attend to and that go into the self-awareness (*prise de conscience*) that is requisite to full-blown corporeality.

The discussion of P frames so far in this chapter has incorporated the simplifying assumption that a frame can be talked about in terms of the participant roles alone, as in Spkr, Adr, Other. This may be justified in order to identify individual components of frames, but speech does not work this way, and pronouns are not isolated. How do native speakers incorporate perceptual, spatial, and discourse context, assumed background knowledge, intentionality, and aspects of the social field into their apprehension of the phenomenal framework? Even holding aside problems of embeddings (see §5.2.1), we still do not know how many dimensions a referential framework contains or what these dimensions are beyond those of the pronouns. This is one of the focal questions of this book, the answer to which will develop over subsequent chapters.

In order to gather metalinguistic evidence of referential practices, my research on Maya included lengthy discussions of the language with several native speakers. These discussions have been described in some detail elsewhere (Hanks 1983; in press) and can only be illustrated briefly here. For present purposes, what is most important is the interdependence between what speakers said about their language and the elicitation context in which the metalanguage was produced. Put simply, they used the face-to-face situation in which I was talking with them as a stage and set of props with which to construct other frames. They described the meanings of shifters by illustrating how they are used, projecting fictitious *Esn* frames to serve as the indexical grounds for hypothetical events of reference. But their hypothetical events and their nonactual grounds were in fact anchored systematically in the corporeal frame of our interaction. Instead of describing what a word like *té ?el a?* 'here (Immed)' meant, they described situations in which it could be used—situations that happened to involve us, the place where we were talking, the objects around us.

This pedagogical strategy seems natural, almost inevitable, given the indexical function of demonstratives and the privileged weighting of the phenomenal frame in discourse. Still, it shows how a current interactive frame can simultaneously ground reference and provide a model on which other frames can be built. It joins the two kinds of evidence of centering processes into a single whole. Rather than describe this in the abstract, I will give an example taken from my first recorded discussion with DP (December 6, 1979).

I had known DP for several years at the time, and he had become accustomed to teaching me how to work, how to live in rural Yucatán, and how to talk Maya. All of our interactions were (and still are) in Maya, and I frequently asked questions such as:

(20)   b'á²aš kut'anik 'x'?
          'What does x mean (say)?'

(21)   b'á²aš uk'aát yá²al 'x'?
          'What does x mean (want to say)?'

(22)   b'iš aná²atik 'x'?
          'How do you understand x (such and such)?'

As is evident in (20–22), there are several relatively simple ways of inquiring as to the significance of speech in Maya. In eliciting commentaries on shifters from DP and others, I purposely posed vague questions, like those cited here, in order to allow speakers to impose their own sense of relevance on the forms. Sometimes I explained that it was an expression I had heard but not understood, and at other times I merely cited the form and asked what it meant. Although my efforts to learn Maya have taken the form of an ongoing 'discussion' between me and my native teachers, some relatively more focused interactions were tape-recorded over a period of several years (approximately 30 hours in 1979–87). These took place between me and speakers with whom I already had well-established relationships, including DP, DC, MC, Man, Margot, Balim, and VI. The setting of talk was always a familiar one, such as sitting in the house after work hours or at a work site during rest periods, and the tenor of interaction was kept informal.

On the day in question, DP and I were sitting in my house, which actually belonged to him. Living in the same walled solar with me was a man named Pablo, with his wife, two children, and dog, who slept in the house structure across the courtyard and shared the kitchen hut and well with me (see the description of Maya domestic space in chap. 7). At the time, we were discussing DLOC expressions for 'there', and I was attempting to get a sense of the difference between *tol o²* 'out there', *té²el o²* 'there', and *way e²* 'here', which I did not yet understand (see chap. 9). After being interrupted by strange noises out in the yard, DP continued his explanation,

(23)   DP: taná²atah b'iših?
              'Did you understand how it is?'

        WH: ²udíferèsia
              'the difference'

DP:

1. siíh → tumèen → kawáaik ti?   kó?oten way e? →
    'Yeah, because, (if) you say to him "Come (to me) here",

2. ?eskeh ?ump'ée maák tak é?eš buká?ah
    it's that, a guy   up to about as far away as

3. na le hòo nah   tú?uš yanó?o ?éstèeh pàabló o? →
    by the front door where, ahh, Pablo (and family) are.

4. ka paáy ti?   kó?oten way e? ?eskeh ak'aát ká ?okokó?
    You call him (to you), "Come here!"   It's that you want them to
                                            enter

5. ?ič nah   way e? → way e? ↓
    inside (the) house here. Here.' (F.1.A.50)

In the opening exchange preceding line (23.1), DP picked up our conversation, asking me if I had understood his preceding explanation. I ask for clarification, saying roughly, 'You mean the difference (between forms)?' In line (23.1), he illustrates by describing a fictional speech event *Esn* with the phrase 'you say to him', which projects the current addressee (me) in the role of speaker addressing some third person. The target form which DP is explaining comes next, in a quotation which indexes the *Esn* he has just established: 'Come here' (to where 'I' am at moment of utterance).

Lines (23.2–3) shift back out of the *Esn* frame and into the corporeal one: DP is once again speaking to me as narrator, describing the *Esn* instead of performing it. The spatial location of this man relative to me in the hypothetical frame is like the actual one between us (DP and me) and Pablo's house on the other side of the courtyard. Given this relation of spatial separation between interactants, line (23.4) goes on to project another utterance of the target form, this time phrased more precisely than the first: 'you call out to him'. The verb *paytik* means to summon an addressee and therefore describes (however minimally) the directive force of the target form. Together with the spatial facts, it projects an *Esn** which then serves as indexical frame for the target. In the second half of line (23.4), DP once again shifts back from quote to direct speech, keying the switch with the Spanish form *?eskeh*.[21] In this last stretch of discourse, he glosses the force of the target utterance relative to its ground as an attempt to get Pablo and family to come 'here' (the current one embodied in our corporeal frame). Thus, DP has assumed the orderliness and intelligibility of our current context and used it to explain a hypothetical one. It might be summarized, 'If you told someone "Come here," it would be like telling them to come here.'

What we see in examples like (23), therefore, is a series of transpositions of the indexical ground of reference, moving from the actual ground of our copresence into the reported one (23.1), back to the actual (23.2), back to the report (23.4), and ending in the actual (23.4–5). For keys to indicate his transpositions, DP uses metalinguistic verbs (23.1, 23.4) to move from corporeal to reported frames and *ʔeskeh* to move from reported frames back into corporeal frames. Although the two frames are fundamentally distinct as footings for DP to take up, they are substantially related: They have in common two participants (me and my neighbor Pablo), albeit in different roles, as well as the spatial setting of the household.

Beyond the obvious shared elements, the two frames have in common something more basic, namely, the unstated but assumed background of knowledge and practices that make our phenomenal framework intelligible. For instance, DP knows and assumes that I know enough about the spatial organization of the household to understand that one can address a person from inside one structure to inside another, since the distances and orientations of doors are appropriate (see chap. 7). He assumes we share an orientation in our corporeal 'here' (line 23.5) tacitly agreeing that it excludes the space outside the walls of the house, and therefore Pablo. If I had been confused and thought that we were currently in the kitchen hut, say, or anywhere other than 'inside the house', then DP's gloss would have been nonsensical or misleading. I could conclude that *way e ʔ* meant 'over there' and that the target utterance was a way of telling someone to visit your sleeping house. Further, he assumes that I know that linguistic forms, at least ones described as *paáy* 'summons', are typically uttered in order to do things of certain kinds, like create an interperspectival engagement by calling out to the interlocutor (line 23.4).

There is a carryover from the corporeal frame to the projected hypothetical frames in DP's discourse, because the commonsense knowledge on which he draws when describing language is rooted in social practices like the one he was actually engaged in. This is another expression of the privileged status of the corporeal frame over nonactual projections. Still, DP describes selected parameters—person, location, conveyed force—and does a tacit analysis of the current framework in the course of it. His glossing strategy reveals as much about how he views our current situation as it does about his views on language. This is a reminder that the phenomenal framework in which speech takes place is not itself simply given as a physical, perceptible reality. Knowledge of the world beyond one's actual reach is part of one's 'here' and 'now' at any point, and even the immediate field is itself structured by practices that go beyond its perceptual horizons.

This availability of schematic knowledge in the local context of speech raises a hard question for the study of interactive frames. Are DP's knowledge and assumptions about my neighbor Pablo part of our simple corporeal frame? Do they attach to his projected hypothetical *Esn*, in the form of unstated 'inferables', to use Prince's (1981) expression? Or does this knowledge pertain to what we called the frame space of possibilities beyond the actual state of talk? These alternatives are not mutually exclusive. DP's background practices and knowledge are part of the immediate speech event (*Es*), insofar as they are an available stock of knowledge that can be drawn on, made explicit (at least in part), and questioned at any point. At the expense of falling into a naive, physical definition of the interactive framework, the stock of knowledge cannot be kept out of it. The line between a framework and a frame space is a fuzzy one. DP grasps his current location in terms of his stock of knowledge, as the reflexive use of the present in his examples illustrates. This implies that the simple mnemonic of the *Es* frame as Spkr, Adr, Other needs to be expanded to include such features as Location, Time, possibly 'utterance form', and other less discretely labelable aspects of routine practice (cf. Hymes 1972; Brown and Yule 1983: §2.2). When we draw a frame containing only participant categories, therefore, it is obviously a heuristic simplification.

Unquestionably, background knowledge can be activated by the description a speaker produces of some event. This means that it can be brought into play by a second-order construct: in (23), my knowledge of the spatial arrangement of the homestead outside the house we were sitting in is activated by DP's making reference to Pablo in the specific context of our interaction. In another context, the same reference could activate other knowledge, for instance, relating to Pablo's religion or work habits, whereas reference to someone else in the current context, say, a neighbor across the street, would lead to a different schematization of our current place. For example, *kó?oten way e?* 'come here' is a fully appropriate way of calling someone into the yard from outside the wall of the homestead and need not make reference to the inside of any structure other than the perimeter (see chap. 7). Thus if DP had mentioned Chio, the neighbor across the road, instead of Pablo, who lived in the same homestead, he would have called into play the schematic division between inside and outside the homestead rather than one structure to another within the yard.

In order to distinguish the general background of schematic knowledge that speakers have available to them from the more limited knowledge in play at any point in any interaction, Brown and Yule's (1983:206) concept of the 'discourse representation' is helpful. A discourse representation is a "specific representation of this particular experience of the world . . . arising from a particular discourse." The emphasis here is on localizing that portion of the stock of knowledge that is most relevant to the point at hand. A related proposal by Brown and Yule is their principle of 'local interpretation', which "instructs the hearer not to construct a context any larger than he needs to arrive at an interpretation" (1983:58 ff.). This principle applies to complex frames, insofar as it guides an interlocutor in constructing a discourse representation of the most recent utterance, and utterances typically combine referential with indexical frames.

If a 'discourse representation' is a complex schema in our terms, then the principle of local interpretation has to do with how speakers draw on the frame space of possibilities in the process of understanding. Given that interactants draw constantly on their background knowledge, in varying degrees of explicitness and detail, it is unlikely that the division between frameworks and frame spaces is neat. In some cases, to be sure, we can say that an actor has adopted one footing and not another, but in others it is less obvious how to distinguish local processes from the background against which they are intelligible. Goffman's definition of frame spaces in terms of participant roles (cf. §5.2.1) must in any case be expanded to a fuller set of coordinates in order to apply to deictics and demonstratives. Once this is done, the amount and variety of knowledge in play in a framework, and therefore potentially in a frame, increases dramatically. Rather than viewing complex frames as boxes within boxes, therefore, one should consider them to be relatively figural structures projected on a background that does not so much 'include' them as 'ground' them in the social context.

The frame space in which metalinguistic discussions took place included the practical knowledge that my interlocutors and I shared of our respective identities, relative positions, and spatial setting. This provided a range of possible frames, while **excluding** others. For instance, it would have been out of the question that I tell them what was correct in Maya, draw on detailed knowledge of Chicago in my statements, ask them to gloss English forms, formulate references as though I were currently in Mérida rather than Oxkutzcab, or claim to be speaking for the winds in the well. Similarly, DP, a senior male who has always described himself as a teacher with patience and willingness to explain, simply could not tell me to stop asking questions, to consult the stars, to learn Spanish instead of Maya, to imagine myself in two places at once, or to put my 'here' in my pocket and speak from the perspective of his foot; nor would he address me in the voice of a young girl or invite me to dance. When I presented him with a linguistic form in mention, he could not respond as though it were a direct utterance, feigning to misunderstand my keyings. As gratuitous as these things might appear, it is important to emphasize that a frame space has limits beyond which positions are out of reach and unlikely to be projected, even in hypothetical frames.[22]

Thus, metalinguistic discourse illustrates the dependency between frames and frame spaces, as well as the tendency of speakers to recapitulate elements of their current framework in the hypothetical ones they have created.

5.3 RITUAL GENRES AND FRAME SPACE

The limits of any frame space are determined by a variety of factors. In the first instance, it should be clear that there is not always a single readily definable range of possibilities available to interactants. To say that there are limits on the roles actors can play is not to say that there is always agreement on what the limits are or that they remain fixed for any specified duration. What is going on, what is most relevant to it, and what can reasonably ensue are things that change over the course of interaction. Moreover, if it is correct to maintain that the difference between local and nonlocal interpretation is a gradual one, then it follows that the indexical frame of an utterance in some sense shades into a vast background of practical knowledge that belongs outside of it. Instead of a volumeless line around the actual frames, there is a zone of decreasing relevance. For DP in example (23), the spatial setting of the household and the teacher-student structure of our relationship were particularly relevant, whereas equally accessible shared knowledge about agricultural practices and vegetation types was irrelevant and never brought into focus. If we fail to account for this difference, the idea of a 'space of possibilities' becomes a rubbish barrel for the totality of speakers' background knowledge.

Part of the answer to this problem lies in the idea of discourse genres.[23] From a formal perspective, genres can be defined as regular groupings of discourse features, such as marked delivery style, characteristic syntactic or morphological structures, conventional themes, and compositional devices. Generic categories determine types, like 'greeting, prayer, ethnic joke', of which actual utterances become token instantiations—provided they display the right arrangement of features. Alternatively, one could define a genre as a set of interpretive conventions (maxims) that orient the production and understanding of an utterance but do not correspond to defining features of its form (Bauman 1986). In the overview of speech around the Maya household in §3.4 above, genres were associated centrally with different footings that interactants adopt relative to one another, such as those of bawling out, sweet-talking, swearing, and baiting in jest. The variety of plausible views is due to the fact that however one defines them, genres have simultaneously formal, pragmatic, historical, and aesthetic dimensions. What is most relevant to our discussion is that the concept of genres applies at the level of the frame space and can help set the limits of the space.

How a speaker applies a principle like 'local interpretation' depends partly upon the genre of speech in which an utterance is produced. It is a platitude that we interpret a wisecrack, a greeting, the instructions for an appliance, and a short story differently, calling on different kinds and amounts of knowledge, requiring different levels of richness or specificity in an appropriate understanding. This variability in what Ingarden (1973) called the "concretization" of discourse is organized, in part, by genre categories. Genres are not only schematic structures but they are modes of local practice as well. On the schematic side, the relative specificity of description in a discourse is tied to its membership in (a) genre(s). In other words, the kinds of frame configurations projected in a text differ according to the kind of sociocultural discourse it instantiates.[24]

Let's take some examples from Maya discourse. Recall the deer stone story, which DC told me under the guise of an experience he had lived. The story contains very detailed descriptions of some things alongside skeletal outlines of others. Events like his hand-to-hoof combat with a large stag on the floor of the forest and the dramatic arrival of the spirits to reclaim the stone are treated with great precision, while things like the forest setting itself, the color of the animals against the vegetation, and the size and weight of his rifle were barely mentioned, if at all. Yet these are all details that could easily draw comment in another context. The story tacitly assumes an enormous familiarity with the forest and hunting practices, and the listener is expected to draw on this knowledge in order to fill in the narrated events beyond what is explicitly projected in the description. Contrast standard greetings exchanged by Maya neighbors passing in the street. These are extremely vague, as in A: 'Hey, where're ya going?' B: 'Yo, just over there', but may rely for their interpretation upon a great deal of shared knowledge and common practice.[25] In other words, the balance between what is said and how much interpretive work is required to derive a discourse representation is variable.[26] In Gumperz's (1982) terms, the processes of 'contextualization' and conversational inference are linked both to the social definition of an interaction as such and such a genre and to the particular circumstances of its occurrence.

As an illustration of the tie between genres and frames, the remainder of this chapter will outline two varieties of Maya ritual performance. In shamanic ritual, the production of frames and frameworks is governed by relatively specific conventions. We can say without qualification that the footings and complex frames generated in the course of these events are highly constrained and derive from a limited array of possible frames. The frame space is constituted by the field of shamanic practice, in which competing specialists perform esoteric tasks for a limited set of purposes, using a definable range of discourse genres. The field of contemporary Maya shamanic practice is relatively complex although not 'officially' institutionalized. It includes specialized personnel, conventionally defined participation frames, and restricted access to positions—although the most obvious restrictions are imposed by the patients, beneficiaries, and other 'consumers', who vote with their feet and pocketbooks rather than by any group of specialists empowered to grant legitimacy. It also intersects with other health care and religious options on which local people regularly draw. This brings into de facto competition agents who attempt to legitimate contradictory paradigms, including 'traditional' *hmèen* 'shamans', proselytizing Protestant sects, magicians, rural health clinics, doctors, and Catholic priests.

In this section, we concentrate on two genres in the practice of DC, a widely recognized *hmèen* 'shaman (lit., doer)'. The participant role configurations in which he performs and the manner of their referential projection are typical of shamanic practice, to my knowledge, and provide a helpful contrast to everyday speech. Shamans systematically produce complex frames in which transpositions and decenterings play a basic role. In the following, I assume that the field of shamanic practice, however one defines its borders, includes an array of discourse genres, which in turn define the limits on footing and frame production for any agent acting in the genre. We will concentrate on the more local aspects of this interdependency, especially the link of genre to the kinds of frames produced in them. The themes introduced in this section will be taken up again in more detail in subsequent chapters, as we look at ritual space in relation to spatial reference.

5.3.1 *Reésar* 'Prayer'

Shamanic practice in contemporary Maya culture includes ritual performances aimed at curing illness and maintaining well-being in humans, cleansing space, achieving success in agriculture, expressing thanks, and

Plate 5.1. DC offering five gourds of *saka²* in his yard.

acquiring knowledge not otherwise available.[27] The verbal components of
these different engagements have a number of features in common, the
most obvious of which is that they are all described in Maya as *reésar*
'prayer'. All forms of *reésar* have the goal of creating an encounter between the shaman, his spirit addressees, and usually some human benefi-
ciary(s). There is virtually always an altar of some kind, which may be
minimally an image of a saint or, in the major ceremonies, a complex
icon of cosmological space (see §7.4.3). The shaman stands facing the
altar with a steady gaze, usually focused down or on an offering being
presented. A premium is placed on the total and unobstructed engagement of the shaman, who does not normally interrupt his prayer or change
his corporeal orientation away from the altar until completion of the performance. The uttered discourse of *reésar* is highly distinctive, being

chanted or intoned in measured breath groups with a repeating intonation contour, bounded at beginning and end by signs of the cross and marked by numerous formal indicators of the restricted style in which it is worded.

Two aspects of ritual genres have special importance to frames, namely, the character of the 'social present' in which they are performed and the kind of represented frames that they project. In those cases where there is a patient or beneficiary present in the framework (the vast majority of rituals), the shaman maintains an engagement with them, at least at certain points but sometimes over long continuous stretches of discourse (say, 45 minutes). At the same time, he maintains contact with the spirits, who are the real effective agents in the event and to whom his prayer is a path.[28] This duality in the shaman's phenomenal orientation, between his engagement with the patient and that with the spirit addressees, is played out in his action, both verbal and corporeal. We will look at this in two kinds of curing discourse, one called *saántiguar* 'sanctify' and the other *tiíč'k'aák'* 'illuminate'. The former is a prayer lasting between about eight and twelve minutes in which an individual human standing with the shaman before the altar is blessed as part of a cure or for prophylaxis against minor illness. 'Illumination' is a practice in which the shaman, using divinatory crystals, acquires knowledge about events and states of affairs beyond his normal access. For example, he may see the location of an illness in the patient's body, locate a malevolent spirit in the distant household of a beneficiary, or learn the whereabouts of a runaway child or the true intentions of a lover. The entire event, which I will call 'divination' for short, lasts anywhere from about five minutes up to nearly an hour.

Both kinds of performance imply distinctive participation frames in which the shaman, a series of named spirits, and a beneficiary are engaged, as well as objectified through reference. The capacity of performance to produce a spatiotemporal present and to extend the shaman's perceptual range through crystals is a function of its embodiment. In performance, the shaman dilates his corporeality into the world and thereby remakes the corporeal field of the patient. While all ritual genres share the kind of language called 'prayer' and operate on the corporeal field of performance, the frames and footings they produce differ. We will start with the *saántiguar*.

5.3.2 Saántiguar

The discourse of *saántiguar* is a paradigm example of *reésar* 'prayer', and many of the properties it displays are found throughout other genres. One of the most important of these is a fundamentally asymmetric participation frame, in which the shaman addresses an omnipotent god, Jesus Christ, and a subset of spirits, all superordinate to humans but with delimited spheres of capacity (i.e., subordinate to God the Father and Son). For the *saántiguar*, a patient must be actually copresent with the shaman during the performance and is enjoined to stand (or sit) facing the altar, gazing on the *santo* image or cross and concentrate on his or her wellbeing. The beneficiary 'helps' the shaman thereby, and his or her involvement is considered to have an impact on the success or failure of the performance. During the performance, the shaman stands behind or off to the right side of the patient and wipes freshly cut flowers or *sip če?* cuttings down the body, holding them in his right hand, and at certain points lightly striking the head and body with them, or holding his right palm over the head. This is said to transfer his *fluúido* 'fluid, energy' to the patient. Delivery style is adjusted to the shaman's perception of the strength of the patient, *peká?an* 'fast' for strong ones and *suave* 'soft' for the weak. The beneficiary remains silent and immobile throughout. If it is a child, it usually sits in its mother's lap (possibly breast-feeding throughout), the woman facing DC who faces her reciprocally (but does not gaze on her) with the altar on his right, leaning forward to touch the child. In all cases, the physical connection between the participants is a focused and sustained component of the phenomenal framework.

Most *saántiguar* performances take place in the home of the shaman, before his personal altar, where he receives patients and conducts divinations. At any given performance of either type, there may be an audience consisting of individuals and groups who have come for treatment and are sitting on the bench or in a hammock behind the altar, awaiting their turn. The patient is often accompanied by a family member who interacts with DC and the patient, discussing the situation before or after the performance or just making small talk. The audience is nowhere mentioned or noticeably attended to by the participants, but there can be little doubt that a shaman is aware of its presence and in some sense oriented towards it. In scores of recorded sessions, I have witnessed only one case in which a person actually addressed DC while he was performing. It was a woman who asked while taking leave when she should return for another treatment. DC was well into another *saántiguar*, focused and engaged with another patient, but he responded *taàrde saáma* 'tomorrow afternoon' instantly and without even breaking the rhythm of his prayer. Patients awaiting treatment do not always pay attention to the performance going on before them, and they may interact and laugh among themselves throughout it without breaching propriety. Thus, although the referential projections in *saántiguar* never focus on the audience, in the corporeal frame of performance, the category may be occupied and become suddenly relevant.

The bodily contact of shaman and patient is asymmetric in the concrete sense that the former speaks over and acts on the latter. They have in common their proximity to the altar, but it is usually the shaman's personal altar, which only he knows intimately. There is a vast discrepancy in the relevant knowledge bases of the participants given by their respective positions. Called a *hmèen* 'doer' or a *hk'iìnil wiínik* 'sun person', the shaman possesses an entire life history of specialized knowledge that allows him to diagnose an illness and properly address scores of spirits by name and according to their spatial order in the cosmos (see chapters 7 and 8). The language he speaks in performing is probably not even intelligible to the patient, since it is a specialized code with a special delivery style.[29] What the patient perceives is the physical contact and the vibration of the voice, coming from near his head but out of his field of vision. Of course, there is a deep-rooted familiarity in all this for the patient, and strips of *reésar,* such as the recurrent signs of the cross, are recognizable, just as the idea of a table with saints' images on it or a shaman with crystals kept in liquor or holy water are familiar to nonspecialists. But to the untrained, the dynamic of the prayer, exactly what it says and why it takes that particular form, remain out of reach. This means that the background frame spaces on which the discourse is grounded, including the inferables and many of the constraints in the immediate situation, are different for the two participants. Despite their coengagement in the corporeal frame, they are occupying different 'here's'. Consequently, the numerous *En* frames projected in the prayer, its discourse representations, are available only to the shaman.

The phenomenal framework of the *saántiguar* changes over the course of the performance, punctuated by the shamans' lightly striking (*haç'ik*) the patient, by the shifting contours of his utterances, the silence-to-sound and sound-to-silence transitions at beginning and end, the breathing. It is not uncommon for a patient to relax visibly during the performance, to weep, and in some cases even sob in relief. But aside from the patient, in that portion of the event frame accessible only to the shaman, equally dramatic changes are effected by the discourse at the level of its projected representation. Moreover, the representation is 'performative' in the speech act sense that it applies reflexively to the *Es* in which it occurs, so that the phenomenal framework is transformed in the image of the represented frames. This is a global process that will be explained in terms of spatial frames in chapter 7 and merits a detailed analysis. Here I will focus selectively on the representation of the speech itself and the coparticipants (shaman, patient, and spirits).

In everyday Maya conversation, speakers rarely utter canonical performative sentences in which they perform a speech act by projecting it as a representation. Utterances like 'I (hereby) promise that S', 'I warn you', 'I agree', 'I assure you', and so forth are rare. In *reésar,* by contrast, explicit performatives are ubiquitous, occurring up to forty or more times in a single prayer of twenty-seven breath groups (Hanks 1984c: Appendix). The forms include the following specialized formulas:

(24)   **k-u-b'in**   **in-t'anik** bakaán šan u-beéyntisyòon
         Aux-Pro3-Vb   Pro1-Vb Prt   Prt Pro3-N
         'It goes (continues) I address evidently   its (the) blessing.'

(25)   **t-u-t'an-ab'al**   **inw-ok'oh?oól** ?in-šolanpìiš ?iŋ-k'aátik . . . .
         Aux-Pro3-Vb-Psv Pro1-Vb   Pro1-Vb   Pro1-Vb
         'It is spoken   I beg weeping I kneel   I request . . . .'

(26)   ?in-yuúm ↑ **k'uč-ik**   **b'ey šan iŋ-k'aátik**
         Pro1-N (Voc) Vb-Prft   Adv Prt Pro1-Vb
         'My lord!   (the time) has arrived too   that I request

         bakaán šan u-beéyntisyòon o
         Prt   Prt Pro3-N
         evidently too the blessings.'

The verbs for address and request are the same ones introduced in §5.2 above, whereas the expression *-ok'oh?oól* 'beg' (lit., 'weep-will'; cf. §3.2.2 on 'will') is apparently archaic and is used exclusively in ritual petitions. The auxiliary verbs are also specialized: 'it goes, is going on' is in my experience never used in self-reference to one's own speech, although the syntactic structure [Aux-Pro3-Vb$_1$ [Pro1-Vb$_2$]] is regular; in it the third person pronoun cross-indexes the rightmost clause and V$_1$ is an auxiliary like 'begin, end, finish'. The passive formation *-ab'-* in (25) is an archaic form common in colonial Maya but rare in modern Maya, and the use of a passivized auxiliary element in reference to one's own action is atypical in nonritual speech. The temporal background of shamanic prayer includes a rich historical foundation, and the auxiliary *k'uč-ik* 'it has arrived' locates the performance as an event whose time has come. What the prayer projects in the first instance is a speech event, an *Esn* frame in which the shaman is the speaker, God is the addressee, and a blessing is what is requested.

The shaman's representation of himself in prayer includes the many first person references attached to metalinguistic formulas, as well as sev-

eral descriptions of himself as a *pékadòor, ?ah k'eban* 'sinner'. Although
the form of the prayer is his own creation, and there is individual vir-
tuosity in performance, he never names himself or describes his own
identity beyond the general terms for 'sinner'. There is an important sense
in which the shaman is anonymous in prayer, standing as an elemental
human before the spirits. Although people describe shamans as powerful,
some of them, like DC, describe themselves as merely facilitating an
event in which the agentive forces are spiritual. It is part of DC's footing
that he merely begs to be given a blessing or enough power (*poder*) to
cure, or begs that the patient be swept by the spirits. He does not banish
the illness with directives or assert that a cure is taking place.[30]

The patient is presented only in the third person, described as an *?ah
siísab'il* 'human' (lit., 'one who has been born'), 'angel' if it is an infant,
as *?a-?iiho* 'your son' if it is a male, and *?a-?iiha* 'your daughter' if it is a
woman. The whole body of the patient is described as his or her 'earth',
and particular parts may be mentioned in accordance with the case, such
as the *k'iík'el* 'blood', *bèenas* 'veins', *hoób'neh* 'abdomen'.

Spirits are represented primarily in the third person, and the sole canonical addressees are God the Father and Jesus Christ. The Holy Spirits
are cited by proper name and described as possessors of grace, agents of
verbs of curing (such as sweeping, cooling, blowing over), and especially
as the possessors of the altar at which the performance takes place. It is
this link of the spirit to the altar that makes the spirit present in the corporeal frame. It constitutes a specialized case of transposition of the second kind, where a referent is brought into the corporeal framework. The
difference here is that the transposition is effected without the use of demonstratives, and paradoxically, it is done in the third person. Instead of
saying to the spirit the equivalent of 'You X are here', the shaman says, 'I
am at the altar of X', and, in the projecting of this spatial frame, X is
made present. Shamans describe this process as 'lowering' the spirits and
'standing them up' around the altar (see chapters 7 and 8). The place is
thereby bound (*k'aš* 'tie, lash'), and in other ritual contexts, DC describes
this as a means of protecting himself from any spirits loosed in the performance by 'raising up fire' around himself.

There is therefore a discrepancy between the actual role of spirits, as
the central addressees of the prayer and agents of the cure, on the one
hand, and their coding as third persons in the discourse, on the other. The
discrepancy is resolved by transposing them from the role of referents
into the actual role of Adr (the pragmatic inverse of the pattern called 'excluded Adr' illustrated above, where a corporeally present actor is commented on in the third person). This new corporeal frame, in which the

spirits provide a perimeter of perspective points all looking inward on the patient, is real only for the shaman; only he knows of its presence.

In DC's practice, the sequential order in which spirits are referred to in *réesar* is governed by strict conventions. The latter relate to the spatial distribution of spirits in the Maya cosmos and specify that the order of references follows the vertical and cyclic order in which the spirits are arranged. Vertical ordering distinguishes high from low, in a series of horizontal planes above and below the surface of the earth (see §7.3.1). The higher spirits are more powerful and uniformly benevolent, some of those associated with the earth are ambivalent (capable of causing harm), and those from below the earth are canonically malevolent. Different genres of performance utilize the fact of vertical organization differently, but it is always relevant, since anywhere from two dozen to fifty or more spirits are cited in any single performance. The major rain ceremony, called *č'aá čaák* 'get rain' (see §8.3.2), proceeds normatively by citing low before high spirits, whereas in the *saántiguar*, the order oscillates (Hanks 1984c:144).

Complementing the vertical principle is a cyclic one based on the distribution of spirits in the cardinal locations, East, North, West, South, Center. At any single level, most spirits are known to be located in a specific cardinal location, so that any individual can be assigned a vertical and a horizontal-cyclic value. Cyclic ordering is more tightly constrained than vertical, being counterclockwise for certain phases of a performance and clockwise for others.[31]

Beyond the details of referent sequence is an important point for the notion of a performance frame. The organization of spirits plus the discourse principles that translate spatial locations into sequential orders are all part of DC's available background knowledge. These facts (virtually) never enter the patient's awareness or representation. From DC's perspective, they are a major part of the third-level frame space, and they literally define the space of possible positions relative to which he orients himself. This already given knowledge governs the referential projections of the prayer, which become a diagram of the cosmos. The diagram in turn acts reflexively on the performance frame, because of the illocutionary force of the utterance, and transforms it. Thus, background knowledge which is initially beyond the local framework of an utterance guides the construction of discourse frames which in turn alter the framework. We might call this double transposition a means of **localizing** background knowledge (from a frame space into a framework).

The process of performing a *saántiguar* can therefore be seen as a systematic elaboration of a complex frame in which a projected *Esn* repre-

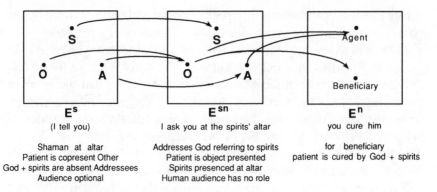

Fig. 5.12. Participant frames in the *saántiguar* performance.

sents the shaman as speaker, God as addressee, and both spirits and patient as Other. From this frame is projected another *En* in which the requested treatments are described, casting the patient as object and as a place where changes are wrought by spirits. The participant frame in the actual *Es* performance is highly asymmetric throughout, a fact embodied in participants' corporeal postures, and is transformed by the superimposition of the *Esn-En* complex onto it: the reported speech events are the very ones being performed, and the described treatments actually take place. The main nexus for the transposition is the altar as a space within which the copresence of spirits and humans can be constructed. Given that 'we are at the altar of X', X is made present. This is (crudely) schematized in figure 5.12.

5.3.3 Divination and Transposition

The divination practice called *tiíč'k'aák'* 'illumination' draws on much of the same background already described but results in a distinctive configuration of frames and tropes connecting them.[32] Like the sanctification, this performance involves the shaman, a subset of spirits, and a human beneficiary. It is typically performed at the shaman's personal altar, where his *saástuún* 'divining crystals (lit., light rocks)' are kept in a bowl of holy water or liquor, and the focal purpose of the performance is to gain knowledge. The knowledge sought is actually described in some detail in the recitation and takes the form of a visual image that the shaman perceives in his divining crystals. He then associates the image before him with the body of the patient or some relevant other, with a residential space, or with some scene of action about which there is a question (for instance, 'Who stole my bicycle?' and the perpetrator appears in the crystals). Whereas the *saántiguar* transforms the spatial setting and participant structure of the performance, making the spirits present, divination transforms the perceptual field of the shaman, bringing into visual access otherwise nonperceivable things, including a patient's inner experiences.

There are clearly demarcated phases in the divination event which must be specified before we proceed. When a Maya person arrives at a shaman's for a divination, (s)he usually tells him little or nothing about his or her problem, leaving it up to him to divine it. In the opening segment, a strip of *reésar* is performed, during which the shaman holds his right hand over the bowl, dipping his index finger into the liquid, and touching the crystals occasionally. The purpose of this is to transfer his *fluúido* 'fluid, energy' to the crystals to awaken them. During the performance, there is always a candle lit right before the shaman, and at the end of the first phase, he picks them up one at a time and examines them in the light. It is not necessary that the target of examination be copresent with the shaman, but if he is (assuming it is an individual), or if any of his kin are present, DC will talk with them during this phase. This is the interactive portion of the event, which may last for nearly an hour if it is a difficult case. During it, the shaman and others converse in routine conversational Maya, while the shaman maintains tactual contact with the crystals. He tells the patient what (s)he is feeling, and what kinds of prior feelings (s)he has had. Once satisfied that he has found the problem, the shaman unilaterally breaks off discussion and starts a brief closing recitation in which the spirits are returned to their axiomatic places and the crystals 'wiped clean'. The stones themselves are then placed back in their customary place on the altar, and the shaman may continue to interact with the interested parties, planning a course of intervention or just talking. Thus, in this event, one can see clearly how the participant frames actual at any given point implicate both prior preparatory ones and subsequent ones in which the knowledge acquired will be put to use (cf. Irvine's [1985] discussion of the temporality inscribed in Wolof insult poetry).

The opening prayer of *tiíč'k'aák'* keys a major transformation in the utterance framework, because it signals the addition of spirit interlocutors to the frame, who are both referred to and addressed. The beneficiary, who had been and will shortly be once again an addressee, is shifted into the role of a nonparticipant object of scrutiny. The asymmetric knowledge base on which the coparticipants in *saántiguar* draw is similar in this event, and is made even more piquant by the fact that the shaman sees and describes the patient's private experiences. He looks into the patient's inner life through the crystals, but the patient cannot peer back the way an interlocutor can respond. In fact, the shaman stands at the juncture of two *Es* frames: one in which he and the beneficiary are coparticipants before the altar; asymmetry is embodied in his superior knowledge and vision, his posture, and his ability to expand his own corporeality into the patient's. In the other frame, he and the spirits interact, leaving the beneficiary as an object of scrutiny. Here the asymmetry consists in the shaman's lowly human status before his more powerful interlocutors, his humble but persistent footing in prayer, his relation to the altar. Insofar as the crystals are the screen on which the representation of illness is projected, they are the concrete nexus between the two event frames that make up the shaman's phenomenal framework. During the interactive portion after the initial recitation, he maintains both footings simultaneously, holding a crystal and gazing at it while talking to his human interlocutor, occasionally addressing a strip of *reésar* to the spirits, imploring them to help, and occasionally averting his gaze toward the patient.

The discourse representation projected by the opening prayer of *tiíč'k'aák'* is more complex than the one for *saántiguar,* because it contains performative components typical of *reésar* but also grammatically overt interrogatives, directives, and conditional statements. The phases making up the opening prayer are as shown in table 5.2, where the upper terms correspond to earlier stages and the crosses key the beginning and ending.

DC systematically constructs a participation frame in his prayer, starting with God as 'you', himself as 'I', his location 'at the foot of your altar', and his activity as informing and asking for the power and the blessing.

(27)   tyá   b'in šan ʔin-maánsik kwèenta bakaán tiʔ tulaákal
            Comp Prt Prt Pro1-Vb   N   Prt   Prt Quant
            'In order that I pass the story (spread the word) evidently to all

            a-sàanto bakaán . . .
            Pro2-N   Prt
            of your saints.' (F.47.A.320)

TABLE **5.2** Phases in the Opening Prayer of *Tiíč'k'aák'*

Cross
Address and presentation of self
Invocation of spirits
Presentation of request
(Pose alternatives)
Presentation of object
(Pose alternatives)
Cross

(28)   tyá   b'in šan in-k'aátik u-poóder e   bakáan ti⁷
              Comp Prt Prt Pro1-Vb Pro3-N   Prt Prt   Prt
              'In order that I request too the power evidently of

              šoó⁷ balan ⁷iik'o b'in šan . . .
              Name   Plur(?) Prt Prt
              Xo Balam spirit reportedly.' (F.47.A.323)

Following this, the spirits are cited by name, not as the possessors of the altar as in *saántiguar,* but rather as those to whom the 'story is passed'. That is, they are coded in the dative as the addressees in reported events of communication.

Given the way *reésar* works, we would expect that this projected *Esn* would performatively alter the actual utterance frame, so that the spirits described as ones to whom things are said are actually being thereby addressed. This expectation is borne out in the following breath groups of the prayer, where the spirits are directly addressed with imperatives and appealed to in the second person, as in (29):

(29)   ⁷é⁷es-é⁷eš   ten té⁷   t-a-sàanto krìistal-é⁷eš a⁷
              Vb-Imper-Pro2Pl Pro1 DLOC Prt-Pro2-Adj N-Pro2P1TD
              'Show me (you all) right here in you sacred crystals,

              ⁷in-yuúm ↑
              Pro1-N (Voc)
              my God!' (F.47.A.328)

The fact that these forms occur indicates securely that DC has constructed a new indexical frame in which the spirits are full-fledged addressees and not just third person referents made present.[33]

The posing of alternatives consists in a stretch of discourse in which the shaman actually suggests possible diagnoses and tells the spirits to show him whether they are accurate. For instance, in the performance from which (27–29) come, he asked:

(30)   wá tumèen ti⁷ suhùuy ⁷ifk' u-tàal e⁷   ⁷in-yuúm ↑
              If Comp   Prt Adj   N   Pro3-Vb TD Pro1-N(Voc)
              'Because if from sacred wind it came, my God!

              k'ub'-é⁷eš   ten   t-a-sàanto kristàal é⁷eš→
              Vb-Imper-Pro2-Pl Pro1 Prt-Pro2-Adj N-Pro2P1
              Deliver it to me in your sacred crystals.' (F.47.A.343)

In this example, there is apparently an ambiguity in the second person forms as to who is addressee, the superordinate God projected in the vocative phrase or this God along with all the named spirits who derive their power from him. It is not obvious to me how to resolve this, or whether it should be resolved.

There is another shift in the shaman's footing relative to the spirits toward the end of the opening prayer, where he switches into the first person plural.

(31)   hé²e tú²uš u-tàal   e² ²in-yuúŋ ↑
            Adv Adv Pro3-Vb TD Pro1-N(Voc)
            'Wherever it comes from, my God!'

            ȼ'-ú-k'učǔl   t-u-k'iini   šan ↓ uti²á **k**-reébisàartik
            Aux-Pro3-Vb Prt-Pro3-N Prt   Comp **Pro1** Vb
            'It has come to its time too, for **us** to review

            le   ²u-lú²umil o²
            DNOM Pro3-N   TD
            that earth (of the patient).' (F.47.A.348)

Who is referred to by the first person plural morpheme (in boldface)? Clearly, this utterance is grounded in the indexical frame in which the shaman is addressing the spirits and the patient is an inactive third person object. Not only is the patient described by the traditional metonymic descriptor 'earth' in reference to his physical aspect, but he is also excluded from the 'we' on the grounds that he does not participate in the act of 'reviewing'. The shaman is teamed up with God and his spirit helpers.

After closing the prayer with the sign of the cross and examining the crystals for a moment (usually between 5 and 30 seconds), DC again shifts footing, this time transposing himself into the alternative *Es* frame in which the addressee is the beneficiary. The ensuing interaction takes place with the shaman examining a representation of the patient in the crystals while simultaneously addressing him. This is the opposite of what was called 'excluded addressee' in (§5.2.2), because in the latter case, we have a speaker actually directing his or her speech at an individual while describing the individual in the third person, whereas in the present case, we have the shaman actually looking at an objectified image of the person, while verbally addressing him in the second person. It is noteworthy that if a shaman were to break into the excluded addressee pattern of address during this event, looking at the individual and asking him about himself in the third person, it would be very weird and probably frightening for the patient. The genre of the event sustains certain frame configurations while ruling others out: the pattern 'excluded addressee' is not available, but what we might call 'participant object' is. This schematized in figure 5.13.

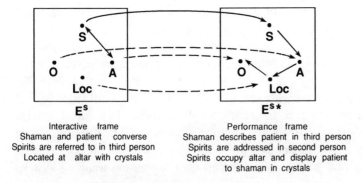

Interactive frame	Performance frame
Shaman and patient converse	Shaman describes patient in third person
Spirits are referred to in third person	Spirits are addressed in second person
Located at altar with crystals	Spirits occupy altar and display patient
	to shaman in crystals

Fig. 5.13. Decentered frames in Maya divination.

The transitions between prayer to the spirits and discussion with the patient is unmistakably keyed by the different delivery styles of the speech. When DC ends his prayer, he pauses and examines the crystals. His next utterance will be addressed to the patient, in this case a senior woman.

(32)   ʔèèe mamá ↑ letiʔ   oʔ ↓ yàan   teč aʔ ↓ máʔ ʔìik'
             Intrj N(Voc) DNOM TD Pro3-Vb Pro2 TD Neg N
             'Aw Mama, that thing that you've got here, it's not a wind that

             cukmahilec iʔiʔiʔ→
             Vb   Trm Trm Trm
             struck you.' (F.47.A.367)

DC assured the woman here that what ailed her was not as serious as if she had actually been struck by a spirit. He went on to explain to her that the natural wind in her body was out of sorts because she was nervous. She thereupon agreed and started talking volubly, recounting the various daily experiences she was having that agitated her—her drunken husband, visits to the doctor and his diagnosis, chest pains, lower back pains. DC listened and reassured, listened, and slipped back into recitation in the middle of one of her utterances. He thereupon closed off the crystals and brought the official event to an end, pausing about five seconds before addressing me and noting that the woman's doctor had diagnosed the case the same way as DC did (F.47.A.428).

During the interactive phase, the displacement of the patient, as alternatively nonparticipant and then addressee, is matched by the alteration in the perceptual field and the posture of the shaman. In all divination in Maya, the visual evidence of states of affairs is central, and the extension of the shaman's visual field is the transformation alluded to in the name of the genre, 'illuminate'. This operates on a spatial metaphor in which the crystal embodies a diagrammatic miniature of the space being examined (see §7.4.3). As a consequence of this, the shaman engages in interestingly transposed deictic references during the interaction that would be impossible or humorous in everyday speech. For instance, he looks at the crystals, points to a mark in them, and says things like, 'see that, here you are, I see what's wrong with you' (F.125.A.090ff.). Recall from §5.2.2 that this sort of reference is usually used to equate the addressee with some object being ostended, for humorous purposes. The difference here is that the device of the crystals provides the basis for an actual image of the addressee, the way a movie screen or a sonograph imaging system might in another society.

Divination therefore illustrates several points of importance to a theory of interactive frames. The switching between frames, and even combining frames simultaneously by the shaman, is a reminder that no simple notion of an *Es* speech event will do. Phenomenal copresence in the sense of 'who is really here now' is not merely a matter of physical presence but is mediated by background knowledge. The context of divination, like that of a 'sanctification', imposes certain modes of frame production on interactants, while ruling others out. For instance, the engagement of the bodily person of the patient rules out having one person go for a divination in another's stead, the way one could seek advice on behalf of another. The patient cannot reveal himself to be representing some other unmentioned party, nor could he reveal his words to actually be a transposition from someone else's speech.[34] The same goes for the shaman, who enters into a very tightly controlled and decentered frame construct, in which his moves must be precise to be effective. In this frame, and in the actual framework of any performance, there is no such thing as a make-believe posture or a 'deferred cure' in which one person's body serves as the medium for another's. These factors further illustrate the necessity of recognizing the frame space within which actual frameworks are definable in terms of genre. The schematization of discourse into genres, like the two treated here, brings with it limits on the range of participant roles and occupancies actors can assume.

5.4 CONCLUSION

We began this chapter with the descriptive problem of how to account for relatively complex participation frames, in which the referents of pronouns were not simply the utterer and his receiver. It is important to recognize that this problem arises with all deictics, not only pronouns. It would be possible in theory either to increase the inventory of participant roles recognized or to maintain a fairly minimal set of roles and P frames, which then could somehow be combined. We chose the latter alternative and used the mechanisms of centering, decentering, transposition, and referential projection to account for some of the complex frames attested in routine Maya interaction. This led us to describe in a unified manner several patterns of speech not commonly joined together in linguistic descriptions, namely, quotation, transposition in the sense of Bühler's theory of deixis, certain forms of creative reference, and a pattern of reference that was called 'excluded addressee'. All of them involve the projection of an alternative indexical ground, either through description or tacit displacement of the speaker's assumed zero point. Pronouns can be interpreted in a simple, consistent way once it is recognized that an utterance may project more than one ground relative to which reference is calculated. In other words, the interpretive complexity of such examples lies not in the participant categories but in the contextualization of the categories in complex frames and frameworks. This contextualization is what determines how frames are to be interpreted and related to the participants (Gumperz 1982:131). The schemata presented in figures 5.1–5.13 were introduced in order to give a graphic representation of this.

It was found that the general form of demonstrative reference as developed in preceding and subsequent chapters, abbreviated as $R(x,i)$, provides a simple, unequivocal way of handling these pragmatic phenomena without positing any new categories or new linguistic processes. Complex frame embeddings, insofar as they effect the interpretation of participant structures, can be explained in terms of indexical-referential chains between frames. These were symbolized as the arced arrows in the schemata, where the R values of the pronouns indicate which portion of the indexical frame is being identified with a portion of the frame projected by description. If the analysis is correct, then it provides strong corroboration for the approach being proposed here, since it will allow us to treat basic-level person reference in the same way as evidently complex or unrelated phenomena such as quotation and transposition.

Parallel to the descriptive problem of characterizing nonbasic participation frames, this chapter has proposed a series of analytic levels needed in order to account for the relation between utterance forms and social contexts. It was necessary to undertake such a leveling in order to give consequences to the commonsense observation that in any social context, the array of participation frames available to interactants is limited, and much of the social *présavoir* that speakers bring to speech is embodied in their appreciation of the alternatives open at any point. Four kinds of frame construct were distinguished: a **simple frame** is one made up of a configuration of categories; a **complex frame** is composed of two or more simple ones in a determinate relation. Frames are the schematic elements corresponding to aspects of the interactive **framework**, where the latter is an actual, historically specific process of communication. Frameworks in turn take place against the background **frame space** of potential moves and footings that could be realized but are not actual in the present. Referential practice always involves complex frames grounded in a sociocultural frame space which has among its organizing principles a system of discourse genres and social fields. As an illustration of how these levels interact, two genres of Maya ritual performance were sketched.

There is in all of this an interplay between two inverse tendencies. The first is the tendency for speakers to recapitulate in their descriptive representations of the world the very conditions of their current utterances. Regardless of the presence or absence of transpositions and embeddings, speech takes place in social contexts, and these impose constraints on what gets said, as well as opening up many possibilities that may never be realized in a given event. The current 'here-now' of any utterance is itself a space of possibilities, not a concrete object immediately given to observation. Utterances may imply multiple 'implicated dialogues', such as the ones described by Irvine (1987) or the ones shown in Maya divination. In all cases, a phenomenal framework implies a frame space of possibilities and background expectancies that is always present, whether brought into play or not. This is why it is unrealistic to attempt to treat participation frames apart from the sociocultural world in which they are generated.

The inverse tendency is that which grants to language the effectiveness to alter the framework in which it is used, so that a descriptive representation of the world is realized, made actual, in its own uttering. The ritual examples illustrate, albeit dramatically and at times by inversion, what goes on constantly in routine conversation. Speakers refer to their own corporeal field in ways that alter it. It is entirely expectable that shifters, being both indexically and referentially focused on participant access to objects, would have an important role in this. The examples of creative reference, excluded addressee, and the displacements in divination meet this expectation.

When speakers use demonstrative elements, they invariably situate themselves in an indexical frame in the very act of making reference to the world. Like corporeal and other kinds of 'position takings', reference and frame projection are constrained and can be disputed. Agents of communication have construable rights, obligations, dispositions, and habitual ways of creating and occupying participation frames. Reference is a way of occupying the sociocultural world, an embodiment of self and meaning in practice.

6 The Perceptual Core of Ostensive Reference

6.1 INTRODUCTION

The category of deictics to be described in this chapter, which we will call the Ostensive Evidentials (OSTEVs), presupposes for its definition the participant structures to which pronouns refer. These forms are functionally complex, with conventional illocution-like forces, including Presentative and Directive, as well as a range of R relations that includes three kinds of perception, reference to discourse, and anticipatory reference to objects not yet present. The indexical grounding of OSTEV utterances works in basically the same way as other deictics, leading us to distinguish relatively symmetrical from asymmetrical grounds, as well as a range of de-centerings analogous to those in chapter 5. The forms are displayed below.

hé?el	a?	'here it is (I give it to you, take it!)'
hé?el	o?	'there it is (I point it out to you, look!)'
hé?e	b'e?	'there it is (I hear it, listen!)'
hé?el	e?	'for sure, indeed'

Like most other deictics in Maya, these are composed of two morphemes each, an initial ID base and a TD terminal. On the face of it, the OSTEVs are composed of a single ID, *hé?e(l)*, which combines with any of four TDs, {*a?*, *o?*, *b'e?*, *e?*}. Of the TDs, the first two are the familiar Immediate and Non-Immediate that recur in all major categories of deictics except the Participant forms (cf. chapters 1 and 9). In the OSTEVs, they retain their relative immediacy values but take on specialized perceptual and actional corollaries. The third TD is of restricted distribution in the deictic system, occurring only with nominal demonstratives and OSTEVs (never with spatial, temporal, or manner deictics). The meaning of the form is invariant: it indexes that the Spkr has perceptual access to the referent at the instant of utterance, **but can neither touch it nor see it.** In the absence of tactual and visual evidence, the Spkr of *b'e?* usually hears the referent but alternatively might smell it (like a fire). We will call this feature 'peripheral sensory' (Prph), since it localizes the referent on the fringe of the perceptual field.

The last form, *hé?el e?*, is significantly different from the others, as the gloss reflects. In fact, this form does not belong fully to the OSTEV category, since it functions grammatically as a modal auxiliary to a verb (DMOD) and is not a referring expression at all. The terminal *e?* occurs elsewhere in the deictic system and never signals relative immediacy or perceptual access of any sort; it is an empty placeholder, used also to mark off topicalized elements and to signal relations across clauses. These differences notwithstanding, the motivations for treating the DMOD together with the OSTEV forms turn on the apparent identity of the ID base. Not only are they phonologically identical, but they have the same morphophonemic variants: *hé?el* ∼ *hé?e* ∼ *hé?* ∼ *hV́*. The loss of final *-l* occurs preconsonantally and *V́?V* is commonly reduced to *V́?* in Maya phonology, so neither of these is particularly distinctive of this deictic category. It is the last reduction that is distinctive, in which the glottal stop is omitted and the root vowel is altered, retaining the high tone of the lexical base. This happens when the ID is followed by a vowel-initial prefixal Participant form, as in the following:

(1)   hé? insukú?un o? ∼ hínsukú?un o?
           'There's my elder brother.'

(2)   hé?intàal e? ∼ híntàal e?
           'I'll come for sure.'

(3)   hé? a b'in e? ∼ háb'in e?
           'You'll go for sure.'

This alternation is parallel to the one between *¢'ó?ok* ∼ *¢'V́* (retaining high tone on *V́*), which occurs in the same context but it is unique among deictics.[1] As additional motivation for assuming a relation between the IDS, it is noteworthy that the DMOD form is occasionally used as a directive, with approximately the same conveyed meaning as standard tokens of *hé?elo?*. Finally, the DMOD and the OSTEVs are in complementary distribution, the former in VC-initial position and the latter in S-initial position, and they never co-occur in the same clause (Hanks 1983: chap. 3; 1984a). For these reasons, we will assume that the ID base *hé?e(l)* is the same in all four forms, which will therefore be treated as a set.

6.1.1 Initial Grammatical Distinctions

The distinction between the three OSTEV deictics and the modal DMOD has a basis in the grammatical distributions of the forms.[2] The former occur in sentence-initial position and may be the sole predicate, as in:

(4)   hé⁷ le b'á⁷al o⁷
             'There's that thing.'

(5)   hé⁷ le máak kinwá⁷alik teč o⁷
             'There's the guy I'm telling you about.'

The DMOD usually co-occurs with a verb or particle (when a verb is recon-structible), but almost never occurs in structures like (4–5) where the ID base is followed by a NP.

(6)   hé⁷ ub'in e⁷
             '(S)he'll surely go.'

(7)   hé⁷ šan e⁷
             '(It) will surely also (be).'

When used to modalize a verb, *hé⁷el e⁷* requires the incompletive stem shape (as in 6), and no syntactic process may separate the ID from imme-diately preverbal position. Thus, whereas (8) and (10) are fine, (9) and (11) are ungrammatical.

(8)   hé⁷ le maák₁ kub'in₂ o⁷
             'There goes₂ the guy₁'

(9)   *hé⁷ le maák ub'in e⁷
             *'the guy'll surely go'

(10)   hé⁷ le maák₁ h b'in₂ o⁷
             'There went₂ the guy₁ (I just saw it)'

(11)   *hé⁷ le maák h b'in e⁷
             *'the guy surely went'

The syntactic constraints on *hé⁷el e⁷* are the same as (or similar to) those that restrict other verbal auxiliaries with aspectlike functions in Maya, including *yàan* 'necessitative, obligative', *¢'ó⁷ok* 'completive', *šú⁷ul* 'terminal', and *k-*'incompletive'.[3] *hé⁷el e⁷* is also mutually ex-clusive with these other auxiliaries and will therefore be treated as an Aux itself.

The linguistic material following the *hé⁷* base of an OSTEV may be a plain noun or a definite NP, with or without further modifiers.

(12)   **hé⁷** siíná⁷an o⁷
             'There's (a) scorpion (Look!).'

(13)   **hé⁷** le nuši⁷ čak siíná⁷an tinwá⁷alah teč o⁷
             'There's that big red scorpion I told you about.'

Furthermore, unlike the DMOD, which occurs in main clauses only, the OSTEVs may be subordinated and function as the sole predicate in a rela-tive clause.

(14)   čeén wá le   hé²el u-b'in   a-ȼ'ó²ok-s-ik   o²
              Prt Q DNOM OSTEV Apro-Vb Apro-Vb-Caus-Inc TD
              'Is that all you've got left to finish?' (BB.4.99)

These initial observations fit into a much larger pattern of grammatical differentiation between OSTEV and DMOD forms, which I have laid out elsewhere (Hanks 1984a) and will only summarize here. The true OSTEVs never co-occur in the same clause with the hypothetical particle *wá* (which marks yes-no questions, the if-clause of conditionals, and both disjuncts of an either-or statement). They never co-occur with the conjectural particle *miín* 'probably, maybe, I suppose', nor can the identity of the referent be questioned.[4] Thus, the following are unattested in speech and refused by Maya informants.

(15)   *hé² wá kubin o²
              'There he goes (look!)?'

(16)   *wá hé² kubin o², má²alob
              'If there he goes (look!), good.'

(17)   *wá tuún hé² kubin o², wá má²
              'Either there he goes (look!), or not.'

(18)   *miín hé² kubin o²
              'I suppose there he goes (look!).'

(19)   *maáš hé² kubin o²
              'Who there he goes (look!)?'

Such utterances are unacceptable because they are pragmatically contradictory: a speaker cannot present or direct attention to a referent while simultaneously calling its existence into question. In every case, the DMOD can be substituted for the OSTEV (with appropriate changes) and the result is a grammatical sentence,

(20)   hé² wá ubin e²
              'Will he go indeed?'

(21)   wá hé² ubin e², má²alob
              'If he'll go, good.'

(22)   wá tuún hé² ubin e², wá má²
              'Either he'll go, or not.'

(23)   miín hé² ubin e²
              'I suppose he'll go.'

(24)   maáš hé² ubin e²
              'Who'll go?'

There is also a distinctive interaction between these deictics and negation. Simple negatives are formed in Maya by the preverbal negative morpheme *má?a,* (which may be accompanied by a terminal *i?* in sentence-final position, depending upon the verb stem and other factors). Any of the OSTEV and DMOD forms can be grammatically negated in this way, but the resulting message is not a negative but instead an emphatic positive. Notice the glosses in the following examples.

(25)   má? ¢'ó?ok ubin i?
         'She has not gone.'

(26)   má? **hé?** ubin e?
         'Of course she'll go for sure.'

(27)   má? **hé?** kubin o?
         'Of course, there she goes (look!).'

The use of negation to express emphasis is relatively common in Maya and by no means limited to deictics. What is special about the deictics formed on the base *hé?,* however, is the fact that they can *never* be semantically negated. This makes sense for the OSTEVs, if one considers the act of directive reference. Speakers do not simultaneously ostend an object while negating its presence; English speakers, for instance, rarely have occasion to say things like, 'there it isn't (look!)', 'here it isn't (making Presentative gesture)', or 'there he doesn't go (look!)'. In the case of the DMOD, it is less evident why it cannot be negated, since negative polarity items (corresponding to nowhere, no one, nothing, etc.) can co-occur with *hé?el e?,* provided they are in focus position. The constraint on *má?* appears relatively arbitrary.

(28)   mištú?uš **hé?** abin e?
         'Nowhere you'll surely go (i.e., you will stay put).'

The expression of emphasis in deictic reference provides a broad field in which to compare and contrast different forms, and will be taken up in chapter 10. Emphatic marking is signaled by reduplication of terminal deictics, of ID bases, combinations of negation with both of these, as well as stereotypical paralinguistic features (nasal, overhigh pitch, expressive *tch!* click). These processes result in the co-occurrence in a single sentence of multiple coreferential deictics, some of them identical in form. The range of emphatic constructions for OSTEV and DMOD deictics provides an additional grammatical differentia between them, since the former is maximal, whereas the latter is more limited. In (29), all eight versions are referentially equivalent, and the conveyed difference between them is the forcefulness and degree of obviousness attaching to the directive.

(29)   hé$^{\textbf{?}}$ kutàal **a**$^{\textbf{?}}$
            má$^{\textbf{?}}$ **hé**$^{\textbf{?}}$ kutàal **a**$^{\textbf{?}}$
            hé$^{\textbf{?}}$ kutàal **a**$^{\textbf{?}}$**a**$^{\textbf{?}}$
            má$^{\textbf{?}}$ **hé**$^{\textbf{?}}$ kutàal **a**$^{\textbf{?}}$**a**$^{\textbf{?}}$

            hé$^{\textbf{?}}$ kutàal **hé**$^{\textbf{?}}$**el a**$^{\textbf{?}}$
            má$^{\textbf{?}}$ **hé**$^{\textbf{?}}$ kutàal **hé**$^{\textbf{?}}$**el a**$^{\textbf{?}}$
            hé$^{\textbf{?}}$ kutàal **hé**$^{\textbf{?}}$**el a**$^{\textbf{?}}$**a**$^{\textbf{?}}$
            má$^{\textbf{?}}$ **hé**$^{\textbf{?}}$ kutàal **hé**$^{\textbf{?}}$**el a**$^{\textbf{?}}$**a**$^{\textbf{?}}$
            'Here (s)he comes (heads up!).'

The DMOD has emphatic variants analogous to the top four in (29) but lacks the bottom four, since it is never copied into sentence-final position as the OSTEVS are.

A final point of significant difference between the OSTEV and DMOD forms is that the former, but not the latter, may be inflected for person. This is related to their respective grammatical functions, since the predicative OSTEVS always take an object, whether an overt NP, a pronominal suffix, or an S, whereas the DMOD, as an Aux element, requires a separate verb, and the latter carries the relevant person marking. Hence, (30) is fine, whereas (30') is ungrammatical.

(30)   **hé**$^{\textbf{?}}$**el**$^{\textbf{?}}$**-ó**$^{\textbf{?}}$**ob a**$^{\textbf{?}}$
            'Here they are (take them!).'

(30')   *hé$^{\textbf{?}}$el-ó$^{\textbf{?}}$ob e$^{\textbf{?}}$
            *'They surely will.'

As might be expected, given the significance of bodily space and participant structure in the OSTEVS, there are interesting restrictions on person marking in these forms. These will be discussed one by one in §6.1.2.

The relation between the OSTEV forms, the R values they may be used to convey, and the communicative functions they perform is not one-to-one. Rather, like most paradigmatic subsystems, the mapping between forms and functions is variable and becomes another dimension on which to differentiate forms. In the OSTEV series, the most marked form by far, is *hé$^{?}$e b'e$^{?}$*, which invariantly conveys Peripheral sensory. *hé$^{?}$el a$^{?}$*, on the other hand, usually conveys Tactual access to the referent but may be used for Visual, Discourse, or Anticipatory as well. We will say that the first of these is the more marked, since it corresponds to a restricted range of variants, whereas the latter is less marked, since it is more variable (cf. §2.2.3). In these terms, the least marked form in this subsystem is *hé$^{?}$el o$^{?}$*, since this OSTEV may be used to convey any of the R values to be discussed. Given the proper communicative circumstances, this form might be a Tactual Presentative, a Visual Directive, a Discourse Directive, a Peripheral Referential, or merely an Expressive item indexing that the Spkr is Certain of his or her assertion. The DMOD, as will be illustrated below, is occasionally used in the Directive function in reference to discourse, giving it a minimum of flexibility not afforded with *hé⁷e b'e⁷*.

In assessing the perceptual features conveyed by given utterances, it is important to observe a distinction between the status of the referent immediately prior to an utterance as opposed to immediately following it. When we speak of different forms indicating different kinds of access, we are not positing an actual sensory link between a participant and an object, but rather a virtual link. An object clearly in sight but not currently in the focus or even visual field of an interlocutor may count as Visual for purposes of individuation. Deictics are used not only to reflect relations of attention already in place, but to direct attention to new objects. When instantiated in a framework, a frame of perceptual reference usually blends into a zone of potentially perceptible objects not currently under attention but available for attention once pointed out. This is a special case of the more global phenomenon addressed in chapter 5: a social present is not only an actual framework of what is in play already but also a frame space in which unrealized but accessible options are present to the interactants. In a multiparty participant framework, actors not currently occupying core P roles can at any moment be projected into those roles through reference to self ('I, we') or others, or through address ('you'). Similarly, in spatial locative deictics, the limits between here and there at any moment in an interactive framework can be redrawn through deictic use—an erstwhile 'over there' can suddenly become a 'right here', even with no change in the corporeal field. Speakers' rights, abilities, and propensities to effect these transformations are of course constrained by their cultural orientations, by the social positions they occupy, their habitual postures in the world, and the kinds of asymmetries that come between them and their present interlocutors.

These last remarks highlight the connection between perceptual deictics and the rest of the deictic system in any language, a tie that becomes even more evident when we consider the R values of these forms and their focus on sensory access. The ability to construct an intersensorial unity out of different modes of perception is at the heart of the *schéma corporel* of actors. Shared, reciprocated, distantiated, and otherwise coengaged perceptual domains are also central in the **corporeal fields** in which action takes place. Deictics like the ones treated in this chapter correspond to finely differentiated referential frames in which aspects of corporeality are combined with other actional capacities through which actors occupy the world in the practice of communication. As such, they provide powerful organizing mechanisms in natural language that help to routinize and tend to schematize sociocultural modes of corporeality. In the process, the body is culturally defined and symbolically projected beyond its own physicality into the conceptual and actional space of communicative practice.

6.1.2 Three Dimensions of Ostensive Reference

The OSTEV deictics are best understood in terms of three primary dimensions, two of which are already familiar. Like all deictics, these forms encode **R values** distinguishing the various relations to ground by which referential objects (x in the standard notation) are individuated. Rather than encoding R values such as Spkr and Adr as the pronouns do, or Immediate, Inclusive as the locative deictics do (see chap. 9), the OSTEVs signal R values defined by perceptual and attentional engagements in the phenomenal field of speech: Tactual, Visual, Peripheral sensory, Discourse, Anticipatory, and Certain. The second dimension is the **indexical ground** of reference, which we will continue to symbolize *i*. Indexical grounds consist in the participation frames relative to which R values are applied. They include what we have called the corporeal frame, the actual relations among interlocutors and referents, against the horizon of a frame space of possibilities open to them. Being deictics, the OSTEVs project complex frames in which the indexical ground is linked to a figural frame of reference. One of the significant conditions of this linkage is the relative symmetry of the ground, that is, the overall sharedness of access to the referent on the part of participants. Quotation, transposition, deferred ostension, and the other kinds of decenterings typical of deictics occur also with the OSTEV forms. These will be described as alterations of the *i* ground of reference, as in chapter 5.

The third dimension of the OSTEV deictics is a **specialized range of functions** that include Presentative, Directive, Referential, and Expressive. 'Function' in this context is used to designate the 'force' or effectiveness of utterances in performing recognizable social acts with certain typical goals, preconditions, and consequences.[5] For example, when a Spkr hands over an object to an interlocutor, saying *hé'el a'* 'Here it is, (take it)', his or her utterance has a Presentative function, in that it is used to focalize and verbalize the presentation of the referent to the Adr, who is within range and able to receive it, with the result that the Adr ends up with the object, and both participants' attention is directed to it. On the other hand, when one points out a passing truck to an interlocutor who is currently engaged in some focused task, such as sharpening a machete, saying, *hé? kubin e maák o?* 'there goes the guy', this utterance has a Directive function. It is issued with the goal of directing the Adr's attention, specifically his focused gaze, on an object not already in his attention. The expectable outcome is that both interlocutors focus visually on the object, for however fleeting a duration. Notice that Presentative entails Directive, since the Adr is directed to focus on and even take up the object; but Directive does not entail Presentative, since the Spkr pointing out a passing vehicle can hardly present that vehicle bodily to an Adr.

As defined here, the Presentative and Directive functions are both predicative in the sense that they designate acts of giving, showing, and pointing out, in which the referent is an object and the participants are agents. Although the forms never take inflection for subject, they do inflect for the person or objects presented. Not all uses of OSTEVs work this way, however, and a description of the pragmatics of these forms must include referential uses as well as predicative ones. For example, when a Spkr asks *?apapah wá e hé?e b'e?* 'Is that your father (audible to us)?' she individuates a sound in the peripheral sensory field in uttering the underlined deictic phrase, but she does not Direct the Adr's attention to that sound.[6] To do this, she would have to say *hé? a papah b'e?* 'There's your father (listen!)', or *hé? leti? b'e?* 'There's the one (Listen!)'. Rather than asserting the sensory availability of the referent, directing attention to it, or presenting it, this utterance presupposes the audibility of the sound and asks about the identity of the individual making it. Similarly, coming to the end of the story about how charcoal and lime are made, DC said, *in swèegro ?é?es ten le meyah o hé?el o?* 'My father-in-law showed me (how to do) those works there (that I've told you about)' (BB.4.87). In this utterance, the underlined OSTEV expression makes reference to the preceding discourse, in which DC had described the 'works' in question. Unlike fully Directive uses of the form, this token is subordinated and used to modify the N 'works', itself a direct object of 'show' in the main clause. As in the preceding example, the OSTEV is used to identify a referent but not to present, demonstrate, or assert its presence. In order to distinguish such cases from the fully Presentative and Directive ones, they will be called Referential. Observe that both Presentative and Directive entail Referential, since they both individuate objects, whatever else they do to them, but Referential does not entail either of the other two. This is not to say that the Referential uses are void of any directivelike function, but rather that the fully embodied Directivity of the main clause OSTEVs is missing in the subordinated ones.

The fourth and final function of the OSTEVs is what we will call Expressive, following Jakobson (1960), that is, the use of language to signal a

Spkr's attitude towards, evaluation of, or expectations regarding what (s)he is saying. It may be less than apparent on first contact what Expressivity so defined has to do with the other functions or with perception, but the relation is a close one. Insofar as a Spkr makes reference to an object by way of its perceptibility, he produces an Expressive act which signals his own current sensory experience at the moment of utterance. This means that all of the preceding functions subsume an Expressive component, probably best represented as a part of the indexical ground to which the R values and functions are joined. Later in this chapter and in chapter 10, we will see that there are productive linguistic processes in Maya whereby speakers can systematically heighten and alter the expressive overtones inherent in deictics. In the present context, analysis of the OSTEV series suggests that the expression of Spkr certainty is linguistically related to the individuation of referents by their perceptual availability. The two are part of a single paradigm, in which perceptual features define the most immediate and concrete form of evidence of the referent, and certainty without perception defines the least immediate. At the lower end is the modal *hé ʔel e ʔ* 'indeed, for sure', containing the same ID base as the OSTEVs but functioning as a verbal auxiliary rather than a referential expression. Figure 6.1 summarizes the three dimensions.

These three dimensions of ostensive reference, the R values, *i* grounds, and communicative functions, combine in a skewed fashion. Certain functions, notably the Directive and Referential, apparently co-occur with nearly the whole range of R values and *i* ground types, which reinforces the independence of the dimensions. Certain others, like Presentative, require a specific R value to be properly instantiated (e.g., Tact), and this value may imply a typical symmetry or asymmetry in the speech event frame. This is the case, for instance, with Tactual, which is more prone to be paired with an asymmetric indexical frame than is Visual. One of the basic facts about this system, then, is that the bundles of features from the three dimensions are limited to relatively few in comparison with the total set of possibilities were the features to combine freely. This selectivity is due to a plurality of factors: definitional limitations of the categories (for instance, one cannot Present a referent assumed not to exist); likely universals of human experience (for instance, although sight, touch, and audition are independent, the body is so structured that a referent within touch is typically within sight and hearing also); and the automatization of certain speech event frames, based on typical perceptual experiences and communicative gestures (cf. discussion of habituation and basic-level participation frames in §4.1). The constitution of reference in such frames, for example, the Tactual Presentative or the Discourse Directive, is a kind

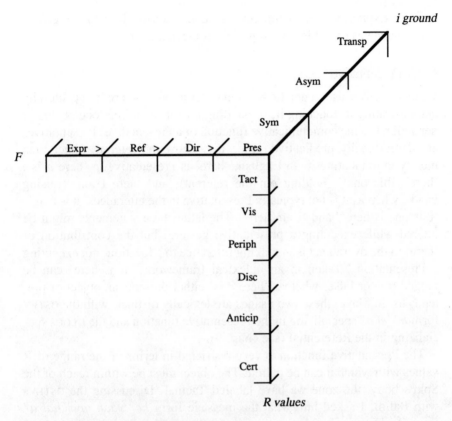

Fig. 6.1. Three dimensions of ostensive reference.

of **embodiment:** the conventional linguistic system is modeled on, and articulated relative to, actionally engaged bodies. At the same time, the link to communicative interaction further selects certain aspects of the entire perceptual apparatus, making visual recognition and touch more relevant than smell or color perception, for example. Moreover, perception enters into practice in relation to other culturally defined corporeal and conceptual capacities of participants, making embodiment once again more general than the body. The OSTEV and DMOD categories therefore provide a further set of links between the language and the phenomenal frameworks with which it is codefined.

6.2 COMMUNICATIVE FUNCTIONS IN THE PERCEPTUAL FIELD

Examples of OSTEV and DMOD usage will be organized in accordance with the three axes in figure 6.1. The first division will be made according to communicative function (horizontal axis), in the order Presentative through Expressive. Each function is subdivided by R values (vertical axis) and states of the indexical ground (diagonal axis).

6.2.1 Presentative

When a speaker uses a deictic form in order to present a referent, literally demonstrating it, touching it, or handing it over to an interlocutor, his or her action has the communicative function of a Presentative. Presentatives are definitionally predicative, since they show the referent rather than merely individuating it. In English, 'here' is Presentative in 'here it is', 'here's this one!' (holding out the referent), and 'here I am' (raising hand), whereas it is not typically Presentative in the utterances 'it is here', 'this one is here', and 'I am here'. The latter three statements might be uttered while executing a presentative gesture, but the contribution of 'here' to the overall act is in making reference to a location, not executing a Presentation.[7] Taken in an indexical framework, 'it is here' can be judged true or false, whereas 'here it is' either presents an object or pretends to. In Maya, these two usages are lexically distinct, with the OSTEV form *hé?el a?* specializing in the Presentative function and the DLOCs specializing in the Referential (see chap. 9).

The Presentative function is very restricted in terms of the range of R values with which it can be paired. The object must be within reach of the Spkr's body, the zone we have labeled Tactual. Discussing the OSTEVs with Balim, I asked him what the message form *hé? yàan tawiknal a?* 'here it is in your bodily space' (see §3.2) would convey if uttered by a Maya speaker. He accepted it as a viable utterance but specified that the Spkr must be right by the Adr and must take the referent in hand, saying:

(31)   . . . péro lelo?   k'ab'eét tí?aneč šan tyiknal i? . . .
             '. . . but that one, you too must   be there in his bodily
             space. . . .

             ?anaȼ'mah ti?, tèeč tiíič'ik
             You've drawn it close to him, you('re the one who) hold it out in
             hand.' (F.19.B.115)

What is interesting about this example and Balim's reaction to it is that the locative expression 'in his bodily space' unavoidably locates the referent in the immediate proximity of the Adr. The OSTEV *hé?el a?* nonetheless is taken to be Presentative, thus unavoidably locating the referent within the focal point of the Spkr's touch. The only way to satisfy both requirements is to locate both Spkr and object within the Adr's bodily space, which Balim promptly does.

6.2.1.1 *Prototypical Presentative*

Prototypical exemplars of the Presentative function are predicative, Tactual, and nontransposed. They are indexically symmetric in the sense that the interlocutors are close enough together for the gesture to be effective and secure the appropriate uptake. For instance, the Adr takes the object in hand or otherwise directs his or her attention and body toward it. Standing outside in the yard of Margot and MC's home, I was washing my hands when Margot, a couple of meters away, picked up the water hose, held it over a small coconut tree, and offered the flowing water to me, saying:

(32)   **héʔel aʔ** p'oʔ ak'ab' i ʔiʔ
          'Here, wash your hands there.' (BB.4.80)

This utterance is a prototypical example of Presentative; I complied by leaning over and washing my hands over the tree.

It was evening and dark inside the kitchen hut, when MC hollered out from inside the main house for Eli to get his sandals and bring them to him. His young son Juan responded by looking around the far end of the kitchen, away from the fire and in darkness. Eli, sitting by the fire about two meters from Juan, offered him a candle so he could see. As she held out the burning candle to him, she said:

```
          »-                               -»
```
(33)   takaštah ⌡ wá má e **hé** kib' **aʔ**→
          'Dj'ya find 'em? If not, here's a candle.' (BB.5.67)

DC was recounting how a man should divide up his wealth among his sons before dying so that there will be no strike among them. Enacting the gesture, he said:

(34)   **héʔ** teč **aʔ** → **héʔ** teč **aʔ** → **héʔ** teč **aʔ** →
          'Here's for you. Here's for you. Here's for you.' (BB.4.50)

Taken in the narrative frame that DC has created, this illustrates three separate acts of presentation, which is a diagram of the kind of equal distribution that DC was advocating in his discussion. Each son is separately addressed in his own presentation. Relative to the indexical frame in which DC was addressing me, the examples are decentered, of course, and thus nonbasic, since DC is quoting the fictional man on his deathbed rather than giving anything to me. At this point in our discussion, it is the direct interpretation relative to the narrated frame that is most relevant, this being a prototypical case.

Sitting with me in his house, DP is describing the importance of making offerings to the guardian spirits of domestic and agricultural spaces. Earlier in the day, he had offered five gourds of *saka?* 'corn gruel' in his yard, and he intended to make a similar offering at his new cornfield once he had cleared and planted it (see discussion in §8.3). Quoting what he would say when addressing the spirits, he said:

(35)   le lú?um ȼ'íntraátartk a?→ **hé?el a?** ?aántené?eš i?
            'This land I've engaged, here it is, help me (with it).' (BB.5.21)

As with the previous example, this one is prototypical only when viewed in the narrative context that DP is animating. Note that in this case, unlike the previous ones, the presentation is preceded by a description of the object, establishing a discourse antecedent for it. On the other hand, the object is too large to be actually held out in his hand—the field in question is about 60 by 120 meters. DP maintains tactual engagement with it nonetheless, since (in the narrative frame) he is standing in the very field being presented. Agricultural ceremonies are performed in the fields themselves (with the exception of communal rituals held in various places).

Tactual access to a referent is fulfilled automatically when the referent is, or includes, the Spkr's own body. For instance, Eli arrived back at her house from an errand, accompanied by a swarm of screaming children. Entering the kitchen where I was sitting, she said to me with a smile:

(36)   **hé?** ȼ'ó?ok ksùut **a?**
            'Here we've returned.' (BB.5.45)

The object of Eli's presentation was her arrival accompanied by the children. In a more narrowly focused example, Is was describing his disapproval of the tight short pants that some girls wear in contemporary Oxkutzcab. By dressing in this way, he said, they show their bodies indecently, as if to say to the world,

(37)   čá?anten i? **hé?elen a?**
            'Look at me. Here I am.' (BB.4.110)

The association between Presentative and the Spkr's body, as a gestural medium or as the object of presentation itself, is borne out in the inflectional pattern of *hé?el a?*, the Presentative form. Example (37) shows the first person singular, and (36) could be roughly glossed with the first person plural (*hé?el-ó?on a?* 'here we are'). On the other hand, combinations of this OSTEV with the second person are exceedingly rare. Offered the form *hé?el-eč a?* 'Here you are', Balim (F.19.B.010) interpreted it as equating the Adr with something the Spkr has in hand. He refused the expression on the reading that the Spkr is Presenting the Adr himself. Ostensive reference to Adr normally requires the *o ʔ* form of the OSTEV and is best interpreted as a Visual Directive rather than a Presentative (see below). While it is possible to imagine interlocutors groping for one another in darkness, making 'here you are' a possible move, the standard indexical context for such an utterance is when the Spkr has in his or her hand an object that (s)he thereby identifies with the Adr. For instance, holding up a photo of the Adr, one could appropriately say 'here you are', showing or giving the image to him or her. With a laugh, Balim also suggested that the Spkr might have in hand part of his own body that he thereby identified with the Adr. Such an utterance would always be demeaning, even if in jest, and probably ribald.[8]

6.2.1.2 *Asymmetrical Presentative*

Not all utterances with a salient Presentative function are prototypical, since one or another contextual feature may be out of place without nullifying the entire act. One common way in which the indexical frame may vary from canonical face-to-face is when the interlocutors are separated by a sufficient distance to make it impossible for the Adr to comply simply by taking the object. Such cases occur commonly in everyday Maya, but are uncharacteristically asymmetric when viewed alongside prototypical examples. MC was standing upon the cargo bed of his truck in his yard, and his wife Eli was off on the other side of the household, within hearing but out of sight. MC had just swept off the truck bed and was about to load up oranges to take to market. Tossing the broom onto the ground so that Eli could get it, he hollered out to her,

(38) **hé ʔ** le miís **a ʔ** → Elena →
'Here's the broom, Elena!' (BB.5.24)

The crucial elements of Presentation are in place in this utterance, since MC has the object in hand and sends it in the direction of the Adr. But the Adr will receive it only later when she responds by coming to this side of the house, and so the presentation is not fully consummated in the act itself.

A similar example arose when I was outside Eli's kitchen one morning, shaving at a small table, and she was inside by the fire, partly out of sight. I called out to ask whether she knew where my towel was, so that I could dry off.

(39) W: kuš tuún intwàaya?
'What about my towel?'

E: **hé** yan yoó sìiyá **a**
   'Here it is on the chair.' (BB.5.41)

The chair in question was clearly within sight and virtual reach of Eli inside the hut but separated from me by a wall and about four meters. As she uttered her response, Eli was walking towards the chair, and she proceeded to take the towel and bring it to me. The utterance is part of the presentation of the towel and not merely a prediction or anticipation, because Eli was engaged in the act during the course of the utterance, and the utterance is the sole linguistic signal of the engagement. Because of the spatial asymmetry between us, however, the time course of the presentation is stretched out more than is the case in canonical instances.

A suggestive example of asymmetric Presentative occurred when DC was narrating an incident from his childhood. As in some of the preceding examples, this one is in quotation, hence decentered, but we will concentrate on the relation between the utterance form and the indexical context in which it is a direct utterance (that is, the narrated E^{sn} frame).[9] It was pitch-dark one evening when DC, then a young boy, was told by his grandfather to open the front door of the house. The boy was inside, fumbling for the front door in the darkness, and his grandfather was outside, trying to lead him to it. Giving him an auditory clue, the old man tapped his cane on the front door, saying as he did so:

(40)   **héel a héel a** way atàal e
            'Here it is. Here it is. Come here.' (BB.4.87)

The DLOC (*way*) in the last sentence of (40) is the Egocentric Inclusive form (see §9.2.1), and this portion of the utterance tells the boy to 'come here to me'. In contrast to the Referential function of the DLOC, the two OSTEV forms present the corporeal location of the Spkr directly. Even without the tapping, the source of the sound would have been embodied in the utterance, making these two OSTEVs fully effective Presentatives. The cane was an auxiliary reinforcement, much as a pointing gesture or directed gaze typically accompanies prototypical Presentatives and Directives.

6.2.1.3 *Anticipatory Presentative*

Anticipatory examples differ from all others in that the object, event, or state of affairs presented does not actually exist at the moment of utterance but is anticipated in the relatively immediate future. Similar examples occur also in English, as in 'Here I come (said just before jumping)', 'this should do it (said just before driving in the last nail)', and so forth. In the Maya examples, we find a distinction between imminent anticipation in these terms and the various future formations in the tense-aspect-mode system of the verb. In other categories of deixis, including the nominal demonstratives and the DLOCs, the relatively nonimmediate *o?* forms tend to be used for retrospective reference, and the *a?* forms for anticipated referents. In the OSTEVs, however, both *a?* and *o?* forms are used anticipatorily. The difference in conveyed meaning evidently hinges not on the perceptibility or relative immediacy of the event in time, as one might expect, but rather on the relation between the interlocutors. The more immediate form *hé?el a?* occurs in messages focusing on the location or experiences of the Spkr, whereas *hé?el o?* occurs in messages focusing on the Adr or common ground. In other words, the distinction between Symmetric (Shared or Adr) and Asymmetric (Spkr only) indexical grounds subcategorizes the Anticipatory uses (cf. §9.2.2 for a parallel subdivision in DLOCs).

One evening after dinner, DC was recounting to me and to his sons the story of his mother's death and final words. She had called him over to the hammock where she was lying, and announced her imminent death.

(41)   ?iího ↑ **hé?** kinkiímil wal **a?**
          'Son! Here I'm dying (Look out).' (BB.4.129)

The woman went on to relate her final wishes to DC and died shortly thereafter.[10] Unlike many examples of Anticipatory Presentative, this one does not involve a verb of motion, and the interlocutors are already immobile next to one another at the time of utterance. Note though that the event presented, the death, will befall the Spkr but not her youthful Adr. The first person singular reference of the event makes it highly asymmetric. Compare this with the following examples, in which the outcome of the Anticipatory Presentative will involve the Adr centrally.

I was sitting in the kitchen of Margot's house, and she was in the adjoining room, engaged in stringing up a hammock, when I called out to her,

(42)   WH: comádre
           'Comadre?'

       Mrg: **hé?e** kintàal **o?**
           'Here I come (I'll be right there).' (BB.4.155)

Several minutes later, she came, obviously unhurried, and said with a smile, *b'e?òora* hé? *¢'íntàal* a? 'now here I've come'. This example might seem to reflect a lesser degree of immediacy in the *o?* form, since Margot came only later. However, examples like the following also occur, in which this interpretation is untenable.

(43)   WH: ¢'ó'ok bakaán atàal
        'You've evidently come.'

        DC: **hé'** kintàal **o'**
        'Here I come.' (BB.4.129)

This exchange took place as DC was walking through the door, entering
the room where I was seated, and he exchanged a glance with me as he
uttered it. Actually, he already had arrived at the time, but he had yet to
take his place at the table beside me. By the time he finished the utterance, he was beginning to sit down, and his anticipation of arrival was
surely more immediate than the old woman's anticipation of death in (41).
The difference, as I interpret it, is that (43) is in response position and
focuses on DC's arrival at the place of his Adr (me)—a goal of motion
also indexed by the verb *tàal* 'to come'.

At the opposite extreme, an Anticipatory Presentative can foresee an
event that will occur much later. I was leaving Cres's soda stand one afternoon, walking towards DP's new cornfield (about 300 meters to the south),
when Sil (DP's grandson) showed up on his bike. He was heading back to
his house, about 250 meters to the west, when we had the following
exchange.[11]

(44)   S: tú'un kabin wiíl?
           'Where're ya' going Will?'

        W: té' 'aák'al o'
           'Over there to the basin.'

        S: **hé'** kintáal **o'o'**
           'Here I come (to where you'll be).'

        W: ah yàan atàal?
           'Oh, are you gonna come (over)?'

        S: yan intàal i'i
           'I'm gonna come there.' (BB.5.57)

Sil's opening question is a routine greeting in Maya, used about as widely
as English 'Hi, how are you?' The basin referred to in my response is a
natural formation in which DP and VC were working, clearing brush to
plant. Sil, DP's grandson and VC's nephew, works with them occasionally, and his second and third utterances assure me that he is heading there
that morning. What is noteworthy is Sil's anticipatory presentation of his
coming to the basin, said as he started off in the other direction. It was
obvious that he would not arrive within a half hour, or probably even an
hour.[12] My interpretation of such utterances is that the presence of the
verb *tàal* 'come', indexing the Adr's location (actual or, as in this ex-

ample, anticipated) is what selects the OSTEV form *hé?el o?* rather than *hé?el a?*. It is possible for a Spkr to say *hé? kintàal a?* 'here I come', in the limiting case in which arrival is imminent and interlocutors already very close together in the goal location, but Maya speakers rarely say this, in my experience.

A final example of Anticipatory Presentation comes from the household of Eli and Pilar (see floor plan fig. 7.6). There are twelve children in this household, and most of them were playing in the yard one February morning after breakfast when Pilar was sprinkling water around to settle the dust. Holding a bucket in one hand, she was tossing scoopfuls of water here and there with the other, circulating in the direction of the children. When she was about three meters from them, and one or two scoops of water at the rate she was going, she warned them to move off so they wouldn't get soaked.

(45)   **hé** kutàal wal le ha? **o?** →
          'Look out, here comes the water!' (BB.5.41)

The children scattered, and Pilar continued her task. Here the anticipated coming of the water was imminent, and one might expect Pilar to have selected the fully Presentative *hé?el a?*, the way Margot had done in example (32) when she offered me running water from a hose. The difference appears to be that Pilar was walking in the direction of the children, as her choice of the verb *tàal* also indexes, and she was telling them to move away, not presenting them water to receive. Her utterance conveys 'here it comes (in your direction)', not 'here it is (take it, I give it to you)'. The association between the *o?* form and the Adr's space is also evident in speakers' reactions to possible deictic forms combining OSTEVS with person marking. Balim, for instance, rejected out of hand as inappropriate both *hé?el-en-o?* 'there I am (look!)' (F.19.B.050), and *hé? yan tinwiknal o?* 'there it is in my place' (F.19.B.110). On the other hand, he found *hé? yan tawiknal o?* 'there it is in your place' transparently intelligible.[13]

6.2.2 Directive

Like Presentative uses, Directive ones function predicatively, pointing out the referent and directing the Adr to look at it rather than simply identifying it in a statement or handing it over in a Presentation. The range of uses of Directives is somewhat broader than that of Presentatives and includes what will be called Prototypical (Tactual or Visual), Peripheral, Discourse, Asymmetric, and Transposed Directives. These are taken up in the order listed.

6.2.2.1 *Prototypical Directive*

Prototypical Directive utterances are those in which the Spkr and Adr share a common visual field which includes the referent, and the Spkr, in uttering the deictic, points out the referent to the Adr with manual indication and directed gaze, saying 'there it is (look!)'. The OSTEV *hé?el o?* is used for the entire range of Directive acts: *hé?e b'e?* for the Peripheral ones and *hé?el a?* for the Asymmetric ones (as we would expect, given the examples in §2.1 above). Pilar, Eli, and I were standing in three different places around the courtyard of their home, each engaged in some task, when we had the following exchange, in which Pilar performs a prototypical Directive.

(46)   P: bihá?an Luis nah le profesor té?el a?
            'Luis has gone to the teacher's place over here.'

       E: ?áam tí? h b'in i? →
            'Oh, that's where he went.'

       W: tú?uš yan le profesor kawáak o? ↓
            'Where's this teacher you're talking about?'

       P: té?el a? a? kó?on iŋwé?es teč →
            'Right here! (pointing) Come here, I'll show it to you.'

At this point, I go over to her, and she points out the little schoolhouse, saying:

       P: **hé?el o?** → tawilik →
            'There it is (look! pointing). Do you see it?' (BB.5.29)

Pilar's last two utterances fit the prototypical Directive usage precisely: in response to my locational question, she establishes a symmetric visual field with me by calling me to her side for the express purpose of showing me. She then directs my gaze to the object of her directed gaze and pointing gesture, saying the OSTEV in so doing and following up to verify the outcome, namely, that we now both see the object.

Tigre, VI, and I were working together at a construction site within the partially erected walls of a stone house. This space was clearly visible to all three of us, although our attentions were directed to different places. VI had misplaced his hammer, and we were all three searching for it. VI, looking on the opposite side of the room from Tigre and me, found the hammer, right in the *saábukàaŋ* 'bag' in which it belonged, which was hanging on the wall. With the bag clearly within his reach and asymmetrically accessible to him but not to Tigre and me, VI could well have

Presented the hammer, taking it in hand and thrusting it up for us to see. Instead, he pointed at it discretely without touching it, and said:

(47)   hé? yàan saábukàaŋ o?
            'There it is in the bag.' (BB.1.94)

In this utterance and the reinforcing gesture, VI indexes the symmetry of the corporeal frame, in which we all share the same visual field and are all engaged in looking for the hammer. The outcome of the act also puts us all on an even footing, gazing on the hammer in unison. Only afterwards did VI take it in hand and return to work with it. This is a significant difference between Directive and Presentative uses, since in the latter cases, the Spkr has asymmetric access to the object, which he takes in hand and gives to the Adr.[14] Prototypical Directives, like this one, do neither of these things.

6.2.2.2 *Peripheral Directive*

Peripheral Directives are cases in which the Directive function of an utterance is fully intact, telling the Adr to pay attention to an object pointed out by the Spkr. What is different, however, is that the object is neither touchable nor visible but only audible (or perhaps, rarely, possible to smell). Eli's four-year-old daughter Manuelita and I were sitting in the kitchen when she heard someone calling my name from outside. To direct my attention to this, she said:

(48)   wiíl hé? kat'á?anal o?
            'Will, there you're being called.' (BB.5.7)

This context is asymmetric in the sense that Manuelita's lived familiarity with the sounds of her home allowed her to recognize the calls to me before I did, but it is symmetric in the significant sense that we are at an equal remove from the sound, and once it was pointed out, both of us would be attending to it together. The same day I was talking with Eli by her fire when we heard the slap of Pilar patting tortillas in her kitchen across the courtyard. Eli remarked that Pilar was making tortillas, and just after she did so, we heard another slapping of corn meal (*hùuč'*, Sp. *masa*) on the table.

(49)   E: pìilar e? tupak'ač →hée b'e? →
            'Pilar's making tortillas. There! Listen! (cocking ear).' (BB.5.7)

As in the previous example, we were at an equal perceptual remove from the referent: both within earshot of the sound, and neither within sight of Pilar.

Whereas the Presentative and prototypical Directive acts engage the bodies of the interlocutors by way of touch, vision, grasping, and pointing, the Peripheral forms are inherently less immediate. The focusing of attention is in play, as Eli's cocked ear gesture reflects, but the rest of the bodily posture and orientation is left undirected, and the referent is never the Spkr's own body or the Adr's. Eli produced an excellent example of Peripheral Directive when she brought her infant son to DC's place seeking a shamanic cure for him. A large inflamed blister had formed on the child's leg, and he had fever and diarrhea. The three of us were standing by the altar, looking at the infant in Eli's arms, when a queasy growl emanated from his gut, and Eli remarked, *t uy ok' ol u nak'* 'his gut is crying'. This was followed immediately by a rush of gastrointestinal sounds indicating a percussive bowel movement, clearly audible to all three of us. Eli summarized our collective deduction,

(50)   ʔaáh ↓ **héʔ** kutaʔ **b'eʔ**
              'Ahah, there he's shit.' (BB.4.95)

6.2.2.3 *Discourse Directive*

Discourse Directives are those that point to a linguistic form or to the import of uttering the form on a specific occasion. Such utterances are true directives in the sense that they function as predicative elements, sometimes a one-word speech act, which direct an Adr to focus attention on the object. As used here, Discourse is a special kind of referential object, requiring a combination of perceptual, conceptual, and social information in order to be interpreted. This is why we do not lump deictic reference to discourse with reference to visible or audible objects, even though the same range of linguistic forms is used in both cases. The typical communicative goals of Discourse Directives in Maya are also markedly different from those of other types of usage. Rather than presenting or localizing talk in a way analogous to other OSTEV usage, these utterances tend strongly to bring to a close units of discourse, concluding statement-response repairs, thematic units in an ongoing description (such as a narrative), or even an entire interaction. Directive reference to discourse shares with standard anaphora (as in 'the man$_1$ . . . he$_1$ . . .') a dependency between the deictic and some preceding unit of expression. Unlike anaphoric coreference, however, Discourse Directives are not coreferential with any antecedent (cf. Hanks 1983:chap. 3). Rather, they individuate the antecedent itself as their object. Unsurprisingly, such utterances tend to occur in response position or after the execution of some act, making them inherently more symmetric than Presentatives and some other kinds of Directives. The prior act or speech is already available for both interactants in the indexical framework at the moment of reference. For example, early on in my research, I was discussing the Maya language with DP when I got sidetracked on a problem of phrasing, and unable to express myself, I said in frustration (and poor Maya):

(51)   W: ʔàah b'éʔorita máʔ inwoheh biš utàal intùukul (sic)
             'Oh, now I don't know how my thoughts were coming.'

       DP: ʔah pwes **héʔ** leti el o ʔ → b'áʔan yàan tiʔ
             'Oh well, there it is (your problem). What of it? (big deal).'

DP's response conveys that he perceives my confusion, agrees with my characterization of it, and encourages me to continue trying. The referent of his OSTEV (in boldface) is my utterance, which is also the referent of the circumfixed *leti el o* 'that one there'. The latter is often used in reference to discourse alone or in combination with other deictics, and in this case, it reinforces the Directive (Hanks 1983:chap. 5).

In many examples, the OSTEV is used alone rather than in combination with other Discourse referential elements, as in Man's explanation of an aspect of Maya language with an example, during which he asked whether I knew a relevant fact before resuming:

(52)   k'aháʔan teč   ká kiím e nohoč maák e ʔ ↑ **héʔel o ʔ** ↑
       'Do you remember when the old man died?   Right,

             hač b'èey . . .
             it was just like it . . .' (BB.4.149)

After Man's question, I had evidently communicated to him my recall of the death in question, and he resumed his explanation, having established this fact and marked the momentary closure with his Directive reference to discourse.

Regardless of what is said in an interaction, speakers can bring it to a close by making directive reference to it. A patient of DC's was taking her leave after a therapeutic session, and as she exited through the doorway, she said, back to DC:

(53)   **héʔel o ʔ** ʔastah viernes
       'There it is, until Friday.' (BB.4.9)

Coming to the end of a verbal listing and display of the merchandise he had bought at market, Lol said to me

(54)   **héʔel o ʔ** → letiʔ binen inman a ʔ
       'There it is. That's what I went to buy.' (BB.4.31)

In this example, there is a combination of the visual availability of the objects purchased with the Disc function of summarizing Lol's display of them. In a parallel example, I was sitting with Eli in her kitchen when a pack of neighborhood dogs appeared outside the back door, milling for handouts. We were accustomed to seeing them, and Eli commonly tossed them a dried tortilla or two, which they snapped up before slinking away. Seeing them arrive, I remarked (without spoken antecedent):

(55)   WH: ȼ'útiípiló?ob'
             'They've shown up.'

        Eli: **hé?el o?** yàan way e?
             'There they are. There (sure) are (dogs) here.' (BB.5.7)

We can see in Eli's response to my remark a combination of the visual evidence of the dogs, since she could see them as well as I could, along with the resumptive force of Discourse Directive.

The next two examples are not Discourse Directive, properly speaking, since the antecedent to which they refer is not speech but some other focused activity. The resumptive function holds constant, however, and the utterance signals the momentary closure achieved by completing an action. Example (56) also occurred in Eli's kitchen, just after she had given a piece of bread to her toddler son, who had been loitering by the fire, making grabs at edibles on the table as she prepared dinner. Giving him the bread, she told him to go away, saying:

(56)   »-   -»
             hé?el o? pero šen kuta té?el o?
             'There it is, but go sit down over there!' (BB.5.5)

As discussed in §9.2.2, Eli's DLOC reference in sentence-final position is nonspecific, whereas her OSTEV reference foregrounds the gesture of giving bread to the boy and conveys roughly 'enough is enough, take this and leave me in peace', which the boy did.

VC had spent about forty-five minutes digging an irrigation canal with a pickax, when his father DP looked on his work and judged it adequate, saying

(57)   **hé?el o?** ȼ'oká?an bey o?
             'There it is, it's finished as is.' (BB.5.31)

The two were clearly within sight of one another at the time, but the crucial fact is that DP was judging as finished a task that VC had performed. By making directive reference to it, he 'summarizes' it and brings it to a close in a way parallel to the standard Discourse examples. Cases like this one make it clear that the Discourse feature must be extended to include focused engagements other than speech, as well.

6.2.2.4 *Asymmetrical Directive*

As the preceding examples make clear, Directives tend to occur in relatively symmetric indexical frames, in which the interlocutors are close together and share a perceptual and attentional field. This is not always the case, however, as asymmetric examples like the following show. DP, VC, and I were working together clearing out irrigation canals in DP's orchard one afternoon.[15] DP was standing on the bank of a canal, with VC on the opposite side behind him, out of his field of vision. He had told VC of his plans to open up a canal in a currently overgrown area that had been a canal in the past. Directing his gaze and pointing at the area before him, DP said:

(58)   hé$^{?}$ le cánal tuún k-inw-áaik teč a$^{?}$
             'Here's the canal I'm telling you about.' (BB.5.31)

Observe that although all three of us were engaged in the work, and DP had told VC of his plans to reopen the old canal, in this utterance he directs attention to it as if it were new information. Both the OSTEV and the first person singular pronoun reinforce the asymmetry of the act, in which DP is boss. Given his seniority and the respect he commands, DP commonly speaks in such a unilateral manner.

In other cases, the asymmetry between interactants can be due mainly to discrepancies in their respective perceptual fields. This was the case in the next two examples. DC was outside in the yard of his home, by the water tank, and Margot was inside the house in room 1 (see floor plan in figure 7.8), when he called out to ask if she had seen his machete:

(59)   DC: má$^{?}$ awil*é$^{?}$eš* wímaáskab' i$^{?}$i$^{?}$?
             'Didn't you see my machete?'

       Mrg: hé$^{?}$ yan yoó$^{?}$ pìilá o$^{?}$
             'There it is on top of the water tank!' (BB.4.88)

At the time of this exchange, DC and Margot were not engaged in talk, and DC's question is actually directed to anyone and everyone within earshot (note the underlined second person plural marking in his question). The water tank and DC himself were both out of Margot's visual field, separated from her by a cinder-block wall, but she knew from prior knowledge where the machete was located and could infer from her knowledge of the domestic space that DC's voice was coming from the same general

area. Thus the object of Directive reference was within sight of the Adr
but not of the Spkr. Relying on the association between *o?* forms and the
Adr's space, Margot selected the OSTEV *hé?el o?* to direct DC's attention
to the referent. Had their respective locations been the inverse, with
Margot outside and DC inside, she would almost certainly have used the
Presentative *hé?el a?* form.

As a final example, consider the situation of passengers sitting in a
crowded station wagon in Mérida, about to depart for Oxkutzcab. The
driver is at the wheel, facing forward, about to pull out of the parking
space, when a passenger in the rear recognizes another Oxkutzcabeño
dashing across the park to catch a ride. The driver is unaware of this new
passenger and cannot see him at the time, when the man in the back of the
wagon announces his imminent arrival, hollering:

(60)   **hé?** kutàal untuúl **o?**
          'Here comes (another) one!' (BB.4.8)

The driver paused, looked, and waited for the last passenger to get in before departing.

6.2.2.5 *Transposed Directive*

With some frequency, one encounters in Maya conversation utterances
which are Directive in function, but which have been transposed, so that
the object of the Directive is located in some indexical frame other than
the corporeal one. These are commonly cases of Bühler's type 1 transposition, in which the Spkr projects himself or herself along with the Adr
into a narrated frame, making objects present in this frame available for
Presentative or Directive reference in the current one (see §5.2.2 for explanation and further examples). In the course of recounting the story of
his dream encounter with a bull and a jaguar, DC produced many transpositions for dramatic effect.[16] In the dream he was taken to a plaza,
bound to a tree, and the animals were set loose to kill him. By a heroic
feat, he broke free and snapped the back of the jaguar, before facing a
rushing bull. At this point in the story DC switched from description to a
transposed Directive.

(61)   sá máareh → **hé?** tuún kutàal ump'é nušií? tòoró **o?**!
          'Holy Mary! Here comes a great big bull!' (BB.4.121)

The OSTEV in boldface in this example directs an Adr (myself) to look at
the referent, the rushing bull, an act that can be performed only in the
narrative frame, since it is only in this frame that the bull exists. The expressive overtones of the transposition are reinforced by the interjection

in utterance-initial position and the concessive particle *tuún* within the transposed portion. This example is not an instance of citation; DC is not reporting anything he said when facing the bull. Rather, he is projecting himself and me with him from our corporeal frame into the narrated one.

Man was telling the story of his feckless cousin who had attempted at one point to become a professional boxer. In the ring, he was arrogant and insulting and tried to strike his opponents with low blows. In his third fight, however, he met his match and was knocked out so quickly and with such ease that the crowd whistled and catcalled at him. When Man reached this point in the story, rather than describing the whistles, he pointed to them with a directive.

(62)   **hé**ʔ tuún kušoóbʼ táʔal **o**ʔ
           'Here he's being whistled at!' (BB.4.97)

Just as the previous example, this one is to be interpreted relative to the narrated frame in which the whistles were a perceivable reality, rather than the context of Man and me talking, from which they could only be described.

6.2.3 Referential

While OSTEVs in their typical Presentative and Directive usages function grammatically as predicates, as I have shown, there is also a full range of Referential uses in which an OSTEV is subordinated and functions as a modifier to a noun rather than as a main clause predicate. These uses are still relatively more directive and more presentative than other deictics, but they differ clearly from the foregoing examples in being subordi-nated.[17] Rather than conveying 'Here it is (take it!)', they convey 'this one here (that I've got in hand)', 'that one there (that we can see)', and so forth. Referential OSTEVs occur with the entire range of R values shown on the vertical axis of figure 6.1.

6.2.3.1 *Prototypical Referential*

Prototypical exemplars of Referential OSTEV usage are those in which the indexical frame is the actual corporeal context or utterance, the inter-locutors share a common field of perception and attention, more or less, and the object is in the appropriate relation of perceptibility, givenness, or anticipation. We will illustrate Referential uses in the standard order of their relational values.

Tactual Referential. Margot and Man were engaged in hanging a ham-mock in the sleeping quarters of their house, he at one end and she at the other end of the hammock. Margot was facing the north wall of the room, with rope and hammock in hand, about to tie it up, while Man was behind her to the south, out of her field of vision but within her focus of attention. He had hung it in a special place the day before, and Margot asked him where to tie her end this time.

(63)   tú ʔuš taȼ 'aá **le héʔ** káʔač **aʔ** ?
             'Where did you put this here before?' (BB.4.157)

The referent of the OSTEV in her utterance was the rope and hammock end that Margot had in her hand at the time, and her choice of the *aʔ* form appears to reflect both this and the asymmetry of access to the object. Notice that she is neither Presenting nor Directing Man's attention to the object but rather precisely individuating it in the course of asking a question about it. The boldface portion functions as an NP introduced by the article *le* and flanking the temporal adverb *káʔač* 'past (finished)'.

Whereas the NP in (63) is a headless relative clause, other examples show that when a lexical noun is included, it precedes the OSTEV.[18] For instance, in the *tiíč'k'aák'* 'divination' events described in §5.3.3, the shaman holds in his hand the crystals in which he can see into the patient's body and private affairs. This specialized indexical frame makes it possible for him to make perceptually specific reference to objects not accessible to a layman. Looking into his crystal just after the opening prayer and speaking to a woman patient standing behind him, DC made reference to her illness as *le k'oháʔanil héʔel aʔ* 'this sickness here (in my hand)' and *lelaʔ* 'this' (F.47.A.382). Such utterances are possible only because of the asymmetry of knowledge and perception in the therapeutic context, along with the symmetry of actual copresence between the interactants. Notice that the former makes explicit DC's Tactual access to the sickness but does not fully Present it to the patient, which he could do by using the nonsubordinated form *héʔ le k'oháʔanil aʔ* 'here's the sickness'.

Visual Referential. Visual Referential uses tend to show the same kinds of symmetry as the Visual Directives do, individuating objects within sight of both interactants. Walking into room 1 from room 2 of her home, on the threshold between the two, Margot responded to a remark made by her husband's cousin, who was standing on outer threshold of room 1 with the yard (see floor plan in figure 7.8). The two were facing one another, separated by the width of room 2 (about 4 meters), and were already engaged in small talk. Man and I were bringing in additional *sahkab'* 'white earth' to resurface the floor. The cousin had just observed that the packed earth floor in room 2 was several centimeters lower than the threshold to room 1, and that it would require a great quantity of earth to fill it in. Margot responded by saying:

(64)   bey anik šan **le hé**ʔ káʔač **o**ʔ
            'That's how this one used to be too.' (BB.4.99)

The referent of her OSTEV was the floor of room 1, equidistant from her
and her interlocutor and visible to both.

Peripheral Referential. Peripheral Referential uses are comparable to
Peripheral Directive except that they are subordinated, and the OSTEV
functions as an argument to some other predicate. Eli was sitting by
the fire in her kitchen one morning, as her daughter Teresita entered the
room, walking towards her. Eli expected her husband MC to stop by the
house that morning during his rounds driving the family truck. Hearing
the sound of a passing vehicle, she asked Teresita:

(65)   Eli: apapa wá **e hé**ʔ **b'e**ʔ?
             'Is that your father (we hear)?'

        Ter: hmʔ ↓
             'Nope.' (BB.5.40)

In this example, the definite article *le* has been reduced to *e,* as often
occurs in rapid speech. Notice that Eli's utterance is a question, whereas
with all fully predicative usages of OSTEVs, question marking is impossible. Eli could not ask, for instance, *hé*ʔ *wá a papah b'e*ʔ? 'there's your
father?'

While the Peripheral terminal *b'e*ʔ tends to co-occur with the OSTEV
base *hé*ʔ, some referential uses show it accompanied by the definite article. One such example arose on the road between Milo's place and the
soda stand (see figure 7.5). Milo was riding his bicycle to work when we
met and paused to greet one another. Hearing the faint sound of a radio
playing, he asked me:

(66)   túʔuš kutàal **le** b'áʔah k-aw-úʔuy ik **b'e**ʔ
            'Where's that sound you hear coming from?' (BB.5.20)

What is revealing about this example is the verb 'you hear (it)' in the relative clause flanked by the deictics in bold print. By using the second
person form, Milo has described the symmetry typical of Perceptual Reference. In other examples, the terminal *b'e*ʔ may be used alone to indicate
that a referent is audible. For instance, Lol, Fi, and I were sitting inside
their home talking when Fi heard a rustle in the yard (in total darkness).
She remarked:

(67)   miín konito kutàal **b'e**ʔ
            'I think the rabbit's coming.' (F.137.B.502)

Note that while this utterance is not a question, it is attenuated with the conjectural particle *miín,* which would be precluded from any Directive utterance. If Fi had said *hé⁷ kutàal konìito b'e⁷* 'here comes the rabbit (listen!)' in order to direct our attention to it, then the conjectural particle could not be used.

Discourse Referential. Discourse Referential uses are very common in everyday Maya and are used to individuate some portion of previous speech, such as an utterance fraction, a temporal frame, or a contrasting member of a set. The pragmatic functions of reference to Discourse are less salient than those of Discourse Directives and closer to standard anaphora. The Referential forms do not bring units to a close in the same way as Directives do. DC was midway through the story of his mother's dying wishes when he remarked that she had told him that he and his younger sister must always care for their elder sister, who was ill. When he told the younger sister of her new responsibility, she was taken aback and saddened. He reported this saying,

(68)   yàah tyoó uúč inwáaik **le** palabra **hé⁷** ti **o⁷**
            'It pained her that I say that word there to her.' (BB.4.129)

The NP containing the OSTEV in this sentence refers back to the words of the mother, which DC had already told me. On a separate occasion, DC was recounting events from his past when he referred back to a specific time saying, *le ⁷òora hé⁷ tuún o⁷* ↑ 'at that time there' (BB.4.123).

In other examples, the Discourse Referential function of an OSTEV is fused with other effects, such as the contrastive separation of two referents. In the course of telling the story of how he acquired a diploma in parapsychology, DC told of a mysterious encounter with a stranger, an event which he saw as related to dreams he had had in the days before. The stranger gave him the diploma without ever explaining to DC why or where he had come from.[19] Next, DC contrasted this with a more standard way of getting a diploma by studying for it or soliciting it, and then, after describing the normal way, he referred back again to his own case, saying:

(69)   DC: pero **le** càaso **hé⁷el a⁷** ↑ bey uúčik ten o⁷
            'But this case (in my case), that's how it happened to me.'
            (BB.4.123)

In addition to making reference back to prior discourse, this utterance foregrounds two additional factors: (i) the case referred to is not the immediately preceding one in DC's description (the normal scenario) but rather an earlier antecedent; and (ii) the case referred to is actually DC's own biography, which gives it an asymmetrically immediate relation to him as Spkr. These two factors, I believe, motivate the selection of the *a*ʔ OSTEV rather than the more typical *o*ʔ form.

6.2.3.2 Nonprototypical Referential

As with other kinds of deictic usage, one finds various nonprototypical examples of Referential OSTEVS. In this section, I will briefly illustrate one case of deferred ostension and one case of transposition.

Deferred Reference. Pilar and I were talking in the courtyard of her house one morning shortly after the death of her mother. She was deeply saddened by the loss of her mother and felt that she needed to get an image of the woman so that she could pray in front of it. Her siblings had converted to Protestantism and could not be counted on to burn candles, keep fresh flowers, and pray for the woman's peaceful passage—a situation of neglect which she described regretfully as *tikin kiímil* 'dry death'. Pilar's dilemma was that she had one photograph of her mother, but in it she was accompanied by her husband (i.e., Pilar's father) and his mother. The latter two individuals were still alive, and their images therefore could not be placed on an altar for the dead. Showing me the photograph and pointing out the two living people in it, she said:

(70)   tumèen **le héʔelóʔob o**ʔ → má kiímen e káʔa tuúl a ʔ aʔ →
        'Because those two there (as I said), they're not dead these two.'
        (BB.5.26)

Needless to say, the OSTEV reference was to the people in the photo and not to the photo itself, as the following comment makes obvious. Pilar had mentioned these individuals just previously and knew that I knew them and that we shared common visual access to the picture. Still, it is unclear to me why she chose the *o*ʔ form rather than the *a*ʔ form for her reference, since the access was tactual, contrastive, and highly foregrounded. The deferred reference to the actual people is a separate problem, I believe, and can be described with a simple principle of identification which says that reference to an image or representation of an individual can serve as reference to the actual person.[20] Discourse accompanying the drawing and explanation of maps is full of similar examples, in which reference to the map is understood as reference to the places it portrays (cf. Hanks 1983:chap. 4). What is special about this case, at least from a cultural point of view, is that the image of a dead person is invested with values and a material connection to the person in a way not characteristic of maps. The same holds evidently for the link between the photo and the living people it shows, since Pilar would not consider placing their image on an altar for the dead.

Transposition. In a few, evidently rare, cases, an OSTEV may be used to make reference to an object that does not exist and is not anticipated in the imminent future. The only example I have found of this was produced by DP while he, VC, and I were working in his fields. We were preparing rows in which corn would be planted, piling up dirt on the low embankments to direct the eventual flow of rainwater. It was mid-February, well into the dry season, and we were arranged as shown schematically below.

$$\begin{array}{c} \hspace{3cm} \text{DP} \\ \rule{8cm}{0.4pt} \end{array}$$

X   Y

      WH   Vic

Vic was standing about five to seven meters on the other side of DP from me, and all three of us were looking at the incline of the land, trying to figure how the rainwater would flow. DP looked in the direction marked X in the schema, pointed, and said:

(71)   **le** ha? kutàal **hé?el a**? →   té? kunaákal o?
         The water coming right here [X], it will reach over there [Y],

         le tú?uš yan vìiktor o?
         where V is.' (BB.5.60)

As he made reference to locations X and Y, on opposite sides of him, DP pointed two times. X marked a patch of high ground from which water would surely flow in the direction DP indicated. What is striking about the example is that the air was bone dry at the time of the utterance, and no rain was anticipated in the near future. The verb 'come' is in the incompletive aspect and can be interpreted either as an ongoing process or as a future event, but the OSTEV can only be interpreted as an ongoing one. Anticipatory Reference does not occur without some further marking, to my knowledge, and in any case DP was not anticipating any imminent rain.[21] What the example shows instead is a transposition of Bühler's second type (see fig. 5.10): DP has projected the eventual rainfall into our current indexical frame, which includes the three of us and our actual perceptual fields.

6.2.4 Expressive

There is a fundamental difference between the category I am calling 'Expressive' and all of the preceding examples. The difference is that while Presentative, Directive, and Referential uses all subsume an Expressive component, Expressive uses are non-Referential and therefore lack any of the other more specific functions. The canonical use of the Deictic Modal (DMOD) particle, which is specialized for Expressivity, does not individuate any object but rather signals that, for whatever reason, it is the speaker's estimation that the proposition in which the modal occurs is true, or will be at some unspecified future time. For primarily heuristic reasons, we will present examples in three sets, prototypical uses, response position uses (which overlap with the preceding), and elaborated uses in which the certainty expressed by the modal is suspended or modified by co-occurring linguistic items.

6.2.4.1 *Prototypical examples*

The central function of the DMOD is to indicate that the speaker considers the validity of the proposition in which the form occurs to be certain, and this is the motivation for our labeling the R value of the form Certain (see fig. 6.1). This R value, although it appears to fit into the scale of OSTEV values, is different from the others, because it actually fails to relate any referential object to the indexical ground. Nonetheless, it does relate the proposition to the indexical frame to the extent that it conveys the speaker's current evaluation of it. It is significant that this certainty is never based on current perceptual evidence but rather on background knowledge or expectation. As the foregoing examples show, when evidence is present, one of the OSTEV forms is the preferred one, and the object is individuated as a presentatum, object of directive, or referent. In metalinguistic discussions with them, Maya speakers cited again and again the precondition that the Spkr of the DMOD 'has made sure' of what (s)he is saying and knows it for certain (Hanks 1983: chaps. 3, 8). This fact points up the relatively presupposing character of the DMOD in its prototypical uses, as well as the close link between the particular certainty it signals and the presupposition of existence accruing to the use of many other demonstratives.

Unlike most of the other nontemporal deictics, the DMOD also has an inherently prospective orientation: the verb with which it co-occurs cannot be in any nonincompletive tense-aspect, nor can it predicate a past event. While the evidence on which the certainty is based may be rooted in the past, the use of the DMOD always indicates the potential for a future occurrence. This is one of the forms canonically used to make predictions, warnings, promises, and statements about forthcoming events. At the same time, unlike the Anticipatory uses, the DMOD gives no indication whether the future occurrence is imminent or in the indefinite future. It is used equally properly for actions on the verge of taking place, such as *hé? inwaántikeč e?* 'I'll help you' (said while starting to help) and actions of generic validity, such as *hé? ukiímil maák e?* 'people die' (they always have and always will), *hé? u žokowtal le k'iin o?* 'the sun gets hot', and

MC's observation that *yàan tak e ¢'ùul ó?ob o? hút'anik màayá e?* 'there are even wealthy people who speak Maya' (F.1.78.178). Part of what is going on in cases with first person verbs is the relatively close association between the DMOD and the expression of a Spkr's intent or willingness to do something. This is another factor motivating the label Expressive for this category.

6.2.4.2 *Response position*

Like the Discourse Directive and Referential utterances illustrated above, Expressive ones tend to occur **after** some other stretch of discourse. In this case, the relevant unit is an utterance by an interlocutor, to which *hé?el e?*, alone or in some larger predication, is an affirmative response. Unlike the OSTEVs, this form is not used to bring thematic units to a close in monologic description; it does not typically make reference to what precedes (although it is occasionally used with quasi-Referential function, as we will see). Rather, it recapitulates what precedes it for the purpose of affirming it. In question-answer pairs, it is commonly in the answer position and so brings closure to the unit. But it is mainly the Expression of affirmation that the form conveys. Not being a fully predicative or referential item itself, *hé?el e?* is not suited for use as a one-word utterance the way all of the OSTEVs are, unless it has an antecedent, nor can it be used in response to a WH question without further qualification (since it fails to encode the appropriate information). In response position, the DMOD is interpreted as an elliptical repeat of what precedes it. For instance, Margot and her four children were about to leave home on a trip to Mérida, when we had the following exchange.

(72)   WH: hé?el o?, pwes kanaánt abaá é?eš
          'There it is, so take care of yourselves.'

        M: **hé?el e?**
          ' "For sure" (turning away to take leave).' (BB.4.26)

My utterance starts with a standard Discourse Directive opening a closing routine in which good wishes are offered to the travelers. Margot's upbeat response conveys unambiguously that she is certain that they will take care of themselves. This interpretation is, of course, reconstructed on the basis of the positional occurrence of the DMOD and is not part of the conventional meaning of the form itself. If I had said 'So you'll be back tomorrow', the same response by Margot would have committed her to that proposition.

As (72) shows, the first pair part, which *hé?el e?* follows, need not be syntactically parallel to a hypothetical full form with the DMOD: my utterance has an imperative, whereas the DMOD would require an incompletive stem. Furthermore, *hé? k kanaántik k baáh e?* 'we'll take care of ourselves for sure' is grammatically fine but awkward and prolix as an utterance. The link between the two utterances is not one of strict grammatical identity, and while a deletion approach to the elliptical response is possible in many cases, in others it is not. For instance, DC was leaving the house one morning to go perform a ceremony in Ticul, when I explained that I planned to stay home and would be there when he returned.

(73)   WH: kán sùunakeč, way yanen e?
        'When you return, I'll be here.'

    DC: **hé?el e?**
    'Sure.' (BB.4.23)

Two things are noteworthy about this example. The first is that while it is clear that DC has assented to my prediction and closed the statement-response pair with an expression of accord, it is not clear exactly how we would fill out his utterance into a full sentence. One possibility is *hé? awantal way e?* 'you'll be here for sure', with or without the preceding when clause. Once again, this would be an odd utterance and seems off the main point of DC's response, which was simply to express his assent and overall positive outlook on my remark. Even though it is not a full sentence, his one-word response is a complete utterance in Maya, and the fact that it receives a situationally contextualized interpretation is not evidence that it has been derived by deletion from some larger statement. The Expressive function is the central one, and it is not elliptical.

Other examples of *hé?el e?* as a one-word response are quite similar to Discourse Directives in that the DMOD expresses the Spkr's understanding of a prior statement. In the following exchange, DC's two responses merely register the names of the people under discussion, without any overtone of futurity or personal engagement.

(74)   DC: b'á?aš a k'àab'a?
        'What's your name?'

    Boy: pèedro
    'Pedro.'

    DC: **hé?el e?** → kuš tuún apapah ↓
    'Right. What about your father?'

    Boy: pèedro šan ↓
    'Pedro too.'

    DC: **hé?el e?**
    'Right.' (BB.2.133)

There is no question in this exchange of DC **agreeing** with the boy's assertions, since he does not know the answers to his questions himself, nor
is there any prediction of a future event. He is merely marking off the
reception of the boy's statements.

6.2.4.3 *Certainty suspended*

Another significant difference between the DMOD and the OSTEVs is that
the Certain figure which is typically conveyed by the former can be
blocked by co-occurrent linguistic items, whereas the evidentiality of the
OSTEVs can never be suspended or blocked. For example, a clause containing the DMOD may be entirely hypothetical, as in Margot's statement:

(75)   múm puúlik ubáa→ čeén hač bey húpulk ubáa **e**ʔ
           'He won't jump,   it's just as if he's going to jump.' (BB.4.58)

We were sitting in the kitchen at the time, watching the pet parrot Cori
swing on the back of a chair, and I thought he would surely jump off.
Margot knew better, but realized that it looked as if he would. The particles *čeén hač bey* effectively cancel any certainty I might have had regarding a jump, just as the preceding sentence explicitly negates the
possibility. Margot's utterance is still a proper one, whereas it would
never be possible to say, for instance, 'it's not really there, it just looks as
if there it is', using an OSTEV. In other cases, it is perfectly acceptable to
say *miín héʔel e*ʔ 'probably for sure', meaning 'probably so', and to
question the possibility of the event predicated, as in *pwes maáš hé*ʔ *yá*ʔ*a
ik* ↓ 'who could say for sure?' or to negate it, as in *miš maák hé*ʔ *yáa k e*ʔ
'nobody could say for sure' (F.17.580, 614). Recall that such utterances
with OSTEV forms are uniformly unacceptable.

Unlike the OSTEVs, the DMOD is commonly used in the if clause of a
conditional and in 'whether clauses', both of which are signaled in Maya
by the 'indefinite' particle *wá*.

(76)   **wá hé**ʔ atàal e ʔ, **hé**ʔ utàal šan leti ʔ **e**ʔ
           'If you'll come (along), he'll come too.'

(77)   kén sa **wá hú** k'učul e ʔ, ʔasta wá ʔòokin
           'Who knows whether he'll arrive, maybe not until nightfall.'
           (BB.4.12)

Finally, the DMOD can be derived with the 'habituative' morpheme *-ili-
(e*ʔ*)*, which affixes to verbs, auxiliary elements, and adjectives and indicates that the state of affairs described by the lexical item is or was in
force at some other reference time. Compare *čak* '(it is/was) red' > *čak-
ili-e*ʔ 'it was already red, it's still red, as usual'; *sùuk ub'in* 'he custom-

arily goes' > *sùuk-ili ub'in e*ʔ 'he was already accustomed to going, he is
still accustomed to going, as usual'; *kinšòok* 'I study' > *kinšòok-ili-e*ʔ 'I
already studied, I still study, as usual'.[22] Interestingly, when this affix is
attached to the DMOD, the result is to suspend the Certain feature, as in:

(78)   **héʔel** im b'óʔotik teč **e**ʔ
         'I'll pay you for sure.'

         héʔel-ili im b'óʔotik teč **e**ʔ
         'I'll pay you some day for sure (tongue in cheek).'

The second of these sentences conveys that the Spkr really has no intention of paying the Adr in the near term. Glossing a parallel example, Margot explained the conveyed meaning well, saying, *yàan* ʔ*ésperàansa . . .,
pero má*ʔ *ta* ʔ*áseguràartik b'á*ʔ*aš k'ìin* 'there is hope, . . . but you don't
specify when (it will occur)' (BB.4.95). It is less than clear exactly how
this semantic effect is achieved, but it appears that the affix signals that
the act (for instance, the act of paying a debt) will remain an unrealized
future possibility for the indefinite future. Expressions like the second one
in (78) are used in a palpably ironic manner in everyday Maya, and convey that the Spkr really has little intention to do what he says. Thus, the
Certain feature is effectively blocked.

   In summary, the Expressive function of the DMOD is related to the range
of functions signaled by the OSTEVS, just as the forms are grammatically
related. From a functional perspective, the certainty canonically conveyed by the DMOD is the epistemic residuum of the perceptual verifiability
which attaches to OSTEVS and gives them an evidential core lacking in the
DMOD. Grammatically, there is credible evidence that the *héʔe(l)* particle
is the same in both cases, despite significant differences in their behavior.
Distributionally, it always occurs in constituent-initial position, unless
subordinated, participates in the *héʔel ~ hé*ʔ *~ hV́ (high tone)* alternation, occurs only once per clause (except in foregrounded structures, to
be treated in chapter 10), and precludes simple negation. What is unique
to the DMOD is the fact that its Expressive meaning, which we have summarized 'Certain', can be blocked or suspended in a variety of ways without any parallel in the OSTEVS.

6.3 CONCLUSION

It is easy to see that there is a relation between sensory evidence of a referent and modal certainty of an event, even if it is difficult to describe
this relation precisely. The features in question are part of the functional
structure of deictic practice in which the indexical frame of utterance is
the ground on which figural referents and events are projected. The key

factor in this projection is not the spatial location of referents but the different kinds of **access** that participants have to them. We can paraphrase the OSTEVS and DMOD only in a vocabulary of sensory, conceptual, and volitional engagements. The corporeal zones of the interactants, each defined by its sensorial reach, are mobilized in communicative acts involving presentation, display, identification, and expression of expectation. The sense of 'space' in play in these forms is based on the Maya -*iknal,* which includes perceptual zones along with relative proximities, the possibility of joint occupation by more than one actor, as well as the agent's habitual way of thinking or acting (see §3.2). That is, the -*iknal* corresponds to what I have called the corporeal field. It is intuitively apparent that one who presents or demonstrates a referent can perceive it, and this commonsensically entails being certain of its existence. On the other hand, if one strips away the perceptual evidence and the referential function of an OSTEV, something like certainty without evidence remains. One objective of this chapter has been to explain the details of this relation.

It is somewhat common that perceptual features show up in deictic systems in natural languages, and visibility, in particular, has been cited for Chinook (Boas 1911), Crow (Graczyk 1986), Quileute and Kwakwaʔla (Anderson and Keenan 1985:288, 290), Malagasy (Anderson and Keenan 1985), and Santali (Zide 1972), among others. Bühler ([1934] 1967) had already worked out the perceptual basis of spatial deixis, and it should come as no surprise that this range of bodily engagements is in play in the Maya system. What is noteworthy about Maya is that perception is irreducibly distinct from space as a domain within the deictic field, as reflected in the formal difference between the OSTEVS and the DLOC adverbs (cf. chap. 9). Further, perceptual features are fused with the distinct communicative functions of Presentative, Directive, Referential, and Expressive in Maya, in a way that reveals the interdependency of these dimensions in natural language. The blending together of sensory evidence with certainty, reference to discourse, and anticipation further reinforces our central thesis: ostensive reference is an actional engagement that agents undertake in accordance with cultural orientations and within a socially defined space of possibilities. Irreducible to physical space and time, the deictic field embodies modes of access to the world that are both preconditions and products of communicative practice.

III Space and Spatial Reference

7 Spatial Orientations and Referential Practices

7.1 INTRODUCTION: SPATIAL GROUNDS OF REFERENTIAL PRACTICE

This chapter outlines the sociocultural constitution of space and time in contemporary Maya culture and thereby provides a critical context for understanding the deictic construction of referential and indexical space and time. We start with two distinctions. First, the familiar one between schematic frames and the emergent engagements that take place in frameworks. Social actors bring the former to interaction as part of their already shared knowledge of the world, whereas they produce and revise the latter in an ongoing, constantly changing process. The second distinction bears on the character of spatiotemporal representations as either 'centered' or 'grid' systems. Like bodily space (see chap. 3), deixis is a centered system, in which spatial relations are defined relative to activities and speech events. On the other hand, cardinal points of a compass and longitude/latitude grids are coordinate systems in which relations among objects are computed relative to fixed axes and dimensions, and no one locus is privileged as 'central', at least in principle.

The purpose of starting from these two basic oppositions is not to isolate the four terms but to better understand their interactions as simultaneous elements of communicative practices. In separating emergent from centered aspects of spatial and temporal orientation, by putting them on different axes, we maintain a distinction between processes as such (definitionally emergent) and the (necessarily centered) agentive perspectives they may include. It would be a mistake to equate the dynamic, processual character of interaction with 'subjectivity', as Saussure did in his treatment of 'parole', and Benveniste (1965) did in his discussion of deixis and human experience. Such an equation obscures the key points that subjectivity is in many ways prestructured and that discourse processes are not all centered on the interactants. It also runs amok of the many points of sociocentricity that are revealed in an empirical study of deixis. The distinction between prefabricated schemata and emergent processes summarizes a series of more specific ones, phrased variously as 'schematic' vs. 'local' knowledge (Cicourel 1985 and literature cited therein), 'objective structure' vs. interactive processes, and conventional semantic structure vs. pragmatics of discourse production. This basic division is encoded in the contrast between frames and frameworks as developed here.

In his brilliant studies of the cultural construction of self, Hallowell made several observations relevant to both of the foregoing distinctions. The first is the idea that individuals must share a common spatiotemporal orientation in order to be able to successfully act in concert (1955:184). Benveniste ([1965] 1974:76) and Gale (1964:97) make the analogous point that successful deictic reference requires that speaker and addressee either share the same perspective or can relate their perspectives to each other. For Hallowell, the common spatiotemporal orientation was made up of two parts. It was "an acquired schema that involves the conscious use of [i] culturally constituted reference points and [ii] awareness of one's position in space' (1955:92; bracket numbers added). The first kind of space is a prefabricated frame of reference that transcends immediate experience (Hallowell 1955:93, 186), whereas the second is anchored in the emergent visual and experiential present of a self-aware actor. The former may be centered or noncentered, whereas the latter is inherently centered (even when decentered; cf. chap. 5). Thus, as Bourdieu ([1972] 1977:114–24), Cicourel (1985, 1986, in prep.), and Evans (1982:162–63) also remarked in different terms, orientation always involves the *combination* of established reference points with the centered, 'local', knowledge and experience of the actor. This has as one of its consequences that deictic reference, an act of orientation par excellence, unavoidably articulates with the broader divisions and relations among regions in sociocultural space and time. It is productive to posit a distinction between the deictic field and the symbolic field, as Bühler ([1934] 1967) and many others have done, but it does not follow that the former can be understood apart from the latter. In order to motivate the communicative choices speakers make in deictic reference, one must first understand the encompassing frame space to which their choices respond.

Talmy (1983:229) observed that linguistic representations of spatial scenes impose a small number of fixed structures upon them, typically picking "one portion within a scene for primary focus and characterizing its spatial disposition in terms of a second portion." The location, orientation, or geometry of the latter is usually already known, so that it provides a ground for specifying the focal object, as in 'The mangos (focal) are in the crate (ground),' and 'The wind (focal) runs through the veins (ground).' The two terms become figure and ground in Talmy's formulation (see chap. 2 above). When the ground of a spatial reference is an individuated object, 'landmark', or portion of a larger spatial scene, then it functions as a **center** relative to which other locations are specified. In the case of deictic reference, the center is the interactional framework of the speech event itself or some portion of it (cf. chap. 2).

This chapter and the next will focus on the spatial and temporal dimensions of interactive contexts in Maya: the locations, orientations, and geometries that speakers already know when they engage in reference. Although clearly extralinguistic in large measure, these sociocultural facts nonetheless organize linguistic practice in significant ways. As I will show, the frames instantiated in spatial deixis are identical to, or homologous with, ones that will be sketched in ethnographic terms here. No less than corporeality, extrabodily spatial and temporal orientations provide a vocabulary in which to describe referential practice. The ones we will review in this chapter are: (§7.2) relative and absolute cardinal orientations, (§7.3) regions, paths, and landmarks, and (§7.4) domestic space, along with its ritual transformations. The first of the three illustrates two distinct patterns of use of cardinal direction terms in Maya, showing how a grid pattern frame can be transformed into a centered one. The significance of this is that when used in a centered way, cardinal terms are semiotically parallel to deictics and can be meaningfully compared (and contrasted) with them. The cardinal orientations are also fundamental in all of ritual practice in this culture and will help to explain ritual discourse later in this chapter and in chapter 8. The local landscape (§7.3) provides many of the referents individuated in deictic usage, as well as generalized schemata that recur in the deictic system. This section will also extend our treatment of frames beyond the household. The description of domestic space in the final section complements the earlier one of social relations in the homestead (§3.3) and adds more fine-grained detail to our account of the schematic knowledge that speakers draw on. The account of rituals operating on domestic space builds directly on previous discussions of ritual discourse in chapters 3–5.

With respect to the study of referential practice, this chapter and chapter 8 will serve a dual purpose. First, they will demonstrate the relations of homology, transformation, and coarticulation that connect frames in Oxkutzcabeño Maya culture. These relations are central to the notion of a frame space. Second, they will fill in some of the fine-grained background knowledge necessary to accurately characterize spatial deictic practice, the focus of chapter 9. Each of the frame constructs dealt with here has temporal as well as spatial properties, in terms of its production, duration, and change over time. Although we will concentrate in this chapter on the spatial arrays implicit in practices, we will return to temporality in chapter 8, and our account of deictic frameworks is definitionally grounded in the temporal dimensions of speech. If we focus selectively on the construction of space, therefore, it is not because it holds any logical priority over temporal orientation but only a heuristic priority with respect to the problems at hand.

7.2 CARDINAL ORIENTATION: RELATIVE AND ABSOLUTE

The basic terms for the cardinal directions in Maya are well known and there is little dispute over their modern meanings: *lak'in* 'east', *šaman* 'north', *čik'in* 'west', and *nòohol* 'south'. Intercardinal points are defined by combining these terms, as in *lak'in nòohol* 'southeast', although speakers use the simple ones much more frequently than the combined ones. As we saw in the 'instrumental' speech illustrated in §3.5, cardinal terms are used to situate objects and locations even in relatively small spatial scenes, such as 'the west side' of a posthole or a tree. Similarly, known places, regardless of their distance, are commonly referred to in Maya simply by direction plus deictic, as in the hypothetical but routine exchange:

(1)   Q: tú ʔuš kabin?
       'Where are you going?'

       A: té ʔe šaman o ʔ
       'There in the north.'

I was sitting in DP's main house one hot afternoon, when DA, in her kitchen and out of sight, hollered to me the following question (2/27/87):

(2)   DA: ȼ'úbin maánwe té ʔ čik'in a ʔ ↑
       'Did MC (already) go there west?'

       WH: ȼ'ó ʔokih→ póoso sèeis h binih
       'Yeah, he went to Well (number) 6.'

       DA: ʔáhàah
       'Oh (yeah).' (BB.5.62)

We both knew that MC drives a truck and that his daily route takes him up the highway to the west. He ferries people and goods along a regular route, making stops at several places, the furthest of which is named Pozo 6. Presupposing this knowledge, DA knows that her formulation of MC's direction is adequate for the purpose of her question, since the direction and the 'going' (in a truck) together imply the whole route with its stops, its typical cargo, and so forth. Her utterance is canonical in its use of the directional term as a metonym for a larger chunk of background knowledge—a path, a region, and a routine activity sequence.[1]

DA's utterance illustrates the important point that in Maya conversation, cardinal terms are used to stand for more than just directions. In order to accurately characterize the semantics of the terms, we need to take account of how they are used. We can begin by observing a distinction between **cardinal directions** and **cardinal places.** The former constitute an abstract coordinate system, presumably fixed by features of the natural environment (terrestrial and celestial), relative to which any actor can orient himself or any other object. The latter are a set of landmark places which define coordinates only by default, when actors orient toward them. In his discussion of spatial orientation, Hallowell (1955:190) made this distinction when he observed that in Salteaux culture, the cardinal points are not true directionals but actually the places of origin of winds. When Salteaux actors travel, they orient from place to place rather than by direction, and their maps show sequences of landmarks more accurately than either path or direction. Similar observations could be made regarding the Maya terms, in some of their uses.

In the context of elemental cosmology and shamanic performance, it is clear that the cardinal points are defined as regions containing specific, named places. *ʔiíkóʔob'* 'winds, spirits' are described as brothers and *maákóʔob'* 'people' who originate from these places, and their qualities depend partly upon their provenance. Ritual discourse creates a point-by-point path, or 'road', as the shaman proceeds from place to place (described in Hanks 1984c). As a corollary of this, there is a great distance between everyday places and the true cardinal locations (which is just what the ritual performance mediates). *čik'in* 'the west' is the place of *ʔah k'iin tùus* and a host of other named spirits, many of whom are malevolent. The cardinal locations are described as *tukantíʔiƈil káʔan, tukantíʔiƈil lúʔum* 'at the four corners of (the) sky, at the four corners of the earth'. They are cited in ritual discourse in rigidly specified order, usually counterclockwise starting with the east in the opening phases of a performance, to *heʔik b'èel* 'open the road', and *k'ašik mèesa* 'bind the altar', then clockwise at the ending, to *waƈ'ik mèesa* 'unbind the altar'.

There is a fifth cardinal place in Maya cosmology, namely *čuúmuk* the 'center, middle'. In both clockwise and counterclockwise sequence, spirits in the center are cited last. They are described as the smallest or youngest of the brothers, yet the most powerful. In most socially significant spaces, including towns, homesteads, plazas, and traditional cornfields, the four corners plus the center define the space as a whole. For instance, in the creation of a cornfield, the corner and center markers are laid down in the forest, and offerings are made in the center before the remaining *šú?uk'* 'boundary markers' are laid out, and before any trees are felled (see §7.4.2 below). Similarly, in the *heé¢ lú?um* 'fix earth' ceremony, which purifies the land within a single bounded *soólar*, the altar is always placed in the *čuúmuk* 'middle' of the yard, and offerings are buried there and at the four corners. The 'middle' of town is often defined by the location of a great *yáašče?* 'ceiba' or *laáwrel* 'laurel' tree.[2]

There are therefore five cardinal places in Maya, the conjunction of which defines a spatial whole. Whether it is a relatively small domestic space, a municipal one, the top of an altar, a cornfield, or the entire world, its four corners plus center define its schematic totality. The corners are connected, not by perpendicular lines intersecting in the middle, but by the perimeter, running point by point E > N > W > S > C, or E > S > W > N > C (cf. §§7.4.3 on domestic perimeter, 8.2.3 on agricultural field, 8.3 on altar arrangements; and see Hanks 1984c on cardinal ordering in discourse of prayer.)[3] This is shown in figure 7.1.

In most everyday usage, this system works differently. The four corner places are used as directional orientations rather than locations. Hence, DP can speak of the 'west' side of a small pit, DA can speak of 'west' of her home, and a person facing east can speak of his right arm as being 'south'. None of these acts would be possible if the cardinal points always

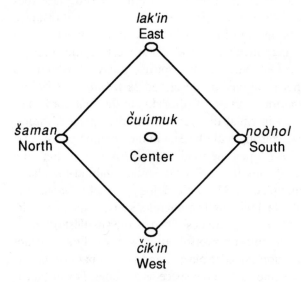

Fig. 7.1. Cardinal places.

denoted places axiomatically distant from 'here'. In everyday usage, there is no fixed sequential order between the cardinal points, analogous to the cyclic ordering of ritual reference. As directions, the terms can be used metonymically to stand for any number of known places, as in DA's usage above, and no fixed evaluative connotations attach to them. The same holds for the nonritual use of *čuúmuk* 'center', which denotes any place within the perimeter of, amid, or between the extremes of a defined region, as in *čuúmuk beh* 'midway (lit., middle road)', *čuúmuk pàarkeh* 'in (the) park', and *taánčumuk* 'half (of a task or material object) (lit., front-mid)'. Whereas the cardinal place frame is invariant, the actual values of cardinal terms in routine conversation are calculated relative to the actor(s) using them or to some situationally designated ground object. This makes the system 'centered' in the strong sense of presupposing a *situationally specific* central place relative to which trajectories are defined. Whereas cardinal places are used to totalize spatial zones by summing up their defining parts, cardinally oriented directions are usually used by speakers individually or in opposed pairs to pick out some focal object or region. 'He went west, not south'. Unlike the cardinal places, the directions have no perimeter but intersect in the center. This can be represented graphically as in figure 7.2, in which the shaded area around the intersection indicates the variable scope of pragmatically determined center zones (cf. concept of *-iknal* 'bodily space', §3.2).

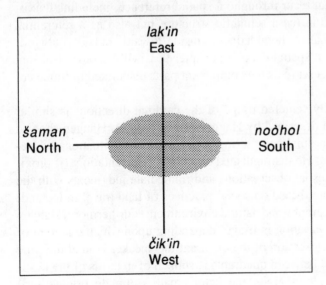

Fig. 7.2. Cardinal directions with indexical center.

There is a substantive as well as a formal similarity between figure 7.2 and the coordinates of body space as shown in figure 3.2 above. In both cases, a central place is intersected by two basic horizontal dimensions: front/back, right/left, and east/west, north/south. In both cases, the center is constituted by the corporeal field currently occupied by the actor. Therefore, it may be defined narrowly within an egocentric or near-object frame, or it may include other interactants or socially defined spaces in an inclusive sociocentric frame, depending on the case. The intersecting dimensions are all directional oppositions defining complementary regions which extend indefinitely beyond the central zone.

The system of cardinal directions, like body space, embodies the basic concept of an actional center out of which vectors extend in opposite and orthogonal directions. Cardinal locations, on the other hand, are connected by a perimeter, as in figure 7.1, not by opposite vectors meeting in the center, as in figure 7.2. The perimeter makes it possible to distinguish what is inside/included from what is outside/excluded. It does not provide vectors of indefinite range or directionality from ground. Even in Maya, where there is a fifth, central, cardinal point that is part of the perimetral schema, it does not function as a relativizing center the way the corporeal field does. This follows from the difference between a schematic midpoint fixed in space and a locally defined indexical ground in communicative practice (cf. chap. 5).

Taken together, these two uses of the cardinal points establish basic logical relations that recur throughout spatial reference, including deixis: the centering relation (as a semantic structure but also as a referential practice), directionality, boundedness, inside/inward, outside/outward. As we work through spatial deixis in chapter 9, it will become clear that these same relations serve as the component parts elaborated in frames of demonstrative reference.

The pragmatically centered usage of the cardinal directions is similar to the phenomenon described by Haugen ([1957] 1969). Haugen showed that in Icelandic, cardinal point terms have a number of situationally specific patterns of use. He distinguished two kinds of orientation: (i) proximate, based on celestial observations and immediate judgments with the eye; and (ii) ultimate, based on social practices of land travel in Iceland, adapting to the topography and natural environment. Furthermore, Haugen identified regional variation in usage, depending upon which quadrant of the island and which section of the quadrant the speaker is in at the time of utterance. Travel between quadrants is spoken of in terms of the destination or next quadrant along the actor's path (ultimate orientation). Hence, when located in the northeast portion of the eastern quadrant, a speaker traveling in the opposite direction from the easternmost valleys is said to be heading 'north' (since this is the quarter towards which he is moving). Someone located in the southeast corner of the eastern quarter heading in the opposite direction from 'east' is said to be heading 'south'. This apparent inconsistency is resolved by the fact that the easternmost valleys of the eastern quarter are an 'orientation area' relative to which directions are defined; and because of the topological shape of Iceland, they are located 'opposite' to both the north and the south regions (Haugen [1957] 1969:334).

As Haugen observes, the significant fact in the Icelandic case is that the cardinal points offer an apparently canonical example of an objectively defined grid, and yet in actual use, this grid becomes a pragmatically conditioned, indexically centered system. Icelandic authors, furthermore, adopt different regional perspectives in the use of these terms in narrative in order to index the regional identity of fictional characters. This is precisely parallel to the transpositions of indexical reference that occur in reported speech (chap. 2 and 5 above; see also Hanks 1986, 1989b). Instead of having a single set of context-free values, the cardinal directions in Icelandic function as a system of shifters whose referential objects differ according to the interactive field from which they are computed. As with the locative-directional terms in Tsimshian (Boas 1911; Dunn 1979) and Tlingit (Story and Naish 1973), this field is defined largely by the socionatural environment. Culturally given knowledge of topography provides a set of schematic regions and landmarks in relation to which trajectories are defined. Moreover, in 'ultimate orientation' we must know the speaker's destination as well as his current location in order to compute directional reference. This is equivalent to saying that we must know the intended goal of his current project in order to interpret his directional 'compass'. The compass is defined not only relative to a frame space of cultural geography but to the practical ends of actors engaged in frameworks as well. Beyond the context sensitivity typical of all locational descriptions (Schegloff 1972:81, 83ff.), these examples show the conversion of a noncentered paradigmatic grid to an indexically centered system of relations.[4] Despite their basic differences, we find an analogous transformation in the Maya case.

The indexicalization of cardinal direction terms brings them into functional parallel with deictics: the actor's current corporeal field (including motion) serves as the ground from which a referential object is projected (an orientation is aligned). Thus, it is an $R(x,i)$ structure in which the directional items encode the R relation. Like deictic frames, cardinal frames further presuppose a sociocultural frame space, a greater 'map'

that is not all currently engaged on any given occasion but that is nevertheless the source and necessary horizon of the more limited frames that
are engaged. Yet deictics are canonically singular definite referring items,
whereas cardinal terms are not, and deictics blend illocutionary force,
evidentiality, and corporeal space in ways unparalleled in other linguistic
subsystems. There is therefore a significant homology between cardinal
orientation and deictic practice, but they remain functionally distinct. This
distinctness, moreover, is why speakers can routinely combine deictics
with centered cardinal orientation without producing any redundancy, as
in examples (1–2).

7.3 REGIONS, PATHS, AND LANDMARKS

The spaces encompassed by the cardinal points and the corporeal schema
are further subdivided into many more finely graded divisions and relations in Maya culture. The purpose of this section is to establish the most
global of these, including (i) the cosmological concept of the world as a
vertically located zone within a spherical universe; (ii) the oppositions between man-made, natural, and intermediary spaces; (iii) ecological zones
characteristic of the region of this study; (iv) roads and pathways; and (v)
landmark places. Not only do the schemata already presented intersect
with these, but speakers routinely presuppose a commonsense knowledge
of them as a resource for reference and interpretation. That is, they are
widely accessible to participants in the frame space of their interactions.

7.3.1 The Place of the Earth

Maps and other symbolic representations of the Mayan universe frequently depict it as a sphere or bubble in which the earth is a horizontal
plane located midway between the zenith and the nadir (e.g., Hanks 1984c,
León-Portilla 1968:140ff., Redfield and Villa Rojas [1934] 1962:205.
Cf. Gossen 1974a:34 on Tzotzil). The most detailed representations of
space at this level are the ones used by shamans. In the course of teaching
me about the spirits addressed and moved in *reésar* 'prayer', DC made a
drawing and produced an explanation of the universe that vividly illustrates the combination of many of the elements discussed so far. Figure
7.3 is a reproduction of DC's map, originally done on three-holed note-
book paper in red pen (F.65.A; October 30, 1980).

The encompassing circle in figure 7.3 represents a globe that defines
the limits of reality. Outside is a void, in which the world is suspended. In
creating the world, God blew it up, filling it with *ʔiik'* 'wind, breath'. At
the top of the heavens are God, *Gloria* 'heaven', and *k'iin* 'Sun', the highest and most mighty agents in the world. This is the east. At the bottom of

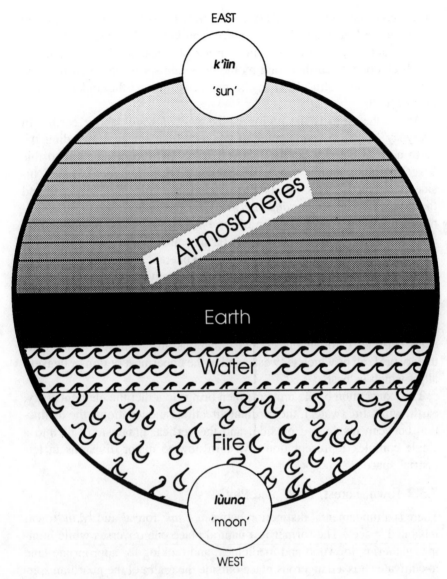

Fig. 7.3. The place of the earth.

the sphere is the west, the moon, and *kó?olebil saásil ?ak'a?* 'Woman light (of) night', a female spirit who resides there. The dark horizontal band roughly in the middle of the sphere stands for *lú?um* the 'earth' we walk on. It marks the divide between 'upper' and 'lower' worlds, a distinction of significance in shamanic practice. Below the earth, westward, is a huge body of water which supports the ground and courses through it in the great underground rivers called *saáyab'ó?ob'*. Driven by earthly winds, these feed the wells and cenotes, providing the water that is ultimately sucked up into the sky in a vortex of celestial winds, to then be cast back down to earth as rain by the *čaák* rain spirits and their helpers. Below the water, still closer to the moon, is fire and the underworld of *metnal* 'hell'.

Above the earth is the region called *yoók'ol kàab'* 'above earth'. In everyday Maya, speakers refer to the world we inhabit, including the earth and visible sky, as the 'above earth'. DC took exception to this usage, pointing out that properly speaking we live *?ičil yoók'ol kàab'* 'inside above earth', which he takes to include the surface of the earth and the sky below the seven *yáaš muúyaló?ob'* 'great cloud layers, green atmospheres'. This is the domain of the *baálam ?iík'ó?ob* 'jaguar spirits' and other earth guardians who assist farmers and protect their cornfields. Above the above earth are the seven atmospheres, layered one upon another, separating humans from the top of the heavens. At each level are located spirits at the five cardinal locations. The higher the spirits, the more powerful they are. Thus, while east and west have vertical corollaries, up and down, they also retain their horizontal values. The divisions between cardinal places and directions are collapsed both in the underworld, all of which is 'west', and in the uppermost region of heaven, all of which is 'east'.

This conception of the universe then brings together the elements (sky, earth, wind, fire, water), the cardinal directions and locations, the distinction between inside and outside, and the vertical dimension, all into a single complex representation. We turn now to major divisions in terrestrial space.

7.3.2 Town, Forest, Field, and Plot

There is a fundamental distinction between *k'aáš* 'forest' and *kàah* 'town, inhabited space'. The former is a natural place one traverses while hunting, gathering firewood and medicines, and looking for appropriate land to cultivate. It is a dangerous place outside the realm of the guardian spirits posted at the cardinal corners of inhabited and cultivated space. It lacks the many internal divisions and marked perimeter of all socially defined spaces. When in the woods, Maya speakers describe themselves as *yàanal k'aáš* 'under (the) forest', a phrasing motivated by the dangerous and unpredictable character of the place. By contrast, one walks *?ič* 'in' or *ti?* 'to, at' a town, a *kòol* 'cornfield', or a *parsela* '(irrigated) field, orchard'. The latter spaces are all bounded by a man-made perimeter, provided with a schematic center, and guarded by spirits posted in the five cardinal places. Fi gave an accurate, if grisly, sense of the danger of the forest in recounting the murder of her grandmother, who was *b'ïsá?ab kíinsbi ič k'aáš ká tuhàantá?a mèen č'om*→ 'brought to be killed in (the) forest, then was eaten by vultures' (F.137.A.330). When shamans banish evil spirits from the human body or domestic space, they cast them away *¢'uú? k'aáš* 'deep into the forest'.

Town is associated with trips to the Catholic church, the doctor, the market, the local *ejido* authorities who dispose of communal lands, the water company, the post office, municipal dances and carnival, and external transportation by train, bus, and taxi. In Oxkutzcab, 'town' lacks the strong economic and ethnic association it apparently had in Ticul as described by Thompson (1974:22–27). Still, it is mainly Maya campesinos who live in the outlying communities where the large orchards and fields are maintained.

Agricultural land, both irrigated and rain fed, lies in an intermediate position between fully social and fully natural space. Traditional cornfields are guarded by a host of spirits, both beneficent and ambiguous. They revert cyclically to forest when the land is allowed to go fallow, after several years of continuous cultivation, and are subsequently reclaimed by felling and burning the vegetation. The milpa is the site on which native strains of corn, beans, and squash are planted, and it is the rhythm of growth and decay of these plots that determines the main ritual calendar of the Maya. *Parselas* are irrigated plots or orchards that stay in cultivation continuously over long periods of time and whose produce is destined mainly for the commercial market. Whereas the *wàahil kòol* 'food of the field' may be performed in the milpa, particularly when it is adjacent to the residential *soólar,* no traditional ceremonies are performed in orchards or commercial plots, to my knowledge. The one exception to this is when a family resides within the boundaries of an orchard, as DP and DA did for years (see residence III in figure 7.5), in which case domestic ceremonies such as the *heé¢ lú?um* 'fix earth' may be held there. I know of no cases of families residing permanently in a traditional milpa, probably because these plots revert to forest after just a few years. In some cases, including DP's second residence (where his sons currently live; cf. §3.3) and Eli's father's residence in Mani, the residential *soólar* adjoins a milpa plot. Under these circumstances, however, there is a wall, fence, or other boundary division between the two. As pointed out in §3.3, these broad divisions between natural, rotating cultivated, permanent cultivated, and residential spaces have many corollaries in the activities that occur in them, who and what can be found there, and how they can be appropriated for human use. They are part of the frame space of referential practice as well. Some more of these will be addressed in §§7.4 and 7.5 below.

7.3.3 Geo-ecological Zones

Being woodsmen and farmers, Maya men possess an enormous stock of knowledge regarding the local ecology, the distribution of soil and vegetation types, the conformation of the land, and the location of specific natural features in the area. The Oxkutzcab region has been continuously occupied (farmed or inhabited) since at least the Terminal Classic period (ca. A.D. 800–1000) (Morley and Brainard [1946] 1983:156; Roys 1957:61 ff.). Today, it is commonly called the *huerta* 'garden' of Yucatán; it encompasses the richest and most diverse vegetation cover in the state, as well as many features of topography and water distribution not found elsewhere. While the vocabulary used to describe the earth and what grows in it includes literally hundreds of terms, a handful of them are routinely used to refer to major **places.** These are shown in figure 7.4, where the shadings indicate regions in which the corresponding features are distributed.

The term *kab'ah če?* means literally 'low tree, wood' but is used as a specialized name for the relatively flat land with low forest that stretches northeast of the Puuc hills. The *pú?uk* consists of high, rolling ground stretching northwest to southeast through Oxkutzcab municipio (county). The town of Oxkutzcab, like the railroad and highway connecting it to Ticul (north) and Tekax (south), lies along and includes the northern base of the Puuc, known as *čùum pú?uk* 'base, trunk of Puuc'. About ten kilometers south of Oxkutzcab (the town), on the other side of the Puuc, is the valley of Cooperativa Emiliano Zapata, known locally as *kóperatìiba,* or just *kopa.* The soil in this valley is extraordinarily rich and supports commercial orchards whose produce is sold by the tons in the Oxkutzcab market and recently through the citrus processing plant opened on the outskirts of town. The deep, dark, fertile soil in parts of the valley is described as *?ék' lú?um* 'black earth'. Among senior men like DP and DC, who have worked the area for scores of years, this descriptor is used as a proper name for the valley as a whole. This practice is clearly a local one, since: (i) adult male native speakers not from the area may fully understand the descriptive meaning of the phrase 'black earth', yet not know that it refers to this particular valley; (ii) the valley contains many other distinct soil configurations which do not fit the description 'black earth', but this does not stop local senior men from following their convention; (iii) women and younger men are either ignorant of the convention, as they are of much of the soil terminology, or consider it a special usage;

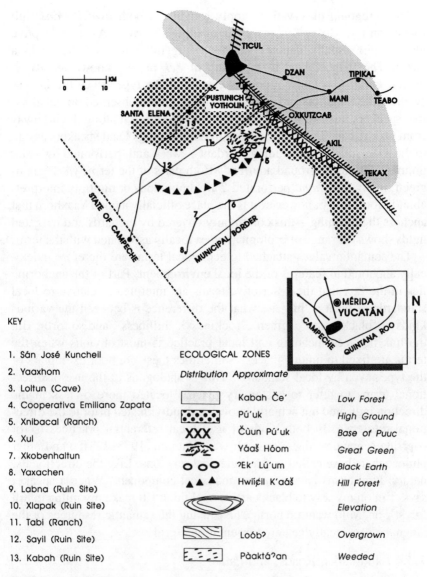

KEY

1. Sán José Kuncheil
2. Yaaxhom
3. Loltun (Cave)
4. Cooperativa Emiliano Zapata
5. Xnibacal (Ranch)
6. Xul
7. Xkobenhaltun
8. Yaxachen
9. Labna (Ruin Site)
10. Xlapak (Ruin Site)
11. Tabi (Ranch)
12. Sayil (Ruin Site)
13. Kabah (Ruin Site)

ECOLOGICAL ZONES

Distribution Approximate

	Kabah Če′	*Low Forest*
	Pú′uk	*High Ground*
XXX	Čùun Pú′uk	*Base of Puuc*
	Yáaš Hóom	*Great Green*
o o o	ʔEk′ Lú′um	*Black Earth*
▲ ▲ ▲	Hwíí¢il K′aáš	*Hill Forest*
		Elevation
	Loób?	*Overgrown*
	Pàaktáʔan	*Weeded*

Fig. 7.4. Ecological zones.

and (iv) although there are pockets of black earth elsewhere in the region, they are not routinely identified by this phrase without further specification. The motivation for the practice is the historical one that this valley has been the focus of intensive development (irrigation, paved roads, electricity, residence) over the past twenty-five years and is one of the main satellites of Oxkutzcab and suppliers of the market.

The foregoing observations apply roughly to both *hwíí¢il k'áaš* 'hill forest' and *yáašhom* 'green, great opening' as well. As a descriptive term, *hwíí¢* usually denotes sharply rising hills, individually or in a chain. The strip of land to the south of *ʔék' lúʔum,* known locally as *hwíí¢il k'aáš,* is actually a poor exemplar of the type, since the land is swelled like Puuc, instead of sharply rising. I have observed nonlocal native speakers mistake it for Puuc when approaching it along the highway from Oxkutzcab. There is variation in the meanings local speakers assign to the term *yáašhom,* including 'verdant', 'wet', and 'perforated by water drainage into underground aquifers'. Both parts of the term, *yáaš* 'great, green, many' and *hom* 'perforated'? are ambiguous or multiply interpretable. In local usage, however, it is the place officially named Yaaxhom that anchors the meaning—this community covered by orchards and irrigated fields shows the range of ecological types locally associated with the term.

The semantic values attached to ecological terms are therefore indexically anchored to features of the local environment. Part of the anchoring lies in the fact that the descriptive terms are interpreted relative to local standards of what a 'hill' is, what the difference is between the various kinds of 'black', 'red', 'green', 'rockiness', 'hilliness', and so forth. But the link between meaning and local practice is most obvious when the terms are fixed to unique places. Sometimes these are poor exemplars of the type, even by local standards. This is analogous to the use of directional terms to refer to customary places, located more or less in the direction indicated but actually known and individuated prior to the directional reference. In both kinds of use, local referential practices fix or override semantic values, through what Putnam (1975:238 ff.) and other philosophers have called 'rigid' indexical relations. Like the directionals, natural kind terms have a hidden indexical component. When a speaker says 'I'm on my way to black earth', or 'I think I'll make my milpa in hill forest', or 'Milo went up north', he is using the semantic resources of the language as a locally centered orientational grid.

7.3.4 Landmarks, Roads, and Paths

The *kaáretèera* 'paved roads' to the southwest of Oxkutzcab in figure 7.4 have been expanded, surfaced, and maintained over the past twenty years as part of the intensive development of the area as a commercial agricultural producer. There is a steady traffic of family-owned trucks ferrying goods and people between the market and the Yaaxhoom-Black Earth farms, up to about twenty kilometers from town. Elders recall years prior to this development, when the only transportation from town over the Puuc was by foot, horseback, or carriage on irregular dirt roads and paths through the woods. In the rainy season, the roads washed out or became treacherously slippery with mud. Still, they represented openings through the forest cover where travel was safe and disorientation unlikely even by night.

Speakers distinguish different kinds of paths, including *noh b'eh* 'open road (lit., great road)', *yam b'eh* 'small path (lit., between road),' and *?ek' b'eh* 'rough trail (lit., black, dark road)'. The first of these were the main pathways through the Puuc prior to the paving of the highway, and they are still used for foot travel today. They are relatively straight and open, provide visual access to a considerable distance, and have been around for as long as anyone can recall. Each of these facts contributes to the sense of 'great' conveyed by *noh*. What I have glossed as 'small paths' means more literally a path which passes between and around objects, such as the way water flows in rivulets down the side of a hill. If great roads are cleared and straightened, tiny paths are overgrown and follow idiosyncratic courses. Natural paths through the low ground between hills such as the Hwiį́ɔ are more precisely described as *b'èekanil* (F.47.B.420). Rough trails are the smallest and least open of all, so that in following one, a person is constantly brushing against overgrowth along the sides. It is tempting to suggest that the descriptor *?ek'* 'black' is motivated by its being the opposite of *sak* 'white', since overgrown footpaths are a sort of antithesis to what the Maya call *sak b'eh* 'white road'. The latter describes the famous paved causeways from preconquest culture, as well as modern roads that have been raised, leveled and covered with a light-color crushed rock.

In all of these cases, an individual walking along a road or path is said to be *yoó? b'eh* 'over road'. This expression makes a neat opposition to *yàanal k'aáš* 'under forest'; it is also used as a metaphor for being 'on the right road', that is, oriented and progressing toward one's goal. Describing people who intentionally give bad advice to others, hoping to see tham fail, Margot said:

(3)   luúgar uhoó?skeč yoó? beh, kuyokskeč ič k'aáš
        'In place of taking you out over road, they put you (deeper) into the woods.'
        (Rather than helping you, they lead you into trouble) (BB.5.140)

A road which 'reaches' some designated landmark is said to 'rise' to it, as in *kunaákal tak Yaaxhom* 'it goes all the way to Yaaxhom', and in the proper discourse context, it can be described as *?ub'èel Yaaxhom* 'the Yaaxhom road' (lit. Yaaxhom's road). When a truck goes out of control 'off the side of the road', it is described as *?éemel pač kaáretèera* 'to go down (the) back of the highway' (F.147.B.551). These apparently isolated bits of usage suggest that roads are themselves raised, and oriented up, front, and towards their destinations.

The root *b'eh* 'road' has far-reaching associations in Maya, beyond the ones cited so far. One of the first expressions one learns in the language is the standard greeting *b'iš ab'èel* 'How are you? (how is your road)', in which the individual's 'road' is his or her general state of being at the time. When people describe their lot in life, their life projects, their daily occupations, they summarize these engagements as their 'road'. One's road is where one has been and is heading. The diurnal path of the sun is its *b'èel* too, as the veins are *?ub'èel k'íik'* 'the path of blood', and the urethra is *?ub'èel wìiš* 'the path of urine'. The articulation between roads, human activity, and time is summarized neatly in the use of *b'eh* as the root for 'day' in the expressions: *b'eh-hé?ela?e?* ~ *b'eh-lá?e?* 'today, nowadays (lit., 'the road right here')', *ká?a-b'eh* 'the day after tomorrow (lit., 'two-road')'.

Landmarks are too numerous and diverse to describe here in anything but the broadest outline. In the forest, any noteworthy configuration such as a *muúl saáy* 'worker ant mound' (sometimes as much as 40 meters square), a large tree of any kind, a promontory or space between promontories, a *muúl* ruin 'mound' from preconquest society, a *krusamiento* crossroad, etc., can serve as landmark. Water sources are especially good points of orientation, because their locations are known to most who traverse the area, and they are vitally important to farmers and thirsty travelers. An *?aák'al* is a semipermanent, rain-fed marsh, with clay-soil bottom, such as the one in Yaaxhom, which no longer fills but used to cover an area of about twenty mecates and has been encoded in the name of the surrounding zone, *yoó? ?aák'al* 'over marsh'. Scattered throughout the Puuc are eroded caverns in the rocks where rainwater gathers, sometimes so small as to hold only a few gallons and sometimes large enough to contain water all year round. These are called *haáltuún*. A *čuúltuún* is a man-made underground water retainer, holding twenty thousand to forty-five thousand liters (Neugebauer 1986:46). These are pre-Columbian ruins found in the Puuc and Hwiią areas. They are not commonly used for water storage today and are considered dangerous.[5] Similarly, there are caves in the Puuc, such as Loltun, whose locations are known by locals and used as points of orientation.

Perhaps the most commonly used landmarks in talk about the region to the southwest of Oxkutzcab are the pump stations that drive the irrigation system on which commercial agriculture depends. These are referred to simply as Pozo *uno* 'Well 1', Pozo *dos* 'Well 2', etc. Along with the paved roads and concrete canals, the layout of these pumps defines a network of landmark places and connecting paths. Speakers describe the locations of their fields and homes, as well as their affiliation with other farmers, in terms of the pumps which draw the water they consume. Sitting over supper in his kitchen, just off the highway from Cooperativa to Labna, MC described his day driving the family truck. Up at 5:00 A.M., he started with two round trips between Oxkutzcab and Cooperativa, bringing full loads of men from town to their fields and orchards. On the third trip he continued farther along the highway, as he put it:

(4)   ká h sùunahen b'ey way a?→ b'in tuún timb'èetah to sèes o? . . .
        'Then I came back this way, (and continuing) I took off for (Pozo)
        6 . . .

        pwes le kuhoó?lo k'iíwik tutàalóo miyah tusòolarób o?→
        Well the ones who go out (from the) market, they come to work in
        their solars,

        pwes désde oóšk'u¢kàab tak koóperatìi tak trèes→
        well from Oxkutzcab to Cooperativa to (Pozo) 3. (F.147.B.331 ff.;
        BB.5.92 ff.)

In usages like these, the numbers of the pumps function as reduced names and stand for whole regions. Whether MC actually arrived at pump stations 3 and 6, what he is saying in the above quote is that he went to the area around the pump, which implies that he followed a certain route and transported certain people familiar to him as the occupants of those areas. The habitual ground of MC's truck route, with all its familiar characters, is recapitulated in his referential practice: becoming schematized, landmarks function as elliptical reference points in a frame that spans a whole region.

7.4 Domestic Frame Spaces and Their Making

Among the many cultural constructions of space, the *soólar* and the milpa stand alongside body space and deictic space as centrally important 'root' constructions. In their internal structure, temporality (development and duration), and symbolic significance, these places embody elementary principles, processes, and experiences. Bourdieu ([1960] 1971) demonstrated the tremendous symbolic value of the Kabyle house as a microcosm of the universe, organized by a series of homologous oppositions. Categories of domestic space in a Thai village were shown by Tambiah ([1969] 1985) to link classifications of animals and humans, as well as embody a moral order regulating conduct. Among the Tswana, the house is an 'atom of structure' that "embodies both a set of primary social values and elementary structural forms, along with the principles of their reproduction and elaboration" (Comaroff and Roberts 1981:49). Comaroff (1985:46–60) further developed this analysis and linked it to a symbolic account of spatial arrangements in the Tshidi house.

These studies of the social and cultural constitution of domestic space have informed my understanding of the Maya homestead, but I am centrally concerned with its properties as a frame space for corporeality and referential practice. Starting from the social relations and interactive patterns among coresident individuals, as described in chapters 3–5, we move here to a direct examination of domestic space as a physical embodiment of the cultural order, as well as a primary locus for communicative activity. The discussion will begin with a sketch of the changes over the past decade in spatial arrangement and buildings of the households in which this research was conducted, along with a narrative account by DP of the process of first selecting and building a home (something I have not witnessed firsthand). Domestic space is constantly (or at least canonically) under construction, and it is apposite to begin by situating it in a developmental process. This will be followed by a brief sketch of the threshold, the layout of main structures, circulation of domestic birds and animals, activity spaces, and maintenance, secular and ritual. The significance of these in the description of referential practice is twofold. First, domestic space is the indexical field in which much of everyday interaction occurs, and its schematic structure is a primary frame of reference, deictic and nondeictic alike. Second, the structure of domestic space embodies as an icon many of the conceptual relations presented already and found in the semantics of deixis as well.

The description of *soólar* units in §3.3 started from the perspective of family development, citing changes that have occurred in the living circumstances of DP, DC, Balim, and Chio over the past ten years. Before resuming the description in terms of production and transformation of frame spaces, it is appropriate to emphasize that changes in domestic structures and family plots are motivated not only by the cyclic growth and fragmentation of the family but also by a purposive engagement on the part of adults in developing the land. Since they are peasant farmers, land and access to water are the key resources for most Oxkutzcabeños, and in order to retain use rights over communally owned ejidal lands, they must use the lands productively. People expand their homes, beautifying them, making different use of the space, building new structures. In the development of homesteads, orchards, and other agricultural land, it is fair to say that producing domestic and agricultural space is a primary life project for most men. The booming citrus and other fruit and vegetable production of the zone makes this engagement all the more intense, as men seek to acquire rights over productive land for themselves and their sons. More significantly for our purposes, the architecture of Maya households embodies a way of segmenting, totalizing, and describing the world that shows deep affinities with habitual practices of reference. Like Gothic architecture and scholasticism in Panofsky's little book, there are mental and corporeal habits in Maya social life that are embodied both in constructed spaces and in the discursive practices of the people who build them. These patterns can teach us a great deal about the culture of Maya language.

There is a very close relation between residential and productive land. Recall that residential space, where whole families (1st, 2d, or 3d level; cf. §3.3) reside semipermanently, is called *kahtalil* or *soólar* if outside of town and *soólar* if within town.[6] In either context, the sleeping home of the individual nuclear family is its *-otoč* 'house', *-iknal* 'place', or *-nahil* 'home, place (the possessed form of *nah*)'. There is no implication with any of these three terms that the space so designated is marked by a stone wall or fence, since most people live in what I characterized in §3.3 as 'second-level' households, in which two or three nuclear families are within a single perimeter. Nonetheless, rights over and ownership of land are possessed by individual nuclear families, and the second-level household is internally subdivided into parts belonging to the adult males. Both *kahtalil* and *soólar* **do** imply a fenced or otherwise physically bounded region. Residents of any fabricated space are described as *ʔotočnal* (< *ʔotoč* 'home', *nal* 'home [ʔinherent nature])'. Whereas *kahtalil*, *-otoč*, and *-nahil* designate residential as opposed to planted lands, *-iknal*, *nah*, and *soólar* are used for both where one sleeps and where one works, even when the two are separated by twenty-five kilometers. *kòol* '(unirrigated milpa) corn plot' and *parsela* '(irrigated) field', specifically designate planted lands.

Sometimes, families reside within or at the edge of their *parsela*, but it is the fact of its being planted that is central to the term: whereas one can describe a small city yard as a *soólar*, even if virtually nothing is planted in it, for a space to be appropriately described as a *parsela*, it must be in some phase of the agricultural process. During key phases of the agricultural cycle, men and sometimes their wives reside temporarily in the milpa in minimal, open-sided shelters called *paásel*. This may lead to a semipermanent move and building a full house and kitchen, but when it does, the domestic space will cease to be called *kòol* and become *soólar* or one of the other terms.

Because productive lands may be located at considerable distance from primary residences and the Oxkutzcab market at which the produce is sold, many families have a secondary residence in addition to their primary one. Is and his father reside near one another in town and work together in a milpa on the far side of Xul, where they stay for up to a week at a time during peak work seasons (especially weeding and harvesting). DP and Milo own houses and a joint kitchen on a *soólar* in Oxkutzcab, but they use them only when business, health care, or parties keep them in town overnight. VI lives in Yaaxhom with his wife and two children, his unmarried brother, and his parents, but has acquired a small *soólar* in Oxkutzcab with a partly built cement house on it. Balim lived temporarily in his wife's father's *soólar* in Oxkutzcab and simultaneously maintained another one at the outskirts of town, with an open-sided structure on it. The latter was not suitable for residence because there was no proximal source of water.

The thrust of these observations is that the line between cultivated and residential space is not a fixed one. Families commonly shift residence between more than one plot, at least temporarily, and a single plot may go through different phases in which it is alternatively a cultivated or residential space. Furthermore, the residential *soólar* is cultivated with as much productive plant life as possible: trees, corn, or garden, depending on the quality of the soil and availability of water. Thus the distinction between residential and cultivated land is a matter of focus and contains a hidden diachronic component—they are different **phases,** not fundamentally distinct **kinds** of space. It is for this reason that we examine the homestead and the milpa in relation to one another, as two embodiments of a single spatiotemporal system.

7.4.1 Diachrony of Domestic Space

DP's lands are currently spread over four discontinuous areas, each of which has been both residential and cultivated at different times during the past ten years. In figure 7.5, a map of DP's lands (except his townhouse in Oxkutzcab), these areas are labeled I, II, III. In 1977, area I was fallow, and there was a single *šáʔani nah* 'palm (roofed) house' there in which some tools were kept. A barbed-wire fence behind the house kept in two Brahman bulls who roamed freely in the wooded backyard of about thirty mecates (120m × 100m). Area II, approximately forty-five mecates (180m × 100m), was partly planted with *k'ušub'* 'achoite' trees, and partly planted with *nal* 'corn'. Both I and II were, and remain today, unirrigated. Area III was within the irrigation network well before 1977 and was covered by mature fruit-bearing citrus, avocado, banana, royal palm, papaya, etc., trees. Set back in the orchard behind an irrigation canal,

KEY

ECOLOGICAL ZONES

Distribution Approximate

	Defecation Area	
	Boundary Marker	
	Spices in Buckets	
	Altar	
	Citrus	
	Mango	
	Achiote	
	Barbed Wire	
	Kitchen	
	Clothesline	
	Poultry	
	Bull	
	Washing Area	
	Unfenced perimeter	
	Rock pit	
	Limestone pit	
	Apsidal Living Structure	
	Rectangular Living Structure	

Symbol	Zone	Type
	Kabah Če'	Low Forest
	Pú'uk	High Ground
XXX	Čùun Pú'uk	Base of Puuc
	Yáaš Hóom	Great Green
o o o	?Ek' Lú'um	Black Earth
▲ ▲ ▲	Hwlíȼil K'aáš	Hill Forest
		Elevation
	Loób?	Overgrown
	Pàaktá?an	Weeded

Key to Figures 7.5 through 7.10.

about twenty meters from the road, was the main residence of DP and DA, their youngest son MC, wife Eli, and first infant MF. The next-older son VC and his wife Pilar lived with their two children farther back in the same orchard. Milo, the oldest son, lived elsewhere in Yaaxhom with his wife and three children. Area IV was also an irrigated orchard (dimensions unknown to me) in MC and VC's names. Neither III nor IV has ever been fenced or walled off, to my knowledge, while I and II have been and remain so. In addition to these areas, MC and DP (and perhaps VC) also maintained individual *kòol* 'cornfield' off in the woods of *Hwiíȼil k'aáš* 'hill forest.' These are not shown in figure 7.5.

By summer of 1978, DP, MC, and VC, along with their families, were residing permanently in area I. They had built, with the help of an urban

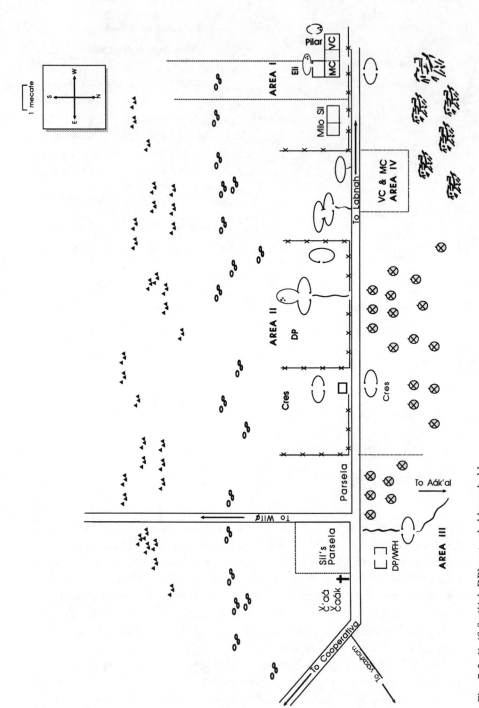

Fig. 7.5. *Yoó? ?aákʼal*: DP's extended household.

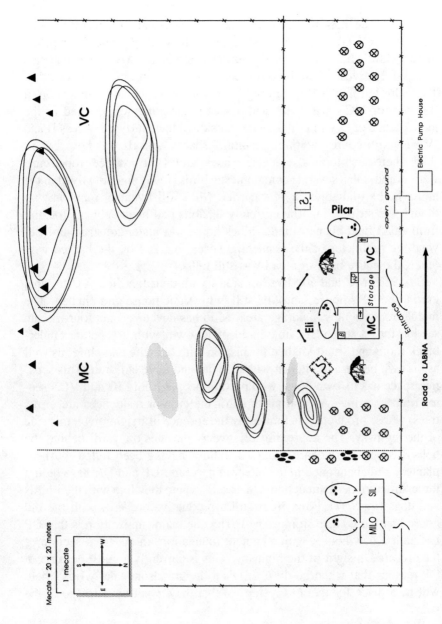

Fig. 7.6. Extended household of Milo, MC, and VC (area I from fig. 7.5).

benefactor, the three-room cinder-block structure that remains there today (see fig. 7.6). DP and DA lived in the rightmost, VC and Pilar in the middle, and MC and Eli in the leftmost structure. MC, who had had successful harvests, had the resources to build two rooms, which he did. The palm hut that had been used as a work shed was now the k'oób'en 'kitchen' of MC's wife, Eli, and a second structure was erected as the joint kitchen of DA and Pilar, at the far side of the courtyard. Areas II and IV were still nonresidential agricultural spaces, and III was now a work shed where such tools as machetes, hoes, crates for produce, rope, etc., were stored. DP's several score domestic birds (fowl, pigeons) lived in the house he had inhabited a year earlier. Milo still lived in Yaaxhom, although the strip of land he currently inhabits had been split off for him from area I, and his new cinder-block home was under construction. Beyond the perimeter of the residential space, marked by the barbed-wire fence, the entire back of area I was still fallow.[7]

By 1987, MC and VC lived in area I with their families, VC in what used to be DP's house, and MC still in his same house and kitchen. The middle room is now a storage area. Milo has developed his four-mecate section into a secondary household of its own, with a separate cinder-block room and small kitchen for his son with his wife and child, as well as his own house and kitchen with his wife and three children. This separate space has its own dogs, who prevent people from MC and VC's sector from entering. Around all three of the current residences are citrus trees, whose production is limited by the absence of irrigation on this side of the highway. The approximately twenty mecates of 'yard' behind the houses is now in the early stages of fallow, having been felled, burned, planted, and abandoned in the intervening years. DP and DA have built a three-structure permanent home in area II, where they live with their birds and dogs (fig. 7.7). Area III is still a productive orchard, with the old house being used as a storage shed. The one major innovation is that DP has built a new house, with a cement foundation, in the front section of the orchard, in sight of the highway. This is currently a guest house, but DP reasons that when he dies, or when the grandsons take wives, there will be a place for them to reside, so that they won't have to 'go in the street'.

When I first met DC in 1979, his home in Oxkutzcab consisted of two living structures, a *nah* and an adjoining *k'oób'en*, along with a pigsty, on a lot measuring sixty by sixty meters. He lived there with his middle son, Lol (then seventeen years old), and his dog Negro 'Blackie'. The kitchen hut was without a fireplace, there being no woman in the household to tend a fire, and contained only a hand mill that DC used (and still uses) to

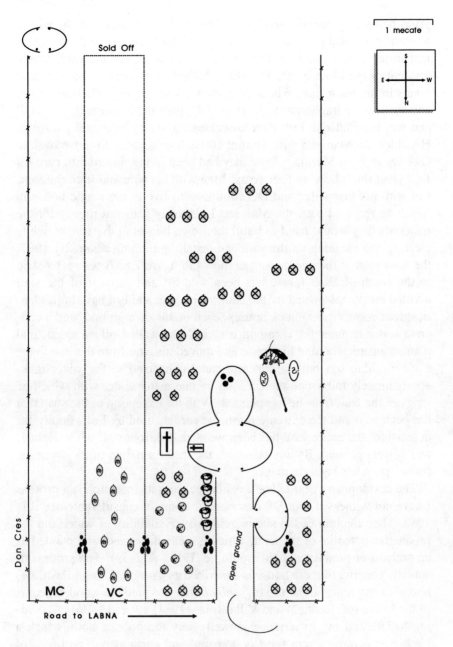

Fig. 7.7. DP's immediate household (area II from fig. 7.5).

grind herbs in preparing medicine. The yard was mostly brush, with a scattering of royal palm and citrus trees, the latter atrophied from lack of irrigation. Twisted paths led out to the back portions of the yard, where residents went to defecate. DC slept, bathed, and received patients and lovers in his main *nah*, which contained his hammocks, clothing, altar, and shamanic paraphernalia. In 1981, DC, then in his late sixties, fell ill and was hospitalized with liver abscesses caused by intestinal parasites. His elder son Man and wife Margot at this time decided to move back to Oxkutzcab from Mérida, where they had been living, in order to care for DC. Over the following four years, Man with his wife and four children, Lol with his first wife, and DC continued to live in the single house in which he received patients. Man and Lol slowly gathered money for the materials they would need to build their own homes in the *soólar*, while clearing and cleaning up the yard and installing running water. By 1987, the floor plan of the *soólar* was as shown in figure 7.8. A ten-meter strip to the south of DC's house has been sold off and the rest of the yard divided into strips owned by the adult men. Man and Lol have built identical four-room cinder-block houses, each on his own ground, and a concrete water retainer for common use. DC has walled off, weeded, and planted a garden behind his house and moved his altar from the *nah* to the *k'oób'en*. Man has built a concrete canal connected to the water tank, approximately thirty-one meters long by one meter wide, with which he irrigates the fruit trees he has planted. With the exception of the strip that has been sold and the extreme northeast corner, used by Lol's family for defecation, the entire yard has been weeded, the front wall whitewashed, and flowers planted. By any standard, the transformation of the domestic frame space has been dramatic.

The development of a *kahtalil* residence from its inception is a process I have not witnessed, but DP described it to me in considerable detail in 1982. The selection of the site is guided by availability of water and the productive potential of the land, which is cleared, burned, and planted as an orchard or productive field would be (F.119.A.2:39). The process of actually constructing the house is described as *k'ašik nah* 'bind (lash, tie) house', a reference to the use of *ʔanikab'* vines to bind the wooden beams of the house (cf. Redfield and Villa Rojas [1934] 1962:33–35). According to DP, and my experience as well, only the poorest houses lack a kitchen structure, where food is prepared and consumed. The result of lighting a fire in the main *nah* is to make it and its contents very smoky. In DP's account, the kitchen is first described as a small *nah* that is the woman's *k'oób'en* (F.119.A.040), a phrasing that suggests that the kitchen is a special kind of *nah* corresponding to the woman's sphere of activity.

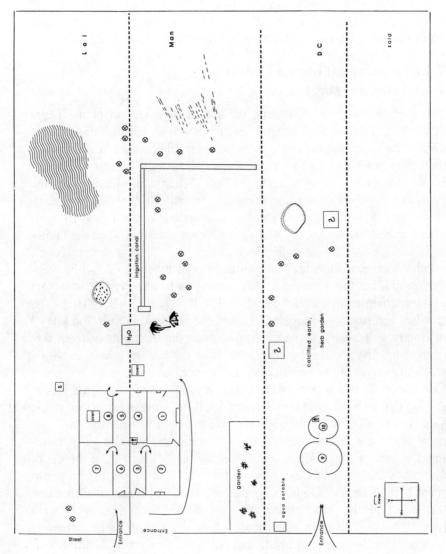

Fig. 7.8. DC's household in town.

Recall that DC's kitchen, lacking a woman to occupy it, also lacks a *k'oób'en* fire. After the two primary living structures, the *so?ih* for domestic birds or *čikèero* 'sty' for pigs is constructed, referred to as *y otoč k ?àalak'* 'our domesticated animals' house(s)'. The *kòot* 'stone wall' is built gradually and is considered a more beautiful division marker than brush fences formed by felled trees and bushes (F.119.A.072).

7.4.2 Perimeter and Internal Divisions

7.4.2.1 *Wall and Division*

The starting point for discussing the spatial organization of the Maya homestead is the *haál* 'perimeter, outer boundary', because this is what divides the inner, private space from the outer, public one. Together with the center point, the four corners which define the perimeter also totalize the domestic space as a unitary whole. When nonresidents enter the yard, they routinely show recognition of its boundary by announcing themselves to resident adults and awaiting instructions to enter (see §3.3.5). This is called 'respecting the *nah*'. People recognize that when the homestead lacks a *kòot* 'stone wall', *?alambréeh* 'fence', *sùup* 'brush fence', or other barrier, visitors may inadvertently cross the threshold without authorization, but this is never strictly proper, and such a visitor is subject to questioning as to his motives (F.119.A.12:04; F.120.B.123 ff.). The standard greeting for strangers in Oxkutzcab is *bwénas días* 'Good day!' or simply *bwéénááas,* delivered from outside the front gate or front side of the yard. Even when the *hòo(l)nah* 'front door of the house' is within reach, it is rare, in my experience, that visitors knock to get a response. One reason for this is perhaps that there is usually no justification for assuming that an adult is inside the house itself, rather than farther off in the yard. For familiar nonresidents who have the right to enter the yard, the usual greeting is a more assertive announcement, such as *tàal telóo* 'Coming in there!' or a question like *tàaken wá té?elo?* 'May I come there?' or *heéy, kulá?aneč wáa?* 'Hey! Are you home?' In all cases, it is proper to speak before entering another's homestead. To any of these, an affirmative response typically includes the imperative *?òoken* 'enter', or *kó?oten* 'come (to me)'. Even in households where there is no barrier, there is always a division between inside and out. This division is a corollary of the completeness of the homestead and is reaffirmed in the ceremonies conducted to purify and protect the place (see §7.4.3 below).

In order to make sense of the internal divisions around the domestic frame space, it is necessary to distinguish three levels of spatial organization, corresponding to (i) nuclear family space, (ii) the shared space of adjoining families headed by brothers, and (iii) the sometimes discontinuous space of adjacent affines (see §3.3.5). First-level divisions are embodied in separate sleeping houses, and often kitchens, but are virtually never marked by fences or other barriers. Second-level ones are canonically marked by barriers along the perimeter. Thus in figure 7.8, DC's second-level homestead is walled in, whereas the first-order divisions are the invisible axes along which the house wall, canal, and gardens are aligned. In figure 7.6, MC and VC form a single second-order homestead, divided from that of Milo by a row of *šú²uk'* 'boundary markers' and by the aggressive behavior of Milo's dogs. The sometimes sprawling domains of affines lack the unitary character of second-order homesteads and are not single places whose perimeters are embodied in threshold greetings, physical divides, or ritual enactments.

In the course of performing a *heéȼ lú²um* 'fix earth' ceremony, DC asked the men of the house how big the place was, and the responses he received demonstrate that the different levels of inclusion are attended to by native speakers.

(5)   A: ²éstee→ ²oóčenta pór ²očenta→
       'Ah, 80 by 80 (meters).'

       B: kwaárenta pór kwaárenta
       '40 by 40.'

       C: má²a→
       'Nope.'

       B: hmm ²aáh sóolar→ bwéeno síi síi→
       'Oh, (the whole) solar, OK yeah, yeah.'

       C: sùut ká²ká²aȼáak
       '2 by 2 mecates all around' (F.78.A.078)

The problem was that B initially understood DC's question to bear on the part of the yard belonging specifically to the sponsor (first-order yard), while A and C correctly understood it to be the entire (second-level) *soólar*.

7.4.2.2 Nah *'House'*

The internal space of the main house of a single marriage unit is described as *²ič nah* 'in (the) house'. It is defined by a conjunction of features, not all of which are invariably present. The *²ič nah* is where at least some residents sleep, where the family *santo* 'saint image' is kept along with fresh flowers and a burning candle, where documents, jewelry, expensive tools, clothing, and other valuables are kept. It is where honored guests are received and offered a hammock or chair to rest on. When it has a finished floor and appropriate drainage, it is commonly, though not always, where members bathe. In traditional *šá?anih nah* 'palm roof house', which are *tú?u¢'* 'apsidal' in shape, the rounded end areas, called *moy,* are often separated by a curtain from the central area. They then become the private spaces in which members sleep, bathe, or dress. This is the case in Is's house, as well as in Toni C's and DC's elder sister's (BB.4.107). In rectangular cinder-block houses, either a separate room or corner by a drain is the typical bathing place, as in Milo's, VC's, MC's, and Man's.

In some cases, residents shift their sleeping places on a seasonal or occasional basis, as do Man, Marg, and their children, who reside in rooms 1 through 4 in figure 7.8. During the winter months, when temperatures drop down to the low sixties, causing considerable discomfort, they sleep in room 2, which retains heat well because of its sheet metal roof and window closures. During the hot season, when daytime temperatures exceed 110 degrees, and the humidity may be sufficient to grow mold on the floor, they sleep in room 1, which is relatively well ventilated with screened windows on two sides. Standing in room 1 weaving a hammock, Man explained that, during the hot season:

(6)   wá té? ká wèenkó?on a? ↑   má? tinwene tub'èel
        'If we were to sleep in there (room 2), I wouldn't sleep right.'
        (BB.4.100–101)

Earlier in the same day, Man had put down a new *sahkab'* 'limestone/clay' surface on the floor in room 1. Standing in room 1, watching Man finish the floor, Margot remarked that she hoped that the next day, the floor in room 2 would be done as well.[8] In her statement, she distinguished the eating room (1), where she was standing, from the front room (2), where valuables are stored and the family currently sleeps, calling the latter *té? ?ič nah o?*.

(7)   saámalili utokar té ič nah o?
        'Tomorrow it's expected come to there inside.' (BB.4.99)

DC formerly slept and stored his medicines in room 9, where his altar was located on the east wall of the south *moy* 'end'. Closest to the street, this room has the only light bulb, drain for bathing, and outside locking door in DC's home. It has fully packed earth and whitewashed walls and is the canonical *?ič nah* 'in (the) house'. Room 10 is referred to as a *k'oób'en* 'kitchen', which it appears to have been originally, although there is no evidence that fire has been lit there since the cement floor was poured. It is smaller than room 9, opens out onto the backyard, facing east, and has no packed earth on the walls, but rather exposed vertical *kolo?če?* 'slats, vertical sticks' (cf. Redfield and Villa Rojas [1934] 1962:33). Today the altar is located on the east wall of the north *moy* in room 10, and DC sleeps in the south *moy* of the same room. As in the past, he prepares *ȼ'àak* 'medicine' in room 10, where his hand mill is fixed to a post permanently planted in the cement floor in the southern *moy*. Sitting in conversation with me in front of his altar in the north *moy*, he explained that he stored the medicines all around the room, atop the door jambs, on the altar, on the wall of the passage connecting rooms 10 and 9.

(8)   le ȼ'àak o? čeén tí?an tée bey o?†→ ?ulaá? té?elo?†→
           'The medicine (under discussion), it's just there† like I say, another
              there†

           ulaá? té?el o?†→
           another there.† †(accompanied by laconic pointing gestures with
              right hand) (BB.4.95)

Thus DC has shifted from north to south and from front to back. He attributed little significance to the transformation when I inquired, saying that despite the cold, he likes to sleep in the more open room since it reminds him of many years ago, when he slept in a poor hovel in the woods. His move, like Man's seasonal shifts, introduces a discrepancy between the physical structure and location of the rooms, whereby *?ič nah* is front and enclosed and *k'oób'en* is back and open, and the activities that occur there. Despite the shift, it is evidently still appropriate to describe room 9 as *?ič nah* 'in (the) house' and room 10 as the *k'oób'en* 'kitchen', suggesting that structure and placement are core features of the terms. Two important features of DC's house that remain constant are that (i) the altar is on the east wall of a *moy* 'end', and (ii) DC sleeps and stores medicine in the same room with the altar. The first of these is apparently motivated by the cosmological values attaching to east as a cardinal location and the second to DC's affective and spiritual bond to his altar and shamanic paraphernalia.

The placement of living structures in the *soólar* appears to follow a few simple principles. The boundary lines of the land belonging to the head of household are the orienting axes of the house walls, with the *taánil, ?aktaán* 'front' wall of the house usually facing the front side of the yard. If one side of the lot lies along a public street or path, that side is usually 'front', and the *hòo(l)nah* 'gate, door, threshold to the house' is there. In figure 7.6, the fronts of the houses of Milo, Sil, MC, and VC are identically aligned with the paved highway; in figure 7.7, DP's house faces the highway, even though it is set back approximately forty meters from it; and in figure 7.8, DC's, Man's, and Lol's places all face the street. If there is a source of water or electricity along the perimeter of the land, it is preferable to locate close to it, to minimize transportation distances. In figure 7.6, the well called Pozo 2 motivated the placement of the cinder-block houses, and in figure 7.7, the availability of city water coincides with the location of Man's and Lol's houses. The unfenced boundaries between individuals' land inside the *soólar* also orient placement of the house. Observe that the wall dividing MC's place from VC's in figure 7.6 lies precisely on the division between their respective parts of the land. In figure 7.8, the wall between Man's and Lol's houses similarly embodies the line dividing their parcels of the yard. The lay of the canal, the placement of the water retainer, and the shape of the gardens in figure 7.8 show a similar orientation.

In recounting how he and Man had moved into and begun developing their father's *soólar,* Lol explained that they first had to *hoók'sik u dokumèentos* 'take out the documents' to the land, which had been repossessed by a bank in Mérida. They were obliged to sell most of their possessions in order to raise the necessary money. After that, they made plans for constructing their houses:

(9)   Lol: kuȼ'ó?ol e?→ká tàal-ó?on bey <u>way</u> o?,   ká t-?á?al e <u>yan</u>
          'afterwards,   then we came around here,   then we said we're
                                                                                                    gonna

          k-bèetk ump'eé nah té?el a?→
          build a house right here.'

    WH: tú?uš
          'Where?'

    Lol: <u>le way a?</u> ↓   'This place right here-'
                  ⌐

    WH: hač 'Really-'
                  ⌐

    Lol: té <u>way</u>→   hàah . . . ȼ'óokok <u>k</u>-bèetk e plàano
                  'Right here, yeah . . . after having finished the
                                                                                    plan,

          bey o? ↑   miná?an ubloki→   péro ȼ'óok k-tukl ik e?
          like I said, we didn't have the cinder blocks. But we had decided,

lel a²→ ump'eé pàarte <u>teč</u> i² ump'eé pàarte <u>ten</u> i²→
'This here, one part (is) for you, one part for me.'
(F.137.A.389–435)

The underlined portions of this strip of talk show Lol's terms of reference
for the placement of the new house in the *soólar*. The first token of *way*
'here' refers to the walled (2d-level) *soólar* as a whole, which belongs by
descent to DC, but by purchase to them. They divided it among themselves, deciding to build a single cement structure in the northwest corner
of the yard, as underscored in the second line of Lol's utterance. In response to my query, he specified that this single structure was then further
split into equal parts according to ownership, a decision realized in the
placement of the middle wall of the house along the divide between their
respective parts of the yard. This segmentation of the whole into first-
level spaces of individual families is reflected linguistically in the combination of *té²* 'there (punctual immediate)' with *way* 'here (regional
inclusive)', and the shift from first person plural (We planned) to first and
second person singular (one for you and one for me), all underlined in
Lol's last utterance. Individual places corresponding to single actors and
their spouses are segmented, physically and linguistically, out of a preestablished common frame space.

7.4.2.3 K'oób'en *'Kitchen'*

In §3.3.4, we observed that the traditional Maya kitchen is a fundamentally female space, the place of fire, water storage, and food preparation
and consumption, usually with a bare earth floor. Because of their linkage
to basic activity patterns of the woman, kitchens are relatively conser-
vative places. While there are many rectangular cinder-block houses
around Oxkutzcab, as these floor plans attest, they are commonly joined
to traditional palm-thatched *k'oób'en*. In addition to these features, the
k'oób'en is virtually always located behind the main house, so that it is
sheltered by it from the outside. Often, though not always, it is physically
connected to the house by a covered passage or paved walkway, as in figures 7.6, 7.7, and 7.8. Figure 7.9 shows the kitchen of VC's wife Pilar in
area I, set behind the main house and truck shelter. Figure 7.10 shows
Eli's kitchen, also in area I. The latter is adjoined to the living house, and
the former is not.

Figures 7.9 and 7.10 show details of the typical layout of Maya kitchens. Both open out onto the courtyard behind the main sleeping houses.
The placement of the three stones forming the cooking fire is identical, in
the *moy* area of the structure. The wall behind the fire is customarily left

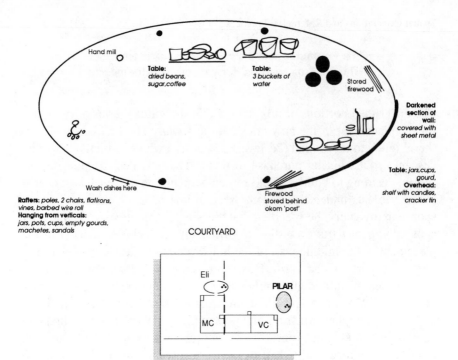

Fig. 7.9. Pilar's kitchen.

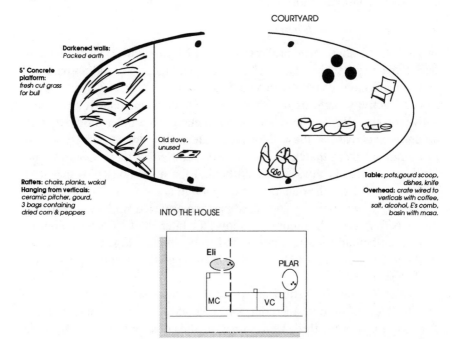

Fig. 7.10. Eli's kitchen.

open, so that smoke and heat can escape in the draft. Within reach of the fire, where the woman of the kitchen spends much time seated on a *k'an če?* 'stool', is a utility table where eating utensils and condiments are stored. Cups, pitchers, *saábukàan* 'shoulder bags' with dried corn, *lèek* 'gourd containers', and tools hang from or are wedged in the vertical *kolo?če* walls. Chairs, planks, fruit crates, rolls of barbed wire, vines, and miscellaneous tools are stored in the rafters over the *moy* opposite the fire (to minimize smoke). In Eli's kitchen, fresh *sú?uk* 'grasses' to be fed to the bull are stored temporarily in the end opposite the fire. The small table at which men eat is placed roughly in the middle ground of the room, within reach of Eli's habitual place by the fire, but away from the heat and smoke. Like DA's kitchen in figure 7.7 and DC's room 10 in figure 7.8, Eli's kitchen opens directly into the back door of the main house. The path between the two is one that members walk routinely in their daily circulation.

There appear to be two canonical relations between the orientation of the kitchen and that of the main house. In households like DC's (figure 7.8), MC's (figure 7.6), Is's (not shown), and Juan C's (not shown), the two structures are identically aligned, both replicating the front face of the *soólar*. In terms of the path of entry, they are arrayed along a single axis leading from outside to inside. In other cases, like VC's and Milo's

Plate 7.1. Eli's kitchen.

(fig. 7.6), DP's (fig. 7.7), DP's Oxkutzcab townhouse (not shown), Chio's (not shown), and Toni C's (not shown), the two have perpendicular orientations. When adjoined, they make a T formation with the house at the top and the *moy* 'end' of the kitchen open to the back door of the house, to permit the free flow of traffic (fig. 7.7). When the two are not connected but open onto a courtyard, they face inward from orthogonal directions. The first kind of orientation is linear-successive, in that the passageways of the structures fall on a single axis, front to back (east to west, north to south, etc.). The second kind of orientation is orthogonal (or perhaps 'lateral'), with the two facing into a single courtyard. Even in orthogonal orientations, there is an unavoidable element of successivity, insofar as the Maya *k'oób'en* is almost invariably behind the house.

7.4.2.4 *Other Minor Places*

Other minor structures around the homestead include the *so?ih* 'coop' for domestic fowl, the *čikèeroh* 'pigsty', the *koóral* 'corral' for bulls, *pìila* 'water retainer', *tàanke* 'water tank', the *baáteyáah* 'scrub basin' at which clothing is washed, and various storage areas. It is a noteworthy fact for the households under discussion that even these minor structures tend strongly to recapitulate the orientation of the major ones. That is, looking in from the front gate, structures are arrayed successively and orthogonally, with very few on the diagonal. Even Man's right-angle irrigation canal in figure 7.8 repeats the perpendicular form of the corner of the yard instead of cutting across on the bias or curving. The same goes for the placement of Margot's scrub basin in figure 7.8, DA's basin in figure 7.7, and Pilar's and Eli's basins in figure 7.6. This is a noteworthy fact, because women spend significant portions of any week washing at the basin, looking out on the yard from its perspective. Usually the basin is covered by a thatch roof or shaded by a tree, to help the women stay cool while laboring at it. Curiously, the two domestic structures that seem canonically askew with respect to the cardinal axes of the yard are the clothesline and the walkways. As is shown in the figures, Maya clotheslines often describe bent or biased trajectories, even cutting through the main courtyard where people walk, forcing them to duck or go around it.

Some of the well-trodden pathways are indicated on figures 7.5 through 7.8. These tend strongly to be curved around major structures. Although straight axes often align structures and their doorways with the entrance to the *soólar*, they do not determine the paths members follow when circulating in the yard. Not only are places private to individual families, but doors are often left closed, obstructing passage. This is the case particularly with front doors, which open into the main living structure where valuables are stored. When the men of the household are out working, and the women are working in the yard, visitors walk around the main house to the courtyard area without going through the house or kitchen. In my experience, strangers are generally greeted at the gate or in the courtyard rather than inside any of the domestic structures. Thus, the cardinal orientations of the household, both linear-successive and orthogonal, are present as a background frame space in which any place can be located, but they do not directly determine the routes people follow in leaving and going to those places. The doorways routinely used by residents in their daily rounds are the inner ones, which face into the common courtyard and tend therefore to function as orthogonal trajectories into the center rather than as successive points along a perimeter.

In the course of preparing herbal medicine to be used for therapeutic bathing, DC gave eloquent evidence of the encompassment of round within rectangular space. Most of his curing and divinatory practice in his capacity as a *hmèen* 'doer, shaman' takes place in his domestic *soólar* (fig. 7.8), where he grinds, dries, and mixes the plant materials that make up his five principal *¢'àakó?ob'* 'medicines'. The drying process involves spreading out the medicine in the sun for several days running, so that it takes on and holds the solar heat. This heat is an important element of the medicine's effectiveness as a means of regulating the hot/cold balance of a patient's body. DC spreads out his medicine on the white path running east-west through his garden, directly behind his altar (fig. 7.8). He shapes the finely ground *pòolßo* 'dust, powder' as a *maák* 'person' consisting of a round belly in the middle with four corner points (limbs) and a round head, oriented to the east. The powdery icon lies on a rectangular sheet of cardboard, in the rectangular garden, in the rectangular yard. The shape in plate 7.2 was formed spontaneously by DC in response to my expressed desire to photograph the medicine. It represents an earlier stage in the preparation of another medicine. The materials are still rough, but the composition is unmistakably a circle with a cruciform, within a quadrilateral.

7.4.2.5 *Activity Fields*

There are significant correlations between major domestic structures and the everyday activities that take place within and around them. Cooking, eating, firewood storage, fire maintenance, and often bathing and dishwashing take place inside the *k'oób'en*, while sleeping, receiving visitors, dressing, and the storing of valuables are usually done *?ič nah* 'inside (the) house'. Beyond these correlations, however, there are a number of daily activities that occur around the yard. For instance,

Plate 7.2. Medicine displayed: cruciform and circle within quadrilateral.

women and children *pàak* 'weed' the grounds around the courtyard, keeping the ground bare and therefore safe from reptiles and vermin. The courtyard and regular pathways, as well as the inside floors of structures, are *miístá ʔan* 'swept' frequently by the women. Around the household in figure 7.6, Pilar and Eli keep water for daily consumption in buckets placed outside in the courtyard, between their kitchens and *baáteyáah* 'scrub basins'. In figure 7.8, Margot keeps water for drinking in a *tinaja* inside room 1, but washing water outside, between the oven and wash-basin. It is here, not at the basins or in the kitchen, that all three women wash dishes and rinse corn in preparation for grinding. Dishes are allowed to dry outside in the sun on a *káʔančeʔ* 'table (lit., elevated wood)' or elevated surface. In all households with which I am familiar, residents defecate, alone and in private, back in the *soólar,* twenty meters or more away from the living area. Often, though not always, there is a single zone designated for this. There is a euphemism in Maya corresponding to the English 'go to the bathroom', and it is *haám b'in ʔič soólar* 'quickly go into (the) yard'. To request the 'use of the bathroom' in Maya, one asks *haán mahaán ten a soólar* 'briefly lend me your yard'. The important point for present purposes is that in such usage, the term '*soólar*' is used to refer to a space inside the perimeter of the yard but outside the living area.

It is worth recalling at this point that conversational interactions take place virtually everywhere in domestic space, whenever two or more appropriate people are within earshot of each other. Sisters-in-law, who spend vast amounts of time working around the same courtyard, frequently talk while performing daily tasks. In figure 7.6, the washbasins and water storage areas of Pilar and Eli are within clear sight of each other, and the women carry on lively conversations while working in their respective places. Margot and Fi share a single water source and courtyard in figure 7.8, and talk while coming and going in their own areas. Coresident adult males, like Man and Lol, work side-by-side or collaboratively on domestic chores and converse while they work. The canonical structures, pathways, and activity spaces form a background frame space, available to residents as a common stock of knowledge against which they define actional and referential foci. When we examine deictic usage in chapter 9, this background will become a crucial schematic context to which speakers attend and which they utilize for communicative effect.

7.4.3 Ritual Transpositions of the Domestic Field

Domestic space is an object of ritual fabrication in at least three distinct modes. In the constitution of the space of ritual performance, *tučùun u mèesa* 'at the foot of the altar (table)', it is an object of iconic elaboration. A performance space is built up through an ordered process in which a diagrammatic icon of absolute cardinal space is erected, step by step, on the altar. By ritual transposition, this cardinal space is the same one that constitutes the perimeter and wholeness of domestic land. In the *tííčʼkʼaák'* 'divination (lit., hold out fire)' process, the *soólar* may be an object of scrutiny, which the shaman visually examines with the help of the *yunȼilóʔob'* 'lords' (cf. §5.3). In the *heéȼ lúʔum* 'fix earth' ceremony, it is an object of transformation which is swept clean of malevolent spirits (cf. Nash [1971] 1975: 17, 151 on house curing in Tzeltal). In this section I wish to suggest that the ritual process in Maya culture also embodies an interaction between two kinds of spatialization. Building on previously discussed features of corporeal space, cardinal orientations, paths and regions of landscape, orientation of domestic structures, and activities around the house, the two kinds are: (i) **Directional organizations** of space, which are approximate, action-centric (i.e., relative to the perspective of an actor), and used to segment objects as successive points along axes. They provide no logical basis for defining a perimeter and therefore cannot determine inclusion/exclusion. (ii) **Locative organizations** are absolute, not perspectival, orthogonal rather than linear-successive, and used to totalize places by their perimeter rather than segment parts relative to one another. They provide no logical basis for defining an action-relative, indexical, perspectival space, except as fixed landmarks. These same fundamental types will be shown to underlie the structure of deictic space, thus providing a nexus between actional body space, ritual practice, domestic space, and referential practice. In the terms employed by Munn (1986:chap 1), ritual action epitomizes the production of spacetime by unifying in a single practice the basic modes of spatiotemporal organization. Moreover, insofar as all Maya ritual performance has a prospective motivation, what is being produced is not only the emergent framework of the ritual engagement but a frame space of virtual outcomes that will follow as a consequence of proper enactment (but are not present in the enactment itself).

7.4.3.1 *Living Space as an Object of Iconic Representation*

In the traditional genres of ritual practice in Maya, the basic dynamic of prayer is the same:[9] spirits, who are located in cardinal places throughout the vertical and horizontal universe, are *ʔeénsáʔal* 'lowered' to the place of performance, actually *peéksáʔal* 'moved' from their appointed places and brought down to an encounter with the shaman and those he presents in the performance space. The space of the altar, referred to in performance as *téʔ tulúʔumil kʼebʼan* 'there on the earth of sin', and *tučùun ʔumèesa X* 'at the base of X's altar (where X is a spirit name)', is constituted in an absolutely orderly process, whereby spirits are lowered in the order of their originative locations. There are differences among types of performance, but in major ceremonies, the opening phases of the ritual, in which spirits are lowered, proceed in the counterclockwise order E > N > W > S > C, whereas the closing phases, in which the shaman *sutikóʔobʼ* 'returns them', the preferred order is clockwise: E > S > W > N > C (Hanks 1984c:138–41). The first phase is called *heʔik bʼeel* 'opening the road', or *kʼašik mèesa* 'binding (the) altar,' and the second is called *wačʼik mèesa* 'untie (the) altar' (cf. §5.3).

Thus in the process of creating the altar as a space, a 'road' is opened between earth and absolute cosmological locations. Recall from §7.3.4 that paths lead 'up' to their destinations, and travelers walk 'over' and 'in front of' them (since 'off the path' in Maya is *pàačil* 'behind' it). The day, state of being, and destiny of the individual is a road, and for it to be 'open', as opposed to *šotá?an* 'cut (off)' or *k'á?alá?an* 'closed, blocked off', *k'aátá?an* 'crossed, blocked', is a sign of possibility. The reference to the opening of the road as a binding of the altar is best seen in relation to the process of building a secure place. House building is described as *k'ašik nah* 'bind house', because of the use of vine lashes to tie the beams together. This is the process of building any lashed domestic structure such as the kitchen, sleeping house, or fowl coop, all of which provide protection and boundaries between inside and out. The altar is secured in the sense that spirits are bound to absolute locations around it, at once protecting the shaman from attack by any marauding spirits in the area and also preventing the lowered spirits themselves from wandering around. Even fully beneficent spirits can cause damage when loosed, and incompetent shamans are often accused of knowing how to move them but not knowing how to secure their place and return them to their *luúgar* 'place (of origin)'.

The fact that in returning the spirits, the altar is said to be 'untied' also accords with an otherwise curious feature of domestic altars like DC's in room 10, figure 7.8: outside the context of performance, the surface used as an altar is not a sacred space but a simple table, on which a random assortment of objects can be found. The process of creating the altar is a reframing of the table in absolute terms, a transformation in which the untied detritus of nonsacred activities, the bits of food, matches, rags, shreds of paper, ants, rodents, and other things occasionally scattered on it are symbolically swept away. The domestic altar is 'bound' temporarily when in performance it becomes an absolute space of the spirits.

There are different kinds of altars, according to the ritual context in which they are used, but all are quadrilateral with a leg at each corner. The domestic altar, of both shamans and nonspecialists, is canonically placed in the east side of the house, in the *moy* 'end' area, as is DC's altar in figure 7.8 and DP's altars in residences II and III in figure 7.5. It is usually on a wooden table that the family *sàantos* 'saints, images', fresh flowers, and a burning candle are kept, in addition to the shaman's divining crystals and other paraphernalia. Divination and much curing takes place at the foot of the shaman's domestic altar, with participants facing the *sàantos* to their east. Major ceremonies in the domestic and agricultural cycles, on the other hand, such as *heéȼ lúʔum* 'fix earth', *čáa čaák* 'get rain', and *wàahil kòol* 'breads of the milpa', take place out of doors at temporary altars constructed or arranged for the event. The construction process is a 'binding' of the altar by lashing fresh-cut branches with vine (or wire). My field notes indicate that these altars tend to face southeast, so that the four corners, rather than the front edge, are aligned to the cardinal locations (F.79–80; F.82.B) or south (F.115.A). The 'front' of the altar is not the side nearest to the shaman, as we might expect, even though this is the direction in which the images face. Instead, it is the far side, nearest to the cardinal location that DC faces as he performs. When lowered to receive the offerings in the *heéȼ lúʔum* 'fix earth' and *čaá čaák* 'get rain' ceremonies, spirits arrive at the 'front' of the altar, and no one except the *bʼóʔol* 'shaman's assistant' is allowed to pass there during the entire event. Spectators remain behind the shaman. Thus there is a dual orientation (of the linear-successive type) in the corporeal field of performance, with the altar serving as pivot: to the east facing west are the spirit addressees, in front of whom stands the *santo* image on the east edge of the altar, also facing west. To the west of the altar surface facing east is the shaman in prayer, with the audience to his back. The audience canonically faces east, recapitulating the shaman's orientation, although there is more flexibility for audience members to sustain other postures and engagements than there is for the shaman to do so.

The process of lowering spirits through prayer combines successive with orthogonal, as well as centered with absolute, orientations. The spirits exist in definitionally absolute cardinal places, and it is to the elemental *lúʔum* 'earth' (see fig. 7.3) of homestead and person that they are lowered. Just as their placement at the four corners plus the center anchors the cardinal directions, their simultaneous union defines totality. Yet in lowering them by *tʼanik u kʼàabʼaʔóʔobʼ* 'speaking their names', the shaman inevitably introduces successivity and segmentation. Successivity because the ritual performance unfolds in real time, and the spirits come down one by one. The clockwise and counterclockwise conventions on spirit citation regiment the shift from simultaneous corners to a sequence of parts. We can speak meaningfully of east being **before** and **in front of** south, instead of just to its side. By the same shift, the totality of the cardinal grid is necessarily split into its five parts, hence segmented. The outcome is a new absolute totality, this one in the performance space, with its own four-corner-plus-center geometry. But in order to transpose absolute space into the emerging performance space, the former must be broken down.

For all its successive and segmenting effect, the citation of spirits in *reésar* 'prayer' is not at all similar to a speaker standing at a table and pointing to the cardinal locations, saying *té'ela' lak'in 'ìik', té'ela' ša-man 'ìik', té'ela' čik'in 'ìik'* 'There east wind, there north wind, there west wind', etc. The locations are in no meaningful sense defined relative to where the shaman is performing; on the contrary, his orientation conforms to their places. Thus the ritual space is not a centered one, as body space and deictic space are. This fact motivates the noteworthy absence of deictic elements in ritual performance. The shaman never directs the spirits to come 'here', in the sense of an egocentric locus, but instead describes his location as 'there on the earth of sin', and 'at the altar of X', where X is a spirit name. Particularly at the outset of prayer, there is no 'here' in the standard sense but only an elemental man on earth in the context of absolute cosmological space. The only locative and nominal deictics that occur are the least marked ones *té'* 'there' and *le* 'the'. As the performance progresses, however, once the spirits have been lowered and *wá'akuntá'al* 'stood up' around the altar, they have essentially constituted a 'here' by their presence. This is the point in *saántiguar* 'blessing' at which the patient is described as *le kwèerpo a'* 'this body', with an immediate deictic (Hanks 1984c:160). Just as the process of prayer results in recreation of absolute space at and around the altar, it also creates the possibility of a centered 'here' in which the spirits, shaman, and patient (if there is one) are copresent. This copresence is what makes the process effective as a way of altering the state of earthly affairs. The basic cosmological principle then combines a diagram of absolute space with the indexical frame of performance, by transposing the former, step by step, into the latter.

7.4.3.2 *Inhabited Space in the Shaman's Gaze*

The dynamic of *reésar* discourse is slightly different in the divination ceremony called *tiíč'k'aák'(-tik)* 'to illuminate (it)', the purpose of which is to gain knowledge rather than alter states of affairs.[10] This involves a combination of prayer, conversation with a patient or beneficiary, and the use of specialized paraphernalia. Unlike major agricultural and curing ceremonies, divination occurs in the shaman's home, at the altar where his divining crystals and sacred images are kept, as in DC's room 10, figure 7.8. The crystals are described as *saástuúnó'ob'* 'lightstones', or *(sàanto) kristaló'ob'* '(sacred) crystals', and the shaman examines them in front of a candle in the course of the performance. Round and clear in the light of the candle, with the help of spirits, they show the elemental earth of the person or land being examined. The event begins with an opening prayer which illuminates the crystals, followed by an interactive phase in which shaman and patient gaze into them to discern sources of illness or evil, and is brought to a close by a final releasing of the spirits. The process articulates the corporeal frame of the participants with the absolute frame of the helper spirits, in order to transform the crystals into an iconic representation of the patient. In §5.3, we outlined the frame decentering involved in this event from the vantage point of participation structures. At this point, we will return to frame transpositions, but from the perspective of lived space and time.

Teaching me how to use the crystals, DC described how they are illuminated. The domestic altar on which they are kept is to the east, which one faces while praying. In addition to the cross or *santo* on the altar, one also scratches a cross on the floor beneath it. There are two circuits of prayer, the first proceeding *šnó?ohi* 'rightward (clockwise)', and the second *š¢'iíkih* 'leftward (counterclockwise)'. When this is completed, *¢'ó?ok ak'ašik* 'you have bound it (the altar)'. In so doing, you erect a perimeter of fire around yourself for protection. It is then time to *saásikuúntik* 'enlighten' the crystals, so that they will *?é?esik* 'show' the source of illness, as a bit of *b'ùu¢'* 'smoke' in the clear light. Without the help of the spirits, or under the influence of evil, the crystals remain obscured, that is, *?éhoč'é?en* 'darkened, blackened' (F.120.B.247ff.). This can be remedied by citing certain very effective spirits *ká paátak u haá¢kab'tikó?ob' e?* 'in order that they might make it (crystal) dawn', an explicit reference to sunrise as an elemental form of enlightenment, implying an analogy between the crystal and the earth (F.132.A.325).

Dealing as it does with events and places on the earth, the *tiíč'k'áak'* engages spirits whose absolute places are within the *yoók'ol kàab'* 'above earth' (cf. fig. 7.3). The five *balamó?ob'* 'jaguars' play a particularly important role:

(10)   DC: tumèen leti? yàan té? h lú?um a?→ taná?atik↑
         'Because they are the ones who are right there on the earth, understand?

         . . . leti? k'almahih   ?esteh le lú?umó?ob' o?→
                                            taná?atik ↑
         . . . they're the ones who shut, aah, the lands, understand?'

     WH: hàah
         'Yeah.'

     DC: lelo? hač wayiló?ob' e?→ hač hač wayiló?ob létíoob' e?→
         'Those (ones) they're really from here. Really, they're right from here.

lú?umiló?ob léetíó?ob . . .   kanaán kòoló?ob b'ey
                                     o?→
They're from the earth those ones . . . they're milpa guardians
                                     like that.

kanaán kaáka? lú?umó?ob→ kalan naló?ob→
They're guardians of ruin-mound land, guardians of corn
   (homes),

kalan maákó?ob→ taná?atik ↑ . . . hàah kalantik kaáh→
guardians of men, understand? . . . Yeah, (they) guard living
   spaces.'[11]

DC's description of the place of the jaguar spirits emphasizes their earthly origin in opposition to other ká?an 'sky' or muúyal 'atmosphere' spirits. Their primary role in the universe is to watch over and protect the earth, which they do by standing at its five cardinal places. In so doing, they impose an absolute spatial order on it, which in turn creates perimeters, 'shutting the lands', as DC put it. He mentions five classes of place over which they guard: kòol 'milpa', kaáhkab' 'land with ruin mounds on it', nal '(land with) living corn plant', maák '(earth of) man', and kàah 'town (semi) permanently inhabited land'. Several features of this list are noteworthy. The fact that these places all fall within the 'jurisdiction' of the jaguar spirits is evidence of their underlying relatedness.[12] In the list, the first and third items denote agriculturally productive land, while the second, fourth, and last denote human inhabited land. The land on which the homestead in figure 7.6 is located is an example of kaáhkab', with ruin mounds rising up beyond the courtyard and continuing throughout the back area.[13] In the course of the prayer, one speaks in order from low to high, to 'the four corners of the earth, the four corners of the sky, the four atmospheres' (F.132.A.036ff.). Ah K'iin Tùus, 'High Priest Deceiver', the guardian of the west temple in the highest sector of the cosmos, is not addressed in this ceremony, because when he moves, all evil in the world moves also, and the crystals will surely deceive.

We can see clearly in this description that the basic mechanism of the crystals is to articulate absolute moral and cosmological space with the fields of human activity. Nowhere is this more evident than in the actual conduct of divination focused on an inhabited soólar. The following notes are excerpted from recordings of an event of tiíč'k'aák' in which two women came to DC's home (room 9, fig. 7.8) requesting a heéç lú?um 'fix earth' ceremony to remedy the constant sickness among the residents and livestock of their common soólar. They show in vivid detail the process of spatialization and visualization underlying knowledge in Maya culture.

DC's first step upon learning that the women sought a *heéȼ lúˀum* was to ask them where they were from and when they wanted the ceremony performed, thus localizing it in everyday space and time. He then explained that there had to be a divination beforehand, in order to see the state of affairs in the *soólar*.

(11)   le heéȼ lúˀum aˀ ↑ k'aáb'eét ureébisàartáal e → ká ˀilak b'iš
                                                                    yanih
         'This fix earth,   it's got to be looked at,   so that it can be
                                                                    seen how it is

         tée solàar oˀ
         there in the soólar.' (how things stand) (F.125.A.011ff.)

Preparing to start, he tells the women to come sit close to the altar, and seeks the name of the head of household.

(12)   kóˀoten tuún way eˀ ↓ huúȼ' aßaá ↓ . . . maáš tíˀal le teérenó
         aˀ→
         'Come here (to me) then. Shove over . . . whose is this plot of land?' (F.125.A.038ff.)

The opening prayer underway (in the fourth breath group), he states his request:[14]

(13)   ˀutíal asaásikuúntkéˀeš ten bãkáan le sùuhuy lúˀum oˀ ˀinyuúm→
         'So that you might illuminate for me the blessed earth, My Lord,'

         le túˀuš bakáãn → kahakbah šan untúl ˀaˀìihoh→
         'where evidently one of your sons is residing.' (F.125.A.051)

The description of the earth as *sùuhuy* is reference to its elemental material as a part of the cosmos (as opposed to its fertility or contour, for instance), and the stipulation that one of God's sons resides there links this elemental substance to the domestic unit as a social whole. The son is, expectably, the male head of household, the metonym of all the residents (cf. chap. 3).

Continuing to send his speech *tyikna* 'to the place' of a number of key spirits, DC addresses them to explain the problem, *ȼikbatik téˀeš b'in šan e? ˀin yùum*→ 'tell you (pl)(about) it, it is said, My Lord'. He then explains, in a separate breath group, that the object of request is specifically the elemental land of the *soólar*. This is worth emphasizing, that while the signs of disorder may be experienced anywhere in the yard in question or its living structures, it is the earth that is in need of treatment.

(14)   ʔuntúul uʔìiha hesukrìisto b'in šan   kutàal uk'aát
          'One of the daughters of Jesus Christ, they say, comes to request

          upoódereh ká ʔu¢kiíntáak usùuhuy lúʔumil usòoláar ↑
          the power that be made better the blessed earth of her soólar.'

DC then shifts from this third person narrative footing onto a performative one in which what gets described is his own current act as it takes place. Notice that the act is a presentative one, of just the kind accomplished with deixis in everyday speech, but it is formulated without deictics. This is because the spatial localization is absolute rather than indexically centered—the 'residential land of a human being' instead of 'over there'—and because the performance context does not constitute a viable spatial ground for deictic reference at this stage in the event.

(15)   le bakáan kutàal ink'aátik b'in šan b'eʔòora ti asàantóiléʔeš
          'which is what I come asking too right now to your saints,

          intuúʔčuʔtikéʔeš b'in šan b'eʔòora awiléʔeš ten uteéreno bakaán
          I point out to you all too right now so you all might see the plot of earth

          e ʔah siísab'ih šan tuseéʔlakih ↑
          of the person as quick as possible.' (F.125.A.051)

It is only in the seventeenth breath group (out of twenty-five in this case) that DC asks the spirits to examine specifically what *kukrusàar* is 'crossing' the land of the *soólar*. As we would expect on the hypothesis that he is constructing the household as an absolute, he asks for the answer in terms of cardinal locations.

(16)   čiíkßes ten ʔukantíʔi¢i le téreno ßakaán oʔ utía ačikßesik ten eʔ
          'Show me the four corners of the plot, so that you show me,

          ʔinyuúm → túʔuš yàan le ßáʔaš kumèentah lòob'
          My Lord, where the thing is doing wrong.' (F.125.A.073)

The evil 'crosses' in the sense that it moves, and when moving, it makes noise and can strike (*heénaántik, ha¢'ik, saáltik*) people or animals, causing them to become sick and perhaps die.[15] Four breaths later, DC requests instructions on what he must offer in the yard in order to *k'aát-behtik* 'block off the path', shut down the evil. What he will do in the *heéȼ lúʔum* is, literally, 'corner' the thing by cutting of the path of its movement.

Once the crystals are illuminated, he begins discussing the case with the prospective beneficiaries, telling them what is happening in their yard and assuring them that he sees what is going on and can remedy it. Looking into the crystals, he dictates what they must prepare in order for the ceremony to work—then suddenly interrupts himself and remarks dramatically:

(17)   maáre ȼ'iík e báʔa yàan tasoólaréʔeš aʔ→ yàan báʔah k'aáb'eét
         'Holy Mary! this thing in your yard is dangerous! There's things
         we've got to

         kluúʔsk iʔ šiíʔ→ ščakk'aáʔteʔ ʔìik'→
         clear out of there, man! Xchackate Spirit (is its name).'
         (F.125.A.051)

Then, pointing into the crystal, he shows the women where it is, saying:

(18)   lèetí e le čan ʔìik' uhoók'ol té h luúgar aʔ tíʔiȼ nòohol→
         'This little spirit that comes out right in this place, the south
         corner,

         kuč'aák tak té hòonah téʔeš oʔ→ kukrusàartik
         it reaches even there at your front door, it crosses,

         tíiȼ nòohol kún uk'u ßeyaʔ→ b'uúhtíʔiȼk e solaár oʔ
         the south corner is where it makes its shrine (nest). It corner-cuts
         the yard.' (F.125.A.138)

As a man *kul* 'sits' in his home, a bird 'alights' on its *k'uʔ* 'nest', and a saint resides in a *k'uʔ* 'shrine', the evil *k'u* 'alights, perches' in the south corner. This stationary aspect is what makes it possible for DC to locate the thing on one day and perform a *heéȼ lúʔum* ceremony only several weeks later, without fear that it has moved. There is a cultural premise that all animates, including spirits, occupy stable places from which they occasionally move. From its place it lops off a corner of the yard as its path, all the way past the front door, itself a metonym for the (first-level) family sleeping quarters.

During another event of divination just days later, DC explained that one must not address the guardian spirits of the *soólar* itself until the evil has been precisely located. To do so would risk moving the evil.

(19)   máʔ tat'anik yìik'al le soólar oʔ . . . kyéesik teč túʔuš yàan . . .
         'You don't address the spirits of the soólar. . . . they show you
         where it is . . .

wá tíʔiȼ yan eʔ ↑ kawilik ukul ump'eé b'ùuȼ' téʔe tíʔiȼ aʔ
if it's in the corner, you see a smoke seated right here in the
corner.' (tapping) (F.132.A.070)

In the miniature, spherical space of the crystal, the noxious *ʔìik'* 'wind'
appears as a blotch of smoke, *kul* 'seated' in the corner. The movement of
the smoke indexes the ambulation of the evil around the yard. DC's spatial representation of the crystal is apparently a rectangular plane, hence
the corners, within a spherical medium. This fits precisely with the placement of the earth within the cosmic globe in figure 7.3, an analogy already implicit in the description of divinatory enlightenment as 'dawn'.

7.4.3.3 *Inhabited Space Transformed*

Because it involves dislodging a malignant spirit seated in the earth of the
household, the *heéȼ lúʔum* 'fix earth' ceremony is dangerous to the
shaman as well as to the residents. Whereas at the agricultural ceremonies, people come and go, play, and socialize in an atmosphere of
good humor, at the *heéȼ lúʔum*, they are likely to be instructed to sit
huddled close together behind the shaman, as DC told the residents of a
sponsoring household in November 1980 (F.78.A.073). Likening it to a
bullfight in which one may perish, DC explained to me that if he makes
an error in the order of spirit invocation, the evil will be loosed and will
charge in on the altar along the diagonal leading from its perch in the
corner of the yard (see fig. 7.11). The ceremony therefore presupposes
the prior performance of *tiíč'k'aák'* 'illumination', to locate the evil, as
well as the cultural frame of domestic space.

The first step in the transformation consists of *liík'sik y iík'al* 'raising
the (guardian) spirits', around the yard in their cardinal places, in order to
k'alik 'lock' the evil in place. The first step is to deprive it of its mobility,
without which it lacks the capacity to strike (F.76.B.340; November
1980).[16] Explaining the same process four years later, DC specified that
he starts his prayer, which he calls *meyah* 'work', in the corner next to the
one in which the evil is lodged, assuming the counterclockwise order of
citation. As you proceed around the perimeter of the yard, *kaw oksik
tuún yunȼilóʔob'* 'you put in lords' (into the yard) by addressing them,
and show them each *šúʔuk'* "boundary stone", except for the one where
the evil is' (F.132.A.095).[17]

After the evil is cornered, the goal of the *heéȼ lúʔum* 'fix earth' is to
get it out of the yard by having the guardian spirits 'drop' it:

(20)   ʔentons kubisáʔa letiʔ→ kuluúʔsáʔa téʔ h teérenó aʔ→
            'So it's taken away, that (evil). It's dropped out of the plot right
            here.' (F.76.B.600)

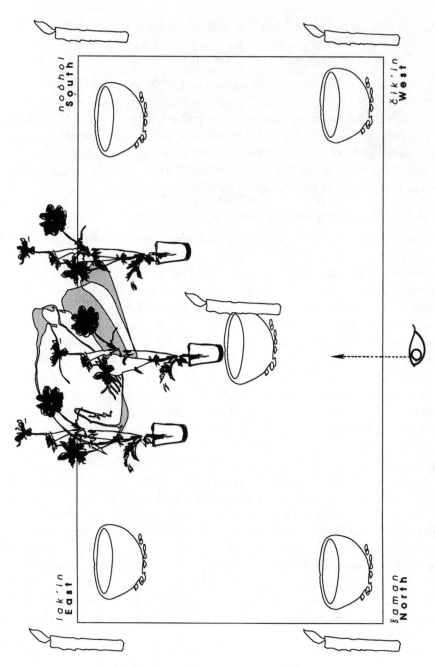

Fig. 7.11. Altar for *heeȼ luʔum* 'fix earth'.

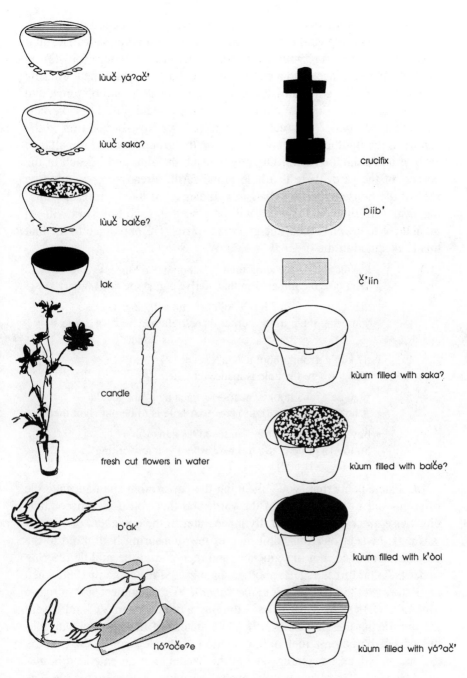

lùuč yáʔač'

lùuč saka?

lùuč balče?

lak

candle

fresh cut flowers in water

b'ak'

hóʔočeʔe

crucifix

piíb'

č'iín

kùum filled with saka?

kùum filled with balče?

kùum filled with k'òol

kùum filled with yóʔač'

Key to Figure 7.11.

Afterwards, when evil has been cast into the woods, locked in an abandoned *čuúltuún*, the yard is pristine, and the offerings are made. The altar is set as in figure 7.11, with *saka?* corn gruel in *lùuč* 'gourd (bowls)' in the five cardinal places and a candle, flowers, and the main meat offering in the middle. The gourd bowls are half-spheres with round bottoms, and each one sits upon a ring of corn kernels which steadies it. These kernels are called *?u k'anče?* 'its seat, placenta' (cf. §3.3.6). In addition to the candle in the middle, there are candles on the ground around the altar in each of its cardinal corners. Directly beneath the altar and in each of the corners of the yard, there is a hole in the earth, already prepared by the men of the house under the shaman's guidance. At the appropriate time, the *saka?* offerings and candles will be placed in each hole and will remain there to *¢eéntik* 'feed' the guardian spirits. DC explained to me that this is executed in the order E > N > W > S > C.

(21)   kač'iík e → le bá?al o? tuún a¢'aáhmah yoó? mèesa
        'You take the things then that you've put on the table (altar),

        kabisik →   té? h tí?i¢ o? ↑ ₣ tukantí?i¢ili a?↑
        you bring them to the corner there, right here to its 4 corners
                                                              as usual,

        tí? kún ¢'á?abil uhòol té?ela?. ↓ ₣
        That's where the hole is made right there.

        yàan u¢'á?aba hòol té?ela?→   yàan u¢'á?aba té?ela?→
        A hole is to be put right here.   A hole is to be put right there.

        b'ey šan té?ela?→ b'ey šan tée tú?uš kameyah a? ↓
        So too right here. So too here where you're working.'
        (F.76.B.600)

DC's statements that 'you', meaning the performing shaman, take the offerings out to the corners of the yard, and that you do so in counter-clockwise order, are both literally inaccurate. In the one event of which I was part, he sent out four adult men of the sponsoring household to the corners all at once, not in sequence, and then placed the middle offering under the altar himself. DB, another shaman, did the same in 1980 when he performed the *heé¢ lú?um* in the *kahtalil* '(rural) homestead' in figure 7.6. Like DP's saying that he was digging a ditch, when VC and I were the ones using the shovels (§3.5), DC's statement that the shaman does the work is based on a metonymic relation. The one running the event is the one who does everything, just as the headman of an extended homestead (second or third level) is the one whose name is given to the place as a whole (as in 'DC's place' for the homestead of his sons). The sequential order he cites is, of course, the one familiar from spirit invocation in prayer. It is this discourse convention which defines what is going on in the ceremony, not the physical fact of carrying objects around the yard (although this enactment is a necessary part of the event). Thus in each case, an individual part or participant in an event is singled out as defining the whole, and the sociocultural hierarchy among participants is what defines the relevant agent.

7.5 CONCLUSION

We started out this chapter with two distinctions among systems of spatial organization, prefabricated vs. emergent representations, and centered vs. absolute ones. Orientation of actors in lived space, and its linguistic expression, always involves a combination of schematic prefabricated knowledge and the emergent awareness of one's own location relative to a context. Deictic reference is an act of orientation par excellence and can be fully understood only relative to the background frame space and schematic frames that speakers share and tacitly respond to in making reference. The frame space is vast and various in content but appears in Maya to be structured according to regular principles.

There are five cardinal points in this culture. They enter into two basic schemata, which I have called **directional** (relative to situational center) and **locative** (absolute, fixed). The former consists of the use of cardinally oriented vectors which originate in the corporeal, domestic, or discourse frame of the actor(s) and lead out of this center towards the cardinal points. This use is approximate or regional in that the directions are 'more or less' accurate, according to the purposes at hand. Objects are segmented and located in succession along these axes, so that one side of a ditch can be said to be east of another, just as it can be 'behind' or 'after' another in one's line of vision. Cardinal locations are absolute in the sense that they are fixed places whose union defines a whole region of space. Instead of being defined relative to a movable center or along a perspectival trajectory, the cardinal center place is fixed, just as the four corners are fixed, within the spatial frame. Altars, yards, cornfields, the earth, the sky, and the highest atmospheres are described in terms of the five-point cardinal frame. Rather than defining relations of successivity, this grid is definitionally simultaneous in that (once completed) places contain all five points at the same time, as a corollary of their being whole. The path connecting the five points defines the perimeter of the space and hence distinguishes inside from outside. Without its perimeter, a place has no unity and is potentially dangerous.

Living structures in domestic space show both successive and peri-metral orientations in their physical layout relative to the front of the yard and common courtyard. They also provide several important illustrations of the interplay between round and quadrilateral space. Recall from fig-ure 7.3 that the earth is traditionally represented in Maya as a quadri-lateral plane contained within a sphere. The same representation recurs in the shaman's use of divining crystals, spherical stones in which he dis-cerns the corners of spaces under study (§7.4.3). Within the household, in the milpa, and on the altars at which shamans perform, the rectangular perimeter encompasses all round shapes, such as drinking and eating ves-sels, the rounded corners of palm houses, bread (everyday and ritual *waáh* 'tortilla'), the divining crystals, and even the shapes in which me-dicinal plant substances are spread out to dry.

Domestic space is **epitomized** in the ritual process in the sense that the underlying processes often hidden but nonetheless attended to in domestic life are given explicit crystalization in the performance. These include mobility and stasis, cleansing, boundary maintenance and infringement, totalization, and segmentation. Munn (1986) showed that Gawan value production is epitomized in certain basic types of acts, including the ex-change of food, which provide a generalized paradigm for other super-ficially dissimilar social practices. In this case, I wish to claim that fundamental spatiotemporal schemata, which recur throughout Maya so-cial life, are constructed in shamanic practice. Like Munn's treatment, furthermore, the present one is focused not only on the structural charac-teristics of basic templates but also on the experiential forms in which they are embodied in action: "not simply a logic of binary oppositions, but a causal-iconic nexus of relations between types of action . . . and certain qualitative . . . signs of positive or negative value" (Munn 1986:508). The five-point elemental schema is an object of iconic repre-sentation in much prayer and in the lowering of spirits to the shaman's altar, located within his home. It is an explicit object of scrutiny in the divination process, in which the shaman sees the domestic space in the crystals as a four-cornered grid. The most dynamic and complex case is the transformation of domestic space effected in the process of the *heéȼ lú ʔum* 'fix earth' ceremony, wherein guardian spirits are projected into the yard through ritual reference and led around its perimeter, step by step, in preparation for cornering and banishing the evil spirit lodged within. In the form of the discourse and the actions of shamanic perfor-mance, the same orientational principles are combined. Earthly, social space is made absolute by the orderly, step-by-step transposition of car-dinal place spirits into the performance framework. The absolute, totalizing, and perimetral functions of the spirits are an explicit part of how performance works. On the other hand, the linearity of speech and action in real time forces the shaman to effect the transposition in a segmented, successive fashion. Whereas cardinal places have no front or back as such, the performance space, including shaman and altar, is directionally oriented, with 'front' to the southeast (and sometimes east).

At the outset of this chapter, I suggested that emergent processes, insofar as they implicate an actor, are unavoidably centered. What Maya ritual discourse shows in its unfolding is an emergent process of spatialization which unifies absolute cardinal space, segmented in a fixed order, with the action-centric field, totalized in the visitation. It is only when this process is *nuúp* 'complete' that the performance space itself is constituted as a zone of proximal copresence of shaman, patient, and the spiritual lords. In binding the altar, opening the road, and standing up the lords, the performing shaman is literally producing a centered space out of an absolute one.

8 Agricultural Processes and Spatiotemporal Frames

8.1 INTRODUCTION

This chapter extends the analysis of spatial and temporal frames in Maya culture from the domestic field to the production, use, and ritual transformations of agricultural land. The Maya men with whom I have worked around Oxkutzcab are all farmers, whatever else they do, and no account of their spatial orientations can fail to address how they work the earth. I will try to show that in the labor practices and ritual attentions paid to productive land, a series of implicit spatiotemporal schemata are habitually instantiated. These include both centered and absolute constructions as defined in chapter 7, and they display specific homologies with the corporeal and domestic frames. They are also coarticulated with the other schemata in the interactive frameworks of deictic reference. As chapter 9 will show, the boundaries, regions, and successions defined in this and the preceding chapter are regularly integrated into spatial reference in both its indexical and denotational components. The first goal of this chapter, then, is to extend our overview of the local sociocultural frame spaces in which communication takes place. The second goal is to summarize concisely the spatial frames presented so far and to illustrate their role in some routine acts of reference.

Section 8.2 begins the synopsis of agricultural frames with the swidden process: its successive phases in the yearly calendar, the placement, preparation, and care of the milpa fields, and the interannual stages in the productive life cycle of land. In local practice, the descriptors of these temporal stages are used as spatial designators, an interesting complement to the use patterns of cardinal terms. Section 8.3 elaborates our account of ritual discourse by describing the performance space and language of major agricultural ceremonies. These epitomize the production of agricultural spacetime, as the divinatory and cleansing rites epitomized domestic frame spaces. Joined to what we have already seen of shamanic practices from the vantage points of corporeal and domestic space, this will complete our overview of ritual frame spaces. We will concentrate on the layout and logic of altars as iconic embodiments of agricultural space. Section 8.4 is a cumulative summary of the spatial frames presented in this book, including corporeal, cardinal, domestic, and agricultural frames, as well as their ritual embodiments. The summary is in three parts: the collection of the schemata in question, the diachronic principles by which they are realized in sociocultural time, and their instantiation in acts of verbal reference.

8.2 THE SWIDDEN PROCESS
8.2.1 Timing in the Yearly Cycle

The seasonal climate around Oxkutzcab is described in terms of variations on three dimensions: relative hotness, wetness, and windiness. The peak hot season, described as *yaáš k'ìin* 'great, green, first sun', begins in late February and increases in intensity through May, with daily temperatures in April and May well over 100 degrees. Maya speakers say that *k u čokowtal le lú?um o?* 'the earth gets hot' (F.151.B.115). Temperatures remain high through August and begin to cool down between then and January, when days in the low 70s are perceived as *ké?el* 'cold'. Whereas *yaáš k'ìin* is definitionally dry, the earth becoming hot and dusty, in June the rains begin; this season is called *há?ahá?al* 'watery-watery' (?). The earth gets *č'uúl* 'soaked', *siískuúná?an* 'cooled', and muddy. From June through September, when the air is still *čokow* 'hot' but the earth is *siís* 'moist, cool' from the rains, the crops of the milpa grow and come to fruition. The *?iík'* 'wind' is strongest during the mid to late *yaáš k'ìin* 'great sun' phase and plays a crucial role in fanning the flames that clean the milpa. As DC explained to me on several occasions, in order to live as a *kolkàab'* 'earth feller, campesino, farmer', one needs the heat of the sun and fire, rain, wind, and earth. The sequence and interplay of these elements underlies the agricultural process in all of its dimensions.[1]

From August through December is *tutyèempo e kòol o?*, the time during which the forest and previously cultivated lands are cleared (F.151.-B.250). Old vegetation is cut back with *b'aát* 'ax', *maáskab'* 'machete', and *loób'če?* 'coa' and then left to dry in the sun. The process of clearing is called *kòol* 'clear, fell vegetation' (transitive *kol-ik*). This is the same stem used to refer to the milpa field as a whole, in any of its phases, as in *má? t im b'èetah kòol* 'I didn't make milpa (e.g., this year).' The exact timing of the clearing depends primarily upon the kind of vegetation involved, according to the anticipated time needed for it to dry out, once cut. Thus, August and September are *?u mèesil u kó?olo nukuč k'aáš* 'the month(s) of the clearing of old forest', which is full grown, and so it requires the longest time to dry before burning. By October, *ȼ'úy oko tiʔ yáʔaš k'aáš* '(the time) has come in for green forest', about fifteen years old, also called *káʔana huúʔčeʔ* 'high young wood'. By December, only very young vegetation can be cleared and still be expected to dry in time for burning by May. As late as March, the previous year's dried out cornstalks can be cleared with a small coa, in a practice called *ʔoóli kolsakaʔ* 'sort of fell stalks', which is closer to *pàak* 'weeding' than true *kòol* 'felling' (F.151.A.3510). The harvest over, one goes along quickly with a large *loóʔčeʔ* 'coa' and clears the land *warašhaȼ'b'il* 'thrashing hitting' (F.27.2206). The process of clearing forest, also called *šot'ik lúʔum* 'cut (up) (the) earth', results in a state of *táʔačeʔ* 'debris wood' (< *taʔ* 'debris, feces, refuse') in the milpa. As it *tiíhil* 'dries out', *k u salk ub'aáh* 'it becomes light (weight)' and ready to burn (F.151.B.414). The drying requires *k'ìin* 'sun', *kuȼ'óʔol eʔ kuk'ab'eéta teč ʔiík'* 'after which you need wind' to burn properly.

The burning of the field, called *toók,* is a cleansing process in which the debris left behind by felling is turned into *táʔam* 'ash', which will then be blown away in the wind. This takes place between March and May, depending upon dryness and wind conditions. Of April, DC said, *ʔič k'ìin yàan, ʔič hòoč yàan* 'it is in (the) sun, it is in the harvest', meaning these activities occur during this month and encompass it (F.-151.A.4400). May is *tuúlis k'ìin* 'whole sun' and windy, therefore good for burning (F.151.A.4606). When the time is right, *k u tàal uy iík'a toók, . . . kutàal uk'ìini utíʔal utiíhi* 'the wind (spirit, animacy) of burning comes, . . . the sun comes for it to dry' (F.151.B.345, 465, 3921). While waiting for this, as the world dries out, people engage in harvesting corn grown during the previous year, left to dry on the stalk. The *nal* 'ears' are broken off the stalks, and the *ʔišíʔim* 'dried kernels' taken off the *bakaál* 'cob(s)' to be stored and consumed over the coming year, or sacked and sold. This process, called *hoóč* 'harvest (corn)', coincides with the burning and precedes planting for the next year, as DC put it, *tíʔan ič toók eʔ* 'it's there in (during) the burning' (F.151.A.4139). During the harvest, with the burning just past, people *paáʔtik haʔ* 'await water (rain)' in order to start *pak'al* 'planting' for the next year (F.151.-B.414). The main period of planting is June through July, although *mehen nal* 'young (short-cycle) corn' can be planted as early as April, and in the Puuc, small plantings take place even in February (F.151.A.-3900; B.020).

As men await the transitions between seasons, marking the onset of different activities, they attend to natural signs announcing changes in the atmosphere. The pods of the *štàak'in če?* tree *wá?ak'al* 'explode' in extreme heat, announcing the arrival of *yaášk'ìin*. The leaves of the *há?abin če?* tree rattle in the wind like a *só?oteneh* 'rattlesnake', making the sound *tiíriš,* indexing that *k'áam le ?iík' o?* 'the wind is strong (loud)', and the time has come to burn. When the earth is at its hottest at the end of May, and rains are expected soon, the *šùulab',* a kind of ground wasp which swarms and destroys beehives for honey, walk the forest floor all night (F.18.B.073ff.). The *pú?uhwih* bird also sings at this time, announcing heat and dryness (F.18.B.563). The coming of *há?ahal* 'rainy season' is indicated by *siínik* 'ants', which enter people's houses four days before the arrival of rain.[2] Dried *k'ùuȼ* 'tobacco' gets soft and moist in the humidity, while *tá?ab* 'salt' and *?aásukàar* 'sugar', which are normally *huehuekil* 'dry and granular' get *ta?ta?kil* 'sticky' (F.18.B.073ff.). After the growing season, when the weather turns cold, the *koós* bird sings, announcing the imminent arrival of storms out of the north, called *šaman ká?an* 'north sky' (F.18.B.498ff.).[3]

8.2.2 Placing the Milpa

There is considerable variation in the distances between the homes and milpas of men in Oxkutzcab. (Cf. Redfield and Villa Rojas [1934] 1962; Thompson 1974; Ewell 1984; Neugebauer 1986). Is and his father, for instance, reside within a block of one another in the town of Oxkutzcab but for years have made milpa together out in the forest near Xul, about thirty kilometers away. In his father's own words, speaking from his house, *to ič kòol o?, naáč* 'Out there in the milpa, it's far away' (BB.4.-98). During intensive activities such as planting, the two may stay out there together, or Is may stay alone, for up to four or five days at a time. They moved to this region some twenty years ago, when their milpa near town was repeatedly trampled by the cattle of wealthy ranch owners, resulting the final time in the near total loss of their crop (BB.4.114).

The first step in making a milpa is to select the plot. Assuming one intends to plant *šnuk nal* 'big (old) corn', *šnùuk ?iib'* 'big white beans', *šnùuk kúum* 'big squash', and *šnùuk b'ú?ul* 'big (black) beans' on a new piece of land, the first step is to go out into the forest, such as *hwiíčil k'aáš* 'hill forest', and find a suitable place (F.19.A.085), preferably free of thorns, *má? ič k'íiši k'aáš i?* 'not in thorn forest'. One then cuts a strip of land in order to *kwaádrartik* 'square off'. The initial cut, and the continuation around the outer edge of the projected field, is called *hoólč'aktik le k'aáš o?* 'perimeter-chop the forest'. The squaring process is begun as early as possible and is done by aligning two straight stakes, called *estàaka,* planted vertically in the ground and lined up by sight (F.27.A.800;

151.A.430). Like the shaman's crystals, the squaring rods extend the corporeal frame by expanding its visual field. In order to assure that the verticals are properly aligned, they are placed at the corners of a square, formed on the ground by placing four more straight sticks of the same length in orthogonal position. If the job is well done, the man *miístik e haál oʔ, kén ȼ'óʔok eʔ, toh u pàač e kòol oʔ* 'sweeps the length of the milpa, after which the outer edge (back) is straight' (F.151.A.1613). If one looks onto a line of boundary markers, they should be perfectly straight and appear as a single one.

In the woods around the town of Oxkutzcab, there are several major boundaries separating the municipio from Yotholim and Ticul to the northwest, Akil to the southeast, and Mani to the north. These boundaries, as well as the property lines of wealthy ranch owners, are called *meénsura* 'limits' and are marked by *ʔu muúltun e k'aáš oʔ* 'the stone-mound(s) of the forest'. These great piles of stones were placed in their locations by *ȼ'ùul* 'foreigners, wealthy men' and by the *kàah* towns, and they define the permanent limits beyond which one cannot go in choosing a place for milpa. If a man were to *piík'č'aktik* 'clear open' right up to or *kruúsàartik* 'cross over' these markers, he would be denounced, *tumèen máʔ kolkàab'iʔ, máʔ uy ohe b'áʔaš ku mèentik* 'because he's no earth feller, he doesn't know what he's doing' (F.151.A.1845). Recall that evil spirits lodged in the house plot are said to 'cross over' the yard, moving without regard to its proper boundaries. Rather than clearing and planting the entirety of the field, one leaves a strip of land to serve as a path for other men working in the area, along the edge of the field. This path is called *ʔu t'óol k'aáš* 'the passage strip of (the) forest', which DC glossed as *ʔu b'èel ká maának maák iʔ* 'the path (road) that people might pass', and *ʔu b'eh k'aáš* 'the forest's path' (F.151.A.2005). From the very outset, then, the farmer must attend to the larger perimeters within which he works and keep straight the sides of his own field. The procedures he follows in so doing are homologous with ritual practices and instantiate many of the frames that form the horizon of reference in everyday discourse as well.

8.2.3 Intra-annual Phases
8.2.3.1 *Measuring and Clearing the Forest*
The cutting open of the edge of the milpa, *hoólč'ak,* and the measuring and laying of boundary stones, called *p'ìis* and *ȼolik šúʔuk',* respectively, are processes that take place concurrently as the farmer is beginning to clear the land. According to DP, men usually cut open two sides of the

milpa, guided by squared and aligned stakes, before proceeding to clear
the interior. If the farmer is experienced and well oriented, he can cut out
the entire field without ever completing the perimetral cut on the remaining two sides (F.27.A.1530). When a sufficient segment of the perimeter
is opened, the farmer *mačik e p'isiʔ čeʔ oʔ* 'grabs the measuring sticks'
(also called *p'isiʔ teʔ* and *walak' čeʔ* 'domesticated wood' (F.27.A.1300)
and begins to lay down boundary markers (F.151.A.450). After beginning to measure, one can return to extend the *hoól č'ak* (F.151.A.1245)
and then return to measuring again.

As the field is measured, the *šúʔuk'* 'markers' are *ȼoláʔan* 'counted
out'. The farmer always assures that they are aligned straight and twenty
meters apart.[4] The first to be put down are the corner markers, called *noh
šúʔuk'* 'great markers' (F.27.A.1245). Along the side between the corners, which might be fifty mecates apart, the markers are placed at the
twenty-meter interval as measured by the *walaʔ čeʔ* 'domesticated stick',
of which six lengths should make one mecate (F.27.A.1300). After cutting out and laying markers along two sides, one begins to count out the
internal divisions, according to DP: he explained, *le kán ȼ'óʔok ap'is
yoóʔl e hoólč'ak oʔ, pwes naká p'is yàanl e k'aáš oʔ* 'when you've measured over the perimetral cut, then you're gonna measure under the forest
(within)' (F.27.A.1333). The verticality embedded in DP's description is
consistent with preceding references to the edge of the milpa as an open
path through the forest cover. DC's account of the stone markers themselves is that, ideally, one *mačik ʔoóšp'eé tùunič, b'ey k'oób'en* 'grabs
three stones, like the kitchen fire' (see chap. 7). After placing them together in a triangular shape, a bigger one *kulkiíntik yoók'ol* 'sat down
above (them)', followed by another one above that (F.151.A.2735). It requires five stones, ideally, like the five cardinal locations (and a great
many other things that come in sets of five in Maya, such as prayers and
ritual offerings).[5] The stones are *ȼoltáʔal* 'counted out (ordered)', just as
are ritual offerings on the altar, and must be *toh toh* 'straight straight'.
The overall process of covering the land with markers DC called *b'óʔon-
tik e lúʔum oʔ* 'tan, cure the earth' (ʔCordemex 64) (F.151.A.2625). The
significance of the *šúʔuk'* markers as indicators of order is nicely reflected
in the slang expression *hutk u šúʔuk'* 'knock down his boundary stones',
used to describe what one does in dominating a foe by disputing or undoing his work.

Once the milpa has been felled and is set to dry, it is called *táʔačeʔ*
'debris wood', which will be burned when it is sufficiently dry. This term
is used only for bush felled after several years' fallow. As soon as it is
burned, it is no longer 'debris wood' but *ʔèele kòol* 'burning milpa'.

Once planted, it is no longer 'burning' but simply kòol 'milpa'. At this point, one can refer to the place as 'my corn plant(s)', as in kim bin ʔič in nal 'I'm going into my corn plant', meaning 'I'm on my way to my field' (F.27.A.1700).

8.2.3.2 Planting, Weeding, and Drying the Corn

Planting follows patterns described as identical to the laying of boundary markers. According to the pattern I have attested, the farmer proceeds along a straight line, poking a hole in the earth with his šúul 'planting stick', a length of wood about four feet long, with hardened (or metal) point, held in the left hand. Hanging on the man's right side, from a string crossed over his shoulders, is the saábukàan 'bag' in which grains to be planted are kept. Taking a few in his hand at a time, he proceeds, poking the earth and tossing a couple of seeds into the hole, then closing the hole over with the end of the stick. This is illustrated in plate 8.1.

The rhythm and intensity of weeding required in a milpa varies considerably with the quality of the soil and the stage of the milpa in the interannual cycle from first clearing to extended fallow. The šnuk nal 'great corn' planted in the more rugged terrain of the Hwii¢ and Puuc requires weeding only in August, provided the forest was nukuč k'aáš 'old forest' when felled and assuming a June planting (F.27.A.1815). Other crops under other conditions require more weeding, which may start as early as June and extend, off and on, throughout the growing season. After a final weeding, one waits until the corn ripens, around October, at which point the process of bending over the stalks, called wàa¢', takes place. This is done in order that the ears will be bent down, so that no rain or scavenging birds will be able to penetrate the husks. One then waits for the kernels to tiíhil tub'èel 'dry properly', at the same time as the freshly felled forest for next year dries out in time for burning.

8.2.4 Interannual Stages and the Use of Descriptors as Place Names

One of the main predictors of the likely productivity of a piece of land is the state of the vegetation growing on it before it is cleared. Time elapsed since prior use for agricultural production is a focal dimension, in which Oxkutzcabeños distinguish several stages: nukuč k'aáš 'great (old) forest', more than twenty-five to thirty years old, is considered new (tumben) for the purposes of milpa, relatively free of weeds and low growth because of the shade of the trees. This is preferred land for planting fruit trees such as citrus and avocado, which will remain for many years and need high-quality soil to grow properly. yaáš k'aáš 'green, strong forest', more than fifteen years old, is lower and therefore has thicker growth.

Plate 8.1. DP (and VC) planting corn in rows, March 1987.

šká?akòol 'second milpa' has been in fallow for approximately fifteen years, after being planted with corn. *taánkelem k'aáš* 'potent, growing (the same term as is used for men from puberty through loss of potency) forest' is four to five years old, while *huú? če?* 'start out wood' is from two to three years old. *pok če?* 'fallow wood' is what results from leaving a cornfield in fallow for a full season, or letting grasses take it over. If the previous planting was the first, and one intends to replant, the same piece of land is *č'akb'é?en sak'ab'* 'chopable cornstalk (land)' (F.26.A.480ff.; B.0ff.), also called *kanyada sak'a?* 'rowed (with rows) stalks', or just *?in sàak'ab'* 'my stalk(s)' (F.19.A.095). Unless modified, the term *č'akb'é?en* denotes forest felled for the first time, or after at least five years' fallow. In all cases, it describes the field as both freshly cut and relatively 'young' in the interannual cycle of productivity (F.19.A052). After the third harvest, the field is simply *šla? sak'a?* 'old stalks'. These descriptive phrases represent only the main distinctions in an extensive vocabulary relating to growth stages and types of soil and vegetation. Without going further into this area, it is important to keep in mind that through their awareness of seasonal cycles and longer-term processes of growth and degeneration of the land, Maya farmers approach agricultural space from a diachronic perspective.

Any of the terms denoting a major phase of the milpa can be used as a descriptor of the place in exchanges such as:

(1)   A : tú?un atàal?
        'Where are you coming from?'

        B : té? ič insàak'ab' a?→
        'Right there in my cornstalks.'

        B': čén htàalen tinšla? sàak'ab' a?→
        'I just came from my old stalks.'

When I discussed this with him, DP justified the B usage by pointing out that *tumèen sak'ab' tatoók i?* '(it is) because stalks you burned there' (F.27.B.2425). So long as there is corn in the field, at any time after the onset of growth in the corn until the harvest, the place can be denoted simply as *?ič innal* 'in my corn', not *?insàak'ab'*. These usages appear to conform to the general tendency of Maya men to denote places by their salient ecological characteristics (cf. §7.3 above). When the characteristics are defined within the milpa process, they imply a succession of work activities, along with their appropriate tools, postures, and motions. The alternative B' response contains the modifier *šla?* 'old, funky, disheveled', which indicates that the field, while perhaps just burned, is nonetheless past its second consecutive harvest and therefore advanced in the sequence of productive years.[6] The descriptors of place not only suffice to indicate where the speaker is coming from but also encode quite precisely the current state of his field, as well as its place in the longer-term cycle from bush to fallow. This is one more example of ecological terms used to denote particular places (cf. §7.3) and of the diachronic implications of spatial frames (cf. sequentiality in domestic and ritual frames, chap. 7).

8.3 RITUAL ARTICULATIONS OF AGRICULTURAL SPACETIME

Like domestic frames, the productive space of the milpa is the subject of various ritual embodiments. These begin in the earliest stages of site selection and continue through the end of the harvest year. Some performances are undertaken by the solitary farmer, out in the yard of his residential *soólar,* in the woods before he ever cuts off the forest, or in the milpa itself. The two most elaborate ceremonies, called *č'aá čaák* 'get rain' and *wàahil kòol* 'bread of (the) milpa', are performed by *hmèen* 'shamans' before a large public. The former is sponsored by the *socios* 'members' of a single irrigation unit in the *ejido* system of land distribution and may therefore involve well over one hundred people, including families. The 'bread of the milpa' is sponsored by a single man and is usually attended by the members of the extended household (third level), as well as neighbors invited to partake of the feast. Our concern here is with the value of the rituals as modes of producing space and time and in particular with the iconic value of the ritual altar. We begin with the prayers of the farmer, which are both simpler than and prior to the public performances.

8.3.1 Requests and Prospects

It is common knowledge among Maya adults that some *lú?umó?ob'* 'lands' can be fruitfully worked only if the farmer feeds the guardians.[7] If one fails to *¢'ik ?uk'ul* 'give drink' to the *yun¢iló?ob'* 'lords', one is sure to encounter venomous snakes or chop one's own leg or arm while working the land. In the past, DP explained to me one day, harvests were certain, because everyone worked reverently, whereas today they no longer believe, and the rain fails to fall. We had spent that morning, February 17, working at a new field that DP had recently burned, helping a hired tractor driver plow rows for the corn he intended to plant. In the afternoon, back at his residence in area II (see fig. 7.7), DP had made an offering of *sìinko lùuč saka?* 'five gourds of gruel'. Standing barefoot and shirtless, facing east, with his right hand raised over the offerings, DP addressed the *yunɕiló ʔob'* asking for their help with his undertaking. He later reported his prayer as:

(2)   le lúʔum ɕ'íntraátartik aʔ→ héʔel aʔ→
        'This earth I've dealt with, here it is (presenting).

        ʔaántenéʔeš iʔ
        Help me with it.' (BB.5.21)

The five gourds were *ʔeɕekbalóʔob'* 'placed, seated' in a straight line (north-south) on a makeshift altar consisting of two stakes lashed in parallel horizontal position in the branches of a citrus tree. To tie up the stakes, DP had used his own *k'aš nak'* 'belt (lit., bindbelly)', a long strip of cloth which is traditionally wrapped around the waist outside the pants to hold them up. After his prayer, which lasted about five minutes, he left the gruel on its temporary altar, and DP and I went into the house to eat. After about an hour, he returned to the altar and began praying aloud. Using a bent leaf as a scoop, he tossed a small amount of gruel from each gourd toward each of the five cardinal locations. This done, he lowered the gruel and poured it back into a single container, from which it was then distributed to all present: to me, DP's wife, VC's wife Pilar, two of her children, and two of Milo's children. DP immediately disassembled the altar. Over the next week, he replowed and leveled the field and commenced planting, dry. He called his endeavor *čeén ump'eé lokùura* 'just a bit of madness', a long shot that might yield a good crop or might be a total loss, depending upon when the rain came and how much fell.

DP's performance of an offering in the early stages of his undertaking is representative of what Maya men mean when they say that a farmer must not only have faith but *manifestartik* 'show, express' his faith and seek the help of the guardian spirits. During the same week in February 1987, DP's son VC offered *sakaʔ* alone in one of his own fields, where he had planted tomatoes. When he first explained the milpa to me seven years earlier, DP emphasized that prayer is a necessary part of the process. It is needed right at the outset, because in the course of felling, one kills the forest (*kiínsik e k'aáš oʔ*). He went on about the need, saying:

(3)   hač koómpromìiso legalmente   kudebeser ubèetk
        'Really (it's a) commitment, by law he has to do it,

        untúu maák meyhi k'aáš eʔ
        a guy   who works (the) forest.' (F.27.B.2900)

Before starting to clear, at the very onset of the *hoólč'ak* 'perimeter cut', five gourds of gruel, a candle, and an Our Father are required to request *u poderile? a meyahtik e lú?um o?* 'the power to work the land'. One subsequently *wá?akuúntik ?uk'ul* 'stand(s) up drink' at the measuring, burning, planting, and when the *yih* 'ears' first sprout from the corn plant.[8] Although he did not list nine occasions when prayer is performed, he summarized his description with the assertion that it occurs nine times (F.27.B.2945). This is doubtless a reflection of the same principle that motivates the placement of nine *lùuč saka?* 'gourds of gruel' on the altar at both *č'aá čaák* 'get rain' and *wàahil kòol* 'bread of the milpa'.[9]

In independent discussions, DC gave an account consistent with DP's, noting that the first *reésar* 'prayer' is *leti e hoól č'ak k'aáš o?* 'that perimeter-cut-forest one'. After the felling, another offering anticipates the burning. Then, *yeét ump'iít uk'ul, na káa pak'a* 'with a little drink, you're going to plant.' This is a process of *loómk e lú?um o?*, *púl a semilla* 'pierce the earth and throw in your seed.' Afterwards, one performs what is called *mak hó?ol šú'ul* 'close hole digging stick', the offering whose function is to close the holes made by the digging stick, so that the plant will take root and come out properly (F.151.B.2545–2850). Since he is a shaman, it is expectable that DC has a more detailed perspective on ritual and a more precise vocabulary for describing prayer than nonspecialists. He added the following details to his account.

The first prayer should be performed before even beginning the perimeter cut, outside the projected *haál* 'edge' of the field, at the corner where one will start work (F.151.A.3250). The perimeter cut made, another offering protects the farmer from snakes during the felling. The intended consequence of these prayers and the thoughts they express, all of which constitute *primisia* 'firstfruits ceremonies' (even though they start long before the fruits exist), is to *wá?akuntik yunȼil* 'stand up the lords' at the five cardinal places of the milpa (F.151.B.820). This is the same term used to describe how one 'stands up' the liquid offerings (see above), and the semantic equivalence is a straightforward result of the iconic equivalence of the two acts in Maya culture. The offerings embody their recipients.

DC listed the classes of spirits addressed after the felling and before the burning (cf. landscape terms in §7.3).

(4)   kanáan k'aášó?ob, kaánan kòoló?ob, ?áa(l)ka? šú?uk'ó?ob,
        'forest guardians, milpa guardians, boundary marker runners,

        kaánan bèekanó?ob → leti e kutàaló?o? ti? čuúltunó?ob
        natural path guardians, the ones who come from *čuúltuúns*

        ti? ?aáktunó?ob o?
        from caves.' (F.151.B.915)

When the *sàanto ʔìik'óʔob hoók'ol* 'blessed spirits (winds) come out'
from their places in the corners, they move around the milpa, *kuhaáhan-
maán yaálkabóʔob'* 'they pass about quickly running.' Particularly, the
moson ʔìik' 'whirlwinds' come up out of the earth and circulate during
burning, helping to fan the flames, and *miístik e kòol oʔ* 'sweep the
milpa'. It should be recalled that while these spirits sweep the *kòol* itself,
the farmer has already 'swept' the outer perimeter of the place, making its
boundaries straight and clean, whereas the 'sweeping' of domestic space
is a task performed only by women. During curing ceremonies, the shaman asks yet other (female) spirits to 'sweep' the earth of the patient's
body, cleansing it of disease (Hanks 1984c). Thus an integral part of
maintaining any socially constituted space is the process of cleaning by
sweeping.[10] When the farmer has made an offering, the spirits are happy,
kíʔimak yoól, and *meyah* 'work' vigorously on their ordained tasks
(F.151.B.1000ff.). Even the term 'work' applies equally well to what the
shaman is doing in performing, what the farmer is doing in burning, and
what a woman does in cleaning the household.

Solitary acts of devotion focus primarily on securing the help of guardians in events that take place after the prayer. Maya men describe their
offerings in terms of the outcomes to which they lead in the agricultural
process. After planting, while the farmer is waiting for rain, the seeds are
burning (*t y eéle*) in the earth. If you give a little drink (*uk'ul*) to the
lords, DC explained, they will *oksik haʔ* 'bring in water' for you (F.151.-
B.1500). This anticipatory focus is a way of trying to secure the outcome
of events in the near future, by binding the framework of practice in the
present. While not nearly as elaborate as a shamanic performance, DP's
simple offering of five gourds of gruel is predicated on the actual visitation of his place by the lords of the five cardinal points. He is totalizing
the same kind of absolute structure as DC did when he performed the
heéç lúʔum in the yard poisoned by an evil wind (cf. §7.4.3). Both kinds
of performance anticipate propitious outcomes and thus seek to bind future events within an orderly system.

Another kind of binding occurs in private prayer but is less significant
in major ceremonies. This is the promissory aspect of the performance.
DC again: When you see that your corn has been plentiful (*ʔanhi* lit., 'it
has been'), you make a *primisia* 'firstfruits' to promise God that when
you *hoóč* 'harvest (dried ears)' you will make (another) *primisia* (F.151.-
B.1645). The second firstfruits to which DC refers is the *wàahil kòol*
ceremony, a major public performance executed by a shaman and
occupying the entire extended family for a day, not counting preparation
(cf. Redfield and Villa Rojas [1934] 1962:134ff.; Villa Rojas [1945]

1978:328ff.). Rather than actually committing the sponsor to a future enactment, this event fulfills a prior commitment and expresses thanks. The
five gourds offered by the farmer establish the promise early in the agricultural process. They are *ʔutʼîin* 'the taut tether' binding a man to
the anticipated fulfillment (F.151.B.1730). In other words, the farmer's

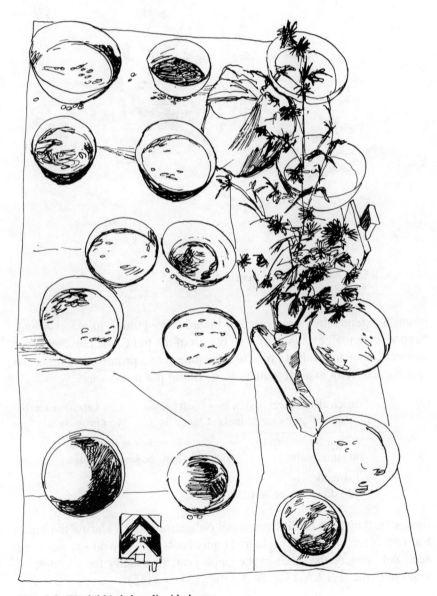

Plate 8.2. *Wàahil kòol* altar: liquid phase.

Plate 8.3. *Wàahil kòol* altar: gruel offering.

promise extends the frame space of his labor by putting in place virtual, but not yet actual, events. Like the 'breads of the field', the rain ceremony delivers on an antecedent promise. Likening it to a promise one makes to sponsor a novena in a subsequent year, Balim put it this way:

(5)   mèen ak'aát abèet ʔesteh le→ č'aáh čáak oʔↆ . . . kaproómetèertik
           'Cause if you want to make a 'get rain', . . . you promise it

           tiʔ wá b'áʔaš sàantó eʔ→   . . . kán učuk e teémporàada . . .
           to some saint   . . . when the season comes, . . .

           kab'èetik
           you do it.' (F.19.A.103)

Insofar as they both fulfill contractual obligations to the spirits, the bread and rain ceremonies are considered equivalent. A man who sponsors one need not sponsor the other in the same year, or usually for a couple of years to come (F.19.A.117; 27.B.3100; 151.B.3115).

8.3.2 Getting the Rain

Whereas the 'breads of the milpa' ceremony takes place at the very end of the agricultural cycle, in fact brings it to a close, the rain ceremony occurs at a critical juncture in the growth of the crop. Between June and August, after the ears have appeared on the stalks, after the field has been weeded, everyone is waiting for rain. Without it, the ears will wither on the stalk. Rather than expressing gratitude for the harvest, the rain ceremony, as its name implies, requests the water necessary for a harvest (cf. Redfield and Villa Rojas [1934] 1962:138 ff. [BB.5.103]; [F.19.A.135; 151.B.2930]). Depending upon the year, it can be a time of tense anticipation. As noted above, this ceremony is the largest-scale performance in local shamanic practice, involving well over one hundred people and

Plate 8.4. *Wàahil kòol* altar: food count.

Plate 8.5. *Wàahil kòol* altar: food offering.

nearly two days to complete. Rather than being confined to the extended family, the sponsors of the rain ceremony are all the *socios* 'members' who make up a unit in the *ejido* system of land distribution. A written tally is kept of individual contributions to the effort, in grain, fowl (usually turkeys, chickens, and roosters), and labor. The altar of the *č'aá čaák* ceremony is similarly the most elaborate of the repertoire, embodying in iconic form most stages in the milpa process.

During the rain ceremony, the altar, in this context called the *ká'an če'* 'elevated wood', is set twice, once relatively early on, when the spirits have been lowered to *'uk'ul* 'drink', and later, when they are offered *piíb'i waáh* 'pit oven loaves', *b'ak'* 'meat', *k'òol* 'soup (sort of)', and *yá'ač* 'squished (cornbreads broken up in broth)'. The first setting consists entirely of liquid offerings contained in *lùuč* 'gourd(s)', which are *¢olá'an* 'counted out' in the configuration shown in figure 8.1.

The first thing to observe about the layout of offerings in figure 8.1 is the regularity with which they are spaced. In fact, they are explicitly intended to represent the laying out of *šú ʔuk'* markers during the process of measuring and perimeter-cutting the milpa (F.79–80). They define the cardinal wholeness of the altar, just as the boundary stones define the entire extent of the cornfield. One salient difference between the two, to which I will return presently, is that whereas the milpa always has a center point, this altar does not. Further, the altar has a front, defined by the cardinal direction which it faces, east or southeast. This is the side on which the *sàanto* is placed, towards which the shaman faces as he performs. To my knowledge, milpas do not have any inherent orientation towards one or another of their cardinally defined sides. The liquid offerings are of two kinds: *saka ʔ* 'gruel' and *b'alče ʔ* 'mead (fermented honey with the bark of the tree of the same name)'. There are nine gourds of the former, corresponding to the nine *ʔarkanheló ʔob'* 'archangels', and five of the latter, corresponding to the sets of five jaguar spirits and other milpa guardians (see below). In the midsection of the altar, one gourd of each liquid is placed inside the perimeter, the front one containing *b'alče ʔ* and the back one (closer to the shaman) *saka ʔ*. Despite the presence of two kinds of liquid offerings, this phase is called *k'ú ʔub'ul saka ʔ* 'delivery of the gruel', indicating that the gruel is the superordinate offering. The whole schematic configuration recurs in both the initial (liquid) and final (food) altars of both the *č'aá čaák* and *wàahil kòol* ceremonies (F.106.B.256). Following the Maya usage, we can call it *ʔuȼol lùuč* 'the gourd count'. It embodies one of the basic schemata of spatial representation in the system.

The gourd count schema is a complex one that can be resolved into constituent parts, starting with the difference between the *saka ʔ* and *b'alče ʔ* offerings. The former define the actual perimeter at the outermost four corners, whereas the latter occur only in the middle row of gourds (where middle means between front and back sides of the altar). In addition to the outer perimeter, there is an inner one defined by the remaining *saka ʔ* gourds, holding aside for the moment the one isolated *saka ʔ* on a direct line between the shaman and the *sàanto*. There are therefore both inner and outer rectangles. Instead of having a marked center, however, as one would expect, the inner rectangle is further divided into two smaller ones by the placement of a *b'alče ʔ* between the corner gourds on each side. This is shown in figure 8.2, which reproduces figure 8.1 along with lines showing the perimeters. This schema is a complex frame in the familiar sense of being composed of several simpler frames. The cardinal location schema, which diagrams the origin points of spirits to whom the offerings are made, governs the structure of both the constituent frames and their combination.

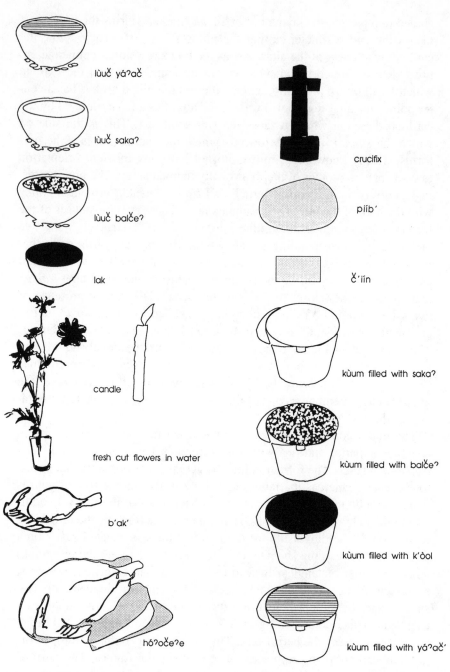

lùuč yáʔač

lùuč saka?

lùuč balče?

lak

candle

fresh cut flowers in water

b'ak'

hóʔoče?e

crucifix

piíb'

č'iín

kùum filled with saka?

kùum filled with balče?

kùum filled with k'òol

kùum filled with yáʔač'

Key to Figures 8.1 through 8.5.

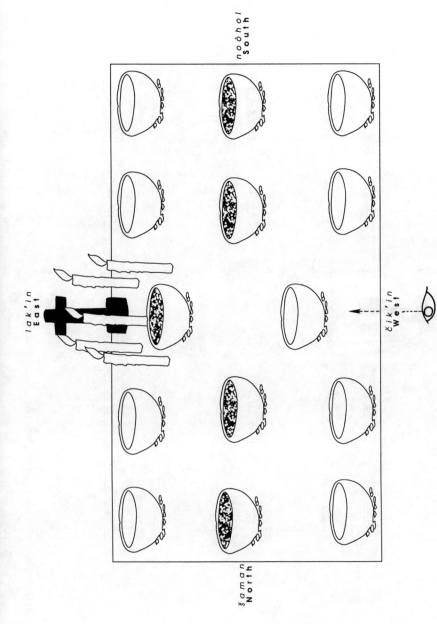

Fig. 8.1. Liquid phase of *čaá čaák* altar.

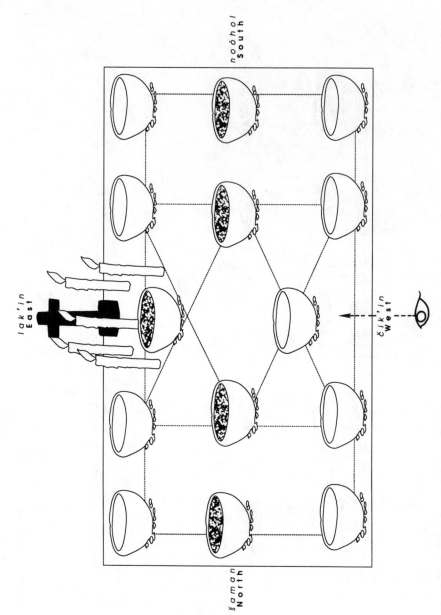

Fig. 8.2. Complex frame: liquid phase of č'aá čaḏk altar.

As figure 8.2 shows, the two gourds that lie on a straight line between the shaman and the *sàanto* also lie almost exactly in the center of the smallest perimeters on the altar. It is only at this level that the placement of these gourds can be accounted for, since they fall on no other lines and cannot be viewed as corners in any other orthogonal composition. Although DC never stated as much explicitly, it is evident that the altar has three levels of inclusion, and that at the lowest level, it resolves into two centers, the front one marked by a *b'alče?* offering, and the back one by a *saka?*. Note that the five candles by the *sàanto,* which *saásikuúntik b'èel* 'light the way', are placed in exactly the same cardinal schema. The motivation for having *b'alče?* in the front was also omitted from DC's various explanations, but I would suggest that the key lies in the fact that the *b'alče?* is offered to the relatively low earth guardians, whereas the *saka?* is directed to the very high archangels. In the discourse sequence of the prayer, the lower spirits are cited **before** the higher ones, making it appropriate for their offerings to lie **in the front** of the space. This is also consistent with the arrangement of the second altar, to which we now turn.[11]

The second-phase altar for the *č'aá čaák* is a composite of three different altars, positioned as in figure 8.3, with a larger main one flanked by a smaller one on either side.[12] The intercardinal direction in which the whole structure faces should be left open, so that when the lords are lowered to the space to be fed, they can pass unobstructed through the open end into the inner area. Connecting the three-part altar is a system of vines that leads into arcs over each structure. Over the main altar, the arcs crisscross in the middle, while over the lateral altars, they form isolated arcs along the perimeter (see insets in figs. 8.3 and 8.4). These correspond to the four *muúyal* 'atmospheres' discussed in §7.3, which are an integral part of the rainmaking process. Hanging from the crossed arcs are five more gourds with liquid offerings, a *saka?* over each corner, and a *b'alče?* over the center. Wrapped around the legs and over the arcs of all three altars are young cornstalks with immature ears still on them. The entire complex frame faces southeast, with the shaman's back to the northwest, where the *piíb'* 'pit oven' in which the breads are cooked is located.[13] That is, it is embedded in the larger frame of cardinal places.

The three altars of the *č'aá čaák* correspond to the three temples of the archangels at the upper level of the cosmos.[14] According to DC's descriptions, the main altar represents the east temple, the place of *Ah k'ìin kolon te? ¢'iíb'* 'High Priest Kolonte Dzib'. When Christ died on the Cross, he left his head in this temple. The left-side altar corresponds to the temple of the north, the place of Ah K'ìin Čan 'High Priest Chan', where Christ left his right hand. The right-side altar corresponds to the south temple,

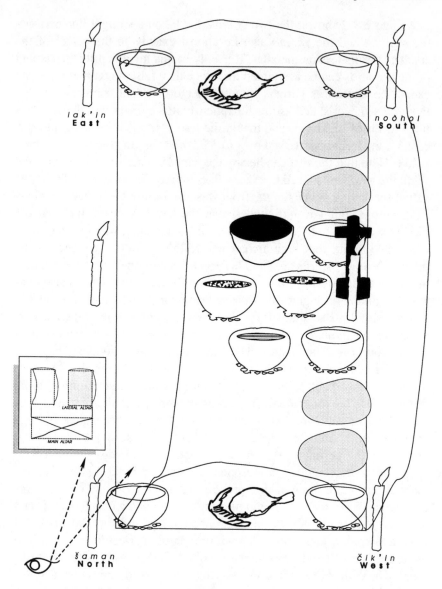

Fig. 8.3. Lateral altar for *č'aá čaák*, with tripartite inset.

the place of Ah K'ìin Koba? 'High Priest Coba', where Christ left his left hand (F.106.B.145). The fourth temple, in the west, is not represented because it is the place of Ah K'ìin Tùus 'High Priest Deceiver', who has no constructive role to play in the agricultural process.[15]

While the surface of the main altar has considerably more offerings in the food phase than in the liquid one, precisely the same gourd count schema is present. Added are the flowers, three more candles, and the food offerings, which follow the lines of the five-point cardinal schema, reproducing the *šúʔuk'* boundary stones as well as the liquid offerings made at earlier stages in the growth cycle. There are twelve *lak* '(ceramic) bowls' that contain *k'òol,* the fatty spiced broth rendered when the fowl offerings are boiled. Ten are placed along the perimeter alternating with the gourds, plus one directly at the *sàanto,* and one in the center formation. The *hóʔočeʔ,* located behind the center formation, consists of the meat offering, a specially designated *noh waáh* 'great bread', and a rectangular bread called *č'íin.* It is located behind the liquid offerings and candles, I believe, because it corresponds to a later stage in the ceremony and in the yearly cycle of agricultural ceremonies than do the liquids in front of it.

Rather than falling within the two smallest rectangles of the gourd count schema, as in figure 8.2, the center of this altar defines its own distinctive quadrilateral: in front a *b'alčeʔ,* to the left a ceramic *lak* full of *yáʔač'* 'soup', to the right a *lak* of *k'òol,* and to the rear a gourd of *sakaʔ.* This inner formation, which summarizes the liquid offerings in all of their forms, occurs in the center of four quadrilaterals: the outermost perimeter of the altar as a whole, the internal perimeter of the four inner *sakaʔ* gourds, the internal perimeter of the four piles of bread offerings, and finally, the overhanging perimeter of the liquid offerings suspended from the arcs. Looking down from above the formation, the center point is actually defined by the *b'alčeʔ* suspended at the crossing of the arcs, a point then reframed by all the quadrilaterals just listed. This superimposition of frames, all defining cardinal perimeters, is a powerful demonstration of the iconic embodiment of the cosmos in the altar, since the spirits to whom it is directed are arrayed quadrilaterally in a vertical universe. When transposed onto the horizontal plane of the altar top, this naturally produces a superimposition. It is unclear to me what motivates the presence of eight candles in the configuration shown, but it is plausible in the light of the foregoing that they can be viewed in terms of two quadrilaterals, one oriented in the same way as the overall perimeter and the other defining a diamond shape around the central (diamond-shaped) grouping of liquids. In figure 8.4 these inferred perimeters are shown as dotted lines.[16]

The lateral altars are considerably simpler than the main altar but are still compositional in the sense of incorporating other more simple structures. The four corners plus center are indicated just as they are in the arcs over the main altar, by four *sakaʔ* plus a *b'alčeʔ* in the middle. Along the edge which defines the front of the altar, a *sàanto* is accompanied by a

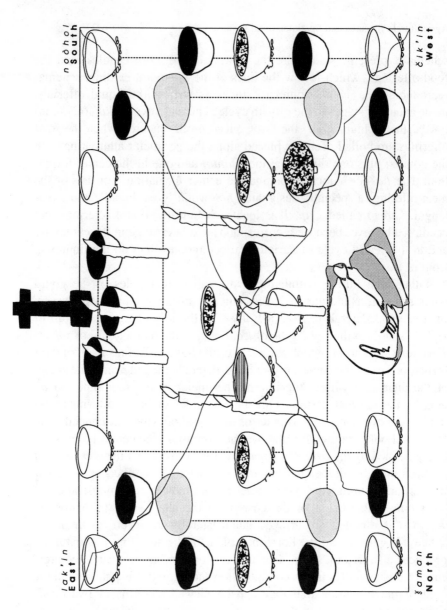

Fig. 8.4. Complex frame: offering count of *č'aá č'ádk* altar.

solitary candle and flanked by two plus two piles of bread offerings. Directly behind the *sàanto* is a five-point grid with two *saka?*, one bowl of broth, one bowl of soup, and a *b'alče?* in the middle. On the ground are five candles, once again in the five-point cardinal arrangement.

These facts substantiate the assertion that the ritual altar is structured by a series of transpositions and combinations of basic visual forms. They include the five point–four corner schema, the perimetral laying of boundary markers on the land, cardinal and intercardinal orientations (both directional and locative), and the vertical dimension distinguishing earth from sky, 'atmosphere' and the top of the heavens. These make up a substantial fraction of the frame space of the schemata instantiated in Maya ritual. The play between liquid and solid offerings has diachronic correspondences too, because liquid offerings are the form of the promissory note which this ceremony fulfills, and they are conventionally described by the same terms used to describe the promissory prayers earlier in the agricultural year. More significantly for present purposes, in addition to the absolute cardinal structures, the altar incorporates their corresponding perspectival functions too. It has a front and back and therefore the potential for successive relations of precedence, a right and left and an over and under, just as body space does. The correspondence is no coincidence, since the altar is designed as the stage on which an exacting kind of activity is carried out by a human specialist endowed with a face, a line of vision, a right side, and a left side. Just as the line of sight is critical in measuring domestic and agricultural space, it is also critical in ritual enactments. Furthermore, the divine addressees of this elaborate performance are considered to be endowed with vision, to have a head in the east facing the west, and to have a right and a left. In other words, they possess the rudiments of corporeality, which are the means by which they are integrated into the corporeal field of ritual practice. One of the fundamental requests of all Maya prayer is that the spirits *sutik awič apaktikó?on té? tulú?umil k'eb'an* 'turn your gaze upon us here on the earth of sin'. Like addressees in a face-to-face interaction, the perspectives of the shaman and the spirits are inverse, but they are ordered by the same axes. Mediated by the absolute spaces of the altar, the sameness makes possible the reciprocity of perspectives presupposed by all ritual address in Maya culture.

8.3.3 Thanks and Retrospects: *Wàahil Kòol*

Whereas the *č'aá čaák* 'get rain' ceremony takes place during a period of anticipation, requesting in the most elaborate terms that the rain fall, the *wàahil kòol* 'breads of the milpa' normatively takes place soon after the end of the agricultural year. It shares the harvest with the lords who helped make the products grow, expressing gratitude and recognition more than a focused request. Nonetheless, it has a prospective component as well, in that it anticipates overall good relations with the spirits in the coming years. It is performed after the *hòoč* 'harvest', when the corn has dried and men are set to burn their fields for the next year. The performance marks the end of the milpa year and delivers the very *nal* 'corn', also called *gràasya* 'grace', that *šíʔiki* 'broke through' the earth of the field. The offerings are distributed on the altar just as the corn plants are in the field, just as the boundary stones are laid down, just as *reésar* 'prayer' unfolds. DC summarized these observations, saying flatly, *ʔu plàan le mèesa, letiʔ e kòol oʔ* 'the plan of the altar, it's the milpa' (F.151.B.1902ff.). Given this correspondence, it is easy to understand his description of the ceremony as *náaksik yoóʔ mèesa* 'raise it [the milpa] over the altar', and *liík'sik e lúʔum oʔ* 'lift up the earth'. The *káʔančeʔ* 'altar (high wood)' stands on four legs, which are the four *yunȼilóʔob'* of the corners of the field (F.151.B.18210).

DC started his description of the *wàahil kòol* 'breads of the milpa' altar with an account of how boundary stones are laid in the forest. After about four minutes, he could see that I was unsure of his direction, not yet appreciating the correspondences. He assured me *núkáʔah koónektàar tuún beʔòora →* 'it's going to connect right away' (F.151.B.345). His utterance accurately reflects his conscious awareness of the connection between the objects and schemata of the altar and the practices and products of labor in the field (BB.5.118–120). While his awareness has the acuity of a specialist with about thirty years' vocation behind him, a more diffuse appreciation of the iconic values is also part of the common sense of nonspecialist adult males.

While the liquid phase altar for the *wàahil kòol* 'breads of the milpa' is the same as that for the *c'aá čaák* 'get rain', the main altar is slightly different. As figure 8.5 shows, it has no arcs, and the layout of offerings is distinct. The inventory of offerings and the perimeter count appear to be identical, while the center arrangement differs. Like the gourd count altar, this one has two centers, a front one nearest the *sàanto*, marked by a *b'alčeʔ* gourd, and a back one closer to the shaman, marked by a *sakaʔ*. One bowl of broth (*kòol*) is added to each center, as was also done in the main altar for the *č'aá čaák* 'get rain'. Behind the liquid offerings, the *hóʔočeʔ* sits closest to the shaman, centered in the rectangle whose front cornerstones are *b'alčeʔ* and back ones *sakaʔ* plus *k'òol*. The front rectangle near the *sàanto* is diachronically antecedent to the back one, for the familiar reasons that the liquids precede the foods both in the larger

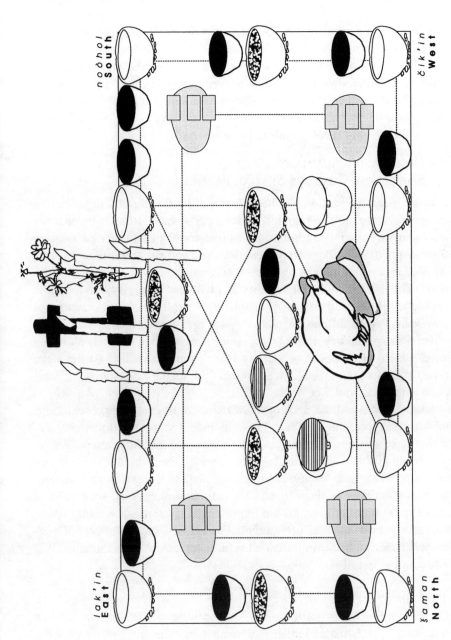

Fig. 8.5. Complex frame: offering count of *wàahil kòol* altar.

yearly cycle of agricultural devotions and in the order of phases in the rain and bread ceremonies.[17] Inset from the outermost perimeter, the breads form their own quadrilateral, each corner marked by the *piíb'i waáh* plus three rectangular *č'iín* loaves. The two round loaves accompanying the meat offering just in front of the shaman are called *u k'anče? waáh* 'the seat (placenta) bread', made of nine layers, and *u hó?oh če? waáh* 'the main offering bread', with thirteen layers.[18]

8.4 CUMULATIVE SUMMARY: SIMPLE AND COMPLEX SPATIAL FRAMES

In this concluding section, the basic forms of spatiotemporal organization in Maya culture are summarized in three parts. First, in a series of schemata showing spatial configurations as line drawings defining elementary forms embodied in altar complexes, domestic and agricultural zones, patterns of succession (counting space), and finally, center-relative orientations. The latter include corporeality and will lead naturally into the topic of deictic schemata, the focus of chapter 9. Next, the different diachronies corresponding to different kinds of space are summarized, in the same order. Phasing and rhythm of succession among spatial units, as in the development of domestic or activity space, temporalizes it. At the same time, it reinforces the analogical potential of spatial descriptors for temporal reference, and vice versa.

Section 8.4.3 will be a synopsis of the main linguistic representations of spacetime presented so far. These include a variety of locational descriptors whose use instantiates one or more schematic frames. As we will see in this section and in chapters 9 and 10, the frameworks of deictic reference instantiate background frames in both indexical and denotational roles. I hope to show that a basic understanding of the sociocultural frame space is not only helpful in linguistic description but actually requisite to a proper account of referential structures and practices. Ethnographic description is more than a useful complement to pragmatics; it is a necessary part of it.

8.4.1 Spatiotemporal Schemata

Our description of spatial frames in Maya culture can be summarized in a limited set of schemata. Rather than recapitulate the order in which these were presented in preceding sections, I will order them here in terms of their conceptual relations. We begin with what appear to be **elementary** forms, that is, ones which function as the units combined into further, **complex** forms (cf. Munn 1966:937). They include the ones shown in figure 8.6.

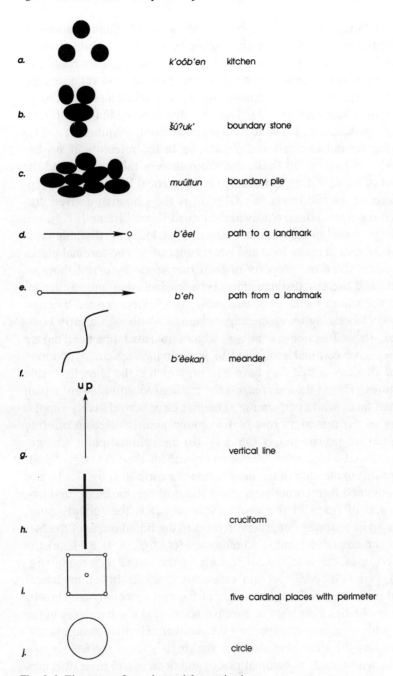

Fig. 8.6. Elementary forms in spatial organization.

The first three schemata in figure 8.6 show simple configurations of stones used to (a) constitute the kitchen fire occupied by a single woman (see §7.4.2); (b) mark the perimeter of domestic and agricultural spaces inhabited by a single man and his kin (see §7.4.2); and (c) mark the perimeter of spaces owned permanently by municipal corporations or wealthy individuals (see §8.2.2). The next three show elongated forms, including a path leading (d) up to, and (e) away from, a landmark; and (f) meandering around one or more objects, as in the referents of *bèekan* 'meander', *ʔékʼbʼeh* 'small trail', and the pathways followed around the household (§7.3.4, 7.4.2). Schema (g) is the vertical line implicit in representations of cosmic levels (§7.3.1); (h) is the Christian-derived cruciform; (i) the five cardinal places in their quadrilateral frame (§7.2); and (j) the circle, found in maps of the cosmos (§7.3.1), in the divining crystals (§7.4.3), and in many food and water containers. The cardinal places and the circle share the property of totalizing space by establishing its perimeter, and thereby distinguishing between inclusion and exclusion.

Figure 8.7 shows forms of considerable complexity, derived by combining and elaborating on elementary schemata. Although clearly compositional, these function as unitary wholes in ritual practice, during which they give cardinal grounding to performance space. A common feature of all altars is that they have a front, which is the uppermost side in the figures. This is the side nearest the cardinal location toward which the shaman faces while performing. The first three are relatively simple, consisting of (a) a straight row of five round gourds, used in offering *saka ʔ* 'gruel' in private prayer (§8.3.1); (b) the cardinal-point arrangement reproduced with candles placed on or beneath altars (cf. figure 8.3), and the gourds in the altar of the *heéȼ lúʔum* 'fix earth' (cf. fig. 7.11); and (c) the combined four corner plus globe shape of the *saástuún* 'divining crystals' and of maps of the world. Schema (d) is the 'gourd count' schema used in counting out gruel offerings in the liquid phase of the 'get rain' and 'breads of the milpa' ceremonies (cf. figs. 8.2, 8.5); (e) the main offering of the *wàahil kòol* 'breads of the milpa' ceremony (fig. 8.5); and (f) the *čʼaá čaák* 'get rain' ceremony (§8.3.2). In (g), the lateral altar, and in (h), the full tripartite altar of the rain ceremony are shown. The latter embodies a diagram of the east, north, and south temples in the cosmos, with vine arcs representing the *muúyal* celestial 'atmospheres' and connecting the altars. Finally, (i) is the single altar of the *heéȼ lúʔum* 'fix earth', with gourds in cardinal places and flowers and meat offerings in front (cf. §7.4.3).

In the next set of forms, we move away from ritual architecture to the everyday shapes of domestic zones (see §§3.3.5 and 7.4). The first three

a. gourd count solitary prayer

b. candles

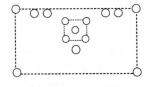

g. food count (lateral altar)
č'aá ča'ak

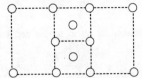

c. divining crystal with
cardinal corners and smoke

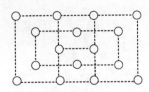

d. gourd count major performance

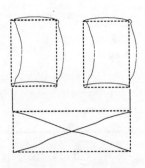

e. food count   wàahil kòol

h. tripartite altar with arcs above
č'aá ča'ak

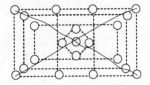

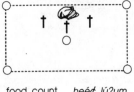

f. food count with arcs above (main altar)
č'aá ča'ak

i. food count   heéȼ lú?um

Fig. 8.7. Altar schemata.

a. single=family soólar with entrance

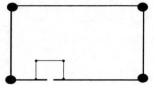

e. kahtalil 'homestead' on edge of milpa

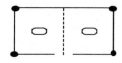

b. two=family soólar with entrance
     and divide

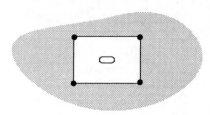

f. residence or milpa surrounded by forest

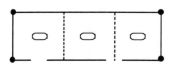

c. three=family soólar with two entrances
     and divide

g. rectangular house with front
     and back entrances

d. soólar with front living space
     and entrance, and 'out back'

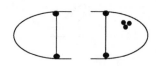

h. apsidal kitchen structure with front
     and back entrance

Fig. 8.8. Domestic zones.

are types of *soólars,* (a) a single family; (b) a double family, with common entrance (to the yard, not to the respective houses); and (c) a three-family household. Schema (d) is the yard divided into a living space in front and an 'out back' behind. Schema (e) is a *kahtalil* 'ranch, homestead' on the edge of a milpa; and (f) is a *kahtalil* or milpa surrounded by (unstructured) forest. Schemata (g–h) are the living structures themselves, the former a quadrilateral cinder-block floor plan and the latter an apsidal kitchen with four *okom* posts, rounded *moy* ends, and three stone *k'oób'en* 'kitchen fire'.

Figure 8.9 displays the shapes engaged in making the milpa a bounded and orderly space (see §8.2 above). It starts with (a) the *?alak'če?* 'domesticated wood', a single straight rod of fixed length used to measure the sides of the field for placement of *šú?uk* 'boundary stone' markers at twenty-meter intervals. Schema (b) is the *kwàadro* 'square' made by laying down four straight rods of equal length in a square, of which two corners on one side are the points at which vertical rods are planted in the earth. Aligning these verticals determines the sight line which will guarantee the straightness of the perimeter. The perimeter itself is evidently often cut along two sides leading away from a common starting point in orthogonal directions (c), leaving the third and fourth sides and the fourth corner unmarked but anticipated. Schema (d) is the milpa perimeter with *t'oól* 'public pathway' separating it from the *muúltun* 'municipal boundary marker'.

Figure 8.10 represents a shift from spatial schemata given as synchronic wholes to patterns of succession between points in the process of *¢ol* 'counting out, ordering' space. In the laying of boundary stones, opening up the perimeter of the field, planting, and ascending in the cosmos through prayer, steps are taken in regimented order. The principles encountered in the foregoing description include (a) the simple progression from one point (∅) to the next (1). This is in play in any directional movement (vertical or horizontal) or ordering of successive objects on a single line, such as measuring rods laid down end over end, or boundary stones along the side of the field. Succession (b) is the shape of a two-sided perimeter, cut out first along side 1 and then along side 2, working out both times from the same point of origin (where the first offering and measurements are made; cf. §8.2.3). It amounts to orthogonal vectors from the same center point, a frame familiar from cardinal directions and corporeal space. Succession (c) is another recursive application of directed movement, showing the parallel lines of men planting a cornfield working down the rows.

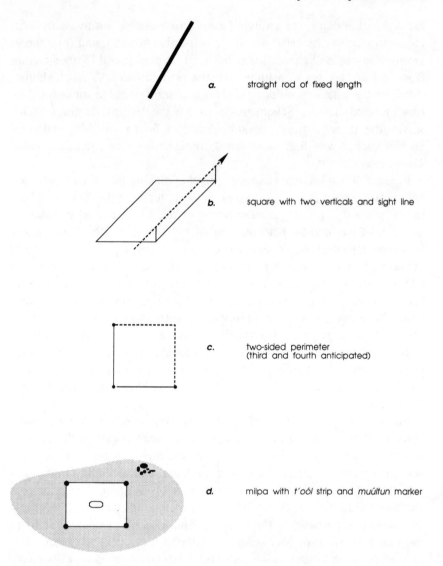

a.   straight rod of fixed length

b.   square with two verticals and sight line

c.   two-sided perimeter
       (third and fourth anticipated)

d.   milpa with *t'oól* strip and *muúltun* marker

Fig. 8.9. Agricultural zones (milpa).

The next three schemata in 8.10 all have ritual functions, although they have obvious analogues in nonritual behavior as well. Schema (d) is a series of *yal* 'layers', stacked from bottom to top along a single axis, such as the levels of the universe (cf. fig. 7.3), the earth below the altar, which is below the sky (cf. §8.3.3), and the nine and thirteen layers of the principal breads in the *č'aá čaák* 'get rain' offering (§8.3.2). Schemata (e)

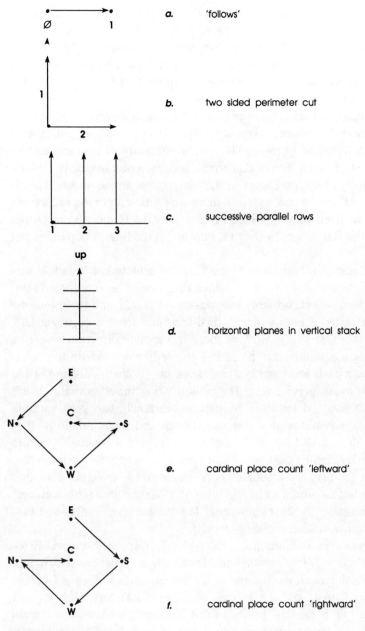

a. 'follows'

b. two sided perimeter cut

c. successive parallel rows

d. horizontal planes in vertical stack

e. cardinal place count 'leftward'

f. cardinal place count 'rightward'

Fig. 8.10. Successions.

and (f) are the schemata embodied in the ordering constraints on spirit reference in shamanic prayer (cf. §7.4.3), the first one 'leftward' (counterclockwise), used to 'bind' the altar, and the second one 'rightward' (clockwise), used to 'unbind' the altar. Note that the left-right opposition centers the successions in the shaman's corporeal frame, since it is his posture that fixes the ground.

These patterns of succession regiment the construction of space stepwise and therefore connect ongoing *meyah* 'work' with its anticipated product in a temporal process. The synchronic unity of a schematically whole place is derived from a diachronic sequence of movements, which itself anticipates later outcomes in the agricultural frame space. This is the reason we are forced to view them as spatiotemporal productions rather than as fixed spatial objects. It also puts the frames in the proper context of the frame spaces they tie into by protending to outcomes not yet actual.

The final pair of schemata in figure 8.11 are centered or 'relative' orientations. Schema (a) shows the cardinal directions when computed relative to a ground object, possibly the speaker (cf. §7.2); and (b) shows the three spatial axes of bodily space, distinguishing front-back, right-left, and over-under (cf. §3.2). Both of these incorporate directional vectors originating at a common zero point and proceeding out indefinitely. Neither provides a basis for drawing a perimeter, nor for distinguishing inside from outside in any precise way. The outer limits of the corporeal field are by definition fuzzy, determined by perception, reach, and such variable aspects of the environment as fog, vegetation, and social relations. It is predictable that in seeking to delimit space lacking a perimeter, actors rely on other available resources. In the case of corporeal fields of interaction, one of the primary resources is deixis, and it is in figure 8.11 that deictic coordinates would fit in this inventory of schemata (although certain deictics appear to convey reference to bounded spaces, thus combining perimetral with directional functions).

Regardless of its configuration, every kind of space discussed heretofore has a *yùumil* 'lord, owner' in Maya culture, to whom it belongs. This goes for the maximal expanse of the cosmos, whose lord is God the Father, Jesus Christ, and the legions of *sàanto ?ìik'ó?ob'* 'Holy Spirits (winds)' with their cardinal positions and zones of guardianship. It goes equally well for land transformed by labor and inhabited by an owner, and also for the field of sensory awareness of an actor, the possession of the one who calls it *tinw iknal* 'my place'. This bond links space to sets of rights and responsibilities among owners of different ranks and kinds. It is reciprocal in the sense that not only do places have owners, but agen-

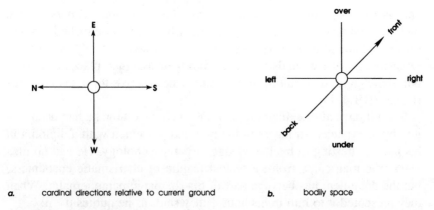

a.   cardinal directions relative to current ground   *b.*   bodily space

Fig. 8.11. Centered orientation.

tive forces, potential owners, have assigned places. It is a matter of common sense for DC, DP, Balim, and most other adult Maya, that all
animates, including spirits and directional winds, occupy relatively fixed
positions. They may move habitually from their places—movement may
be one of their defining features—yet they remain anchored to them and
return there. Spirits in their cardinal locations, birds in their *k'uh* 'nest', a
man or woman *y oó?l u meyah* 'over his-her work', and *kulá?an* 'seated,
at home' are examples of this. After we had walked a few hours in the
forest one afternoon, while I was being eaten alive by mosquitos and
sweating profusely, DP assured me that, even though I was having such a
good time, *má? ?u tí?aleč k'aáš* 'you don't belong to (the) forest.' The
forest belongs to the Maya and they belong to it, in DP's view and that of
most other adult Maya Oxkutzcabeños.

The concept that agents belong to places receives special elaboration in
DC's shamanic practice, where it plays a central role. The logic of prayer,
with its vertical and quadrilateral reference, lowering of spirits and returning them, is based squarely on the premise that the spirits are to be
found where they belong. When they move, things happen, whether the
orderly visitation of prayer with its beneficial consequences or the chaotic
meandering of a spirit, nested in the corner of the yard, whose movement
strikes people and animals, leaving them sick (see §7.4.3). Venomous
snakes, among the best exemplars of *k'àak'as b'á?ah* 'very bad, evil
things', are as bound to their assigned places as are the winds and spirits.
DC explained that a snake may live its entire life within a small area in the
woods, say four by four meters, never venturing beyond it. When it once
strays out of this area, it will surely die or be killed by a man. The great
wind beneath the sea obeys the same constraint: its place is under water

and its role is to drive the seawater into the *nukuč saáyab'ó'?ob'* 'large underground water currents' in the earth, where it will be rushed through the ground and filtered into sweet water to be found in the *č'é'?en* 'well(s)'. Occasionally, these winds dislodge from their assigned places and come out above ground, resulting in potentially destructive tornados and hurricanes (BB.4.85).

Several days after explaining this, DC recounted how he had been visited by unexpected strangers in the past and presented with a diploma in his name, attesting to his knowledge of parapsychology. He had no idea where the men came from, a typical feature of charismatic encounters, but the document has become part of his shamanic paraphernalia. When they presented it to him in his house, they said, as he quotes them:

(6)   way kameyah e'?, yàan teč derečo, pero má ahoó'?l amaán
            'Here you work, you have a right, but you're not to go out

            hòo nah hòo nah
            door to door.' (BB.4.123)

The concept of working and living in a place to which one has a right and which one must *por ley* 'by law' occupy is epitomized in DC's practice, but is also a widely encountered one. It means, among other things, that speakers frequently have as part of their schematic knowledge of individuals the places they frequent, and of places, the people to whom they belong.

8.4.2 Space in Time and Time in Space

All space in Maya is embedded in one or another diachronic process, and different kinds of place correspond to different rhythms of change, from the kinesis of the corporeal schema to the long-term developments of the forest. Boundary stones locate a milpa or yard within the historical sphere of a single family (the more inclusive, the wider the temporal zone), while *muúltun* 'stone pile' markers imply a longer duration. Not only do altars embody the sequence of steps by which they are created, but they are also saturated with the diachronic corollaries of the gifts themselves. The front offerings on altars correspond to earlier phases in the agricultural process and are addressed to relatively lower spirits than the back offerings (§8.3.2). The solitary *'?uk'ul* 'drink' offered by a farmer is timed and directed towards certain anticipated outcomes, from which it takes its name, such as *mak hò'?ol šú'?ul* 'close digging stick hole'. Insofar as different phases in the development of families place different demands on the living space, the domestic frames in figure 8.8 can be translated into statements about the likely life stage of the inhabitants.

Moreover, since the household is usually under construction, its state at any point in time is a temporary one. The same can be said of the agricultural zones in figure 8.9, whose configurations anchor them indexically in a certain stage in the process, particularly the initial measuring and cutting.

The successive and centered schemata in figures 8.10 and 8.11 are all readily adapted to the purpose of temporal reckoning insofar as they incorporate sequential relations of order or relative distance on an axis. In addition to this potential, bodily space in Maya, as I have presented it (§3.2), unavoidably articulates with the processes of ordered perception, kinesis, memory, and anticipation, all of which give the place temporal as well as spatial contours.

These observations suggest that the divide between schematic and emergent knowledge, with which we began chapter 7, is a relative rather than absolute one. Spatial frames are produced through time, and the places they refer to have history. The microdiachrony of an activity field, changing from one instant to the next, is an extreme example, but what is most distinctive of it is not the fact of its changing but the different rates and dimensions in which it changes, depending upon what kind of activity is in course and who the participants are. The more fixed, broad-stroke developments of forest growth and the interannual milpa cycle (§8.2.3) take place in a different rhythm, as do the changes in domestic space. For native actors, this means that a series of partly overlapping cycles is going on at any point in time, in the course of which the spatial world is mutating at different rates. Events are seen to take place when *ȼ'úk'uȼul ʔuk'ìinil* 'their time has come', implying that they have temporal as well as spatial boundaries. Some of the best examples of the intermingling of temporal and spatial orientations come, not surprisingly, from language use.

8.4.3 Spacetime and Verbal Reference

Language use is not coordinate with any of the embodiments so far discussed, because it is the one system that encompasses the principles of nearly all the others. Talk about place implies one or another of the subsystems of orientation presented or a combination of them. A good example is the convention on ordering spirit reference in prayer, which transposes the function of drawing the perimeter (cutting through the forest, walking, laying stones) from the material level of a path between landmarks to a series of verbal references. When a speaker identifies a referent as inside, outside, over, under, after, or in front of some other object, (s)he mobilizes schemata also embodied in other kinds of practice, such as ones involving the perimetrical function of cardinal places, the vertical planes of the altar, the directionality of a path to a landmark, and the orientation of altars and domestic structures. When a referent is identified with a deictic expression, such as *le hé?elo?* 'that one (pointing to object in sight)', the corporeal frame is one of the relevant schemata making the act intelligible. In most deictic usage, not only the emergent framework of the interaction but also the schematic divisions of the larger frame space are part of the communicative process. When a Maya woman tells a visitor to the house that her husband *miná?an way e?* 'he's not here', she conveys that he is not within the *soólar* perimeter. A proper interpretation of her statement identifies the referent of the deictic with the *soólar* as a bounded place. Such examples demonstrate that linguistic subsystems are not only partly homologous with nonlinguistic ones, but that they also combine with them in the process of interpretation and discourse 'contextualization' (Gumperz 1982:chap. 6).

One way in which this combination functions is through a metonymic principle of reference, which says that an activity, event, or place can be referred to as being done by, pertaining to, or belonging to its 'head'. The *soólar* is referred to by the name of the senior male, as in *nah don Pil* 'at Pil's house', which may encompass two or three subordinate homes as well as that of the head. As the officiating *hmèen* 'shaman (lit., doer)', DC says without hesitation that he is the one doing the *heé¢ lú?um* 'fix earth' ceremony, despite the fact that he is directing the adult male residents as they do much of the work. DP adopts the same stance when he describes projects he engages in with his son VC as things **he** is doing (cf. §3.5). In these cases, the application of metonymy is guided by rank asymmetries among coparticipants (or coresidents): the highest rank stands for the whole. This seems to be the motivating principle also when the gourd count offering in *wàahil kòol* 'breads of the milpa' and *č'aá čaák* 'get rain' ceremonies is described as *k'ú?ub'ul sak'a?* 'delivery of gruel', even though both gruel and *b'alče?* 'mead' are offered (cf. fig. 8.1). Similarly, a man's main sleeping house, the *nah* proper, may be only a small fraction of the land he occupies for living and agriculture (cf. §7.4 above). When referring to his lands from outside, however, any part of the total expanse, even a milpa twenty-five kilometers away from his house, can be referred to simply as his *nah*. The core structure stands for the whole. Finally, the totalizing function of the five cardinal places, like the 'earth' of the person as the whole body, results from the application of a metonymic extension whereby key parts of an object stand for the whole.[19]

Place-names cast another light on the combination of linguistic schemata with nonlinguistic context. Many consist of phrase-length descriptions of the natural environment, focusing on selected features, such as Hwiíɟil k'aáš 'Hill Forest (esp. to the south of Cooperativa)', ʔék'lúʔum 'Black Earth (esp. the valley southwest of Cooperativa)', and Yoók' ʔaák'al 'Over (the) Marsh'. The names have conventional semantic and grammatical structure, which local Maya men share as part of their schematic knowledge of their language. The semantics can be misleading, however, since the lexicon of ecological descriptors is grounded in local linguistic practice: on one hand, specific places around the area serve as standards for categories, which can be confusing to an outsider who nonetheless understands the 'dictionary definition' of the description (see §7.3.3). On the other hand, the places named by phrases like the above could be described in any number of other ways, meaning that the description is a highly selective one. It is easy enough to go to the place called Black Earth and find pockets of land that do not fit the description but do fit some distinct descriptions. This can be plausibly explained as another instance of metonymy, in which the most salient feature of the area is used as the name of the whole.

Such examples force us to view the conventional semantics of the expressions in relation to the actual environment and referential practices around Oxkutzcab. Moreover, the use of such terms may persist even after they cease to be descriptively accurate, something particularly evident with place-names describing man-made features of the setting. In the mid 1970s, there was a lot on the road going west out of Cooperativa, where communally owned heavy machinery was kept, called the *kaámpamento* 'encampment'. By the early 1980s the same plot of land had been cleared and was an irrigated field, with the machinery stored at a different location. Despite this, the stretch of road where it used to be continued to be called *šlaʔ kaámpamento* 'old encampment', or just *kaámpamento*. A neighborhood in Oxkutzcab around the building that formerly housed a *rastro* 'slaughterhouse' continued to be referred to as *ràastro*, even years after the building had been converted permanently into a primary school. The name ceased to be descriptively accurate and has become an index of the prior history of the place. By persisting, descriptive names take on diachronic corollaries. The terms used to describe temporary phases in the milpa process are also used to refer to the place itself (§8.2.4). By saying that he is going to his *šlaʔ sàakab* 'old stalks', a Maya farmer indicates the developmental state of the place in both the yearly cycle (postharvest, preclearing) and in the interyear one (after the second harvest in succession).

The use of spatial terms to characterize diachronic relations is commonplace in linguistic systems, and Maya is unexceptional in this regard. The terms for 'in front of', 'behind', and 'inside' have both spatial and temporal uses:

(7)   (yaáš) taánil
            '(first) in front, before, earlier'

(8)   pàači ti
            'behind, after, later'. Cf. infix -pača?- probably same root.
            (BB.4.76)

(9)   ?ič(il)
            'inside, during'. Cf. ?iči ti b'á?até?e 'during battle', ?ič hòoč
            'during harvest', ?iči sìinko diáas 'within (before lapse of) five
            days'.

Time itself is described as a road, as in b'ehelá?e? 'today (lit., road here)', and ká?ab'eh 'day after tomorrow (lit., two road)' (cf. §7.3.4), and the movement of the sun is the main focus of many temporal descriptors, including:

(10)   tumaán le k'ìin o?
            'time passes (lit., the sun travels)'

(11)   há?a¢kab'
            'dawn (lit., strike earth)'

(12)   ?òok'in
            'evening (lit., enter sun)'

(13)   ¢'úk'učul uk'ìinil
            'the time has come (lit., the sun has arrived)'

The succession of temporal units larger than the day, such as the month, season, and year, also involve the concepts of entering and going out, but have the inverse meanings, le ?àaño hoók' o? 'last year (lit., the year gone out)', kuy okol yaášk'iin 'Yaaxkin (hot season) enters (starts)'. Not surprisingly, one of the spatial deictics is the root of a temporal one, tol-akhéak o? 'then (distant past known by both interlocutors) (lit., out there past)'. Such examples give evidence of the interpenetration of spatial and temporal schemata in referential practice.

8.4.3.1 The Specific Relativity of Deictic Frames

More subtle cases of the imbrication of spatial and temporal reckonings show up in the pragmatics of indexical particles, including deictics. By way of foreshadowing issues addressed in the coming chapters, we can illustrate this point with a few examples.[20] One of the temporal particles is *ká'ač ih* 'in the past', which indicates that the state of affairs or event referred to in the clause took place prior to the moment of utterance (or some other ground established in discourse). The form encodes no indication of how long ago the event took place but only that, at the time of utterance, it is over. In some contexts, the boundary between these two times, 'now' and 'then', is calculated relative to changes in location.

Sitting in room 1 (fig. 7.8) after supper, Man told me about a man who used to live in our neighborhood but who had since moved to another area of Oxkutzcab, called the Mejorada, about fifteen blocks away.

(14)   tí'an té' yoók'ol eskìina i média kahakbaló'ob' ká'ač a'†
        'There there at (over) a block and a half they used to live.' († pointing)

Anticipating a question from me, he added spontaneously,

(15)   ká'ač a' ↑ tumèen behlá e' ↑ h maánó'ob té' bàanda té'el o'
        '*ká'ača'* because nowadays they've moved over in that area over there.' (BB.4.100)

The question Man answered was why he had chosen to utter the past particle, and his reason was that the state of affairs described by the sentence failed to correspond with the current situation. The distinction between current and past is not a fixed measure, however, but is drawn relative to a frame, which in this case is movement from one place to another. This relativity to the current frame of reference is a crucial component in all centered orientation, including cardinal directional orientation as well as deictic (cf. §7.2).

Another temporal particle with spatial corollaries is *saám* 'a while ago (earlier in same day)'. Man and I had been sitting together at the table in room 1 (fig. 7.8) for a couple of hours discussing the Maya language, when he compared something I said with an utterance I had made earlier:

(16)   wá čeén tawá'ak hé'eš 'uúčik má' saám a'a' . . .
        'If you just say it, as you did not long ago . . .' (BB.4.105)

He continued, again without prompting, by explaining that his choice of 'not long ago' reflected the fact that we were still engaged in conversation at the same table. There had been no break in our location to motivate referring to an earlier utterance as having occurred in the past.

(17)   saám a'a' tumèen má' saáŋ kuyuúču ičiló'on a'.
        '*saám a'a'* because not long ago it occurred among us.

miš untuúl luk'uk iʔiʔ.   Entonses, ká luk'óʔon téʔel aʔ,
Not one (of us) has left (here). Now (for example), if we left
                                                here,

ká b'inóʔon té nah le háʔas oʔ,
and went over there by the banana tree,

ká hoóp'óʔon kȼikbaléʔeš le ʔásuntó oʔ,
and we started talking about the event,

entonses yan awáʔak le saámeak oʔ
then you'd have to say that 'a while ago' (form).'

For Man, the break between 'not long ago' and 'a while ago' is best illustrated by a break in the conversation along with a spatial displacement of
one or more of the participants.[21] In other words, because the participants
are still in the same place, the two utterances can be described as (almost)
contemporaneous.

The important point here appears to be that both temporal and spatial
successions presuppose boundaries between units. Under the proper circumstances, spatial boundaries and displacements can determine the calculation of temporal ones. A conversation stretching over time is like a
field stretching over space: the limits of the former can define the difference between now (included) and then (excluded), and the limits of the
latter can determine here (included) vs. there (excluded). In cases like the
one cited, a spatial inclusion motivates a temporal one.

The relativity of deictic reference is equally important in straightforward spatial usage. Recall from the summary of forms in §1.3 that the
locatives include an opposition between regional Inclusive *way eʔ* 'here'
and Exclusive *tol oʔ* '(out) there', as well as a pair of (relatively) punctate
forms distinguishing *téʔel aʔ* 'Immediate' from *téʔel oʔ* 'Non-Immediate'. In rough and ready terms, the Inclusive and Immediate forms indicate proximal space, and the other two less proximal space. *tol oʔ*, in
particular, is used for reference to things far off, out of sight, vaguely
known.

Consider now the futility of attempting to explain these expressions in
terms of fixed relations of relative proximity, according to which 'here'
should be closer than 'over there'. The Inclusive/Exclusive pair is naturally suited to the distinction between first-level households within the
soólar. The difference in male family heads, the boundary between their
respective parts of the yard, and the many consequences of these things
all reinforce the division. Sitting in room 1 (fig. 7.8), my comadre Margot asked me whether I planned to sleep that night there (in 1) or over at

DC's (room 9). On previous nights, I had slept at DC's, but earlier that afternoon had moved my hammock over to room 1 for a siesta. With this in mind, she asked:

(18)　　　　way kán a p'at ak'àan e ʔ,　　　　wá yan amáansik tol o ʔ
　　　　　　'Will you leave your hammock here, or are you taking it over
　　　　　　　　　　　　　　　　　　　　　　　　there?' (BB.4.67)

The divide between her home and her father-in-law's is a central aspect of the schematic frame of this reference and was made more acute by her desire to have me be honored guest in her home. The Inclusive/Exclusive pair maps right on to this context. On an earlier occasion, still in room 1, Margot contrasted a hammock over at DC's (room 9) with one hanging here in room 2:

(19)　　　　maʔa to tak'àan o ʔ, téʔe k'àan téʔel a ʔ
　　　　　　'Not in your hammock over there, here in the hammock right
　　　　　　here.' (BB.4.60)

This usage follows the same logic of locating DC's house as outside but refers more punctually to the location of the hammock in the next room of the house we were in instead of the inclusive 'here' of the house as a whole.

　　When Margot asked me whether I would leave my hammock 'here' or bring it 'over there', I answered that I wanted to hang it at DC's. Moments later, she and I were setting it up in the north *moy* 'end' of room 9, she on one side and I on the other, tying the ropes. Standing back, I suggested that we raise it higher, so the fleas couldn't jump in. She stood back on her side, both of us now equidistant from the two ends, facing each other. She looked at it, pointed to one end, and said *tolo ʔ* '(raise it) over there (at that end)' (BB.4.67). At about five feet from Margot, punctual and in clear view, the end of the hammock was by any measure 'close', and qualified well for *téʔela ʔ* 'right here'. Several days later, Man was repairing a door jamb (between rooms 1 and 2), pounding on one of the hinges. Standing about ten feet away across the room, Margot observed that when he got one side in place, the other one popped out:

(20)　　　　péro hoók'áʔan tol o ʔ
　　　　　　'But it's popped out over there.' (BB.4.93)

Both examples illustrate narrowly defined referential segmentations within the proximal zone of interaction, yet the speaker selected a deictic usually used for distant regions, outside and of great extent. Observations of other speakers confirm that these uses are neither odd nor uncommon.

Recall from §3.5 that DP referred to the far end of an irrigation canal as *tolo?*, despite its being part of the very work site.

The inverse case also arises, in which a referent in fact far off is treated as though it were proximal. Sitting in Is's house, Is's father referred to his home, two blocks away from where we were, as *té?el a?* 'right here'. He was telling how he had moved from out in the Puuc region into the town of Oxkutzcab (BB.4.98). At a remove of two blocks and out of sight, the place could well have been treated as far off instead of close. Man told of something he had seen in Mérida, a very different social setting 100 kilometers away from our conversation, referring to the city as *tée Ho? a?* 'right here in Mérida' (BB.4.156).

Such examples are utterly routine but difficult to square with any description claiming that 'here' is close and 'there' far. Like the Icelandic directionals (see §7.2) and the relative uses of cardinal directions in Maya, the problem here is that deictic schemata incorporate an **indexical ground.** Any metric statement of distance between 'here' and 'there' is meaningless unless paired with an indexical frame. In Margot's first two utterances, the frame was her interest in seeing me sleep at their house as opposed to her father-in-law's, a simple Inclusive/Exclusive relation reinforced by an entire series of kinship and spatial schemata. When one is engaged in a focused task involving proximal segmentations, the indexical frame is much more constricted, allowing the Exclusive deictic to be used properly in reference to the 'other' end of an object, perhaps no longer than one's arm. When one is narrating the development of one's third-level household in Oxkutzcab, contrasting it to the Puuc outside of town, the frame is expanded, and a member house in the larger group is segmentable as 'right here' (cf. Bühler's transposition types in chap. 5). Finally, Man's reference to Mérida as *tée . . . a?* 'right here' involves two distinct indexical components, by my analysis. The first is his familiarity with the city, where he goes several times a month to visit affines. This draws the place within the sphere of his routine experience, making it 'closer'. The second is the fact that in the utterance in which the token occurred, Man was launching into a story about what he had seen. The normally proximal terminal deictic *a?* is motivated at least partly by the anticipatory function of introducing a new narrative line.

This illustrates one of the basic characteristics of indexical frames in deictic reference: they are multidimensional. A simple metric approach fails not only because distance scales expand and contract situationally but also because spatial location is only one of many dimensions activated in most phenomenal frameworks. Standing apart from absolute, cardinal spacetime, with its measuring rods and prefabricated schemata, the indexical framework of reference is constituted in the ongoing interactive process. Therefore it includes verbal discourse, corporeal frames, and the social relations among participants. Whether we see the deictic field as a 'patchwork of moments' or just a more complex kind of system, the analysis begins with an account of the linguistic forms and immediate details of deictic practice, to which we now turn.

9   The Spatial Frame
of Deictic Reference

Recall from chapter 1 that spatial deictics in Maya consist of five lexical items, each containing two morphemes, in the familiar Initial Deictic (ID) plus Terminal Deictic (TD) shape:

> way eʔ 'here (around me)'
> tol oʔ 'there (out, excluding me)'
> téʔel aʔ'Right there (specific point nearby)'
> téʔel oʔ'(Right) there (point or region at intermediate remove)'
> tíʔ iʔ 'there (anaphoric)'

I will argue that the conventional relational features of these forms, by which they individuate referential objects, are organized along three axes: Regional (top two) versus Restricted (middle two), Egocentric (top two) versus Sociocentric (middle and lower three), and Concrete (top four) versus Non-Concrete (bottom one). The latter distinction is needed to capture the fact that the anaphoric deictic encodes no characterization of the perceptibility, spatial location, or extent of the referent whatsoever, except that it is known. This form is semantically lean and only minimally corporeal, while the others are relatively richer in information and embody the corporeal frame more fully.

Several larger issues arise naturally in giving an account of the structure and use of these forms. The most obvious is the role of egocentricity as a distinctive parameter, an issue that arose already in relation to corporeality (§3.2) and participant roles (chap. 5). Here we will see that this component of the participant structure has a more central function in some categories than in others. This is not surprising, given the range of variation in the *-iknal* 'bodily space', sometimes limited to the individual and sometimes including other interactants (see §3.2). Still, it will illustrate once again that a feature commonsensically associated with deixis as a whole in fact pertains only to some expressions under certain circumstances. Such is the case with directivity and corporeality, as well as egocentricity. Less obvious from the forms but no less central to the practice of reference, spatial deictics are implemented relative to indexical frames, as was exemplified in §8.4. This relativity has two consequences: (i) the extent of the current frame of reference may be relatively **expanded** (e.g., 'here on earth') or relatively **contracted** ('here on the tip of my finger'); and (ii) the frame may be indexically grounded in the current participant structure, as in **standard direct** referential usage, or it may be **transposed,** as in quoted speech and transposed reference, where some established point other than the current participant frame is the 'pivot' relative to which the referent is identified. Because of these basic variations in usage, any metric statement of the distance values of deictics is meaningless unless paired with a pragmatic frame.

The last major issue that underlies my account is the relation between deictic space as an orientational schema implemented in communicative practice and the other culturally embedded systems detailed in previous chapters. Two relations predominate: (i) acts of deictic reference presuppose the prefabricated schematic divisions in space and time that were summarized in §8.4. The referents individuated by deictic tokens typically coincide with places already segmented by one or more extralinguistic cultural systems, such as the perimeter of the homestead and the interior of the *nah* house. As a corollary of this, deictics may be productively combined with lexical descriptions of location in referring expressions; (ii) the categorial structure of spatial deixis is related to other schemata, both centered and noncentered, by homology and selective elaboration. Contrasts between inclusion and exclusion, totalized and segmented, locative and directional spatial arrays, which arose in such systems as the cardinal points, agricultural practice, and corporeal orientation, are also embodied in the deictics. This fact provides powerful evidence of the underlying unity of deictic with other cultural systems. Referential practices arise out of the interplay of language with lived space, and both bear the trace of their joining.

9.1 SPATIAL DEICTICS AND OTHER LOCATIONAL EXPRESSIONS IN MAYA

Virtually all of the spatial information set forth in chapters 7 and 8 is represented in standard locational descriptions in everyday Maya. Typical ways of making reference to places include (i) place names, both official and unofficial; (ii) descriptors of the natural environment, commonly associated with unique places; (iii) known landmarks, including features of the social as well as natural environment, such as the church, the market, and the well; (iv) places characterized as the locus of some temporally circumscribed activity or event, as in *tinč'akb'é?en sak'ab'* 'my freshly cut stalks', *té? tú?uš k uy uúčul pàak o?* 'there where weeding is going on'; (v) relational expressions identifying referents relative to some ground point. For purposes of description, we can distinguish four subvarieties: (a) Simple relations of contiguity, inclusion, and exclusion, such as *nàa¢' tinw otoč* 'near my house' (cf. also far, at, inside, outside). (b) Directional relations, which define a vector from one place to another: *lak'in ti?* 'east of it' and *taáni ti?* 'in front of it' (cf. also behind, above, below, to the right, to the left). These often rely on ground objects endowed with inherent orientations, such as bodily space, moving vehicles, and domestic structures. (c) Relational expressions in which the ground is a human actor, including many of the cases in (a) and (b) but also expressions like *nah maánweh* 'at Manuel's place' and *tukòol feélis* 'at Feliciano's milpa'. (d) Deictics, which encode relations between indexical and referential objects. Insofar as they localize places relative to a centering participant frame, deictics are akin to expressions designating human-grounded spaces, but there is a key difference among them: the center for deixis is an actional framework, not an individual human or an enduring place.

If we borrow the notation originally used by Jakobson (1957) in his early treatment of shifters, these kinds of expressions can be summarized as: L^n 'narrated locations' (i–iii); L^n/E^n 'locations identified relative to narrated events' (iv); L^n/L^n 'location identified relative to another location' (v.a, v.b); L^n/P^n 'location relative to a participant in some narrated event' (v.c); and L^n/E^s (or L^n/P^s) 'location identified relative to the current speech event (or its participants)' (v.c–d). While deictics fit quite clearly into the last group of expressions, this summary notation needs to be refined, as we shall see, in order to reflect the different relational features that mediate between the indexical ground and the referent.

There are no case markers, prepositions, or relational nouns in Maya that distinguish consistently between the locative adverbial functions of Location, Source, Goal, and Path. Subject to independently motivated semantic and grammatical constraints, expressions of any of the types outlined in the preceding paragraph may occur in any of the four functions.

(1)   hwàane? kumeyah {h k'iíwik, tukòol, nàa¢'č'é?en, tinwiknal,
       té?el o?}
       'Juan works {(at the) market, at his milpa, near the well, at my
       place, there}.'

(2)   hwèelo kutàal {teritòoryo, ?aák'al, ¢eél Cres, tuyiknal usukú?un,
       té?el o?}'
       'Manuel comes (from) {(the) territory (Quintana Roo), the water
       hole, beside Cres, his brother's place, there}.'

(3)   kubin félis {h k'iíwik, tusoólar, pàači ti? Xul, tinwiknal,
             té?el o?}.
             'Feliciano goes {(to the) market, to his plot, behind Xul, to my
             place, there}.'

(4)   kumáan hwàan {pú?uk, tuhaál uč'akb'é?en, ?ič hwiíȼ, tawiknal,
             té?el o?}.
             'Juan traverses {Puuc, the boundary of his new milpa, among
             steep hills, your place, there}.'

As the above examples show, a noun phrase functioning as a locative
descriptor normally needs no special marking, in the form of case affixes
or prepositions, unless it meets one of three criteria.
         (i) If a noun phrase is overtly possessed, it requires the relational
particle *ti?* when used in any of the four locative functions.

(5)   kimbin {*∅, t-} uk'àašil Akil
             'I'm going to the Akil woods.'

         (ii) If a noun phrase is overtly marked for definiteness, the ex-
pected demonstrative or article is replaced by the appropriate DLOC.

(6)   tinkonah * le k'iíwik o?
             'I sold it (at the) market.'[1]

(7)   tinkonah * {ti?, té?} le k'iíwik o?
             'I sold it (at the) market.'

(8)   tinkonah té? k'iíwik o?
             'I sold it (at the) market.'

Constraint ii implies that when making reference to overtly marked definite locations in Maya, speakers are obliged to specify the Relation (R
value) linking the place referred to and the current interactive framework.
In linguistic terms, the field of choice includes all four of the concrete
deictics, any of which could occur in place of *té? . . . o?* in (8). The
conditioning factor is naturally the type of access participants have to the
referent.
         (iii) If the noun phrase is [+Animate] or [+Human], it requires a
DLOC or other marker of locative adverbial function.

(9)   yàan amaán {* tìigréeh, nah tìigrée, té? h tìigré o?}
             'You've got to swing by {* Tigre, Tigre's place, there (at) Tigre}.'

Within Locative phrases, the order of elements is [DLOC Adv NP]$_{LOC}$
with the Terminal Deictic particle occurring in sentence-final position
(which may or may not coincide with locative-phrase final).

(10)   té⁷ nàag̣' č'é⁷en o⁷
         'There near (the) well'

(11)   té⁷ ⁷aáktáan tuyotoč hwèeló o⁷
         'There in front of Manuel's house'

(12)   té⁷ tubak' pàač hk'iíwik o⁷
         'There all around (lit., at the wrapped back of) the market'

(13)   to naáč tú⁷uš kbin o⁷
         'Out there far off where we go'

(14)   way tú⁷uš kinmeyah e⁷
         'Here where I work'

(15)   té⁷ yoó⁷ pak'i nah tusutó⁷ob e b'á⁷a tuyokló⁷ob' o⁷
         'There above the walled house they returned the thing(s) they (had)
         stolen.' (BB.4.100–101)

(16)   té⁷ tusutó⁷ob yoó⁷ pak'i nah o⁷
         'There they returned it above the walled house.'

(17)   *yoó⁷ pak'i nah tusut ó⁷ob té⁷el o⁷

(18)   tí⁷an té⁷ ⁷ič kòol o⁷
         'There('s where) it is (right) there.'

In cases like (13–14), a subordinate clause may be embedded in the locative phrase, with the DLOC base occurring in initial position as the head
of a relative clause. In nonlocative usage, the definite article plus WH-
question word would be expected, as in (19):

(19)   le tú⁷uš kinmeyah e⁷ → má⁷alob'
         '(The place) where I work, (it's) good.'

Examples like (15–18) foreshadow the focus constructions to be described in chapter 10 and illustrate that when all or part of the locative
phrase is fronted into preverbal position, the order DLOC Adv N remains
fixed. Lexical description of location cannot precede a coreferential DLOC
in the same sentence (17), but in several kinds of focus constructions, two
or more DLOCs may jointly specify the same spatial referent.

    Unlike the Ostensive Evidential particles (chap. 6), which are typically
predicative, the DLOCs are typically referential in function. Locative
phrases show no marking for tense, aspect, or person, as do predicative
elements in Maya (verbs, predicative adjectives and nouns, certain particles). They can be used predicatively by inserting an appropriate form
of the verbal stem ⁷an 'to exist, be (in a place)'. Tense, aspect, and person inflection are signaled according to the standard pattern for this verb.[2]

(20)   *tikul-ó?on
            'We are in Ticul.'

(21)   *nohoč kàah-ó?ob'
            'They are in (a) large city.'

(22)   *way-en e?
            'I am here.'

(23)   tikul ?anil-ó?on
            'We're in Ticul (temporarily).'

(24)   yàan way e?
            'He's here.'

(25)   way yàan-en e?
            'Here (is where) I am.'

Two more preliminary contrasts are needed before we turn to a detailed description of the conventional meanings of these deictics. The first separates two surface shapes in which the DLOCs occur: **continuous,** where the two parts of the compound are immediately adjacent, and **discontinuous,** where they are separated by intervening lexical material. Examples (10–18, 25) all illustrate the discontinuous shape, while (24) shows the continuous shape. In continuous shape, DLOCs invariably appear in the full canonical form, as cited at the outset of this chapter. When discontinuous, however, *té?el-* and *tol-* usually undergo morphophonemic reductions similar (but not identical) to the ones cited for the Ostensive Evidentials (chap. 6).[3] The second contrast sets **prolocative** uses, where the DLOC is the sole element in the locative phrase, apart from **adlocative** uses, where it is lexically elaborated. Examples (10–14) are adlocative, because they all contain a combination of lexical description of the location along with the deictic. In (24, 25), however, there is no further description in the locative phrase of the place referred to. While all adlocative uses are discontinuous, since the Initial DLOC base precedes and the Terminal follows, not all discontinuous DLOCs are adlocative in function. One reason for this is that lexical material not belonging to the locative phrase may immediately follow the Initial Deictic, as in (26):

(26)   kimbisik té?e šan o?
            'I take it there **too.**'

Also, the Initial DLOC base may be fronted into preverbal position in a couple of different ways, to be discussed in chapter 10.

9.2 DIMENSIONS OF DEICTIC SPACE

The central analytic problem in describing the use of the DLOCs is to characterize their referential-descriptive potentials. Special illocutionary effects are on the whole less determinate and more weakly associated with these forms than was the case with Ostensive Evidentials (chap. 6). Furthermore, while the OSTEVs can be scaled in terms of the relative richness of perceptual evidence of the referent, it is unclear that any single scale, such as relative immediacy, can be fruitfully applied to the DLOCs. Rather, the system incorporates several basic relations found also in the cultural schemata described in chapters 7 and 8, and it is in relation to these that my description will proceed. The evidence for my interpretations comes from three principal kinds of data (see chap. 2). The first is observations of actual use, where tokens are embedded in communicative frameworks whose schematic aspects are configured in frames. The second is observations of the ways in which native speakers describe the meaning and use of the forms, giving further clues to their standards of reference and interpretation. And the third is observations of the grammatical consequences of functional relations. These include the many co-occurrence restrictions that govern the distribution of deictics relative to selected constructions, other lexical items, and so forth. The last kind of evidence can help in determining whether or not some feature of an interactive framework is part of the language.

9.2.1 Egocentric Boundaries

9.2.1.1 *Inclusive: 'Here' is the Perimeter around Me*

The deictic feature Inclusive, encoded in *way e?* 'here', is most closely associated with the concept of bounded space, in which a perimeter distinguishes inside from outside. The most typical referents individuated with this form include the interactants' *-iknal* 'bodily space' (including the perceptual and kinetic field of corporeal engagements), the space of a single walled room, the first-level *soólar* space of a single marriage pair with unmarried offspring, the second-level, walled *soólar* as a whole, the agricultural plots or orchards worked by a single man or 'team', the region frequented by the interactants, and the earth inhabited by man, as opposed to the sky inhabited by gods (see chaps. 7 and 8). Despite the great differences among these spaces in terms of their extent and the kinds of boundaries they involve, all are routine referents of *way e?* 'here'. We can summarize them schematically as in figure 9.1.

Fig. 9.1. Perimetral frame of *way e?* 'here (Inclusive of ego)'.

The core feature of 'here' as characterized by *way e?* is that it invari-ably includes the speaker. Wherever the interactants are in relation to one another, each one is inalienably *way e?*, just as each one inalienably in-habits his own corporeal schema. Sitting in a crowded bus, a girl got up and offered her seat to a woman with a child in her arms, saying,

(27)   hé? **way** akutalé?eš e?
          'Here you can sit right here.' (3/3/81)

It is significant to this utterance that the girl was offering the seat she was herself sitting in, since if this were not the case, the boldface DLOC would not be present in her utterance. When one enters a Maya house and is offered a chair or hammock to sit in, a strict rule of Maya etiquette, the presentative offering is *hé? b'á?al a kutal a?* 'Here's something to sit on', not *hé? way a kutal e?* 'Here's (where) you sit here.' Conversing over supper, DC recounted an incident from his childhood, when, in pitch darkness, he was groping around the house looking for the front door in order to let his grandfather in. The old man directed DC towards the door, tapping on it and saying:

(28)   hé?el a? hé?el a? **way** atàal e?
          'Here it is, here it is. Come here (to me).' (BB.4.87)

In general, when interactants are separated by spatial, perceptual, or major social divisions, each refers to his own location as *way e?*, and

DC's grandfather knew that in simply following the sound of his voice, DC would come to him.

During major ceremonies such as the *č'aá čaák* 'get rain' and *wàahil kòol* 'breads of the milpa', DC as senior shaman stands apart from all spectators and helpers. While the altar space is rarely referred to as *way e?* in ritual language, because of its decentered status (see §§5.3, 7.4, 8.3), it is the main 'here' of the shaman when he addresses the people behind him, for instance, when he issues instructions or solicits information. Depending upon his current engagement, his phenomenal corporeal field is either available as a focal referent or elided in the reframings of ritual genres. He recounted the story of a rain ceremony in which one of the sponsors had brought him a dead rooster to offer up, already beginning to rot. When he got to the point in the ceremony of presenting the thing, he called out to the men behind him to summon the one who was responsible, saying:

(29)   maáš tí?al le t'eél a? ↑ t'àan ten **way e?**
         'Whose rooster is this? Call him here to me.'

When the man stepped forward, DC told him that whatever is brought to him, he presents, implying that it was the man's responsibility if he really wanted to offer a rotten rooster instead of a fresh turkey or chicken.

(30)   ten e? le kutàas á?al **way e?**, kink'ub' ik
         'Me, what's brought here (to me), I deliver it (up).' (BB.4.120)

The important point for understanding the DLOC is that the altar is both a bounded space in the full cosmological sense (see §§7.4, 8.3) and the privileged location of the shaman, in contrast to the human beneficiaries and spectators. These culturally constituted facts motivate the form of DC's reference.

It is also the association between 'here' and the corporeal field that motivates the use of this form with the indexically grounded verbs *tàal* '(to) come', and *tàasik* '(to) bring it' (causative derivation from 'come'), as in (30).[4] *kó?oten* 'come (to me)', a suppletive imperative form, refers unequivocally to the speaker's egocentric location and is very commonly paired with the Inclusive DLOC, as in:

(31)   kó?oten way e?
         'Come here (to me).'

The conventional gesture accompanying this summons is a downward and inward flick of the hand and forearm, palm down, in front of the speaker.

When interactants cannot hear one another or eschew speech for any reason, this gesture invariably conveys the summons by itself. As a corollary of its grounding in the speaker's corporeal schema, *way eʔ* is not used to pick out places **in contrast to** the speaker's location, nor is it used to refer to destinations where (s)he **anticipates** arriving in the near future, nor is it used to **segment** parts of the speaker's own body. These narrowly contrasting referential functions, as we shall see, are achieved with other deictic categories. Thus, it is never appropriate to utter the form in (32), in which this DLOC functions as the speaker's Goal.

(32)   *kóʔoš way eʔ
             'Let's go here.'

We saw in §3.2 that in practice, the *-iknal* 'bodily space' of an actor reaches beyond the individual to include other interactants and the corporeal field of their current engagement. This same expansion applies to the 'here' of *way eʔ*, which consists of the work site in utterances like (33). This occurred at a site where the speaker, Tigre, and the addressees were building a masonry house. They had labored for a week and had nearly completed the outer wall of the structure. One afternoon, several tools fell off a ledge where they had been leaned. Tigre looked up, chuckled and said:

(33)   **way** yàan k'àasi báʔal eʔ
             'There's evil hereabouts.' (3.B.408)

The DLOC in this statement does not refer to the specific ledge or to the outer regions of the neighborhood or Oxkutzcab but to the work site, within a walled *soólar,* where we were jointly engaged. Recall DC's narrative of the dream in which he was to be killed by a jaguar (chap. 4, 1–4). Tied up and about to be mauled, he said:

(34)   háʔali b'eʔ kíʔičkelem hahal dios, **way** kin ȼ'óʔokol eʔ
             'That's all, Beautiful True God,   here (is where) I come to an
                                                 end.' (BB.4.121)

In what appears to be an extension of the bodily grounding of this DLOC, the form is commonly used in reference to 'the near side' of an object or place, even when it is objectively far away from the speaker. Sitting in her kitchen in area I (fig. 7.6), Eli explained to me the location of a store in town, about fifteen kilometers away, where I could purchase fresh meat for the family. She described the place as:

(35)   hač **way** taánil eʔ →   máʔ tak'uč uk'iíwik →
             'Right here in front of it. You don't arrive (at the) market.

hač **way** taánil **eˀ** →
Right here in front

téˀ kukóˀonol oˀ →
that's where its sold' (BB.5.45 2/19/87)

In other words, along the path leading between her current location and
the landmark Oxkutzcab market, the intermediate ground on 'this side' is
described as 'here in front'. This description in no way depends upon the
inherent orientation of the landmark, which may or may not itself have a
front and back. Rather, it is the fact that the landmark situationally defines an endpoint for the trajectory leading away from the speaker; objects
along the way are represented as a fixed succession in which earlier is
front and later is *pàačil* 'back'. Expectably, a place beyond the market,
on 'the other side' of it, is referred to as *téˀ pàačil oˀ* 'there in back',
never * *way pàačil eˀ* 'here in back'.[5]

VC's wife Pilar used a similar form on another occasion when, standing in front of her kitchen (see fig. 7.6), she told me we were going to
pick the oranges off the trees on her side of the homestead.

(36)   čeén le yan **way** hòo nah → le kún t'okb'il oˀ →
             'Only the ones here by the entrance are to be picked.' (BB.5.10)

As figure 7.6 shows, there are citrus trees on both sides of the domestic
compound, corresponding to the parcels belonging to VC and MC (DP's
two younger sons). I was initially uncertain as to which trees she was referring to, but understood shortly later, when we picked all the ones 'on
the near side' of the entrance, belonging to her and VC. Within the
second-level homestead, as a frame split in half by the entrance placed on
the divide between the two owners, Pilar was contrasting all of the trees
'on this side' of the entrance to the ones on 'the other side'. In distinction
to the more typical locative use of *way eˀ*, diagrammed in figure 9.1, the
'near side' use can be represented as the schema in figure 9.2. This
schema incorporates the ego as ground point for a region between 'me'
and a landmark. The landmark functions as a perimetral boundary (much
like the more permanent stone markings of chaps. 7 and 8), the near side
of which is Included and the far side Excluded.

As would be predicted from its association with the *-iknal*, *way eˀ* may
also refer to the enclosed space of a single room in a multiroom house,
where the walls coincide with perceptual boundaries as well as activity
spaces. Sitting one evening at Lol's table in room 5 (see fig. 7.8), he and I
were being consumed by mosquitos; he decided to light a fire in the corner of the room and smoke them out. Feeling the effect of the smoke my-

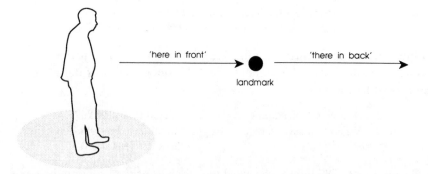

Speaker's corporeal schema

Fig. 9.2. Landmark frame of *way e?* 'here (near side to ego)'.

self, I wondered whether he thought it would waft into room 7, where his infant was sleeping in the hammock. No, he said, he didn't think so,

(37)   čeén puro **way** bey o?, má?ateč
            'Just only here like that, no way.' (BB.4.29)

In other situations, the DLOC is properly used to refer to the entire single family home, as in (38), which also occurred in room 5 of Lol's house.

(38)   WH: hay p'eé kwàartos yàan **way** → bwéno
             'How many rooms are there her— well,'

       Lol: **way e?** ↑
             'Here?'

       WH: hàah
             'Yeah.'

       Lol: **way e?** ?oóšp'ée kwàarto →   ?oóšp'é kwàarto ten i? →
             'Here, (there are) three rooms. Three rooms of mine.'

             ?oóš p'ée t in sukú?un o?
             Three of my elder brother's.' (F.137.A.465)

Lol carefully distinguishes here between his own portion of the *soólar* and that of his brother Man, whose house actually adjoins his (about one foot away from where we are sitting) but is nonetheless beyond the relevant 'here'.

First-time visitors to the homes of DC and Lol often mistakenly go to Man's door in search of them, only to be informed by his wife Margot that it is 'the other house'. She routinely tells them:

(39)   má⁷ **way e**⁷ → té⁷ tulaá⁷ ump'é nah **o**⁷
             'Not here.   Over there at the other house.' (F.137.B.0ĺ5)

Sitting with DC in room 10 (see fig. 7.8), he told me about a patient who had just left after having her infant treated. He quoted himself, telling me that he had told her:

(40)   ká tawil e k'ohá⁷anil o⁷,   déser ahaán tàas **way** ká⁷ač **e**⁷
             'When you saw that sickness, you should have brought him here
                                          right way.' (BB.4.95)

In this utterance, DC lightly chastised the woman for not promptly bring-ing the child to him for treatment. The bold face DLOC refers not to the entire walled homestead, since she could not have received care at either Man's or Lol's places, but precisely to DC's house, where the utterance occurred.

No less common are uses of *way e*⁷ 'here' in reference to the entire walled *soólar* in which the speaker finds himself or herself. Such tokens pass over the internal segmentation of domestic zones and totalize the second-level place as a unitary whole. Sitting in Man's house and explain-ing the fact that the plot of land on which he and his sons live belongs to them, DC said:

(41)   le lú⁷um **way** a⁷, máa tupaáhtal utàal č'aáb' i⁷
             'This land here can't just come and be taken away.' (BB.4.65)

What he was saying was that the whole place is owned by him and his sons. Lol made the same spatial reference on another occasion, when, also at Man's table, he recounted to me his comings and goings around Oxkutzcab that day. Finishing up with his return to the household, he uttered (42):

(42)   ká sùun ahen tàal **way e**⁷
             'then I turned around to come back here.' (BB.4.78)

Note that it was not to his current location that Lol returned exactly but to his own house next door. His deictic reference resolves this discrepancy by including both houses within the totality of the yard. I asked him if it would be equally acceptable to use the Immediate DLOC *té⁷el a*⁷ 'right here' instead of *way e*⁷, and he responded that it would be understood to refer to the very table we were sitting at. I then asked about *té⁷el o*⁷ '(right) there', which he said would convey that he had returned to DC's house next door or elsewhere in the yard. Finally, I asked if he could have used the Exclusive form *tol o*⁷ 'out there', and he told me:

(43)   **tol o**ʔ kawáʔaleh,   čeén wá túʔuš ič solàar oʔ
            ' "Out there" were you to say, (it's) just anywhere out in the yard.'
                                    (BB.4.78)

Rather than maintain the entire homestead as its referential frame, this
utterance would index the inner space of the room in which we were talking, in respect to which the rest of the yard can be treated properly as
'outside.' It differs from *téʔel oʔ,* the Non-Immediate 'there', in that it
lacks the specificity of reference to a coresident house. Example (43) illustrates what I call the 'throwaway' use of the Exclusive, to which we
will return presently.

Early on in my fieldwork, I tried to ask DP how large his yard was,
where we were working. I erroneously used the Immediate DLOC *téʔel aʔ*
'right here', eliciting a correction:

(44)   WH: hay ȼ'àak yàan **téʔel a**ʔ
             'How many mecates (of land) are there here?'

       DP: le wá ti e **way a**ʔ ↓
             '(You mean) This one here?'

             le wá tiʔ e soólar aʔ ↓
             'This one yard (we're in)?' (16.B.543)

As we shall see, the problem with my utterance is that the DLOC I chose is
not typically used to refer to whole social regions, as the Inclusive one is.
Several months later, as we were talking in the living quarters of a local
hacienda, where DP occasionally worked as caretaker, he explained to me
that his responsibility consisted in staying there in case anything came up.

(45)   le ʔaásyèendá aʔ, **way** yanen eʔ
            '(As for) this hacienda, I'm here.' (29.A.48)

Seven years later, as we sat in his new house in the same *soólar* as in (44)
(area III on the map in fig. 7.5), DP referred to the place in the same
terms again.

(46)   komo **way e**ʔ yàan túʔuš inmeyah **way e**ʔ → . . . **way ič**
            Since here, there's places for me to work here . . . here in

            insoólar nàaȼ' eʔ
            my solar nearby.' (BB 5.34)

The discourse context for (46) was a contrast between DP's land and a
plot nearby which he was preparing to plant. He had waited fruitlessly
that day for Feliz to come with the tractor to plow the rows. But he was
able to work productively while waiting, since he had other things to do

'around here'. The first two tokens of 'here' refer to the *soólar* as a whole (area III of fig. 7.5). The spot referred to by the third token, however, where he had actually spent the day, was on the far side of the *soólar* from where we were at the time of utterance, about 100 yards away through the orchard (nearer to the marsh). Why does he not switch to the typically segmenting DLOC *té?el o?* '(right) there', which would also reflect the distance? I think the answer lies in the fact that the work site to which he refers is within the limits of DP's land, between us and the plot he hopes to plow. Schematically, the first two tokens mobilize the perimetral 'here' of figure 9.1, and the last token either the same one or the landmark schema shown in figure 9.2

In addition to the demarcated zones of domestic and agricultural frame spaces, the Inclusive 'here' is used to refer to the less precisely bounded region in which the speaker routinely circulates. This includes the neighborhood or town along with its main pathways and landmarks, as in Margot's reference to the public clinic in Oxkutzcab as *way e?* 'here' in contrast to the towns of Mani and Ticul. We were in her home at the time, and having established Oxkutzcab as her frame, she went on to indicate the direction of the clinic, saying *té?el a?* 'right there', with a point (BB.4.138). Riding in the back of a truck along the road out of Cooperativa, Bert and a friend were assisting other passengers as they got off at their stops by passing their belongings down to them. Coming to a crossroad leading towards Yaaxhom, the truck stops, and Bert's friend gets down, saying as he does:

(47)   pwes **way** ten e? →
            'Well, here ('s where) I (get off).' (BB.5.4)

This utterance makes reference to the general zone of the crossroads, where the speaker habitually gets off the truck, a fact known by the driver. It conveys in effect, 'It's my turn here (to get off the truck)', with the first person reference contrasting the speaker with all the other people who had already disembarked or would do so further along the road.

Given the right context, more extensive regions still make proper referential objects of *way e?*. In contrast to the United States, DC refers to Yucatán as 'here' and then goes on to segment a particular town up the road from us in (48):

(48)   WH: kuyuúčul le k'ohá?anil o? tak ti? tó?on té?el o?
               'That illness occurs even among us there (in U.S.).'

        DC: **way e?** →   té? Mayapan o?, tinwilah . . .
               '(Around) here, over there in Mayapan, I saw ↑ ' (BB.4.120)

In shifting from the more extensive frame of reference to the more specific segmentation of it, DC plays out a very common discourse pattern, which can be summarized as 'establish a region and then segment it'. If we ignore the shift in frame of reference established by the contrast between 'us' in the United States and the 'here' of Yucatán, then we are led to infer that this exchange equates Mayapan with the United States, since the same DLOC is used to designate both. This absurd inference fails to account for the fact that Mayapan is within the regional scope of DC's *way e?*, but the United States is not. On the other hand, when contrasting the earthly world to that of the spirits, speakers use this same form, including the whole terrestrial world within its referential scope.[6]

(49)   tó?on **way** yanó?on **way** tulú?um **e?**
              'Us, we're here,   here on the earth.' (F.17.606)

Taken together, examples (27–49) illustrate the entire range of typical extensions of the Inclusive DLOC *way e?*. They demonstrate that this linguistic form routinely articulates with the culturally defined schemata that were described in ethnographic terms in chapters 7 and 8. This implies that all Inclusive spatial reference is relatively presupposing in the sense developed by Silverstein (1976b, 1979, 1985), since utterances link up with previously established spatiotemporal divisions. On the other hand, the very fact that the entire array of perimetral schemata can be mobilized for reference imposes upon speakers the choice among frames. The choice, and the possibility (if not unavoidability) of shifting frames during discourse, is the source of many 'creative' or 'entailing' acts of reference. With the exception of the 'near side/far side of landmark' uses, all of the ones that native speakers cite as typical, and in fact perform daily, are interpreted as characterizing recognized sociocultural places. Starting with bodily space and leading through cardinal locations, walled-in domestic and agricultural spaces, regions of routine experience, out to the earthly world as a whole, all of these uses turn on a division between the speaker's current location and some place **outside** it. The special link between this DLOC and the egocentric zone of the speaker is evidenced also in a tendency for the form to co-occur with first person participant deictics in the same clause, explicitly binding the place to the speaker (cf. 29, 30, 34, 38, 45, 46, 47, and 49 above). These examples all totalize the Ecogentric Inclusive zone, rather than segmenting it or picking out successive points along trajectories. In terms of the other spatiotemporal orientations, *way e?* defines a perimetral schema (cf. fig. 8.8), not a directional one (cf. fig. 8.11). This raises an interesting question as to why it should be that the perimetral schema is centered on egocentric space, whereas, as we shall see below, the directional is centered on the social ground of an interaction.

9.2.1.2 *Exclusive: 'There' beyond the Perimeter*

The referential range of the Egocentric Exclusive deictic *tol o?* '(out) there', is the complement of *way e?*, namely, the relatively boundless space beyond the limit of the current here. It varies in extent just the way the Inclusive form does, with the added feature that *tol o?* commonly fails to identify any unique place at all. This is the 'throwaway' use, which conveys nonspecificity and absence of visual access. The referential use of *tol o?* can be represented as figure 9.3, where the speaker's corporeal schema (on the left) is removed from, or excluded by, the place referred to (shown on the right). Nonreferential, throwaway uses rest on the same schema but lack any specific referential space.

Wherever an actor finds himself or herself, *tol o?* 'out there' is elsewhere. It rarely makes sense to summon another person to this space using the egocentric imperative, as in *kó?oten tol o?* 'Come (to me) out there.' The only possible interpretations for this peculiar utterance entail indexical transpositions. It could be heard as a directive to the addressee

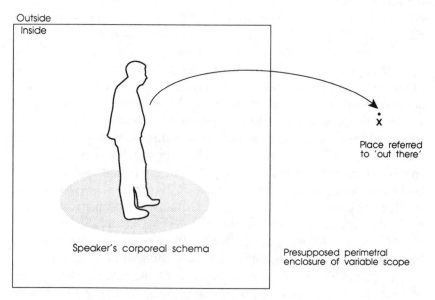

Fig. 9.3. Perimetral frame of *tol o?* '(out) there (Exclusive of ego)'.

to meet the speaker at some distinct location apart from the place of utterance. This would involve a transposed indexical ground for the imperative, meaning roughly 'Come (to me when I am elsewhere).' Alternatively, it could be construed as a transposed DLOC usage, making reference to the speaker's actual location from the perspective of some other person or place. Either way, Maya speakers consider the phrase weird or nonsensical, and I have never noticed it used spontaneously. In general, this DLOC is very rarely paired with a first person reference the way the Inclusive form is, tending to rule out collocations such as, # *tol t inw iknal o ?* 'out there in my place', # *tí ?an en tol o ?* 'I'm out there', # *tàas ten tol o ?* 'bring it to me out there', and so forth (cf. corresponding examples with *way e ?*). Such utterances could be interpreted assuming implicit transpositions of the indexical ground, with 'my place' referring not to where I am but to my homestead, or 'me' referring not to me at the time of utterance but to me in the past or future. While it would be false to say that such forms do not occur, therefore, they are surely atypical.

Any place outside the speaker's current corporeal and actional frame can be referred to as 'out there'. This begins with the initially perplexing cases of *tol o ?* in reference to places metrically very close to the speaker, such as the far end of a hammock or the far end of a door jamb, as illustrated in the utterances of Margot, cited in §8.4.3. In such cases, the assumed frame of reference is contracted down to a single object, with its two extreme ends polarized into a 'near side' (implicit *way e ?*) and a 'far side' *tol o ?*.

Back at the work site where we were digging irrigation ditches, DP was seated beside me on the north bank of the canal we had just dug out (see figs. 3.5 and 3.6 with discussion). Addressing me, he made reference to the far end of the canal, approximately twenty-five meters from us.

(50)   b'ey šan le kutàa **to** šùul o ? →
         'Also the one (canal) that comes from the end over there.' (BB.5.32)

In immediately prior discourse, DP had been discussing more proximal sections of the canal, and this utterance has a slightly contrastive function. Still, it is the fact of its being the far extremity of the canal that motivates DPs phrasing. Showing me how to hoe a corn row properly several days later, he made the same kind of reference to the far end, this time about twenty meters away.

(51)   ?ésale → ?ásta uhoók'o **to** tušùul o ?
         'Right (that's it), until it comes out over there at the end.' (BB.5.58)

It is important to appreciate that in these cases the referent of the DLOC is perfectly visible, and sometimes even tactually available to the speaker. Although they are not rare in conversation, such uses are not considered typical by native speakers, who even tend to reject equivalent examples if they are offered to them in the abstract. For speakers, one of the core features of this form is that its referent is not in sight, a corollary of its being characterized as outside the speaker's corporeal frame.[7]

When making reference to one area of a single-family household from the vantage point of another, *tol o?* is one of the appropriate deictics, especially if there is an intervening wall or other visual obstruction. Sitting at the table in room 1 late at night (fig. 7.8), Margot told me that a mouse we had chased during the day had come back out of the wall and gotten up on the table. I knew there were two tables in the house, the one we were sitting at and another in room 2, in darkness at the time.

(52)   Mrg: naák e č'o? yoó? mèesa
                'The mouse got on the table.'

        WH: le ti e mèesa hé?el a? ↑
                'This table here?'

        Mrg: má? ↓ **tol o?** ↓
                'Nope. Over there.' (BB.4.143)

Margot's choice of DLOC indexes a complex frame of reference that includes the binary contrast between the two tables, the perceptual and social boundary between room 1 and room 2, and the discourse contrast between my Ostensive Evidential reference to 'this' table and her maximally distanced reference to the other one.

The next level of inclusion in domestic space, beyond the single-family household, is the joining of two or more households within the same walled *soólar*. We called this a 'second-level' household in §7.4. This constitutes a larger whole subdivided by parts, each owned by a male head (usually father and sons). Just as one's own plot is a 'here', the adjacent plot within the same *soólar* makes a proper *tol o?* 'over there'. This is especially so when an act of reference identifies a place in the backyard of the next home. Back at the familiar table in room 1 with Man, I told him of how I had spent part of the day digging stones from a pit in the yard (see fig. 7.8). We then had the exchange in (53).

(53)   Man: tú?uš tahoó?sah tùunič ?
                'Where did you take out the stones?'

        WH: té?el o?
                'There.' (pointing towards east)

Man: ʔah **tol** oʔ
        'Oh, out there.' (BB.4.74)

It was late at night, and the yard was in darkness; the pit to which we referred was on the far side of a group of trees, on the far side of the boundary line of Man's own property and close to the area where residents defecate. These aspects of the relation between referent and indexical ground establish the schematic boundaries that motivate Man's preference for the Exclusive DLOC over the Non-Immediate.[8]

Household members very commonly refer to the adjacent *nah* 'house (main sleeping structure)' with which they share the *soólar* as simply *tol oʔ* 'over there'. Recall Marg's practice of fending off DC's visitors while he is eating in her house (see chap. 3), telling one young man who arrived at the door:

(54)   šén **tol** oʔ → taán uyuk'ul, šeén **to** ič nah oʔ
           'Go over there. He's having supper, go over there in the house.'
           (BB.4.129)

Similarly, DC refers to his own house as *tol oʔ* 'over there' when speaking in room 1 in Man's house, next door.

(55)   WH: yan wá teč le čamal oʔ?
             'You got the cigarettes?'

       DC: tíʔan **tol** oʔ
             'They're over there.' (BB.4.75)

As he uttered the response in (55), DC tossed his head in the direction of his house. He had left the cigarettes on his altar in room 10. All of these uses presuppose the socially constituted boundaries between coresident houses within the same *soólar*.

The next more inclusive frame in sociocultural terms is the extended 'third-level' household, encompassing all inhabited space under the authority of a senior head and his (or, less commonly, her) sons. This typically includes parcels of land at some distance from one another, as in the DP family holdings labeled I–IV in figure 7.5. Sitting in Eli's kitchen in area I, I explained to Pilar's ten-year-old daughter that I had slept the last night at her grandfather's house (area III, about 500 meters down the road). She laughed mischievously and assured me that spooks would come awaken me 'over there'.

(56)   yàan atàal ahsbi **tol** oʔ ⌢ mèen h waáy
           'You're gonna come awakened over there, . . . by a witch!'
           (BB.5.7)

Several days later, Pilar and I were talking in the courtyard of area I about the orchard in area III. She remarked that she and VC used to live over there,

(57)   tíʔanóʔon **to** káʔač **o**ʔ
             'We used to be (live) over there.' (BB 5.42)

This way of formulating reference to area III was typical for Pilar and occurred on other occasions as well (BB.5.65).

The set of uses that native speakers appear to consider the most typical of this form are the ones in which the referent can be described as *naáč* 'far away'. In (58), the milpa to which Is's father refers is about twenty-five kilometers out of town, where we were, a place to which he and Is travel by truck and stay sometimes for up to a week during peak work times.

(58)   **to** ič kòol **o**ʔ → naáč
             'Out there in the milpa, it's far away.' (BB.4.98)

The hill forest behind MC and VC's household (fig. 7.6) is far removed from the living space in the sense of being wild, unprotected, and uninhabited. This is all the more true from the perspective of MC's wife, Eli, who used to go into the forest to gather firewood prior to the birth of her youngest child six months earlier. We were planning to go out for wood together with the boys one day when she explained to me that she hadn't been doing so recently, saying:

(59)   E: máa čimbʼin siʔ
                 'I don't (really) go for firewood.'

             W: mát awáal ten yàan abin ↓
                 'Didn't you tell me you're going?'

             E: niŋkáʔa → pero máa čimbin **to** naáč **o**ʔ
                 'I am going, but I don't really go far out there.' (BB 5.48)

Eli's second utterance makes clear that what she intends to convey is that she does not usually go out into the forest for wood; she subsequently explained that she usually gathered dead wood from the orchards in front of the house. The absence of routine familiarity with the referent, along with its being off in the woods, motivate her choice of DLOC.[9]

Another usage that native speakers consider exemplary is what I have called throwaway *tol o*ʔ. The distinctive characteristic of this usage is that the speaker conveys that (s)he doesn't really know where the place referred to is. That is, unlike most acts of demonstrative reference, this type fails to individuate any specific object and conveys, on the contrary, that such individuation is impossible or irrelevant. You heave a piece of rotten fruit over the trees into the woods to be rid of it and report this act as:

(60)   timpiík'č'intah wá tú?uš **tol o**?
         'I chucked it somewhere out there.'

Recall Lol's gloss on this form as *čeén wá tú?uš ?ič soólar* 'just anywhere in the yard', in (43) above. This is consistent with glosses elicited from DP, Balim, and VI over several years, in which they affirmed that one who localizes an object as *tol o*? is really conveying that (s)he does not know where it is or is unwilling to tell the addressee. As a hypothetical response to a where question, this DLOC is judged uninformative, and DP actually told me that it is used for things *pulb'il* 'thrown away' (F.17.A.297; 119.A.490).

On other occasions, the same individuals have affirmed that the speaker who uses *tol o*? must in fact know where the referent is and so must the addressee (F.16.A.268; 122.A.640; DC spoken 7/7/82). The reasoning here is that the DLOC itself gives little or no indication of the place, and therefore in order to preserve the assumption that the speaker is being reasonable, one must assume that (s)he knows where it is, assumes the addressee knows too, and simply leaves it unstated. This Gricean scenario is in fact what is going on in most of the foregoing examples, where quite specific places are identified with the Exclusive DLOC, such as the house next door or the far end of a hammock. Routine, shared experience in a place provides a background frame space of symmetric knowledge that interactants rely on. The common ground is particularly necessary with this DLOC, since perceptual and other immediate forms of access to the referent are missing. Because it presupposes preestablished frames, furthermore, the form is ill suited for use in introducing new spatial segmentations in discourse, a function carried mainly by the Sociocentric DLOCs (see §9.2.2).

The relation between the throwaway uses and the fully referential ones is therefore a matter of knowledge and prior experience more than of physical space. Since it is defined negatively as outside the zone of interaction, the referential space of *tol o*? is boundless and nonspecific unless incremented by common background knowledge. To put it in graphic terms, the referential space on the right of figure 9.3 can be specified only on the basis of indexically engaged symmetric knowledge of the sociocultural surround. In the absence of that horizon, there is no canonical frame of spatial reference and no individuated referent.

The two Egocentric DLOCs *tol o*? and *way e*? form an equipollent opposition in the semantic system of Maya. I am aware of no linguistic contexts in which the distinction is neutralized, nor is either form (impressionistically) more frequent in discourse than the other. A referential region either includes or excludes the speaker dichotomously, and there is rarely, if ever, a possibility of interchanging the two. The forms are never combined in a single reference, although each may be paired with other DLOCS (see below), and combination is generally productive in the deictic system (yielding a repertoire of deictic constructions far outnumbering the basic lexicon). The gestures routinely used with the two DLOCS are almost exactly inverse: hand held palm down, flicked inward and downward towards the speaker looking straight ahead for the Inclusive form; hand held palm down flicked outward and upward away from the speaker, simultaneously turning the line of vision away from the trajectory of the hand, for the Exclusive. No other deictic is associated with either of these gestures, nor are the forms ever switched so that the Inclusive lexical item gets the Exclusive gesture or the Exclusive word gets the Inclusive gesture.

In discourse practice, however, both Egocentric DLOCS enter into pragmatic contrasts with other deictics as well. We have seen several of these, starting with Margot's contrast between a hammock *té?el a?* 'right here' in the next room of her house and another one *tol o?* 'over there' in DC's house in the same *soólar* (BB.4.60; see §8.4.3). Shortly later she contrasted her house as a whole *way e?* 'here' with DC's as a whole *tol o?* 'over there' (BB.4.67). In (52) she opposed the table we were sitting at, which I had characterized as *hé?el a?* 'right here', to the one *tol o?* 'over there' in the next room. The Maya equivalent of English 'this and that' as a summary report of speech is *ké bey a? ké tol o?* 'that like this, that over there' (BB.4.10). Similarly, *way e?* 'here' enters into contrast in speech with the Non-Immediate form *té?el o?* 'there', as in example (39), where Margot contrasts her house with the adjoining one, and (48), where DC contrasts the United States with Yucatán. Such contrasts arising in discourse are not motivated by the structural oppositions of the categories alone, or the frames they correspond to, but by these factors joined with an interactively produced indexical framework. It matters, for instance, whether in fact one pole in a contrast is regional or relatively punctual, familiar to the addressee, or newly presented, regardless of the features of the other pole. Inclusive vs. Exclusive and Tactual vs. Visual are minimal oppositions, whereas speakers often cut nonminimal contrasts such as Exclusive vs. Tactual. This merely reflects their ability to shift attention focus among frames in the space of possibilities, to transpose indexical centers and referential targets, thereby expanding the universe of their discourse.

9.2.2 Sociocentric Points and Directions

While both the Inclusive and Exclusive deictics are paired with egocentric grounds, in relation to which they refer to perimetralized regions, the Immediate and Non-Immediate forms are paired with sociocentric grounds, in relation to which they segment points and places of restricted extent. While the egocentric forms refer to whole regions, the sociocentric ones focus on successive relations among points on a situationally defined scale of relative immediacy. Like the relative and fixed values of the cardinal directions in Maya (see §7.2), spatial deictics therefore also incorporate both perimetral and directional schemata. One difference is that whereas a single set of cardinal terms enters into both uses, the two are categorially distinguished in the deictics. The schema corresponding to the sociocentric space of *té'el a'* 'right here' is shown in figure 9.4, in which the indexical ground is the relation between speaker and addressee, and the referential object is one of a scatter of alternative possible points instead of a region with a perimeter.

The independence of the sociocentric deictics from the speaker's corporeal schema is clear in the range of fully proper uses of these forms. Whereas neither *way e'* 'here' nor *tol o'* 'out there' may be used to segment the speaker's own body, both *té'el a'* 'right here' and *té'el o'* '(right) there' may be so used. Furthermore, both of the latter forms are used to individuate places **in contrast to** the speaker's current location but still within the (roughly) proximal zone. Instead of the inward vs. out-

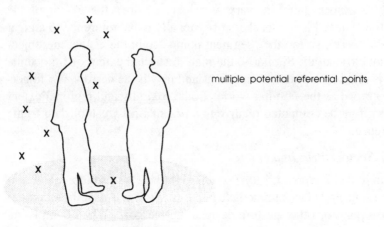

multiple potential referential points

Sociocentric *'iknal* of participants,
weighted towards Speaker

Fig. 9.4. Punctual frame of *té'el a'* 'there (Sociocentric, Immediate)'.

ward full-hand gestures of the egocentric forms, the sociocentric ones, especially the Immediate member of the pair, are canonically accompanied by pointing gestures. This is indicative of two things: (i) without a preestablished link to the speaker's corporeal schema, the gesture is necessary to further identify where the referent is; and (ii) gestures are communicative only if perceived, which implies that the interlocutors must already share a perceptual field at the time of utterance. This means that the sociocentric forms, especially the Immediate one, tend *not* to be used in situations where interactants are separated by perceptual barriers. When pointing out the cardinal directions relative to an actional ground, it is the sociocentric forms that are used, since these are functionally suited to successive, directional orientation rather than absolute location. The forward path, goal of motion, and places anticipated are treated as Immediate, while ground already covered, the source of motion and places recalled, are Non-Immediate. Neither of these successive relations is characterized with egocentric regional expressions, which index where the speaker is at the moment, not where (s)he was or will be. Finally, the Immediate form tends to be the one used for introducing new spatial segmentations into the discourse, while the Non-Immediate form maintains already established referents.

Acts of punctual, sociocentric reference usually take place in communicative situations whose relevant perimeters are already defined. Given a sense of their current placement relative to surrounding boundaries, speakers can then go on to individuate points within regions. The different degrees of metrical proximity associated with Immediate and Non-Immediate frames therefore vary as widely as does the extent of the perimetral frame. Just as speakers occasionally make reference to a great expansive 'here', so too they segment points 'right there' that are objectively not close at all. Similarly, the more restricted extent of Immediate 'there' is relative to practical situations and may be as narrow as a fingertip or as broad as the familiar world. Both proximity and regional extent must therefore be computed relative to a pragmatically established frame of reference.

9.2.2.1 *Sociocentric Immediate*

As a summons, *kó?oten té?el a?* 'come right here' is used to call an addressee to specific places immediate to the speaker. It is usually accompanied by a point or other gesture designating the goal. When contrasting this phrase to the corresponding one with *way e?*, DP and VI consistently claimed that the *té?el a?* form can be properly used only if the interactants are **already** close together prior to the utterance. If the directive issues from the other side of a major boundary, the preferred form is with *way e⁷*. This pattern reflects the distinction between sociocentric and egocentric reference. For example, DP was in the kitchen hut of his house in area II, while I was in the main *nah* room adjoining the kitchen (see fig. 7.7). He called me to the table for lunch, saying, without eye contact or prior discussion:

(61)   **té⁷** atàal **a⁷** wiíl → kó⁷oš hana
           'Come right here Will. Let's eat.' (BB.5.22)

He proceeded to offer me a seat next to him at the table. It is significant to DP's utterance that it was not his own seat he was offering me, since if it were, his deictic reference would have been phrased in egocentric terms (cf. 27, 28). Further, we were both in the house, albeit in different rooms, waiting for lunch prior to his utterance.

When I was discussing the relation between *-iknal* 'body space' and the DLOCs with VI, we came up with a hypothetical scenario in which a man brings a package to the speaker, who must tell him where to place it. According to VI, one says *tàas té⁷ t inw iknal a⁷* 'Bring it here by me', with a point, provided the man is close by at the moment of address. If he is still twenty meters or so off, then the proper phrasing is *tàas way t inw iknal e⁷* 'Bring it here to me.' No gesture is necessary, since the Adr is still far away, and the locative phrase in any case refers to the speaker's bodily space. I then asked VI whether one could say *ȼ'taá way t inw iknal e⁷* 'Put it here where I am' to a delivery man who was already close at hand, say at the door to the room. The man would question the spatial reference, VI said, because he would know better than to put the package *right on* the speaker, but this is just what he would have been told to do. The speaker would have to add *té⁷el a⁷, té⁷el o⁷* 'Right here, (or) there' to clarify (F.123.A.250).

On the other hand, *kó⁷oš té⁷el a⁷* 'let's go here' is a perfectly routine utterance, used to lead an addressee along a path. This would not be possible if the referent were unavoidably linked to the speaker's location, since he would already be 'here', rather than on his way. Glossing *kó⁷oš té⁷el a⁷*, DP made the observation in (62).

(62)   ⁷óli b'ey ka⁷iínbitàarte → . . . teč e⁷ ⁷awohe tú⁷uš
           'It's sort of like you invite him. You, you know where

           ken ab'is i⁷ → leti⁷ e⁷ má⁷ uyòohl i⁷
           you're gonna take him. Him, he doesn't know.' (F.16.A.247)

So unlike the Inclusive 'here', where a speaker **is,** the Immediate 'here' is a place to which (s)he can **go.** DP has put his finger on the main basis of contrast between the Immediate DLOC, ending in *a⁊*, and the two DLOCS ending in *o⁊*, *té⁊el o⁊* and *tol o⁊*, both of which also co-occur with the imperative 'let's go.' The Immediate form indexes an asymmetric knowledge of the referent—the speaker is taking the addressee to a place which only (s)he can identify. The systematic interplay between new information and already-shared knowledge is a dimension to be taken up in detail below. At this point, I wish to foreground the difference between *way e⁊* and *té⁊el a⁊*, since not only do they refer to places of different extent, but they presuppose quite different indexical frames: the question of whether interactants share knowledge of the place referred to only arises because this place must be **sociocentrically** specified in the interaction. This in turn is a consequence of its not being egocentric by convention.

Not being tied to the corporeal schema as a whole, *té⁊el a⁊* is the preferred DLOC for segmenting this space into points and small regions. One speaker asks another whether (s)he has any money, as they prepare to depart for the market,

(63)   A: kuš tuún seéntavo
        'What about money?'

        B: yàan **té⁊el a⁊**
        'There's some right here' (tapping change in pocket). (7/9/82)

In this exchange, which I witnessed, the referent was the microspace of B's pocket, flat on his thigh, indicated by touch and an audible gesture. Demonstrating the unit of measure called a 'quarter', DP extended the thumb and index finger of one hand and touched each tip in succession with the index finger of his other hand, saying:

(64)   bey a⁊ ⁊ump'eé kwàartoh, **té⁊el a⁊** tak **té⁊el a⁊**
            'Like this, a quarto (is) right here to right here.' (7/9/82)

When Maya speakers complain of bodily aches and pains, the most proper DLOC for localizing the pain is the Immediate one, as in (65), in which a woman explains to DC how her husband hurt his leg, demonstrating on her own:

(65)   mèn le hé⁊el a⁊ . . . bey tún uúčih **té⁊e** bey a⁊
            cause this thing, . . . So then it happened right here like this.'
            (BB.4.9)

With the same motivation, this is the DLOC used to refer precisely to an object in hand, as in DC's instructions to the same woman as he handed her a small packet of herbal medicine minutes later.

(66)   DC: káʔap'é kén ahoóʔs **téʔel aʔ** → tayik ↑
        'Two (baths) you're gonna get out of (this) here, got it?'

    Wm: ʌhʌʌ →
        'Ahah.' (BB.4.10)

In all of the preceding examples, corporeality is in play as a frame space
of possible points, but the referential foci picked out are actually distinct
from the corporeal frame of the actor.

It is within the typical range of *téʔel aʔ* also to segment places within
frames more extensive than bodily space, including the home or work
site. Working with VC and me at the site of the irrigation ditches discussed in §3.5, DP remarked that it would be easy to open up another
small canal in a place right before him, currently covered by weeds. DP
addressed us, from about four meters behind VC and in front of me, looking directly at the spot where he intended to open another canal, saying:

(67)   máʔ ⇀ má abèetk ulaák' kaána **téʔ** wá ak'aát **aʔ** →
        'Hah! Couldn't ya make another canal right there if ya wanted to?'
        (Sure you could!) (BB.5.32)

His deictic reference to the location of a potential ditch illustrates well the
individuation of a restricted focus upon a background of possibilities
available to interactants. Relative to the current framework of our engagement, the reference is novel—the spot he denoted was not among the
ones we were working on—rather than maintaining a focus we already
shared. This fact, along with DP's status asymmetry, motivates his choice
of DLOCs.

On a separate occasion, Lol and I were sitting in his house (I in room 5,
he in room 6 about two meters away within view; cf. fig. 7.8), when I
asked him if he had seen Victor, his younger brother. Lol responded that
he hadn't seen him, because:

(68)   máʔ luk'en **téʔel aʔ**
        'I haven't left right here.' (BB.4.36)

He was sitting at his sewing machine at the time, and his utterance conveyed that he had continued working, never leaving the precise place
where he was at the time. When recounting the story of how he and his
brother had moved back to their father's *soólar* 'yard', Lol produced another apt illustration of the Immediate DLOC used to individuate a specific
place within the broader expanse of domestic space.

(69)   kuȼ'ó?ol e? → ká tàaló?on bey **way** o?, ká t?á?al e yan
            'In the end, then we returned here, like I say, and we said, "We're
            gonna

            kbèetk ump'eé nah **té?el a**? →
            make a house right there."' (F.137.A.389)

In (69), *way e?* bears the same relation to *té?el a?* that the entire three-
family yard bears to the piece of ground on which Lol's house is built
(cf. chap. 7, (9)).

DP explained years earlier how he would confront strangers were he to
find that they had entered his yard without an invitation. Finding them
lurking by the door, he would approach them and ask:

(70)   b'á?an kakaštik **té?el a**? →   maáš   ?á?al teč ká ?òokeč šan
            'What are you looking for there? And who told you to come in?'
            (F.119.A.137)

The locative reference cuts off from the surrounding household the specific
spot occupied by the intruder, while indexing the asymmetric relation between the interactants; it is DP who, as authorized head of household,
segments the reference space in word and act (walking to it, looking at it),
and demands a response.

Other uses of *té?el a?* make reference to places not physically immediate to the speaker but well within his or her routine experience. When one
is speaking in the home, the locations of neighbors make exemplary objects of Immediate deictic reference. Is's father was sitting in Is's house,
just around the corner from his own place. He was narrating to me how he
had come to live there, starting with the point at which he first moved in,
which he phrased:

(71)   taánt inmaán **té?el a**?
            'I (had) just come there.' (BB.4.98)

The Immediate DLOC neatly fits the indexical frame: the place referred to
is close by but does not include our current location; as addressee, I know
where he means, more or less, but we have never been there together, nor
were we already discussing the place. The reference makes a new individuation relative to an ongoing face-to-face conversation and rests on
asymmetric knowledge; therefore it is accomplished with *té?el a?*.

Talking around the house (see fig. 7.8), Man and Margot routinely
made reference to neighbors' places using the Immediate DLOC. Man arrived back from Mérida several days after a death had occurred at the
neighbor's across the road. Having been told by Margot of the event and

the public *velorio* 'vigil' celebrated at the house, he asked me whether many people showed up, saying:

(72)   ?áh→ čob'anah velòorio **té?el a?**
         'Oh, did the vigil get crowded there?' (BB.4.149)

On another occasion, Man was telling of a former neighbor who used to live around the block, but had since moved to another neighborhood.

(73)   tí?an **té?** yoók' ol eskìina i média kahakbaló?ob' ká?ač **a?**
         "There it is there at a block and a half they used to live.'
         (BB.4.100–101)

Whereas in (72) we both know the place Man refers to, right close by, in (73) he is making a first-time reference to a place I never saw and still could not locate. The former was performed without any accompanying gesture, whereas the latter was accompanied by a manual point. While the household in question was objectively a location, Man's reference functions partly as a directional in (73), 'over this way'.

A more complex example was produced by Lol in the course of explaining to me how he and Man had gathered the money necessary to purchase materials to build their house. They had sold their valuable possessions to neighbors:

(74)   ?insukú?un e?   tukonah ti e maestro tàal **waya? a** → . . .
         'My elder brother, he sold (a machine) to the teacher who comes
                                   here . . .

         ten e? tinkonah tiinbesìino yàan   **té?el a?** →
         Me, I sold to   my neighbor (who) is right here

         le ?estèerio   kupàaš **té?el o?** →
         the stereo that plays there.' (F.137.A.389–435)

What is most revealing about this example is the sequence of spatial references. The teacher across the way comes to visit the household as a whole, which is reflected in the Inclusive DLOC in the first line. Lol was referring for the first time to the neighbor in the second line, individuating him apart from the teacher and from his own household. Note that the second and third lines are a single sentence with two relative clauses, and that the two DLOCs, despite their formal difference, are coreferential—the neighbor who is 'right here' is the one who plays the stereo 'there'. The motivating factor for the switch is obviously not the spatial relation, since it is the same place in both cases. It is this: the reference to the neighbor is contrastive and highly asymmetric, since I don't know who Lol is talking about; the relative clause of which 'the stereo' is head maintains coreference to the neighbor's place. It also invokes shared background knowledge, since we had been hearing the stereo play daily prior to this exchange (without my knowing that it had belonged to Lol).[10] The former is asymmetric and the latter symmetric, while both segment the place apart from our current location.

As an extension of the 'neighborly' uses of Immediate reference, places objectively quite distant can be treated referentially as if they were close at hand. DC was performing a *tííč'k'aák'* 'divination' for a woman who was trying to find her son, who had run away from home (see §7.4.3). DC was gazing into the crystals in silence with the woman sitting at his side. At one point, he asserted that the boy had headed south, then moments later that he was at a place called Plan Chac, an irrigation zone on the south side of town (about 5 kilometers away).

(75)   tíʔan le šíʔipa **téʔ** plančaák **aʔ**
            'The kid's right here at Planchac.' (108.A.511)

DC's reference is asymmetric, in that it presents a new localization, which he derived from looking at the crystals in his own hand. This helps motivate the choice of the Immediate DLOC.[11] Equally important is his reassurance to the woman that the boy has not gone far; he is 'right here' at the edge of town, rather than off at the Caribbean coast or lost in the forest. Sometimes speakers refer to places as far away as Quintana Roo, the neighboring state (formerly a territory, associated with high forest, fugitives, and danger; several hours away by bus), with the Immediate form, as in *téʔ teéritorió aʔ* 'right here in the territory'. While not infrequent, such uses are considered less than typical by native speakers, if asked out of context. VI, for example, explained that 'right here in the territory' is an acceptable phrase spoken in Oxkutzcab, but that it is 'adorned', whereas *téʔ teéritorió oʔ* is more suited to the geographical distance (F.122.A.524). The sense of 'adornment' apparently consists in presenting the territory as if it were right next door. In any case, these relatively remote uses of Immediate are not representative of its standard distance values, which are more proximal and more restricted in extent. In referring to the boy's location with *téʔel aʔ*, DC foregrounds its relative proximity compared to other alternatives in the frame space of reference.

Not all uses of *téʔel aʔ* 'right (t)here' pick out places, regardless of distance or extent. Two very common uses are based on directional and successive relations. The first is the routine use of this DLOC when pointing out the cardinal directions, as in (76):

(76)   té?el a? lak'in $\xrightarrow{}$ té?el a? šaman → té?el a? čik'in →
'There is east.   There is north.   There is west.

té?ela? nòohol →
There is south.'

As far as I know, no other demonstrative is ever used to point out cardinal directions in everyday Maya. In discourse contexts in which directionals are combined with deictics to pick out some particular place or path, either *té?el a?* or *té?el o?* may occur, depending upon other factors. Recall DA's question to me about whether MC had gone west yet:

(77)   ¢'úbin maánwel **té?** čikin **a?** ↑
'Has Manuel already gone westward?' (BB.5.62)

Among the factors motivating DA's choice of deictic are that we were in her house at the time, which is on the road that MC drives when heading west from town. Also, she is referring not to a specific place at the end of his road but to an entire succession of stops that he makes as he continues westward. Both of these factors help focus on the direction rather than the goal of MC's movement.

Whenever interactants are moving or anticipating movement, the forward path is referred to with the Immediate DLOC *té?el a?*, as in (78).

(78)   beh?òora kbin **té?el a?**
'We're going there right away.' (BB.1.104)

This utterance was addressed to me by the driver of a truck as we stopped briefly at a crossroad before resuming our trip towards my destination. I was in the back of the truck, he was in the cab, and he was assuring me that we would proceed shortly. We were about three kilometers from my destination, but the most relevant fact is that we were en route. The directional use of *té?el a?* is diagrammed in figure 9.5.

In the much smaller zones of domestic space, speakers walking from area to area in the house make the same directional usage. As DC walked from room 1 to room 4 in Man's house in search of a piece of firewood (see fig. 7.8), he told Man:

(79)   DC: p'ínč'ík ump'eé če? **té?el a?**
'Let me grab a piece of wood right here.'

Man: aháa ↓ yàan wá **té?el o?**
'Ahah, is there (some) there?' (BB.4.86)

DC's spatial reference is to his own forward path, the trajectory connecting him alone to his destination. Man, who is standing by the table in

Sociocentric *?iknal* of participants,
weighted towards Speaker

Fig. 9.5. Forward path of *té?el a?* '(t)here (Sociocentric, Immediate)'.

room 1, refers to the same goal but from an external perspective. He
shares fully in the knowledge of where DC is going but is himself stationary. Rather than segment a new place, his deictic maintains coreference
with DC's just preceding one. These factors in the indexical framework
motivate his switch from the Immediate to the Non-Immediate deictic;
from a focus on 'my destination' to 'a well-known and just mentioned
spot in the next room'.

I was sitting at a table in the courtyard of MC and VC's place (see
fig. 7.6), when Eli walked out of her kitchen, about fifteen feet away. She
said she was going to pick some *čáay* 'chaya' (a leafy green vegetable),
and I asked her where. She responded:

(80)   **té?el a?** → nah pìilar
              'Right here, at Pilar's.' (BB 5.46)

She pointed vaguely towards Pilar's kitchen as she uttered the deictic and
proceeded to walk towards her goal. A few days later I was sitting in the
same spot in the courtyard, and Eli was coming out of the kitchen carrying my lunch. The smoke and heat in the kitchen had driven me to try to
eat outside, but I was sitting in full sun at the moment; not a good solution. Coming out of the kitchen, Eli pointed to the shade at Pilar's wash-
basin and suggested I eat there, saying only:

(81)   **té?** bo?y **a?** → hač čokow k'ìin **té?el o?**
              'Here in the shade. The sun's really hot there.' (BB.5.61)

It is worth emphasizing that the washbasin was farther away from Eli
(about 20 feet) than I was at the time; yet she still referred to the basin

with the Immediate form, and to my location with the Non-Immediate. The difference is that she is en route to the former and introducing it as a new referent, whereas I am in my habitual place, already preestablished in the interactive field.[12]

Sitting at the same table on another occasion, I was addressed by Pilar's son Luis, who was standing next to Eli as she washed dishes in her habitual place. He told me there were pictures of me in his house, on the other side of the courtyard.

(82)   L: tí'an afòoto **té'el o'**
         'There's your photo there.'

      W: tú'uš → 'ič nah?
         'Where? in (the) house?'

      L: tí' i' → **té** yan **té'el a'**
         'Yup, there they are right here.' (BB.5.28)

Luis's first utterance refers to his house as a moderately remote place known by both of us. The remoteness consisted in the facts that the house was out of our field of vision and on the other side of the property divide between VC (Luis's father) and MC (Eli's husband). His second reference indexes quite a different pragmatic frame, since he had begun walking towards the house as he uttered it. It had become the goal of his movement. Note that this factor (location vs. forward path) overrides the division between first time and Anaphoric reference. On the basis of the latter, we would expect the *a'* form to precede the *o'* (cf. (79)).

In addition to its directional and restricted locational uses, *té'el a'* 'right here' is also consistently associated with the introduction of new information into the discourse. This has come up in several of the preceding examples, in combination with directionality and relative immediacy. Recall (62), in which DP asserts that the imperative *kó'oš té'el a'* 'let's go right here' is used when the speaker knows where (s)he is going, but the addressee does not. This asymmetry in participant knowledge is preparatory to the speaker's act of informing by pointing out a new direction or individuating a new referent as destination. The same utterance with the Non-Immediate *té'el o'* could convey that both interactants know where they are going, as a matter of common ground. When drawing maps of places, with pictures or words, new points are introduced as *té'el a'*, and already established ones are maintained as *té'el o'*. VI diagramed the road leading past his house:

(83)   lel a' kaáretèera tak tabi ↑ tí'anó'on **té'el a'**
        'This is (the) highway to Tabi. We're (living) right here.'
        (F.4.B.191)

Shortly later, having described the curve in the road just before his place, he realizes that I had not retained the information:

(84)   yàan ʔòora kuyoko bùus **téʔ** kùurbá **oʔ** →   **téʔ** kùurba awoh
            'Sometimes the bus enters there at the curve. There at the curve,
                                                                    ya know.

            tinwáʔa teč **téʔel aʔ** → lel aʔ čʼéʔen   lel aʔ tíʔ kùurbá eʔ
            I told ya right here.   This (is the) well. This, it's there at
            (the) curve.' (F.4.B.314)

The first boldface deictic pair indexes the symmetric ground of information preestablished in the discourse; it's the curve he's already talked about. The following deictics are coreferential, but they break out of the normal anaphoric chain to reestablish the referent as though for the first time. Right after the switch to the Immediate DLOC, he goes on to redefine the location of the curve yet again, in relation to the well, a landmark we both know. Thus the Non-Immediate form is preferred when the referent is being maintained as part of the common ground, and the Immediate is preferred when the referent is segmented for the first time or in order to introduce new information.[13]

In narrative accounts of site choice and the building of houses, the perimetral reference of Egocentric *way eʔ* 'here' is used to refer to the household site as a whole, and *téʔel aʔ* is used to individuate the locations of specific structures. DP's account shows a familiar pattern of reference.

(85)   pwes **way** kén inkʼaš inwotoč eʔ → **téʔel aʔ** → kʼoóbʼen →
            'So here's where I'll bind my house. Right here, (the) kitchen.'
            (BB.5.4)

We saw the same sequence of Egocentric Inclusive reference, establishing the overall frame, followed by segmenting Immediate reference, picking a spot within it, in example (69) above. Comparable uses are shown in (42, 43, 48, and 67) as well, where an Inclusive frame is established and then analyzed into a set of restricted parts. Just as the new informational uses of the Immediate form blend with the anticipation of the forward path, so too the segmenting function blends with high informational focus: objects are often individuated because they are new to the discourse or for the purpose of introducing new information about them.

These blends and associations between functions notwithstanding, some examples are less complex. In (86) Man has made reference to Mérida from Oxkutzcab (100 km distance). He cannot be framing it as a goal, since he has just returned and is not planning another trip for several weeks. He cannot be proposing to individuate Mérida as though it were a new referent, since we were already talking about it (a fact indexed by the deictic particle *laáyli* 'still'). What seems to be in play rather is the placement of the reference in initial position in a story, into which he launched as he said (86).[14]

(86)   sí tumèen yan ump'eé tinwilah   laáyli **tée** Ho? a?, . . .
            Yeah, because there's one(thing) I saw, still right here in
            Mérida, . . . (BB.4.156)

Given its introductory force, the conveyed meaning of (86) might be glossed as a presentative, 'Here's one I saw in Merida', although there are other more direct ways of saying this in Maya, using Ostensive Evidential forms.

Passengers riding in moving vehicles announce their desire to get off at an upcoming spot by using *té?el a?* 'right here'. Working her way through the crowded aisle of a bus, a woman hollers to the driver that she wants to get off *té?el a?*, meaning, roughly, as soon as he could stop the vehicle to let her off (BB.1.49). A large truck backing carefully into the narrow entrance to a yard inches along to avoid knocking down the stone wall or hitting a post. A man standing on the back of the truck watches intently and tells the driver when to stop, shouting:

(87)   **tée** ká wáalakéeš **a**?
            'Stop right there!' (BB.4.135)

And the driver responds by stopping short. These examples appear to combine the forceful announcement of new information, the place to stop at, with the anticipatory sense of the forward path, since the location is characterized as a destination.

In summary, the Immediate locative deictic has a spectrum of uses overlapping with both Inclusive *way e?* 'here' and Non-Immediate *té?el o?* '(right) there', yet clearly distinct from both of them. Unlike the Egocentric form, it can be used to segment both the speaker's own body and his or her immediate field of action. It can pick out the ground an intruder in the yard is standing on, a spot in the next room or in the neighborhood. Detached from the speaker's actual position in space, it is used in reference to the goal of his or her motion, to the forward path, and to places anticipated but not yet present. It is the deictic most closely associated with cardinal directional orientation, where the current framework is the ground out of which paths are defined as vectors with cardinal values. On the dimension of background knowledge and information in discourse, it is the DLOC most closely associated with presentation of new referents and descriptions. It is segmenting rather than totalizing, directional rather than just fixed, and foregrounding rather than backgrounding in discourse. Like other highly figural deictic categories, it tends to require an already ongoing face-to-face interaction, in which participants have a common perceptual field and mutual access at the time of utterance (Hanks 1989b). If this is lacking in the interactive framework, if the addressee is engaged in other things on the other side of the yard, then the potential for pinpointing objects cannot be implemented without further lexical description. The gestural corollary of this is that Immediate reference is typified for native speakers by the pointing finger. As Man remarked of one of his own utterances, referring to the neighbor's place as *té'el a'*, with a point:

(88)   k'ab'eét intuču'tik,   tumèen má' čuká'an i' →
          'I've got to point to it, because it's not complete (by itself),

          le dèedo le čukb'esik
          the finger (is what) makes it complete.' (BB.4.101)

9.2.2.2 *Sociocentric Non-Immediate*

The Non-Immediate deictic *té'el o'* '(right) there' shares with its Immediate counterpart the function of segmenting the proximal frame of reference. Both forms may point to places included within the regional scope of 'here', as VI put it:

(89)   té'el a', **té'el o'** laáyli way e'
          'Right here, there, they're still (around) here.'

This usage distinguishes the Sociocentric forms from the Egocentric ones: *way e'* can be used to indicate points in the proximal frame only clumsily and with further lexical description (e.g., *way yoó' mèesá e'* 'here on the table'),[15] while it cannot be used to segment the speaker's own body. Its basic uses are perimetral and landmark reference. *tol o'* is rarely used to refer to points in the immediate zone of the Spkr unless a very restricted frame of reference is already established, and it is never used to indicate parts of the body. Its range of reference starts outside the corporeal schema and preferably outside a sociocultural perimeter. Unlike *way e'* and *té'el a'*, *té'el o'* cannot be equated with the speaker's immediate bodily space; *kó'oten té'el o'* 'Come (to me) there' is not normally said and is judged weird by native speakers (F.1.A.101 DP; F.6.A.163 VI). Similarly, *té' t inw iknal o'* 'there in my place' is pragmatically odd, since it commits the speaker to being in two places at once; in his or her *-iknal* 'body space' right in front of the addressee and at a remove sufficient to motivate the Non-Immediate deictic. VI suggested

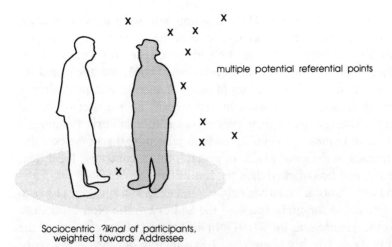

multiple potential referential points

Sociocentric *ʔiknal* of participants,
weighted towards Addressee

Fig. 9.6. Punctual frame of *téʔel oʔ* 'there (Sociocentric, Non-Immediate)'.

that it would be more correctly phrased *téʔ t inw otoč oʔ* 'there at my
house', indicating that the DLOC forces the 'home' rather than 'bodily
space' reading of *-iknal* (F.123.A.303). The spatial schema corresponding to Non-Immediate reference is the one in figure 9.6, which differs
from figure 9.4 in two details: (i) the relative remoteness of the points
standing for possible referents, and (ii) the foregrounding of the addressee
rather than the speaker. The second feature is motivated by the fairly consistent association between the 'there' of *téʔel oʔ* and the addressee's
location.

Like its Immediate counterpart, *téʔel oʔ* combines productively with
'let's go': *kóʔoš téʔel oʔ* 'let's go there.' However, whereas the Immediate form implies that the speaker alone knows where (s)he is going,
the Non-Immediate form implies that both interactants already know
(F.16.A.257). The Non-Immediate form is paired with the maintenance
of preestablished knowledge, and the Immediate with the introduction of
new information into the discourse. In contrastive contexts where one or
more places is already established and the speaker wishes to define some
other one, the preferred form is *téʔel oʔ*. This is particularly the case
if the contrasting referent can be considered the more remote alternative. For instance, sitting in Oxkutzcab, VI interpreted *téʔ t aw otoč oʔ*
'there in your house' as his home in Yaaxhom, not his nearby townhouse
(F.123.B.105). Within the preestablished frame of his two residences, the
more distant is the preferred referent.

These summary remarks suggest several distinctions between *téʔel oʔ*

and the other related deictics. The discussion will begin with the relation between *téʔel oʔ* and the corporeal schema of the addressee and will proceed with segmentations of domestic and work space (at what we have called first, second, and third degrees of inclusion), the town and region.[16] Next is *téʔel oʔ* as the origin point of motion and path already traversed, then as a place known by interactants as a matter of shared knowledge. The last set of examples shows it in anaphoric function, a special case of common knowledge, where preceding discourse contains overt reference to the same place. In general, this form is less focal, less asymmetric, and less marked than the Immediate one.[17]

When interactants are relatively close together, and a speaker wishes to make reference to the body space of the addressee, the Non-Immediate deictic is the one used, as in (90, 91). In the former, MC scolds one of the children in room 1 of his house (fig. 7.8), singling out the child's space along with him.

(90)   mak ači⁈ **téʔel oʔ** paál!
            'Shut up over there, kid!' (BB.4.60)

(91)   ¢'aá e b'áʔah **téʔel oʔ**
            'Put the thing down there.' (BB.5.66)

In (91), Eli tells her daughter Chiki to put down a thermos that she is playing with. All three of us were in the kitchen at the time, the girl only about four feet away from her mother. She responded immediately by putting the object down right where she was standing. Early on in my research, I asked VI to explain the meaning of the expression *téʔ nàa¢'il oʔ* 'there nearby', and he created a dialogue:

(92)   A: b'áʔaš kakaštik?
          'What are you looking for?'

       B: báaldéeh
          '(A) bucket.'

       A: **téʔ** nàa¢'il **oʔ** → **téʔ** nàa¢' teč **oʔ**
          'There nearby, there near to you.' (F.5.B.292)

All of these examples share the feature of making reference to the bodily space of the addressee as distinct from that of the speaker. In (92), VI has interpreted the adverb 'near' in relation to the addressee, not to the speaker or some other ground. This focus on the interlocutor's space arises most commonly in the context of an ongoing face-to-face interaction, as VI also suggests with his hypothetical example.

Around the work site, as people collaborate in the transformation of space, an addressee's placement relative to the whole field of engagement may be used as an orientation. Working with DP and VC at a field soon to be planted, we all participated in estimating the incline of the land for purposes of water runoff. Standing along a canal going north-south, VC is about fifteen feet north of DP, who asks him whether he figures the incline is from north to south.

(93)   téʔ wá šaman kawik oʔ
         'There in the north as you see it?' (BB.5.59)

Here the extremity of the canal nearest the Adr is denoted with the same form that is used for reference to the Adr's corporeal schema.[18] Shortly later at the same site, DP addressed me, giving his prediction that the water would flow from the high ground at the south end of the ditch up to the spot where VC was standing, about fifteen feet away. Looking towards the south, he said:

(94)   le haʔ kutàal héʔel aʔ→ téʔ kunaákal oʔ le túʔuš yan vìiktor oʔ
         'The water coming right here, it will reach over there, where V is.'
         (BB.5.60)

   In other situations, the association between this form and the location of an addressee may be extended to his or her habitual places or those of some other actor. Commenting on the greeting form b'iš abèel téʔel oʔ 'How are you there?' VI noted that it can be interpreted in reference to the individual's current location or to any of his or her habitual places,

(95)   yàan ink'aátik teč túʔuš, tumèen tulaáht'anik
         'I'd have to ask you where (you mean), because it says everything.'
         (F.122.A.460)

   The Non-Immediate deictic includes the entire range of the addressee's nah 'place' and -iknal 'place', starting at the corporeal schema and perceptual field and extending to his or her entire household and routine work sites. Unavoidably, these different spatial frames imply different sets of other actors with whom the individual coresides and co-works. Thus it is unsurprising that the related question b'iš aw ani téʔel oʔ 'How are you there?' can be properly interpreted as asking about the family or co-workers as well as the addressee himself. VI stated simply that the question is about letiʔóʔob' 'the ones' at home or work. The spatial reference implies a larger set of socially related others, thus expanding the personal reference accordingly. The fact that an addressee can question the referent of téʔel oʔ, whereas it makes little sense to ask where the referent of way eʔ is, is a feature shared with its Immediate counterpart.[19] In order to narrow down the possible referents, pointing gestures or further verbal description are needed.

The association between *té'el o'* and the position of an addressee is likely part of the reason why this form is the preferred one for greetings into a house from outside. Recall the standard *tàa telóo* 'Coming théere!' that visitors holler to announce themselves and seek permission to enter (BB.4.59, 66, 82). The corresponding form with *té'el a'* is not used and would imply that the speaker is already within the perimeter of the yard, walking towards a specific destination. Margot laughed at a woman who hollered the standard greeting to DC after having already entered his yard, precisely because she had already transgressed the division. The Exclusive *tol o'* '(out) there' would reflect nicely the major boundary between inside and outside, but it is less commonly used and judged clumsy by native speakers. This may be because the speaker is preparing to **enter** the yard, while *tol o'* represents it as outside. The close association between the place and the addressee who lives there is another motivating factor, since *té'el o'* is often grounded in an addressee's space and *tol o'* rarely is (unless the interactants are quite remote from one another, for instance, in the forest). A further reflection of this is that when asking me about life in the United States, local Maya speakers virtually never ask about *to t a kàahal o'* 'over there in your town', but almost always *té' t a kàahal o'* 'there in your town'. Despite the experiential remoteness of the place, its link to me, the addressee, makes it *té'el o'* instead of *tol o'*.

Like the Exclusive form, the Non-Immediate has an interesting set of throwaway uses in which the deictic fails to identify any particular place, pointing instead to an ill-defined or undefined, region. Throwaway uses of the form have the distinctive feature that they retain their association with the addressee's place rather than just any place 'out in the woods' (cf. (60) above). The result is that it is the person himself or herself who is told to 'get lost'. Consider the following routine examples.

(96)   šen **té'elo'**
          'Go over there.' (BB.4.8)

          ᷉‿   ‿᷉
(97)   tiít abáa **té'el o'** 'iho →
          'Shake yourself over there, son!' (BB 5.34)

          »‿   ‿»
(98)   hé'el o' pero šen kuta **té'el o'**
          'There it is, but go sit down over there.' (BB.5.5)

In (96), DC hollers to one of the children behind him, who was making a racket, telling him to 'beat it'. In (97), Eli uses the slightly more idiomatic phrase 'shake yourself' to convey the same directive with an added urging to hurry up. We can say with confidence that the boldface DLOCs do not refer to the **current** location of the addressees, for two reasons: (i) in (96) the combination of the adverb with the verb 'to go' can only be interpreted as a goal/direction rather than a source of motion; (ii) in (97) the boy was within arm's length of Eli at the moment of utterance, too close for standard reference with Non-Immediate. In both cases, the children understood the directives quite clearly and went elsewhere to play. Example (98) is an identical use by Eli, addressing another of the boys as she sat by the fire and he loitered at the table, playing with food. She finally gave him a piece and told him to beat it.

Discussing with Margot ways of *tohoč'iíntik* 'sending away' people to whom one does not want to talk, she cited several expressions with the Non-Immediate deictic, including the foregoing and the expressions:

(99)   kintuúštik
            'I send him (away).'

            kinwá'aik ti' ká ší'ik
            'I tell him to go.'

            tiít abáah **té'el o'** ↓
            'Shake it over there (Beat it!).'

            yuún tabaá **té'el o'**
            'Swing yourself over there (scram!, take a hike!).'

            šeén **té'el o'**, má' asùut
            'Go over there, don't return.'

Although we will not enter into the pragmatics of each of these phrases, it is clear that they all direct an addressee to leave the speaker in peace, without indicating where (s)he is to go. Listening to Margot's examples, Man observed that in none does the speaker have any specific place in mind, saying *čeén leti y ohe tú'uš k u bin* 'Only (s)he (the addressee) knows where (s)he'll go' (BB.4.107). In other words, wherever the interlocutor goes, so long as it is away from the speaker, it is for practical purposes *té'el o'* 'there'. The difference between these uses and throwaway *tol o'* 'out there' is that it is the addressee's corporeal schema that grounds the Non-Immediate deictic, not only the exclusion of the speaker.

Speakers routinely individuate sections of the house, homestead, and work site with *té'el o'* 'there'. The communicative difference between these and the corresponding utterances with *té'el a'* 'right here' or *tol o'* 'over there' is often a subtle one. In many of its occurrences, *té'el o'* has a contrastive function, setting off a unique object or segment of space from the immediate surroundings. The referent is usually a stationary location rather than a trajectory or goal, and is often preestablished among interactants as the habitual place of some referent already under discussion.

In §3.5, the examples of 'instrumental speech' illustrated contrastive *té'el o'* around a work site at which DP, VC, and I were digging irrigation ditches. At one point, VC was digging a hole in which to plant a tree, with DP standing almost directly over him, within a meter of the hole. Pointing to the west side as VC worked, DP told him to dig out a little more *tée čik'in o'* 'there (on the) west' (BB.5.30). Recall Margot's reference to the other end of a hammock as *tol o'* (see §8.4.3), a similarly proximal reference to 'the other side' of an object. My hunch as to why DP used the DLOC he did is that: (i) the objective distances between speaker, addressee, and referent are too small for the Exclusive (even smaller than the length of a hammock); (ii) he was pointing to a particular section of the hole, not just 'the other side'; (iii) the added qualifier 'west' makes the Exclusive deictic quite unlikely, since *to čik'in o'* 'out there west' would normally refer to an objectively distant place. On the other hand, *té' čik'in a'* 'right here (on the) west', would have been equally proper and typical of DP's instrumental speech. The difference is that it would have been an asymmetric reference, segmenting the west side of the hole as if for the first time, when in fact, the indexical frame was highly symmetric: the addressee (VC) was already engaged in the digging and all parties were focused on it together.

Another symmetric example on the same work site was DP's statement that *té'el o'* → *yan cánal té' pàačil o'* 'there, there's a ditch back there' (see fig. 3.6 and discussion). We were sitting side by side on the bank of a ditch looking upon the work site, and DP's referent was a patch of land overgrown in weeds about four meters away, on the other side of the ditch, behind a dirt pile several feet high (BB.5.32). In our line of vision, there was a succession of objects, with the ditch in the foreground, the dirt pile defining the high point, and the overgrown ditch behind it (cf. 'near side' uses of *way e'*, fig. 9.2). The combination of relative proximity and separation by a sequence of objects, along with our shared sight line on the place, made up an indexical frame well suited to the Non-Immediate deictic. With respect to the symmetrical ground of our interaction, the referent was 'just over there, on the other side'.

I was getting water to drink from one of two *p'uúl ó'ob'* '(ceramic) jugs' standing side by side in Pablo's wife's kitchen as she tended the fire several feet away. When I reached for it, she corrected me, saying:

(100)   **té' kán ač'aáh o'**
             'There's where you'll take it from.' (BB.1.48)

She pointed to the other jug, on the far side from her. Her directive individuates the other alternative of a preestablished pair (the jugs), contrasting it to the choice I had obviously made. Seven years later, as we were about to be seated for lunch at Margot's table in room 1 (fig. 7.8), the food was laid out and I addressed Fi, who was joining us, saying:

(101)   WH: má²a takutal señora?
       'Won't you sit, Señora?'

   Fi: yàan, **té²el o²**
       'I will, right there.' (BB.4.26)

I was offering a place to sit, and Fi was referring to the other end of the table, to which she pointed as she spoke. She later sat down in the place she had chosen. Both of these examples make a contrast between a place that I, the addressee, had selected and some other restricted spot in the proximal zone of interaction. Fi might well have used *té²el a²* 'right here', particularly if she were heading for her seat as she spoke. But she was not yet going to her seat, and her referent was on the far side of the table, just as the jug Pablo's wife referred to was the farther of the pair. Had Fi used the Exclusive *tol o²*, on the other hand, the effect would have been to emphasize the exclusion of her seat, representing it as outside the convivial 'here' of the meal table.

When not functioning as contrastive places, the referents of *té²el o²* are often fixed by habitual experience. They are where objects are customarily kept, hence identifiable on the basis of knowledge already available to both interactants. One day after DP had chided his daughter-in-law Eli for leaving a large piece of firewood outside the kitchen door, Eli's daughter Chiki was about to bring it inside the kitchen. DP had left, and Eli made fast work of his instructions, telling Chiki to leave the thing where it was (where it had been for several days), saying from inside:

(102)   p'at **tée** b'ey o²
           'Leave it there as it is.' (BB.5.6)

On a different occasion, DC and I were sitting by his altar discussing his medicines, and he recounted how a group of outsiders had asked him to teach them the preparation (see §7.4.2.2). He refused, saying that God gave him something by which he lives, and if he gave it away, he would go hungry. His medicines are still around the room, stored where they are always kept, he said to me, pointing vaguely with his right hand:

(103)   le ¢'àak o² čeén tí²an **tée** bey o² → ²ulaá² **té²el o²** →
           'The medicine, it's just there like (usual). (points) Another there,
           (points)

ulaá⁷ **té⁷el o⁷** →
another there.' (points) (BB.4.95)

Although I did not yet know the locations of the medicines, I had frequented the room and discussed medicine with DC for seven years, off
and on. His references focus not on the asymmetry in our respective
knowledge but on the fact that the well-known objects were still in their
normal places around the room, not in the possession of some outsiders.

Several days before, Man had spent a day resurfacing the packed-earth
floor of room 3 (see fig. 7.8). Walking out of room 1 into the courtyard
where Margot and I were talking, he addressed me, saying:

(104)   lìisto ani le **té⁷el o⁷** kompádre →
             'It's ready (in) there, compadre!' (BB.4.77)

I had worked with him that day and was fully familiar with the task he had
just finished, although the room was separated from us by three doorways
and as many walls. These facts, plus the fact that he had just come from
there (making it a source of motion) make up a complex frame that motivates his choice of the symmetric Non-Immediate deictic.

Reference to the 'next' house within the confines of a walled *soólar* is
often made using the Non-Immediate DLOC. This was illustrated in Margot's routine directives to visitors looking for DC or Lol, in which she
contrasts the *way e⁷* 'here' of her house to the *té⁷el o⁷* 'there' of the adjoining ones (see (39)). Lol was sitting talking with me at the table in
Man's kitchen, when Man walked out of the room looking for the pickax
to work in the yard. Lol tossed his head in the direction of his house,
saying:

(105)   miín tí⁷an ti⁷ ten **té⁷el o⁷**
             'I think I've got it over there (in my place).' (BB.4.93)

It is relevant that Lol made no motion to go over to his house himself, but
simply located the tool there, tacitly inviting his brother to go to get it. In
this indexical frame, several factors are in play: the boundary between the
two houses, the fact that the pick was where he had left it (like the habitual uses), and the fact that his brother was going to get it, putting it in the
addressee's field of action (cf. (79) for identical usage).

In the more inclusive frame of the entire (third-level) household, linking sometimes distant domestic and agricultural places to a senior owner
and his sons, *té⁷el o⁷* is very commonly used to refer to one area from the
vantage point of another. For Pilar and Eli, who reside in area I of DP's

extended household (see fig. 7.5), areas II and III are standardly characterized as *té?el o?* 'there'. Loading a roll of firewood onto a tricycle in area I, VC said he was taking it to his mother in area II:

(106)   kimbisik tinmàama **té?el o?**
           'I'm taking it to my mother there.' (BB 5.46)

Similarly, speaking in her home in area II, DA refers to area III the same way. Telling me that DP and VC were not at the house, she said (without antecedent):

(107)   miná?anó?ob' **té?el o?**
           'They're not there (area III).' (BB.5.20)

Speaking in area I, DP and VC were discussing their plans to make a mango snack for the tractor driver scheduled to plow their field, a customary prestation. VC informed DP that there were ripe ones on his trees in area III, saying

(108)   màango → yàan teč **té** ič soólàar o? →
           'Mangos, you've got there in the solar.' (BB.5.24)

Clearly, all such uses are interpreted relative to the habitual experience of the participants, who know the places referred to intimately and recognize the boundaries of ownership, as well as the ties among places belonging to a single family. Within the frame space of the extended household, subframes are bound to members by ownership.

The regional frame space extends outward into the zone of routine and even remote familiarity. Uses of Non-Immediate in reference to ecological zones around town (see §7.3.3), neighboring towns, or even more distant ones are standard. For instance, Oxkutzcabeños conversing in town can virtually always presuppose that their interlocutor is familiar with the Puuc hills, which can then be referred to simply as *té? pú?uk o?* 'there in the Puuc'. Similarly, the 'low forest' section north of town is *té? kabah če? o?* 'there in low wood' to local men who work, hunt, or traverse the area.[20] If one takes the southern part of Yucatán state as a frame of reference, Oxkutzcab is *way e?* 'here', and Mayapan, about twenty-five kilometers away, is *té? maáyapàan o?* 'there in Mayapan' (BB.4.120).

The remaining examples show Non-Immediate reference to the source and path already covered by the speaker, to places known by both interactants, and to places referred to in preceding discourse (i.e., anaphoric). These share the feature of being rooted in the past experience of the speaker or the speaker and addressee and make a point-for-point contrast with the use of *té?el a?* for the goal and forward path, places not known by the interlocutor, and places newly introduced into the discourse. Like *héʔel aʔ* in some uses, *téʔel aʔ* is anticipatory; *téʔel oʔ*, like *héʔel oʔ*, is based on recall. The link between *téʔel oʔ* and past experience is strong enough to lead Margot, generally an excellent commentator on her language, to reject the hypothetical sentence *hb'inen téʔel aʔ* 'I went right here.' With the past tense verb marking, she preferred the *téʔel oʔ* deictic form (BB.4.59).

Eli and I were sitting in her kitchen one night, she by the fire and I at a small table within an arm's length from her. After walking around the far *moy* 'end' of the kitchen structure looking for her cutting knife in semi-darkness, she had found it more or less where it should have been on the table just to her left by the fire (see fig. 7.10). Without a gesture, she remarked ironically:

(109)   b'áʔaš ʔòora hóop' inkaštik → kinmaán **téʔeloʔ** →
           'When did I start looking for it? I go around there,

           téʔel oʔ → **téʔel oʔ** →
           there,   there.' (BB.5.34)

I was facing her with my back to the places to which she referred. Arguably, this use could be treated as throwaway reference, since Eli never really individuates places for me. The main conveyed meaning is that she had looked in several spots in a sequence completed prior to her utterance and leading to her current location. The use of Non-Immediate reference to the path covered prior to utterance can be diagramed as in figure 9.7.

Sociocentric *iknal* of participants

Fig. 9.7. Source frame of *telʔel oʔ* 'there (Sociocentric, Non-Immediate)'.

In §7.4.2 I outlined the changes that have taken place in the residence of DP's family over the past ten years. Commenting on DP's move away from area I, directly across from a pozo 'well', Cres's elder brother said:

(110)   luk'ó?ob' **té?** na č'é?en o? →
          'They've moved from there by the well (Pozo 2).' (BB.5.7)

We were talking in Cres's store just down the road from area II, where DP lives presently. Not only is the referent where DP used to reside, but also it is a place where I have resided at various times in the past, and Cres' brother knows this. Thus, it is simultaneously the farther of two known residences, familiar in some detail to both of us and linked to the past from which DP has moved. This combination of factors in the indexical frame reinforces the man's choice of the Non-Immediate deictic.

Comparing the size of Fi's brother to that of a foreigner named Pedro who used to reside in one of DC's lots on the outskirts of Oxkutzcab, Lol asserted:

(111)   mas bek'eč ti? Pedro ⟿ leti yàan **té** ká?ač **té?** párselá o? →
          'He's thinner than Pedro, the one who used to be over there in the parsela.' (F.137.A (050))

We were sitting in his house at the time, and the lot in question was around the corner. As Lol's use of the past particle *ká?ač* indicates, Pedro no longer lives there; but it is common knowledge among us that he once did. While the phrasing introduces the reference to the lot as a relative clause identifying Pedro, Pedro also helps to specify the deictic reference as the particular lot in question, since DC has had several lots, but we all know that Pedro only resided in one of them.

Anaphoric coreference with a preceding expression in discourse is a special case of shared background knowledge, in which the source of the knowledge is given in an antecedent utterance. It is therefore unsurprising that the same deictic forms that specialize in reference to places already known are also used for anaphoric coreference. These are *té?el o?* 'there' and *tí? i?* 'there' (see §9.2.3). Lol's description of how he raised money for the house by selling his stereo to the neighbor illustrated a combination of anaphora and knowledge based on habitual experience. Having identified the man with the *té?el a?* 'right here' standard for neighborly reference, he then referred to the stereo as *le ?estèerio k u pàaš té?el o?* 'the stereo that plays right there' (see (74)). Making me a map of the Yaaxhom area years earlier, VI described a spot, which led to this exchange.

(112)   WH: **té?el a?** ↓ ?inwohe tú?uš
        'Right here. I know where (you mean).'

VI: ʔawohe túʔuš ↑ héʔel oʔ → **téʔel oʔ** ↓
      'You know where? OK then, right there.' (F.4.A.155)

My utterance shows proper use of the Immediate form to localize the place, and VI makes certain that I know where he means and then switches conclusively to Non-Immediate. Again, there is a confluence of anaphora and background knowledge of the place.

DC told the story of a ceremony he had performed for a man in Mexico City, who had suffered a series of major thefts from his house. Having described the house, which I had never seen and would not recognize, he then explained how the thieves had taken the objects through a skylight in the roof and had escaped by climbing to another building. After his performance, they began bringing the things back the same way:

(113)   **téʔ** yoóʔ pak'i nah tusutóʔob' e b'áʔa tuyoklóʔob' **oʔ**
            'There atop the walled house they returned the things they had
            stolen.' (BB.4.100–101)

This utterance shows a spatial frame preestablished in discourse, without any overlay of common background experience of the place. A similar, though less extreme case arose in Eli's instructions to me on where to purchase beef in town (see (35)). Having established the frame in which to locate the place, she individuated it with the phrase _téʔ_ k u kóʔonol _oʔ_ 'that's where it's sold.'

9.2.3 A Place of Common Knowledge

The final member of the basic DLOC series is _tíʔ_ _iʔ_ 'there'. This form is the least informationally rich of the set, in that it provides no characterization of the locus of the referent with respect to interactants' corporeal or other spatial fields, or with respect to the perimetral or directional aspects of speech context. The referent can be literally anywhere, a fixed place of a trajectory, and still properly fit the conditions for _tíʔ_ _iʔ_ 'there'. For its lack of relational concreteness compared to the other forms, this one can be represented as Non-Concrete. This is not to say that in practice speakers do not individuate highly concrete places and trajectories with the form, since they routinely do. Rather, the perceptual, spatial, or actional concreteness of the referent is derived entirely from elsewhere in the adjacent discourse or extralinguistic setting. Rather than being negatively marked (−Concrete), as _tol oʔ_ '(out) there' is negatively marked for inclusion, _tíʔ_ _iʔ_ 'there' is unmarked for concreteness.

At the same time, to say that it is unmarked on this dimension is not to say that it has no relational value whatever. On the contrary, when used without further lexical description, the form requires that the interactants **both already know** the locus of the referent or have available in the joint discourse frame a fuller description of it. One of its core uses is as an anaphoric device, often reasonably paraphrased (for heuristic purposes) 'there, where we said'. In view of these factors, I represent the core feature of the form as Specified, meaning that the referent is specified by some other linguistic description or bit of shared knowledge currently available to the interactants in the framework of speech. It is unclear how best to represent the spatiotemporal schema on which *tíʔ iʔ* 'there' rests, since it lacks the 'geometric' properties of the other forms. For the sake of contrast, we can represent it as a point of shared knowledge between interactants, without perimeter, proximity, or extent. This is shown in figure 9.8.

In light of the functional differences between the Concrete and Non-Concrete forms, it is not surprising that they also differ grammatically. The Initial deictic *tíʔ* is a specialized focus marker that occurs only in preverbal position in the sentence, as in:

(114)   **tíʔ kumeyah iʔ**
             'There('s where s)he works.'

(115)   **tíʔanóʔob' iʔ**
             'There('s where) they are.'

Sociocentric *iknal* of participants

Fig. 9.8. Non-Concrete frame of *tíʔ iʔ* 'there (Sociocentric, Specified)'.

One consequence of this is that the form does not co-occur with the imperative verb forms *šen* 'go', *kóʔoš* 'let's go', and *kóʔoten,* since none of these can take a locative focus, and *tíʔ iʔ* is always focal. Unlike the Concrete forms, it does not occur in relative clauses or as the head of a relative clause:

(116)   *timp'atah yoóʔ le mèesa **tíʔan iʔ**
           'I left it on the table there it is.'

(117)   *timp'atah **tíʔ** túʔuš kinmeyah **iʔ**
           'I left it there where I work.'

While previous examples illustrate the form in prolocative function, adlocative uses are also routine, as in:

(118)   **tíʔan h k'iíwik eʔ**
           'There it is (in the) market.'

(119)   **tíʔ** timp'atah yoóʔ mèesá **eʔ**
           'There I left it on the table.'

Observe in (118–19) that the terminal deictic particle *iʔ* normally coupled with *tíʔ* has had *eʔ* substituted for it. The rule accounting for this says that if the DLOC is coreferential with a lexical description in the same sentence, then the expected *iʔ* terminal is replaced by *eʔ*.[21] Observe also that while the initial deictic base *tíʔ* occurs in preverbal position, the lexical description follows the verb, as locative phrases usually do. Corresponding examples in which the *tíʔ* and the lexical description are immediately adjacent on the surface are all ungrammatical.

(120)   ***tíʔ hk'iíwik** yan eʔ

(121)   ***tíʔ yoóʔ mèesa** timp'atah eʔ

These sentences can be repaired by shifting the lexical descriptions into postverbal position or switching the DLOC to one of the Concrete forms. We will return to focus constructions and the grammatical constraints on DLOCs in chapter 10. At this point, I emphasize that there are detailed and systematic differences in the grammatical behavior of the Non-Concrete deictic, as opposed to the Concrete ones. These differences reflect the functional distinctions among the forms.

Lacking concrete relational information in its encoded semantics, the DLOC *tíʔ iʔ* 'there' can be used freely with locative antecedents of all types. Making a map of the Yaaxhom area, VI defined a landmark place using the expected Immediate deictic, after which the Non-Concrete maintains coreference:[22]

(122)   **lel a**ʔ tyèenda → **tí**ʔ ku¢'aáh bwèelta le b'ùus kawáʔak oʔ
            'This is (the) store. There's where the bus you're talking about
            turns.' (F.4.B.499)

DC explains to a woman who has come to him for treatment that this evil
thing bothering her, he'll cast it off into a cave in the forest.

(123)   **té**ʔ aáktuún kén impul le b'áʔal **a**ʔ, **tí**ʔ kint'aŋk **i**ʔ
            'There (in a) cave will I dispose of this thing, that's where I address
            it.' (BB.4.9)

When I was talking with DC after the woman left, he assured me that the
cave to which he had referred and pointed was not close by, but far out in
the woods. It didn't matter what cave it was, so long as it was off in the
forest. His use of the Immediate deictic instead of throwaway *tol o*ʔ or
*té*ʔ*el o*ʔ is consistent with the asymmetric and anticipatory aspects of the
indexical frame: the woman can have no idea of where he intends to throw
the spirit or how he does it, really, since this is esoteric knowledge. He
hasn't performed the act of throwing yet and apparently is not individuating a specific cave but is anticipating the performance and indicating the
trajectory on which he will send the spirit. The Immediate deictic refers
to his forward path in this situation, which he will follow not by actually
walking but by speaking and moving spirits (see discussion of ritual
speech in §§7.5 and 8.3). The Non-Concrete *tí*ʔ *i*ʔ in the next sentence
maintains this frame without adding any new spatial information to it.

Antecedents of *tí*ʔ *i*ʔ 'there' are often established by expressions containing Non-Immediate deictics as well. Describing the meaning of *kahtalil* 'homestead' to me, Margot created the example *té*ʔ *kahtalil o*ʔ ↑
*tí*ʔ *kahakbal en i*ʔ 'there in that homestead, there('s where) I reside'
(BB.4.134). DP explained the conveyed meaning of *kó*ʔ*oten té*ʔ*el a*ʔ
'come here' as

(124)   **le** túʔuš yàan wáakbal **o**ʔ →   **tí**ʔ kuna¢'eč **i**ʔ
            'The (place) where he's standing, there('s where) he draws you
                                                              near,

            ká wáʔalakeč **i**ʔ
            for you to stand there.'
            (F1.A.18)

In both cases, the preceding spatial reference is maintained by the Non-
Concrete DLOC as the thematic focus of a new sentence. The antecedent
need not be uniquely identified, in that it makes no difference where the
hypothetical speaker is standing for (124), or where the smokestacks turn
out to be in (125).

(125)   **hé⁷ tú⁷uš** yàan le čìiminyá o⁷ **tí⁷an** y otoč le maákina ká⁷ač o⁷
               'Wherever there's the chimney, there('s where) there used to be a
                                        machine.' (F.29.A.98)

In this utterance, DP was explaining that the remains of smokestacks
around the ranch where he worked were evidence of the sugar processing
plants that had been there in the past. Note in these examples that what
motivates the use of *tí⁷* is the discourse-internal relation of anaphoric cohesion. Even if an antecedent fails to identify a referent (as in 125), it can
still serve as the initial ground in an anaphoric chain.[23]

As I was about to leave area I to walk to the field where DP and VC
were working (see fig. 7.5), Pilar asked me where I was off to. I responded simply *té⁷el o⁷* 'there', and she guessed my destination:

(126)   nal inswèegro→ ⁷áhàa tyikʌn inswèegro → **tí⁷anó⁷ob i⁷**
               '(To) my father-in-law's place. Ahah, to my father-in-law's place.
               There('s where) they are.' (BB.5.54)

As in other cases, the Non-Concrete deictic occurs after the location has
already been established in the discourse. 'My father-in-law' refers to DP,
and his 'place' is anywhere in his residential or agricultural lands.

In many cases, the antecedent occurs not in immediately preceding discourse but in talk that occurred minutes before, as in (127).

(127)   lel a⁷ → má⁷ **tí⁷** kubin i⁷
               'This one, there's not (where) it goes.' (BB.1.49)

This utterance was addressed to me by a woman with whom I was waiting
for a truck out of the Oxkutzcab market. We had established that we were
both heading for Cooperativa and were thus waiting for the same truck.
For about five minutes prior to her utterance, however, we had sat in silence as other vehicles came and went. For the purpose of identifying a
referent for the DLOC, what is important is not that there be an easily identifiable antecedent but that if there is not, the interlocutors both know
where the place is.[24] DP produced a clear instance of this when he used
the Non-Concrete form in the opening utterance of an exchange. Standing
in MC's yard, he hollered over to Milo's next door to see if he was home,
saying:

(128)   heéy→ **tí⁷an** wá mìilo → ⁷á⁷al ti⁷ nukáa naáksb'i le čìiná o⁷
               Hey! Is Milo there? Tell him that the oranges are going to be
               picked up!' (BB.5.24)

DP was speaking to whoever in Milo's house heard him, and the spatial
referent of the underlined DLOC is no more specific than the addressee. It

refers to anywhere in the homestead in which an addressee is located. Note that Milo need not even be in the same place as the one who hears and picks up on the directive; his wife in the kitchen could hear it and pass the word on to Milo on the far side of the living house (see fig. 7.6). Since there is no other description in the prior or accompanying discourse, it is the link between the addressee and the place that makes it eventually identifiable. Though far from uniquely identifying the place referred to, it is adequate for the practical purpose of getting Milo's attention.

The coreferential complement of *tí? i?* 'there' need not precede it in discourse if the two occur in the same sentence. Just as common as the anaphoric cases are cataphoric ones, in which a following expression is the descriptive complement. This is the case in all 'split focus' constructions (see chap. 10) in which the preverbal deictic base is paired with a postverbal locative description, as in:

(129)   **tí?an té?el a?** → way yan ič nah e?
           'There it is right there. Here it is inside the house.' (BB.5.21)

DP uttered (129) lying in his hammock in the main sleeping house just after DA, in the kitchen, had asked him to pass her the bottle of honey (see fig. 7.7). In (129), DP conveys the instruction for VC to fetch it from its storage spot in the rafters in the main house, which he did. At the time of utterance, VC was sitting behind DP in the same room, thus sharing his auditory and actional field but not his visual one.

Fi and I were sitting at her table in room 5 (fig. 7.8) about to peel some oranges, when I asked her for the knife, and she told me it was over at Man and Margot's place, using the split-focus construction in (130):

(130)   WH: kuš tuún cuchillo?
            'What about (the) knife?'

        Fi: **tí?an té?e** ti? leti? o?
            'It's theirs over there.' (BB.4.28)

Fi's utterance, as she explained subsequently, conveys two quite distinct propositions, namely, that the knife is in the next household and that it belongs to them as well. The precise location of the thing is something neither Fi nor I know, but the reference to 'them (lit., 'the one')' links it to the space of the adjoining house. On the other hand, I was sitting in area I talking with Pilar about DP's place in area III, about 500 meters away (see fig. 7.5), when she remarked that she and VC used to reside there.

(131)   **tí?anó?on to** ká?ač o?
           'We used to be (live) over there.' (BB 5.42)

In split-focus constructions, *tí?* may co-occur with any of the Immediate, Non-Immediate, or Exclusive locative deictics, but not with the Inclusive form (for reasons not entirely clear to me). I have not attested *tí? an way e?* 'there('s where) it is here' in actual conversation, and native speakers reject it in favor of *way yan e?* 'here('s where) it is', or *tí? an té?el a?* 'there('s where) it is right here.' In pairings that do occur, the terminal particle *i?* is replaced by either *a?* or *o?*, according to the requirements of the accompanying Initial Deictic base. The mechanisms for such replacement, along with the other focus constructions, will be taken up in chapter 10. At this point two factors are central. (i) *tí?* may be accompanied by a postverbal locative expression in the same clause, with which it is automatically coreferential (an utterance like *tí? k u bin té?el o?* 'there('s where s)he goes right there' can never be taken to refer to two different places). (ii) When the postverbal locative is itself a deictic adverb, then the *i?* terminal associated with *tí?* is automatically replaced by *a?* or *o?*. It was shown in examples (118–21) what happens when the postverbal locative is a lexical description rather than another deictic: the *i?* is replaced with *e?*.

Fi was telling me of her family who live about twenty kilometers by road from Oxkutzcab, in a place called Tekax. I asked her where her older sisters were living, and she said they too were there, using the Non-Concrete form, which led me to request further clarification.[25]

(132)   WH: kuš tuún akìik ó?ob→ tú?uš yàan→
        'What about your elder sisters? Where are they?'

        Fi: **tían** o
        'There('s where) they are.'

        WH: tek'aš ↑
        'Tekax?'

        Fi: **tían** tek'ašó?ob e? → čeén ten ⇗ way e?
        'There('s where) they are in Tekax. It's just me here (in Oxkutz-
        cab).' (F.137.A.263)

In Fi's final utterance, the Non-Concrete base is complemented in postverbal position by the place name plus the plural morpheme *tek'aš ó?ob*, and the terminal particle is *e?*.[26]

Similarly, when Man explained to me the temporal deictic *taánte?* 'just', he created the example and gloss in (133).

(133)   hač taánt ukiínl e?→ ká h b'inen i?, hač tukiímil e? ↑
            ' "Really she just died, when I went there", (conveys that) right at
            her death,

k'ab'eét **tí**an eč tyiknal **e**ˀ
you've got to be there.' (BB.4.150)

Examples (119–33) show that the terminal *i*ˀ is paired with the deictic base *tí*ˀ only when there is no other specification of the place referred to in the same clause.[27] Any other terminals following it in the same sentence override it (*i*ˀ→ {*a*ˀ, *o*ˀ}), and nondeictic lexical description triggers the *i*ˀ→ *e*ˀ substitution. Thus, *i*ˀ is the residual case: what relates the referent to the participant ground is preestablished shared knowledge, not co-occurrent verbal description. We can say, then, that the anaphoric function of the Non-Concrete locative deictic attaches primarily to the *i*ˀ terminal. What is the semantic contribution of the initial base?

All of the examples cited in this section (114–33) reflect the pragmatic fact that locative focus constructions occur in frameworks in which the location of some object is already established as a theme in discourse. A 'where' question has been asked, or the whereabouts of some thematic object has been raised for commentary. This is distinct from saying that the structure tends to have an anaphoric function, since many examples (cf. 129, 130) have no coreferential antecedent, yet fit snugly in the response position to a 'where' question. Insofar as it is restricted to focus position, the Non-Concrete base therefore encodes the thematic information that the referent is to be interpreted as the one best suited to fit the question or description in prior talk. Thus in its canonical uses, *tí*ˀ *i*ˀ 'there' is both anaphoric and focal. The combination of the two is of course not totally arbitrary, since both anaphora and focus on theme are kinds of presuppositions linking the deictic to preceding discourse and therefore to a relatively symmetric ground of shared information. DP's call for Milo in (128), occurring without any prior interaction, is the exception that proves the rule, since he used the initial base alone, without any terminal *i*ˀ. This is just what we would expect, given the common knowledge that Milo resides where he does, and that speakers call each other from the edge of the yard, coupled with the absence of any recoverable antecedent. DP uses the linguistic devices of deixis to achieve his referential ends, while at the same time positioning himself precisely within the frame space of coresidents.

9.3 SUMMARY OF DEICTIC SPACE

We began this chapter with the observation that deictic space is linked to other cultural frames of spatiotemporal orientation in two primary ways. Necessarily, because deictic reference occurs in social contexts, it **must**

articulate with the many other prefabricated and emergent schemata simultaneously in play in any interactive framework. When a speaker refers
to her father-in-law's former residence as 'there', speaking inside her own
home, she relies quite directly on common knowledge of the social relations and boundaries between her current location and the one referred to.
Whatever the encoded relational value of a deictic type—Inclusive, Exclusive, Immediate, Non-Immediate, or Non-Concrete (Specified)—the
value is computed pragmatically relative to other available systems of orientation. This is evident in the variety of uses documented for each of the
forms and the ease with which speakers shift among orientational perspectives during talk; the body, the forward path, the addressee's location, the common ground of shared knowledge. At the level of tokens in
use, therefore, the indexical ground of deictic reference articulates the relational value to an ongoing social framework in which other, logically
independent frames are in play.

The second primary relation between the deictic frame and other frames
of understanding connects the encoded structure of deictic types to the
structure of other systems. Embedded in the conventional meanings of
spatial deictics in Maya are the following schemata:

    i. The perimetral frame which defines an inside and an outside, en-
        coded in the Egocentric DLOCs

    ii. The landmark frame which defines a near side and a far side

    iii. The directional frame of centered orientation, encoded in the
        Sociocentric DLOCs

    iv. The forward path frame, one of the core uses of the Immediate DLOC

    v. The source frame, one of core uses of the Non-Immediate DLOC

    vi. The Non-Concrete frame of the Specified DLOC

All of them function also in the extralinguistic contexts of corporeal, domestic, agricultural, and ritual orientations (compare §8.4). While they
are unquestionably grounded in universal features of cognition, a problem
to which we return in chapter 10, these schemata derive their specific
forms from Maya culture, of which the language is a part.

Rather than attempt to reduce the spatial deictic system to a single abstract structure, we will summarize it in three perspectives: the hierarchical relations among categories, the axial relations among intersecting
dimensions, and the geometric relations among the corresponding reference spaces.

9.3.1 Hierarchical Relations

The DLOCS make up a closed set of paradigmatically opposed forms in the grammar of Maya, and the relations among them can be described in terms of a branching diagram like the one in figure 9.9. What such a diagram shows perhaps most clearly are the relations of superordination among the categories. The highest-level split in the paradigm is the one separating the Concrete from the Non-Concrete forms. As was shown above, the Non-Concrete deictic is grammatically, as well as semantically, different from the others. It is a specialized locative focus device whose only relational value is to indicate that the referent is specifiable in context, from background knowledge, antecedent, or accompanying description. Its separate status will become even clearer in chapter 10, when we examine focus constructions in more detail.

It is within the informationally richer Concrete category that the next opposition is established, between Egocentric and Sociocentric localizations. The Egocentric localizations relate a referent to the speaker's corporeal schema as a whole. They tend strongly to refer to total regions rather than restricted points and are further subdivided into the Inclusive zone (occupied by the speaker) and the Exclusive one (not occupied by the speaker). The Sociocentric category is divided into Immediate and Non-Immediate poles. What they share in opposition to the Egocentric forms is that (i) they are computed relative to the interactive field rather than the speaker alone, so that they may segment, include, exclude, overlap, or contrast with the speaker's corporeal schema; (ii) they tend to refer

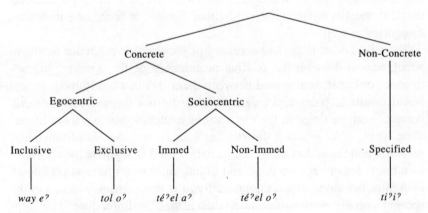

Fig. 9.9. Hierarchical structure of spatial deictic categories.

to relatively punctate spaces rather than zones, particularly the Immediate pole; and (iii) the opposition is a relative one rather than an absolute dichotomy. Regardless of background knowledge, contrasts being drawn, or participant attention focus, a place is either Inclusive or Exclusive of the speaker, but not both at the same time. Relative immediacy, on the other hand, is a scalar judgment, and a spot in the proximal zone can be treated either way, or one way and then the other, depending on other situational factors in the framework, such as attention focus and the knowledge base of participants. Further evidence of the independence of Egocentric and Sociocentric categories will emerge in chapter 10, when we see that they may be combined in a single complex localization.

These basic categories of deictic space have further corollaries in referential practice. Both Egocentric forms tend to be used in reference to stationary, fixed regions rather than paths or movement along them. One way to understand the difference is to recall the two main senses of -iknal 'place': (i) the highly mobile bodily space of the individual, and (ii) the relatively enduring domestic space of residence and agricultural practice. While the Egocentric forms **index** the speaker's current footing in the first sense, they tend strongly to **refer to** places of the second kind. Hence, the functions of totalizing a perimetral space, fixing referents to a stationary zone, and locating oneself are lumped together in the Egocentric 'here' and 'there'. The Sociocentric forms, by contrast, are associated with the successive relations of movement from the current place towards a goal, and from some other place of origin towards the current one.[28] The former gets the Immediate form, the anticipatory 'here', and the latter the non-Immediate 'there' of recall. Thus, the logical division between perimetral and directional spatial practices, which we have seen in corporeal, cardinal, domestic, agricultural, and ritual frames, is embodied in deictic categories as well.

There is another important corollary of sociocentric reference in Maya, which has to do with the relative prominence of the speaker, the addressee, or the shared ground between them. While both Immediate and Non-Immediate poles can be distinguished from the respective bodily space of each participant, there is a strong association between the Immediate form, té'el a', and the speaker's zone, and the Non-Immediate, té'el o', and the addressee's. The former is used to segment the speaker's own body, his or her own goal, and to introduce new information known by him or her alone. Impressionistically, it is more strongly linked to the speaker's bodily gesture of pointing than is the Non-Immediate. The latter is used to refer to the addressee's corporeal schema or routine places, if distinguished from the common ground, and to the undirected path (s)he

SPEAKER   ADDRESSEE

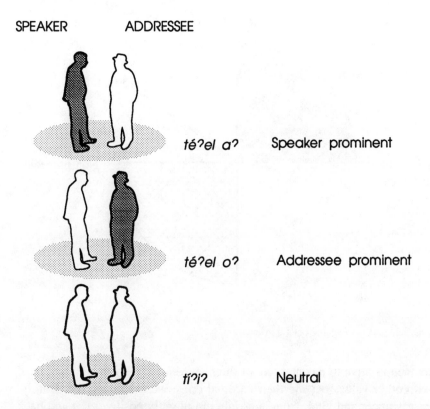

té?el a?   Speaker prominent

té?el o?   Addressee prominent

tí?i?   Neutral

Fig. 9.10. Variable weighting of indexical ground.

will follow when told to 'beat it'. It is used to maintain information already shared by interactants. Thus while both are Sociocentric in opposition to the Egocentric categories, one is weighted towards the speaker and the other towards the addressee. In the context of this variable weighting, the Non-Concrete form *tí? i?* 'there' is relatively neutral. When unelaborated by further description, it requires a shared knowledge of the place or some antecedent characterization of it, while it can go either way when coupled with another deictic. These alternatives are pictured in figure 9.10.

9.3.2 Axes of Deictic Orientation

From the perspective of deixis as a system of centered orientation, the DLOC categories are best represented as intersecting dimensions computed relative to an actional center. The similarity between the schema in figure 9.11 and the ones for bodily space and cardinal directional space in figure 8.11 is not arbitrary. Like corporeal and cardinal directional space, the deictic axes form a grid on which both places and trajectories can be

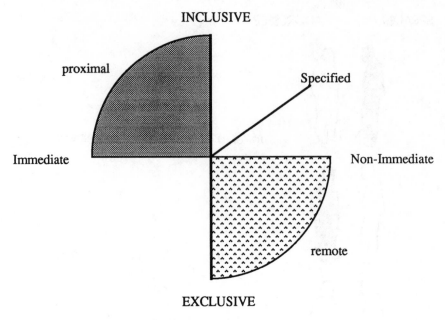

Fig. 9.11. Axes of spatial deictic orientation.

defined relative to a center. In all three systems, the poles are associated with other values beyond their cardinal ones: west is under and deathly, east is upper and vital, front and right are morally positive, left and back are negative (see §§3.2, 7.2, 8.4), Inclusive and Immediate are proximate, Exclusive and Non-Immediate are remote, Immediate is speaker-weighted, and Non-Immediate is addressee-weighted. Unlike either of the other two, the deictic system categorially distinguishes between the successive and segmenting orientation of relative immediacy as opposed to the fixed and totalizing orientation of inclusive/exclusive. Thus while incorporating the same schemata that recur in other fields in Maya culture, deixis incorporates them in a distinctive way.

9.3.3 Composite Geometry of Deictic Space

Viewed as a geometry of the actional field of practice, the locative subsystem of deixis in Maya combines the perimetral division between inside and outside regions with the punctate segmentation of restricted places on both sides of the boundary. The Non-Concrete form has the spatially null but interactively significant function of activating shared knowledge to identify places. In figure 9.12, these coexistent spaces in the deictic field are represented schematically. The patterned, unbounded area in the center is the Indexical ground, which may consist of the speaker's corporeal schema or of the symmetrical framework of an ongoing interaction. The perimeter is the rectangular box encompassing the Indexical ground and defining thereby an Inclusive zone and an Exclusive one. I have used a quadrilateral perimeter rather than the more standard oval or round shape, for the ethnographic reason that most perimeters in Maya culture are in fact four-cornered, as we have seen.

The final point I wish to reiterate before turning to more complex cases of combined and derived deictics bears on the phenomenon of transposition. Starting with Bühler and leading through modern studies by Fillmore and Levinson, among others, scholars have recognized the significance of transposed deictic reference. The distinctive feature of transposition is that the relational value of a deictic is computed, not relative to the typical indexical ground of speaker, or of speaker cum addressee, but relative to some other. Quoted speech is one of the clearest examples of this, as in, 'He said "I won't stay here with you."' In the quoted utterance, 'I', 'here', 'you', and the future marker are not computed relative to the corporeal frame—the speaker of the quote is not telling his addressee that he won't stay with him—but to the narrative frame projected by 'He said.' Sometimes speakers also transpose their references in direct speech, when they adopt the perspective of an addressee or character being described (see chap. 5). The evidence presented in this chapter demonstrates that speakers are frequently, if not constantly, in the process of repositioning themselves in deictic reference. Not only do they extend and contract their frame of reference, but they switch among different di-

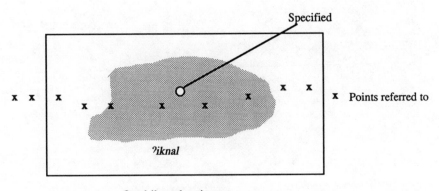

Fig. 9.12. Composite geometry of deictic space.

mensions with different indexical corollaries, implying different kinds of pragmatic grounds as well. The important insight that indexical transposition in fact takes place is most productive when applied to the utterly routine and ubiquitous practice of perspectival centering through deixis. Only some of the transpositions take on the highly foregrounded character of "creative" indexicals (Silverstein 1976b) or "breakthroughs" (Friedrich 1966), but the undramatic cases are an automatic part of the referential process. We return at this point to what was earlier dubbed the 'constantly shifting indexical ground' (chap. 5).

IV Structure in Referential Practice

10 System and Utterance:
The Elements of Maya Deixis

10.1 INTRODUCTION

The main objective of this chapter is to draw together into a single system the categories of deictics presented separately in preceding chapters. Having examined in some detail the properties of deictic utterances in Maya, I want to reassert at this point the unity of deixis as a linguistic and cultural system which, while it is defined relative to use, nonetheless transcends it. This unity can be constituted at different levels, starting with the linguistic types, each of which stands for an open-ended series of token instantiations, all unrepeatable and potentially novel, yet all recognizable as tokens of the type. Any type, as we have seen, has a consistent range of uses, summarizable as its inherent functional potential, just as it has a consistent range of morphophonemic variants.[1] At a more inclusive level, the unity of a set of types in a single grammatical category, such as the OSTEVs or the DLOCs, is constituted on the basis of properties shared consistently by members. Such properties include the morphosyntactic distributions which define the category, in some cases a range of semantic constraints, and even formal similarity or identity among forms, as in the *hé*? and *le* ID bases definitive of the OSTEVs and DNOMs, respectively. Categories in turn are not autonomous codes floating about randomly in the language but fit together in regular ways. As we observed in §2.2, many linguists have noted the tendency for these forms to fall into regular paradigms of proportional oppositions. The key descriptive question, it seems to me, is which aspects of deixis are systematic in this sense, and to what degree of regularity. Put slightly differently, at what level of specificity does the interrelatedness of the categories emerge clearly, and at what level does it dissolve into category-, type-, or token-specific idiosyncrasies? If we can answer these questions, then we can ask the explanatory one of why the system is as it is. Why, given the spectrum of possibilities, did Maya culture develop this communicative resource and not some other? This is one of the questions to which the present chapter leads.

There is another kind of unity that will figure prominently in the latter part of this chapter, based not on the conventional resources of the linguistic system but on the emergent articulation of parts of this system with interactive frameworks. The components of this unity are not linguistic types in a grammatical system. Nor are they (complex) frames in a frame space. Rather, the components are token messages composed of a plurality of simultaneous functions and connected to a corporeal field.[2] In actual frameworks, the frames and roles are occupied by real people and particulars. Here the key problem appears to be how we characterize the local, contingent processes of **integration** that take place in language use, which accumulate and organize relatively large quantities of independent and often fragmentary information, some of it linguistic and much of it not. If the first kind of unity reasserts the linguistic system as a total object with boundaries and its own inner logic, the second kind of unity reasserts the **embodiment** of language in the social world, as a fragmentary resource with extremely permeable boundaries, subject to the logic of historically contingent practices. An overall theory of linguistic practice would have to bring together these two kinds of unity, it seems to me, rather than attempt to assert the priority of one over the other.

The discussion will proceed in three main sections, beginning with the regularities of structure across deictic categories in the Maya language in §10.2. While the PART, DNOM, OSTEV, DMOD, and DLOC categories are by no means identically structured, they are nonetheless parallel in significant, nonobvious, ways. This provides a basis for describing the cross-categorial **iconicity** of the forms. In §10.3, the **overlap** among categories is explored through a discussion of the terminal deictics (TDs), which make up a single series whose members combine with IDs from all categories. The existence in Maya of this series, along with the regular rules by which the forms are combined with IDs, provides some of the most compelling evidence of the linguistic unity of deixis in the language. The final section §10.4, draws together the total frame space of Maya deixis, including the system of conventional functions, general properties of the indexical ground, and the interpretation of complex deictic acts.[3]

10.2 ICONICITY ACROSS CATEGORIES

10.2.1 Prima Facie Similarities

Maya deictics share a number of obvious, prima facie similarities which suggest that they form a single system.[4] The first of these is the fact that nearly all deictics in this language are made up of two morphemes, which we have called the ID (initial deictic) and the TD (terminal deictic). In all categories except the PART forms, the ID element is the one that bears the grammatical category feature of the type, for instance, NP for the DNOMs, Loc Adv for the DLOCs, and OSTEV for the OSTEVs (these forms have no nondeictic analogues). Holding aside the foregrounded constructions to be presented later in this section, only one ID base from any category may occur in a single constituent, to be accompanied by only one TD in S-final position. OSTEVs and the DMOD are also mutually exclusive, as was shown in chapter 6. The TDS {*a?, o?, b'e?, i?, e?*} form a single series, of which the first two are the most widely distributed, the middle two are the most specialized, and the last occurs with DTEMP, DLOC, and DMOD compounds. The TDS make up a tight paradigm whose members are usually mutually exclusive and occur only in S- or topic-final position.

All deictic constructions except the PART forms occur in two characteristic shapes, which we have called continuous, where the two forms are immediately adjacent to one another in surface structure, and discontinuous, where they are separated by intervening lexical material which they circumfix. Despite important differences between PART suffixes and TDS, there is a deep similarity between them as well, which we will attempt to make explicit, and PART forms also have discontinuous variants, falling into what we called set A and set B. There are also noteworthy phonological similarities among forms such as the OSTEV ID *hé?e(l)* and the DLOC *té?e(l)*, and among TDS, although it is less than clear how to integrate these facts properly in a linguistic description.

Recall from chapters 4, 5, 6, and 9 that in each category of Maya deictics there is at least one construction whose conventional R value is noticeably more abstract than the others. In the PART category, we find the third person, nonparticipant forms, while in the DNOMs there is *leti?* (lacking any value for relative immediacy), in the OSTEVs there is the DMOD *hé?ele?* (lacking any evidentiality), and in the DLOCs there is the Non-Concrete *tí?i?* lacking any properly spatial value. In the TDS, the semantically empty form *e?* fits the same description. In every case, the form which is the least specific in terms of information is also the most diverse in terms of functions outside the category. This is a standard corollary of markedness asymmetries among semantic features, but it works out in a highly regular way in Maya. Thus, the non-PART pronouns have an array of grammatical functions apart from referring to individuals (see chap. 4). The DNOM *leti?* functions as a clefting device quite distinct from the other forms in its category (see below). The DMOD *hé?el e?* is bleached of all evidentiality and functions instead as a nonreferential verbal auxil-

iary (see chap 6). And the DLOC *ti⁷* is in all likelihood the source of the
relational particle *ti⁷*, which is the only root preposition in Maya, used
for 'to, for, at, from, on, . . .'[5] Among TDS, *e⁷* is the most commonly
attested in nondeictic functions, serving as an S-final marker and general
connective. Comparing categories in this way, one gets a sense that each
category is constructed along similar lines, with a grading of informational richness. At the bottom end of the scale, the least informationally
rich forms tend to migrate outside the category, picking up grammatical
functions only tenuously related to the core communicative and referential values of the category.

These facts point to a level of proportionality in the structuring of Maya
deixis that goes far beyond the standard notion that all deictic categories
have proximal and distal subcategories. In the framework of this book,
we can make more specific and revealing statements which separate the
fact of proportionality from the idea of spatial proximity or any other
single relational dimension, while also allowing us to bring into focus the
absence of regularity in some key areas. In §10.2.2, we concentrate on
the resources for foregrounding deictic functions, which provide some
particularly revealing proportionalities.

10.2.2 Foregrounding Deictic Functions

Nearly all of the deictic expressions in Maya are distinguishable from
nondeictic elements by the kinds of foregrounded constructions in which
they may be used. These constructions occur only in main clauses, to my
knowledge, and involve moving deictics from their usual S-medial positions into initial or final position, as well as copying both IDS and TDS.
Foregrounded sentences may contain several coreferential deictics, with
the communicative effect of increased emphasis, focus, or specificity.
In most cases, these constructions are referentially equivalent to nonforegrounded ones, but indexically distinct. For instance, they may be
relatively more Expressive than the simple forms, or relatively more presupposing of discourse antecedents or of symmetrical participant access
to the object at the time of utterance. Yet the modes of access by participants to referential objects remains the same as the nonforegrounded expressions. It is important to appreciate that these means for foregrounding
deictic functions are specific to deictics in Maya grammar, and they have
no obvious analogues among standard lexical items. Furthermore, they
provide the resources whereby speakers can retain a given grammatical
category of a deictic while nonetheless increasing the salience of its indexical ground. For instance, a maximally foregrounded DLOC, like *má⁷*

té? yàan té?ela? a? 'it's right there! (obviously, look!)' approaches the Directive force normally conveyed by an OSTEV like *hé?el o?* 'there it is (look!)' while still focusing on the spatial location of the referent rather than its perceptibility. In terms of relative elaborateness of alternatives, the major categories treated can be graded from least (DNOMS) to most (DLOCS) elaborate, with the OSTEVs in the middle. They will be described in that order.[6] TDS also contribute to foregrounding in each category but will be discussed separately in §10.3.

10.2.2.1 *DNOM Incrementation*

Nominal deictics in Maya can occur in incremented structures like the following:

(1)   **leti? e maák kawá?alik o?**, ?iŋk'ah?oól
        'That guy you're talking (about), I know him.'

(2)   **leti? el o?**, haȼ'uȼ
        'That one there, it's nice.'

(3)   **leti? ?insukú?un** b'èeteh
        'That one my brother (is the one who) did it.'

(4)   b'ey u?estilo **leti e way a?**
        'That's how it is around here.' (BB.4.144)

Incremented NPs may occur in topical (1–2), focus (3), or S-final position (4), and always begin with the DNOM *leti?* 'the one', followed immediately by some other noun or noun phrase. To my knowledge, they do not occur S-medial. Constraints on the accompanying nominal expression are that it cannot be another instance of *leti?* (*leti? eti?* is ungrammatical), nor can it be a pronoun or a nondefinite noun. It must be either possessed or preceded by the definite article and may be a complex NP (1). The presence or absence of a TD in final position in the incremented NP is optional and depends upon the conveyed meaning.

The ordering relations between DNOMs in incremented constructions are invariant, with *leti?* preceding all others.[7] This rules out examples such as:

(5)   * le ?insukú?un leti? b'èeteh
        'My brother is the one (who) did it.'

(6)   * lelo? eti? haȼ'uȼ
        'That one there, it's nice.'

(7)   * b'ey ?u?estìilo le way leti? a?
        'That's how it is around here.'

Whereas foregrounded locative constructions occur in which the DLOCs are separated by lexical material, the two deictics in an incremented DNOM are obligatorily adjacent. Examples like the following are either ungrammatical or the deictics are interpreted as non-coreferential.

(8)   *leti^ʔ b'èet ʔinsukúʔun oʔ

(9)   *leti^ʔ haȼ'uȼ el oʔ

(10)   *b'ey ʔuʔestìilo leti^ʔ way lel aʔ

Taken out of context, incremented DNOMs are ambiguous between a single NP or an equational S with ∅ copula.

(11)   leti^ʔ el oʔ
           'that one,' 'that's the one'

(12)   leti^ʔ ʔinsukúʔun
           'that one my brother,' 'that one's my brother'

(13)   leti^ʔ el oʔ haȼ'uȼ
           'that one there, it's good,' 'that's the one. Good'

The proper use of incremented NPs is subject to the referential and indexical conditions on both DNOMs. As was shown in §4.2.3, the form *leti^ʔ* tends strongly to be used in reference to unique objects already known by both interactants. This knowledge may be based on preceding discourse in the same indexical frame or on background knowledge assumed by participants. Example (4), for instance, is an actual utterance produced by DC in the course of discussing the composition of the neighborhood in which he lives. He had just said that many local people actually moved to Oxkutzcab from Mani, a nearby town, and this utterance has the function of summarizing and reasserting his statements. Notice that the DLOC *way* 'here' is flanked by the further DNOM *(l)e(l)a^ʔ* 'this', giving it the conveyed meaning 'this here', namely, the place asymmetrically inhabited by DC (but not by me, his interlocutor). The token *leti^ʔ* can be interpreted in either of two ways: (i) it is coreferential with the nominalized DLOC, in which case it merely adds to the referential specificity already inherent in the phrase, meaning roughly 'this here (as opposed to any other)'; or (ii) it refers back to the preceding talk which DC was thereby summarizing, in which case it is cointerpreted with the manner deictic *b'ey* 'like (that)'. The former is by far the more likely interpretation, given that the entire incremented NP can be used properly without any antecedent, whereas the simple form *leti^ʔ* cannot be used in reference to prior discourse in this context (DC could not have said *b'ey leti^ʔ* 'that's how it is').

leti? el o? 'that's the one' is very commonly attested in response posi-tion as a way of making reference to a preceding utterance (by either interlocutor), in order to register understanding or convey agreement. In this usage, it is very similar pragmatically to Discourse Directive *hé?el o?* as described in §6.2.2. Thus, (13) could well be uttered in response to a statement by an interlocutor which the Spkr has understood and posi-tively evaluated. Of the two incremented DNOM constructions *leti? e . . . o?* and *leti? e . . . a?*, the former is the more commonly attested (speak-ing impressionistically), which is as would be expected, given the mark-edness values of the TDS.

10.2.2.2 OSTEV *Foregrounding*

It was noted in chapter 6 that the expressive load of OSTEVs may be increased in three ways: by negation (which is never interpretable as se-mantic negation), by copying the ID base into penultimate position in the S, or by lengthening the TD. All three processes may be combined, fur-thermore, yielding eight possible renditions of a single Presentative or Di-rective sentence. In this section, we will be concerned only with the copying of the ID; TDS will be described in §10.3. Recall that this involves primarily *hé?el a?* 'here it is (take it! look!)' and *hé?el o?* 'there it is (take it! look!)'. The DMOD *hé?el e?* never occurs in double ID construc-tions, and the Peripheral Directive *hé?e b'e?* rarely does, if ever.[8]

(14)   hé? yàan hé?el a?
          'Here it is here (take it!).'

(15)   hé? kub'in leti? hé?el o?
          'There goes the one there (look!).'

(16)   *hé? yàan hé? leti? o?

(17)   *hé? kub'in té?el o? hé?el o?

There are several noteworthy constraints on these forms. (i) The sec-ond instance of the OSTEV must be in absolute S-final position; there are no grammatical examples like (16). (ii) The two instances of the OSTEV must be separated by a lexical verb or by a lexical N. Despite the fact that the Presentative is fully predicative and can be used as a one-word utter-ance, the verb *yàan* 'is' in forms like (14) can never be omitted. (iii) There can be no DLOC in the same sentence with the OSTEV. Thus whereas *hé? kub'in té?el o?* 'there he goes over there (look!)' is fine, the form in (17) is gibberish and cannot be repaired so long as the DLOC is retained and the OSTEV doubled. (iv) Doubled OSTEVs are never used in subordinate clauses. (v) Whereas the OSTEVS which enter into this construction are used elsewhere with the entire range of Relational values in the category (see §6.2), doubled structures tend strongly to be used for Tactual and Visual reference. Discourse, Anticipatory, and Certain uses were unattested. (vi) Finally, these forms tend strongly to be used in brief, pointed utterances. The more elaborate the description that intervenes between the two token OSTEV bases, the less likely the utterance becomes. Thus, while _hé? k u b'in le ká?atuúl ?oóȼi maák k aw á?alik ten hé?el o?_ 'there go the two poor men you're talking about right there (look!)' is grammatical in theory, it is unlikely and prolix in practice.

Typically, doubled OSTEV constructions are used in relatively symmetric indexical frameworks, in which coparticipants are already oriented to the referent and share a perceptual field. The most characteristic examples occur in response to locational questions and are accompanied by high-focus gestures, such as handing over or pointing to the referent. The expressivity of such utterances is often reinforced by special prosodic features, particularly in the forms combining negation, ID doubling, and TD doubling. At the maximum, these features include (i) contrastive stress on the normally atonic TDs; (ii) uncharacteristically high pitch on the first of two TDs; (iii) very high pitch on the negative and the first OSTEV element (_má hé_), verging on falsetto; (iv) high pitch and nasality throughout the utterance; (v) distinct, maximally clear articulation of all glottal stops except the one in the negative morpheme _má?_, (which is usually lost entirely, merging the negative with the OSTEV particle), resulting in a jerky rhythm; (vi) finally, the utterance may be preceded by an apical click, conveying mild exasperation. Example (18) shows all of these features.

(18)   A: kuš tuún ?inmàaskab' ↓
        'What about my machete? (where is it?)'

        B: tch! má hé? yàan hé?el a?a? → ?oómeŋ
        'Tch! Here it is right here, man! (what are you blind?)'

This example is hypothetical, but the utterance type illustrated is very common in everyday Maya, in speech of men, women, and children. The expressive effect is consistently that of indicating that the Spkr takes the referent to be obvious, beyond question, sometimes to the point of exasperation.

10.2.2.3 DLOC *Foregrounding*

As was noted above, the possibilities for foregrounding deictic reference are nowhere as elaborately developed as in the DLOCs. In this category, it is necessary to distinguish three major types of focus constructions, which can be called simple, split, and double ID focus. The distinctive feature shared by all three is that some portion of the locative phrase in a sentence occurs in immediate pre-VC (verb complex) position: in **simple focus,** the entire locative phrase precedes the verbal auxiliary (i.e., the leftmost element in the VC). In **split focus,** the ID base of the DLOC **precedes** the verbal auxiliary, but any lexical descriptors which elaborate the reference **follow** the verb in the normal, nonfocal position (see §9.1). In **double ID focus,** two initial DLOC bases occur in the same clause, one in pre-VC position and one in post-VC position. The two may be identical but need not be, and the presence of further lexical description is grammatically optional. Beyond these three focal constructions and their variants, there is also a nonfocal variant of the double ID construction. We will take these up in the order cited.

Simple DLOC focus. Simple DLOC focus appears to work in the same way as nominal focus, the distinctive feature of which is that the focal element occurs in immediately pre-VC position. Corresponding to the nonfocused *k im bin té?el o?* 'I go there', we get *té? k im b'in o?* 'there (is where) I go', and from *k im b'in hk'iíwik* 'I go to market', we get *hk'iíwik k im bin* '(to) market (is where) I go'. Any element which can function as a nonfocal locative may be focused in this way, without any special morphological marking on the verb or elsewhere.[9] If the locative phrase is a DLOC without any further lexical description, the ID base occurs in focus position and the TD in S-final position, as usual. All DLOCs occur in simple focus constructions (recall from chapter 9 that *tí?i?* 'there [Non-Concrete]' is used only for focus).

(19)   **té?** kimbin a?
        'Here('s where) I'm going'.

(20)   **way** kinwèenl e?
        'Here('s where) I sleep.'

(21)   **to** naáč kub'in o?
        'Out there far away (is where) he goes.'

(22)   **té? k'oób'en** kán awuk' awó?oč kàafe o? → wá **té?el a?**
        'There in the kitchen you'll drink your coffee, or (out) here?'
            (BB.5.27)

The utterance in (22) was produced by Eli while she was standing in the courtyard outside her kitchen. It was addressed to me, while I was seated at a small table writing. Moments earlier, I had asked her to heat some water for coffee, and she was inquiring whether I would have it outside, where I was, or inside the kitchen. As expected, given the spatial configuration, the inside of the kitchen was treated as 'there' (Non-Immed Sym) from our shared vantage point, and my current location was treated as 'here' (Immed, Asym). Notice that the entire locative phrase 'there in the kitchen' has been fronted.

DC produced a structurally similar utterance while describing a trip he and his sons had taken to central Mexico to ritually protect a man whose possessions had been stolen repeatedly. After the ceremony, DC observed, the property was returned anonymously, evidently brought back to the rooftop from which it had been stolen through a skylight.

(23)   té⁷ yoó⁷ pak'i nah tusutó⁷ob' e b'á⁷a tuyokló⁷ob' o⁷
             'There atop the house they returned the things they had stolen.'
             (BB.4.100)

As this utterance illustrates, the focused locative may contain a prepositional phrase. To my knowledge, it may not contain an embedded relative clause, which would result in a verb crossing over the main verb, as in *té⁷ tú⁷uš kinmeyah k a b'in o⁷ 'there where I work (is where) you'll go' (Cf. nonfocal kab'in té⁷ tú⁷uš kinmeyah o⁷, 'you'll go there where I work', which is fine). On the other hand, a DLOC associated with a subordinate verb may precede the verb of the main clause, as in:

(24)   tak tée   kubin   šiímbal o⁷ →
             'Even there he goes walking.' (F.137.A.277)

(25)   té⁷ tutuúštah b'èetb'il o⁷
             'There ('s where) he sent it to be done.'

Focused locative phrases may also be questioned, cast in the optative-subjunctive mode, or in the *if* clause of a conditional, as in the following.

(26)   té⁷ wá yan a⁷ ⇝ eléna↑
             'Is it here, Elena?' (BB.5.28)

(27)   tée ká wáalakéeš a⁷
             'Stop right here!' (BB.4.135)

(28)   wá té⁷ ká wèenkó⁷on a⁷ ↑ má⁷ tinwene tub'èel
             'If there we were to sleep, I wouldn't sleep right.' (BB.4.100)

The first of these was produced by Luis as he was looking at a photo album and was addressed to Eli (his father's brother's wife), who was about

two meters behind him. The selection of the Immediate DLOC form reflects this asymmetry in his own and his addressee's access to the referent.
Number (27), on the other hand, was produced by a man standing on the
open bed of a truck as it backed through the gate into a yard. The Spkr
was watching as the truck inched towards the wall, and his utterance told
the driver where to stop before hitting it. The verb is in the optative mode,
subordinated to the particle *ká*. This is a relatively common way of expressing a wish, possibility, or, as in this case, a directive. In (28) the
focused DLOC introduces an irrealis clause within the scope of the indefinite particle *wá* marking a counterfactual *if* clause. This was produced by
Man in room 1 of his house (see floor plan in fig. 7.8) and addressed to
me in the same room. He had told me shortly before that he and Margot
sleep in room 2 during the winter months, because it is warmer, and the
remark in (28) adds that, were they to do otherwise, he would not sleep
properly (because of the cold).

Split DLOC focus. In split focus constructions, the DLOC is in focal position, and the lexical descriptor remains in its usual post-VC position. This
results in two coreferential locative elements, one initial and one final in
the clause. All of the DLOCs occur in this construction, and for *tí?i?* 'there
(Non-Concrete)', it is the only way to lexically elaborate the locative reference (cf. §9.2.3). Examples (29–31) illustrate the split construction.[10]

(29)   **tí?an t-y-iknal e?**
         'It's in their place.' (BB.4.28)

(30)   **way** kup'aá?tal **t-inw-iknal e?**
         'Here ('s where) it stays in my place.'

(31)   **té?** kimb'in **hk'iíwik o?**
         'There ('s where) I'm going (to) market.'

While the deictic ID in such examples is fronted alone, leaving the
lexical phrase in post-VC position, the lexical phrase cannot be fronted
leaving the ID behind. There are no grammatical split focus sentences
like *tyiknal tí? an e?*, *hk'iíwik té? kimb'in o?*, or *hk'iíwik kimb'in té?el
o?*.

Double DLOC focus. Whereas **simple locative focus** corresponds to the
template [LOC VC X] (where the LOC element may be either a DLOC or a
nondeictic locative phrase), and **split focus** corresponds to [DLOC VC X
LOC Y] (where X and Y are possibly null variables), **double DLOC focus**
corresponds to [DLOC VC X DLOC Y], where the second DLOC may be
further elaborated by a lexical description and may be followed by certain
adverbial elements.

Although both simple and split focus constructions are transparently related to nonfocused sentences, with the DLOC in its usual post-VC position, double constructions often have no obvious nonfocused counterparts. The reason is that Spkrs rarely use more than one DLOC base unless one is in focal position, and there is only one construction type (to be discussed presently) in which DLOCs occur immediately adjacent to one another.

Both of Luis's utterances in (32) contain doubled constructions. He was standing in the courtyard of his house at the time, and I was sitting at a small table writing. His first DLOC reference combines the Non-Concrete form in focal position with the Non-Immediate one S-final; he knew that I knew where his house was and was familiar with the inside as well, although I was unaware that he had a picture of me, and so the predication as a whole presented new information. Unsure of where he meant, I asked, and he then recycled with another doubled construction, in which the ID *té?* occurred both pre- and post-VC. This last utterance was spoken as Luis was beginning to walk to the house to get the photo, and his choice of the Immediate form reflected this forward trajectory.

(32)   L: **tí?**-an afòoto **té?el o?**
            'There's your photo there.'

        W: tú?uš→ ?ič nah?
            'Where? In (the) house?'

        L: tí? i?→ **té** yan **té?el a?**
            'Yup, there they are right there.' (BB.5.28)

Whereas both of Luis's locational references show the post-VC deictic in continuous shape, other examples show that it may also circumfix a lexical description of the referent, as in the next two.

(33)   ?òoken i?→ **tí?**-an **té?** ič nah **o?**
            'Go in there. There he is there in the house.' (BB.4.82)

(34)   **tí?**-an **té?** yoók'ol eskìina i média kahakbaló?ob' ká?ač **a?**
            'There (is where) there at a block and a half they used to live.'
            (BB.4.100)

Example (33) was uttered by Margot as she was standing at her oven in the yard (see fig. 7.8) and was addressed to a visitor who had just arrived at the gate to DC's place next door in the same household. Example (34) was uttered by Man as he was telling me the story of a former neighbor who had moved away from the immediate neighborhood. Note that the two IDs are separated by the inserted verb 'to be', and that the second is elaborated by the lexical description 'at a block and a half', which is in turn followed by the stative positional verb 'they live', itself modified by the temporal adverb *káʔač* 'in the past'. The TD as always occurs in absolute final position. Examples like this one make it clear that the second locative phrase need not be in S-final position for the sentence to be grammatical.[11]

The fact that a sentence contains a double ID locative focus does not preclude its simultaneously predicating a possessive relation. Recall from §4.2 that one of the ways that possession is predicated in Maya is by using the locative-existential verb *ʔan* 'to be', as in *y àan ¢iímin tiʔ ten* ~ *y àan ten ¢iímin* 'I have (a) horse' (lit., 'there is a horse to me)'. This is the same verb used for locative predication in the foregoing examples, and in the following two examples, it serves both functions at once.

(35)   miín **tíʔ**-an tiʔ ten **téʔel** oʔ
            'I think I've got it over there.' (BB.4.93)

(36)   WH: kuš tuún cuchillo?
            'What about the knife?'

        Fi: **tíʔ**-an **téʔe** tiʔ oʔ
            'There it is theirs over there.' (BB.4.28)

Sentence (35) was uttered by Lol and addressed to Man after Man had asked Lol if he knew where the family pickax was. Lol was sitting in Man's house at the time (room 1, fig. 7.8), and tossed this head in the direction of his own home (rooms 5–8) as he spoke. The utterance locates the ax both spatially and in terms of current possession. The two relations are linguistically distinct but converge in the fact that the spaces around the household all have owners, and the occupants all have distinct subspaces. The possessive phrase *tiʔ ten* 'mine' can therefore be seen as a further specification of the location referred to.

In (36), a similar convergence is effected, but in a more truncated form. Fi (Lol's wife) and I were sitting in her house (room 5, fig. 7.8) about to peel oranges to make juice, when I asked her whether she had the knife. As with the pickax, the family shares a single cutting knife, which belongs to Man and Margot next door. Fi's utterance initially surprised me, and I asked her to repeat it, not having heard such a compressed statement of possession and location before. In response to my request, she said *tíʔ an téʔe tiʔ letiʔ oʔ*, which is structurally identical except for the addition of the independent Non-Participant form. She then explained that both utterances convey *both* the location of the knife (next door) and the fact that it belongs to Man and Margot. The double DLOC construction is purely locational, and the *ti⁷* (*leti⁷*) phrase purely possessive. Notice that, unlike the preceding example, Fi's utterances show the possessive element after the second DLOC base rather than before it. It is tempting to suggest that this is motivated by the difference between first and third persons (the former precedes circumstantial elements, and the latter follows), although this interpretation would require further evidence.

In other examples, temporal or manner adverbs may also follow the second DLOC base, giving further evidence that it need not necessarily occur S-final. This is significant, because in most examples, the postverbal DLOC is S-final (followed only by the TD), and furthermore, it is a point of difference between DLOCs and OSTEVs. Recall that in doubled OSTEV constructions, the second token must be final, ruling out sentences such as **hé⁷ yàan hé⁷ ti leti⁷ o⁷* 'there it is his (look!)'.

(37)   le ȼ'àak o⁷ čeén **tí⁷**-an **tée** b'ey **o⁷**
            'That medicine, just there (is where) it is there like that.' (BB.4.95)

(38)   **tí⁷** anó⁷on **té** ká⁷ač **o⁷**
            'We used to be (live) over there.' (BB.5.42)

In (37) the post-VC DLOC *tée* 'there' is followed by the manner deictic (DMAN) *b'ey* 'like that (as I said, as usual, as we can see)', and in (38) it is followed by the temporal adverb *ká⁷ač* 'in the past'. The former was produced by DC sitting before his altar, and he was telling me that he stores medicines around the room. We were already discussing the medicine, as indicated by the Non-Immediate DNOM, and there was a question as to where he kept it.

Sentence (38) was uttered by Pilar as we were talking in the courtyard of her house. We were already discussing the most distant of DP's houses, which is located in an orchard where Pilar and her husband VC formerly lived. All of these examples share the significant feature that the question of location had already been raised in the discourse at the point at which the focal construction is produced. This is evidently a constant property of the indexical frame of locative focus and is indeed one of the motivations for calling them 'focal'.

As the foregoing examples show, the two DLOC bases in a doubled construction need not be identical, but they may be. All of the DLOCs except *tí⁷i⁷* can be coupled with themselves, yielding examples like the following.

(39)   **to** kimb'in **to** nukuč k'aáš **o⁷**
            'Out there (is where) I go there in (the) high forest.'

(40)   **way** kup'aá'tal **way** e'
            'Here (is where) it stays here.'

Of the nonidentical couplings, the most common is *tí'* . . . *té'*, as in examples (32–38), although *té'* . . . *tol o'* occurs as well.

(41)   **té'** kimb'in **tol o'**
            'There (is where) I go out there.'

(42)   ****to** kimb'in **té'el o'**
            'Out there (is where) I go there.'

(43)   ****té'** timp'atah **way a'**
            'There (is where) I left it here.'

(44)   ****way** tinwilah **té'el a'**
            'Here (is where) I saw it right here.'

It is unclear to me precisely what difference is conveyed when a speaker selects between the alternatives summarized by {*tí'*, *té'*} . . . *té'*, or {*tí'*, *té'*, *to*} . . . *tol o'*. Note in (42–44) that *to* cannot precede *té'*, and *way* cannot be combined with *té'* in these constructions. In fact, *way* is unique in that it combines only with itself (although see below).

Whatever the nuances of conveyed meaning may be, there are clear constraints on co-occurrence and linear ordering of the DLOCs in doubled constructions. *tí'* occurs only in DLOC$_1$ position (pre-VC), and may be followed in DLOC$_2$ position (post-VC) by any of the others except itself or *way* e'. *té'* occurs in DLOC$_1$ position, followed in DLOC$_2$ position by itself or *tol o'*. Both *way* and *to* occur in DLOC$_1$ position and can be followed only by themselves.

These ordering relations can be captured in a simple hierarchy stating *tí'* > *té'* > *to*, where 'X > Y' indicates that X precedes Y. Any ID can be used as DLOC$_1$ in a construction with those which it precedes in this ordering, but not with those which precede it. Recall that an analogous order governs the combination of DNOMs, *leti'* > *lel a'*, *lel o'*.

Although this hierarchy is a relatively arbitrary fact of Maya grammar and does not correspond precisely to the hierarchy of R values conveyed by the forms, these R values can nevertheless help make the ordering intelligible. Focus and anaphora both entail a relation between an utterance token and the discourse which precedes it. The Non-Concrete DLOC *tí'* is the one form in the locative category which is specialized in both functions. Being restricted to DLOC$_1$ position furthermore, *tí'* functions as a 'thematic' device in the sense discussed by Halliday (1985) and Brown and Yule (1983:126ff.). That is, it defines the point of departure of the utterance, in distinction to the rheme, or commentary, which follows it. *tí⁷* thematizes space, then, but adds no further information unless elaborated.

The other two DLOC bases are inherently richer in information than the Non-Concrete one. They may or may not signal a relation with prior discourse and may or may not be used to thematize space, but they always convey some qualitative information regarding the relation between the space under discussion and the space of the utterance. These considerations also appear to bear out the (admittedly vague) Praguean notion of communicative dynamism, whereby already established information tends to precede relatively newer contributions.[12]

There is an obvious analogy to be drawn between double DLOC and the emphatic OSTEV constructions. Both involve two deictics of the same category, one before and one after the verb, and both tend strongly to be used in relatively presupposing frameworks, in which the relevance of a locational statement is already established. *tí⁷i⁷* and *hé⁷el e⁷* are the most informationally impoverished forms in their respective categories, and neither can occur in second position. Exclusive *tol o⁷* 'out there' occurs in doubled constructions, whereas the Peripheral Directive *hé⁷e b'e⁷* 'there it is (listen!)' apparently does not. The remaining forms, *hé⁷el a⁷*, *hé⁷el o⁷*, *té⁷el a⁷*, *té⁷el o⁷* are equally susceptible of entering into doubled constructions. Whereas the combination of negation with doubling of the ID provides a range of alternative OSTEV constructions (see chap. 6, (29)), the alternatives for DLOCs are the ones listed below. Note that these do not show either emphatic negation or doubling of the Terminal Deictics, both of which **also** apply to DLOCs and multiply still further the number of constructions.

(45)   kimb'in **h k'iíwik**   'I go (to) market.' (plain)
          h k'iíwik kimb'in   Simple locative focus
          kimb'in **té⁷ h k'iíwik o⁷**   Plain with DLOC
          té⁷ h k'iíwik kimb'in o⁷   Simple locative focus with DLOC
          to⁷ h k'iíwik kimb'in o⁷   Simple locative focus with DLOC
          tí⁷ kimb'in **h k'iíwik e⁷**   Split locative focus
          té⁷ kimb'in **h k'iíwik o⁷**   Split locative focus
          to⁷ kimb'in **h k'iíwik o⁷**   Split locative focus
          tí⁷ kimb'in **té⁷ h k'iíwik o⁷**   Double DLOC focus
          tí⁷ kimb'in **to⁷ h k'iíwik o⁷**   Double DLOC focus
          té⁷ kimb'in **té⁷ h k'iíwik o⁷**   Double DLOC focus
          té⁷ kimb'in **to⁷ h k'iíwik o⁷**   Double DLOC focus

The range of constructions in (45), along with their negated and double TD counterparts, make up a formidable resource for spatial reference.

What is striking is that these formal variants involve only limited changes (if any) in the R values of the references, whereas they signal outstanding differences in the expressive force and overtones. In our terms, they elaborate the indexical ground of spatial reference, providing systematic means of differentiating among indexical frames. Moreover, there is an iconic relation between the relative weight of the utterance form (complexity, redundancy, length, prosodic features) and the degree of expressive foregrounding. The fact that OSTEV and DNOM categories show analogous repertoires reinforces the other homologies in the linguistic structure of deixis that we have already seen.

It is tempting to suggest that this cross-categorical iconicity among sets of deictics (and its limits) is motivated by the practical and functional parallels among the frames of indexical reference. Among the common features of deictic frames that we have seen are the relational structures, engagements of corporeality, participation frameworks, and the possibility of transposed reference. It is because all deictics fit into this matrix of functions connecting language and lived space that they display the formal parallels that they do. Some of the commonalities, such as the bimorphemic structure ID-TD appear to be directly connected to functional bifurcations (see §10.3), whereas others may derive from analogical formations involving arbitrary facts of grammar (the loss of (el-) in OSTEV and DLOC bases).

Further combinations of DLOCs. In addition to the foregrounded constructions described in the preceding sections, DLOCs occur in two more distinctive configurations. These are less commonly attested than the others, and native speakers are prone to reject them if presented with them for metalinguistic commentary. One of them involves the combination of *té?el a?* and *way e?*, and the other involves the use of more than one DLOC base in postverbal position. The latter are simpler than the former and will be taken up first. Examples (46–47) show the two instances I have recorded of doubled DLOCs which do not fit the standard template for doubled focus constructions.

(46)   má?a to tak'àan o?, **té?e k'àan té?el a?**
        'Not over there in your hammock, right here in the hammock
        here.' (BB.4.60)

(47)   Fi: bey ukwèerpo ti? Pedro . . .
        'His body is like Pedro's . . .

        Lol: mas bek'eč ti? Pedro ⌣, leti yàan té ká?ač té? párselá o?→
        'He's thinner than Pedro, the one who used to be there there in the
        (family) plot.' (F.137.A.050)

The peculiar feature of both of these examples is that there are two tokens of *té?* which are not separated by a verb. In (47), in particular, the DNOM *leti?* 'the one' defines the grammatical focus and discourse theme of the sentence, to which the locative phrase is a rhematic complement. Sentence (46) was addressed to me by Margot as we sat at her table in room 1 (fig. 7.8). I was about to take a nap, dressed in filthy clothes after working in the yard, and she offered me an old hammock in the next room. Thus, the question of where I would rest was already in play in the interactive framework, and Margot's utterance sets off the two alternatives.

In (47), Lol and Fi were describing Fi's brother to me and comparing his physical stature to that of a third party we all knew, named Pedro. I had only met Pedro once, years earlier, and Lol's locative phrase specified for me who he and Fi were referring to. In (46), the two DLOCs occur in flanking positions in a single, continuous locative phrase. Given that the simpler form corresponding to this is *té? k'àan a?* and not **k'àan té?el a?*, the best description appears to be that the DLOC has been copied to the right of the lexical locative. This makes it a close parallel to the doubled OSTEV constructions, in which the second deictic base is copied into S-final position (that is, at the end of the syntactic constituent conventionally circumfixed by this category of deictic). Example (47) is grammatically distinct from (46), since the two DLOCs do not form a single continuous constituent: *té? pàarsela o?* is a routine locative phrase, whereas *té? ká?ač pàarsela o?* is not (to my knowledge). The temporal particle evidently precedes the locative in *ká?ač té? pàarsela o?*, since focus and movement rules cannot shift it along with the locative.[13] What appears to be going on in the example is that a second copy of the DLOC is inserted before the temporal particle, as a way of 'staging' the locative reference. It is my sense that this is related to focus formation, and that other DLOCs occur in parallel constructions, although, in the absence of further evidence, these will have to remain unsubstantiated hunches.

The combinations of *té?el a?* with *way e?* pose more interesting problems from a semantic perspective, since these two forms are associated with distinct R values and indexical frames. Consider first some examples.[14]

(48)   hé? uluúb'ul maák **té? way h b'eh a?**
        'One (can) surely fall(s) (around) here on this road.'

(49)   **té? way hoó? kàah,** kàasi lòote? kàahiló?ob yàan i?
        '(Around) here (at the) outskirts of town, pretty much (only) people
        from other towns are here.'

(50)   **té⁇ way nàaç'il** kahá⁇anó⁇on **a⁇**
             'Right there near here (is where) we reside.'

Utterances like these are relatively rare, as I have noted, and several Maya speakers have rejected them outright as 'not Maya' when asked to comment on them in the elicitation context. These three examples were attested in everyday speech by native speakers. In each of these examples, the DLOCs are further elaborated by some lexical description, although this is not always the case. Observe that when they are, the two DLOCs must remain immediately adjacent to one another, ruling out phrases like *té⁇ hoó⁇ kàah way a⁇* and *té⁇ b'eh way a⁇*. The presence of the TD *a⁇* in final position is grammatically optional, but no other TD can be used, which indicates that it is only the Immediate DLOC which may combine this way with the Inclusive *way e⁇*. No other DLOCs may be so combined, and the linear order of the parts is invariant. Furthermore, although the doubled phrase may itself be thematic (49, 50) or not (48), it is not usually associated with another DLOC in the same sentence.[15] Thus, these constructions do not combine with split or doubled DLOC focus as presented previously.

Number (48) was addressed to me by a woman as we walked towards each other on a muddy path. We were both slipping about and I had just avoided falling, throwing out my arms and lurching to the side to stay afoot. The force of her utterance is that the whole road was potentially slippery, and especially the part on which I was struggling to keep my footing. Sentence (49) was uttered by MC in the course of describing his neighborhood on the outskirts of Oxkutzcab. The referential scope of the locative includes his own home, where we were at the time, as well as others around the area. Sentence (50) was produced by a man with whom I was talking at a party, and the referent of the locative phrase is his own home nearby but outside the one in which we were sitting.

These examples are troublesome, and the inability of native speakers to discuss them makes the interpretation still more delicate. I wish to suggest, however, that they actually correspond to two different locational schemata: (48, 49) project a relation of inclusion, whereby the region to which *way* refers includes the more restricted point to which *té⁇el a⁇* refers. Examples like (50) project two spatial locations in a relation of contiguity to one another. These alternatives are shown graphically in figure 10.1.

If this characterization is correct, it implies that in both cases, the R values of both DLOCs contribute to the overall interpretation but in slightly

INCLUSION   CONTIGUITY

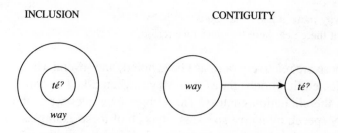

Fig. 10.1. Complex frames of spatial reference: *té? way.*

different ways. In the case of Inclusion, there appears to be a single complex spatial reference whch entails both an encompassing region and a point segmented within it. With the Contiguity cases, however, it is more tempting to posit a two-step interpretation in which the region referred to by *way* (which includes the current location of the utterance) serves as a transposed indexical ground relative to which some second place is described as 'nearby'. It is only in this case that the descriptor *nàaȼ'il* 'near' can be used (although it need not be), and this term applies precisely to the relation between the two frames. For instance, if the woman slipping on the road had qualified her spatial reference by 'nearby', then her utterance would have activated the Contiguity rather than the Inclusion schema and unambiguously conveyed that the road was slippery **somewhere else** nearby but not where we were at the time. This is clearly not what she intended.

Another example of the Inclusion schema occurred in the course of Lol's description of how he and his brother had moved into their current household and planned to develop it. This was presented as example (9) in chapter 7, to which the reader is referred. Recall that in the immediately preceding discourse, Lol had described the arrival of him and his brother 'here' at the homestead we were currently sitting in. Once established, this region was then subdivided by the Immediate DLOC into a specific place for the building itself. In response to my question, he then combined the two references, inclusive and segmenting, into a single complex reference.

(51)   WH: hač
          'Right-

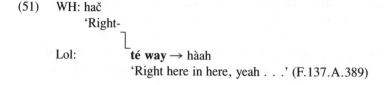

        Lol: **té way** → hàah
                      'Right here in here, yeah . . .' (F.137.A.389)

Lol's choice of spatial reference reflects nicely the duality of the homestead as a single inclusive whole that is internally subdivided by places
corresponding to each family. Had he added a descriptor like *nàaȼ'il* and
forced the Contiguity rather than the Inclusion interpretation, he would
have conveyed erroneously that the place where they built the house was
somewhere other than our actual location.[16]

The next example shows the Inclusion schema again. Note that unlike
the preceding example, this one entails a division between the location in
which the utterance is performed and the location referred to.

(52)   Lol: tubèetah le ti? té?el o?
         'She made it there.'

         WH: b'iš té?el o?→
         'How so, "there"?'

         Lol: le ti? b'èet **tée** → h **té way** bey a? ↓
         'She('s) the one (who) made it there, there here like I said.'
         (F.137.B.165)

At the time of this exchange between Lol and me, we were sitting inside
his main house (room 5, fig. 7.8), and he was explaining that although
each nuclear family pays for its own food separately, still, on occasion
they share. That day his wife Fi had prepared the food for the children of
Margot and Man next door, who had gone to Mérida on some errands. In
Lol's first utterance, he used the DNOM *leti?* without antecedent for reference to his wife and referred to her cooking area with the Non-Immediate
DLOC. This is a standard usage which reflects the boundary between the
(male, public) receiving area in which we were sitting (area 7 in fig. 7.8)
and the (female, private) cooking area at which Fi works (area 8 in
fig. 7.8). In response to my query as to where he meant, Lol produced the
incremented DLOC construction in the last line. Unlike the previous examples, this one actually shows three DLOC bases in a row, separated only
by the locative proclitic *h* and followed by the manner deictic *b'ey* (which
is glossed nonliterally 'as I said'). The most significant features of the indexical frame of this example are the following two: (i) There are just two
cooking areas in the household, one belonging to Fi and one to Margot.
Thus my question is interpretable as a disjunction, 'here or over there?'
(ii) Although the cooking area is outside the room where we were at the
time, as reflected in his first utterance, it is also part of the same nuclear
household belonging to Lol as distinct from that of Margot and Man.
Therefore, I take the utterance to index our current corporeal frame

within room 7, while referring to Fi's cooking area (8) just beyond our perceptual field but still included in the larger frame space.

The clearest examples of the Contiguity schema involve more than a distinction between two reference spaces, like the foregoing. They involve a **disjunction** between the referent of *way* and the referent of *té'el a'*. Eli and I were sitting in her kitchen in area I (see fig. 7.6) as I explained to her that I would sleep that evening in the secondary residence of DP (area III, fig. 7.5). She then described this place in contrast to DP's main residence. Recall from figure 7.5 that the three households form a single, third-order household spread out discontinuously along a road, such that area I (where we were) is separated from area III by area II. Eli said:

(53)   tí kawene màas pàačil o'→   'oóšp'ée yotoč leti'→
           'There (is where) you're sleeping behind. Three houses he has,

           má' **té' way nàac̣'il a**ɂ **a**ɂ→ té' pàačil o'
           not the one nearby here,   (but the one) there behind (it).'
                                                (BB.5.7)

Once again the qualifier 'nearby' is combined with the DLOC reference and confirms the disjunction between the current location of our conversation (included within the referential frame of *way*) and the location of the focal referent. Reinforcing the three-way contrast among the places is the opposition between 'nearby' and 'behind', a standard way of formulating places on the far side of a landmark (cf. fig. 9.2). What Eli's complex referential frame does precisely is individuate the landmark midway between our corporeal field (area I) and the distant 'out back' of area III.

One of the significant implications of the *té' way* constructions is that the two basic axes of deictic space in this language are combined. These axes, as they were developed in chapter 9, were called Sociocentric (Restricted) and Egocentric (Regional). On the basis of routine usage and grammatical distributions, they were shown to be complementary parts of the deictic frame space, along with the isolated *tí'i'* on its own, Non-Concrete axis. On each of the former axes, a pair of terms is opposed, by relative Immediacy on the first and by Inclusivity on the second. It is noteworthy that of all the DLOCs, only the Immediate and the Inclusive combine in this way. We find no analogous *té' tol o'* in the nonproximal region. Why? One reason is probably that the nonproximal forms combine productively in the double focus constructions outlined in the preceding section, whereas the proximal ones happen not to combine there.

Thus, the development of *té? way* creates a functional parallel between the two regions that would not otherwise be present.

Why is there no analogous combination of Inclusive with Non-Immediate, given that we know *té?el o?* can be used in reference to places within the scope of *way e??* In fact, there is no construction in which these two are combined, even though they may be juxtaposed and have overlapping reference in discourse. I take this gap to be a relatively arbitrary fact of Maya grammar, but consider the combination of Immediate with Inclusive to be the product of two tendencies. The first is *the tendency towards proportionality* across categories, which plays a basic role in the structuring of the Maya system. The second, equally basic, is *the tendency for the proximal zone to be more delicately differentiated* than the remote zone. Recall that in all of the double focus constructions, the two DLOCs are interpreted as coreferential. It is the indexical frame of the reference which is elaborated in these forms (through thematization and Expressivity) and not the semantic complexity of the reference itself. If my analysis is correct, the *té? way* constructions involve a real increase in semantic complexity, corresponding to two distinct spatial frames, the Inclusion and the Contiguity. Each one subsumes two reference points, in addition to the indexical ground relative to which they are interpreted. This means that in the proximal zone of reference relative to coparticipants, there are two complex schemata available that are not available for remote reference.

If we look at the repertoire of categories, this kind of discrepancy is repeated again and again: there are six categories of Participant (Spkr, Adr, sg, pl, Inclusive, third person Inclusive) but only two Non-Participant (sg, pl). In the OSTEVs, there are three types of Perception, plus Discourse, Anticipation, and the communicative functions of Presentative and Directive, all of which are lacking in the remote regions beyond ostensive reference. In the DLOCs, Inclusive, Immediate, and Non-Immediate are all used singly in reference to the proximal zone, and the first two are combined in complex references. Although we have not attempted to analyze the temporal deictics in this book, a similar skewing is immediately apparent in the proliferation of terms for proximal temporal reference as opposed to the spotty, more vague coverage of temporally distant zones.

If we look at the totality of referential values (R values) in the deictic system, there is a strong bias towards the proximal region. The closer we get to the immediate corporeal frame of reference, the finer and more numerous are the distinctions among deictic categories. We can call this skewing the principle of **proximal differentiation.** This fundamental feature of the system is motivated by its roots in the phenomenal field of linguistic practice. It is obscured in standard approaches to deixis which take as their touchstone 'real' space rather than social interaction.

Looking at the indexical effects of foregrounding as described in this section, the question arises as to why the deictics should show such a proliferation of formal resources for foregrounding, most of them without obvious parallels outside the deictic system. One reason for this falls out naturally from the analysis of demonstrative reference as presented in this book: the articulation of an interactive indexical ground with a referential figure, summarized in the $R(x, i)$ notation, along with the overlay of communicative functions (Presentative through Expressive) together set up the necessary semiotic frame for foregrounding. They unavoidably link the utterance into the very interactive coordinates that are brought to the fore through focus, expressive reduplication, and double deictic constructions: the Spkr, the relation to Adr, the prior discourse, the relative certainty of reference. This amounts to an increase in the number of distinctions in already-established categories rather than a proliferation of new categories or new combinations of them. The regularity of the foregrounded constructions across categories also enhances the iconicity of the language in two ways. Internal to the system, the similarity of structuring among categories is increased. In the relation between the system and the kinds of embodied acts it is used to perform, the similarity between elaborateness of message form and elaborateness of functional structure is increased; the heavier the form, the greater the foregrounding.

10.3 Overlapping Deictic Categories

In addition to the deep-seated similarities in the structuring of deictic categories, there are in Maya several forms that help bind the system together by occurring in more than one category while nonetheless remaining functionally consistent. The most significant case of this is the Terminal Deictics (TDs). In this section, we examine the behavior of TDs across categories and attempt to describe the constraints on their surface shapes. In addition, we will try to make explicit the parallel between these enclitics and the Participant suffixes. To the extent that this parallel can be established, we will have another large piece of evidence for the underlying unity of the deictic system, including the pronouns. This then leads to a new set of foregrounded constructions, in which TDs are doubled.

10.3.1 TDs and the Unity of Deictic Categories

Each of the Initial Deictic bases bears a grammatical category feature, and each is associated with a core dimension of the deictic frame. The

PART forms are all nouns, and their core dimension is Participation, as defined in chapters 4 and 5; the OSTEVS are all sentential adverbs, and their core dimension is Perception, as defined in chapter 6; the DLOCS are all circumstantial adverbs, and their core dimension is Space. Recall that the 'core dimension' of a category is that dimension in the total deictic frame which the forms in the category subdivide most finely. Perceptual access to referents is almost always a relevant feature of the phenomenal framework of deictic utterances, but no deictics in the system subdivide the perceptual screen so finely as the OSTEVS. Spatial relations are virtually always part of the actional context of deictic reference, but it is the DLOCS alone that distinguish five spatial relations. And so on for the other categories. The IDS, then, encode two crucial kinds of information: (i) the **grammatical features** which govern how the deictic referent will be integrated into a linguistic message, and (ii) the **metapragmatic features** which govern how the referent is to be localized within the indexical and referential frames projected in deixis.

The Terminal Deictics work differently. TDS have no grammatical category features apart from the TD category itself. While there are co-occurrence restrictions between TD and IDS, for the most part, the TDS combine with every category of ID (holding aside the PART category). Similarly, there are some associations between given TDS and dimensions of deictic frames (such as the fact that *b'e?* is invariantly Peripheral Perceptual), but for the most part the TDS cut across the dimensions rather than coinciding with them. What they differentiate instead are values within the dimensions, such as relative Immediacy in Space, relative fullness of Perceptual access (Tact, Vis, Periph), and relative role within the Participation framework (Spkr, Adr, Other). These are what we have called Relational values, which are metapragmatic features at a lower, finer level of definition than the dimensions. In some cases, IDS are specific to Relational values, such as the Exclusive and Inclusive DLOCS, but for the most part, it is the TDS which distinguish values at this level.

Not all TDS combine with all IDS, and this means that there are implicational relations holding between the two series.[17] Complexes such as *hé?el i?*, *tol a?*, *té?el e?*, *way i?* do not occur and are uniformly rejected by native speakers in elicitation. In some cases, there is apparently a functional motivation for the gap, as for *tol a?*, where the ID and TD are intuitively incompatible. For the most part, however, the formal gaps are best treated as arbitrary facts of the Maya language, since it is virtually always possible to create a distinction for an additional form or to associate it functionally with some already existing distinction(s). The TDS *a?* and *o?* are the most fully implemented, since they figure in all categories except PART. *b'e$^?$* and *i$^?$* are on the opposite extreme, since the former occurs only in the OSTEVs (and marginally in DNOMs), and the latter occurs only in the DLOCs.[18] *e$^?$* figures only in the DMOD, DLOC, and temporal categories.

There are therefore significant differences among the TDs in terms of their privileges of combination with IDs. When they do recur, however, they are consistently associated with certain ranges of R values, and this consistency anchors the dimensions into a single, repeating pattern.

All *a$^?$* forms are associated with high-focus gestures, such as extending the referent in hand, touching, or pointing to it with directed gaze, all of which imply that the Spkr is in a relation of contiguity with the object. These are the preferred deictics for segmenting the Spkr's corporeal schema, current performance, or immediate region, and all of them tend to be indexically asymmetric. That is, they focalize the Spkr's zone as opposed to the shared ground, new information in discourse as opposed to what is already known, and anticipated objects rather than ones already passed by.

All *o$^?$* forms are associated with relatively less focal gestures, such as a vague toss of the hand or a less ostentatiously directed point. In many cases, there is no gesture at all. These are the forms used to make reference to objects in the Adr's zone or in the common field. They are relatively symmetric in our terms and are used for reference to prior discourse, or coreference with it, as well as for resumptive closing of discourse or actional units. Thus, we can say that the formal similarities between categories correspond to functional ones as well: *hé$^?$el a$^?$* : *hé$^?$el o$^?$* :: *té$^?$el a$^?$* : *té$^?$el o$^?$* :: *lel a$^?$* : *lel o$^?$* :: *b'ey a$^?$* : *b'ey o$^?$*.

The remaining TDs are more specialized but can be regularly graded in terms of the richness of information they convey. *b'e$^?$* is by far the most specific TD in the language, since it invariantly conveys presence of Peripheral and absence of Tactual or Visual evidence of a referent. It tends to be used in symmetric indexical frames in which both participants can perceive the referent, although it is also used when only the Spkr has access to it. *i$^?$* and *e$^?$* are both Non-Concrete, indifferent to relative perceptual or spatial immediacy.[19] The former is used to convey unique individuation of a referent (individual or place) in the symmetric frame of background knowledge or prior discourse. The latter is an empty placeholder with a variety of syntactic functions. It adds no sensory evidentiality to *hé$^?$* in the DMOD and apparently adds no information to the already specific DLOC *way* 'here'. There is a contrast in the DLOCs between simple focus *tí$^?$* . . . *i$^?$* and split focus *tí$^?$* . . . LOC *e$^?$*, where the former is anaphoric and the latter is not. We can phrase this as follows:

when the locative reference is identified solely by the DLOC, the interpretation is anaphoric and the TD is $i^{\textipa{?}}$; when the referent is identified by a lexical description, the description overrides any anaphoric interpretation, and the TD is $e^{\textipa{?}}$. I take this to be a neutralization of the privative opposition between $i^{\textipa{?}}$ [+Specified] and $e^{\textipa{?}}$ [Ø Specified], with the unmarked term occurring in the neutralizing context.

The relative ordering which emerges from these observations is $a^{\textipa{?}} > o^{\textipa{?}} > b'e^{\textipa{?}} > i^{\textipa{?}} > e^{\textipa{?}}$. This hierarchy is based on the relative immediacy of access to the referent conveyed by the TDS, with more immediate preceding less immediate. It also provides one of the main governing factors in the grammatical derivation of the TDS. There are two major constraints on the normal syntactic distribution of TDS: (i) they occur only at the final boundary of a topic phrase or sentence, and (ii) only one TD occurs at any boundary. This means that sentences containing a plurality of ID bases nonetheless have only a single TD associated with them, ruling out examples like the following.

(54)   *hé?el **e?** ub'in lel **o?** maák
         'That man will surely go.'

(55)   *tí? **i?** an lel **o?** ší?ipal tinwiknal
         'There ('s where) that boy is at my house.'

(56)   *way **e?** yàan lel **a?** ?insukú?un
         'Here ('s where) this brother of mine is.'

(57)   *té?el **o?** ?ič k'í?iš
         'there in (the) thorns'

The correct forms for these sentences are of course (58–60).

(58)   hé?el ub'in le maák **o?**
         'That man will surely go.'

(59)   tí?an le ší?ipal tinwiknal **o?**
         'There ('s where) that boy is at my house.'

(60)   way yàan le ?insukú?un **a?**
         'Here ('s where) this brother of mine is.'

(61)   té? ?ič k'í?iš **o?**
         'there in (the) thorns' (F.137.A.115)

The first constraint, that TDS occur only at the final boundary of a sentence or topic, will properly rule out medial TDS, as in (54–57), and the second constraint, that only one occur per boundary, rules out (62–63).

(62)   *hé?el ub'in le maák **o?** **e?**

(63)   *tí? kub'in le hé?el **a?** **a?** **i?**

When a sentence contains an embedded clause, the TDs occur at the final sentence boundary and not at the internal clause boundary. In (64), the complement clause 'to work' is separated from the matrix verb 'I went' by the DLOC base *té?*, indicating that the DLOC is part of the matrix clause (cf. *té? h b'inen meyah a?* 'there (is where) I went to work'). This fact notwithstanding, the TD obligatorily follows the subordinate clause.

(64)   tulaá? ?àaño ká   hb'inen té?   meyah a?
          RN   N   Comp VC   ID Immed VC   TD
          'The next year when I went to work there' (BB.4.76)
          (cf. *tulaá? ?àaño ká hb'inen té?el a? h meyah)

Similarly, in (65), the ID base separates the verb of going from its complement, but the TD must follow the complement, not precede it.

(65)   kó?oš té?   šiímb'al o?
          VC   DLOC Ølmmed VC   TD
          'Let's go there walking.' (F.137.A.115)
          (cf. *kó?oš té?el o? šiímb'al)

Given only the two syntactic constraints on TDs, it is impossible to predict which one from a potential *n*-tuple will appear in final position in the sentence or topic. The constraints operate uniformly on all TDs, regardless of their identity or the identity or syntactic placement of an ID with which they are cointerpreted. Yet it is clear that the selection of one or another from a possible set of TDs is not random. This is where the functional hierarchy comes into play. The correct generalization appears to be that in any potential *n*-tuple of TDs, the one which is highest (leftmost) in the hierarchy is the one that will appear on the surface. Alternatively stated, any member in the ordering $a? > o? > b'e? > i? > e?$ is automatically overridden by all those to its left.

This is equivalent to saying that the most immediate deictic subframe projected in any act of reference takes precedence over all others. The relatively arbitrary syntactic constraints on these deictics force Maya speakers to choose, and the normal expectation is that they will choose the highest values available. Note that this is one more expression of the basic tendency in the system for the immediate, more concrete zone to take precedence over the remote, less concrete zone.

In the following routine examples, the (simplified) lexical version of the sentence is on the left and the actual attested forms, conforming to syntactic constraints, are on the right. The precedence relations at play in each example are shown in parentheses after the English gloss.

	SEMANTIC: [ID ——]	SYNTACTIC: [ID X ——##]
(66)	tol o$^{?}$ tinkaštah lel a$^{?}$ b'á$^{?}$al DLOC Excl VC N Immed N 'Out there (is where) I found this thing.'	→ tol tinkaštah le b'á$^{?}$al a$^{?}$ (a$^{?}$ > o$^{?}$)
(67)	hé$^{?}$e b'e$^{?}$ kutàal lel o$^{?}$ maàk Dir Periph VC N ∅Immed N 'There goes the guy (listen!).'	→ hé$^{?}$ kutàal le maák o$^{?}$ (o$^{?}$ > b'e$^{?}$)
(68)	tí$^{?}$ i$^{?}$ kub'in lel o$^{?}$ maàk DLOC Spec VC N ∅Immed N 'There (is where) the guy goes.'	→ tí$^{?}$ kub'in le maák o$^{?}$ (o$^{?}$ > i$^{?}$)
(69)	b'ey o$^{?}$ lel o$^{?}$ bíida Adv ∅Immed N ∅Immed N tó$^{?}$on way e$^{?}$ Part DLOC Incl TD 'That's how life (is) for us (around) here.'	→ b'ey le bìida tó$^{?}$on way o$^{?}$ (o$^{?}$ > e$^{?}$)
(70)	má$^{?}$ i$^{?}$ way e$^{?}$ kutàal Neg Trm DLOC Incl VC 'Here (is) not (where) he comes.'	→ má$^{?}$ way kutàal i$^{?}$ (i$^{?}$ > e$^{?}$)

These simple generalizations will account for the selection and place-ment of the vast majority of TDs in routine Maya, but there are complica-tions. If an Initial deictic base occurs in S-final position, as they often do when not foregrounded, then the constraints on continuous combinations of the base with TDs may override the hierarchy. In other words, the lexical gaps in the paradigm of canonical citation deictics reassert them-selves, ruling out superficial forms like *tol a$^{?}$, *hé$^{?}$el i$^{?}$, *way b'e$^{?}$, and *way i$^{?}$, regardless of the syntactic environment in which they might be expected to occur. Thus, the nonfocused version of (66) is tinkaštah le b'á$^{?}$al tol o$^{?}$, not *tinkaštah le b'á$^{?}$al tol a$^{?}$; the nonfocused version of (70) is má$^{?}$ tutàal way e$^{?}$, not *má$^{?}$ tutàal way i$^{?}$. There is a further snag, however, since in some cases, the syntactic constraints on TD selec-tion override the citation forms nonetheless, as (69) shows: way o$^{?}$ is not a valid citation form and does not arise unless the TD has a lexical source elsewhere in the sentence, but it is the standard form in cases like this one. The most I can say of these facts is that they are irregularities in the system. Alongside their systematic connections, deictics display idio-syncratic features of structure as well as use.

The other major source of nonautomatic TD configurations is fore-grounding, which is a pervasive feature of Maya usage and accounts for numerous departures from the standard pattern. As with the foregrounding possibilities for IDs, the ones for TDs involve something akin to copying or reduplication, along with combinations of nonidentical forms. These constructions are fairly common in talk and are clearly intelligible and purposeful for native Maya speakers. They must therefore be taken into consideration as part of the overall system. Before turning to them, however, I want to establish the analogy between TDs and the PART categories, in order to show that the subdimensions signaled by these deictics are functionally, as well as grammatically, linked to the categories of person.

10.3.2 TDs and Suffixal Participant Deictics

The strongest similarities between TDs and the PART forms involve the suffixal series commonly called the 'B set pronouns' (see §4.2 for more detailed discussion). Like the TDs, these pronouns follow the lexical material which they modify, in this case some predicative element (verb, adjective, or predicate N), or the ID base of the PART category, *t(i?)*, as in *t-en*. And like the TDs, the pronouns are (often) cointerpreted with another PART form in the same clause. This is the case in the plural forms, *k-X-é?eš* 'us (Incl Pl Adr)', *a-X-é?eš* 'you (pl)', *u-X-ó?ob'* 'they', where the prefixal and suffixal pronouns join in a single reference. An important point of difference is that whereas TDs are canonically limited to one per sentence, the PART suffixes commonly occur in noncoreferential pairs, where one member identifies a Subject, Agent, or Possessor, and the other refers to an Object or equational Subject. Furthermore, whereas the TDs are frequently doubled for foregrounding (see §10.3.3), there is *never* more than one non-null pronominal suffix of the same category attached to the same word.

The possibility of combining nonidentical suffixes is motivated by the fact they are referentially distinct, and it is governed by two constraints: (i) under no circumstances can a single constituent have more than two B set pronouns, even though semantically plausible candidates exist, as in **kuyilik-ó?on-é?eš-ó?ob'* 'they see us (Incl Pl)'; and (ii) the superficial linear order of the pronouns is governed by the PART hierarchy Spkr > Adr > Other, regardless of the grammatical role of the argument relative to the predicate and regardless of the placement or role of a cointerpreted A set or independent pronoun (see examples 27–29, chap. 4). This hierarchy is homologous with the one that governs normal TD selection and is a basic point of contact between the two subsystems.

It is important to bear in mind that while both TDs and pronouns are linked to the Participant frames of deictic reference, the linkage is not the same: the PART deictics **refer to** participants and project P frames in their figural component, whereas the TDS **index** participant relations and project P frames in their background component. The expectable consequence of this discrepancy is that the PART forms provide a more finely subdivided set of participant relations than do the TDS, since they focalize them as their core dimension. Thus in the PART forms, speakers can readily distinguish Spkr sg (*-en*) and Spkr pl (*-óʔon*) from Spkr Incl (*-óʔon-éʔeš*), whereas number plays no role whatsoever in the TDS. On the other hand, the TDS distinguish Perceptual values, which index corporeal frames, but play no role in the PART forms. Thus, the relation between the two subsystems is one of functional overlap, not identity, and it is further mediated by the distinction between (focal) referential and (subsidiary) indexical modes of deixis. Put in these terms, the two subsystems can be seen to complement rather than duplicate one another. For the reasons sketched in §10.3.1, the closest correspondences are: *aʔ* (asymmetric; Spkr), *oʔ* (symmetric; Spkr + Adr, Adr), *b'eʔ* (symmetric; Spkr + Adr), *iʔ* (symmetric; Other), *eʔ* (null). These correspondences are shown graphically in figure 10.2.

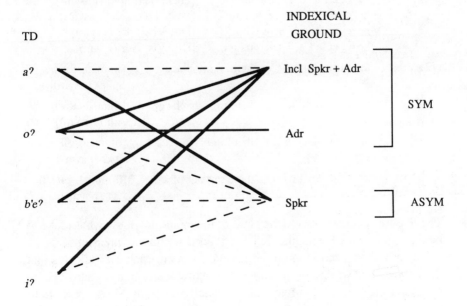

Fig. 10.2. Indexical corollaries of terminal deictics.

Figure 10.2 is a simplification and overlooks the phenomena described in chapter 5 under the rubric of 'decentering' and 'footing'. The bold lines indicate the most typical corollaries of each TD, whereas the dashed lines indicate other commonly attested but less central uses. Thus, for instance, the *a*^{2} forms *can* be used in reference to objects symmetrically accessible to interactants, as we have seen repeatedly in the preceding chapters, but are most typically used to create a new segmentation asymmetrically available to the Spkr. *o*^{2} forms *can* be used in reference to objects more accessible to the Spkr than the Adr (asymmetric), but their most typical usage is for things accessible to both participants (symmetric).

One class of evidence for the generalizations represented in figure 10.2 is the co-occurrence constraints holding between TDs and pronominal affixes in certain deictic constructions. In particular, the OSTEV and DLOC categories provide us with a series of minimal pairs combining first and second person with *a*^{2} and *o*^{2} TDs. These examples were cited in the chapters focused on OSTEVs and DLOCs, respectively, and we will not review here the contexts in which they might be used appropriately. What is important is the complementarity between the two series.

(71)   hé^{2}el **en a**^{2} 'Here I am.' $_s$[Pres, Tact, Spkr (*i* asym)]
        #hé^{2}el **eč a**^{2} 'Here you are.' $_s$[Pres, Tact, Adr (*i* asym)]
        #hé^{2}el **en o**^{2} 'There I am.' $_s$[Dir, Vis, Spkr (*i* sym)]
        hé^{2}el **eč o**^{2} 'There you are.' $_s$[Dir, Vis, Adr (*i* sym)]

(72)   té^2 t **inw** iknal **a**^{2} 'here in my place' $_{Loc}$[Immed, Restr,
                                                              Spkr (*i* asym)]

        #té^2 t **aw** iknal **a**^{2} 'here in your place' $_{Loc}$[Immed, Restr,
                                                              Adr (*i* asym)]

        #té^2 t **inw** iknal **o**^{2} 'there in my place' $_{Loc}$[ØImmed, ØRestr,
                                                              Spkr (*i* sym)]

        té^2 t **aw** iknal **o**^{2} 'there in your place' $_{Loc}$[ØImmed, ØRestr,
                                                              Adr (*i* sym)]

The feature specifications to the right of the examples show what I take to be the conventional semantic values encoded in these expressions.

The crosshatch marking on the middle forms in each set indicates that the expression, while not unusable, is pragmatically nonstandard. Thus, recall that *hé^{2}eleča*^{2} 'here you are' is usually taken by Maya speakers to be an insulting equation between Adr and some part of the Spkr's body; *té^{2}e tinwiknal o*^{2} 'there in my place' might be usable on the reading of *-iknal* as 'residence' and not body space, but this is unlikely and was rejected by native speakers. The important point, as I said, is that the complementarity gives evidence that the TDS are conventionally associated with Participant domains: whereas the medial pronouns **refer** to the participants, the TDS **index** them; the two modes are unified in the act of deictic reference.

The correspondences summarized in figure 10.2 corroborate another basic generalization about Maya, and I believe all deictic systems, namely, that they are skewed towards relatively symmetric indexical frames. Recall from the discussion of indexical grounding in §2.1.3 that the indexical frame in which an act of deictic reference is performed partially governs the range of referential categories that can be mobilized in the act. On the basis of this interdependence, a pragmatic 'principle of relative symmetry' was proposed, which is repeated below for convenience.

> The more symmetric the indexical ground (the more interactants already share at the time of utterance), the more deictic oppositions are available for making reference (the greater the range of choice among distinct deictics).

This principle says that the more interactants already share at the moment of utterance, the more precisely they can individuate referents. Observe in figure 10.2 that the Symmetric ground conjoins with four of the five TDS, while the Asymmetric conjoins with just two. When interactants are face to face, engaged, and share a great quantity of relevant information, any TD is usable, whereas when they are separated by perceptual, spatial, or conceptual boundaries, the possibilities are more limited.[20] The properties of the indexical frame set limits on the referential projections for which it can adequately serve as ground.

10.3.3 TD Foregrounding

There are two main kinds of construction in which the functions of TDS are foregrounded, those involving the expansion of a single TD by way of stretching or reduplication and those involving the combination of two nonidentical TDS in a continuous bundle. For heuristic purposes, I will call the former **TD stretching** and the latter **TD$_1$ TD$_2$ couplets.** Both of them entail departures from the constraint that only one simple TD may occur at any boundary, but it is likely that they require different explanations. The former combines with ID foregrounding, whereas the latter evidently does not. I prefer 'stretching' to 'reduplication', because in the scant few cases of foregrounded *b'e?* that I have attested, it was *b'e?e?* that was said, and never *b'e? b'e?*. For all of the *V?* terminals, a reduplication analysis would be possible and may be preferable, although I will not address the question directly. To my knowledge, there are never more than two TDs (or one stretched once, as the case may be) at the end of a single sentence, a constraint as arbitrary as the one limiting PART suffixes to a maximum of two. The constraint that TDs occur at the final boundary of topic or sentence is evidently not violated for communicative purposes.[21] TD stretching is by far the more common of the two kinds of foregrounding, and the functional motivations for it are quite diverse. We take these up first, before proceeding to the more exotic TD_1 TD_2 couplets.

10.3.3.1 *TD Stretching*

TD stretching is illustrated by sentences such as the following.

(73)   hé? yaálka? le ha?   b'ey a?a?
             DMOD VC   ∅Immed N Adv Immed
             'The water will surely run (off) this way.' (BB.5.60)

(74)   lel a? č'é?en→ . . . yan keš dyèes mekàates i?→ tí?an lel a ？ a?
             ↓ le k b'èel o?
             'This (is the) well. . . . There's about 10 mecates there. There's this. Our path.' (F.4.B.292)

(75)   lela? nah dón alpòonso ⇨ lel a? a? ⇨ č'é?em ↓
             'This is Don Alfonso's place. This (pause) is (the) well.'
             (F.4.B.203)

The central question for examples of TD stretching for our purposes is their functional motivation. If my analysis of the constraints on TDs is correct, then these forms must be foregrounded, but since they involve only a single TD, it is not always clear what is being pushed to the fore. My data include three distinguishable sorts of case: **expressive stretching,** where the Spkr conveys an intense involvement in the utterance, and special emphasis on some aspect of it (73); **stretching as a staging device,** marking a topicalized element, a member of an ongoing list, or an utterance fraction otherwise preparatory to some further statement (74); and **stretching as a pause filler,** or hesitation devide that may build some dramatic tension or merely hold an interlocutor's attention in preparation for some imminent continuation (75). The latter two are obviously related and may be the same, while the former seems distinct from both and akin to ID doubling (particularly the variety that does not involve pre-VC focus).

What I am calling Expressive stretching commonly arises in discourse contexts in which the expressive utterance responds to a previous question or to some other aspect of the interactive framework. In (73), DP was looking at the lay of the land in his field, and the question of how the rainwater would run was already established; he was answering it. In other cases an explicit question is voiced, as in (76–79).[22]

(76)   DP: máʔ klàaro iʔ ↓
              'It's not clear.'

         WH: máʔ klàaro iʔ ↑
              'It's not clear?'

         DP: máʔ klàaro íʔistak o ʔ oʔ→
              'Of course it's not clear.' (F.1.A.895)

(77)   DB: kuȼonik č'iíč' ⇗ b'ey → (laughter) máʔa tub'èel i ʔ iʔ
              'he shoots birds, like so.' (pause, laughter) 'It's not correct.'
              (F.92.A.280)

(78)   b'eéyli eʔ ↑ ken teč→ kinkáʔa k'aátik teč eʔ→ kawáak eʔ b'aáyli
              o ʔ oʔ→
              ' "It's still so?" I say to you. I ask you again. You say, "It's still
              so." ' (F.92.B.478)

(79)   máʔ sùuk utàal e wiíl ↑ tch!   tíʔili sùuk ukutal eʔ eʔ→
              'Doesn't he customarily come, Will?' 'Tch! (Of course) there('s
              where) he customarily sits.' (F.1.A.804)

In (76), DP once again asserts his authoritative opinion, this time a metalinguistic judgment informing me that a previous example utterance was poorly constructed. When I ask for confirmation, he makes the definitive judgment, marking it formally with the emphatic enclitic *íʔistak oʔ*. This form is functionally specialized in two ways: it signals forceful assertion but only in response position. That it, it answers some previous utterance with an assertion—as opposed, for instance, to another question, a directive, a mitigated suggestion, or a hypothetical statement. The fact of its occurring in response position is indexed by the TD *oʔ* (which, as we have seen, is the one for anaphoric and preexistent, symmetrically accessible referents), and it is noteworthy that this is the only TD that normally co-occurs with *íʔistak*. The emphasis already inherent in the enclitic is then bumped up another notch of intensity by the stretched TD; there was no need to seek a second confirmation after this one.

Example (77) also occurred during metalinguistic discussion, this time with Balim. In the first portion of his utterance, he is attempting to repeat an example I had presented to him for glossing, namely, *kuȼ'onik b'ey čiíč' le maák oʔ* 'the man shoots like birds'. He found it so garbled and laughably bad that he was unable to repeat it accurately. By stretching out the TD, he foregrounds the certitude of his opinion.

Balim was also the speaker of (78), in which the stretched TD is again in response position, this time in a hypothetical exchange. Note that the

TD from the target utterance *b'eéyli e$^?$* has been shifted to *o$^?$* in the answer, a conventional index of its status as response. The stretching indexes the emphasis of the assertion.[23]

Example (79) is another hypothetical exchange created by DP showing the same configuration of emphatic assertion in response position. The ingressive click, tch! is the same expressive type used in conjunction with OSTEV foregrounding and reinforces the emphasis of the TDs.

Another class of TD stretchings is associated with topicalization and what Brown and Yule (1983:134), following Grimes and others, called 'staging'. As used here, the notion of staging is loose and heuristic and meant to be more inclusive than 'thematization', but still focusing on the function of some utterance fractions to foreground one portion of a scene as the point of departure for what follows it. Although these examples often occur in response position, staging is rather the function of the utterance to anticipate and set up the conditions for further commentary. In my metalinguistic discussions with Maya speakers, the hypothetical forms I offered them for glossing prepared the ground for their comments and were commonly repeated by them at the outset of their response. This is the case in (80–82).

(80)   W: čeén té$^?$ le hé$^?$el o$^?$ ↓
            'Just *té$^?$ le hé$^?$el o$^?$?* (what does it mean?)'

         DP: čeén té$^?$ le hé$^?$el o$^?$ o$^?$ ↑ miš b'á$^?$ah kyáaik
            'Just "*té$^?$ le hé$^?$el o$^?$*"? It means nothing.' (F.1.A.354)

(81)   B: tumèen bey → bey kub'in e maák saánsamal o ႃ o$^?$ ↑ kyere desir
            e$^?$ . . .
            'Because "So, so goes that man every day", it means . . .'
            (F.92.A.460)

(82)   WH: tí$^?$ atàal i$^?$ → b'á$^?$aš u k'aát y á$^?$ale
            ' "There (is where) you come from" What does it mean?'

         DP: pwes uk'aát yá$^?$al tí$^?$ atàal e$^?$ e$^?$ → pór ehemplo . . .
            'Well, "There is where you come from", it means, for
            example . . .' (F.1.A.774)

Note in (82) that the TD of the target form I had offered DP has been switched in his response from *i$^?$* to *e$^?$*. The motivation for this is the shift in status of the phrase from an isolated utterance in the mention mode to a topical element on which DP is beginning a commentary. In his response, it is still 'mentioned' rather than directly used, but it has been partially integrated into the direct discourse of his gloss. We will return to the relation between TD foregrounding and decentering in §10.3.3.3.

In (83) the utterance fraction mentioned initially is part of a list of alternative utterances that DP was making to illustrate the form *tí? ili e?*. Observe that immediately afterwards, as he launches into a gloss, he shifts the TDS from the citation form to the *o?* form. This is a standard index of the anaphoric relation holding between the form he is glossing and the one mentioned in the immediately preceding discourse. The flanking *le . . . o?* is a direct, fully referential DNOM whose indexical ground is the corporeal frame that DP and I were occupying.

(83)   DP: <u>tí?ili sùuk uhàanl</u> **e** ʕ **e**?→ le <u>tí? ili</u> **o o**? ↑
        ' "There('s where) he customarily eats", that '*tí?ili*',

        ?éskeh tut'àam pero . . .
        it's that it speaks (is meaningful), but . . .' (F.1.A.735)

(84)   DP: . . . uȼ'iík teč ump'ée bá?al akutal e?→ kuliíkl **e**? **e**? ↑ kiyá?aik
        teč e?
        ' "(he could) give you a thing to sit on. He stands up, he says to
        you,

        kó?oten té?el a?→
        "Come right here." ' (F.1.A.22)

Example (84) shows a case of staging without any decentering between mention and direct commentary, DP is sketching a scenario in which the underlined form could be used, and each new piece of information he adds is set off with a topicalization *e?*. It is unclear to me why the TD in this clause is stretched and the others are not.

10.3.3.2 *TD₁-TD₂ Couplets*

It is noticeable that most of the foregoing examples of TD stretching are taken from metalinguistic commentary by three adult male Maya speakers. This is an accidental feature of my recorded data and does not reflect the limitations of the phenomenon in Maya speech. In my experience, all kinds of speakers use stretched TD forms under a wide variety of everyday circumstances. The same cannot be said for the next set of examples, which involve TD_1-TD_2 couplets. These forms are highly specialized functionally and are not encountered in routine Maya, to my knowledge. I found in working with them that they are rejected straightaway as ungrammatical by DP, the very speaker who produced the most florid examples. Given these facts, why include them at all? The main motivation is that they were produced repeatedly and purposefully by DP, a senior head of household (third-level) and monolingual Maya speaker. Furthermore, they are not simply garbled utterances without sense but follow the functional patterns of the language, while casting into sharp relief the capacity of a Maya speaker to adapt the system to uncommon circumstances.

We were discussing the meanings of deictic expressions, and DP was producing glosses that combined mention with direct use, as well as what appear to be semidirect shadings between the two. In (85), he repeated verbatim the citation form I offered for commentary while simultaneously marking it as a topical item in the current utterance. The shift in footing from mention to direct use is an indexical transposition signaled by the pairing of TDs.²⁴ Note that the superficial order of TDs preserves the integrity of the cited form, as it does also in the next example. I had offered the citation form *hé?el eč e?* in order to see whether the DMOD could be directly inflected for person, and DP assured me that it cannot (a judgment corroborated by my observations of direct use). His utterance preserves the boundary between the two footings and embeds the citation within the DNOM *le . . . o?* 'that', itself the standard way of signaling anaphoric identity.

(85)   WH: b'á?aš u k'aát yá?al <u>tí? ili o?</u>→
        'What does <u>tí?ili o?</u> mean?'

        DP: pwes . . . čeén <u>tí? ili o?</u> e? → mišb'á?ah kut'anik→
        'Well, . . . just *tí?ili o?*, it means nothing.' (F.1.A.788)

(86)   DP: le <u>hé?el eč e?</u> o? → miš b'á?ah kiyáaik →
        'That *hé?el eč e?* (that you've said), it means nothing.'
        (F.1.B.168)

Example (87) is parallel to the preceding two in that a citation form (underlined) is reproduced intact and embedded within a direct utterance. DP was listing alternative ways of saying what he took to be my intended meaning, marking off the hypothetical status of these utterances with the indefinite particle plus TD *wá . . . e?*. The circumfixing particles are part of the direct discourse, and what is circumfixed is part of the citation.

(87)   DP: . . . ?áwra <u>tí?ili e?</u> → tí?ili sùuk e maákó?ob' o?
        '. . . now (if you say) "there customarily," "there('s where) those
        guys customarily (are)",

        wá <u>tí? ili sùuk ub'in i?</u> e? → wá tí? sùuk umaán i?→ . . .
        or "there('s where) they customarily go", or "there('s where) he
        customarily passes" . . .' (F.1.A.733)

The next example is more complex, because the boundary between the citation and the direct commentary is partly effaced. Note that the citation form ends in the TD *e?*, whereas in DP's utterance, this has been replaced by the couplet *a? o?*. By my analysis, both of these TDs are indexically grounded in the basic corporeal frame of my interaction with DP. The $e^{\textipa{P}}$ terminal of the citation has been treated as part of the direct speech and overridden by the other two hierarchically superordinate forms, just as would be expected under normal circumstances.

(88)   WH: tí? ili e? ↑ b'á?aš uk'aát iyá?aleh →
             '*tí?ili e?* What does it mean?'

        DP: pwes uk'áat iyá?al le tí? ili a? o? →
             'Well, this *tí?ili* (that you've said), it means,

             ?óli ká k?á?al ump'eé b'á?a sùuk →
             it's sort of like if we were to say a customary thing.' (F.1.A.685)

The $o^{\textipa{P}}$ terminal in this utterance is motivated by the anaphoric relation to my utterance, since DP is repeating what I have just said. The motivation for the $a^{\textipa{P}}$ is more elusive. There appear to be two factors at work. (i) The target form had just been introduced into our interaction by DP, as I was in the course of asking about a different series of citation forms, and he suggested this one on his own. This contrastive asymmetry is consistent with the TD. (ii) There is an overtone of anticipatory reference, in that DP, having introduced his new form, then goes on to explain to me how it is used. Although the form is too rare for me to make secure generalizations, it is also noteworthy that the two TDs are in the linear order that would be predicted by the hierarchy $a^{\textipa{P}} > o^{\textipa{P}}$.

The final example of TD_1-TD_2 couplets occurred during elicited metalinguistic discussion but does not involve decentered discourse. Once again, the linear order of the forms is consistent with the hierarchical ordering. DP had explained that the underlined expression required a pointing gesture in order to be used appropriately, and I double-checked this by repeating his judgment. His response was the emphatic assertion that, obviously, what he was saying was so. The $o^{\textipa{P}}$ TD is once again an index of the relation to what precedes, reinforcing the response position *í?istak*. The $e^{\textipa{P}}$, by my reckoning, is added in order to index that this assertion of DP's is not the last word but will be followed by another illustration. In other words, it is a staging device, combined with an anaphoric one.

(89)   WH: ?àah ?eske k'ab'eét awé?esik ti? →
             'Oh, it's that you've got to show it to him.'

        DP: klàaro pwos b'eyí?istak o e? → [ingress] tí? atàal té?el a?
             ?oómeŋ ↓
             'Clearly, well of course that's how it is, "Come right here,
             man!"' (F.1.A.82)

Despite the admittedly exotic character of these utterances, they reveal an important property of the Maya deictic system, namely, its flexibility and potential for novel forms. Automatic constraints provide resources for purposely nonautomatic utterances. Messages are virtually always plurifunctional, and in many cases a plurality of TDs could be motivated. As we have seen, the automatic grammatical constraints on TD distribution serve to reduce the plurality to the one highest value. But the reduction is not always called for, and speakers like DP can have occasion to foreground the fact that more than one function is salient in their current frame of reference. This is what is going on in the couplet forms, each of which shows two TDs, each associated with a distinct function. In some cases, the duality corresponds to two separate indexical grounds that are being combined in the decentered frame utterance, while in others, there is a single indexicai frame which nonetheless has more than a single salient feature. It is not surprising that the TDs, of all the deictics, are the ones mobilized to signal these complex indexical matrices, since it is the TDs that encode the most indexical information, without any overlay of grammatical category features to limit their distribution. Furthermore, this is one more parallel between TDs and PART affixes, since the latter are another central resource for signaling decentering and footing shifts (see chapter 5).

10.4 THE FRAME SPACE OF MAYA DEIXIS

At the outset of this chapter, I suggested that a comprehensive account of linguistic practice in any society must bring together two kinds of unity, one defined by the linguistic system as a total object with its own inner logic and the other defined by the situated embodiment of language in utterances whose intelligibility depends upon a combination of extralinguistic with linguistic information. The overall frame space of Maya deixis is built on both of these planes, and my treatment of deictic forms and activities has reflected this duality. By way of concluding this chapter, we will review the Maya system of deixis in three steps: (i) the linguistic frames of reference, (ii) generalized properties of the indexical ground, and (iii) the interpretation of complex frames of deictic reference that combine (i) and (ii).

10.4.1 The Linguistic Frames of Ostensive Reference

Maya deictics form a system of interrelated categories organized in accordance with regular principles. The categories that we have explored most directly in this book are the PART (participant) deictics, the OSTEVs, and the DLOCs. The nominal deictics (DNOMs) overlap with the PART series and have figured in many examples, although we did not examine them as thoroughly as the others. These four series make up a central portion of the total system and can be directly compared in terms of the three semiotic axes of communicative Functions, Relational values, and Indexical grounds.

The communicative Functions of an utterance, as we have used this term, are the projective ends, goals, and realized outcomes of the act. Like 'illocutionary force' in speech act theory, communicative Functions are defined in terms of the socially recognized acts executed in the saying of certain linguistic forms under certain circumstances. The Functions we have distinguished include Presentative, Directive, Referential, and Expressive. In order to complete the list, we will add to it Predicative and Phatic, to be explained below. What Austin treated as felicity conditions have as their analogues the indexical constraints on performing these Functions in Maya, that is, that the circumstances must be appropriate, that the act must be executed properly and completely, that participants must engage in the act with the proper intentions, and that they must in fact follow through.

Two significant points of difference between Functions and illocutionary forces are: (i) Functions as viewed here are interactively constituted and executed; and (ii) they need not be acts achievable only through speech. Austin's commitment to the formalist doctrine that the effectiveness of speech can be treated as inhering in the words themselves led him to emphasize the boundary between language and nonlanguage in a way we have rejected. Acts of ostensive reference unavoidably rest on the interaction between coparticipants, as we have shown, and engage relatively large quantities of obviously nonlinguistic knowledge. It would be blatantly erroneous to claim that Presentative or Directive acts cannot be achieved through nonlinguistic means, but this fact does not contravene the observation that deictic categories in Maya and other natural languages have these Functions as part of their conventional potentials.

It was in relation to the OSTEV category (chapter 6) that this notion of a Function was first introduced, but it is clear that it has application beyond this category. The Expressive Function is in play in most deictic utterances insofar as the Spkr, in performing an act of demonstrative reference, indexes his or her current access to the object (perceptual, spatial, conceptual), thereby displaying the certainty that it exists and is available for individuation. This inherent Expressivity is residual when compared with the more pointedly Expressive Function of the DMOD *hé?el e?* 'for sure, indeed' and the array of emphatic foregrounded structures into which most Maya deictics enter (with different degrees of freedom). Similarly, all deictics have what can be called a Phatic Function, whose focus is the **contact** between coparticipants in the current framework: the role of relative indexical symmetry as a conditioning factor in most deictic usage assures that the contact between coparticipants is a pervasively relevant feature of use. However, in the Discourse Directive and Referential uses of OSTEVS, DMOD, and DNOMS, this Phatic component is relatively more central than elsewhere. Recall that these utterance types convey further communicative effects beyond reference to prior discourse, including agreement with and understanding of an immediately preceding utterance and the closing of conversation. These interactive moves operate on the relation between coparticipants, and in this way are saliently Phatic.[25]

The Referential Function is the central one for deixis in that it is the prototypical core by which the phenomenon is defined. It is also the function to which the widest range of forms contribute. We have defined the Referential Function of deixis in terms of the pairing: figure = referential object, ground = indexical frame. The use of the asymmetric figure-ground model of categorization has allowed us to take account of the relational structure of deictic reference while not falling into a morass of unordered contextual details. The Referential focus is the sharp point of the deictic act and is clearly at a different order of conceptual salience from the indexical frame relative to which the reference is nonetheless unavoidably interpreted. The figure-ground structure provides a mechanism for incorporating both the diffuse, relatively extensive indexical frame and the narrowly tapered spike of ostensive reference. Given its centrality, it is unsurprising that the Referential Function is the most delicately calibrated of all, with as many subdivisions as there are relational (R) values in the system. Working only with the PART, OSTEV, and DLOC categories, we have shown that nearly twenty R values are distinguished in Maya. There is little reason to think that the language is atypical in this respect.[26]

While only the OSTEV category is inherently predicative in its core uses, it is descriptively helpful to distinguish a Predicative Function from both Referential and Directive. The reason is that certain deictic constructions in Maya are conventionally used to predicate relations of identity, manner, or location, while nonetheless not achieving the force of a Directive. For instance, the array of focus constructions treated earlier in this chapter are Predicative in the sense that they say that the object **is the one** (the individual, the place) that fits the description. The PART deictics have a distinct paradigm of derived forms that are inherently Predicative (the

ʔin tíʔal series; see §4.2.2). Similarly, although the DLOCs require insertion of the existential verb *ʔan* 'to be' in order to be used predicatively, they are very commonly used this way. The manner deictics, based on the ID *b'ey* 'like that, so' also are routinely used as the sole predicate in a sentence and may even be directly inflected for person (without any inserted verb form or morphological derivation).

The canonical Presentative and Directive Functions are centrally associated with the OSTEVs *héʔel aʔ* and *héʔel oʔ*, *héʔe b'eʔ*, respectively. Directive utterances tell an Adr to turn his or her perceptual or attentional focus to the object and are typically associated with high-focus gestures such as pointing, directed gaze, and cocking of the ear. These differ from other Predicative deictic constructions in that they are relatively more Directive, with the force of verbal imperatives, and they have a range of distinctive co-occurrence constraints that reflect this fact. Presentatives have the distinctive feature that they are executed in order to present the referent to the Adr, by holding it out in hand (if possible), enacting it, or otherwise 'connecting' with it in the immediate corporeal field. The Adr in turn is directed by a Presentative to take the object in the appropriate corporeal manner. While many utterances with deictic components are used to Presentative ends, it is only the OSTEVs that are functionally specialized in this way.

The communicative Functions outlined here are not all coordinate, as we observed in chapter 6. Rather, they can be arranged in a scale of ascending **functional density,** starting from the Phatic Function at the low end and working towards Presentative, in the order:

Phatic > **Expressive** > **Referential** > **Predicative** >
Directive > Presentative

Any Function in this scale subsumes all those to its left.[27] It is noteworthy that the mid-range of the scale (boldface) is the region of most elaborate subcategorization, in terms of distinct R values and distinct linguistic constructions (including foregrounded forms). Both the upper and the lower end are more specialized, in that there are relatively few deictic forms with these as their main conventional functions. I take this as corroboration of the hypothesis that this range in the scale is the basic level for deixis, that is, the level at which the categories of the system correspond most closely to the structure of the world as perceived by Maya speakers. For deixis, the relevant portion of the world is the sociocentric field of referential practice. This includes the corporeal field of interactants, the background frame space of possible but not actual moves and references and the routine practices in which speakers individuate referential objects. The more general level of Phatic Function is underspecified, since all deictic use has a Phatic component, guaranteed by the sociocentric basis of the indexical ground. The level of Directive and Presentative is overspecified, since (as used here) these Functions correspond only to the OSTEVS.

The relational (R) values which mediate between the referential object and the indexical frame of an utterance have been extensively illustrated in the foregoing chapters. The key concept behind R values is that deictic reference is achieved by a vector starting in the indexical frame of utterance and ending in the referential frame. The magnitude and direction of the vector is determined by the R value, while the character of the endpoint depends primarily upon the grammatical category of the deictic form. In the PART category, we distinguished eight R values (see fig. 4.1): Spkr is subdivided by sg, pl (ØIncl, +Incl (Adr, Other)); Adr is subdivided by sg, pl, and Other is subdivided by Øpl, pl. In the OSTEV category, we distinguished five plus one for the DMOD: Tactual, Visual, Peripheral, Discourse, Anticipatory, and Certain (see fig. 6.1). The DLOCS are subdivided by five R values, arrayed on three axes: the Egocentric (regional) axis is dichotomized by Inclusive and Exclusive; the Sociocentric (restricted) axis distinguishes +Immediate from ØImmediate privatively; the Non-Concrete axis shows only a single R value, which we designated Specified. This corresponds to the Anaphoric and Background Knowledge uses of *tí'i'*. Thus, looking at only three major categories and holding aside the most richly divided of all (the Temporal category), we have a total of nineteen R values. It is noteworthy that the bulk of these values fall in the relatively proximal zone of interaction. As suggested in §10.2 above, this skewing towards the immediate corporeal frame of participants is a fundamental feature of Maya deixis and, I believe, of ostensive reference in other languages as well.

There is little question that some of these distinctions among R values could be collapsed in a more abstract approach to deixis than the one adopted in this book. In particular, it is possible that the relatively Non-Concrete R values in each category could be conflated: Other (PART), Certain (OSTEV), and Specified (DLOC) could be treated as a single feature, say Non-Concrete, with category-specific implementations. For the remaining Concrete R values, there is little point in attempting to lump in order to achieve a more simple account. The simplicity gained by such an exercise is entirely internal to the system and results unavoidably in a **loss** of simplicity in the empirical interpretation of the system. It is imperative in the study of language use to distinguish **intrinsic** simplicity, which strives for a small number of very abstract primitives, from **extrinsic** simplicity, which concentrates more on streamlining the application of the system to actual cases.[28]

One could propose a more abstract set of features, such as Proximal vs. Distal, to account for many of the R values proposed in this study. However, the intrinsic simplicity of such an account gives little indication of how we are to interpret the features in any particular case. Short of a complicated set of correspondence principles to get from the primitives to the extrinsic contexts in which they are implemented, one is left with a simple system that sheds little light on how deixis works in use. This is the legacy of traditional approaches to deixis which take as their goal the reduction of all deictic categories to a small set of primitives. It is not accidental that more recent extensionally oriented semantic theories, which focus on the relation between language and the world (including native typifications of language), lean more towards extrinsic simplicity. The approach to which this book seeks to contribute shares this orientation.

There is an ambiguity in the way the indexical frame of ostensive reference has been treated in this study. On the one hand, we have attempted to specify for a large number of attested utterances in Maya the precise aspects of utterance context that are indexed. This is not an easy task, because of the backgrounded status, and frequently diffuse boundaries, of the indexical ground relative to the referential focus. Still, by working through the details of examples, we are able to get a relatively clear idea of which aspects of utterance context are most relevant to individual uses. Thus, while *hé?el o?* and *té?el o?* are in many ways parallel, including their relative indexical symmetry, the former canonically indexes perceptual contact between coparticipants and the referent, whereas the latter does not. On the other hand, we have also sought to characterize indexical frames by a more abstract measure, which we have called 'relative symmetry'. Thus, in summarizing sets of examples involving more than one deictic type and in describing the typical indexical corollaries of TDS, the more abstract division between relatively symmetric and relatively asymmetric provides an appropriate measure of intrinsic simplicity, whereas for the description of individual cases, it is the extrinsic simplicity of a more detailed account that is required.

The three axes of communicative Functions, Relational values, and Indexical grounds are unified in the complex frames of ostensive reference. The main organizing principle in deictic frames is relative **salience.** As used here, the notion of salience merges relative focality of the speech act with relative immediacy of participant access to the referent. The former is inherently ordered in terms of **functional density,** as outlined above. The latter, as shown throughout the preceding chapters, is organized by the principle of **proximal differentiation,** which says roughly that closer equals more finely distinguished. The proximal zone of the deictic field offers the widest range of relational R values for identifying referents, as well as the most functionally dense types of ostensive acts.

The axis of salience, including now proximity and functional density, interacts with Indexical grounds in two ways. From the intrinsic perspective of the system, the indexical potentials of deictic types show a strong correlation between **high salience and asymmetry:** the most focal, most immediate forms in any category are also the most likely to identify a referent as novel, precisely bounded, and within the bodily reach of the Spkr.

From the extrinsic perspective of indexical grounds as the preparatory conditions for ostensive acts, the inverse is true: the more symmetric a given indexical frame (the more relevant knowledge interactants already share at the moment of utterance), the more distinctions are available to participants for the purpose of individuated reference. Any symmetric indexical framework can be treated as if it were asymmetric for the purpose of foregrounding a portion of it, while the opposite does not hold. Thus, there is a basic correlation between high salience in reference and the requirement of a symmetric indexical frame in which to perform the reference. In the first case, we start from functional categories and attempt to predict how they are combined in the conventional structure of the language. In the second case, we start from a social situation and attempt to predict what kinds of ostensive acts can be performed in it.

10.4.2 Indexical Frames and the Interpretation of Deictic Acts

The concept of the Indexical ground of deictic reference, as it has been developed in this study, has certain general properties. Any utterance, regardless of how many deictics it contains, typically has only a single indexical frame relative to which they are all interpreted. This is why TDs, with their indexical loadings, are usually limited to one per utterance. Unless otherwise indicated, this frame is the interperspectival one in which coparticipants are corporeally present to one another and acting 'for themselves'. Although any indexical frame is singular in this sense, speakers almost always have the possibility of **decentering** through transposition, quotation, and creative acts of reference. This provides a means of abstracting from, or building upon, the corporeal field. Given its nonbasic status, decentering is usually (but not always) formally signaled. It results in rapid shifts between different indexical frames. Within the complex framework of interaction then, more than one indexical ground may well be in play, but any single utterance is anchored to just one.[29]

To say that indexical frames are singular is not to say that they are without internal differentiation. Different categories of deictics require slightly different indexical features as ground, and the phenomenal framework is virtually always made up of several different subframes. For instance, *tèen, héʔelaʔ*, and *téʔelaʔ* are reasonably similar in terms of their gross asymmetry, but they place different demands on utterance contexts, corresponding to their core dimensions, Participant, Perceptual, and Spatial, respectively.

Deictic frames can be defined at three different levels of inclusiveness. The first level corresponds to the immediate corporeal frame occupied by coparticipants, apart from the narrated scene projected by the referential and descriptive elements in a message. The second level corresponds to combinations of frames, such as the pairing of the speech event (E^s) with the narrated event (E^n), that is, the context of utterance with what the utterance says about the world. Deictic reference always engages a second-order frame by this definition, because of its relational structure.

Simple and complex frames as we have encountered them are actualized in interactive frameworks. In citing examples throughout this study, I present the residua of such frameworks. Beyond what actually happens in a framework, however, is a frame space of possibilities, most of which are not actualized. What interactants do at any point in talk is contingent on local considerations and background knowledge, without being a matter of pure chance. By my analysis, the 'phenomenal field' of an utterance, the social present in which reference is produced, is a framework emerging on the background of a frame space. Far from the apparent simplicity of here-now, the indexical context of an utterance is therefore (i) **internally complex,** since it includes different axes; (ii) **dynamic,** since it is subject to ongoing revision in talk, through recentering; and (iii) **inclusive,** since it encompasses both the actual footings and the messages of participants, in union with the socially defined space of possibilities from which actual moves are selected and relative to which they are intelligible. This space is partly constituted by the system of deictic categories and partly by the schematic structures learned and reinforced in social experience. Neither a fleeting jumble of particulars nor a fixed structure, communicative context is a sociocultural framespace that is both objective and emergent.

The understanding of any act of ostensive reference involves a judgment as to 'what is going on here'. This is often a difficult question, almost always requiring conversational inferences that can be disputed or defeased. Given what we know of the semantic structure corresponding to simple deictic constructions, what can we say about the overall interpretation of deictic acts? I have argued repeatedly that the indexical frame of speech and the conventional categories of deictic systems are less simple than is usually assumed. At the same time, there are many simplifying factors which work together to schematize and reduce the complexity of any utterance and to reinforce a coherent interpretation. These factors are both intrinsic and extrinsic.

Factors intrinsic to deictic systems that tend to simplify their functioning include: (i) the figure-ground structure, which provides a means of integrating a large amount of diverse information in a single structure without losing the focus on the referent; (ii) the widespread *iconicity* that binds different categories into repeating sets of homologous oppositions; (iii) the *overlap* among categories resulting from shared forms and combinations of mutually reinforcing forms; (iv) the partial *correspondence* between values in deictic dimensions and Participant roles; and (v) the organizing principle of relative *salience* according to which both Functional categories and Relational values are graded.

Linguistically extrinsic factors in the organization of deictic practice include (i) the pervasive tendency towards *habituation and basic level categorizations* which embody a correspondence between routine experience of language in the world and the conventional categories of linguistic systems; (ii) the constraint that any utterance have only *one indexical frame,* unless otherwise indicated; (iii) the pervasive reinforcement of verbal acts by *bodily gestures;* and (iv) participants' access to, and ability to mobilize, *socially constituted schematic knowledge.* This encompasses the embodied categories of corporeal frames, including perception and actional engagement, as well as domestic, agricultural, cardinal point, and ritual spatial frames, along with the repeatedly experienced participation frameworks in which they arise. These various schemata display significant **homologies** to deictic categories and provide a preconstituted frame space with which the referential values of deictics **articulate** in speech.

In trying to say why the Maya system is as it is, all of these factors, both intrinsic and extrinsic, come into play. It is unlikely that any adequate response can be offered without further comparative and historical research, which goes beyond the purposes of this study. Still, the split between Initial Deictic bases and Terminal Deictic complements stands out as a specific feature of modern Maya that requires comment. Two questions arise: Why are the two series distinguished? And why do most deictic constructions combine them? The answer to the first question is elusive, but involves the kinds of information encoded in the forms. IDS encode grammatical category features that integrate the deictic into a message structure, along with core dimensions that integrate the focal object into the total frame of reference. TDS encode values within dimensions, along with communicative functions and standard indexical co-efficients. They specify the precise location of the referent in the network of deictic dimensions, at the same time as they bind it to its indexical ground in the Participation framework. Deictic constructions in Maya usually combine the two, because the act of ostensive reference, which is the core engagement mediated by these linguistic resources, itself requires a combination of these kinds of information: a coherent message structure (whether fragmentary or grammatically complete), a frame of reference with multiple categories subdivided by values, and an indexical ground with its basis in the relation between coparticipants and the schematic knowledge on which they draw in speaking and understanding. Although this study has focused solely on synchronic, language-specific analysis, I believe the approach and principles developed here can help shed light on the structure and evolution of other systems as well.

11 Conclusion

My main conclusions regarding the principles of Maya deixis were summarized in chapter 10. Those regarding the background of schematic knowledge relative to which the system is intelligible were drawn together in chapters 3, 7, and 8, and their implementation in referential practice was examined in chapters 4, 5, 6, and 9. Rather than recapitulate the specific points made in the course of this study, I want, by way of ending, to place the issues addressed here in a larger perspective. I started from the suggestion that a research focus on referential practice could make a significant contribution to our understanding of language structure and use, by providing a framework in which to systematically describe communicative processes, without our falling into subjective, naively concrete, or mechanistic views of speech. I think the present absence of any comprehensive theory of deixis, the relative paucity of sustained empirical description in the contemporary literature, and the significant advances made by a variety of scholars in the study of language use warrant the attempt to develop a new synthesis.

My main proposal can be summarized in a few sentences. Deictic reference is a communicative practice based on a figure-ground structure joining a socially defined indexical ground, emergent in the process of interaction, and a referential focus articulated through culturally constituted schematic knowledge. To engage in referential practice is to locate oneself in the world, to occupy a position, however fleetingly, in one or more sociocultural fields. The horizon of schematic knowledge (in the mind and in the body) that practice presupposes is also produced in practice, through incipient habituation, the regularities of language structure, and the predisposition of actors to schematize their experiences in the very process of living them. The organization of deictic categories incorporates relatively arbitrary grammatical features, as do all linguistic systems, but deixis is ultimately inseparable from the habitual practices in which it is embodied. This widely recognized fact has consequences that have yet to be accorded their proper weight in either linguistics or anthropology.

From the social bases of reference, it follows that demonstrative usage can never be adequately described from the egocentric or speaker-centered perspectives that have dominated linguistic pragmatics until recently. The same holds for corporeality, which enters the communicative process as a field occupied by coparticipants, not as an individual possession. Egocentricity is a special case of sociocentricity, which is more basic and provides a more powerful approach to pragmatic description. From the existence of a plurality of conventional features encoded in deictic systems, it follows that deixis cannot be assumed always and everywhere to be grounded in space and time in any useful objective sense. Spatial and temporal contiguity are special cases of the access that participants have (or fail to have) to each other and to objects in the world. This means that descriptions of deictics based on features like 'proximate' and 'distal' may inconsistently lump together significantly different phenomena and thereby obscure the actional bases of linguistic subsystems.

It follows from the fact that indexical features are elaborately encoded in languages such as Maya that indexicality cannot be equated with that which is inherently situated, purely emergent in action, and unstructured. Indexical relations are no less susceptible of conventional structuring and schematization than nonindexical ones and cannot be grasped apart from symbolic and ideological values that go beyond the immediate zone of utterance. Hence we can speak of indexical frames and not only of indexical frameworks. Moreover, what we called the 'principle of relative symmetry' governs the relation between referential projections and indexical frames, by narrowing or broadening the range of choices a speaker has according to the indexical ground which (s)he is currently occupying.[1] In other words, there are systematic indexical requisites for reference. As a corollary of routinely attending to these requisites, speakers tend to schematize indexical processes, to simplify and focalize aspects of them. We find compelling evidence of this in the regularities of usage across a range of discourse genres, in native metalanguage, and in the grammaticalization of indexical differences. By routinely engaging in referential practice, speakers not only portray a world out there, but reflexively, naturally, schematize the ground in here from which the portrayal arises.

The ongoing tendency to schematize indexical frameworks of reference is abetted and guided by what we call the 'principle of proximal differentiation' (chap. 10). This says simply that the immediate zone of interaction is more finely subdivided by deictic distinctions than is the distal zone outside it. The practical range of deixis is centered in the proximal zone, where there are many available contrasts among reference points and they attain a level of delicacy unparalleled in the distant.[2] It is not surprising that there is a proliferation of functions and R values in Maya that focalize the engagements of core participants and their corporeal fields. By providing the categories in which reference points are projected onto the immediate indexical ground, deictics are structurally predisposed to **produce schemata that embody emergent interactive processes.** The standard uses of shifters actually produce context, by converting an emergent framework into a frame of reference. The semiotic power of deixis is that it governs the conversion while categorizing the relation between the two phases of context.

'Here-now' is never a sheer physical reality to which we can meaningfully apply objective measures. As the ground and by-product of communicative practices, it is inevitably a **lived space** made up of perspectival subspaces, costructured with the corporeal fields of human actors, and located within a broader sociocultural frame space. Frame spaces provide the field of possibilities from which the actual conditions of linguistic practice are derived and against which the present is commonsensically understood.

Taken as a comprehensive whole, the deictic frame space in Maya is a fundamental sociocultural construct. It stands alongside corporeal, cardinal directional, domestic, productive labor, and ritual frame spaces. Like these, it is made up of a range of potential positions and occupancies, configured in frames and combinations of them. Its constituent frames display specific and detailed homologies with those of the other sociocultural spaces, and they are coarticulated with them in the course of talk. It follows that deixis has a significant contribution to make to ethnographic description.

Because they index relative symmetries of knowledge and experience among interactants, words like 'this' and 'there' may have as much social resonance as a second person pronoun which codes a status asymmetry. Demonstratives appear more neutral because their referential foci are in many cases distinct from the participants, but this appearance misleads. In the routine act of referring, a speaker takes up a social relation to his or her context as surely as (s)he does in the act of address or in a public performance.

Because of the dynamic character of indexical processes, an ethnography capable of encompassing the native 'here' must take the details of interaction as its point of departure. Yet it cannot stop there, since the status of details as cultural facts is contingent on their place in larger meaning contexts, most of which do not show up in a transcript. The objective realities with which indexicals connect are themselves social products with meaning horizons. In deictic practice, we have to do with the production of objectivity, not with the verbal reflection of what is always already there.

The distinction between intrinsic and extrinsic simplicity, put forth in chapter 10, was one way of locating the specificities of actual language use in relation to the generalities of linguistic theory. I have been concerned throughout this book with describing the material specificities of things said and places occupied by real people on actual occasions in the community of Oxkutzcab, Yucatán. The abstractness inherent in most theorizing about language has produced important insights, and will continue to do so. For the study of deixis, however, it has also been a liability that has helped to shield theory from the real complexities of actual language use. Ironically, the seductive abstractness of 'spatial proximity' has sustained an unrealistically concrete view of the deictic 'here'.

By sifting through the minutiae of a mass of particular examples, we work towards more revealing generalizations. Our disciplinary languages provide more than ample resources for reducing many of the details of speech to their common factors, but the reduction sometimes distorts. The logical conclusion to such a process of abstraction applied to deictics is the proposal that indexicals can be translated into nonindexical terms, so that a centered reference space can be substituted by a Cartesian coordinate space (as in Gell 1985; Lyons 1977). The payoff to such an exercise is the unification of reference in a single, acentric framework and the reassurance that in ostensive reference, we really do lock into objective reality 'out there' after all. The down side is that this approach utterly fails to explain why *all* human languages have deictic and centered referential terms, why they have the recurrent features they do, how corporeal engagement pervasively grounds reference, and how the everyday concepts of space and time are rooted in people's habitual interactions with the world. Such an approach mistakenly tries to understand deixis in relation to an anonymous, memorial space, whereas the real challenge is to incorporate it into lived space.

Beyond the ethnographic rationale for increasing the specificity of description, I have also tried to show the kinds of linguistic evidence that are needed in order to describe a system of shifters. Given the scope of 'context' with which we must be concerned, it has not always been obvious how to proceed. There are enough examples in the foregoing chapters to challenge my interpretations, hopefully, and to give a clear picture of the kinds of evidence that would be relevant to analogous cases in other languages. This is critical in the study of deixis, in which existing empirical descriptions are relatively few and incomplete. By piecing together what a group of speakers actually say, what they say they say, and the conditions under which they say it, we get a sufficiently explicit account to serve as a starting point for further research.

In chapter 1, I suggested that by combining cultural anthropology with frame semantics and interpretive sociology, we could get a better understanding of reference as a kind of practice. Such an approach directs our attention to cultural schemata, habitual modes of producing and receiving speech, and the embodiments of language in corporeally experienced communication. It also helps to draw attention to the limits of these factors, the nonschematic, decentered uses and modes of embodiment in media other than the body. The study of deixis can in turn make important contributions to the development of these overlapping fields. In examining ostensive reference, one gets a privileged view of the corporeal engagement of agents in talk. Sometimes the object referred to and nearly always the geometer that orients reference to the world beyond itself, the corporeal frame enters into practice at levels of both figure and ground. While it is clear that in collections of terms for body parts, we can construct a more finely categorized **descriptive representation,** it is only in the centered categories of indexical-denotational expressions that we find representation interpenetrated so systematically with direct **engagement.** This duality is one of the key properties of referential processes in natural language, and no anthropology of verbal practice can be complete without some account of it.

The same mechanisms that center reference in the corporeal field provide the means whereby speakers can submerge or break away from corporeality. The relational structure of deixis is a simple, elegant device for projecting references off an indexical ground. Whether the ground is bodily or transposed into some other frame, the relational structure works the same way. This constancy allows participants to produce remarkably abstract frames of reference with little apparent effort, complete with embeddings and transpositions, and rarely lose their way.

The grammatical organization of Maya deixis into sets of proportional opposites and analogical constructions displays the 'inner logic' of a linguistic system to a striking degree. In arguing against the objectivist notion of a pure abstract system, contemporary anthropology must not allow itself to claim that linguistic systems do not exist apart from ongoing practices. None of the hundreds of utterances adduced in this study could be explained without reference to the categorical structure of the Maya language, which defines an important part of the total space of possibilities for verbal action. At the same time, the indexical ground of deixis connects it to an immediate present as unavoidable and compelling as the conventional system of language. Deixis shows in its duality that whatever synthesis we adopt in describing communicative practices, both orders must be accorded their proper weight; neither can be brushed aside or relegated to the status of an epiphenomenon of the other.

Speakers in the course of deictic usage do not create their frames of reference from nothing but occupy frames in frameworks, combine and juxtapose them in contingent ways, and produce schematic representations, some of which get repeated. This touches on another key question for the description of communicative practice. How can we characterize the open-ended, fragmentary, and 'locally negotiated' aspects of social activities, the freedom of actors to improvise, while still recognizing the constraints? How can we give consequences to the platitude that utterances are situationally contingent without being random? Here deixis provides a really valuable case study for anthropology. The figure-ground relational structure of ostensive reference makes possible a variety of decenterings, as analyzed in chapter 5 and illustrated throughout the book. These have in common that the participants engaging in decentered speech adopt as indexical ground a frame other than the actual one in which they corporeally positioned. From the analysis of deixis, it follows that the 'actual' framework of speech is a relational construct, minimally a pairing of the immediate corporeal zone of speech with the referential-descriptive frame projected by the message. Deictics mediate precisely between the speech event (Es) and the narrated event (En), to put it in Jakobsonian terms, and this mediation inherently alters the former. What is actual prior to an utterance and what is actual after it are not the same, since reference reflexively alters the context of its own production.

Processes of decentering account for a great deal of the plasticity and creativity in routine reference, and they can be described with considerable detail in light of the structure of deixis. But the figure-ground pairing fails to address the issue of contingency, because it tells us only which frames of reference and indexicality are *currently occupied* by the interactants. It sheds no light whatsoever on the broader space of possibilities of which the currently active framework is a part. Following practice theory and some leads of Goffman, we posited a 'frame space' to talk about the *virtual* frames to which speakers have access, whether or not they mobilize them on given occasions. Here the idea of habitus is helpful. One can appreciate how the durable, habitually engaged orientations to action that communities of speakers share can constitute for them a space of possibilities automatically available as a resource and automatically constraining. The study of everyday deictic usage can contribute in return a richly detailed understanding of how a space of possibilities is embodied in usage, and how interactants move about in that space.

The foundation of deixis, as I have treated it, lies in the sociocultural practices of communication to which it contributes. These practices rest on a background frame space of habitual engagements and schematic knowledge, with which deictic frames are partly homologous and with which utterances articulate in interactive frameworks. In cases in which practices are saliently spatial or saliently egocentric, we can accurately describe language in these terms. But the blatant inadequacy of these as universal postulates leaves us with the difficult question of what the universal basis of natural language deixis *is*. Put slightly differently, what motivates the specific features of Maya, and what can this language contribute to an understanding of other languages, or language in general? To argue for a socially based account is by no means to assume a radical relativism, any more than symbolic anthropologists assume that different cultural systems have nothing in common. The difficulty of the comparative question is that most (although not all) of the existing literature on the topic of deixis embodies the assumptions of spatiotemporal egocentricity, and the evidence supporting claims about conventional meaning is too rarely spelled out in detail. Beyond notes on the structure of categories or the apparent presence of such and such a distinction in given languages, it is not obvious how to compare the facts of usage and native typification adduced here with descriptions of other systems. The problem is once again that lived space in its phenomenal and sociocultural dimensions is the basis of deixis, and this makes comparison difficult. In trying to do a linguistic ethnography of lived space, one is repeatedly struck by how simple things look and how involved they turn out to be.

It is unclear to me whether any set of diagnostic tests could be devised that would allow one to say with confidence which dimensions of context are in play in an utterance and which ones not. It would have been reassuring to find such criteria. My solution has been the laborious but deeply rewarding one of learning to speak Maya language reasonably well, listening to it for a long time in a variety of contexts, teasing out linguistic distributions, and talking with native speakers to get a sense of their views. The problem is as acute in the case of familiar languages like English and French as for unfamiliar ones like Maya or Malagasy. It turns out to be prodigiously easy to occupy the vantage points of one's own common sense, to assume the self-evidence of thisness and hereness, especially in one's own culture. Few things could be more obvious to a Maya speaker than his or her unreflective ways of occupying communicative spaces. But this image of transparency is part of what needs to be explained, not part of the explanation. A major aim of this study has been to show empirically how language, lived space, and common sense are costructured in the lives of a group of Maya people. The difficulties of analyzing this costructuring are considerable and doubtless carry over into the reading, as they have into the writing. Despite its length and density, this book has dealt closely with a mere handful of words in a single language, and even so, I have skirted many issues. The results are not likely to be uniformly convincing. If I have accurately represented the practices of DP, DC, and other Maya friends and teachers and if I have managed to return some of reference to its ground in human experience, then at least it is a start.

Notes

CHAPTER 1: Introduction

1. I will follow the standard practice of Mayanist linguists, designating Yucatec Maya, the language under study, as Maya, and all other related languages as 'Mayan', accompanied by a qualifier, such as Quiché Mayan, Tzotzil Mayan, and so forth. Yucatec is the only language of the family in which the native speakers describe themselves as *màaya* and their land as *mayab'*. It is spoken in the Mexican states of Yucatán, Campeche, and Quintana Roo, as well as parts of Belize. There is a great deal of bilingualism in the region, and the number of native speakers can only be estimated. It seems safe to guess that somewhere over one half million people speak Maya in a large portion of their daily activities, while many more are capable of doing so when necessary, and still more exhibit various degrees of understanding and ability to interact in Maya. In Oxkutzcab, where my main research has been conducted, Maya is the language of home, work, marketing, medical care, political speeches, and religious observance for a large part of the population, including all of my informants.

2. Throughout this book, I adopt a purposely narrow interpretation of the words 'deixis' and 'deictic', restricting them to the contribution of a limited number of linguistic forms to acts of reference. In more technical terms, 'deixis' designates the **indexical denotational** function of linguistic forms, whereby they contribute to the individuation of referential objects relative to indexical contexts (Hanks 1989b). Hence, I exclude what Levinson (1983) calls 'social deixis', which is the indexical potential of speech to signal social aspects of utterance context, apart from the denotational values of the utterance. This I treat as 'nonreferential indexicality', following Silverstein (1976b). Given these definitions, I will occasionally use the expressions 'ostensive' or 'ostensive reference' to describe the use of deictic categories. Unless otherwise indicated, no special meaning is intended in such usage.

3. It will become clear in chapter 2, I use the term *semantic* to designate the conventional (in the Gricean sense) functional potentials of linguistic expressions, whether or not the function is reference and description.

4. In addition to more specific developments to follow in this book, interested readers are referred to Brubaker (1985), de Fornel and Encrevé (1983), Encrevé (1988), Hanks (1987a), Lave (1988), Ortner (1984), as well as the writings of Bourdieu.

5. Gricean implicature is a notable exception to this but has other limitations stemming from its objectivist roots. This framework will be discussed, and adopted in part, in chapter 2.

6. As will become clear in chapter 2, I refer at this point primarily to research by Cicourel, Fauconnier, Fillmore, Johnson, Lakoff, and their collaborators.

7. These often unexplained terminological differences provide ample opportunities for equivocation, but it would require a separate study to sort them out. In this book, I will use the term **schema** (pl **schemata**) (adj **schematic**) to designate prefabricated social constructs. These may have the status of mental structures or physically embodied forms, synchronic states or diachronic successions, stereotypes discussable by native actors, or tacit aspects of their practice. Rather than propose a new formalism, I will try to specify with further description which sense of the term is intended in given passages. The alternative of developing a distinct terminology would be potentially cleaner, but is beyond my purposes. When discussing the work of other scholars I will use their terms.

8. The virtually total absence of phenomenological references in works like the two cited is fully comprehensible in view of the scholarly provenience of cognitive studies, but it is ironic, because many of the key arguments put forth against objectivism, in favor of experience, the body, typification, and situated interpretation, were made some time ago by phenomenologists and figure prominently in the writings of Husserl (1978), Merleau-Ponty ([1945] 1967), and Schutz ([1932] 1967, 1970, 1973), among others (see, for instance, Kellner in Luckmann 1978).

9. I assume a distinction here between what might be called 'ego involvement', the engagement of a speaking ego in the act of utterance, and true 'egocentricity', where the speaker is the orientational center relative to which the reference is computed. All deictic use involves the ego, but only the two DLOCs encoding Inclusive and Exclusive are properly egocentric in Maya. The evidence for this assertion is spelled out in chapter 9.

10. The indexicalization of meaning in recent semantic theory could be said to go in the same direction, by uncovering a hidden deictic dependency in the meaning of many apparently nondeictic expressions, such as Putnam's (1975) treatment of natural kind terms and Searle's (1979) discussion of literal meaning.

CHAPTER 2: A Relational Approach to Demonstrative Reference

1. Kripke ([1977] 1979:14) makes the stronger claim that Donnellan's distinction is merely a special case of Grice's notions of conventional and natural meaning, but the justification for this is unclear to me.

2. I mean here to distinguish mention from quotation and reports of speech attributed to authors, as well as from hypothetical or fictional speech not attributed to any speaker. For more detailed discussion of this distinction, see chapter 5 and Hanks in press.

3. This is a convenient shorthand. It is the speaker or interactive dyad that make reference, and only derivatively do the words they use in so doing (Linsky [1967] 1971:76).

4. I am assuming that actual identity of meaning is vanishingly rare in natural language, and that synonymy could be defined relative to minimal oppositions among terms (cf. Weinreich 1980:77). Such oppositions play an important role in the structure of deictic systems, which form closed sets of near synonyms.

5. Note that this is distinct from Donnellan's definition of 'semantic meaning', which is what the speaker's words mean *on a particular occasion of use*.

6. Fillmore's position here appears to be most closely in line with Grice's (1967, 1975, 1978) distinction between what is **said** (encoded, conventionalized) and what is **conveyed** (encoded plus implicated) in an utterance. One important difference is that Fillmore's interpretations are built directly on the conventional meanings of linguistic forms uttered,

not on the logical semantics of the proposition (fragment) corresponding to the forms (Fillmore 1985:234). Langacker (1984:172) starts from the more radical and problematic assumptions that semantics and pragmatics are *not* distinct, nor are linguistic and non-linguistic knowledge. Fillmore's position is more consistent with the one adopted here.

7. It is appropriate to recall at this point that the terms of description will evolve as we work through the Maya material, and in particular that a distinction between schematic frames and local frameworks will be introduced in §2.3.1 of this chapter and refined in chapters 4 and 5.

8. Putnam (1975:230ff.) argues that the general meaning of a linguistic form like 'water' is based on what it typically refers to in ostensive contexts (H_2O with certain typical attributes). This implies that ostensive definitions are a necessary part of a semantic investigation (even level 1 in present terms). Weinreich (1980:302) takes a similar approach to lexical definition, incorporating an ostensive component along with a descriptive one. For an extensional approach to semantics, a descriptively accurate account of ostensive reference is an unavoidable requirement.

9. Kaplan ([1978] 1979:391) is undoubtedly right in asserting that such an approach loses its appeal if one attempts to force all demonstrative phenomena into one or the other of sense and denotation, with sense alone comprising propositions. But it is not my proposal that all phenomena be handled this way, only certain components in the paradigmatic structure of lexical deictics. What Kaplan slights from a natural language perspective is the overbearing fact of paradigmatic structure. It won't do to replace the ostensive component of all demonstrative utterances by 'dthat' in a language like Maya, with several score alternative deictic phrasings. It is possible that such an analysis could work, but it would do so by distinguishing a range of d-like operators, not by lumping them into a single one. For further discussion of ostension, see also Baker and Hacker (1980:168–227, 1984:140ff., 197ff.).

10. Such a definition of the index as a set of dimensions is implicit in the way ethnographers of speaking have described speech events, as a set of simultaneous dimensions; Es → {Spkr, Adr, Time, Place, Key, . . .} (see Jakobson 1960; Hymes 1974; Bauman and Sherzer 1974; Silverstein 1976b; Hanks 1983; Sherzer 1983).

11. I abbreviate here a topic developed at length elsewhere. Hanks (1989b) focuses on the distinctiveness of deictic reference and the role of figure-ground structuring in the semantics of deictic expressions.

12. I do not wish to suggest that paraphrases could provide an adequate account of the linkage between expressions and frames, but rather that they can do a useful part of working out the interrelations among the forms.

13. The preceding paragraph is abbreviated from Hanks 1989b. Some of the precedents for describing semantic structure in terms of the Figure-Ground relation are cited there, with particular reference to work by Charles Fillmore, Leonard Talmy, and Stephen Wallace.

14. See Anderson and Keenan (1985:280), Bloomfield (1933:284), Bühler ([1934] 1967:175), Lyons (1977:646), Russell (1940:114).

15. In a study of spatial orientation, Gell (1985:278ff.) takes a position evidently consistent with that of Evans when he argues that token indexical spatial propositions logically presuppose non-token-indexical ones. Just as Lyons (1977) suggested that natural language reference could be achieved without any indexical elements, Gell goes on to argue that token indexicality is reducible to a more basic set of nonindexical coordinates that actors represent in mental maps. From the perspective of this book, both Lyons and

Gell overemphasize the conceptual as opposed to the practical, and the Cartesian as opposed to phenomenological conditions on reference. If indexicality really were a dispensable part of language and orientation, then we would be hard-pressed to explain why all human languages have indexical terms and why they are ubiquitous in speech.

16. One confronts on this point the tradition of looking at speech acts as essentially one-man productions consisting of intentions acted out. But see Hancher (1979).

17. This is a fairly drastic summary of Schutz's thesis of the reciprocity of motives. A slightly longer discussion is in Hanks 1983: chapter 2. See Schutz ([1932] 1967, 1970, 1973).

18. This is too simple, since interactants may well, even canonically, share a common 'here' and 'now' in speech, and different deictic forms differ in terms of the kinds of reciprocity that they require. The point is simply that perspectival relations are an integral part of the structure of deictic categories.

19. Cicourel (1986) discusses in depth the relation between knowledge and domination in the context of language use in medical settings.

20. Labov's ([1970] 1972a:299ff.) division between A, B, and AB events in discourse is a close analogue. For a fine-grained and ethnographically rich treatment of indexical symmetry, see Errington 1988.

21. Silverstein (1976b) noted this when he observed that demonstrative reference tends to be relatively presupposing compared to the creative potential of address. This section of the discussion is developed in Hanks (1989b).

22. These generalizations rest on three assumptions: (i) speakers seek to achieve mutuality; (ii) they do so on the basis of reciprocal access and the ability to identify referents; and (iii) the relational structure of deixis forces a pairing of identifying features with indexical origos, which makes interaction between the two components unavoidable.

23. On this point, see §§3.4–3.6 and chapter 5, as well as Hanks 1987a and 1989a.

24. The term 'situated' is intended in the strong sense of those aspects of meaning that arise **only in situations.** The weaker sense, what Goffman called the 'merely situated,' pertains to features of conveyed meaning that are encoded **in the language** (or some other cultural code) and are merely instantiated in use.

25. There is a very substantial literature on the topic of implicature in linguistic pragmatics; it is reviewed clearly and critically by Levinson (1983: chap. 3).

26. It does not demonstrate whether the form is ambiguous or unmarked with respect to the specificity of location, however (see Sadock 1978). Like the other kinds of evidence outlined here, this one must be used in conjunction with others.

27. Gumperz (1982: chaps. 2, 6, 7) presents a thorough treatment of conversational inference from a broadly sociolinguistic perspective.

28. I have omitted Grice's nondetachability criterion, which is meant to reflect the fact that implicatures are interpreted on the basis of the semantic content of what is said, not the linguistic form itself. In this view, implicatures cannot be detached from an utterance simply by changing the words for synonyms. There are well-known problems with this formulation (Sadock 1978; Levinson 1983:119), the most serious from my perspective being that Grice assumes that, in general, languages have different forms with identical meanings and implicatures. We find limited equivalences among certain deictic expressions, but to claim they are identical is problematic. Without this claim, the idea of nondetachability loses its force. I have also omitted nonconventionality as a feature of conversational meaning, because, as Morgan (1978) showed and sociolinguists have long

known, language use is in important ways conventional. If there are conventions of use as well as conventions of semantics, then conventionality is not what distinguishes the two levels.

29. For simplicity at this point, I overlook the fact that if X is not in S-final or topic-final position, then the TD will be discontinuous, since it is always S- or topic-final.

30. There is actually a pretty thorny question here as to whether co-occurrent deictics are coreferential, overlapping in reference, or in a relation of inclusion or contiguity to one another. The simplest cases are clearly coreferential, but more difficult examples arise and can be constructed. These will be ignored at this point and will be treated only with examples.

31. Use of negation for positive emphasis is common in Maya speech but reaches exceptional proportions in deictic reference.

32. The English and the Maya appear quite dissimilar on first view but share some important features: each is an irreversible binomial (speakers don't say 'we talked about that and this', or 'that, this, and that there', or their analogues in Maya). The first part in the pair is the more immediate form.

33. Various criteria for judging markedness relations were proposed by Prague School linguists, beginning with Trubetskoy and Jakobson. Baltaxe (1978:50ff.) presents a very clear and thorough account of markedness in phonology, in which equipollent and privative relations were first distinguished. Khlebnikova (1973) explores oppositions in morphology, including the notions of invariance, zero, neutralization, and microsystems, all of which figure in our treatment of Maya deixis. Friedrich's (1974) study of Homeric aspect introduces the notion of degrees of markedness and provides a classic demonstration of the necessity of analyzing oppositions in terms of a network of interacting semantic subcategories rather than isolated pairs. Markedness theory has been fruitfully applied to the study of language universals, particularly by Greenberg (1966) and, in a more detailed study, by Silverstein (1976b). These are among the works that have had most influence on the approach to paradigmatic structure in this book.

34. I have left out of the discussion the question of the kinds of evidence needed to demonstrate private oppositions, as well as the application of markedness in language universals. These topics are important, and I have addressed them elsewhere (Hanks 1987b). In the present context, my goal is to introduce privative and equipollent oppositions in relation to certain aspects of certain pairs of forms, not as a unifying vision of the whole language or deictic system.

35. For instance, Bloomfield (1933:258), Fillmore (1982:48), Frei (1944), Kuryłowicz (1972), Weinreich (1980:51). Russell (1940) and Reichenbach (1947:284) do not claim explicitly that indexicals are all proportional, but their attempts to reduce all of them to a single one, egocentric for Russell and token-centric for Reichenbach, make sense only if one assumes the forms to be regularly interrelated. Lyons (1977:646) makes the same assumption in his proposed paraphrases. If one starts from the position of structural variety rather than uniformity, such attempts lose their appeal.

36. This statement is consistent with the claim in cognitive grammar that the conceptual organization of the language is of a piece with the organization of thought and experience beyond the language (see Lakoff 1987; Langacker 1984; Fillmore 1985). Without going so far as to claim that no division exists between language and the socially constituted world, I will attempt to show substantial links between them. The empirical demonstration of this is in chapters 3, 7, and 8.

37. The direct relation between language and the world associated with this kind of semantics is addressed by Coleman and Kay (1981:36–42), Kronenfeld, Armstrong, and Wilmoth (1985:97), Rosch (1978:31ff.), and Lakoff (1987).

38. These features are discussed in Hanks (1989b) and in chapters 6 and 10 of the present work.

39. Although I see it as a natural use for the idea of 'core' dimensions, it should be clear that I am using the concept of core in a slightly different sense than the prototype theorists discussed in preceding sections. For one thing, I am applying it at the level of a set of linguistic expressions, not a single construction.

40. It also fails to provide values under the Temporal dimension, which is still under investigation.

41. This question has been addressed by nearly all major theorists of language. My treatment of it is aimed only at laying the groundwork for the subsequent discussion.

42. The point that categories are culturally constituted is made by Fillmore and Lakoff in several places but merits reiteration because of its global significance to the kind of semantics one envisions. Linguistically naive statements that semantics derives from the natural realities of the 'objective world' run amok in the face of the overwhelming evidence that in at least some features, languages are arbitrary systems, and cultures are as well.

43. Schutz foreshadows the phenomenon of 'defeasibility' here, whereby the descriptor applied to some referent on one occasion may be proven inaccurate in light of subsequent experience, as in Putnam's (1975:225) "This is water," pointing to a glass of clear liquid. It may take an indefinite amount of research to determine that in fact the liquid is not H_2O. Because it can be proven wrong, the definition is 'defeasible'. Applied to language use more generally, defeasibility denotes the fact that meanings that arise in one context of use may fail to arise or be precluded in another (see Levinson 1983 for an extended discussion).

44. This section draws heavily on Hanks In press and summarizes empirical conclusions demonstrated there and in Hanks 1983:part 3.

45. Cf. Schutz's various descriptions of the "recipe-like" character of common sense.

46. Cf. Silverstein (1979:202) for a general statement of this problem.

47. See Lakoff's (1987:301) interesting remarks about objectivity in relation to perspective.

CHAPTER 3: Foundations of Indexical Context: Social Mediations of the Body

1. Stated in semiotic terms, even indexicals, which are defined by their actual contiguity with objects, come in conventional types. They are, as Peirce put it, "indexical legisigns." Thus an expressive particle in Maya like *bakaán* 'evidently, apparently', conventionally indexes that the proposition with which it occurs is unexpected or only apparently true.

2. Remarks on the esoteric knowledge of Maya shamans are based on in-depth experience with a single shaman in the region of this research, along with impressionistic observations of the practice of other shamans.

3. The perceived relation between swarming ants and the animacy of a person is perhaps also reflected in the description of rage in a person as *p'uúhul usíinik* 'his ants are stirred up, his Mongolian spot excited'. One adult female speaker explained that the *síinik*

is actually the Mongolian spot at the base of the spine, but that *p'uúhul* describes the swarming of ants (BB.4.134). According to the Cordemex dictionary, the former term meant 'pulse' during the colonial period. The verb *p'uúhul* is described in the Cordemex as "to make a din, cause a racket" and also denotes the collective hunts that Maya men conduct, in which they fan out in the forest making a racket to drive the game towards men posted along known paths. The analogy between the body with its nerves and pulse and the earth with its living inhabitants is patent here.

4. Nash ([1971] 1975:13) cites a close analogue in Tzeltal culture, in which body and homestead are symbolically equated. As in Tzeltal culture, Maya creation myths posit the derivation of man from earth in combination with God's breath.

5. Turner (1980:120ff.) describes a similar divide between hearing and seeing in Kayapo: the former is associated with passive understanding and conformity, a basic part of the political process, complemented by active understanding associated with seeing, speaking, and making things happen.

6. Cf. Tzeltal *š?awai* 'feel, hear' used to describe a shaman's understanding of the messages in the pulse of a patient (Nash [1971] 1975:xxiii).

7. This point was driven home to me forcefully during my first fieldwork among Maya people in 1977. DP's family, with whom I lived and worked for three months, had a newborn son in the household (the first child of MC and Eli). The child, later to become my *ahijado* 'godchild', was kept in a hammock out of my sight, further covered with a white cotton cloth. At the time, the family lived in what I have labeled area III of DP's current homestead (see maps in chapter 7), while I slept and ate in area I, then a small hut (*šá?anih nah*) on the edge of the woods. It was nearly two months before I learned of the child's existence and only in my last week that I actually saw him. When I first saw him we had just returned to the house from the fields, where we had been weeding for several hours. We were filthy and sweaty in the August afternoon sun when DA came walking out of the house with an infant in her arms. She handed the child to me, to my shock, and told me to wipe the sweat from my arms and torso on the baby, then to walk around the yard carrying him in my arms, then to hold a pen in his hand and write on a sheet of paper. I followed her instructions and only learned at the end that I had just become the baby's *padrino* 'godfather' by the Maya rite of *heȼ meék* (lit., 'fix-embrace', or perhaps 'forkedleg-embrace' after the position of the child's legs). Prior to that, the baby had been kept from my sight so that I would not inadvertently give it *ojo*, transferring my body heat to it by way of my gaze and thereby causing a thermal breakdown in the child. As DA explained it, the positions in which I carried the child were meant to insure that he would grow into a man who stays cool while working under the intense sun (hence transference of sweat), a man not afraid to walk about the woods (hence meander around the yard under the trees with him), and a good student (hence writing). By having me touch the child upon first seeing him, DA neutralized the danger of my giving him *ojo* with my unaccompanied gaze.

8. The role of gaze in shamanic practice recalls Merleau-Ponty's ([1945] 1967:81ff.) striking discussion of gaze as a mode of constituting and actually occupying objects.

9. These terms were pointed out to me by three Maya speakers in the course of a conversation in which I was trying (unsuccessfully) to explain the peculiar look a woman had given me in the market. As I was reaching for ways to describe her look, they suggested the terms and demonstrated them as they did.

10. The following discussion is abstracted from a longer comparison of the concept of

-iknal with the referential space of 'here' (Hanks In press). The data on which my statements here are based include many attestations of uses of the term by native speakers, as well as extended discussions with several adults.

11. The youngest son is currently fifteen years old and known to steal, lie, and use vulgar language. The older brothers see this is a negative reflection on themselves and an eventual negative influence on their children.

12. Comaroff and Roberts (1981 : chap. 2) describe a contrasting, more extreme case of tensions among agnates in the Tswana household, where agnatic bonds embody rivalry, hostility, and sorcery, in opposition to matrilateral bonds, which embody supportive and privileged relations. Unlike the Tswana, the Maya do not usually describe the agnatic bond in terms of its ambivalent characteristics but rather cite the prescription of solidarity.

13. The presence of an inner wall would surely be a sign of fractured relations. DC's older son, Man, speaking in bitter frustration of the behavior of his younger brother, Victor, said that if Vic grows up as a good-for-nothing and brings shiftless types to the house, Man would 'slap up a goddamn cement and cinder-block wall' to keep him out. Is's wife, Bal, recounted the arguments she had had with SC, her neighbor to the east, over SC's turkeys wandering into Bal's yard. Bal got so fed up she wanted to put up a wall, to which SC objected violently (BB.4.101).

14. Thompson (1974:29) observed that in Ticul, sharing the kitchen of the senior woman was a sign of subordination to her, but this is not entirely accurate for the Oxkutzcabeño households that I know. In fact, in at least some cases, it is the most senior daughter-in-law who shares with the husbands' mother, and this is a sign of alliance rather than subordination (the case of Pilar with DA).

15. Room numbers are shown in figure 7.10. Room 1 is Margot's eating area, 5 is the eating area of Lol and Fi, and 6 the front receiving and work area of Lol.

16. My data are insufficient to indicate how many *solars* an individual family may go through and perhaps retain as property in the course of its career. In the case of DP's sprawling homestead, none of the currently inhabited areas was the childhood home of his oldest son, although rights over these lands have been gradually acquired by the family over some thirty years.

17. As men acquire *solar* space and move in the course of their careers, they commonly keep poultry and fowl, which they call simply *ʔinwàalak'* 'my domesticated (animals)' in a *solar* separate from the one in which they actually reside. Balim kept his birds in a *solar* about 1 km away from the one in which he resided in 1979–81; Milo keeps his in a *solar* about 3 km away, in Yaaxhom; DP, while residing with MC and VC, kept his fowl in area III. In such cases, only the men go to feed the birds. They describe this simply as *kimbin tinsoólar* 'I'm going to my *solar*', letting context disambiguate between the *solar* where they sleep and the one where the birds sleep.

18. Cf. Comaroff (1985:56) for a partly parallel case of a close symbolic relation between the Tshidi woman's body and the house structure.

19. Nash ([1971] 1975:292ff.) makes an analogous demonstration of the schematic arrangement of activities and spatial arrays according to rank and custom in Tzeltal society.

20. My use of the term 'asymmetry' in this discussion is guided primarily by two sets of readings, one focused on participant structure in verbal interaction (including the works cited in the text) and one focused on social systems more generally. Along these lines, Comaroff (1985:48) describes the symmetric relation between genders around the Tshidi household, as opposed to their asymmetric participation in the sociopolitical process beyond the household. Munn (1986:279–91) describes the role of asymmetry as a principle

unifying objects of kula exchange (necklaces and armshells), with their gender corollaries (female and male, respectively) and their motion corollaries (slow, enduring, arriving from the northwest vs. fast, arriving from the southeast). My focus here is naturally on the interactive and specifically verbal consequences of social asymmetries among household members.

21. These remarks abbreviate a longer discussion of the problem of speech genres presented in Hanks (1987a), where I suggest that the components of genre include the orientation of the speech form (i) to structures of power and authority; (ii) to the process of reception; (iii) to historically specific courses of action; and (iv) to the indexical centering of the performance in a field of participation. It is primarily the first and fourth that I focus on here.

22. Alternatively, the expression *tí'an té'el o'* could be motivated by the shared orientation of the two to the task of digging the poseta, and so DP could be referring merely to the part of the task left to do without there having been any previous discussion of it.

23. Merleau-Ponty's attempt to derive everything from the self-possessed subject is no more distorting than the opposite claim, made by scholars such as Lyons (1977) and Gell (1985), that the actional orientations of deictic reference could all be translated into nonindexical Cartesian terms. Study of actual deictic usage in its cultural context leads away from the excesses of both objectivist and subjectivist semantics. What is needed is a combined approach in which the subject-object dichotomy is replaced with the relational terms of social practice.

CHAPTER 4: Participants and Persons

1. This statement bears on the semiotic function of pronouns in linking what I will call 'frames' in talk. The actual relation between a speaker and the events (s)he narrates goes far beyond person reference and is subject to a whole range of ambiguating moves and interactive pitfalls not discussed here.

2. I use the term 'phenomenal field' to include both the corporeal field of engagement among coparticipants and the narrative frames they project through talk. This combines the 'speech event' and the 'narrated event' in traditional terminology. I will occasionally use the phrase 'phenomenal framework', and this should be understood to designate the emerging configuration of frames produced in interaction—both through the referential projections of utterances and through corporeal changes in the bodily field.

3. The best discussion of this problem that I am aware of is to be found in Ingarden's (1973) study of the structure of literary works, where he articulates a theory of schematic partiality that accounts for many features of deixis and ellipsis in spoken language.

4. Although Goffman never stated the figure-ground duality of person reference, to my knowledge, his term 'figure' happens to designate the referential pole in contrast to the indexical pole of deixis.

5. There is a strong likeness between Goffman's idea of footing, the task-oriented *prise de position* of Merleau-Ponty's *schéma corporel* and the orientation of Bourdieu's ([1972] 1977) "body as geometer."

6. On the discrepancy between literal sense and the larger conveyed meanings communicated in discourse, we could also cite Ingarden's (1973) important discussion of the concretization of literary works or Grice's theory of conversational implicature. For further references, see Hanks (1989a).

7. I state these defaults in the conceptualist language of 'assumptions,' but as far as I

can see, the same kinds of facts could be stated in terms of preconceptual *schémas corporels,* as Merleau-Ponty proposed.

8. It seems to me that this is one of the points on which the approach to participant categories taken by Levinson (1987) is open to question. Levinson's proposed features do not distinguish focal person values as these are encoded in the R values of linguistic forms from indexical distinctions, which may remain underspecified in linguistic terms even if they are demonstrably in play in given contexts. For instance, most of Goffman's examples of animators distinct from authors and principals are merely cases of indexical transposition without any variance in the Spkr, Adr, Other values of the pronouns. In 'You told me "I won't go"', both first person forms make reference to Spkr; the first one is untransposed, and the second transposed from direct to reported speech frame. It would be inaccurate to say that the pronoun means Animator sometimes and Principal others, since this is a division in indexical frames, not in the referential categories.

9. I purposely avoid the standard cognitive description of linguistic expressions as **category labels,** since this term falsely implies that there is a one-to-one mapping between categories and expressions. This obscures the fact that verbal forms relate to functional categories in a variety of ways, rarely one-to-one (see §2.2.3).

10. See, for instance, DuBois (1987) for a discourse-based analysis of ergativity (illustrating from Sacapultec), Bricker (1978, 1981) on the evolution and structure of Yucatec Maya pronouns, Robertson (1980, 1984, 1987) on comparative Mayan and Yucatecan.

11. In certain cases, a prefixal pronoun may fail to glide insert before a vowel-initial word, provided this word is not the noun base, as in *ʔin oóšp'eé maáskab'* 'my three machetes'. Some nouns also fail to trigger glide insertion, as in *ʔin-ʔòon* 'my avocado', but not * *ʔinw-òon.*

12. Plurality is rarely marked more than once in a clause and may be left entirely unsignaled if interpretable in context. Still, it could be marked on a Vb as well as its adjunct NPs, as in *k-u-b'isik-óʔob' ʔin-nuúkul-óʔob' le maák-óʔob'* 'the men bring my tools.' In such cases, any of the three may be the sole plural marking, or all may be omitted. In poetically regimented discourse, redundant plural marking is used as a device for creating rhyme and repetition (Hanks 1990).

13. An alternative interpretation would have the simple pronoun forms on the right in (35) be interpreted as the dative series in its reduced variant. Recall that first and second person forms *t-en* and *t-eč* (etc.) can be interpreted either as dative forms, alternating with *tiʔ t-en, tiʔ t-eč,* etc., or as standard forms for nondative case roles. The alternations in (35) might be best analyzed as possessive alternating with dative forms. This would then explain the ungrammaticality of the third person forms in (36), since the reduced dative form in this person is simple *tiʔ ∅,* not simple *le tiʔ.*

14. To my knowledge, the term *iglesia* 'church' (Sp.) is used only for the Catholic place of worship.

15. The persistent grounding of person reference in spatial reference is a feature of many domains of Maya life, in evidence in the earliest colonial Maya discourse (Hanks 1986, 1988), as well as in the contemporary culture.

16. It is uncertain to me at present how a Spkr would formulate reference to the group consisting of himself along with his current interlocutor and some third party. The only phrasings I am aware of are the ones presented. The *-óʔon* suffix is unmarked for inclusion of Adr, and the comitative phrase merely amplifies the identifying description of the third party. I would expect the *-óʔon yeétel x* phrasing to be unmarked for Adr.

17. Notice that since the superordinate verb of thinking is first person plural, it is un-

certain which of the brothers is 'you' and which one 'we' in the reported speech event. The point seems to be that both play both roles. This reciprocal interchangeability in their participant perspectives is an embodiment of their solidarity as brothers and co-owners of the household.

18. This fact separates the example from ones like Lol's statement that not even he would enter his brother's house without announcing himself:

té?el o? → miš **tèen** hé **inw**-okol bey sín ké **in**-t'àan o?
'There, not even I enter without announcing myself.' (F.137.A.614)

In this utterance, the individual referred to by the independent Pro (Lol) is also cross-referenced as subject of the two verbs. This is a straightforward case of negative focus.

19. The three lines as laid out in the example can be readily scanned as a parallel couplet followed by a third structurally dissimilar but semantically related line. This is a recognized pattern in Mayan literary discourse (Tedlock 1983; Hanks 1989a).

20. This is essentially Levinson's (1987:192) definition stated in the present terminology.

21. This part of the discussion excludes uses of third person forms which are not referential.

22. It would be more accurate to say that the referents overlap. *le lo?* 'that' refers to our activity of discussing Maya language and *le ti?* refers to the Maya language itself.

23. Actually, in sustained metalinguistic discussion with Maya speakers, in which they created and commented on examples of routine use, they showed a strong propensity to create examples in which the individuals, places, and actions were taken from the real social surround rather than some purely hypothetical realm. In the present example, Man may well have had some particular individuals or events in mind, although if he did, he never let on.

24. In attested cases of this construction, the initial /l/ of *le la?* and *le lo?* is always elided. On syntactic grounds, it is clear that this is the form, since it can introduce an NP, as in *leti? e maák o?* 'that man'. This ID is often susceptible of reduction from *le* to *e*, but what is distinctive in these constructions is that the reduction appears to be obligatory.

25. There appear to be other constraints on this construction whose motivation is unclear to me. For instance, I have never attested the construction lacking the subordinate clause of (69), as in ? *le ti? e hé?el o?*.

26. The one apparent counterexample to this is the 'imperial I' of a *nukuč maák* 'great (old) person', who can stand for an entire collectivity. For instance, DP, father of three, grandfather of twelve, great grandfather of three, and compadre of eighty (by his count), stands at the head of a large household which he automatically represents in his singularity. However, this is not a fact of the pronouns but of the social organization of Maya households (see chapter 3). Furthermore, it has equal consequences for reference to household residents in all three persons and therefore gives no evidence for markedness distinctions among them.

27. It may appear awkward to label the entire domain 'participant categories', given that it subsumes the nonparticipant, Other category along with the first and second. The same awkwardness arises if we call the domain 'person' and subsume the nonperson Other category within it. I take this to be a terminological difficulty that need not confuse us: the global category derives its label from its core members (the participants) but quite naturally includes other non–core members at the periphery.

28. It is likely that this putative frame is made up of at least two subframes, corre-

sponding to the participant contact between the interlocutors and their common spatial displacement along the forward path.

CHAPTER 5: Complex Participation Frames in Social Context

1. Given the focus of this chapter on issues of participation, I state the problem of complexity and the alternative solutions in terms of participant categories, but it should be clear that precisely the same set of problems arises in respect to spatial, temporal, and other types of deixis.

2. Goffman did not distinguish what I am calling 'frames' and 'frameworks', and his terminology could be confusing. At certain points he used the apparently more specific term 'framework' in reference to participation; e.g., 1981:3, 137, 226. On the grounds that what he called 'production' and 'reception' are organically linked in interaction, I have lumped them together under the term participant 'frame' and distinguished this schematic structure from local frameworks of reference (on this distinction, see also Gumperz 1982:21-22, 36, 130ff.). At various junctures, Goffman also uses the term 'frame' (1976, 1981:230). Unless otherwise indicated, usage of these terms in this book conforms to the descriptive apparatus I am trying to construct. See also introductory remarks in §2.1 above.

3. In addition to works cited in the text, this section draws liberally on seminar presentations by Bourdieu at the University of Chicago and the Center for Psychosocial Studies, Chicago, during March 1986.

4. Recall Merleau-Ponty's ([1945] 1967) description of the space of possible postures that makes up the *schéma corporel*. What Bourdieu calls field shares the virtuality of the *schéma corporel* but is mediated by social divisions that never entered into Merleau-Ponty's model.

5. The relation between frame space and field suggested here would also fit well with Goffman's example of radio talk, since the individuals who engage in this discourse are surely players in a field of broadcasting.

6. This usage is more narrow than the one proposed in Silverstein (1987:157), in which 'decentered' designates a universe of reference given 'out there' independent of any observer and any communicative event, much like what Bühler (1982) called the 'symbolic field'. For this more global phenomenon of nonindexical dependency, 'noncentered' seems more accurate, if more clumsy.

7. Even in these cases, it could be claimed that the deictic unavoidably projects an indexical ground relative to which it is commented on and interpreted. For instance, '"here" means where I am when I utter "here."' The first instance of the DLOC in this utterance is a case of mention; the Spkr does not thereby make reference to his current location. However, the relation to a current location is still in play in the gloss.

8. The distinction between simple and complex frames is entirely relative, and it should already be clear that the corporeal frame is a composite of participant perspectives, psychophysical modes of access to context, and the reflexive *prises de conscience* of the occupants.

9. Unless we consider the separate problem of how to describe utterances performed in order to be subsequently reported, a sort of anticipatory embedding.

10. This statement is hedged because indirect discourse is a kind of direct usage itself, and it is not true that the devices listed are 'excluded from it'. The current, reporting speaker can express himself with them. The proper generalization is that they cannot be

used in indirect report so as to be attributed to the original Spkr reported on. The following discussion draws heavily on Hanks In press.

11. The *E, Es, En,* and *Esn* notation for describing Events, the Event of Speaking, the Event narrated, and the Event of speaking narrated are taken from the ethnography of speaking, where they are standard (cf. Hymes 1972; Jakobson [1957] 1971; Silverstein 1976b).

12. Because the quotative particle in Maya always follows the quoted discourse instead of preceding it, there is a strong tendency for the metalinguistic description 'he said to me', etc., to be encoded after the quote. This fact of superficial order does not alter the logical priority of what the metalinguistic device describes: any shifters found in the quoted speech will be interpreted **relative to the reported event,** not to the current retelling of it.

13. The example is hypothetical, but Pablo is a real individual who happened to live in a separate house in the same *solar* with me—a *solar* that belonged in fact to DP. Thus both the reference to Pablo and the description of his house as 'right there' are accurate descriptions of our actual context (*Es*).

14. I am not proposing that this explicit version with the boldface clause would be truly equivalent to what DP said but that it does not distort the import of his hypothetical affirmation, which **is** an answer from him to me.

15. This example is fictitious but realistic. Speakers sitting in the market in Oxkutzcab do make reference to the Puuk in the terms cited, and the Puuk is an ecological zone that actually does stretch out for (over) fifteen kilometers. See §7.3 for a description of the ecological context.

16. Field recording and current transcription by WFH, drawing on close transcription by Anne C. Rendahl.

17. This example could be analyzed alternatively as an example of deferred ostension, in which the demonstrative refers to the bodily gesture and the bodily gesture is the trigger for a second reference to the actual event. Alternatively, it could be claimed to involve neither transposition nor deferral of reference—the demonstrative simply refers to DC's gesture, and our ability to connect the gesture to the narrated event it represents is independent of the first-order reference. The result in stylistic terms is to make the narrated event vivid and perceptible to me, DC's audience, in the telling, and for this reason, I see it as a transposition. Moreover, the interjection in line (15.1) is understood as issuing from DC when he is faced by the deer and hence it indexes the narrated frame without deferral of reference.

18. There is an additional factor that may be relevant to his usage, namely, that he knew that I did not know where he lived, and the deictics ending in the Immediate TD *-aʔ* are often used to index asymmetric knowledge of the referent by the interlocutors (see chap. 9).

19. Or something like it; the example is recalled without notes.

20. This is a general case of the observation by Bourdieu ([1972] 1977), Evans (1982), Gale (1964), and Hallowell (1955) that in order to orient themselves spatially, actors must share both a system of coordinates and a knowledge of where they are currently located relative to them. The fact of sharing such knowledge and the localization of self in it are both linked to the actual conditions of an interactant, hence to the phenomenal frame.

21. This is a commonly attested use of Spanish borrowings for keying frame embeddings (discussed in Hanks In press).

22. The same point arises in relation to the limits on corporeal engagements; we could

list indefinitely many bodily engagements with himself or his situation that DP simply could not adopt in my company or that of his housemates.

23. My discussion of 'genre' summarizes a longer treatment in Hanks 1987a.

24. By 'kind' I mean socioculturally valued, historically produced genres. These are not reducible to types of structure in the manner of formalist theory, but they do have structural components. 'Instantiate' is intended to cover production of novel genres, as well as reproduction of already existing ones (Hanks 1987a).

25. The rough pragmatic equivalent of this exchange is also routinely performed in gestures in Maya—a shrug with tossed out hand, palm up, for the question and a directed nod or toss of the hand for the response. It is noteworthy that speakers rarely provide informative answers to this question, which has basically been desemanticized through routine use as a mere greeting.

26. Brown and Yule (1983) mention genres many times in their discussion of discourse without developing a focused approach to them. They do suggest a connection with 'local interpretation' (1983:63), which is consistent with the one posited here.

27. This section draws on more complete discussions in Hanks (1984) and another paper presented at the AAA annual meeting (1984b).

28. The image of path is DC's standard way of describing the sequence of reference frames projected in his prayer. Through its spatial references, prayer has *b'èel* 'road, way, path', and this becomes the way by which the spirits descend from the cosmos to the altar. This spatial transformation will be treated in chapter 8.

29. Many men who are not practicing shamans have nonetheless studied with a shaman in the past, or assisted one, or talked at length with one or more. The knowledge of Maya shamans diffuses through repeated performance, discussions with senior men, and patients of all ages. Many women regularly participate in novenas held in houses, in which prayers are recited in groups. For all these reasons, it is inaccurate simply to say that shamanic recitation is unintelligible to nonspecialists. The people with whom I have spoken about it nevertheless claim that it is unintelligible and esoteric and display only a splintered ability to recognize, but not analyze, the familiar. Shamans, on the other hand, analyze and rationalize their practice.

30. In colonial texts like the Ritual of Bacabs (Roys 1965) one does find these modes of address, illustrated in Hanks (1990). Similarly, in other forms of modern *reésar* I would expect to find examples, as in the *pa? ?iík'* 'exorcism (lit., drop wind)' which is much more aggressive than the *saántiguar*.

31. For the sake of brevity, this section of the discussion leaves much unexplained regarding the order and citation of spirits. See Hanks (1984c) on modern prayer and (1988) for colonial examples from the Chilam Balam. There is every reason to believe that these principles have great time depth in Maya culture, being in use prior to the conquest. See also Fought (1985), MacLeod (1990).

32. This section draws heavily on unpublished research reported in papers at the AAA annual meetings in 1984 and 1988.

33. In the intervening discourse, he describes the crystals as belonging to the spirits, and this relation lends support to the claim that the second person in (29) is actually the spirits, and not, say, God the Father and the Son.

34. Actually, similar happenings are cited by shamans as ways in which individuals acting in bad faith come to trick them. DC is proud of his ability to recognize such cases quickly and convince the trickster despite himself (or herself).

CHAPTER 6: The Perceptual Core of Ostensive Reference

1. It is true that the relational particle alternates *ti?* ~ *t,* as is shown in chapters 4 and 9, and this is analogous to the alternation in question. An important difference, however, is that in the present case, there is a high tone involved in the alternation, and this would usually block the collapse of the root vowel. Cf. the locative deictics *té?el* ~ *té?e* ~ *té?* and *ti?* never alternates with *tV* (chapter 9). For convenience, I will cite the *hé?* variant henceforth, unless there is reason to do otherwise.

2. The present introductory remarks on the grammatical properties of these forms are abbreviated from Hanks (1984a), a condensed version of Hanks (1983: chap. 3).

3. The sources of these auxiliary elements and their grammatical distributions in embedded clauses, for instance, vary widely. The two key properties for present purposes are their occurrence in immediately preverbal position and the fact that they determine the stem shape of the verb.

4. These constraints hold only for co-occurrence in the same clause. If the OSTEV is subordinated, as in *le hé?el o?* 'that one right there', then it may function as an NP to a higher predicate which may be questioned or called into doubt in any of the standard ways.

5. See Silverstein's (1987) important discussion of different kinds of functions. In Silverstein's terms, Presentative, Directive, Referential, and Expressive are pragmatic functions$_1$, although they also have typical indexical function$_2$ corollaries, which we are attempting to spell out with the *i* ground.

6. Example from (BB.5.40), spoken by Margot February 19, 1987.

7. This statement oversimplifies for the sake of making a clean distinction. Depending upon circumstances and the prosodic and gestural performance of the utterance, any of the Referential expressions could be used as a true Presentative. For instance, a magician could say, 'it's (long pause for dramatic effect) here! (pulling rabbit from hat).'

8. Examples like this do occur, especially in verbal banter among males. It is unclear to me whether a proper analysis would treat them as incorporating an equational statement identifying the presentatum with the Adr (i.e., the object of the OSTEV with the object of the pronoun), or whether they involve a deferred ostension. One can say 'here you are', holding a photo, the way one can say 'here's the problem', pointing to a gage indicating an overheating engine. In either case, the basic relation between the OSTEV form, the act of presentation, and the direct object is evidently intact.

9. Given the distinctions established in chapter 5, we can treat deixis in quoted and direct discourse in a consistent manner, separating the interpretation of the R values from the decentering of the indexical ground relative to which they are interpreted. The use of quoted examples to illustrate direct uses need not pose any special problems.

10. The particle *wal* in penultimate position is 'adversative' here, adding to the utterance an overtone of foreboding. See Hanks (1984a) for fuller discussion.

11. The places referred to in this example are described in more detail in chapter 7 and are shown in maps in figures 7.5 and 7.6.

12. In fact, he never showed up at all, although this outcome is nowhere foreseen in his utterances.

13. See §9.2.2 for the same weighting in the DLOCs. Balim's rejection of the forms cited should not be misread as evidence that such forms cannot be used under any circumstances. Given technology like film and audio recording, decentered contexts can be constructed in which such forms are perfectly appropriate. What Balim's reaction tells us is that in routine usage, the conditions for saying these things do not arise.

14. The **asymmetry** of tactual contact with the object, which is typical of Presentatives, rests on the relative **symmetry** of interactants' copresence. In face-to-face contact, these utterances index very small, though communicatively significant, differences.

15. See sketch maps of this location in figures 3.5 and 3.6, along with further discussion of this and adjacent utterances.

16. This dream narrative is briefly discussed in §4.1.2, examples (1–4).

17. This remark is meant to emphasize the fact that the functions of Presentative and Directive are not merely present or absent in a binary fashion but are graded. The main clause OSTEVs define the highest point in the functional scale, but the subordinated forms are still higher than many other Referential deictics. In chapter 10, when we take up foregrounded and elaborated deictic structures, the functional scales will be still more finely subdivided.

18. For the sake of brevity, I am skipping over many grammatical details in these examples, as well as the evidence for my claims about subordination. These matters are taken up in more detail in Hanks 1983:chap. 3.

19. Encounters with strangers are a significant theme in Maya storytelling, and it is often in the form of a stranger that spirits first contact humans. DC in particular has had several such encounters at important junctures in his development as a shaman.

20. Compare Fauconnier's (1984, 1988) more systematic development of what he dubs the Identification Principle, which accounts for various kinds of identifications whereby reference to one object can trigger reference to another.

21. The only example I have recorded of Anticipatory Reference (as opposed to Anticipatory Presentation) involving *hé?el a?* is the expression *le saábado hé? kutàal ká?ab'eh a?* 'this Saturday coming the day after tomorrow', in which the temporal expression makes the anticipation clear (BB.1.111; April 22, 1980).

22. The semantics and pragmatics of this affix are clearly more complicated than is suggested by my label 'habituative', and would require more evidence and discussion to make it explicit than can be devoted to it here. For further discussion, see Hanks 1983: chap. 3. The main point here is that the affix can be used with the DMOD but not with the OSTEVs.

CHAPTER 7: Spatial Orientations and Referential Practices

1. As we will see in chapter 9, DA's choice of the deictic *te? . . . a?*, rather than *té? . . . o?*, focuses on the path MC takes, in contrast to the destination he will arrive at.

2. Nash ([1971] 1975:3–10) describes the importance of the 'center' in Tzeltal (Tzo'ontahal).

3. Gossen (1974a:chap. 1) discusses comparable configurations in Tzotzil, and Nash ([1971] 1975:292–96) shows the pervasive presence of the square, four corners, and four sides in Tzeltal.

4. Fillmore (1982:36, 39ff.) also observed that some linguistic expressions with apparently straightforward semantic values, such as 'in front of ——', may actually be used in such a way as to presuppose a deictic center.

5. Shamans cast off evil spirits from the human body and domestic space, throwing them down into *čuúltuúns* deep in the forest. Neugebauer (1986) repaired and used one in Cooperativa in 1982 as part of his research. Before his workmen would begin repairing it, they felt it advisable to have a shaman come and cleanse it of any spirits. DC and I performed the ceremony in August 1981.

6. Margot described a *kahtalil* as a 'little ranch where milpa is made, about one to five

homes (nah) are there, like off in the Puuc' (BB.4.134). It should be pointed out that the root *kah* underlies *kàah* 'town', *kahtalil* 'homestead, ranch', as well as *kahakbal* '(to) reside'.

7. VC's area on figure 7.6 appears to be double the size of his two brothers' areas, but this is because he owns it jointly with his father, DP, with whom he works.

8. The process involved extracting *sahkab'* with pickax and shovel from the pit shown on DC's land in figure 7.6, carrying it into room 1, spreading it around evenly, and tamping it down with the flat surface of a cinder block.

9. The 'traditional' is meant to exclude from consideration the novena and other centrally Catholic practices. While these are an irreducible part of the universe of sacred practice in contemporary Maya culture, they are not articulated with spatialization in the same way as the practices under discussion here. They are part of the native category of *reésar* 'prayer', but not part of *payalči'* t'àan 'summons speech'.

10. From *tíč* 'to hold out in hand, present, demonstrate in a single stroke (Cordemex 791.1)' + *k'aák'* 'fire, heat, light'. See also §5.3 above.

11. What I have glossed as 'living spaces' includes both productive land and homesteads where people live and labor.

12. In fact they are part of an elaborate schema in which other kinds of place are under the influence of other classes of spirits (see Hanks 1984c).

13. The root *kaáh* in this compound is the same as the one in *kahakbal* 'reside', *kahtalil* 'homestead', and *kàah* 'town'.

14. Maya performance style involves regimented breathing, prayer being spoken in integral breath groups. For a fuller description, see Hanks 1984c.

15. The verbs used to describe the action of spirits all focus on their mobility and ability to bump into, hit on, and knock over people. The association shows up also in the semantics of the term *yiík'al* 'its spirit, animacy', and 'momentum'.

16. Munn (1986: chap. 6, 283 ff.) analyzes the relation between motion and stasis in Gawan culture, showing, among other things, that the immobility of agricultural land, enhanced by tightly arranged planting, is the precondition of the mobility associated with growth. For Maya, it is above all the perimetral fixing of domestic as well as agricultural land which is the precondition for the 'safe conduct' of daily labor and locomotion. Further, the concern in Gawan political process with controlling motion through immobility and recalcitrance, which Munn describes, has a functional analogue in the Maya shamanic practice of first immobilizing an intruding spirit and then throwing it away. The two cases differ, however, in that in Gawan, two rates of motion are distinguished, and the entire dimension of movement is articulated with an opposition between female (recalcitrant, slow moving) and male (persuading, fast moving). Neither of these statements obtains in the Maya case.

17. Many of the quotations from DC are in the second person, because he was teaching me to perform the ceremonies, not merely describing his own performances. There is also an impersonal use of the second person, as in English.

CHAPTER 8: Agricultural Processes and Spatiotemporal Frames

1. For comparison, see descriptions of the yearly cycle by Thompson (1974:53–60), Redfield and Villa Rojas ([1934] 1962:43–46, 81–86), Ewell (1984), and Neugebauer (1986:§2.2). My own description is informed by these but based mainly on descriptions produced by Maya men, along with impressionistic observations.

2. Perhaps the most famous illustration of this bit of Maya common sense occurred at

the end of the Indian offensive during the war of castes in nineteenth-century Yucatán. Having driven the Spanish-speaking troops from the countryside, the Maya farmer-soldiers abandoned their front lines when the ants arrived in June in order to return to plant their fields (Reed 1964).

3. Another case is recorded in (F.80.B), in which DC reviews the yearly cycle.

4. If one is *k'àak'as maák* 'bad person', he will cheat on the measuring, making the milpa bigger than it is supposed to be by adding to the perimetral length. This is called *tip'ik* and is considered a theft of land and labor as well (F.151.A.930).

5. There is variation on this point. While DC claims five stones, DP described the ideal boundary marker as consisting of four stones, in the same basic configuration as DC described (BB.5.21). In point of fact, markers are used that consist of anything from the ideal form to a single large boulder or a small pile of stones with a stick stuck in the middle.

6. I have not attempted to give the maximum number of years a milpa can produce in the Oxkutzcab region, because I believe there is significant variation according to the inherent quality of the soil. And since there are scores and scores of soil types conventionally distinguished by men of the region, to attempt a summary would lead the discussion off the path.

7. Or at least it is common knowledge that many people hold that belief. Many others repudiate it in favor of the tenets of any of the numerous strands of evangelical Protestantism in Yucatán today.

8. Recall that *wá?akuúntik* 'stand up (caus)' is the same verb DC uses to describe his placing of the spirits around the perimeter of the altar. The frame of offertory ritual is basically the same in a layman's practice, albeit greatly simplified in comparison to DC's.

9. The number nine is of great significance in Maya cosmology.

10. The great age of this belief is attested in the books of Chilam Balam, where ritual sweeping is described (Edmonson 1982; Hanks 1988).

11. An alternative interpretation is plausible, in which the *b'alče?* is masculine and the *saka?* is feminine. Note that I resolved the liquid phase altar into a complex frame that includes three levels of complexity, just as domestic space is made up of three levels of complexity, corresponding to nuclear, coresident, and extended agnatic households. The homology between altar and household establishes an equivalence between the central *b'alče?* and *saka?* offerings and the space of a single nuclear family. Recall that the individual house has two main parts, the sleeping house, called the *nah,* and the kitchen, called the *k'oób'en.* The former is canonically in front of the latter, just as the *b'alče?* is in front of the *saka?.* Moreover, the *nah* is a predominantly masculine (or unmarked) space, as opposed to the clear feminine valence of the *k'oób'en.* Similarly, the offertory *b'alče?* is prepared by the shaman (canonically male), whereas the *saka?* is prepared by women.

The implication is that there is a tacit correspondence between the liquid altar and the organization of domestic space. Both incorporate an elemental pairing of complementary parts which code a gender asymmetry.

12. This drawing, and my discussion, simplifies the actual altar used by DC in his rain ceremony at Yoó? Ak'al. The men of the area prepared a four-part structure, closing off the front end. DC considers this a well-intentioned mistake on their part, which he works around by presenting the main offering, not on the main altar where it should be, but on the altar at the front side.

13. This is a point of fundamental importance to the event, since the fire of the pit

oven, if placed to the east of the altar, would burn the spirits. It is to the west, just as the flames of the underworld are.

14. They also reproduce the same three-sided figure as the medicine laid out to dry by DC. Cf. plate 7.2.

15. This set of correspondences, which DC produced without hesitation, poses conceptual problems I have not addressed in the text. DC believes that God is located in the east but faces west in vigilance over evil originating from there. Hence the left-right orientation of the altar is for the shaman the opposite of what it is for his divine addressee. In addition to the inversion of perspective, there is a rotation in the symbolic values. DC's descriptive order would fit the actual altar at which he stands if once flipped over, the main altar were rotated counterclockwise until it aligned with cardinal east.

16. Not shown is the incense burning on the ground in front of the main altar, whose stated function is to perfume the way of the lords. Recall also that smoke is the form taken by spirits in DC's divining crystals. It is also the form of the heavenly lords when still in their upper places.

17. The same order of *ʔuk'ul* 'drink' preceding *hanal* 'eat' is embodied in the eating habits of Maya people, for whom the former describes morning 'breakfast' (as well as evening snack), and the latter describes the mid-day main meal.

18. *Wàahil kòol* 'breads of the milpa' performances by DC, recorded: (F.102–3.A) January 29, 1981, in Oxkutzcab, of which figures 8.1 and 8.5 are diagrams; (F.121–22.A) July 3, 1982, a combination *primisia* and blessing of the family well in Mani. Further discussion on (F.152.A) March 4, 1987.

19. These remarks on metonymy could be considerably extended were one to introduce the use of parallelism and *difracismo* (semantic couplets with a veiled meaning) in Maya discourse (Bricker 1974; Edmonson 1973; Hanks 1990). As Lakoff (1987:77) observes, "metonymy is one of the basic characteristics of cognition," and is very common in speech. My purpose at this point is to summarize the particular metonymic effects observed in the data under discussion, focusing the general phenomenon on the particulars of spatiotemporal reference in Maya.

20. The following discussion took shape largely in response to reading Bourdieu's analysis of the Kabylia agrarian calendar (1977:chap. 3), in particular, the proof that *lyali* is not a period of forty days (105ff.). 'Here' is not a zone of metric proximity.

21. I pass over the fact that Man has also slipped in the past marker *e ak*, which only reinforces the perceived pastness of talk that occurred in another place.

CHAPTER 9: The Spatial Frame of Deictic Reference

1. Sentence (6) is acceptable under the extremely unlikely reading 'I sold the market.'

2. The form *tíʔan* is probably best viewed as a derived verb form and not a deictic followed by a verb, since none of the particles that normally intervene between a verb stem and any preverbal elements can intervene between the DLOC base and the verb: *tíʔan wá letiʔ iʔ* 'Is he there?' but never *tíʔ wá ʔan letiʔ iʔ;* cf. *tíʔ wá k u bin iʔ* 'Is that where he's going?' The same constraint holds for *šan* 'too, also', *bakaán* 'evidently', *bʔin* 'reportedly', preventing them from intervening between the deictic and the verb. In the rare cases where something does intervene, the verb form is *yàan,* a freestanding incompletive verb form 'it exists.'

3. The most common variant of both DLOCs and OSTEVs, both prevocalic and preconso-

nantal, lacks the base-final *-l*, as in *té?e-, to-*. Unlike *hé?*, the root vowel of the DLOC bases are never assimilated to a following vowel, and hence one says *té? ič k'aáš o?* 'there in the woods', but never *tíč k'aáš o?*. Cf. *hé? insukú?un o? ∼ hínsukú?un o?* 'there's my brother.'

4. It is not my claim that *tàal* 'to come' invariably indexes movement toward the speaker. Rather, it always indexes movement toward, or accompanied by, one of the interactants. In many cases it happens to be the speaker. The imperative form *kó?oten*, on the other hand, is specifically egocentric, 'come here to me.'

5. 'Here in back' is a proper phrasing of a different spatial arrangement, in which the speaker's location is represented as behind some other landmark, which must therefore have an independently defined front-back orientation in this context.

6. The presence of two instances of *way* 'here' in (49) is due to the focal construction, described in chapter 10.

7. Another very nice example occurred in the context of a scholarly meeting in a conference hall in Mérida, on July 13, 1982. Among the audience was a group of native Maya speakers who work together in public education. One member of the group chose a seat in the row directly behind the others, which elicited the query from his friend, *yàan a kutal tol o?* ↑, 'Are you gonna sit (back) there?' At the time of the utterance, the interactants were no more than three feet apart, but the division created by the row of chairs and their forward orientation put the one speaker at a sufficient practical remove to motivate the DLOC choice.

8. It is also possible that Man switched from Non-Immediate to Exclusive DLOC in order not to repeat my utterance verbatim, a conversational practice he likes to avoid (see chap. 3). Even if this is the case, the stone pit out in back makes a fully appropriate *tol o?* 'out there' because of its separation from Man's living space.

9. Milo mobilized the same schematic opposition between routine social and non-routine wild space when he described the hunting grounds where he and his brothers go once a year as *to nukuč k'aáš o?* 'out there in high forest'. We were sitting in his house outside Cooperativa, and the place he referred to was the sparsely inhabited woods southeast of the Hwííȼ hills. As he uttered it, he made the typical 'out there' hand gesture: hand open, palm down and in, flicked outward and upward at about eye level, while simultaneously turning the line of vision away from the trajectory of the hand (Hanks 1983:190).

10. The example is perhaps more transparent if one has in mind that Maya customarily listen to music at what many North Americans would consider extremely loud levels. Music coming from the neighbor three doors over is perfectly audible, if not intrusive.

11. A reasonable alternative explanation is that it is to the representation in the crystal that DC is referring, and only derivatively to the actual place Plan Chac. Since the crystal is a very restricted space, held in the hand, he naturally chooses the segmenting Immediate DLOC. This is plausible and consistent with other deictic reference involving divining crystals (see §7.4.3). Unfortunately, this forces us to claim that the word *plančaák* in his utterance also refers to the crystals rather than the place at the edge of town, since it would normally be coreferential with the DLOC flanking it in the phrase. This is unlikely, since the crystals, to my knowledge, do not provide that level of representational detail. Further, the overall thrust of DC's remark was that the boy was not far away, and we lose a basis for this conveyed meaning if we claim that DC is referring, not to the boy's location, but to the crystals in his own hand.

12. It will become clear in §9.2.2.2 that one of the standard uses of the Non-Immediate

deictic is in reference to the addressee's current location, when speaker and addressee are not face to face.

13. A basically identical usage occurred years later when I was sitting with Eli in her kitchen and a bunch of dogs were milling outside the door. Knowing they have no dogs, I asked her where one standing right in the doorway came from. The exchange was as follows,

> WH: kuš tuún el a⁷ ?
> 'What about this one?'
>
> E: čeén yàana pèek' kutàa **té⁷** besìiná o⁷→
> 'It's just another dog that comes there from the neighbor's.'
>
> WH: pero maáš tíal
> 'But whose is it?'
>
> E: tíal le besìina **té⁷el a**⁷→
> 'It belongs to the neighbor right there (pointing down road).' (BB 5.39)

Eli starts off assuming I can figure out who she is referring to, using the symmetric Non-Immediate DLOC indexing shared knowledge. When I question her again, she recycles to identify the neighbor with a new ostensive identification.

14. And possibly the kind of 'adorned' reference which emphasizes proximity.

15. The preferred DLOC for this usage, assuming the speaker is standing by the table, is with *té⁷el a⁷*.

16. Recall from chapter 3 that we are distinguishing the **corporeal schema** of the individual body space of Spkr or Adr from the **corporeal field**, which is occupied by an entire participant framework.

17. These features are an expectable corollary of the difference between *a⁷* and *o⁷* Terminal Deictics, the former being always more asymmetric and high focus than the latter. This will be addressed in chapter 10.

18. In the Landmark frame, *té⁷el a⁷* is of the form used for the region 'on the near side'.

19. It is, of course, often possible to question the **extent** of the region the speaker refers to with *way e⁷*. What is not possible is to question reasonably where the region is, since wherever the speaker is, he is *way e⁷*.

20. In conversational context, such phrases often refer to specific places in the Puuc and Low Wood zones, such as an interlocutor's cornfield, bee colonies, or hunting areas.

21. The motivation for this is that *i⁷* is an anaphoric device, indicating that the locative reference is coreferential with a preceding description, while *e⁷* is a referentially empty placeholder. The presence of lexical description in the same sentence overrides any anaphoric relation to a preceding one, making the *i⁷* particle inappropriate.

22. The TD *i⁷* is replaced by *o⁷* according to a regular rule. See chapter 10.

23. Such examples seem to show that one can have discourse coreference even without reference.

24. We have already seen that if there is a verbal antecedent, the requirement that the referent be known by both participants no longer holds.

25. The absence of the *i⁷* terminal particle, and the presence of *o⁷*, indicates that the 'replacement' process, whatever its form, can apply to structures even when there is only

one DLOC base present. A corollary of this is that the terminal particles must be available in the grammar independent of the initial bases, a problem to which I will return in chapter 10.

26. Interestingly, the plural inflection that would normally attach to the verb in the locative phrase has floated rightward to the periphery. We would normally expect *tí?a-nó?ob' tek'aš*.

27. An immediately preceding description in another sentence (or fragment) makes an ideal antecedent, while the same one triggers *i?* → *e?* substitution if it occurs in the same clause; compare 126 with 133.

28. It should be clear from the description that I am not claiming these corollaries to be characteristic of all uses of the deictics in question, but only some of them. At the same time, in concrete contexts, they may restrict a speaker's choice of deictic quite strictly. When a person is walking towards a goal or is on the verge of setting out, *té?el a?* 'right here' is really the only DLOC available for making reference to the forward path.

CHAPTER 10: System and Utterance: The Elements of Maya Deixis

1. Recall that we have emphatically **not** claimed that types must be functionally invariant but rather than they fit into an array of referential and indexical frames in a consistent manner, which we have sought to describe in terms of relative markedness.

2. The corporeal ground can be effaced or abstracted away from in transposition. Also, it is occupied by coengaged interactants, not just by an individual.

3. More accurately, the final section summarizes the portion of the system that has been investigated in this book. We have made no attempt to treat temporal or manner deictics, which would considerably extend and possibly force revision of the functional space.

4. These preliminary remarks are taken in summary from Hanks (1983:27ff.).

5. The suggestion that the DLOC and the relational particle are at some level the same is not an accepted interpretation in Mayan linguistics, to my knowledge, and should not obscure the fact that they are phonemically distinct, differing by the presence or absence of the high tone. It is nonetheless a reasonable suspicion on the basis of the rest of the deictic system. Moreover, the high pitch on the DLOC could be motivated by the independent constraint in Maya that *V?V* sequences tend to acquire high tone on the first *V*.

6. As was made clear in chapters 4 and 5, the PART forms have analogous structures involving double person marking (affixed to the predicative element, as well as independent PART forms). These will not be discussed in this chapter, since they appear to work somewhat differently from the DNOM, OSTEV, and DLOC categories. On the other hand, the normal use of the DNOMs has not been discussed in detail in this book, but the foregrounded versions will be presented, nevertheless, in the aim of bringing out the parallel between this category and the others. I draw in this section on Hanks (1983:260ff.).

7. Utterances such as *le leti? o?* do in fact occur, but are not standard incremented NPs. Instead, they occur in metalinguistic discourse in which the medial *leti?* is quoted, as in 'that *leti?* that you've said'.

8. It is unclear to me whether the Peripheral form never occurs in double constructions or whether it is vanishingly rare (and never attested by me). In either case, its R value Peripheral is not conducive to the expression of obviousness usually conveyed by these constructions.

9. This absence of special marking distinguishes locative focus from both nominal and manner adverbial focus: the former triggers loss of prefixal person marking if the focal NP is an agent of a transitive verb; the latter triggers voicelike suffixal morphology if the man-

ner adverb is focused with an intransitive nonincompletive verb. Locatives never get any special marking other than the fronting of the adverb.

10. As pointed out in §9.2.3, the expected TD *i*? that complements the ID base in (29) alternates automatically with *e*? in the presence of a lexical description.

11. Contrary to the erroneous claim made in Hanks (1983:218) that the second locative element is always in final position.

12. This explanation leaves unaccounted for the ordering relation between *té*? and *to*, the motivation for which escapes me. On the other hand, it does cast some light on why *leti*? always precedes the other DNOMs in the NP category, since *leti*?, like *tí*?, is a thematic device.

13. Cf. *té*? *pàarsela kub'in o*?, **ká*?*ač té*? *pàarsela kubin o*?, *té*? *pàarsela kubin ká*?*ač o*?

14. The first three examples are taken from Hanks (1983:215), where this construction was first noted but was left essentially unexplained for lack of sufficient data.

15. One example recorded in my notes contradicts this generalization, but may be interpreted as two phrases separated by a brief pause. See example (52).

16. A revealing example occurred in DP's house one afternoon when DA called out from the kitchen hut asking for someone to bring her the honey. DP was resting in his hammock at the time and VC was sitting on the other side of the same room. In response to his wife, DP told VC where the honey was, implying that he should get it and bring it to DA. He said,

> tí?an **té**?**el a**?→ **way** yan ič nah **e**?
> 'It's right there. It's here inside the house.' (BB.5.21)

This pair of utterances does in sequence what the others do in a single utterance: they locate a point within the more inclusive region.

17. The following generalizations bear on **continuous** deictic constructions, and particularly canonical citation forms. When TDs and IDs occur in **discontinuous** shape in connected discourse, where they circumfix some non-null lexical material, combinations such as *té*? . . . *i*?, *tol* . . . *e*?, and *way* . . . *o*? do occur. This is indicative of the partial independence of the two series, since isolated TDs and IDs also occur in connected discourse but are in most cases rejected in citation.

18. At this point, I hold aside other functions of the TD *i*? when it is without an accompanying ID, such as partitive anaphoric (e.g., give me some of it), negative (*má*? . . . *i*?), and anaphoric locative (*kub'in i*? 'he goes there').

19. Where there is a minimal contrast between one of these and the other TDs, such as *hé*?*el e*?, the *e*? form conveys absence of immediacy. This is expectable if *e*? is unmarked for immediacy, as I am suggesting.

20. This skewing towards symmetric frames is distinct from the principle of **proximal differentiation** proposed in §10.3.1. The former is a fact about the way deictic systems are used by speakers in the course of communicating, while the latter is a fact about the way these systems are paradigmatically structured.

21. I have attested a few possible examples of medial *o*?, but it is unclear to me whether it is actually the TD or the residuum of another morpheme, such as plural *ó*?*ob'* that has been phonologically reduced. Alternatively, a microslight pause at the TD may indicate that these examples actually involve a hesitation or boundary which is absent in a subsequent recycling. What we call these cases is a judgment call, and for the present my judgment is that they are not medial TDs, which means that the constraint on positioning these forms at S or topic boundaries stands unqualified.

22. Underscored portions of the Maya text are the 'target' forms that I asked speakers to comment on in the course of metalinguistic discussions.

23. The shift from *b'eéyli* to *b'aáyli* is an independent variable, the conditioning factors for which are unclear to me.

24. These remarks are abbreviated for the sake of brevity. A more complete analysis of such examples would follow along the lines of the complex and transposed frames in §5.2.

25. It is noteworthy that none of the deictics is associated with opening an interaction the way several are with closing moves. Only the Spkr and Adr PART forms and the Ø Immed DLOC *té?el o?* (in reference to Adr's location) are routinely used in first utterances in interactions, but it is the whole utterance, rather than the deictic as such, which executes the opening. For instance, in the greeting at the gate, *tàal té?el o?* 'coming in there', it is because the Spkr says he is coming in that the utterance works as a greeting, not merely because he makes reference to the Adr's location. In Discourse Referential *leti el o?* 'that's the one' and *hé?el o?* 'there it is', the deictics themselves embody the Phatic move of closing a discourse unit. Although we did not examine the Manner deictics (*b'ey* 'like that' series), these forms have especially salient Phatic functions, used routinely as back-channel devices.

26. Because of the sheer quantity of description required to portray Maya referential practice, I have not addressed comparative evidence in this book, except glancingly. For further references on this point, see Anderson and Keenan (1985) and Hanks (1989b).

27. The Function of Address has been omitted from the scale because it is specialized to the Adr PART forms and because it is ambiguous. Vocative Address, executed at the outset of an interaction, would figure in the Directive, Presentative range, whereas simple Address during talk is, by my analysis, a species of Reference, in which the object happens to be the Adr.

28. This distinction comes from Nicod's ([1923] 1962: vi) study of geometry in the perceptible world.

29. Some of the decenterings in metalanguage fail to follow this generalization, which is why we discussed them in detail (see §10.3.3).

CHAPTER 11: Conclusion

1. This is usually the corporeal field, but for a storyteller, the current indexical frame could very well be a narrative scene projected in a previous description or reconstructible by familiarity with the genre. The widespread incidence of decentering requires that we recognize a difference between 'current footing' (which can be transposed) and 'current corporeal engagement' (which by definition is nontransposed).

2. Nondeictic description, of course, provides encyclopedic resources for reference beyond the proximal zone, but this another matter. Deixis is specialized in the proximal zones, where communicative functions other than reference (directivity, phatic, expressivity) are multiplied.

References

Agar, M., and J. Hobbs. 1985. How to Grow Schemas out of Interviews. In J. Dougherty, ed., *Directions in Cognitive Anthropology*, 413–31. Urbana: University of Illinois Press.

Anderson, S. R., and E. L. Keenan. 1985. Deixis. In T. Shopen, ed., *Language Typology and Syntactic Description*. Vol. 3, *Grammatical Categories and the Lexicon*, 259–308. Cambridge: Cambridge University Press.

Atkinson, J. M., and J. Heritage, eds. 1984. *Structures of Social Action*. Cambridge: Cambridge University Press.

Baker, G. P., and P. M. S. Hacker. 1980. *Wittgenstein: Understanding and Meaning*. Oxford: Blackwell.

———. 1984. *Language, Sense, and Nonsense*. Oxford: Blackwell.

Bakhtin, M. M. 1981. *The Dialogic Imagination: Four Essays*. M. Holquist, ed., M. Holquist and C. Emerson, trans. Austin: University of Texas Press.

Baltaxe, C. 1978. *Foundations of Distinctive Feature Theory*. Baltimore: University Park Press.

Banfield, A. 1982. *Unspeakable Sentences*. London: Routledge and Kegan Paul.

Barrera-Vasquez, A., et al., eds. 1980. *Diccionario maya cordemex*. Mérida: Ediciones Cordemex.

Bauman, R. 1986. Contextualization, Tradition, and the Dialogue of Genres: Icelandic Legends of the Kraftaskáld. Paper presented at the annual meeting of the American Anthropological Association, Philadelphia, Pennsylvania.

Bauman, R., and J. Sherzer, eds. 1974. *Explorations in the Ethnography of Speaking*. Cambridge: Cambridge University Press.

Benveniste, E. 1965. *Problèmes de linguistique générale*. 2 vols. Paris: Gallimard.

———. [1956] 1966a. La nature des pronoms. In *Problèmes de linguistique générale*, Vol. 1, 251–58. Paris: Gallimard.

———. [1958] 1966b. De la subjectivité dans le langage. In *Problèmes de linguistique générale*, Vol. 1, 258–66. Paris: Gallimard.

———. [1965] 1974. Le langage et l'expérience humaine. In *Problèmes de linguistique générale*, Vol. 2, 67–78. Paris: Gallimard.

Bergsland, K. 1951. Kleinschmidt Centennial IV: Aleut Demonstratives and the Aleut-Eskimo Relation. *International Journal of American Linguistics* 17:167–69.

Berlin, B. 1978. *Tzeltal Numeral Classifiers*. The Hague: Mouton.

Berlin B., and P. Kay. 1969. *Basic Color Terms: Their Universality and Evolution*. Berkeley: University of California Press.

Bloomfield, L. 1933. *Language*. New York: Holt.

Boas, F. 1911. *Handbook of American Indian Languages*. BAE Bulletin 40, pt. 1.

———. [1911] 1966. *Introduction to the Handbook of American Indian Languages*. Washington, D.C.: Georgetown University Press.

Bodding, P. O. 1929. *Materials for a Santali Grammer II, Mostly Pedagogical*. Dumka.

Bolinger, D. 1965. The Atomization of Meaning. *Language* 41(4): 555–73.

Bourdieu, P. [1960] 1971. The Berber House. In M. Douglas, ed., *Rules and Meanings*, 98–110. London: Penguin.

———. [1972] 1977. *Outline of the Theory of Practice*. Cambridge: Cambridge University Press. Originally published in French.

———. 1980. *Le sens pratique*. Paris: Les Éditions de Minuit.

———. 1983. The Field of Cultural Production, or, the Economic World Revisited. *Poetics* 12: 311–56.

———. 1984. *Questions de sociologie*. Paris: Les Éditions de Minuit.

———. 1985. The Social Space and the Genesis of Groups. *Social Science Information* 24(2): 195–220.

Brenneis, D., and F. Meyers, eds. 1984. *Dangerous Words: Language and Politics in the Pacific*. New York: New York University Press.

Bricker, V. R. 1970. Relationship terms with the Usative Suffix in Tzotzil and Yucatec Maya. In *Papers from the Sixth Regional Meeting*. Chicago: Chicago Linguistic Society, 75–86.

———. 1974. The Ethnographic Context of Some Traditional Mayan Speech Genres. *Social Science Information* 24(2): 195–220.

———. 1978. Antipassive Constructions in Yucatec Maya. In N. C. England, ed., *Papers in Mayan Linguistics*. University of Missouri Miscellaneous Publications in Anthropology no. 6, 3–24. Columbia: University of Missouri.

———. 1981. *The Indian Christ, the Indian King: The Historical Substrate of Maya Myth and Ritual*. Austin: University of Texas Press.

Brown, G., and G. Yule. 1983. *Discourse Analysis*. Cambridge: Cambridge University Press.

Brown, R., and A. Gillman. [1960] 1972. The Pronouns of Power and Solidarity. In Sebeok 1960, 253–76. Reprinted in P. P. Giglioli, ed., *Language and Social Context*, 252–82. New York: Penguin.

Brubaker, R. 1985. Rethinking Classical Theory: The Sociological Vision of Pierre Bourdieu. *Theory and Society* 14: 723–44.

Bühler, K. [1934] 1967. *Teoría del lenguaje*. Madrid: Revista de Occidente. Original German reprinted as Bühler 1982.

———. 1982. *Sprachtheorie: die Darstellungsfunktion der Sprache*. Stuttgart: Gustav Fischer Verlag.

Carrithers, M., S. Collins, and S. Lukes, eds. 1985. *The Category of Person: Anthropology, Philosophy, History*. Cambridge: Cambridge University Press.

Cicourel, A. 1985. Text and Discourse. *Annual Review of Anthropology* 14: 159–85.

———. 1986. The Reproduction of Objective Knowledge: Common Sense Reasoning in Medical Decision Making. In Böhme, G., and N. Stehr, eds., *The Knowledge Society*, 87–122. Dordrecht and Boston: Reidel Publishing Company.

———. In prep. The Interpenetration of Communicative Contexts: Examples from Medical Encounters. In A. Duranti and C. Goodwin, eds., *Rethinking Context: Language as an Interactive Phenomenon*. Cambridge: Cambridge University Press.

Clark, H. H., and D. Wilkes-Gibbs. 1986. Referring as a Collaborative Process. *Cognition* 22(1): 1–39.

Cole, P., ed. 1978. *Syntax and Semantics 9: Pragmatics*. New York: Academic Press.

Coleman, L., and P. Kay. 1981. Prototype Semantics: The English Verb *Lie*. *Language* 57(1): 26–44.

Collinson, W. 1937. Indication: A Study of Demonstratives, Articles, and Other 'Indicators'. *Language* monographs no. 17, April–June.

Comaroff, J. 1985. *Body of Power, Body of Spirit: The Culture and History of a South African People*. Chicago: University of Chicago Press.

Comaroff, J. L., and S. Roberts. 1981. *Rules and Processes: The Cultural Logic of Dispute in an African Context*. Chicago: University of Chicago Press.

Conklin, H. C. 1973. Review Article: Color Categorization. *American Anthropologist* 75(1): 931–42.

Denny, J. P. 1984. Semantics of the Inuktitut (Eskimo) Spatial Deictics. *International Journal of American Linguistics* 48(4): 359–84.

Donnellan, K. S. [1968] 1971. Reference and Definite Description. In Steinberg and Jakobovits 1971, 100–114.

———. [1978] 1979. Speaker Reference, Descriptions and Anaphora. In Cole 1978, 47–68. Reprinted in P. French, ed., *Contemporary Perspectives in the Philosophy of Language*, 28–44. Minneapolis: University of Minnesota Press, 1979.

Douglas, M., ed. 1973. *Rules and Meanings: The Anthropology of Everyday Knowledge*. Harmondsworth: Penguin.

Dreyfus, H. L., and S. E. Dreyfus. 1987. From Socrates to Expert Systems: The Limits of Calculative Rationality. In P. Rabinow and W. M. Sullivan, eds., *Interpretive Social Science: A Second Look*, 327–50. Berkeley: University of California Press.

DuBois, J. W. 1987. The Discourse Basis of Ergativity. *Language* 63(4): 805–55.

Ducrot, O. 1984. *Le Dire et le Dit*. Paris: Les Éditions de Minuit.

Dunn, J. A. 1978. *A Practical Dictionary of the Coast Tsimshian Language*. Ottawa: National Museum of Canada.

———. 1979. *A Reference Grammar for the Coast Tshimshian Language*. Canadian Ethnology Service Paper 55. Ottawa: National Museum of Canada.

Duranti, A. 1984. Lauga and Talanoaga: Two Speech Genres in a Samoan Political Event. In Brenneis and Meyers 1984, 217–42.

Eco, U., et al., eds. 1988. *Meaning and Mental Representation*. Bloomington: Indiana University Press.

Edmonson, M. 1973. Semantic Universals and Particulars in Quiche. In M. Edmonson, ed., *Meaning in Mayan Languages*, 235–46. The Hague: Mouton.

———. 1982. *The Ancient Future of the Itza: The Book of Chilam Balam of Tizimin*. Austin: University of Texas Press.

Encrevé, P. 1988. "C'est Reagan qui a coulé le billet vert." La dérivation généralisée. *Actes de Recherche en Sciences Sociales* 71(2): 109–28.

Errington, J. J. 1988. *Structure and Style in Javanese: A Semiotic View of Linguistic Etiquette*. Philadelphia: University of Pennsylvania Press.

Ervin-Tripp, S. 1972. On Sociolinguistic Rules: Alternations and Co-occurrence. In Gumperz and Hymes 1972, 213–50.

———. 1976. Is Sybil There? The Structure of American English Directives. *Language in Society* 5: 25–66.

Evans, G. 1982. *The Varieties of Reference.* Edited by J. McDowell. New York: Oxford University Press.

Ewell, P. T. 1984. *Intensification of Peasant Agriculture in Yucatan.* Ithaca, N.Y.: Department of Agricultural Economy, Cornell University.

Fauconnier, G. 1984. *Espaces mentaux: Aspects de la construction du sens dans les langues naturelles.* Paris: Les Editions de Minuit.

———. 1988. Quantification, Roles and Domains. In Eco 1988, 61–80.

Fillmore, C. 1978. The Organization of Semantic Information in the Lexicon. In D. Farkas, W. M. Jacobsen, and K. W. Todrys, eds., *Papers from the Parasession on the Lexicon,* 1–11. Chicago: Chicago Linguistic Society.

———. 1982. Towards a Descriptive Framework for Spatial Deixis. In R. Jarvella and W. Klein, eds., *Speech, Place, and Action: Studies in Deixis and Related Topics,* 31–59. New York: John Wiley and Sons.

———. 1985. Frames and the Semantics of Understanding. *Quaderni di Semantica* 6(2): 222–53.

Foley, W. A., and R. Van Valin. 1984. *Functional Syntax and Universal Grammar.* Cambridge: Cambridge University Press.

de Fornel, M., and P. Encrevé. 1983. Le sens pratique, construction de la référence et structure de l'interaction dans le couple question/réponse. *Actes de Recherche en Sciences Sociales* 43:3–30.

Fortes, M. 1958. Introduction. In J. R. Goody, ed., *The Developmental Cycle in Domestic Groups.* Cambridge: Cambridge University Press.

Fought, J. 1985. Cyclical patterns in Chorti (Mayan) literature. In M. S. Edmonson, ed., *Supplement to the Handbook of Middle American Indians.* Vol. 3, 147–70. Austin: University of Texas Press.

Frei, H. 1944. Systèmes de déictiques. *Acta Linguistica* 4:111–29.

Friedrich, P. 1966. Structural Implications of Russian Pronominal Usage. In W. Bright, ed., *Sociolinguistics,* 214–59. The Hague: Mouton.

———. 1974. On Aspect Theory and Homeric Aspect. *IJAL* memoir 28, 40(4/2): 1–44.

———. [1970] 1979a. *Language, Context and the Imagination.* Selected and introduced by A. S. Dil. Stanford: Stanford University Press.

———. [1964, 1970] 1979b. Semantic Structure and Social Structure: An Instance from Russian. In P. Friedrich, *Language, Context, and the Imagination: Essays,* 126–67. Stanford: Stanford University Press.

———. 1985. Review of P. J. Hopper, ed., *Tense-Aspect: Between Semantics and Pragmatics. Language* 61(1): 182–87.

Gale, R. M. 1964. Is It Now Now? *Mind* 73(289): 97–105.

———. 1968. Indexical Signs, Egocentric Particulars, and Token-Reflexive Words. In P. Edwards, ed., *Encyclopedia of Philosophy.* Vol. 4, 151–55. New York: Collier Macmillan.

Garfinkel, H. 1967. *Studies in Ethnomethodology.* Englewood Cliffs, N.J.: Prentice-Hall.

———. [1962] 1972. Studies of the Routine Grounds of Everyday Activities. *Social Problems* 11(3). Reprinted in D. Sudnow, ed., *Studies in Social Interaction,* 1–30. New York: Free Press.

Garver, N. 1965. Varieties of Use and Mention. *Philosophy and Phenomenological Research* 24:230–38.

Gell, A. 1985. See How to Read a Map: Remarks on the Practical Logic of Navigation. *Man* n.s. 20:271–86.

Goffman, E. 1974. *Frame Analysis*. New York: Harper and Row.
――――. 1976. Replies and Responses. *Language in Society* 5:257–313.
――――. 1981. *Forms of Talk*. Philadelphia: University of Pennsylvania Press.
――――. [1979] 1983. Footing. *Semiotica* 25(1/2): 1–29. Reprinted in Goffman 1981, 124–59.
Goodwin, C. 1981. *Conversational Organization: Interaction Between Speakers and Hearers*. New York: Academic Press.
――――. 1984. Notes on Story Structure and the Organization of Participation. In J. M. Atkinson and J. Heritage, eds., *Structures of Social Action: Studies in Conversation Analysis*, 225–46. Cambridge: Cambridge University Press.
――――. 1987. Embedded Context. Paper presented at the eighty-seventh annual meeting of the American Anthropological Association, Phoenix, Arizona.
Goodwin, M. H. 1982. Processes of Dispute Management among Urban Black Children. *American Ethnologist* 9:76–96.
――――. 1985. Byplay: The Framing of Collaborative Collusion. Paper presented at the eighty-fourth annual meeting of the American Anthropological Association, Washington, D.C.
――――. In press. *HE-SAID-HE-SAID: The Interactive Organization of Talk in an Urban Black Peer Group*. Bloomington: Indiana University Press.
Gossen, G. H. 1974a. *Chamulas in the World of the Sun: Time and Space in a Maya Oral Tradition*. Cambridge, Mass.: Harvard University Press.
――――. 1974b. To Speak with a Heated Heart: Chamula Canons of Style and Good Performance. In Bauman and Sherzer 1974, 389–413.
Graczyk, R. 1986. Crow Deixis. Department of Linguistics, University of Chicago. Manuscript.
Greenberg, J. 1966. Some Universals of Grammar with Particular Reference to the Order of Meaningful Elements. In J. H. Greenberg, ed., *Universals of Language*, 73–113. Cambridge: MIT Press.
Grice, H. P. [1957] 1971. Meaning. *Philosophical Review* 67. Reprinted in Steinberg and Jakobovits 1971, 53–59.
――――. 1967. Logic and Conversation. William James Lectures, Harvard University.
――――. 1975. Logic and Conversation. In P. Cole and J. Morgan, eds., *Syntax and Semantics 3: Speech Acts*, 41–59. New York: Academic Press.
――――. 1978. Further Notes on Logic and Conversation. In Cole 1978, 113–28.
Gumperz, J. 1977. Sociocultural Knowledge in Conversational Inference. In Saville-Troike 1977, 191–212.
――――. 1982. *Discourse Strategies*. Cambridge: Cambridge University Press.
Gumperz, J., and D. H. Hymes, eds. 1972. *Directions in Sociolinguistics*. New York: Holt, Rinehart and Winston.
Halliday, M. A. K. 1985. *An Introduction to Functional Grammar*. Baltimore: Edward Arnold Press.
Halliday, M. A. K., and R. Hasan. 1976. *Cohesion in English*. London: Longman.
Hallowell, A. I. 1955. Cultural Factors in Spatial Orientation. In A. I. Hallowell, *Culture and Experience*. Philadelphia: University of Pennsylvania Press.
Hancher, M. 1979. The Classification of Co-operative Illocutionary Acts. *Language in Society* 8(1): 1–14.
Hanks, W. F. 1983. Deixis and the Organization of Interactive Context in Yucatec Maya.

Ph.D. diss., Department of Anthropology and Department of Linguistics, University of Chicago.

———. 1984a. The Evidential Core of Deixis in Yucatec Maya. In Drogo, J. et al., eds. *Papers from the Twentieth Regional Meeting of the Chicago Linguistic Society,* 154–72. Chicago: Chicago Linguistic Society.

———. 1984b. The Interactive Basis of Maya Divination. Paper presented at the eighty-third annual meeting of the American Anthropological Association, Denver, Colorado.

———. 1984c. Sanctification, Structure, and Experience in a Yucatec Maya Ritual Event. *Journal of American Folklore* 97(384): 131–66.

———. 1986. Authenticity and Ambivalence in the Text: A Colonial Maya Case. *American Ethnologist* 13(4): 721–44.

———. 1987a. Discourse Genres in a Theory of Practice. *American Ethnologist* 14(4): 64–88.

———. 1987b. Markedness and Category Interactions in the Malagasy Deictic System. *University of Chicago Working Papers in Linguistics* 3:109–36.

———. 1988. Orientations spatiales et pratiques de référence. Ms., Department of Anthropology, University of Chicago.

———. 1989a. Text and Textuality. *Annual Review of Anthropology* 18:95–127.

———. 1989b. The Indexical Ground of Deictic Reference. In B. Music, R. Graczyk, and C. Wiltshire, eds., *Papers from the Twenty-Fifth Annual Regional Meeting of the Chicago Linguistic Society, Part Two: Parasession on Language in Context,* 104–22. Chicago: Chicago Linguistic Society.

———. 1990. Elements of Maya Style. In W. F. Hanks and D. S. Rice, eds., *Word and Image in Mayan Culture: Explorations in Language, Writing, and Representation.* Salt Lake City: University of Utah Press.

———. In press. Metalanguage and the Pragmatics of Deixis. In J. Lucy, ed., *Reflexive Language: Reported Speech and Metapragmatics.* Cambridge: Cambridge University Press.

Harman, G. H. [1968] 1971. Three Levels of Meaning. *Journal of Philosophy* 64:590–602. Reprinted in Steinberg and Jakobovits 1971, 66–75.

Haugen, E. [1957] 1969. The Semantics of Icelandic Orientation. In S. A. Tyler, ed., *Cognitive Anthropology,* 330–42. New York: Holt, Rinehart and Winston.

Havránek, B. [1932] 1964. The Functional Differentiation of the Standard Language. In P. L. Garvin, ed., *A Prague School Reader in Esthetics, Literary Structure, and Style,* 3–17. Washington: Georgetown University Press.

Heath, J. 1980. Nungubuyu Deixis, Anaphora, and Culture. In *Proceedings from the Parasession on Pronouns and Anaphora,* 151–65. Chicago: Chicago Linguistic Society.

Husserl, E. 1978. The Origin of Geometry. In Luckmann 1978, 42–70.

Hymes, D. 1972. Models of the Interaction of Language and Social Life. In Gumperz and Hymes 1972, 35–71.

———. 1974. *Foundations in Sociolinguistics: An Ethnographic Approach.* Philadelphia: University of Pennsylvania Press.

Ingarden, R. 1973. *The Literary Work of Art: An Investigation on the Borderlines of Ontology, Logic, and Theory of Literature.* G. G. Grabowicz, trans. Evanston: Northwestern University Press.

Irvine, J. 1985. Review Article: Status and Style in Language. *Annual Review of Anthropology* 14:557–81.

———. 1987. The Implicated Dialogue: Structures of Participation in Discourse. Paper presented at the conference "Decentering Discourse," eighty-sixth annual meeting of the American Anthropological Society, Chicago, Illinois.

Jacobson, S. 1984. *Yup'ik Eskimo Dictionary.* Fairbanks: Alaska National Language Center.

Jakobson, R. 1957. Metalanguage as a Linguistic Problem. In *The Framework of Language.* Michigan Studies in the Humanities, 81–92. Ann Arbor: University of Michigan Press.

———. 1960. Concluding Statement: Linguistics and Poetics. In Sebeok 1960, 350–77.

———. [1936] 1966a. Beitrag zur allgemeinen Kasuslehre. In E. P. Hamp, F. W. Householder, and R. Austerlitz, eds., *Readings in Linguistics* 2, 51–89. Chicago: University of Chicago Press.

———. [1939] 1966b. Signe zéro. In E. P. Hamp, F. W. Householder, and R. Austerlitz, eds., *Readings in Linguistics* 2, 109–15. Chicago: University of Chicago Press.

———. [1957] 1971. Shifters, Verbal Categories, and the Russian Verb. In *Selected Writings of Roman Jakobson* 2, 130–47. The Hague: Mouton.

Jesperson, O. [1924] 1965. *The Philosophy of Grammar.* New York: W. W. Norton.

Johnson, M. 1987. *The Body in the Mind: The Bodily Basis of Meaning, Imagination, and Reason.* Chicago: University of Chicago Press.

Kaplan, D. 1978. Dthat. In Cole 1978, 221–43.

———. [1978] 1979. On the Logic of Demonstratives. In P. A. French, et al., eds., *Contemporary Perspectives in the Philosophy of Language,* 401–12. Minneapolis: University of Minnesota Press.

Katz, J. J. 1971. Semantic Theory. In Steinberg and Jakobovits 1971, 297–307.

Kellner, H. [1973] 1978. On the Cognitive Significance of the System of Language in Communication. In Luckmann 1978, 324–42.

Khlebnikova, I. 1973. *Oppositions in Morphology.* Paris: Mouton.

Kripke, S. [1977] 1979. Speaker's Reference and Semantic Reference. In P. A. French, et al., eds., *Contemporary Perspectives in the Philosophy of Language,* 401–12. Minneapolis: University of Minnesota Press.

Kronenfeld, D. B., J. D. Armstrong, and S. Wilmoth. 1985. Exploring the Internal Structure of Linguistic Categories: An Extensionist Semantic View. In J. W. D. Dougherty, ed., *Directions in Cognitive Anthropology,* 91–110. Urbana and Chicago: University of Illinois Press.

Kuryłowicz, J. 1972. Universaux linguistiques. In L. Heilman, ed., *Proceedings of the Eleventh International Congress of Linguists.* Bologna.

Labov, W. [1970] 1972a. The Study of Language in its Social Context. In P. P. Giglioli, ed., *Language and Social Context.* New York: Penguin.

———. 1972b. Rules for Ritual Insults. Chap. 8 in *Language in the Inner City,* 297–353. Philadelphia: University of Pennsylvania Press.

Lakoff, G. 1984. There Constructions: A Case Study in Grammatical Construction Theory and Prototype Theory. *Berkeley Cognitive Science Report* no. 18.

———. 1987. *Women, Fire, and Dangerous Things.* Chicago: University of Chicago Press.

Langacker, R. W. 1984. Active Zones. In C. Brugman and M. Macaulay, eds., *Proceed-*

ings of the Tenth Annual Meeting of the Berkeley Linguistics Society, 172–88. Berkeley: Berkeley Linguistics Society.

Lave, J. 1988. *Cognition in Practice: Mind, Mathematics, and Culture in Everyday Life.* Cambridge: Cambridge University Press.

Leonard, R. A. 1985. Swahili Demonstratives: Evaluating the Validity of Competing Semantic Hypotheses. *Studies in African Linguistics* 16(3): 281–95.

León-Portilla, A. H. de. 1968. *Tiempo y realidad en el pensamiento maya.* Mexico City: Universidad Nacional Autónoma de México.

Levinson, S. 1983. *Pragmatics.* Cambridge: Cambridge University Press.

———. 1987. Putting Linguistics on a Proper Footing: Explorations in Goffman's Concepts of Participation. In P. Drew and A. Woolton, eds., *Goffman: An Interdisciplinary Appreciation*, 161–227. Oxford: Polity Press.

Linsky, L. [1967] 1971. Reference and Referents. In Steinberg and Jakobovits 1971, 76–85. Previously published in L. Linsky, *Referring.* New York: Humanities Press, 1967.

Logan, M. H. 1977. Humoral Medicine in Guatemala and Peasant Acceptance of Modern Medicine. In D. Landy, ed., *Culture, Disease, and Healing: Studies in Medical Anthropology*, 487–95. New York: Macmillan.

Lounsbury, F. [1964] 1969. A Formal Account of the Crow- and Omaha-Type Kinship Terminologies. In W. H. Goodenough, ed., *Explorations in Cultural Anthropology*, 351–44. Reprinted in S. A. Tyler, ed., *Cognitive Anthropology*, 212–54. New York: Holt, Rinehart and Winston.

Luckmann, T., ed. 1978. *Phenomenology and Sociology: Selected Readings.* New York: Penguin.

Lucy, J. 1985. Whorf's View of the Linguistic Mediation of Thought. In E. Mertz and R. Parmentier, eds., *Semiotic Mediation: Sociocultural and Psychological Perspectives*, 73–97. New York: Academic Press.

———. ed. In press. *Reflexive Language: Reported Speech and Metapragmatics.* Cambridge: Cambridge University Press.

Lyons, J. 1977. *Semantics.* 2 vols. Cambridge: Cambridge University Press.

———. 1982. Deixis and Subjectivity: Loquor, Ergo Sum? In R. Jarvella and W. Klein, eds., *Speech, Place, and Action: Studies in Deixis and Related Topics*, 101–24. New York: John Wiley and Sons.

MacLeod, B. 1990. The 819-day Count Verb: A Soulful Mechanism. In W. F. Hanks and D. S. Rice, eds., *Word and Image in Mayan Culture: Explorations in Language, Writing, and Representation.* Salt Lake City: University of Utah Press.

Merleau-Ponty, M. [1945] 1967. *Phénomenologie de la perception.* Paris: Editions Gallimard.

Morgan, J. 1978. Two Types of Convention in Indirect Speech Acts. In Cole 1978, 261–80.

Morley, S. G., and G. W. Brainard. [1946] 1983. *The Ancient Maya.* Stanford: Stanford University Press.

Morris, C. W. 1971. *Writings on the General Theory of Signs.* The Hague: Mouton.

Munn, N. 1966. Visual Categories: An Approach to the Study of Representational Systems. *American Anthropologist* 68:936–49.

———. 1986. *The Fame of Gawa: A Symbolic Study of Value Transformation in a Massim (Papua New Guinea) Society.* Cambridge: Cambridge University Press.

Nash, J. [1971] 1975. *Bajo la mirada de los antepasados: creencias y comportamiento en una comunidad maya*. Mexico City: Instituto Indigenista Interamericano.

Neugebauer, B. 1986. *Der Wandel Kleinbäuerlicher Landnutzung in Oxkutzcab-Yucatán*. Freiburg: Harald Reimann.

Nicod, J. [1923] 1962. *La géométrie dans le monde sensible*. Paris: Presses Universitaires de France.

Ortner, S. B. 1984. Theory in Anthropology since the Sixties. *Comparative Studies in Society and History* 26(1):126–66.

Panofsky, E. 1976. *Gothic Architecture and Scholasticism: An Inquiry into the Analogy of the Arts, Philosophy, and Religion in the Middle Ages*. New York: New American Library.

Partee, B. 1973. The Syntax and Semantics of Quotation. In P. Kiparsky, and S. Anderson, eds., *A Festschrift for Morris Halle*. 410–18. New York: Holt, Rinehart and Winston.

Peirce, C. S. [1955] 1940. *Philosophical Writings of Peirce: Selected Writings*. J. Buchler, ed. New York: Dover.

Platts, M. 1979. *Ways of Meaning: An Introduction to a Philosophy of Language*. London: Routledge and Kegan Paul.

Prince, E. F. 1981. Towards a Taxonomy of Given-New Information. In Cole 1978, 223–56.

Putnam, H. 1975. *Mind, Language and Reality*. London: Cambridge University Press.

Quine, W. 1971. The Inscrutability of Reference. In Steinberg and Jakobovits 1971, 142–54.

Redfield, R. 1941. *The Folk Culture of Yucatan*. Chicago: University of Chicago Press.

Redfield, R., and A. Villa Rojas. [1934] 1962. *Chan Kom: A Maya Village*. Chicago: University of Chicago Press.

Reed, I. et al., eds. 1977. *Yup'ik Eskimo Grammar*. Fairbanks: Alaska Native Language Center, University of Alaska.

Reed, N. 1964. *The Caste War of Yucatan*. Stanford: Stanford University Press.

Reichenbach, H. 1947. *Elements of Symbolic Logic*. New York: Macmillan.

Robertson, J. 1980. *The Structure of Pronoun Incorporation in the Mayan Verb Complex*. New York: Garland.

———. 1983. From Symbol to Icon: The Evolution of the Pronominal System of Common Mayan to Modern Yucatecan. *Language* 59:529–40.

———. 1984. Colonial Evidence for a Pre-Quiche, Ergative 3sg *ru-*. *International Journal of American Linguistics* 50(4): 452–56.

———. 1987. The Origins of the Mamean Pronominals: A Mayan/Indo-European Typological Comparison. *IJAL* 53(1): 74–85.

Rosch, E. 1978. Principles of Categorization. In E. Rosch and B. B. Lloyd, eds., *Cognition and Categorization*, 28–49. Hillsdale, New Jersey: Lawrence Erlbaum Associates.

Roys, R. 1957. *The Political Geography of the Yucatan Maya*. Publication 613. Washington, D.C.: Carnegie Institution.

———, ed. 1965. *Ritual of the Bacabs*. Norman: University of Oklahoma Press.

Russell, B. 1940. *An Inquiry into Meaning and Truth*. London: Allen and Unwin.

Sacks, H., E. A. Schegloff, and G. Jefferson. 1974. A Simplest Systematics for the Organization of Turn-Taking in Conversation. *Language* 50(4): 696–735.

Sadock, J. 1978. On Testing for Conversational Implicature. In Cole 1978, 281–98.

Sahlins, M. [1976] 1977. Colors and Cultures. *Semiotica* 16:1–22. Reprinted in J. L. Dolgin, et al., eds., *Symbolic Anthropology*, 165–80. New York: Columbia University Press.

Sapir, E. 1921. *Language: An Introduction to the Study of Speech*. New York: Harcourt Brace.

———. [1931] 1949. Communication. In D. G. Mandelbaum, ed., *Edward Sapir: Selected Writings in Language, Culture, and Personality*, 104–9. Berkeley and Los Angeles: University of California Press.

Saville-Troike, M., ed. 1977. *Linguistics and Anthropology*. Georgetown University Round Table on Languages and Linguistics 1977. Washington, D.C.: Georgetown University Press.

Schegloff, E. 1972. Notes on a Conversational Practice: Formulating Place. In D. Sudnow, ed., *Studies in Social Interaction*, 75–119. New York: Free Press.

———. 1982. Discourse as an Interactional Achievement. In D. Tannen, ed., *Analyzing Discourse: Text and Talk*. Georgetown University Round Table on Languages and Linguistics 1981, 71–94. Washington, D.C.: Georgetown University Press.

Schutz, A. [1932] 1967. *The Phenomenology of the Social World*. G. Walsh and F. Lehnert, trans. Evanston: Northwestern University Press.

———. 1970. On Phenomenology and Social Relations. H. R. Wagner, ed. Chicago: University of Chicago Press.

———. 1973. Collected Papers. Vol. 1, *The Problem of Social Reality*. M. Natanson, ed. The Hague: Mouton.

Searle, J. 1969. *Speech Acts: An Essay in the Philosophy of Language*. Cambridge: Cambridge University Press.

———. 1979. *Meaning and Expression*. Cambridge: Cambridge University Press.

Sebeok, T., ed. 1960. *Style in Language*. Cambridge, Mass.: MIT Press.

Sherzer, J. 1973. Verbal and Nonverbal Deixis: The Pointed Lip Gesture among the San Blas Cuna. *Language in Society* 2:117–31.

———. 1983. *Kuna Ways of Speaking: An Ethnographic Perspective*. Austin: University of Texas Press.

Silverstein, M. 1976a. Hierarchy of Features and Ergativity. In R. M. W. Dixon, ed., *Grammatical Categories in Australian Languages*, 112–71. Canberra: Australian Institute of Aboriginal Studies.

———. 1976b. Shifters, Verbal Categories and Cultural Description. In K. Basso and H. Selby, eds., *Meaning in Anthropology*, 11–57. Albuquerque: School of American Research.

———. 1979. Language Structure and Linguistic Ideology. In P. Clyne, et al., eds., *Papers from the Parasession on Linguistic Units and Levels*, 193–247. Chicago: Chicago Linguistic Society.

———. 1985. The Functional Stratification of Language and Ontogenesis. In J. Wertch, ed., *Culture, Communication and Cognition: Vygotskian Perspectives*, 205–35. Cambridge and New York: Cambridge University Press.

———. 1987. The Three Faces of "Function": Preliminaries to a Psychology of Language. In M. Hickmann, ed., *Social and Functional Approaches to Language and Thought*, 17–38. Orlando: Academic Press.

Steinberg, D., and L. Jacobovits, eds. 1971. *Semantics: An Interdisciplinary Reader in*

Philosophy, Linguistics, and Psychology. Cambridge: Cambridge University Press.

Story, G. L., and C. M. Naish. 1973. *Tlingit Verb Dictionary.* Fairbanks: Alaska Native Language Center, University of Alaska.

Talmy, L. 1978. Figure and Ground in Complex Sentences. In J. Greenberg, et al., eds., *Universals of Human Language.* Vol. 4, 625–54. Stanford: Stanford University Press.

———. 1983. How Language Structures Space. In H. L. Pick and L. P. Acredolo, eds., *Spatial Orientation: Theory, Research, and Application,* 225–82. New York: Plenum Press.

Tambiah, S. J. [1969] 1985. Animals Are Good to Think and Good to Prohibit. Chap. 5 in *Culture, Thought, and Social Action: An Anthropological Perspective,* 169–211. Cambridge, Mass.: Harvard University Press.

Tedlock, D. 1983. *The Spoken Word and the Work of Interpretation.* Philadelphia: University of Pennsylvania Press.

Thompson, R. A. 1974. *The Winds of Tomorrow: Social Change in a Maya Town.* Chicago: University of Chicago Press.

Timberlake, A. 1982. Invariance and the Syntax of Russian Aspect. In P. J. Hopper, ed., *Tense-Aspect: Between Semantics and Pragmatics,* 305–34. Philadelphia: Benjamins.

Turner, R., ed. 1974. *Ethnomethodology: Modern Sociology Readings.* Harmondsworth: Penguin.

Turner, T. 1980. The Social Skin. In J. Cherfas and R. Lewin, eds., *Not Work Alone.* Beverly Hills: Sage Publications.

Turner, V. 1967. *The Forest of Symbols.* New York: Cornell University Press.

Villa Rojas, A. [1945] 1978. *Los Elegidos de Dios: Etnografía de los Mayas de Quintana Roo.* Série de Antropología Social, 56. Mexico: INI.

Vološinov, V. N. [1929] 1986. *Marxism and the Philosophy of Language.* L. Matejka and I. R. Titunik, trans. Cambridge, Mass.: Harvard University Press.

Weinreich, U. 1963. On the Semantic Structure of Language. In J. Greenberg, ed., *Universals of Language,* 142–216. Cambridge, Mass.: MIT Press.

———. 1980. *On Semantics.* Philadelphia: University of Pennsylvania Press.

Whorf, B. L. 1941. The Relation of Habitual Thought and Behavior to Language. In J. B. Carroll, ed., *Language, Thought, and Reality: Selected Writings of Benjamin Lee Whorf,* 134–59. Cambridge: MIT Press.

Zide, N. 1972. A Munda Demonstrative System: Santali. In J. M. C. Thomas and L. Bernot, eds., *Mélanges Haudricourt.* Vol. 1, 267–72. Paris: Editions Klincksieck.

Zipf, P. 1971. On H. P. Grice's Account of Meaning. In Steinberg and Jakobovits 1971, 60–66.

Zwicky, A. 1974. Hey, Whatsyourname! In M. W. LaGaly, R. A. Fox, and A. Bruck, eds., *Proceedings from the Tenth Regional Meeting of the Chicago Linguistic Society,* 787–801. Chicago: Chicago Linguistic Society.

Name Index

Index of Subjects